Praise for

T0024607

BUSH

"Smith is particularly good on the nuances of Bush's character. . . . [A] carefully researched portrait."

—David M. Shribman, *The Boston Globe*

"Anyone prone to romanticize the old GOP should take a bracing shot of *Bush,* a hefty biography of our 43rd president by the prolific and acclaimed biographer Jean Edward Smith. Written in sober, smooth, snark-free prose, with an air of thoughtful, detached authority, the book is nonetheless exceedingly damning in its judgments about George W. Bush's years in office. . . . Authoritative and trustworthy."

—David Greenberg, *The Washington Post*

"Harsh though the book is, overall it is well-researched, well-written and convincing."

—Morton Kondracke, *The Wall Street Journal*

"A swift and damning judgment on the 43rd president. . . . Smith writes with a deft sweep and sense of history."

—Ray Locker, *USA Today*

"Pulls no punches. . . . A fair, comprehensive and highly readable account of a critical period that is sure to be reassessed by historians over the coming decades."

—Ray Harkavy, *Associated Press*

"A thought-provoking book that anybody who wants to understand the opening years of this millennium must read."

—James M. McPherson, author of *Battle Cry of Freedom*

"A well-rounded portrait of Bush as president. . . . Smith's account is necessary and valuable."

—Erik Spanberg, *Christian Science Monitor*

"Makes a voluminously detailed—and compelling—case that vindication is unlikely to come for the Bush administration anytime soon."
—Glenn C. Altschuler, *San Francisco Chronicle*

"An excellent initial assessment of a presidency that began in controversy . . . and ended with the international and domestic failures that saddled Bush with the most sustained negative ratings of any modern president."
—Carl P. Leubsdorf, *The Dallas Morning News*

"Hard-hitting. . . . A shrewd, nuanced view of Bush. . . . Smith embeds this portrait in a lucid, highly readable narrative, balancing rich detail with clear delineation of the larger shape of policy through the chaos of politics. This is a superb recap and critical analysis of Bush's controversial administration."
—*Publishers Weekly*

"A compelling examination of George W. Bush's unlikely ascent to the White House and his calamitous administration of it. . . . A masterful retelling."
—Craig Offman, *The Globe and Mail* (Toronto)

" 'Rarely in the history of the United States has the nation been so ill-served as during the presidency of George W. Bush'. . . . Having laid out that thesis in his opening pages, *Bush* goes on to comprehensively, meticulously and persuasively back up [Smith's] assertions."
—Dale Singer, *St. Louis Post-Dispatch*

"A relentlessly hard-hitting assessment."
—*Kirkus Reviews*

"Magisterial."
—*Richmond Times-Dispatch*

"Smith's portrait is fascinating."
—*Booklist*

BUSH

Jean Edward Smith

SIMON & SCHUSTER PAPERBACKS

NEW YORK
LONDON
TORONTO
SYDNEY
NEW DELHI

Simon & Schuster Paperbacks
An Imprint of Simon & Schuster, Inc.
1230 Avenue of the Americas
New York, NY 10020

First Simon & Schuster paperback edition July 2017

SIMON & SCHUSTER PAPERBACKS and colophon are registered
trademarks of Simon & Schuster, Inc.

For information about special discounts for bulk purchases,
please contact Simon & Schuster Special Sales at 1-866-506-1949
or business@simonandschuster.com.

The Simon & Schuster Speakers Bureau can bring authors
to your live event. For more information or to book an event
contact the Simon & Schuster Speakers Bureau at 1-866-248-3049
or visit our website at www.simonspeakers.com.

Interior design by Joy O'Meara

Manufactured in the United States of America

10   9   8   7   6   5   4   3   2   1

The Library of Congress has cataloged the hardcover edition as follows:

Smith, Jean Edward, author.
    Bush / Jean Edward Smith. — First Simon & Schuster hardcover edition.
       pages cm
    Includes bibliographical references and index.
       ISBN 978-1-4767-4119-2 — ISBN 1-4767-4119-0   1. Bush, George W.
(George Walker), 1946–   2. United States—Politics and government—
2001–2009.   I. Title.
    E902.S59 2016
    973.931092—dc23   2015034690
PP

ISBN 978-1-4767-4119-2
ISBN 978-1-4767-4120-8 (pbk)
ISBN 978-1-4767-4121-5 (ebook)

To John and Sandy

friends . . . colleagues . . . mentors

There's not going to be any question about who's in charge. Decisions are going to come to my desk, and I'm going to be the one making them. I am THE DECIDER.

GEORGE W. BUSH

Contents

	Preface	XV
ONE	The Wilderness Years	1
TWO	Turnaround	28
THREE	"Don't Mess with Texas"	54
FOUR	Governor	80
FIVE	The 2000 Election	99
SIX	The Rule of Law	123
SEVEN	Inauguration	148
EIGHT	March of the Hegelians	175
NINE	Asleep at the Switch	204
TEN	Toppling the Taliban	228
ELEVEN	*L'État, c'est moi*	253
TWELVE	The Torture Trail	279
THIRTEEN	Waging Aggressive War: The Prelude	300
FOURTEEN	Invasion	326
FIFTEEN	"Mission Accomplished"	356
SIXTEEN	Four More Years	381
SEVENTEEN	Katrina	416
EIGHTEEN	Perils of a Second Term	444
NINETEEN	The Mess in Mesopotamia	472

TWENTY   Rummy Walks the Plank   499

TWENTY-ONE   Bush Takes Command   524

TWENTY-TWO   AIDS   549

TWENTY-THREE   Quagmire of the Vanities   576

TWENTY-FOUR   Financial Armageddon   606

TWENTY-FIVE   *Finis*   633

                  Acknowledgments   661
                  Notes   663
                  Bibliography   747
                  Index   759
                  Illustration Credits   809

BUSH

Preface

Rarely in the history of the United States has the nation been so ill-served as during the presidency of George W. Bush. When Bush took office in 2001, the federal budget ran a surplus, the national debt stood at a generational low of 56 percent of gross domestic product (GDP), and unemployment clocked in at 4 percent—which most economists consider the practical equivalent of full employment. The government's tax revenue amounted to $2.1 trillion annually, of which $1 trillion came from personal income taxes and another $200 billion from corporate taxes. Military spending totaled $350 billion, or 3 percent of GDP—a low not seen since the late 1940s—and not one American had been killed in combat in almost a decade. Each dollar bought 1.06 euros, or 117 yen. Gasoline cost $1.50 per gallon. Twelve years after the Berlin Wall came down, the United States stood at the pinnacle of authority: the world's only superpower, endowed with democratic legitimacy, the credible champion of the rule of law, the exemplar of freedom and prosperity.[1]

Eight years later the United States found itself in two distant "wars of choice"; military spending constituted 20 percent of all federal outlays and more than 5 percent of the gross domestic product. The final Bush budget was $1.4 trillion in the red and the national debt was out of control. The nation's GDP had increased from $10.3 trillion to

$14.2 trillion during those eight years, but a series of tax cuts that Bush introduced had reduced the government's revenue from personal income taxes by 9 percent and corporate taxes by 33 percent. Unemployment stood at 9.3 percent and was rising; two million Americans had lost their homes when a housing bubble burst, and new construction was at a standstill. The stock market had taken a nosedive, the dollar had lost much of its former value, and gasoline sold for $3.27 a gallon.[2] The United States remained the world's only superpower, but its reputation abroad was badly tarnished.

Was Bush responsible? Perhaps not for the housing bubble or the disastrous collapse of high-risk investments in derivatives, except that he equated the American dream with home ownership and loosened oversight of the securities industry. Otherwise the answer is a resounding yes. Unprepared for the complexities of governing, with little executive experience and a glaring deficit in his attention span, untutored, untraveled, and unversed in the ways of the world, Bush thrived on making a show of his decisiveness. "I'm not afraid to make decisions," he told a biographer. "Matter of fact, I *like* this aspect of the presidency."[3] But his greatest strength became his worst flaw. His self-confidence and decisiveness caused him to do far more damage than a less assertive president would have.

The critical turning point came on September 12, 2001. Al Qaeda's attacks on the United States on 9/11 violated the universal norms of civilized society, and the immediate global outpouring of empathy for the U.S. was unparalleled. Accordingly, September 12 was a defining moment in American history: the United States was not only an economic powerhouse and a military superpower but also enjoyed unprecedented moral authority. Bush could have capitalized on that support but instead he squandered it. He strutted around like a cowboy and then picked a fight with Iraq.[4]

By conflating the events of 9/11 and Saddam Hussein, Bush precipitated the deterioration of America's position abroad, led the United States into a $3 trillion war in Iraq that cost more than four thousand American lives and an unwinnable conflict in Afghanistan, promulgated an egregious doctrine of preventive war, alienated America's allies, weakened its alliances, and inspired young Muslims throughout the world to join the jihad.[5] If Saddam and his secular regime had remained in power, the so-called Islamic State of Iraq could not have been created and the ISIS we know today would not exist. Domestically, the hysteria unleashed by his administration undermined civil liberty, eroded the rule of law, and tarnished respect for traditional values of tolerance and moderation.

"I am the war president," Bush once boasted, asserting sophomoric delight in military braggadocio.[6] Neither Dwight Eisenhower nor Harry Truman would have called themselves "the war president," even though a nuclear war between the United States and the Soviet Union could at any moment have taken 150 million lives in a few hours.[7] George W. Bush had lived in his father's shadow all of his life: at Andover and Yale, in the oil business, and in politics. To crush Saddam Hussein, which George Herbert Walker Bush had declined to do, would afford him the rare opportunity to succeed where his father had failed.

George W. Bush's legacy was a nation impoverished by debt, besieged by doubt, struggling with the aftereffects of the worst recession since the Great Depression, and deeply engaged in military conflicts of our own choosing. His tin ear for traditional conservative values, his sanctimonious religiosity, his support for Guantánamo, CIA "renditions," and government snooping have eroded public trust in the United States at home and abroad. For eight years Bush made the decisions that put the United States on a collision course with reality. To argue that by taking the actions that he did, the president kept America safe is meretricious: the type of *post hoc ergo propter hoc* analysis that could justify any action, regardless of its impropriety. The fact is, the threat of terrorism that confronts the United States is in many respects a direct result of Bush's decision to invade Iraq in 2003.

Bush was the decider. But he did not wrestle with the details of policy, particularly foreign policy. By contrast, FDR and Eisenhower determined every nuance of America's global stance. Roosevelt had no foreign policy adviser. Harry Hopkins was the president's personal emissary with foreign leaders, and Secretary of State Cordell Hull was relegated to diplomatic housekeeping. Under Eisenhower, the director of the NSC staff was merely an assistant to the president, not the national security adviser, and Ike always kept Secretary of State John Foster Dulles on a short leash.

Bush took a different view of the chain of command. Not since the days of Warren Harding, Calvin Coolidge, and Herbert Hoover—the Republican hands-off-the-ship-of-state trinity of the 1920s—had a president been so detached from the detailed, day-to-day determination of policy alternatives. Bush saw issues in terms of black and white. There were no subtleties and no shades of gray. The war in Iraq was a biblical struggle of good versus evil—something from the pages of the Book of Revelation. His decision to bring democracy to Iraq was equally arbitrary and unilateral. Bush's religious fundamentalism often obscured reality. And he expected his cabinet to fall into line, not debate possible alternatives.

Bush was supported by a phalanx of subcabinet appointees, conservative in outlook, crisply articulate, and powerfully motivated to provide the intellectual justification for policies the president had decided upon: men like I. Lewis "Scooter" Libby, Paul Wolfowitz, Elliott Abrams, and Douglas Feith. Never before in American history has an administration come to power with a subcabinet echelon of likeminded ideologues, friends over the decades, dedicated to a common purpose, and armed with a game plan ready to be implemented. All had served in the administration of George H. W. Bush, and during the Clinton years formed a veritable government in exile. Their seminal policy statement had been drafted in 1991 by Wolfowitz and Libby, then serving as Secretary Dick Cheney's deputies in the Department of Defense, calling for American military superiority, emphasizing the power of the president to act unilaterally "when international reaction proves sluggish," and advocating preemptive attack against rogue states seeking to acquire weapons of mass destruction.[8]

In 1997, they, along with Cheney and Donald Rumsfeld, founded the Project for the New American Century, dedicated to increasing defense spending, challenging "regimes hostile to U.S. interests and values," and explicitly advocating regime change in Iraq. Had it not been for 9/11, their manifesto would have been little more than a footnote in intellectual history. But with the terrorist attack, the administration's second echelon dusted off their agenda, Bush signed on, and the direction of the administration was defined. When George W. Bush left office in 2009, the U.S. defense budget exceeded the combined defense budgets of every major country in the world and was clearly unsustainable.[9]

But the Bush administration was not without its accomplishments. Because of his Texas roots and his admirable freedom from racial prejudice, Bush was far more sympathetic than Clinton or his father to the plight of illegal immigrants, particularly those of Hispanic origin, and he pioneered the nation's first prescription drug program for seniors. No Child Left Behind may not be a perfect solution, but it reflected the president's concern to improve the nation's schools. And Bush led the international fight against AIDS and malaria. On the other hand, the Bush administration turned a blind eye to the growing environmental problems confronting the country and the globe, showed little interest in improving the nation's infrastructure, and downgraded federal regulatory activity, particularly in relation to Wall Street, noxious emissions, and mine safety.

This book relates the life of George W. Bush—his family heritage of investment banking and public service, his childhood in Midland, Texas (which by the late 1970s had the highest per capita income of any city in the United States), Andover, Yale, Harvard Business School, the Air National Guard, oil business, and the Texas Rangers baseball team. At Andover, George was a Big Man on Campus, and at Yale a solid fourth-quartile student. "We need good men in the bottom quartile," an Ivy League dean of admissions once said. "Men who won't jump out of a window if they get a D, and who might leave the university five million dollars."[10]

Bush's personal life was at times unglued. Out of college and at loose ends, he often drank too much and was no stranger to prohibited substances. A premature and unsuccessful run for Congress in 1978 caused him to hesitate about entering politics. His marriage to Austin librarian Laura Welch in 1977, and his reentry into life as a born-again Christian in 1985, led him back to the straight and narrow.[11] Bush's

embrace of evangelical Christianity helped anchor him in the fundamentalist culture of contemporary Texas, and facilitated his effort to
distance himself from his New England origins and Ivy League education. "The biggest difference between me and my father," George W.
was fond of saying, "is that he went to Greenwich Country Day and
I went to San Jacinto Junior High." [12]

Bush flaunted his Texas roots while profiting from his family's establishment connections. For a dozen years he struggled to make a go
of it in the oil business, and then struck pay dirt as the public face of
the Texas Rangers. Dressed in cowboy boots and blue jeans, chewing tobacco and speaking with a West Texas twang, Bush became the
J. R. Ewing of the American League West. In 1994 he rode his public
prominence into the governor's mansion, defeating incumbent Democrat Ann Richards in a banner year for Republicans across the country.

The Texas governorship is primarily a ceremonial post with virtually no executive responsibility—scholars of government consider it the
weakest in the nation—and Bush thrived as a consensus builder and
state cheerleader. Reelected overwhelmingly in 1998 in what had become the second most populous state in the nation, Bush was poised to
seek the Republican presidential nomination in 2000. In 1930, Franklin Roosevelt's overwhelming reelection as governor of New York,
then the nation's most populous state, made him the odds-on favorite
for the Democratic nomination in 1932. Bush's victory in Texas served
the same purpose. After overwhelming John McCain in the primaries, he was nominated virtually without opposition on the first ballot
at the Republican convention in Philadelphia. Vice President Al Gore
received the Democratic nomination in Los Angeles two weeks later,
also on the first ballot.

The election was Gore's to lose. The nation enjoyed unprecedented
peace and prosperity, and Bush's slogan of "compassionate conservatism" initially fell on deaf ears. The country suffered Clinton fatigue,
exacerbated by the Monica Lewinsky affair, but the president had survived impeachment efforts, and the issue seemed to be fading. If Gore
could mobilize the Democratic base, he seemed a shoo-in.

Whether it was overconfidence or incompetence, the Gore campaign got off to a shaky start. The selection of Connecticut's neoconservative Joe Lieberman as the party's vice presidential nominee found little resonance among African American and Latino voters, and Gore's failure to protect the party's left flank allowed third-party candidate Ralph Nader to siphon off almost three million traditional liberal voters. On the campaign trail, Gore appeared as lifeless as a wooden Indian. He refused to appear on the platform with President Clinton, and muffed his three debates with Bush.

Even with Gore's miscues and an almost flawless campaign waged by Bush and vice presidential nominee Dick Cheney, the election was a cliffhanger. When the dust settled, Bush won thirty states with 271 electoral votes, although Gore enjoyed a slight plurality in the popular vote. In Florida, which Bush ultimately won by 537 votes out of the almost six million that were cast, the Democrats were again asleep at the switch.

It was evident on election night that the Florida vote totals would be contested. The Republicans rushed more than one hundred lawyers to the state and spent over $12 million in legal fees. The Democrats made do with $3 million. The decision was fought out in the courts, and ultimately the Republicans prevailed. Given the complexities of the American electoral system, there can be no question that George W. Bush was legitimately installed as the nation's forty-third president. What is less clear is why President Clinton did not step in—as Ulysses Grant had done in the contested Hayes-Tilden election of 1876—to organize a special electoral commission to determine the electoral vote from Florida. It would have been a political solution to a political question and would have removed the taint that the Bush administration initially suffered from.

I was not permitted to interview George W. Bush for this book. Vice President Cheney set up an interview for me with the former president, but just before it was to take place I received a telephone call from Logan Walters, Bush's personal assistant. "The president does not wish to see you," said Walters. "You have written a book critical of his father, and because of that he does not wish to see you." Walters was correct. In 1992, I wrote *George Bush's War*, highly critical of George H. W. Bush's decision to commence the first Gulf War.*

Ironically, in 1997 the University of Toronto decided to award George H. W. Bush an honorary degree for his role in ending the Cold War. This decision was highly unpopular in Toronto, largely because of Bush's earlier role as head of the CIA, and over a thousand demonstrators appeared on campus to protest the award. Our university president, Rob Prichard, said, "Jean, you're going to introduce Bush at the convocation because you wrote a book about him."

"But the book is critical," I replied.

"Doesn't matter," said Prichard.

So I introduced former president Bush at the ceremony, and two dozen of my faculty colleagues stood up and walked out. That evening at dinner at the university president's house I gave Bush a copy of my book. He read it on the plane back to Houston, and several days later I received a two-page single-spaced letter from him. "I have read your book," said the former president. "Having done that I must tell you that I am surprised you were able to be so darn pleasant to me there at Toronto University . . . Your introduction negated the charges of 'murderer' heard outside and set a positive tone for my remarks." [13]

Jean Edward Smith

---

* Jean Edward Smith, *George Bush's War* (New York: Henry Holt, 1992).

CHAPTER ONE

The Wilderness Years

It's great to return to New Haven. My car was fol-
lowed all the way from the airport by a long line of
police cars with slowly rotating lights. It was just like
being an undergraduate again.

President George W. Bush

Yale Commencement, 2001

George W. Bush was born in New Haven, Connecticut, July 6, 1946. His father, George, known to the Bush family as Poppy, had just completed his freshman year at Yale. His mother, Barbara, then twenty-one, had cut short her studies at Smith to marry George. She described herself as a housewife. "I play tennis, do volunteer work and admire George Bush."[1] She also worked part-time in the Yale Co-op to pay for her cigarette habit.

At this point, the Bush family was not involved in politics. Prescott Bush, George W.'s grandfather, the family patriarch, lived in Greenwich, Connecticut, and was managing partner of Brown Brothers Harriman, the prestigious New York investment firm. Prescott and his wife, Dorothy, were staunch Republicans but watched from the sidelines. Prescott hated Franklin Roosevelt and Dorothy felt the same

Dorothy and Prescott Bush

about Eleanor. Yet their partisanship was tempered by a commitment to public service. For more than a decade Prescott had been moderator (presiding officer) of the Greenwich Town Meeting and a major fundraiser for charitable causes. After Pearl Harbor he headed national drives to raise money for the USO— the United Services Organization, which was charged with boosting the morale of the armed forces— and the American Birth Control League. (Birth control was illegal at the time in Connecticut.*) In 1947, he became treasurer of the first national fundraising campaign of Planned Parenthood. He also headed the United Negro College Fund in Connecticut, and was a member of the Yale Corporation (the university's governing body) from 1944 to 1956. An avid golfer, he had served as president of the United States Golf Association (USGA) in 1935.

In 1950, four years after George W.'s birth, Prescott Bush yielded to entreaties from Republican leaders in Connecticut and agreed to contest the United States Senate seat held by Democrat William Benton. Bush's role raising money for Planned Parenthood was used against him effectively during the campaign in Catholic precincts, and the election came down to the wire. When the votes were counted, Benton won by a mere 1,102 votes out of the more than 860,000 cast, a margin of .13 percent.[2]

Two years later Prescott Bush ran as an Eisenhower Republican for the vacant Senate seat of the late Brien McMahon. His Democratic

---

*   An 1879 Connecticut statute made it a crime for any person to use any drug, article, or instrument to prevent conception. It remained in effect until overturned by the United States Supreme Court in 1965 in the leading case of *Griswold v. Connecticut*, 381 U.S. 479, establishing a constitutional right to privacy.

opponent was Hartford congressman Abraham Ribicoff, described by *Time* magazine as "the best Democratic vote-getter in the state."[3] But Ike's coattails were remarkably long in 1952. Bush accompanied Eisenhower when he campaigned in the state, and introduced him to a crowd of six thousand at Yale wearing a raccoon coat, an Eli boater, and leading the audience in a rousing rendition of "Boola, Boola," the Yale fight song.[4]

When Senator Joseph McCarthy, then at the height of his popularity, visited Connecticut to campaign for the Republican ticket, Bush, as the head of the ticket, was dragooned into introducing him at a major GOP rally in Bridgeport. To his eternal credit, Prescott Bush did not succumb to the hysteria of the moment. After a few perfunctory remarks, Bush told the crowd that "in all candor, I must say that some of us, while we admire his objectives in his fight against Communism, we have very considerable reservations sometimes concerning the methods which he employs." Bush's remarks were greeted by a crescendo of boos and hisses. The state's GOP national committeeman rebuked him, and the *Hartford Courant* reported the story with a banner headline, "GOPs Boo Bush's Anti-Smear Stand."[5]

Prescott Bush was a man of principle—a fact the Eisenhower campaign did not forget. Ike carried Connecticut easily, and Bush beat Ribicoff by almost thirty thousand votes.[6] In Washington, Prescott Bush voted consistently with the liberal wing of the Republican Party. He was stalwart on civil rights and a staunch advocate of repealing the discriminatory provisions of the McCarran-Walter Immigration Act. Prescott Bush also became a favorite golfing partner of Ike (Bush was the better golfer), was reelected easily in 1956, and retired from the Senate in 1962. He died ten years later, when George W. was twenty-six.

Poppy Bush, George W.'s father, graduated from Yale in 1948. Like most returning servicemen, George H. W. Bush—who served as a Navy pilot during World War II—had followed an accelerated schedule and finished his studies in three years. Before the war at Andover, Poppy was a mediocre (C+) student, but excelled at athletics and in leadership: captain of the soccer team, captain of the baseball nine, president of the fraternity council, and president of his senior class. "George was not an intellectual, or even intellectually curious," said his roommate George "Red Dog" Warren. "He was more of an achiever, a doer."[7]

The commencement speaker at Poppy's Andover graduation was Secretary of War Henry L. Stimson, an Andover old boy, president of the board of trustees, the epitome of public service. Secretary of state under Herbert Hoover, secretary of war under William Howard Taft, and a lifelong Republican, Stimson had returned to Washington in 1940 to become FDR's secretary of war in Europe's darkest hour. Pearl Harbor was now six months past, and the military situation looked grim. Secretary Stimson focused on the war, but urged the boys graduating to complete their education before undertaking military service. The country would call them when they were needed, said Stimson. Poppy long remembered the elderly secretary's admonition that a soldier should be "brave without being brutal, self-confident without boasting, part of an irresistible might, but without losing faith in individual liberty."[8]

Poppy ignored Stimson's advice to wait. He had already been accepted at Yale, but four days after commencement, on his eighteenth birthday, he went to Boston and enlisted in the Navy. By the end of the year, sixty-eight of his Andover classmates had entered the service, but Poppy had been the first to join.[9] On August 6, 1942, George H. W. Bush reported for duty at the Navy's preflight training center at Chapel Hill, North Carolina. Ted Williams, the baseball immortal, was in the same flight class. Bush was commissioned an ensign and went into the Navy's air arm. He was assigned to the carrier USS *San Jacinto* in the Pacific,

George H. W. Bush as a Navy fighter pilot, 1943.

part of Admiral Marc Mitscher's Task Force 58. Bush flew Avenger torpedo planes from the flight deck of the *San Jacinto*, saw action off Marcus and Wake Islands, was shot down over Chichi-Jima near the Japanese home islands, and was rescued by an American submarine. Altogether, Poppy Bush flew fifty-eight combat missions and won the Distinguished Flying Cross, the Navy's second highest combat decoration.

The *San Jacinto* returned to the West Coast for refitting in December 1944, and Poppy spent his Christmas leave with the family in Connecticut. He and Barbara had been "secretly" engaged for a year and a half, but as he later wrote it was "secret to the extent that the German and Japanese high commands did not know about it."[10] They were married on January 6, 1945, in the Rye Presbyterian Church in Rye, New York. After the honeymoon, Bush reported to Norfolk and spent the remainder of the war on stateside training assignments. He was discharged September 18, 1945, and entered Yale as a freshman with the class of returning servicemen at the beginning of November.

Poppy and Barbara set up housekeeping in New Haven, and shared a house with two other families. The veterans on campus—there were eight hundred on the G.I. Bill in George's class—were intent on making up for lost time, and Bush was no exception. Majoring in economics and sociology, he finished in the top 10 percent of his class and graduated Phi Beta Kappa. But it was in athletics where Bush excelled. He led Yale to the NCAA College World Series championship games in Kalamazoo, Michigan, in both 1947 and 1948. (Yale lost to the University of California in 1947, and USC in 1948.) Poppy played first base, and according to the *Yale Daily News*, was "one of the flashiest fielding first basemen in collegiate circles."[11]

Franklin Roosevelt is alleged to have said that his greatest disappointment in life was not being invited to join Porcellian as a Harvard undergraduate, Porcellian being the most prestigious of Harvard's final clubs.[12] George H. W. Bush suffered no similar disappointment at Yale. While Skull and Bones is not precisely the same as Porcellian, admission to the secret society is considered by many to be the ultimate distinction for a Yale undergraduate. Bush, in fact, was tapped last of the fifteen men inducted into Skull and Bones in May 1947, making him the leader, or "king," of his class, after the biblical injunction that the last shall be first.*

George W.'s maternal forebears hail from backgrounds similar to the Bush family. His grandmother Dorothy, Prescott's wife, was the daughter of George Herbert Walker, a legendary Wall Street tycoon (G. H. Walker and Company), a millionaire many times over, and the financial enabler of the Bush family, much as Joe Kennedy was for several generations of Kennedys. Walker was a bare-knuckles competitor (Senator Harry Truman once castigated him for "rampaging greed"), and he passed that competitiveness on to his offspring. Walker's Point in Maine bears his name, as does the Walker Cup in amateur golf. An avid sportsman, Walker owned a stable of race horses, and preceded Prescott as president of the USGA in 1920. His daughter Dorothy, a graduate of Miss Porter's School in Farmington, Connecticut, and a postgraduate year mingling with European society in Paris, was a natural athlete and a gifted tennis player. Her uncle, Joseph Wear, was captain of the U.S. Davis Cup teams in 1928 and 1935, and Dorothy was runner-up in the first National Girls' Tennis Championship

George Herbert Walker

played in Philadelphia in 1918. She and Prescott were married at the Walker estate in Kennebunkport, Maine, in 1920, and lived a relatively modest life in Greenwich, raising five children.[13]

"We were well-off, but we weren't considered rich. Not by Greenwich standards," said George W.'s uncle, Prescott Bush, Jr. "Mother was a stickler for saving," Jonathan Bush, another uncle, re-

---

* "So the last will be first, and the first will be last; for many are called, but few chosen." *Matthew* 20:16.

members. "They sold
Cokes at the tennis club,
but we weren't allowed to
buy any there. We had to
get ours at home because
they were cheaper."[14]
Dotty, as she was called,
was also fervently reli-
gious and began each
morning by reading
personal devotions to
her family at breakfast.
"These were little moral
stories, three to five minutes, about how to live
your life," said "Bucky"
Bush, Dotty's youngest

George W. Bush at nine months with
his parents in New Haven.

son. "Every Sunday, the whole family went to church [Episcopal]. It
wasn't an option."[15]

When Prescott died in 1972, Dorothy wrote a tribute for his funeral.
"When he stood at the altar 51 years ago and promised to 'Keep thee
only unto her as long as you both shall live,' he was making a pledge to
God that he never forgot, and gave his wife the most joyous life that any
woman could experience."[16]

Barbara Pierce Bush, George W.'s mother, was cut from the same
cloth: competitive, outspoken, direct, and devoted to her husband and
family. Barbara was the third of four children of Marvin and Pauline Pierce, and grew up in the affluent Indian Village section of Rye,
New York. Her father, Marvin, was a senior executive on his way up
at the McCall Publishing Company (*McCall's* and *Redbook*)—and
would soon become president. He was a distant descendant of Franklin Pierce, the fourteenth president of the United States. Her mother,
Pauline, was the daughter of an Ohio Supreme Court justice and an as-
piring New York socialite who raised prize-winning lilies for the Garden Club of America. Barbara was a self-described tomboy growing

up, large-boned, athletic, scarcely as ladylike as her mother would have preferred. "I was five feet eight at the age of twelve and already weighed 148 pounds."[17] Before entering Smith, Barbara attended Ashley Hall in Charleston, South Carolina, played soccer and tennis, and was known to be able to hold her breath for two laps while swimming underwater. George (Poppy) met Barbara at a Christmas dance at the Round Hill Club in Greenwich during his senior year at Andover. They were drawn to each other immediately. "George recognized the type of person Barbara was when they first met," said his friend Fitzhugh Green. "He had seen the same characteristics in his mother: a woman of strong character and personality, direct and honest, one who cares about the outdoors and people, especially children, and is oriented to home life. Anyone who has met both mother and wife can see they belong in the same category."[18]

George W. Bush was two when the family moved from New Haven to Texas. When Poppy had indicated that he did not want to follow his father and maternal grandfather into the investment business in New York, Prescott Bush approached his Yale classmate and fellow Bonesman Neil Mallon ("Uncle Neil" to the family) to secure a trainee position for him with Dresser Industries—an oil conglomerate controlled by Brown Brothers Harriman, which Mallon headed. Prescott Bush not only sat on the board of Dresser Industries but was Mallon's chief adviser and consultant.[19] When Prescott asked, Mallon quickly found a trainee position for Poppy at the International Derrick and Equipment Company (Ideco), a Dresser subsidiary in Odessa, Texas. In 1948 the oil boom was just beginning, and Odessa, in the heart of the Permian Basin, was the epicenter. Dresser Industries and its subsidiaries were the nation's leading supplier of oil-drilling equipment, and Mallon saw Poppy as his protégé and possible successor. Poppy would be exposed to every aspect of the oil business from the bottom up, and Odessa was the best place to begin. "I've *always wanted* to live in Odessa, Texas," Barbara deadpanned when Poppy told her of his assignment.[20]

George H. W. Bush was scarcely starting from scratch in the oil business. He might be a trainee at Ideco earning $375 a month ($3,530 currently), but he was going to Texas with the full support of the Bush family network. "My stay in Texas was no Horatio Alger thing," Poppy later acknowledged, "but moving from New Haven to Odessa just about the day I graduated was quite a shift in lifestyle."[21]

The Bushes remained in Odessa for less than a year. Poppy worked long hours doing manual labor in Ideco warehouses, and in the spring of 1949 was transferred to California to learn the sales end of the business. The family lived in makeshift quarters in Whittier, Ventura, Bakersfield, and Compton, and George sold drill bits for Security Engineers Company, another Dresser subsidiary. Later he claimed he drove a thousand miles a week peddling his wares.

After a year in California, Bush was ordered back to West Texas, this time to Midland, where he worked for Ideco as a salesman, calling on oil companies headquartered in the city. Odessa was the blue-collar capital of the Permian Basin, the place where oil companies set up their warehouses and workshops—"the hardscrabble, hard-drinking, honky-tonk underbelly of West Texas" in the words of one knowledgeable observer.[22] Midland, thirty miles to the east, was where the company headquarters were located, where deals were signed and men had deep pockets—a white-collar oasis populated by geologists, engineers, doctors, lawyers, and young men from elite East Coast backgrounds who had come to make a fortune in the oil business. The average age in Midland in the 1950s was twenty-eight. Poppy later wrote that it was like "Yuppieland West."[23]

Using an FHA loan of $7,500, the Bushes bought a small frame house in a new housing development known as Easter Egg Row—so labeled because each of the houses was painted a different color. The Bush house was light blue, with a small yard, adjacent to two dozen similar houses all occupied by eager young couples with small children more or less the same age as George W. It was a time of optimism and financial speculation, and in late 1950 Poppy "caught the fever" as he called it. He resigned from his salaried job at Ideco and formed a partnership with his Easter Egg neighbor John Overby to buy oil leases on undeveloped West Texas property. "I really hate to see you go [from Dresser Industries]," Neil Mallon told Poppy, "but if I were your age, I'd be doing the same thing."[24]

The concept behind the Bush-Overby Oil Development Company was simple enough. Bush-Overby would lease the mineral rights on property adjacent to land where someone was planning to drill. If the drilling company struck oil, the value of the leases held by Bush-Overby would increase exponentially.[25] Overby was a West Texas veteran who knew land, and Bush undertook to raise the capital that would be necessary to purchase the leases. Back east, the Bush family endorsed the scheme. Herbert Walker, Jr., Poppy's uncle, rounded up $300,000 for the enterprise, Prescott kicked in an additional $50,000, as did *Washington Post* publisher Eugene Meyer.

The Bush-Overby partnership rocked along for three years, never making much money but never losing much, and in late 1953 Poppy and Overby threw in with Hugh Liedtke, a fellow Navy veteran— Amherst, University of Texas Law School, Harvard Business School— to found Zapata Petroleum Company and actually drill for oil. Liedtke, who would eventually found Pennzoil, was sometimes called the "boy genius of West Texas Oil." He believed that a vast reservoir of oil lay untapped in Coke County, some seventy miles east of Midland. It was an all-or-nothing gamble. Bush undertook to raise the $850,000 necessary to lease an eight-thousand-acre tract in what was known as the West Jameson field, and Liedtke handled the drilling. The results were spectacular. By the end of 1954, Zapata had drilled seventy-one wells in Coke County without hitting a dry hole. The field averaged 1,250 barrels a day, and eventually there would be 130 producing wells. The price of a single share of Zapata Oil went from 7 cents to $23. Poppy and Barbara were now on easy street.

The Bushes moved to a more desirable subdivision, and then in 1955 to an imposing, custom-built three-thousand-square-foot home with the first residential swimming pool in Midland. The house bordered on Cowden Park where the children played Little League baseball and soccer. George W. was joined by a sister, Robin, in 1949 (she died of leukemia at the age of four); a brother John Ellis (Jeb) in 1953; a second brother, Neil Mallon, in 1955; and a third, Marvin Pierce (named for Barbara's father), eighteen months later. George W.'s sole surviving sister, Dorothy, or Doro as she was called, was born in 1959. "Those were comfortable, carefree years," wrote George W. Bush. "On Friday nights, we cheered on the Bulldogs of Midland High. On Sunday mornings, we went to church. Nobody locked their doors. Years later, when I would speak about the American Dream, it was Midland I had in mind." [26]

As Zapata Oil prospered, Poppy was increasingly on the road pushing Zapata's interests. Raising the children became Barbara's responsibility. "Dad wasn't at home at night to play catch," Jeb remem-

The Bush family in Houston, Texas, in 1964. Neil, Jeb, and George W. behind. George H. W., Doro, Barbara, and Marvin sitting.

bered. "In a sense, it was a matriarchal family." [27] Barbara doled out the rewards, administered the punishment, and taught the children how to behave. In August 1959, with Zapata heavily engaged in offshore drilling, the family moved to Houston to be closer to the rigs in the Gulf of Mexico. George was enrolled at the nearby Kinkaid School, one of the most generously endowed prep schools in the South, and would complete the eighth and ninth grades there. Summers were spent at the equally upscale Longhorn Camp in the lake district northwest of Austin. George was popular at school, said Charles Sanders, a longtime faculty member at Kinkaid. "He was very good looking—he wasn't what I would call incredibly handsome, but he was popular." [28]

When it came time for high school, Poppy and Barbara decided that George should go to Andover. "I don't think George chose to go to Andover because his father went to Andover," his cousin John Ellis recalled. "I think George went to Andover because his parents said, 'You should

George W. as head cheerleader at Andover.

go to Andover, that's a good school, that's a good place to go.' "[29]

Andover was a shock to George W. The Kinkaid School had not prepared him for the academic rigor of one of the world's leading preparatory schools, and growing up in the openness of life in Texas had not readied him for the snooty, buttoned-up attitudes of an exclusive all-male school like Andover. Students wore coats and ties, class attendance and daily chapel were mandatory, schedules were rigid, meals were spartan, and competitive athletics provided almost the only emotional outlet. "Going to Andover was the hardest thing I did until I ran for president almost forty years later," George W. wrote in his memoirs.[30]

At Andover, Bush struggled academically and lacked his father's athletic prowess. "He used his audacity and chutzpah to entertain us," said his classmate Torbert Macdonald, son of a Democratic congressman from Massachusetts. "He was gregarious, verging on goofiness. Very sarcastic but without malice. He did not have a lot of respect for authority, so he was not afraid to mouth off. We called him 'The Lip.' There was a small party everywhere he went."[31]

Another classmate, Bill Semple, a star hockey player from Grosse Pointe, Michigan, recalled that George rose to a certain prominence in the class "for no ostensible reason. He was an attractive guy, very handsome, he had a presence to him, he had a cool look. He had a way about him, and he fit easily in. You know the cool guys. . . . He really came on as 'to the manor born.' "[32]

As at Groton and Exeter, athletics were mandatory at Andover. There were varsity teams in seventeen sports and students were expected to go out for everything whether they were talented or not.

"George and I played junior varsity basketball together and spent a lot of time warming the bench," said Conway Downing. "He could only dribble with his right hand, so he was useless on the court and I wasn't much better. And as a baseball player, unlike his father, George always seemed to have his foot in the bucket . . . and football . . . well, forget it."[33]

To compensate for his athletic ineptitude, Bush became a cheerleader and by his senior year was head cheerleader, which was something of a leadership position at Andover. Dwight Eisenhower, after he injured his knee playing football, became head cheerleader at West Point, Ronald Reagan was head cheerleader at Eureka College, and Franklin Roosevelt, who was a world-class sailor and gifted golfer but hopeless at baseball and football, was head cheerleader at Harvard his senior year. For Bush, it was a prestigious position at Andover, but not something he talked about back in Houston. Going to an all-boys school was already suspect to many of George's Texas buddies, said Randall Roden, a childhood friend from Midland. "They would have had a field day had they known he was head cheerleader. In Texas a cheerleader is a girl with big hair, a twirly skirt, and pretty legs."[34]

George graduated from Andover in June 1964, near the bottom of his class. Once again, he was popular among his classmates—the senior yearbook called him a BMOC (Big Man on Campus)—but his admission to university hung by a thread. His SAT score (1206) was unimpressive, his grades were poor, and he was not the outstanding athlete his father had been. So shaky were his credentials that Andover's dean of students suggested he not bother applying to Yale. Bush ignored the advice. He was a legacy many times over, and as the grandson of Prescott Bush his admission was more or less assured. (In 1964, few Yalies stood higher in New Haven than Senator Prescott Bush—who was often referred to as the "Senator from Yale.") George W. assumed he was entitled to admission.* He told his classmate Robert Birge that

---

* In the early 1960s when George W. Bush applied, the admissions office at Yale accepted well over 50% of the legacy applicants. That often resulted in freshman classes composed of at least a quarter of alumni sons—almost three times that of Harvard and Princeton. The pattern

what irritated him about "Ivy League Liberals" was their sense of guilt about being born to privilege.[35] And Bush was indeed admitted that spring, along with twenty-nine of his classmates. Forty-nine were off to Harvard, twenty to Princeton, and a smattering to Columbia, Dartmouth, and Brown. "Leaving Andover," said Bush, "was like ridding myself of a straitjacket."[36]

Yale was scarcely more congenial. A rough-edged Texan among preppies, and a privileged preppy among the highly motivated young men from the nation's high schools who had been admitted to Yale, Bush found intellectual life a burden. He took gut courses, coasted by with gentleman Cs, and earned a reputation as a hard-drinking, good-time guy who loved to raise hell. Later he would tell family members that he didn't learn "a damn thing at Yale."[37] After graduation he never looked back. He did not attend class reunions, did not contribute to Yale's annual alumni fund drives, and in 1993 submitted only his name and a post office box address for his twenty-fifth reunion yearbook. He did not return to the campus in New Haven until 2001 when his daughter Barbara graduated and he was awarded an honorary degree.

George W.'s cultivated anti-intellectualism stems in many respects from his four years at Yale. He detested what he considered the "intellectual snobbery" on campus and placed himself at the center of those who sought to make the college years enjoyable. "George was a student of people, not subjects," said his classmate Robert McCallum. "He knew everything about everyone and you could see him making a conscious effort to learn about others. He decided pretty early on to be people smart, not book smart."[38]

In his sophomore year, George pledged Delta Kappa Epsilon, one of six fraternities at Yale, and was elected president his junior year. DKE

---

changed when Kingman Brewster became president, and by the late 1960s Yale was more or less in step with its Ivy League compeers. "I do not intend to preside over a finishing school on Long Island Sound," Brewster said shortly after assuming office. George W. Bush's three younger brothers were not admitted to Yale, although their legacy credentials were identical to his and their secondary school records were at least as good if not better. Geoffrey Kabaservice, "The Birth of a New Institution: How two Yale presidents and their admissions directors tore up the 'old blueprint' to create a modern Yale," *Yale Alumni Magazine*, December 1999.

was regarded as a less-
than-sober jock house
with the longest bar in
New Haven, possibly in
Connecticut, and its par-
ties on football weekends
were legendary. But fra-
ternity life was in serious
decline at Yale by the mid-
1960s. Less than 15 per-
cent of the student body
belonged, and unlike the
frat houses at most uni-
versities, students did not
live there.[39] Bush was also
among the fifteen mem-
bers of his class tapped for
Skull and Bones, which

George W. at Yale

was also in decline, but he was never immersed in the society as his father and grandfather had been. Each member of Skull and Bones was
given a special nickname. George's was "Temporary." "I didn't take it
all that seriously," he later told Walter Isaacson of *Time* magazine.[40]

On campus, Bush developed a reputation for coasting, not because
he was less bright than his classmates, but because he cultivated a dis-
dain for scholarship. His habitual smirk is a by-product. In a story
George W. often told on himself, Calvin Hill, the great running back
for Yale and the Dallas Cowboys, who was a DKE fraternity brother,
once spotted him at the beginning of the school year shopping for
courses. "Hey! George Bush is in this class," Hill shouted to his team-
mates. "This is the one for us."[41]

The 1960s were years of change on university campuses, and Yale
was no exception. Women were admitted to the all-male bastions of
the Ivy League, admission standards were tightened, the number of
legacies drastically reduced, and for the first time preppies became a
minority at Princeton, Harvard, and Yale. Culturally it was a time of

Woodstock, long hair, and student protest. "When we were freshmen," one of Bush's classmates recalled, "we would ask seniors to buy liquor for us. When we became seniors, we would ask freshmen to buy marijuana for us." [42]

The spring of 1968, George's senior year, was a time of unprecedented turmoil. On March 31, following the Vietcong's Tet Offensive, Lyndon Johnson shocked the country by announcing he would not seek reelection. Johnson also said he had halted the bombing of North Vietnam. [43] Several days later Dr. Martin Luther King was assassinated in Memphis. Demonstrations swept the country. In Los Angeles and Washington, D.C., the demonstrations turned violent. On college campuses students took to the streets. Yale was in the forefront, except that in New Haven student protest focused on the death of Dr. King and the war in Vietnam. Unlike student unrest at Berkeley, Columbia, and Cornell—where the issues pertained primarily to internal university matters—the demonstrations at Yale were triggered by events in the nation at large. The assassination of Dr. King was the precipitating factor, but the war in Vietnam was in many respects the root cause.

For the Class of 1968 the issue of Vietnam was particularly acute. Their student deferments would soon expire and the reality of combat was upon them. "If you didn't get into the Reserve or the Guard, or get a deferment, or become a conscientious objector, or go to Canada, then you were headed for downtown Da Nang," said George W.'s classmate Mark Soler. [44]

Like all of his classmates, Bush had registered for the draft when he turned eighteen, and had been classified II-S, the normal student deferment. At Yale he mostly avoided discussions about Vietnam, did not participate in student demonstrations, and kept his views on the war to himself. In Houston, during the vacation between his junior and senior years, he often talked with friends about what would happen when his student deferment expired. As his friend Doug Hannah recalled, "George and I used to talk all the time that there has to be a better alternative than being a lieutenant in the Army." [45] On the other hand, Poppy Bush had just been elected to Congress from Houston, and was a staunch supporter of the war effort. George W. was torn. As his DKE fraternity brother Roland Betts put it, "he felt that in order not to derail his father's political career he had to be in military service of some kind."[46]

Looking back on that period thirty years later, Bush summarized his feelings as follows—an insight that is particularly pertinent given more recent history. "I knew I would serve," he wrote in 1999. "Leaving the country was not an op-

In the Texas Air National Guard

tion for me; I was too conservative and too traditional." Bush said his inclination was to support the government and the war until that cause was proven wrong, "and that only came later, as I realized *we could not explain the mission, had no exit strategy, and did not seem to be fighting to win.*"[47] [Emphasis added.]

The record of George W.'s military service is murky and controversial. What is clear is that at Christmas of his senior year his father suggested the Texas Air National Guard as a possible option. There was a waiting list of over 100,000 men hoping to get into the Guard and over 150 pilot applicants for the Texas unit. Nevertheless, Poppy told George W. to consult with his friend from the oil industry Sid Adger, a former pilot well connected with the Guard. Adger was a mover and shaker on the Houston social scene and the first stop on an underground railroad that quietly moved the sons of privilege from the Selective Service system to safe havens in the Texas Guard.[48]

George W. followed Poppy's advice and told Adger of his interest in flying, at which point Adger placed a call to Ben Barnes, speaker of the Texas House of Representatives, the second stop on the underground railroad. Barnes, although a Democrat, required little coaxing.

When told that Congressman Bush's son needed a spot in the Texas Air National Guard, he promptly called Brigadier General James M. Rose, who commanded the Air Guard, who in turn called Lieutenant Colonel Walter Staudt, commander of the 147th Fighter Group at Ellington Air Force Base in Houston—stations three and four on the underground railroad. According to the later testimony of Major General Thomas Bishop, who was the overall commander of the Texas National Guard in 1968, the Guard was full at that time and there were no vacancies.[49] Nevertheless, a place was found for George W. in the 147th. There is no question that Bush received preferential treatment. There is also no question that Poppy did not contact anyone on his son's behalf. He knew how things worked in Houston and simply left it to others.

George W. was not alone in receiving preferential treatment. The 147th Fighter Group was known locally as a "champagne unit" because of its privileged roster. In addition to Bush, the unit included the sons of Senator John Tower and Governor John Connally, two sons of future senator Lloyd Bentsen, two of oilman Sid Adger, and a grandson of billionaire H. L. Hunt. Clint Murchison, Jr., the owner of the Dallas Cowboys, placed seven of his players in the unit to avoid Vietnam. Admission to the 147th, as one scholar of the period has written, "was like getting into Yale as a legacy."[50]*

George W. Bush's brief military career provides a case study in preferential treatment. After completing six weeks of basic training at Lackland Air Force Base in San Antonio in August 1968, he was discharged as an enlisted man in the Air Guard and immediately recommended for a direct commission as a second lieutenant and for flight training to commence in November. In the interim he was granted a two-month leave of absence to work in the Florida senatorial campaign of Congressman Edward Gurney, a close friend of Poppy. It was the military equivalent of a trifecta. Direct commissions in 1968 were reserved primarily for doctors because the Air Guard needed

---

* General Colin Powell offers a different perspective. "I am angry that so many sons of the powerful and well-placed managed to wangle slots in Reserve and National Guard units," Powell wrote in his memoirs. "Of the many tragedies of Vietnam, this raw class discrimination strikes me as the most damaging to the ideal that all Americans are created equal." *My American Journey* (New York: Ballantine Books, 1995), 148.

flight surgeons. To become a second lieutenant ordinarily required either completion of Officer Candidate School (OCS), eighteen months of prior military service, or four years of ROTC in college—none of which Bush had. Assignment to flight training, which was expensive, was normally reserved for those with prior experience or who had a background in navigation, mathematics, physics, and electronics. On the Air Force qualifying exam, Bush had scored in the 25th percentile for pilot aptitude—the absolute minimum for acceptance. And to receive a two-month furlough at the height of the war in Vietnam to work on a political campaign in Florida was truly extraordinary.

When Bush reported for flight training at Moody Air Force Base in Valdosta, Georgia, on November 25, 1968, he was the only guardsman in his class. The other sixty-four members of the Consolidated Pilot Training Program were experienced fliers from the Air Force and the Navy, as well as a sprinkling of military men from NATO allies. "Basically we knew George was there on a special deal," said his classmate David Hanifl. "It was unheard of that a taxpayer would be paying that much to train someone. Normally you don't send someone who is totally green."[51]

Despite his preferential treatment, George W. did well in flight training. "Everybody knew who he was and who his father was," said Norman Dotti, a fellow officer. "They knew he was there from the Texas Air National Guard. If anybody felt negative about that, nobody said anything. He was certainly competent. He didn't put on airs."[52] Ralph Anderson, another classmate, told the *Los Angeles Times* that Bush was "a real outgoing guy, a good pilot, and lots of fun. He was a leader. He took things on and got them done. I liked him a lot."[53] Jim Wilkes, his flight instructor, agreed. "I gave then-Lieutenant Bush two of his check rides, including his final instrument and navigation check," said Wilkes. "He was an excellent pilot and so graded."[54] Colonel Maurice Udell, who later taught Bush to fly jets, said much the same. "I would rank him in the top five percent of the pilots I knew," Udell told author Kitty Kelley. "And in the thinking department, he was in the top one percent. He was very capable and tough as a boot."[55]

There is no question that Bush stood out during his year of flight training at Valdosta. When President Richard Nixon dispatched an Air

Force plane to fly George W. to Washington for a date with his daughter Tricia, it was evident that he was moving in different circles than his
classmates. George and Tricia did not hit it off. "We went to dinner,"
Bush told *The Dallas Morning News* many years later. "It wasn't a very
long date." [56]

When George W. graduated from flight training in December
1969—only twenty-eight of the original sixty-five members of his class
made it—the commencement speaker was his father. Poppy was billed
as a former war hero and Navy pilot, and his record in Congress as a
staunch supporter of the administration's policy in Vietnam was widely
advertised. After speaking to the assembly, a beaming George H. W.
Bush pinned the silver wings of a pilot on the uniform of his son.

Following completion of his year of flight training at Moody Air
Force Base in Valdosta, George W. returned to Houston for an additional six months of active duty learning to fly F-102 interceptors, a top-
of-the-line fighter jet. Bush proved a gifted pilot and became a poster
boy for the Texas Air Guard. After his first solo flight in an F-102 in
March 1970, the Guard issued a glowing press release with a dazzling
photo:

> George Walker Bush is one member of the younger generation
> who doesn't get his kicks from pot or hashish or speed. Oh, he gets
> high all right, but not from narcotics. . . . As far as kicks are concerned,
> Lt. Bush gets his from the roaring afterburner of the F-102. [57]

Bush completed jet training on June 23, 1970, and was released
from active duty at that point. He would become a weekend warrior in
the Guard, reporting for drill once a month, and spending two weeks
each summer on active duty. His final performance report, written by
his commanding officer, Lieutenant Colonel Jerry B. Killian, called
Bush "a dynamic, outstanding young officer. He clearly stands out as a
top notch fighter interceptor pilot. Lt. Bush is possessed of sound judgment, yet is a tenacious competitor and an aggressive pilot. . . . He is a
natural leader with outstanding disciplinary traits and an impeccable
military bearing." [58]

After his release from active duty, Bush went to work in his father's 1970 senatorial campaign against Democrat Lloyd Bentsen (Bentsen had defeated incumbent Ralph Yarborough in the Democratic primary). George W.'s principal duty was to serve as Poppy's surrogate at lesser speaking engagements around the state. "The funniest part of the whole thing was watching George try to be his father," said his friend Doug Hannah. "Talk like him, picking up the mannerisms. He ultimately did it perfectly." [59]

Freed from his military duties, George W. moved into a one-bedroom apartment at the hilariously named Chateaux Dijon, an exclusive, garden-style apartment complex with 353 units fanning out around six swimming pools. The Chateaux was the favorite playground for Houston's upwardly mobile young professionals. "The scene around the pool was awe inspiring," a friend of Bush told *U.S. News & World Report*. "Lots and lots of great-looking girls and people barbecuing and drinking beers." [60] Bush drank heavily and partied heavily, but no more than anyone else. "It was our social niche," said another friend, like a college campus without classes or deans or proctors. [61]

Election day in November 1970 was a day of profound disappointment for the Bushes. Lloyd Bentsen, whose World War II combat record rivaled that of Poppy, won handily with 53.5 percent of the vote. Like Yarborough six years earlier, Bentsen nailed George H. W. Bush as an Ivy League import out of touch with the concerns of ordinary Texans. Richard Nixon, who had encouraged Bush to run, later said that Poppy was a poor campaigner. "You can see it all over him. It's not that he doesn't like people; it's just that he is not very comfortable out there on the stump trying to connect with them." [62]

Nixon rescued Poppy by appointing him United States ambassador to the United Nations, and elevating him to cabinet rank. Bush and Barbara moved to New York, took up diplomatic quarters at the Waldorf-Astoria, and flourished in the cosmopolitan setting. "I would pay to do this job," Barbara told a reporter for the *Washington Evening Star*. [63]

Poppy's defeat and his move to New York marked the beginning of George W.'s descent into the wilderness, what he later called his "no-

madic years." He applied for admission to the University of Texas Law
School but was rejected. "I am sure young Mr. Bush has all the many
amiable qualities you describe," the dean informed one of the VIPs
who had recommended George, "and so will find a place at one of
the many fine institutions around the country. But not the University
of Texas."[64] George W.'s free pass had expired, his entitlement lapsed,
and his life cratered. "I don't think he was used to not doing what he
wanted to do," said his mother.[65] With no job and no school, George
idled his time around the pools at Chateaux Dijon, living off the res-
idue of the educational trust fund his grandfather Prescott had established for him. "There are some people who, the minute they get out of
college, know exactly what they want to do," Bush said later. "I did not.
And it didn't bother me. That's just the way it was."[66]

As the saying goes, the devil finds work for idle hands, and George
W. was no exception. He began to drink too much, smoke substances
other than tobacco, and party too often. Alcohol, drugs, and unpro-
tected sex can cause a myriad of problems, and Bush suffered accordingly.* His flying skills deteriorated and his girlfriend became
pregnant. Using his connections once again, Bush arranged for her
to have a D&C [dilation and curettage]—often a euphemism for an
early-term abortion—at Houston's Twelve Oaks Hospital, and broke
off the relationship.† According to friends, he did not visit the young
woman in the hospital and never saw her again.[67]

By the late spring of 1971, Poppy and Barbara were sufficiently concerned about the dissolute life George W. was leading at the Chateaux
Dijon that they convinced him to move to more modest quarters in a
garage apartment behind the house of family friends in a residential
neighborhood of Houston. They also arranged for a roommate who

---

*   "Dad was shy," said George W. Bush. "We never had 'the talk.' He never told me to wear a
raincoat [condom] or anything." "In the Fishbowl with Little George," *Chicago Tribune*, May 1,
1992.

†   In 1971 the Texas statute prohibiting abortion was one of the most restrictive in the nation
and was not overturned until the Supreme Court's decision in *Roe v. Wade*, 410 U.S. 113, a Texas
case, two years later. Given the statutory prohibition, a D&C, which a doctor might perform after
diagnosing a "miscarriage," was often used to terminate a pregnancy.

could keep an eye on him: Donald Ensenat, a Yale classmate of the younger Bush who had worked on Poppy's senatorial campaign.[68]

George W. also needed a job, and Poppy convinced another old friend, Robert H. Gow (Yale '55), to hire him as a management trainee at Stratford of Texas, a global agricultural firm that Gow headed. Gow had succeeded Poppy as president of Zapata Off-Shore Drilling, and had founded Stratford in 1966. The family ties between the Bushes and the Gows were deep, going back to Yale, where Gow had roomed with Bush's cousin Ray Walker. And like the Walkers and the Bushes, he was also Skull and Bones. Stratford of Texas was located in downtown Houston's financial district and George W.'s duties were vague. "I'm now wearing a coat and tie and selling chicken shit," he joked to friends.[69] Bush remained at Stratford for almost a year, but quit abruptly in early 1972 saying he was bored. Later he called it a "stupid coat-and-tie job" that he considered beneath him.[70]

Bush was also having trouble in the cockpit. He continued to report for scheduled drills at Ellington, but on several occasions was unable to land his F-102 on the first attempt. In February 1972 he was relieved from flying the sophisticated F-102 and shifted back to a basic T-33 training jet. His last recorded flight was April 17, 1972. After that date, George W. Bush dropped from the Guard's radar screen. It has been suggested by more than one writer that Bush's abrupt departure from flying coincided with the Air Force's introduction of drug testing for flight crews.[71]

Once again the senior Bush came to the rescue. Winton Blount, Nixon's postmaster general, had resigned from the cabinet to run for the Senate in Alabama against Democratic incumbent John Sparkman, who had been Adlai Stevenson's running mate in 1952. Blount's campaign was being run by Poppy's former aide and political assistant Jimmy Allison. Bush called Allison from his office at the United Nations and asked him to put George W. to work. "He's killing us in Houston," Poppy said. "Take him down there and let him work on the campaign." As Allison's wife, Linda, recalled, the tenor of Poppy's message was, "George W. is in and out of trouble seven days a week, and would you take him down there with you."[72]

Bush departed for Alabama in early May 1972. He was hired by the Blount campaign for $900 a month as a campaign coordinator, and was told to stay in contact with the Republican campaign managers in each of Alabama's sixty-seven counties and distribute campaign material. Fellow campaign workers remember him as someone who would come to work around noon, prop his cowboy boots on a desk, and start bragging about how much he had drunk the night before. "He just struck me as a guy who really had an idea of himself as very much a child of privilege," remembered Blount's nephew, C. Murphy Archibald. "He wasn't operating by the same rules as everyone else."[73]

In September Bush applied for a nonflying transfer from his Reserve unit in Houston to the 187th Tactical Reconnaissance Group in Montgomery. His request was approved, yet there is no record that George W. ever reported for duty. "I'm dead certain he didn't show up," Colonel William Turnipseed, who commanded the 187th told *The Boston Globe*. "Had he reported in, I would have had some recollection and I do not. I had been in Texas, done my flight training there. If we had a first lieutenant from Texas I would have remembered."[74] Other than the approval of his transfer to the 187th, neither the Texas nor the Alabama Guard has any record of George W. Bush reporting for duty in 1972.

In November, Nixon carried Alabama with 72 percent of the vote, while Sparkman trounced Blount by almost the same margin. Ticket splitting in the South was now a common phenomenon. After the election, George W. returned to Houston, but again there is no record of his reporting back to the Texas Air Guard as he was required to do. On his annual efficiency report covering the period from May 1, 1972, to April 30, 1973, his commanding officer, Lieutenant Colonel William D. Harris, noted that "Lt. Bush has not been observed at this unit during the period of this report."[75]

Following his reelection that autumn, President Nixon asked George H. W. Bush to leave his post at the United Nations, where he had performed ably, and assume the chairmanship of the Republican National Committee in Washington. The Watergate scandal was unfolding, and the president needed a fresh face to head the party. Poppy and Barbara moved to Washington, and the children joined them for Christmas. One evening, George W., who was twenty-six, took his sixteen-year-old brother, Marvin, with him to visit the Allisons, who also lived in Washington. The Christmas cheer flowed freely and the two were soon intoxicated. Driving home erratically, George W. mowed down a neighbor's garbage cans before turning into his parents' driveway. He staggered into the house drunk and boisterous, and was confronted by his father. When Poppy began to chastise him, George W. challenged him to a fight. "You want to go mano a mano right here?" [76]

Tempers cooled, but Poppy recognized that W needed help. Friends of the Bushes say the family's frustration with George W. was no secret. "I remember the old man saying he didn't ever think young George would get it together," said syndicated columnist Cody Shearer.[77] For the third time since W's graduation from Yale, Poppy intervened, this time placing a call to his friend John White, the former tight end of the AFL champion Houston Oilers. White and his Oiler teammate the legendary Ernie Ladd had founded an inner-city youth program in Houston designed to mentor underprivileged boys. Known by its acronym PULL (Professional United Leadership League) the organization brought leading professional athletes to blighted neighborhoods to provide examples for minority kids. George H. W. Bush had been a major fundraiser for PULL, and in 1973 served as the organization's honorary chairman. "John White was a good friend of [George H. W.] Bush," said Muriel Henderson, a senior counselor at PULL. "He told us that the father wanted George W. to see the other side of life. He asked John if he would put him in there." [78]

Bush commenced work at PULL in January 1973 and remained for seven months. He was thrust into the heart of Houston's black belt, working daily with underprivileged kids seventeen and under. "My job gave me a glimpse of a world I had never seen," he wrote many years later. "It was tragic, heartbreaking, and uplifting all at the same time. I saw a lot of poverty. . . . I saw children who could not read and were way behind in school. I also saw good and decent people working to try to help lift their kids out of their terrible circumstances." [79] By all accounts Bush acquitted himself admirably. "He was a super,

super guy," Ernie Ladd recalled. "Any white guy that showed up on McGowen Street was going to get caught in some tough situations . . . but he handled it well. He had a way with people. They didn't want him to leave."[80]

Various authors, including Kevin Phillips, have suggested that George W.'s stint at PULL was in part a plea bargain that Poppy negotiated with a sympathetic magistrate in Houston.[81] Rather than face charges for possession, it was agreed that W would do community service in the ghetto. PULL was located in the headquarters building of the probation office for Harris County (Houston), and according to Althia Turner, John White's administrative assistant, "George had to sign in and out. I remember his signature was a hurried cursive. But he wasn't an employee. He was not a volunteer either. John [White] said he had to keep track of George's hours because George had to put in a lot of hours because he was in trouble."[82] Fred Maura, a close friend of White, confirmed as much to the Knight Ridder news service in 2004. "John didn't say what kind of trouble 43 was in—just that he had done something and he [John] made a deal to take him as a favor to 41 to get some funding."[83]

In the spring of 1973, George W. received word that he had been admitted by Harvard Business School for the class entering in September. Bush had applied just prior to Christmas in the normal manner but did not inform his parents. In the early 1970s, Harvard Business School accepted only one in four applicants, and he did not want to be embarrassed if he was turned down. Before accepting Harvard's offer, George W. discussed the matter with John White, who had become somewhat of a mentor. "John encouraged me to go," Bush recalled. " 'If you really care about these kids as I think you do [said White], why don't you go and learn more and then you can really help.' "[84]

Before matriculating at Harvard in September 1973, Bush requested a discharge from the Texas Air National Guard. His request was approved on September 18, and he received an honorable discharge one month later. There is no evidence that he received preferential treatment in the approval of his discharge. On the other hand, there is also no evidence that he fully complied with his statutory obligation to serve six years in the active Reserve.

George W. Bush brought the same swagger to Cambridge that he had carried to New Haven. "He was trying to figure out what to do with his life," said his classmate Al Hubbard. "He was there to get prepared, but he didn't know for what."[85] Bush habitually wore cowboy boots and a flight jacket to class, and lived off-campus in a one-bedroom bachelor pad near Central Square in Cambridge (in the vicinity of MIT). Professors remember him as an unpretentious, good middle-of-the-road student, but without gravitas.[86] Professor Yoshi Tsurumi remembers that George W. was exceptionally opinionated. "This has nothing to do with politics," said Tsurumi. "Most business students are conservative [but] unlike most of the others in class, George Bush came across as totally lacking in compassion, with no sense of history. Even among Republicans his kind was rare. He had no shame about his views, and that's when the rest of the class started treating him like a clown . . . I did not judge him to be stupid, just spoiled and undisciplined."[87]

George W.'s record at Harvard was uninspiring. "He had fifty-three job interviews with Fortune 500 companies," said fellow Harvard Business School graduate Bill White, but no job offer. "He is the only Harvard Business School graduate that I know of who ever left there without a goddamned job."[88]

George W. Bush's years after Yale were scarcely memorable. "When I was young and irresponsible, I behaved young and irresponsibly," Bush acknowledged on the eve of his run for the presidency. "I made some mistakes years ago."[89] That pretty well says it all.

CHAPTER TWO

Turnaround

I'm damn serious, pal. In our family, if you go to war,
we want you completely on our side.

George W. Bush

Geoge W. Bush made a virtue of necessity. With no job offer at Harvard, he returned to Midland to seek his future in the oil business. "The barriers to entry in the industry were low," he wrote, "and I loved the idea of starting a business on my own. I made up my mind: I was headed back to Texas."[1] In his two memoirs, and in early biographies, his decision to return to Midland is depicted as his absolute, unfettered preference. "West Texas was in my blood."[2] The fact is he had little choice.

In Midland, Bush moved into a modest alley apartment behind the house of family friends, drove a beat-up five-year-old Oldsmobile Cutlass, and latched on to Poppy's old associates in the oil business. Friends of his father saw to it that he was admitted to the Petroleum Club and the Midland Country Club, and provided him with a rent-free storage room in a downtown office building that he could use as a business address. As Poppy had done twenty-five years earlier, George W. began his career in the oil business as a landman, someone who researched land titles and mineral rights in county courthouses and then went door-to-door representing oil companies trying to lease those rights from the owners.

The price of West Texas crude was soaring in the mid-1970s, touched off by the OPEC oil embargo of 1973, and Bush was earning upward of $100 a day working freelance as a landman. It was an ideal way for him to enter the oil business. "You get a lot of exposure without putting up a lot of money," said his childhood friend Robert McCleskey.[3]

Bush worked hard and partied hard. Vacationing at the family compound in Kennebunkport over the Labor Day weekend in 1976, he was arrested one evening for driving under the influence. He had been out drinking beer with friends and was spotted by a local constable driving erratically. "When I failed the straight-line walk," said Bush, "he took me to the station. I was guilty and told the authorities so." W was fined $150 and his driving privileges in Maine were suspended for a year. Much has been made of Bush's DUI conviction, and he has acknowledged that he made a serious mistake. "I was fortunate I hadn't done any harm to my passengers, other drivers, or myself."[4]

Back in Midland at the beginning of 1977, Bush had done sufficiently well as a landman to organize his own company, Arbusto (Spanish for "bush") Energy, to invest in leases for himself—a move similar to Poppy's early partnership with John Overby. Initially Arbusto was simply a private holding company that allowed Bush to dabble in mineral rights on his own account and did not begin active operations as a corporate investment vehicle until March 1979.[5]

As Bush continued his apprenticeship in the oil business in Midland, an unexpected political opportunity arose. On July 6, 1977—his thirty-first birthday—Congressman George Mahon, the dean of the House of Representatives and chairman of the Appropriations Committee for the last thirteen years, announced his intention to retire. Mahon had been elected to Congress from West Texas in the Democratic landslide of 1934, and had served for twenty-two consecutive terms. He was now seventy-seven and still unbeatable at the polls. But he was ready to step down. Mahon's decision sent shock waves across the nineteenth congressional district, a sprawling expanse of seventeen West Texas counties including the cities of Lubbock, Midland, and Odessa. Nominally Democratic, the area was staunchly conservative, and with Mahon out of the picture the Republicans had a fighting chance to capture the seat.

The obvious GOP candidate was forty-eight-year-old Jim Reese, former mayor of Odessa, an ultraconservative Republican who had won 45 percent of the vote against Mahon in 1976. The most likely Democratic candidate was thirty-five-year-old state senator Kent Hance from Lubbock. Both Reese and Hance had deep Texas roots, mingled easily with the country folk, and spoke with a pronounced Texas twang. But two weeks after Mahon revealed his decision to retire, George W. Bush stunned the local Republican and Democratic establishments by announcing his candidacy. "Out of nowhere—and I mean nowhere—comes George Bush," said V. Lance Tarrance, a Republican pollster in Texas.[6]

"My friends were a little surprised why I was doing this," Bush later told *Texas Monthly*, "but at the time, Jimmy Carter was president and he was trying to control natural gas prices, and I felt that the United States was headed toward European-style socialism."[7] The fact that Reese and Hanse were equally committed to resisting "European-style socialism" suggests that Bush's decision was somewhat more personal.

George W. Bush was a political animal—from a family of political animals. He had already worked in three of his father's campaigns in Texas: twice for the United States Senate and once for the House. He had been on the campaign staffs of Republican senatorial candidates in Florida and Alabama, and in 1976 had headed Gerald Ford's search for convention delegates from the nineteenth congressional district in the Texas primary. "The campaign lifestyle was a perfect fit for me," Bush wrote many years later. "I enjoyed moving around and meeting new people. I thrived on the intensity and competition of the races. . . . I hadn't planned it this way, but by the time Congressman Mahon retired, I was a relatively seasoned political operative. . . . I was having my first experience with the political bug, and it was biting hard."[8]

Ten days after Bush announced his candidacy, his longtime friends

Joe and Jan O'Neill invited him for a backyard cookout at their home in Midland. They also invited another old friend, Laura Welch, a Midland native who was working as a school librarian in Austin. The O'Neills were matchmaking. Bush was thirty-one and at loose ends. "I don't think he was shopping around," said Joe O'Neill, but "he was at an age when it was getting awkward to be a bachelor."[9] Laura Welch, who was four months shy of thirty-one, was also unattached. "The timing was crucial," noted Dr. Charles Younger, another old friend. "Both of them were at a crossroads in their lives. He was ready to settle down and think about a family and have a decent lady to make a life with. Call it fate, destiny, whatever, but they came along and crossed at the right time."[10]

George and Laura were unacquainted, although they had grown up within ten blocks of each other in Midland. They had gone to different elementary schools, but had been in the seventh grade together at San Jacinto Junior High before the Bushes moved to Houston. They had also lived briefly in the Chateaux Dijon in Houston at the same time when Laura was working in the city. But they had not met. "I had a vague memory of George from the seventh grade, almost twenty years before," Laura recalled. "I knew that his dad had run for the Senate and lost in 1970, and I assumed that George would be very interested in politics, while I was not."[11]

Both Laura and George were swept away that evening. "She was gorgeous," wrote Bush. "She had stunning blue eyes and moved so gracefully. She was intelligent and dignified, with a warm and easy laugh. If there is love at first sight, this was it."[12] For Laura it was much the same. "I loved how he made me laugh. Our childhoods overlapped so completely, and our worlds were so intertwined, it was as if we had known each other our whole lives. I knew in my heart that he was the one."[13]

Laura was the only child of Harold and Jenna Welch of Midland. Her father was a prosperous developer and home builder, and her mother was active in local civic organizations. Laura was a popular, straight-A student in high school who dated regularly and was considered mature by her classmates. Her life was shattered badly one evening

in November of her senior year when the car she was driving struck
another at an unregulated intersection, instantly killing the driver of
the other vehicle, who, as fate would have it, was a high school chum
of hers. "I can never absolve myself of the guilt," Laura wrote many
years later. "And the guilt isn't simply from Mike dying. The guilt is
from all the implications, from the way those few seconds spun out and
enfolded so many other lives. . . . I lost my faith that November, lost it
for many, many years."[14]

In September 1964, Laura entered Southern Methodist University
in Dallas, the same year that George entered Yale. SMU, in a Texas setting, was much like Yale at the time—a privileged sanctuary for scions
of the establishment. Laura majored in education, joined the top so-
rority, Kappa Alpha Theta, and like George, graduated in 1968. After
traveling briefly in Europe she began her teaching career at Longfellow
Elementary in Dallas, a predominantly African American school,
where she taught the fourth grade. After a year in the classroom she
flirted with moving to Boston or Washington, interviewed with Congressman Mahon for a job in his Capitol Hill office ("Can you type?"),
and moved to Houston, where she worked briefly in a brokerage house.
By the beginning of 1970 she was back in the classroom, this time at
the John F. Kennedy Elementary School in Houston's black ghetto. She
remained at JFK three years, and then enrolled in graduate school at
the University of Texas in Austin, where she earned a master's degree
in library science.

After graduating from UT in 1972, Laura returned to Houston,
worked for a year in a neighborhood library, and then moved back to
Austin where she found a job as the school librarian at the Molly Daw-
son Elementary School in a largely Hispanic neighborhood. The University of Texas cast a spell, and Austin was a liberal oasis in Texas.[15]
A left-of-center Democrat who admired Lady Bird Johnson, Laura felt
more at home in Austin than in Dallas or Houston, and was living
there when she and George met. After a brief courtship they were married in Midland, November 5, 1977.

The wedding was small by Bush standards, seventy-five relatives
and close friends in Midland's United Methodist Church. "We had no

ushers, no bridesmaids, and no groomsmen," George recalled. "It was just me, Laura, and her dad to walk her down the aisle." [16]

Many were surprised that Bush and Laura had hit it off. W.'s younger brother Marvin said Laura's entry into the Bush family was like "Katharine Hepburn starring in *Animal House.*" [17] Poppy's sister, Nancy Bush Ellis, offered a more reflective judgment. "George saw that Laura's feet were firmly

George and Laura at their wedding with Rev. Jerry Wyatt, November 5, 1977.

planted on the ground," she told Frank Bruni of *The New York Times.* "I think after all the transitions in his life, he wasn't interested in marrying someone like himself. He wanted someone steady and calm." [18]

Bush said much the same. "We were a perfect match," he wrote many years later. "I'm a talker; Laura is a listener. I am restless; she is calm. I can get a little carried away; she is practical and down to earth. . . . I provoke people, confront them in a teasing way. She is kinder, much more measured, arriving at a conclusion carefully." [19]

After a brief honeymoon in Cozumel, Laura and George hit the campaign trail. The Republican primary was six months away, and Reese was the odds-on favorite. They moved into a small townhouse that Bush owned on Midland's Golf Course Road (Laura said the weeds were as tall as the roofline), and began the arduous process of making themselves known. "Campaigning in West Texas is an exercise in retail politics," said Laura. "We drove up and down the back roads and asphalt highways of the Texas panhandle, from Midland in the south

Campaigning for Congress, 1978.

to Plainview and Hereford in the north. We spent nearly a year on the road, and in many ways the bonds of our marriage were cemented in the front seat of that Oldsmobile Cutlass."[20]

Bush had found his calling. On the stump he was a natural. He had an exceptional talent for memorizing names and faces, and flattering ordinary people with his attention. And unlike Poppy, he enjoyed every minute of it. Up at the crack of dawn, he and Laura would head out to meet the voters. They never missed a morning coffee gathering or a chili supper, and would knock on more than sixty doors a day, always leaving a polite note if the residents were not home.

When Reese realized that Bush was a serious candidate, the campaign intensified. Reese's ultraconservative supporters attacked George as a New England liberal out of touch with rural life in Texas. Some suggested that he was a tool of the Rockefellers, sent out to buy up farmland for the family. Poppy's name was brought into the campaign, and he was castigated for his U.N. service and as a member of the ominous-sounding Trilateral Commission, a group of international political and corporate leaders seen by right-wing critics as a sinister gang of elitists plotting to establish world government. Reese had headed Ronald Reagan's 1976 campaign for the Republican presidential nomination in the district, and the campaign took on the aspects of a battle between conservative Reaganites and the more moderate Bush faction of the party, with the 1980 presidential nomination looming in the background. Reagan's political action committee contributed $1,000 to Reese's campaign, and Reagan himself wrote a letter to the district's registered Republicans endorsing Reese.

But Reese's efforts were no match for Bush's personal appeal. On primary day, May 6, 1978, George W. led the three-man field with six hundred more votes than Reese but failed to win a majority. A third candidate, a retired Air Force colonel, had won enough votes to force Bush and Reese into a run-off. The run-off was set for June 3, less than a month away, and Reese stepped up his attacks. Reagan contributed another $2,000 to Reese's campaign, and on Friday before election day Reese produced a copy of Bush's birth certificate to prove that he had been born in New Haven, Connecticut, not in Texas. Bush agreed that was so. "No, I wasn't born in Texas," he said. "I wanted to be close to my mother that day."[21]

When the votes were counted, Bush defeated Reese 6,787 to 5,350. Reese carried sixteen of the district's seventeen counties, but Bush's enormous majority in Midland put him over the top. The following day Reagan called George W. to offer his congratulations. "He was gracious and volunteered to help in the general election," wrote Bush. "I was grateful for his call and bore no hard feelings."[22]

Bush's opponent in the general election was state senator Kent Hance, described by Poppy's friend Bob Strauss, former chairman of the Democratic National Committee, as "smart as a whip and mean as a snake."[23] The nineteenth congressional district in Texas was traditionally Democratic. It had occasionally voted for Republican presidential candidates (Eisenhower and Nixon), but at the state and local level almost all of the officeholders were Democrats. Registered Democrats outnumbered Republicans six to one, and George Mahon had held the seat for forty-four years. Bush recognized that it would be an uphill struggle to beat Hance.

The Bush family fundraising network shifted into high gear. With the Republican nomination secure, donors flocked to the cause. Poppy held fundraisers for George W. in Washington, Dallas, and Houston. Former president Gerald Ford sent a check, as did baseball commissioner Bowie Kuhn, Mrs. Douglas MacArthur (who had been a neighbor of the Bushes at the Waldorf-Astoria), and Donald Rumsfeld. Oil industry executives such as Hugh Liedtke of Pennzoil lined up to contribute, as did the senior Bush's friends from industry and finance. Altogether the Bushes raised $406,000 ($1.4 million in today's dollars)

compared to $175,000 raised by Hance. That was a record for a con-
gressional campaign in Texas at the time.

Bush's outside fundraising made him vulnerable to charges that he
was trying to buy the election. Hance painted Bush as a Yankee carpetbagger and constantly reminded voters that while Bush was at Andover
in Massachusetts, he was attending Dimmit High School in Dimmit,
Texas, and while George was at Yale, he was at Texas Tech. "When
I graduated from the University of Texas Law School—get this folks—
he was attending Harvard. We don't need someone from the Northeast
telling us what our problems are." [24]

Aside from the attacks on Bush as a carpetbagger, the tone of the
general election was higher than in the Republican primary. Democrats might be parochial, but they were not paranoid and they did not
think Bush was part of a global conspiracy to foist world government
on the United States or a dupe of the Rockefellers. Hance had the police
record of Bush's conviction in Maine for DUI, but chose in the gentle-
manly tone of the campaign not to release it. Bush for his part declined
to make an issue of Hance's ownership of property on which a bar was
located that sold alcohol to students at Texas Tech. "Kent lives here
[in Lubbock]," Bush told his staff. "I'm not going to ruin a guy in his
hometown. He's not a bad person." [25] On policy matters there was little
difference between the candidates. Bush recognized that Hance held
the trump cards as a native son of the nineteenth congressional district
and deep down he understood that it was a fight he could not win.

On election night, Hance won going away. Bush carried Midland
by five thousand votes, but that was not enough to overcome Hance's
lead in the other sixteen counties. Final results gave Hance 53,917 votes
to Bush's 47,497—roughly 53 to 47 percent. Bush had run a credible
race and had lost in large measure because Hance had out-Texased
him—a lesson he would take to heart. "Hance deserved to win that
race," Bush wrote many years later.* "Frankly, getting whipped was

---

* Kent Hance served three terms in the House of Representatives, and then lost his bid for the
Democratic senatorial nomination to succeed John Tower. He became a Republican in 1985, ran
unsuccessfully for several statewide offices, and was later chancellor of the Texas Tech university

probably a pretty good thing for me. . . . I discovered that I could accept
defeat and move on. That was not easy for someone as competitive as
I am. But it was an important part of my maturing."[26]

Bush finished the campaign with a slight surplus. He opened a
small office in Midland's Petroleum Building, and again as Poppy had
done, went east to consult with the family about raising money for Arbusto. Working through Uncle Jonathan, his father's younger brother,
who had followed family tradition and become a Wall Street money
manager, W converted Arbusto into a limited partnership catering to
East Coast investors seeking an entry to the oil business. The price of
petroleum was spiking, and as Jonathan later told *The Washington Post*,

> George was an easy sale. The people who met him would say, "I'd like
> to drill with this guy." He had run for Congress. He was an upstand-
> ing guy. They figured he knew what he was doing, but mostly they
> figured they'd get a fair shake from him. . . . The only people who go
> into [these investments] are people that aren't going to miss the money.
> If they could have a shot at a big payoff and still take a huge [tax] write-
> off, they considered it a gamble worth taking.[27]

Arbusto began active operations in March 1979. In his first year
as president of the company, Bush raised $565,000 from twenty-eight
limited partners. The fact that Poppy announced his candidacy for
the Republican presidential nomination on May 1, 1979, was scarcely
an impediment. "It didn't hurt him that his father had been in the oil
business," noted Jonathan.[28] In 1980, with oil moving up to $30 a bar-
rel, Bush raised another $1.24 million from thirty-six investors, and
in 1981 an additional $1.72 million. The list of investors in Arbusto
reads like the roster of George H. W. Bush's A-Team of campaign
contributors. Lewis Lehrman, the founder of the Rite-Aid drugstore
chain who would spend $7 million of his own money unsuccessfully
running for governor of New York against Mario Cuomo in 1982, in-

---

system. "He is still the only politician ever to beat me," wrote Bush in his memoirs. *Decision
Points* (New York: Crown, 2010), 41.

vested $140,500; George L. Ball, then head of E. F. Hutton and later
Prudential-Bache, put up $300,000; California venture capitalist Wil-
liam H. Draper invested $93,000; and John D. Macomber, an old Yale
buddy of Jonathan who chaired the Celanese Corporation of America,
$79,000. Draper and Macomber would later take turns as president of
the U.S. Export-Import Bank under Reagan and George H. W. Bush,
and Lehrman was awarded the Medal of Freedom by George W. Bush
in a White House ceremony in 2005. James A. Baker, who ran Poppy's
presidential primary campaign and became Reagan's chief of staff in
the White House, also pointed investors in W's direction.

By 1984, Bush's limited partners had invested $4.66 million and
had received $1.54 million in cash distributions in return. They also
received $3.89 million in tax write-offs, which would have netted them
another $2.91 million. George W., who owned 80 percent of Arbusto,
invested $102,000 of his own money during the same period and re-
ceived $678,000 back in administrative and management fees as well
as cash distributions. Arbusto drilled an average of ten wells a year,
spending $250,000 to $500,000 for each, and averaging a 50 percent
success rate. "I was slowly but surely building a solid, small producing
company and I thought we'd developed a reputation as honest opera-
tors who worked hard and gave people a fair shake," said Bush. "But
I'm not going to pretend that it was any huge success at the time." [29]

During their early years of marriage, George and Laura tried des-
perately to have children. "We were approaching our mid-thirties,"
Bush wrote, "and began to feel the pressure of our ages." [30] In the fall of
1980, as the Carter-Reagan presidential race was drawing to a close—
Reagan had beaten Poppy in the primaries but then chose him as his
vice presidential running mate—Laura still had not become pregnant
and they decided to begin adoption procedures at the Edna Gladney
adoption home in Fort Worth. At the same time, Laura began fertility
treatments with a gynecologist in Houston. In April 1981 she discovered she was pregnant. "I was thirty-five years old," said Laura, "which
in those days was considered old for a first-time mother." [31]

As Laura anticipated, it was a difficult pregnancy. An early sono-
gram revealed twin girls, and George gave her two dozen roses. Early

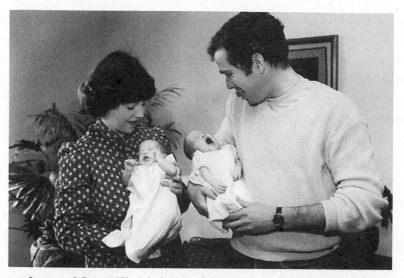

Laura and George W. with their newborn twins, Jenna and Barbara, 1981.

in her third trimester, Laura was diagnosed with preeclampsia, a serious condition involving dangerously high blood pressure and possible kidney failure. She was admitted to Baylor Hospital in Dallas, kept in bed so as not to induce early labor, and her condition temporarily stabilized. But after two weeks of bed rest the attending physicians decided they had no choice but to perform a cesarean and take the babies. George was in Midland when the doctor called.

Bush asked about the twin girls and was assured they would survive. "They will be premature, and they will be fine. But the time to move is now." [32]

He rushed to Dallas and was in the delivery room the morning of November 25, 1981, when the girls were born. "It was the most thrilling moment of my life. Laura was in bed and sedated. I stroked her head. Barbara came first, then Jenna, and they were large for twins, five pounds, four ounces, and four pounds, twelve ounces, both healthy." [33] The girls were named in honor of their grandmothers, Barbara Bush and Jenna Welch. "We did it alphabetically and democratically," said Laura. "The baby who arrived first would be Barbara, and the second would be Jenna." [34]

In the spring of 1982, Bush took Arbusto public and changed the name to Bush Exploration Company. The rechristening took advantage of the fact that Poppy was now vice president and the Bush name had increased appeal. Bush Exploration would also appear more serious to public investors who might be leery of a firm sometimes parodied as Ar-*bust*-o. Bush hoped to raise $6 million for expanded operations but drummed up only $1.2 million, less than he had raised privately in each of the past two years. "Going public was a mistake," he told reporters for *The Dallas Morning News* years later when he was running for governor. "We weren't prepared for it. We didn't raise any money, we weren't able to get enough exposure. . . . I made a bad mistake." [35]

In 1983 Bush's problems intensified. "We didn't find much oil and gas," said Michael Conaway, the company's financial officer, "and we weren't raising much money." [36] The American Petroleum Information Corporation ranked Bush Exploration 993rd in Texas with sixteen wells producing a total of 47,888 barrels a year. With oil prices plummeting from their OPEC-induced high, the entire industry was in trouble and Bush Exploration was hit particularly hard. [37]

Once again fortune came to Bush's rescue, this time in the form of a partnership with two well-heeled Cincinnati investors who needed a Texas head for their oil and gas operations, a firm known as Spectrum 7. At the time, Spectrum 7 operated 180 oil wells, mostly in West Texas. The company was owned by William O. DeWitt, Jr. (Yale '63), and Mercer Reynolds. DeWitt's father, William O. DeWitt, Sr., a longtime baseball executive, had owned successively the St. Louis Browns and the Cincinnati Reds, and had sold the Reds after a championship season. He invested the profits in the oil business, hit a gusher on his first attempt, and formed Spectrum 7 with Reynolds, the family's broker.* When the senior DeWitt died, William Jr. took over. (He currently owns the St. Louis Cardinals.) DeWitt and Reynolds also owned

---

* Reynolds later served as George W. Bush's principal fundraiser in Ohio in 2000 and 2004. People living in Reynolds's Cincinnati zip code contributed more to the Bush campaign than in any other zip code except Manhattan's Upper East Side. Reynolds was subsequently appointed United States ambassador to Switzerland and Liechtenstein. Russ Baker, *Family of Secrets: The Bush Dynasty, America's Invisible Government, and the Hidden History of the Last Fifty Years* (New York: Bloomsbury, 2009), 332.

Coca-Cola distributorships in Cincinnati and Dayton, a string of restaurants, radio and TV stations in the Midwest, and a brokerage firm. They needed someone to handle the oil operation and Bush—Yale grad and baseball fan—fit the bill. Despite the mediocre performance of Arbusto and Bush Exploration, Bush was regarded as a straight shooter.

"We wanted Bush's leadership abilities, and his operational ability which we didn't have," said DeWitt. "He actually operated wells. We owned wells, but we never operated wells." [38] The fact that Poppy was vice president may have made Bush an even more attractive associate, but DeWitt downplayed the fact. "There was obviously some notoriety because of who Bush was, but it didn't open any doors for us. Our doors were already opened." [39]

On February 29, 1984, the merger of Bush Exploration and Spectrum 7 was consummated. DeWitt and Reynolds each retained slightly more than 20 percent of the new Spectrum 7, and George W. was given 16.3 percent—1.166 million shares worth $530,000 at market value. Bush became chairman and CEO of Spectrum 7 with an annual salary of $75,000, plus $120,000 in consulting fees. The price of oil, although down from its $34-a-barrel high, had stabilized in the mid-20s and the next eighteen months were relatively prosperous for Bush and Spectrum 7.

In the summer of 1985, with Spectrum 7 holding its own, George, Laura, and the twins took their annual visit to the family compound in Kennebunkport. Since the birth of the twins, Bush had stopped smoking and was running three to five miles every day at the Midland Y. His drinking continued, but only in the evening, and did not affect his work or family life. "Each step was another exercise in discipline,"

George W. and Laura at Kennebunkport.

said Laura. "He likes that. It makes him feel good to give up bad habits."[40]

At Kennebunkport that summer Bush experienced an epiphany of sorts. The Reverend Billy Graham and his wife, Ruth, visited the Bush family for a weekend in Maine every year. Graham would preach at the Bushes' two churches—St. Ann's Episcopal and the First Congregational—and then at night the family would gather for dinner and discuss spiritual values. In 1985 the discussion focused on belief in Christ. Poppy asked Graham whether his mother, Dorothy, who was deeply religious, but an Episcopalian, would go to heaven since she had no born-again experience—the classic conflict between good works and a born-again belief in Christ. Graham, who had fielded that question many times, was ready with an answer. "George," he said, "some of us require a born-again experience to understand God, and some of us are born Christians. It sounds like your mom was just born a Christian."[41]

George W. was captivated by Graham. "Billy Graham didn't make you feel guilty; he made you feel loved."[42] The following day he and Graham took a walk on the beach. Graham asked him about his life in Texas. "I talked to him about the girls and shared my thought that reading the Bible could make me a better person." Graham was skeptical. There was nothing wrong with reading the Bible, he said, but self-improvement was not the point. "The center of Christianity is not the self. It is Christ."

"Billy explained that we are all sinners, and that we cannot earn God's love through good deeds. . . . The path to salvation is through the grace of God. And the way to find that grace is to embrace Christ as the risen Lord."[43]

For Bush it was a watershed moment. "These were profound concepts," he wrote, "and I did not fully grasp them that day. But Billy had planted a seed."* Back in Midland, Bush began to take religion more

---

* I have accepted Bush's version of his born-again experience with Billy Graham as laid out in his memoirs *A Charge to Keep* and later in *Decision Points*. But there is a considerable body of evidence suggesting that the experience occurred a year earlier in Midland thanks to a lesser

seriously. He joined a Bible study group and worked his way through the New Testament. "At first I was troubled by my doubts. . . . Surrendering yourself to an Almighty is a challenge to the ego. But I came to realize that struggles and doubts are natural parts of faith.

"Prayer was the nourishment that sustained me. As I deepened my understanding of Christ, I came closer to my original goal of being a better person— not because I was racking up points on the positive side of the heavenly ledger, but because I was moved by God's love."[44]

By the spring of 1986, Bush needed all the faith

Rev. and Mrs. Billy Graham with George W. and his twin girls at Walker's Point, Kennebunkport, Maine, 1983.

known evangelist named Arthur Blessitt, "The Man Who Carried the Cross Around the World." Billy Graham, when interviewed about Bush's conversion by NBC's Brian Williams, said he never felt he had turned W's life around, and there is a strong possibility that the Graham connection was devised for electoral purposes by Karen Hughes, who coauthored *A Charge to Keep* on the eve of Bush's run for the presidency in 1999. Most biographies repeat the Graham account. Like the reporter in John Ford's *The Man Who Shot Liberty Valance*, "when the legend becomes fact," I have chosen to "print the legend." For the details of Bush's earlier encounter with Blessitt, see Craig Unger, *The Fall of the House of Bush* (New York: Scribner, 2007), 79–85. Also see http://www.blessitt.com/praying-with-george-w-bush/. Blessitt's diary entry for April 3, 1984, calls it "A great and powerful day. Led Vice President Bush's son to Jesus today. George Bush Jr. This is great. Glory to God." This was a year prior to Bush's encounter with Graham at Kennebunkport.

he could muster. The price of oil, which had held steady in the mid-20s, had begun a precipitous decline. Within six months it would plummet to $9 a barrel. Drilling stopped. Banks failed and people with debt went under overnight. Spectrum 7 reported a net loss of $1.6 million for 1985, due primarily to the declining value of its assets. In the first three months of 1986, it lost another $402,000. The company owed $3.1 million in bank loans, and the threat of foreclosure appeared imminent. "It's very slow out here," Bush told *The New York Times*. "Times are tough. We are using cash to survive. I'm all name and no money."[45] Rather than reduce staff, Bush asked his employees to take a 10 percent pay cut. He reduced his own salary 25 percent.

As the situation in the oil patch worsened, Bush faced two choices. He could hunker down, cut expenses to the bone, and try to hang on in the hope that oil prices would recover before the banks foreclosed; or he could find a larger, more solvent company that was bottom-feeding— a firm that was absorbing smaller oil companies because it was cheap to do so. After a frantic search, Bush found Harken Oil and Gas, a big Dallas-based company that was aggressively taking over troubled competitors. It was the commercial equivalent of love at first sight. Spectrum 7 was hemorrhaging money and Bush needed a transfusion; Harken, for its part, liked to attach itself to stars, and despite his lackluster track record, Bush had a name to be reckoned with. "One of the reasons Harken was so interested in merging," said Paul Rea, a geologist who had been president of Spectrum 7, "was because of George. They believed George's name would be a big help to them. They wanted him on their board."[46]

Harken Oil and Gas (later, Harken Energy) was described by *Time* magazine in 1991 as "one of the most mysterious and eccentric outfits ever to drill for oil."[47] The company had been taken over in 1983 by a group headed by New York lawyer Alan Quasha, and the principal investors included billionaire George Soros (46.8 percent), Saudi real estate magnate Abdullah Taha Bakhsh, and the Harvard Management Corporation, the investing arm of Harvard University. Jeffrey Laikind, who was on Harken's board at the time, said that Spectrum was an attractive purchase because the price was right. Bush's name drew attention because he "had been in the oil patch, somebody who had experience, although his status as the vice president's son was not a fact you could ignore." [48]

Another board member allowed as how George could be very useful to Harken. "He could have been more so if he had had funds, but as far as contacts were concerned, he was terrific. . . . It seemed like George knew everybody in the U.S. who was worth knowing." [49]

Negotiations with Harken continued through the summer of 1986. The pressure was intense, and Bush had resumed drinking heavily. According to Laura, George drank the three Bs—bourbon before dinner, beer with dinner, and then the sweet liqueur B&B (brandy and Bénédictine) after dinner. "It was lethal, and it was completely accepted because that, or some version of it, was the drinking life of most men.

"Maybe it's funny when other people's husbands have too much to drink at a party, but I didn't think it was funny when mine did. And I told him so. But I never said the line 'It's either Jim Beam or me.' I was not going to leave George. But I was disappointed." [50]

"Laura wasn't afraid to tell me what she thought," Bush agreed, "but she couldn't quit drinking for me. I've been asked if I consider myself an alcoholic. I can't say for sure. I do know that I have a habitual personality. I was drinking too much, and it was starting to create a problem." [51]

Matters came to a head in July 1986 during an excursion to the Broadmoor Hotel in Colorado Springs. The Bushes, along with two other couples from Midland, the O'Neills and the Evanses (Don Evans would later serve as Bush's campaign finance chairman and then as secretary of commerce), were off for a collective celebration of their fortieth birthdays, and were joined by George's younger brother Neil, who lived in Denver. The Broadmoor, with its three golf courses a stone's throw from Pikes Peak, was a favorite resort of the Bush family. Built originally as a casino during Colorado's Gold Rush days, it had been converted in 1918 to a lavish hotel. During the weekend, the men golfed while the women sunned by the pool. Dinner on Saturday night, July 26, was an extravagant affair with numerous courses, ample bottles of expensive California cabernet, and repeated toasts to the birthday celebrants. "I heard the same toast repeated twenty times," Laura remembered. [52]

Reckoning came the next morning. Bush woke up with an incredible hangover—which was not unusual—looked at himself in the mirror, and resolved to quit drinking. "There had been many drunken and half-drunken weekends," Laura recalled. "There was nothing particularly out of the ordinary about this one, except that it was one weekend too many."[53] Joe O'Neill, who had a similar drinking problem and would eventually check himself into the Betty Ford Clinic, thought the upcoming 1988 presidential campaign was decisive for Bush. "He looked in the mirror and said, 'Someday I might embarrass my father. It might get my dad in trouble.' And boy, that was it."[54] Laura agreed. "None of the Bush children ever wanted to do anything to embarrass their dad," she wrote. There was a lighter side to W's resolve. When he told Laura of his decision, she quipped that it was because he got the bar bill for that evening's celebration.[55]

Bush credits Billy Graham and his newfound belief in God. "At age forty I finally found the strength to do it," he wrote. "I could not have stopped drinking without faith. I also don't think my faith would be as strong if I hadn't quit drinking. I believe God helped open my eyes, which were closing because of booze."[56]

In September, the deal with Harken closed. Harken assumed Spectrum 7's $3.1 million bank debt and absorbed its operations. It was strictly a stock transfer. No money changed hands. Shareholders in Spectrum 7 received one share of Harken stock for every five shares of Spectrum. Harken acquired the untapped oil reserves that Spectrum had failed to exploit, and placed George W. Bush on its board at a time when his father was planning to run for president. "We were buying political influence. That was it," said George Soros.[57]*

---

* In January 1990, well into the G. H. W. Bush presidency and one year before Desert Storm, Harken Energy cashed in on its ties to the Bushes when the government of Bahrain granted it an exclusive thirty-five-year contract to drill in the offshore waters of the Persian Gulf. Harken had no international or offshore experience and was too small to undertake the project until it brought in the Bass brothers of Houston, major GOP contributors and also friends of the Bushes. *Forbes* magazine called the deal "hard to imagine. A tiny company with no international experience drilling in the Middle East." *Time* said the emirate of Bahrain was "unabashed in its desire to foster a warm relationship with the U.S." Asked by *The Wall Street Journal* whether

The takeover by Harken ended Bush's eleven years in the oil business. He found jobs for all of his employees at Spectrum, and moved on. Unlike Poppy, Bush had failed to make a big score. Once again success eluded him. He profited personally, but lost money for most of his investors. As critic Molly Ivins pointed out, Bush's oil patch career "had more to do with selling investments than drilling for oil. . . . Don't look for his portrait to be hanging in the Petroleum Hall of Fame anytime soon."[58]

Bush would not disagree. "I learned a lot of lessons in the oil business," he wrote many years later. "I learned the perils of entrepreneurship. I learned that sometimes you can do most things right, manage risk carefully, use resources responsibly, make good decisions, but still never hit the big gusher. . . . Some people in the oil business hit grand slams, but like baseball, success in the energy business is primarily a game of singles."[59]

The merger of Spectrum 7 with Harken left Bush free to join Poppy's campaign for the Republican presidential nomination. The year before, shortly after his inauguration for a second term as vice president, George H. W. Bush had convened a family conclave at Camp David to discuss the 1988 campaign. "This is my best shot," said Poppy, "but I am not going to do it if we don't have 100 percent behind me."[60]

At the time, each member of the Bush family was marching to his own drummer. George W. was running Spectrum 7 in Midland and drinking heavily. Jeb, who had graduated Phi Beta Kappa from the University of Texas, was married to Columba Garnica Gallo, whom he had met as a young man in Mexico, prospering in Florida real estate, and beginning to dabble in Miami politics. Neil, thirty, who had struggled with dyslexia as a child, had graduated from Tulane with a BA

---

having the president's son on its board facilitated Harken's chances, George W. quipped, "Ask the Bahrainis."

Russ Baker, *Family of Secrets: The Bush Dynasty, America's Invisible Government, and the Hidden History of the Last Fifty Years* (New York: Bloomsbury, 2009), 353–54; J. H. Hatfield, *Fortunate Son: George W. Bush and the Making of an American President* (New York: Soft Skull Press, 2000), 99–100; Bill Minutaglio, *First Son: George W. Bush and the Bush Family Dynasty* (New York: Times Books, 1999), 246–47; Molly Ivins and Lou Dubose, *Shrub: The Short but Happy Political Life of George W. Bush* (New York: Vintage, 2000), 28–32.

and an MBA and was living in Denver where he was flying high. Like
Poppy and George W., he had started in the oil business, organized his
own firm, and had recently joined the board of directors of Silverado
Savings and Loan. Marvin, the youngest son and the least political, was
working as an investment banker following his graduation from the
University of Virginia and was suffering from an inflammatory bowel
disease. (He would shortly have emergency surgery to remove his large
intestine.) Dorothy, who was twenty-five, had recently graduated from
Boston College, married, and was living in Cape Elizabeth, Maine, as a
housewife. Closest of all the children to her father, Doro called the vice
president almost daily.

In addition to the family, the meeting was attended by the campaign staff the elder Bush was beginning to stitch together: Lee Atwater, *l'enfant terrible* of Washington political consultants, as campaign
manager; Marlin Fitzwater as press secretary; Roger Ailes (who later
became head of Fox News) as media consultant; pollster Robert Teeter,
and his chief of staff, Craig Fuller. As campaign manager, Atwater led
the discussion that day and emphasized the importance of Super Tuesday, March 8, 1988, when seventeen states would choose their convention delegates. Atwater had a deserved reputation for self-confidence,
and eventually his pontificating became grating.

"How do we know we can trust you?" interjected George W.—
a veiled reference to the fact that Atwater's partners would be working
for Jack Kemp and Bob Dole, two of Poppy's principal opponents.

"Are you serious?" Atwater replied.

"I'm damn serious, pal. In our family, if you go to war, we want you
completely on our side."[61]

The imagery is from *The Godfather*, a favorite film of the Bush
family,* and W was voicing the sentiment of the Corleones' hotheaded

---

* When Francis Ford Coppola's *The Godfather* was released in March 1972, George H. W.
Bush, who was United States ambassador to the United Nations at the time, was so captivated
by the film that he rented a theater in New York for a private showing and invited a hundred
guests. The film was sold out all over New York City and it was difficult to get tickets. Bush's
sons shared his affection for the movie and often recited lines from memory. Bill Minutaglio,
First Son: George W. Bush and the Bush Family Dynasty (New York: Times Books, 1999), 134.

eldest boy, Sonny. If the family was going to the mattresses, they needed to know that everyone would be loyal.

Atwater was unfazed. "If you're so worried about my loyalty," he shot back, "then why don't you come in the office and watch me, and the first time I'm disloyal see to it that I get run off."[62] Atwater assumed Bush would take him up on the offer, and he knew he could handle him. As he later told friends (quoting Lyndon Johnson), "I'd rather have him inside the tent pissing out than outside the tent pissing in."[63] It was now a year later, Bush's consulting contract with Harken did not require his presence in Midland or Dallas, and he had time on his hands. Atwater's offer was too good to turn down.

Initially, Bush commuted. Campaign headquarters was located in the Woodward Building on Fifteenth Street, two short blocks from Poppy's office in the West Wing of the White House. Bush was given an office between Atwater and Ailes, and for the next eighteen months received a crash course in practical politics from two of the profession's most gifted practitioners. Atwater and Bush became soul mates: both were reformed drinkers, voluble, iconoclastic, and ruthlessly devoted to Poppy's cause. Bush had no job title. "You don't need a title," the vice president told his son. "Everyone will know who you are."[64] At first, Bush filled in as Poppy's surrogate at events too distant to fit the vice president's schedule. Then he became the front man and chief liaison with the powerful evangelical wing of the party. Above all, he was a handy conduit between the campaign staff and Poppy. "He was an assessor of problems," said staffer Mary Matalin. "If they were real, he did something. If they weren't, he at least made people feel better. He was a general morale booster." Others remember that like Sonny Corleone, he was a ferocious defender of family prerogative: "the enforcer from hell," in the words of the vice president's deputy chief of staff.[65]

American politics underwent a sea change during the presidential primary season in 1987. Colorado senator Gary Hart, a notorious skirt chaser, was confronted during a press conference in Hanover, New Hampshire, by a reporter from *The Washington Post*. "Have you ever committed adultery?" the reporter asked. Hart was dumbfounded. The question shattered the long-standing rule that a politician's philandering was off-limits for reporters. The question to Hart turned American politics on its ear. The once unmentionable subject of a politician's personal life was now fair game for reporters. It was a measure of a candidate's character. Hart refused to answer the question, and withdrew from the campaign for the Democratic nomination on May 8, 1987.

After Hart's withdrawal, every Democratic candidate was asked the same question. Forewarned is forearmed, and they had their denials ready. The best came from Senator Fritz Hollings of South Carolina. When asked if he had ever committed adultery, Hollings said he had been trying for the last thirty-one years but had never succeeded.

On the Republican side, George H. W. Bush had a problem—"the Jennifer problem" as it would come to be known. Jennifer Fitzgerald, a young English woman, had been Poppy's executive assistant since he chaired the Republican National Committee under Richard Nixon. Like many executive assistants, Jennifer ruled the elder Bush's office with an iron hand, and regularly traveled with Poppy on his many jaunts to foreign countries. That inevitably led to speculation that he and Jennifer had more than a professional relationship. After the Hart affair broke, *Newsweek* reporters focused on the rumors. Atwater and George W. were aware of the magazine's interest, and put their heads together. Both were firm believers in addressing dangerous issues head-on. It was better to lance the wound immediately and let the poison run out rather than allowing it to fester. They met with Poppy and press secretary Marlin Fitzwater.

W was blunt. "You've heard the rumors," he said to his father. "What do you say?"

"They're just not true," Poppy replied.

Fitzwater and the elder Bush thought they should keep a low profile, say nothing, and hope the story would disappear. George W. and Atwater disagreed. After the meeting, George W. phoned *Newsweek*'s Howard Fineman. "The answer to the Big A question is N-O," he said. "I didn't ask permission," Bush told Jon Meacham. "I just did it." [66]

Newsweek ran the story under the headline, "Bush and the Big A Question." Other publications picked it up, and in a week the issue

disappeared.[67] George W.'s snappy one-liner saved the day.* The episode carries significance beyond the election of 1988. Bush had not only
confronted his father as an equal but had overridden his objections and
spoken directly to the press. "If there was any sort of leftover competition with being named George Bush and being the eldest, it really at
that point was resolved," said Laura.[68]

Shortly after the Hart story broke, George and Laura sold their
house in Midland and moved to Washington. "I had never lived outside
of Texas for more than a few weeks," said Laura. "We left Midland,
but never truly left it behind."[69] They bought a house on Massachusetts
Avenue near American University, about a mile from the vice president's residence at the Naval Observatory, and enrolled the twins at the
Horace Mann public school in northwest Washington.

Poppy announced his candidacy for the Republican presidential
nomination on October 13, 1987. As vice president, Bush had a built-in
advantage, but his campaign was off to a slow start. In the Iowa caucuses, Bush finished a poor third, well behind Kansas senator Bob Dole
and evangelist Pat Robertson. But in New Hampshire, assisted by Governor John Sununu and baseball immortal Ted Williams (his classmate
from flight training forty-six years earlier), Bush pulled ahead, trouncing Dole by 9 percentage points. The Dole campaign never recovered.
Super Tuesday was a rout. Bush carried sixteen of the seventeen states
(Robertson carried Alaska), and effectively cinched the nomination.
When the Republican convention met in the New Orleans Superdome
on August 15, Poppy had the support of forty-one states and was nominated by acclamation following the roll call on the first ballot.

At the convention, George W. came into his own. He was chosen
honorary chairman of the Texas delegation, and announced the Texas
vote on the roll call: "One hundred and eleven votes for Texas's favorite son and the world's best father, George Herbert Walker Bush."[70]
George W. told the family that after the convention he would be re-

----

* At the insistence of James Baker, who later became campaign chairman, Jennifer Fitzgerald
was removed from the vice president's staff and shifted to the New York campaign office where
she would be less visible. The elder Bush paid her salary out of his own pocket. Herbert S. Parmet, *George Bush: The Life of a Lone Star Yankee* (New York: Scribner, 1997), 241.

turning to Texas, and it was generally assumed that he would be entering public life. "I want to make it clear that I'm not running for anything right now," he told reporters from the *Houston Chronicle*, "but if I decide to do so in the future, I have to work to establish my own identity."[71] Bush later said that he had "zero interest" in remaining in Washington as a hanger-on in his father's administration.[72]

The general election against Massachusetts governor Michael Dukakis was scarcely a walkover. Early opinion polls gave Dukakis a 16-point lead, but a combination of Democratic miscues and the skillful GOP campaign engineered by Atwater and Ailes narrowed the gap. Dukakis was in many ways his own worst enemy. When Kansas farmers complained about the price of wheat, the Massachusetts governor suggested they grow arugula, and the film footage of Dukakis with an ill-fitting Army helmet on his head waving from the turret of an M-1 battle tank did nothing to assure voters he was ready to be commander in chief. Atwater and Ailes painted Dukakis as weak on crime and pollution, and GOP television ads (Willie Horton and a polluted Boston Harbor) drove the point home. By mid-September the gap between Bush and Dukakis had closed, and by October, Bush was well ahead. As one Democratic official put it, "Atwater was the Babe Ruth of negative politics."[73]

George W. spent the campaign shuttling between Dallas and Washington. He spoke at election rallies in dozens of Texas cities and continued to act as Poppy's intermediary with the evangelicals and the Christian Right. Shortly before the election, George W. received a phone call from William DeWitt, Jr., his former partner in Spectrum 7. Because of his father, DeWitt was well connected to Major League Baseball and had learned that the Texas Rangers were up for sale. Eddie Chiles, the Fort Worth oil baron who owned the Rangers, and who was an old friend of the Bushes from the 1950s in the Permian Basin, was in poor health and wanted to unload the team. DeWitt also said that baseball commissioner Peter Ueberroth insisted that the team be bought by investors from Texas. He wanted no absentee ownership. DeWitt asked Bush if he would be interested in helping him put together a group of local investors to buy the team. "This could be a natural for you," said DeWitt. "I know you want to get back to Texas, and you've always loved baseball." [74]

"I almost jumped out of my chair," said Bush. "Owning a baseball team would be a dream come true. I was determined to make it happen." He and DeWitt agreed to talk about it after the election. [75]

During the waning weeks of the campaign, Bush pressed his father to name Lee Atwater chairman of the Republican National Committee. No political consultant, no hired gun, had ever been named to head either party, but George W. argued they owed it to Atwater. There was also a personal dimension. During his eighteen months in Washington, Bush had served a political apprenticeship under Atwater. He had become his alter ego. Sometimes, observers said, it seemed as though they could read each other's mind. They didn't need to finish their sentences. [76] Bush had learned more about conducting a national political campaign than most candidates would ever know. And he understood that Atwater was unique—a rock star political consultant and an inspiration to young party workers around the country.

Pressed relentlessly by George W., Poppy yielded. On election day in November, jogging with Atwater in Houston's Memorial Park, the vice president made the offer and Atwater accepted. That evening, George H. W. Bush carried forty states with 426 electoral votes and won 53.4 percent of the popular vote. George W. spent the day house hunting in Dallas.

CHAPTER THREE

"Don't Mess with Texas"

Baseball should always be played outdoors, on grass,
with wooden bats.

George W. Bush

In the second week of November 1988, Bush closed on a property at 6029 Northwood Road in the affluent Preston Hollow neighborhood in the north end of the city.* His neighbors included Tom Landry, Ross Perot, and Stanley Marcus (of the Neiman Marcus department store chain). The house, typical for the area, was a ranch-style dwelling with a circular drive and a swimming pool, set off by a grove of scrub oak. The family moved from Washington in early December, and the girls, Barbara and Jenna, were enrolled first in public school, and later in the nearby Hockaday School, the preeminent private school for girls in Texas.

Bush's purpose in moving to Dallas was two-fold: to put together a consortium to buy the Texas Rangers, and to run for governor. The

---

* According to Dallas County records, the Bushes purchased the house at 6029 Northwood Road from Hervey and Ellen Feldman for $320,000. Official records also indicate that the Bushes put none of their own money into the house and took out a 100 percent mortgage with the United Bank National Association, the holding company that had absorbed the United Bank of Midland.

goals were mutually reinforcing. As Bush's political adviser Karl Rove told reporters in Dallas, "Ownership of the Texas Rangers anchors him clearly as a Texas businessman and gives him name identification and exposure that will be easily recalled by the people."[1] Rove at the time was running a flourishing direct-mail operation in Austin for the Republican Party.

Bush pursued both goals simultaneously. "He always possessed an amazing amount of energy," said younger brother Marvin. "Today I think he's learned how to channel that energy in positive ways."[2] Lee Atwater, who was the incoming chairman of the Republican National Committee, passed the word to party operatives in Texas to pave the way for his friend and benefactor, and Bush undertook an extensive speaking tour throughout the state. In the second week of February, he delivered nine "Lincoln Day" speeches to the Republican faithful in key Texas cities, always making it clear to well-wishers that he had not ruled out running for governor in 1990.

When Kent Hance, who had defeated Bush in 1978 and was now a former congressman, considered a bid for the Republican gubernatorial nomination, he tried to smoke out Bush in a private conversation. Bush equivocated.

"I owe you one," Hance confided. "If you want to run for governor I will support you. But if you are not going to run, I want to run."

"Well, I'm not in a position to tell you right now," Bush replied. "But let's stay in touch."[3]

In Washington, Texas senator Phil Gramm beat the drum for Bush. Interviewed by John McLaughlin of *The McLaughlin Group*, Gramm said there was a good chance Bush would run in 1990. "He has good political tools," said Gramm, "in some way, as good or better than his dad's. He's smart and, remarkably, after having gone to Yale and Harvard, he still is a redneck with a good common touch."[4]

On the other hand, Bush's mother, Barbara, let it be known that she thought George W. was biting off more than he could chew. "When you make a major commitment like that [to baseball]," she told reporters at a White House luncheon, "I think maybe you won't be running for governor."[5]

Barbara's remarks were widely reported. When Bush was asked to comment, he exploded. "Mother's worried about my daddy's campaign affecting my race," he said. "Thank you very much. You've been giving me advice for forty-two years, most of which I haven't taken.

"I love my mother, and I appreciate her advice, but that's all it is, advice. . . . I don't know what I'm going to do yet."[6]

Bush's campaign for governor marched in step with his quest for the Texas Rangers, and again he was helped enormously by family connections. Baseball Commissioner Peter Ueberroth was not only a long-standing friend of Poppy, but was widely touted as a top cabinet appointee in the incoming administration. Before the convention, Washington columnist George Will, always reliably informed on GOP maneuverings, had placed Ueberroth on the short list of possible vice presidential candidates. American League president Dr. Robert W. Brown, better known as the Yankees' flashy third baseman Bobby, was also a close friend of George H. W. Bush, and the investors who were being rounded up all had ties to the family. "It certainly helped that he [George W.] was the president's son," Brown told Nicholas Kristof of *The New York Times*. "It wasn't just a strange happenstance that things fell into place."[7]

The Texas Rangers were a mixed bag. On the positive side, they were the *Texas* Rangers. The team played in Arlington, a suburban community between Dallas and Fort Worth. But they were not the Arlington Rangers, or the Dallas-Fort Worth Rangers, they were the *Texas* Rangers—evoking state pride in the legendary lawmen who had maintained order since 1823. For a budding politician seeking statewide office, nothing could be better than to identify with historic icons of Texas.

On the downside, the Rangers were scarcely pennant contenders. The team played in the old Turnpike Stadium that had been built in 1965 to house the Dallas-Fort Worth Spurs in the Texas League, a Double A minor league. Attendance was spotty, the summer heat made Turnpike Stadium the hottest in the majors, and the team consistently lost more games than it won.

The franchise began in 1961 as the Washington Senators, an American League expansion team awarded to Washington after the original Senators moved to Minneapolis and became the Minnesota Twins.

After eleven dismal years in Washington, during which the team lost an average of ninety games a year, the franchise moved to Arlington in 1972. As the Rangers, the team had a series of successful seasons in the late 1970s, but again fell on hard times. During the 1980s, the team finished last in the Western Division of the American League three times, and posted only two winning seasons, one of which was in 1981 when the season was shortened by a players strike.

The team was owned by seventy-eight-year-old Texas oilman Eddie Chiles, a self-made multimillionaire who was in failing health. Chiles was the founder and owner of the Western Company, a vast offshore oil operation and the world's largest supplier of oil rigs. But he was in financial difficulty. The collapse of the oil market had sent the price of Western shares tumbling from $32 to $1.75, and Chiles faced bankruptcy. He had no choice but to sell the franchise. "I can last two more years," Chiles told the *Dallas Times-Herald* in 1986. "If this goes on any longer, I don't know whether any of us will be around." [8] It was now two years later and the price of oil showed little sign of recovering. Chiles had tried to sell the team in the summer of 1988 to out-of-state purchasers who wanted to move the franchise, but the major league owners committee had rejected the deal and told him to seek local buyers. That opened the door for Bush and DeWitt. The Chiles and Bush families had been friends for many years, and Eddie had been a major contributor to all of the senior Bush's campaigns. Mrs. Chiles was the Republican national committeewoman from Texas for much of the 1980s.

As soon as he was settled in Dallas, Bush visited Chiles. He walked into Chiles's house and said he would like to buy the team, that he would put together a syndicate to buy it. "I want you to give me serious consideration," Bush said." [9]

"I'd like to sell it to you, son," Chiles replied, "but you don't have any money." [10] Chiles was asking $80 million for the Rangers, and it was clear that Bush and DeWitt had nowhere near that amount. Chiles reported the conversation to American League president Brown, noting that he would keep the door open, but repeating his doubts about Bush's financial resources.

Negotiations with Chiles went forward in early winter, and Bush

worked feverishly to line up investors. His first call was to his Yale classmate and DKE buddy Roland Betts, who headed a film investment
company called Silver Screen Management. Betts, who was one of his
closest friends at Yale, was also a fourth-generation legacy but there the
similarity ended. After graduation, Betts had secured a draft deferment
by becoming a public school teacher in Harlem, wrote a book about the
plight of inner-city schools, attended Columbia Law School, joined the
liberal Manhattan law firm of Paul, Weiss, Rifkind, Wharton & Garrison as an entertainment lawyer, and then had gone into the business
of providing money for filmmakers. His investment company had financed sixty-three Walt Disney Company movies, including *The Little
Mermaid, Beauty and the Beast, Gandhi, Pretty Woman*, and *The Killing
Fields*. Betts was also a staunch Democrat, his wife was African American, and he had built the 1.7-million-square-foot health club fantasyland
known as Chelsea Piers on the Hudson River in lower Manhattan. Initially Betts was concerned about Bush's plans to run for governor, but
ultimately agreed to invest $3.6 million in the Rangers, making him the
largest single investor in the team. His partner at Silver Screen, Tom
Bernstein, agreed to invest $2.4 million. Bush also convinced his cousin
Craig Stapleton with Marsh & McLennan, and Marriott executive Fred
Malek, a former Nixon aide, to invest. Comer Cottrell, an African
American businessman in Dallas, agreed to put up $500,000.

"The first time I met George," said Cottrell, "he came up to my office and told me he wanted to have a true American diverse team partnership. He said I would be the black partner, Afro-American. George
brought a lot to the table just by being the president's son," said Cottrell.
"Everybody wanted to know him." [11] Bush initially invested $500,000,
later raised to $606,302, based on a loan from the United Bank National
Association against which he pledged his Harken stock as collateral.

DeWitt worked simultaneously to recruit investors in Ohio. By
mid-February, the Bush-DeWitt team had raised close to $40 million,
still too little to make a serious offer to Chiles. At that point, Ueberroth
and Brown flew to Dallas to talk to potential investors on Bush's behalf.
Their principal target was billionaire Richard Rainwater, a Wall Street
legend who, as investment manager for the Bass family, had converted

Eddie Chiles announcing the sale of the Texas Rangers to a syndicate
led by "Rusty" Rose (left) and George W. Bush (right).

a $50 million fortune into $4 billion over a fifteen-year period. Bush
had previously approached Rainwater but had been turned down. Ueberroth and Brown pressed Rainwater to reconsider joining W's syndicate "out of respect for his father."[12] Rainwater eventually agreed to
round up another $40 million, providing his friend Edward "Rusty"
Rose, president of Cardinal Investments and known locally as "The
Mortician" because of his ability to profit from short-selling companies
in distress, would join him. "The commissioner is a better salesman
than you are," Rainwater told Bush.[13]

Under the deal that was finally hammered out, Chiles agreed to
sell his 86 percent ownership in the Rangers for $75 million. Bush and
Rose would become the managing partners, Bush taking the outside
role as the public face of the Rangers, Rose working inside. "Being the
president's son puts you in the limelight," Bush told a reporter for *Time*
magazine. "While in the limelight, you might as well sell tickets."[14]

The sale was announced on March 17, 1989. Bush's share of the
Rangers amounted to 1.8 percent. Asked by reporters why he was made
a managing partner when his share of the team was so small, Bush
snapped back, "Because I put the deal together. I thought of it, worked
it and I was the one Eddie wanted to sell to."[15] In the moment of vic-

tory, Bush can be excused for a bit of self-promotion. Years later, Peter
Ueberroth corrected the record. "George W. Bush deserves great credit
for the development of the franchise," he told *The New York Times*.
"However, the bringing together of the buying group was the result of
Richard Rainwater, Rusty Rose, Dr. Bobby Brown, and the commis-
sioner [Ueberroth]." [16]

For Bush, the Rangers became an obsession. "Buying the baseball
team was a financial risk for me," he wrote on the eve of his run for the
presidency. "I put $600,000—almost a third of my entire net worth—
into a team that had a twenty-five-year losing streak, sagging attendance, and an inferior ballpark. On the other hand, owning a Major
League Baseball team was a dream come true." [17] Bush continued
to flirt with running for governor, but his heart was now in Arlington. And on August 1, 1989, he officially took himself out of the race.
Speaking to the annual meeting of the lawyers division of the Dallas
Jewish Federation, he told the surprised attorneys, "I've decided at this
time that I will not run for governor of Texas in 1990. For now I want
to focus on my job as the managing general partner of the Texas Rangers and more importantly as a good father and good husband." [18]

Later, he told the press, "I'm sure my mother will be happy." [19]

Bush was paid $200,000 a year as managing partner of the Rang-
ers. He also received $10,000 a month from Harken Energy as a board
member and consultant. Bush's duties with Harken were minimal. He
described himself as an adviser to the president, sat on the eight-man
board of directors, and was a member of the three-man audit committee. Basically, Harken wanted Bush because of his name, and in
January 1990 cashed in when the government of Bahrain awarded it an
exclusive offshore drilling contract. Press coverage was favorable, and
shares of the company soared.

Later that spring, Bush was approached by a Los Angeles broker
representing an institutional investor seeking a large block of Harken
stock.* Bush initially declined to sell, but soon had second thoughts

---

* Tangential evidence suggests the investor was the Harvard Management Company, the investment arm of Harvard University. Harvard's holdings in Harken stock increased by 212,750

and on June 22 agreed to sell his original holding of 212,140 shares of Harken for $4 a share, netting him $848,560. Bush said he decided to sell because he wanted to pay off the bank loan he had obtained to buy his slice of the Texas Rangers. "I didn't need to pay it off," he said in an interview. "I did it because I just don't like to carry debt."[20]*

Eight days after Bush's stock sale, Harken finished the second quarter of 1990 with an operating loss of $6.7 million. When nonrecurring expenses were added, Harken lost a total $23.2 million in the quarter. The price of Harken stock plunged to $2.37 a share. Was George W. Bush guilty of insider trading? Did he know of the impending losses before he sold his stock? He was a member of Harken's three-member audit committee as well as its board of directors, and had been warned by financial consultants from Smith Barney of Harken's rapidly deteriorating financial situation.† Bush also failed to file the required notice of sale until eight months after the transaction took place. As numerous critics have suggested, the sale "does not pass the smell test."[21] Bush has denied having any insider knowledge of the impending losses— "I wouldn't have sold if I had"—and a subsequent investigation by the Securities and Exchange Commission ended in 1993 with no charges being filed.[22] But as Bruce A. Hiler, the SEC's associate director for enforcement, noted, that "must in no way be construed as indicating that the party has been exonerated."[23] Like Bush's military service, the 1990 sale of his Harken stock remains shrouded in controversy.

At the ballpark, Bush was in heaven. He became a public figure in his own right, sitting behind the Rangers dugout, handing out baseball cards with his picture on them, autographing scorecards for fans. Bush

---

shares in 1990, essentially the number of shares Bush sold. See Russ Baker, *Family of Secrets: The Bush Dynasty, America's Invisible Government, and the Hidden History of the Last Fifty Years* (New York: Bloomsbury, 2009), 355, and the sources cited therein.

* Considering that Bush had a 100 percent mortgage on his house on which he had made no payments, his comment must be taken with a grain of salt.

† On June 11, 1990, Bush and his two colleagues on the audit committee met with auditors from Arthur Andersen & Co., Harken's accountants, to review the company's books. Harken declined to make the minutes of that meeting available. George Lardner, Jr., and Lois Romano, "Bush Name Helps Fuel Oil Dealings," *Washington Post*, July 30, 1999.

emphasized his Texas roots: the swagger, the twang, the cowboy boots, the chewing tobacco—the J. R. Ewing of the American League West.*

The fact is Bush loved baseball. As a child he had collected baseball cards, could recite the lineups of each major league team, and knew the batting averages and ERAs of most players. But unlike Poppy, he was not an accomplished player. Bush often told the story of his days on the diamond at Yale as a relief pitcher on the freshman team. It was late in the game, Yale was behind by ten runs, and he was warming up in the bullpen. The freshman coach went onto the field and signaled that he wanted to make a pitching change. Bush thought it was his big moment. But the coach called the second baseman to the mound, even though he had never thrown a pitch. "That's when I figured my aspirations of becoming a major league player might not be achieved," said Bush.[24]

He enjoyed socializing with the players in the clubhouse. "I liked him from the get-go," said pitching ace Kenny Rogers.[25] Bush and base-ball immortal Nolan Ryan were especially close. At the age of forty-two Ryan joined the Rangers the year the Bush syndicate purchased the team, threw his 5,000th strikeout that season, and remained for an-other four years, the oldest player in baseball. "Nolan and I often ex-ercised together," said Bush. "I would run on the warning track or on the streets around the ballpark, and then go to the clubhouse to lift weights. He was almost always there. I marveled at Nolan's work ethic and intensity. . . . God gave him the talent to be a good player, his hard work and drive made him great."[26]

And it was not just the players. Bush got to know the ticket takers and hot dog vendors at Turnpike Stadium by their first names, and kept up a steady banter with fans and reporters. "If you're going to a baseball game, you had better go with someone you like," said Bush, "because you have ample time to talk." Laura went to most games, and the twins went to many. "Our girls grew up at the ballpark. It was a time of family and friends."[27]

---

* Bush was a baseball purist. Twice he was outvoted 27–1 by major league owners on signif-icant rule changes. First, Bush opposed adding a wild-card team to league playoffs; second, he opposed regular season interleague play. In both instances, Bush favored tradition over profits. Lou Cannon and Carl M. Cannon, *Reagan's Disciple: George W. Bush's Quest for a Presidential Legacy* (New York: PublicAffairs, 2008), 229.

As owners, Bush and Rose took pride in not micromanaging. Both proved astute businessmen, set the agenda for the Rangers, but left the baseball details to the professionals. Bush learned to delegate. Sometimes he made mistakes, and sometimes monumentally so, most notably when he approved a decision made several levels below him to trade a young Sammy Sosa to the Chicago White Sox for an aging Harold Baines. Right or wrong, Bush thrived on making decisions, a trait he would carry into the White House. But according to everyone associated with the Rangers at the time, Bush's hands-off management style won him fierce loyalty. "You know, this guy fired me," former Rangers manager Bobby Valentine told reporters for *The Washington Post* in 1999. "The honest truth is I would campaign barefoot for him today." [28]

The most pressing problem for the Rangers was the minor league ballpark they played in, which had been expanded when the team came to Arlington in 1972, but was still a far cry from a major league facility. "The first time I went down there, I was shocked," said principal owner Roland Betts. "At our first meeting we agreed that to turn this thing around we were going to build a new stadium." [29] Cost was estimated at $200 million, and the owners did not want to inject more money into the franchise. The solution was to get the city of Arlington to build the ballpark. Point man in the negotiations was Thomas Schieffer, a former Democratic member of the Texas legislature and brother of CBS News correspondent Bob Schieffer. Behind the scenes, it was Bush and Rose who called the shots.

Under the deal that was finally worked out, Arlington agreed to put up $135 million, raised by increasing the city's sales tax by a half cent, and the team's owners undertook to provide the balance, generated primarily by a $1 increase in the price of tickets. The city would initially retain title to the stadium, which the Rangers would rent for $5 million annually. After twelve years, the team could take title if they wished, with no additional money changing hands.* Critics savaged the project as "local socialism," but when the proposal was placed before the citizens of Arlington in a referendum in January 1991, a record 65 percent

---

* Later owners of the Rangers surrendered the option to own the stadium since it was far less expensive to rent it than it would have been to pay property taxes as the owner.

turnout voted in favor of the deal by a margin of two to one. "I was comfortable with this type of public-private financing," said Bush, "so long as the taxpayers of Arlington knew all the facts and were allowed to vote on the proposal."[30]

The day after the referendum, Bush and his fellow owners sat down to plan the stadium. "We agreed that all seats should face the mound, and the field had to be outdoors and grass. We wanted an old-style park. . . . We wanted unpredictable corners in the outfield [similar to the old Ebbets Field] to enhance triples, one of the game's most exciting plays."[31] The stadium, which seats fifty thousand, was designed by David Schwarz of Washington, D.C., and its towering walls of red brick and Texas granite make it one of the most attractive in baseball. The scoreboard in the left field wall evokes memories of Boston's Fenway Park, and the field itself is one of the most hitter-friendly in the majors with the left field foul pole just 332 feet from home plate. Bush chose the name for the stadium—The Ballpark at Arlington—and the first game was played April 1, 1994. That year the Rangers had an average attendance of 40,374 for sixty-two home games—which remains a team record.

"Our partners had a vision," said Bush. "The Ballpark in Arlington is an unqualified success, a win for everybody involved." According to Bush:

> Baseball was a great training ground for politics and government. The bottom line in baseball is results: wins and losses. It's a people business. . . . We had to create trust with the fans that we wanted to win. From baseball I developed a thick skin against criticism. I learned to overlook minor setbacks and focus on the long haul.[32]

National politics rarely intruded. In April of 1991, at the conclusion of the Gulf War, George H. W. Bush's approval rating stood at 89 percent. Six months later it had dropped to 29 percent. The economy was in the doldrums, the president seemed curiously detached from domestic matters, and his partisan nomination of Clarence Thomas to the Supreme Court eroded much of the senior Bush's credibility with independents. With the election one year away, the administration seemed adrift. To add to Poppy's woes, he had recently been diagnosed with Graves' disease, a thyroid ailment that sapped his energy and required continued medication. Finally, and most serious of all, Lee Atwater, the architect of victory in 1988, died of brain cancer in the spring of 1991, leaving a vacuum in the campaign that could not be filled.*

By the autumn of 1991 the situation was critical. On Halloween, Poppy reached out for advice and sent a confidential letter to eight of his most loyal supporters asking their opinion. "I have asked son George to very quietly make some soundings for me on 1992. I'd appreciate it if you'd visit with him on your innermost thoughts about how best to structure the campaign." The president said he planned to wait a while before making any decisions, "but there seems to be a fair amount of churning out there."[33]

Out of the blue, as it were, George W. was back at the center of action in Washington. "He is the number one troubleshooter, the number one confidant of his father," said Republican strategist Mary Matalin. W allowed as how his father saw him as someone who could perform whatever was asked with total loyalty. "He relied on me to do things. I'm not a 1,000 pound gorilla, but do I talk to my dad? You bet. Does he do everything I suggest? No way. But he can always be sure that my agenda is his agenda."[34] When the chips were down, the Bushes, like the Corleones and the Kennedys, preferred to keep things within the family.

Bush remained in Dallas, and his father's friends consulted with him by phone. The unanimous opinion was that White House chief of staff John Sununu must go. Poppy was deeply indebted to Sununu for his primary victory in New Hampshire in 1988, but in three years as chief of staff the imperious former governor had alienated many mem-

---

* "The White House is in total disarray," former president Nixon told his policy assistant Monica Crowley. "It still believes it has a communications problem and if it could just put together a slick photo op, he [Bush] will be back to seventy percent approval. The problem is deeper, it's something that Lee Atwater could sense. I knew him. He was a tough southern son of a bitch, and we needed him. Bush will miss him this election: He doesn't have it without Atwater." Monica Crowley, *Nixon Off the Record: His Candid Commentary on People and Politics* (New York: Random House, 1996), 279.

bers of Congress, the press, and a good portion of the White House staff. As *The New York Times* columnist William Safire put it, "He is widely perceived to be a pompous ass . . . because he has repeatedly demonstrated arrogant asininity."[35]

When the results were in, George W. flew to Washington to meet with Sununu. "Tell him to take the fall," said Poppy, who preferred to leave the beheading to his son.[36] It was the day before Thanksgiving. Sitting in the chief of staff's office in the West Wing of the White House, Bush delivered the message. "John, a lot of people are saying you are the problem. It might be in everybody's interest if you stepped aside."

"Is this request coming from the president?" asked Sununu.

"Let me put it this way, John. I'm not freelancing."[37]

Sununu submitted his resignation on December 3. Poppy wrote a gracious letter in reply, praising Sununu's contributions to the administration. "You have never wavered in your loyalty to us," said the president, "and more importantly, your loyalty to the principles and goals of this administration."[38]

Shortly afterward, George W. told the Texas magazine *D* that wielding the ax against Sununu was one of the highlights of his life. "It's just not that often that you can do something really meaningful to help the president of the United States."[39]

Like 1988, the Bush campaign got off to a slow start. But this time Atwater and Ailes were not there to pick up the slack. George W. remained in Texas (baseball season was under way) and commuted monthly to Washington where he "hung people out to dry" for not responding quickly enough to fast-moving political developments. "I think I can bring an added dimension by staying out here and staying in touch with folks like the Athens [Texas] Rotary Club," said W. He described his job as troubleshooter and loyalty checker. "I had one agenda, and that was what was in the best interests of George H. W. Bush. I told some people in the '92 campaign that I didn't appreciate them trying to climb off the good ship George Bush before it docked."[40]

Aside from the economy and the absence of Atwater and Ailes, the principal problem in the campaign was George H. W. Bush himself, who could not accept the possibility that he might be defeated. Despite constant warnings from W—who could see for himself the mood in Dallas—Poppy dismissed Ross Perot's independent candidacy as loony, and saw Bill Clinton as a clown and a scoundrel. "A guy like that doesn't deserve to be president," he told his sister Nancy Ellis. Barbara Bush agreed. "Bill Clinton and I have something in common," she gloated in a television interview. "Neither of us served in the military. Ha. Ha."[41]

In October, as polls showed Clinton clearly ahead, Bush became shrill. He called Clinton a bozo. "My dog Millie knows more about foreign policy than that clown."[42] Al Gore became "Ozone Man," a mocking reference to the Democratic vice presidential nominee's concern for the environment, and the Democratic ticket was "Governor Taxes and Ozone Man." By the end of October it was clear that Bush was going down—clear that is, to everyone except George H. W. Bush. "I don't want to hear about polls," he told Mary Matalin. "I don't care about the polls. I know I am going to win and I know why I am going to win. It has nothing to do with these numbers."[43]

The final blow was delivered by a federal grand jury on October 30, 1992, less than a week before the election, when former defense secretary Caspar Weinberger was indicted for his role in the Iran-contra affair. Among the documents released by federal prosecutors were handwritten minutes by Weinberger of an off-the-record meeting showing that Bush had strongly supported the arms-for-hostages deal, while Weinberger and Secretary of State George Shultz had opposed. For the last five years, George H. W. Bush had maintained he was "out of the loop." Press coverage was devastating. "It's all over," George W. told Mary Matalin on Poppy's campaign plane.[44]

On election day, November 3, 1992, voter turnout (55.9 percent) was the highest in twenty-four years. Clinton carried thirty-two states and the District of Columbia, won 370 electoral votes, and polled 43 percent of the popular vote. Bush trailed with eighteen states, 168 electoral votes, and 37.5 percent of the popular vote—the lowest percentage of any Republican candidate since William Howard Taft in 1912. Billionaire Ross Perot, running as an Independent, won 18.9 percent of the popular vote (nearly twenty million), the greatest of any third party candidate since Theodore Roosevelt's Bull Moose bid, also in 1912. Poppy, always a good sport, conceded gracefully at 10 p.m. "Watching a good man lose made 1992 one of the worst years of my life," George W. said later.[45]

Poppy's defeat in 1992 cleared the way for George W. to run for office. If George H. W. Bush had been reelected, W would not have been comfortable running in 1994—it would have been on his father's coattails, as it were. Or as Laura put it, "As painful as it was for the family, George H. W. Bush's loss had finally freed his own children to say what they thought and to go after their own objectives."[46]

Bush's target was the governor's mansion in Austin. Meanwhile his brother Jeb set his sights on the governor's mansion in Tallahassee. There was no coordination. Each bid was independent. The two brothers were not close, and never became friends growing up. As adults competing for their father's attention they became even more distant. George had his father's name and his mother's temperament. Jeb was more like his father, married early, settled down, and carved out a political life for himself in Florida, becoming chairman of the Miami-Dade County Republican Party and secretary of state for commerce. Jeb was considered the smarter of the two and was his parents' pride and joy. George W., especially during his first forty years, was often an embarrassment and reveled in his bad-boy reputation. He once introduced himself to Queen Elizabeth at a White House reception as "the family's black sheep." Jeb was the more serious; George the more likable.[47]* Jeb would be running against Democratic incumbent Lawton Chiles and would be favored to win. George W. would be taking on Ann Richards, the best known governor in the country, and was expected to lose.

---

* Elsie Walker, the granddaughter of George Herbert Walker and a cousin of the Bush boys, often summered at the family compound in Kennebunkport as a young girl. She recalled one day she accidentally broke a chandelier while roughhousing with the boys. Jeb ran to tell his mother, and Barbara was not amused. "What the hell is going on here," she exploded. "Jebbie tells me that you've broken the chandelier." Elsie broke into tears, at which point George W. stepped forward. "I broke it," he said, taking the blame and ending the conversation. If people liked George better than Jeb, as most did, Elsie's story helps explain why. Kitty Kelley, *The Family: The Real Story of the Bush Dynasty* (New York: Random House, 2004), 540.

Ann Richards was more than a formidable candidate. She was an iconic figure in Texas politics. Elected state treasurer in 1982, her keynote address to the Democratic National Convention in 1988 electrified the country. "Poor George. He can't help it. He was born with a silver foot in his mouth."[48]* She went on to score a stunning upset victory over Republican Clayton Williams in 1990, becoming the first woman elected governor of Texas since "Ma" Ferguson sixty years earlier.[†]

Texas governor Ann Richards in 1992.

Clayton Williams, a multimillionaire rancher from Midland and Fort Stockton, had been a heavy favorite, at one point leading Richards by 20 points. But his blunders on the campaign trail cost him heavily, particularly among women voters and "new Texans" in the suburbs of Dallas and Houston. He refused to shake hands with Richards in full view of the cameras

---

* George H. W. Bush, always a gentleman, had a silver pin in the shape of a foot made and presented it to Richards, who often wore it. Molly Ivins and Lou Dubose, *Shrub: The Short but Happy Political Life of George W. Bush* (New York: Vintage, 2000), 47.

† Miriam Amanda Ferguson ("Ma"), the wife of Governor James Ferguson ("Pa"), was first elected governor of Texas in 1924 and again in 1932, and was widely considered to be a surrogate for her husband, who had been impeached in 1917 and was no longer eligible to run. On the campaign trail, Ma Ferguson assured voters that she would always follow the advice of her husband. T. R. Fehrenbach, *Lone Star: A History of Texas and the Texans* (New York: Da Capo, 2000), 646–47, 651.

at a television debate, and then threatened to "head her, hoof her, and drag her through the mud." He boasted publicly about going to bordellos across the Mexican border "to get serviced," and followed up by comparing rape to the weather: "If it's inevitable, relax and enjoy it."[49] Richards kept her composure throughout the race and defeated Williams by a hundred thousand votes. As governor, Richards consistently recorded approval ratings of over 60 percent, crime in Texas was down, students' test scores were up, the economy was becoming increasingly diversified, and tax rates were among the lowest in the nation. Her reelection seemed certain.

Bush decided to run in the spring of 1993. Like his decision to run for Congress in 1978, he decided on his own. "I didn't take a poll," said Bush. "I didn't sit around with focus groups or travel around the state."[50] The family and the Bushes' close friends were taken by surprise. Barbara was appalled. Not only did she think George could not win, but his campaign would divert funds from the family network that would otherwise have gone to Jeb. Poppy was equally dismayed, but less outspoken. "George was doing very well in business with the Texas Rangers baseball team," the former president told Hugh Sidey of *Time* magazine. "It surprised me a little when he decided to run for governor."[51]

But the biggest critic was Laura. George was making a good income as the managing partner of the Rangers, he enjoyed his work, and their lifestyle in the Preston Hollow neighborhood left little to be desired. Laura enjoyed the friends they had made in Dallas and was active in philanthropic causes. The twins, who were now eleven, were happily enrolled in the Hockaday School with a full array of friends and extracurricular activities. Why upset such a happy existence to undertake an uphill struggle to unseat Ann Richards?

"Laura was the last person to sign on," Bush told an interviewer on the eve of his run for the presidency. "She wanted to make sure this was something I really wanted to do and that I wasn't being drug in as a result of friends or 'Well, you're supposed to do it in order to prove yourself, vis-à-vis your father.'"[52]

Laura soon recognized that George was serious and that the political bug was biting once again. But she drove a hard bargain. She made it clear the family came first: she was not going to play the role of a typical politician's wife; she was not going on the campaign trail with him, and he must agree to be home every evening for the twins, regardless of where he might be campaigning that day. True to her word, Laura rarely left their home in Dallas for the next year, and George, for his part, returned home every evening. Later in the campaign, Laura spoke occasionally at Republican women's club luncheons, but usually about personal matters and family.[53]

"I wanted Laura to do only what she wanted to do," said George. "I didn't push her to make speeches or public appearances. I didn't want my decision to enter public life to dictate her choices."[54]

During the summer of 1993, Bush was a stealth candidate. He began to organize his campaign staff, set up a fundraising operation, and clear the Republican field so that he might go head-to-head against Richards in the general election. Molly Ivins, who was scarcely an admirer of the Bushes, once wrote, "Don't underestimate George W. Bush," and W's skill at working his way to a virtually uncontested Republican nomination more than justifies Ivins's judgment.[55]

Bush had three potential opponents for the nomination: wealthy Dallas attorney Tom Luce, former campaign manager for Ross Perot; the even wealthier Rob Mosbacher, son of oilman and Bush family friend Robert Mosbacher (who had been Poppy's secretary of commerce), and state legislator Tom Craddick from Midland. Bush held the trump cards: family, ready access to campaign funds, and name recognition. He played them aggressively. On August 30, Bush met with Mosbacher for ninety minutes at the oilman's downtown office and advised him of his intention to seek the nomination. Mosbacher immediately took himself out of the race. He told W that he wasn't interested in spending $15 million and going to war with the Bush family and then Richards.[56] Two hours and several phone calls later Tom Luce announced he too was out of the race. Both men told reporters they were reluctant to run a "tough, expensive race against their long-time good friend."[57] Tom Craddick withdrew later that evening. It was, as Texas pundits put it, "the only one-day gubernatorial primary in Texas history."[58]

By the end of summer, Bush had his campaign staff organized. Karl Rove would handle policy; Joe Allbaugh would manage the campaign, and Karen Hughes would deal with the press. In Allbaugh's words they were "the brain, the brawn, and the bite."[59] The closest parallel is the team Franklin Roosevelt assembled before he made his bid for the New York governorship in 1928: Louis Howe for policy, James A. Farley to manage the campaign, and Missy LeHand for everything else. Without Howe and Farley, FDR could not have won the election that year, and it is doubtful if Bush could have done so without Rove, Allbaugh, and Hughes. Roosevelt kept his team together for four years and they helped usher him into the White House. Bush did the same.

Like Louis Howe, Karl Rove was the eminence gris of the Bush campaign. Nothing happened he was not aware of. For twenty years Rove had been at the center of a political realignment that had transformed Texas from a solid Democratic stronghold to a bastion of Republican power. Now he had a candidate who could make his dreams come true. "Bush is the kind of candidate political hacks like me wait a lifetime to be associated with," Rove told Miriam Rozen of the *Dallas Observer*.[60]

Rove was not a native Texan. He was born on Christmas Day 1950 in Denver, Colorado, the second of five children. His biological father abandoned the family when the children were young, and Rove grew up in Nevada with his mother's second husband, a Norwegian geologist whose name Rove adopted. In 1965 the family moved to Salt Lake City, Rove entered the University of Utah, but left after three years and moved to Washington where he became executive director of the College Republicans. In 1973 the College Republicans were investigated by the Republican National Committee (Poppy was chairman) for dirty tricks during the Nixon campaign against George McGovern, but Rove was exonerated. George W. met Rove at that time. "I assumed he would be another one of the campus political types who had turned me off at Yale," Bush recalled. "I soon recognized that Karl was different. He wasn't smug or self-righteous, and he sure wasn't the typical suave campaign operator. Karl was like a political mad scientist—intellectual, funny, and overflowing with energy and ideas."[61] Louis Howe always called FDR "Franklin"; Rove called Bush "Sir."

Joe Allbaugh, a giant of a man, was recruited by Bush from Oklahoma to make the trains run on time. Allbaugh looked and sounded

like General H. Norman
Schwarzkopf, had run
the successful gubernato-
rial campaign of Repub-
lican Henry Bellmon in
1986, and had served as
Bellmon's chief of staff
in Oklahoma City. Bush
wanted a campaign man-
ager who could enforce
discipline and make his
decisions stick. "Fortu-
nately, that's one of my

Bush's "Iron Triangle": Karl Rove,
Joseph Allbaugh, and Karen Hughes.

strengths," Allbaugh told *The Washington Post.* "I'm the heavy, in the
literal sense of the word." [62]

Karen Hughes, an Army brat, was born in Paris on December 27,
1956. Her father, Major General Harold Parfitt, was the last American
commander of the Panama Canal Zone. After graduating from SMU
in 1977, Hughes went to work as a television journalist and gravitated
into politics. She was the press coordinator of the Reagan campaign in
Texas in 1984, and since 1992 had been the executive director of the
state Republican Party. Of the three principal aides, Hughes was the
closest to Bush. "People have either got good instincts or they don't,"
said George W. "Karen has got good instincts. She can spot a phony
a mile away. Her voice is one of reason and honesty. Plus, Karen is
someone who knows that it's important to be proactive as opposed to
defensive. . . . The day she signed on with the campaign was one of the
best of my political career." [63]

Hughes was equally complimentary. "When you're together for
long days in very high-stress situations, you either end up not liking
each other or liking each other a lot, and we ended up liking each other
a lot. He is funny, he is irreverent, and he has a great big-picture view of
things so he doesn't take himself too seriously. If there is a minor glitch,
he has a great sense of humor about letting it roll off." [64]

Bush can scarcely be faulted for his early campaign efforts. He had

preempted the GOP nomination, tapped into an endless reservoir of
financial contributions (one evening on the telephone Bush raised over
a million dollars), and assembled a campaign team of unrivaled competence. Rove, Allbaugh, and Hughes formed what came to be known as
the Iron Triangle—the core of Bush's election effort. "I run a baseball
team," Bush told them. "I don't pick up the phone and criticize players
when they screw up. That's my manager's job. I'll let you run the campaign. But I'm in charge." [65]

Bush waited until after baseball season to announce his candidacy. On November 8, 1993, exactly one year before election day, Bush
flew to Houston to launch his campaign before an enthusiastic crowd
of three hundred supporters at the Hyatt-Regency hotel in the Gal-
leria shopping mall, less than a mile from where Poppy and Barbara
lived.* "I am not running for governor because I am George Bush's
son," W declared. "I am running because I am Jenna and Barbara's father." Bush went on to lay out a four-point program stressing education,
juvenile justice, welfare reform, and tort reform—the bedrock of his
campaign. These issues had been prominent in Texas politics for the
last decade, and Bush made them his own. "What I offer the people of
Texas is a modern-day revolution. It's a revolution of hope, change, and
ideas. It can only be launched by a new generation of leadership taking
responsibility, and it can only succeed with your support." [66]

As he would do throughout the campaign, Bush refrained from attacking Richards directly. "We're never going to attack her because she
would be a fabulous victim," he told Rove. "We are going to treat her
with respect and dignity. . . . I don't have to erode her likeability. I have
to erode her electability." [67] Bush's discipline on the campaign trail was
exceptional—a reflection not only of his growing maturity, but what
he had learned from Atwater and Ailes. "Years ago George's emotions
related to Ann Richards's statements about my father would have been

* The former president and his wife were noticeably absent when George W. made his an-
nouncement, having been requested not to attend for fear they would steal the spotlight.
J. H. Hatfield, *Fortunate Son: George W. Bush and the Making of an American President* (New
York: Soft Skull Press, 2000), 123–24.

transparent," said his brother Marvin. "It may have gotten to him. He may have said something publicly that he would regret. By the time the election rolled around in 1994, he was a different guy. He was disciplined. I think he surprised a lot of people who did not know him."[68]

For the next year Bush barnstormed across Texas without deviating from his message: education, juvenile justice, welfare and tort reform. "I would travel all day, visit a school or a factory or a courthouse, and then have a fundraiser. I love campaigning, especially in small-town Texas. I enjoy meeting people and shaking their hands and listening to their stories about their lives."[69]

Not everything went according to plan. Both Bush and Richards mounted appeals to the state's vast population of hunters, and Richards was pictured on the cover of a Texas magazine, shotgun in hand, at the opening of dove season. Not to be outdone, Bush organized a dove hunt in Harris County, outside Houston. When the guide shouted "Dove. On your left," Bush fired his shotgun and hit a bird. Bush picked it up, held it for photographers, and the picture was flashed across the state. The problem was the bird was not a dove, but a killdeer, a protected songbird. "I have a confession to make," Bush told Ken Herman of the *Houston Post* as soon as his mistake was discovered. "I am a killdeer killer." He immediately paid a $130 fine and went to the next event on his schedule, a press conference in Dallas. Bush repeated his confession and added, "Thank God it was not deer season. I might have shot a cow." Bush was the butt of jokes across the state, but in the end his candor worked to his advantage. "I think it showed a side of me that voters had not seen. I was able to laugh at myself, to make a mistake, admit it, and poke fun at it. People watch the way you handle things. They like and trust you, or they don't."[70]

Ann Richards, like Poppy in 1992, had difficulty gearing up for the campaign. She too thought she was entitled to be reelected. Richards had also stumbled in a statewide referendum pertaining to education funding, and she refused to take Bush seriously. "I tell you, he is just like your brother-in-law who was supposed to help with the moving," she joked. "They show up after it's done and tell you that the furniture is not in the right place."[71]

The problem of education funding was a long-standing issue in Texas. With over one thousand school districts, the disparity between those that were rich and those that were poor was enormous. Under Texas law, the state provided the funds to assure each child a minimum education, and local districts then enriched that basic education with money derived from property taxes. As a result there were significant differences in per-pupil expenditures from district to district. The issue reached the Supreme Court in 1973 in the case of *San Antonio Independent School District v. Rodriguez,** and a sharply divided Court (5–4) held that education was not a fundamental right guaranteed by the equal protection clause of the Fourteenth Amendment. That threw the issue back to Texas, and in the decade that followed the legislature wrestled with the problem of providing educational equality but failed to come up with an answer. Finally, in 1989, the Texas Supreme Court, in a unanimous decision, held that the existing system was unconstitutional under Article VII of the Texas constitution.[†]

Ann Richards was elected governor shortly afterward and attempted to ram legislation through Austin that would have equalized expenditures from school district to school district. Dubbed "Robin Hood" by the press, the proposal would have taken from the rich and given to the poor. When that failed, Richards and the legislature submitted the proposal to a referendum. The "Robin Hood" scheme would take the revenue from property taxes and distribute it equally throughout the state. Texans voted on the referendum in a special election on May 1, 1993, and voted it down by almost two to one.

Richards was still smarting over that defeat, and on August 20, 1994, speaking before a packed audience of over a thousand teachers in Texarkana, she let her frustration show. "You work like a dog, do well, the test scores are up, the kids are looking better, the dropout rate is down, and all of a sudden you've got some jerk who's running for public office telling everybody it's all a sham."[72] It was a major gaffe. "We knew we had her," said Rove afterward. "As long as we kept our discipline not to be provoked, we were in great shape."[73]

---

*   411 U.S. 1 (1973).

†   *Edgewood Independent School District v. Kirby*, 777 S.W. 2d 391 (Tex. 1989).

Bush fielded the insult flawlessly. The last time he had been called a jerk, he told a Houston PTA group, was "in fourth grade at Sam Houston Elementary School. I didn't think that fellow knew what he was talking about then, and I don't think she knows what she's talking about now."[74] Bush later told *The Washington Post* that Richards's goof was a turning point in the campaign. "I think the dynamics changed when she called me a jerk. People didn't like that. I think it undermined the 'Re-elect-Ann-Richards, she's larger than life' feeling."[75] And indeed, by September, opinion polls showed Bush and Richards were even.

The question of Bush's drinking and drug use did not become an issue in the campaign. Richards had similar problems in her past, and both candidates avoided the matter. When a reporter for the *Houston Chronicle* asked Bush about rumors of his drug use, Bush said, "Maybe I did, maybe I didn't. What's the relevance?"[76] Speaking later to an audience in Lubbock, Bush put the matters to rest. "What I did as a kid I don't think is relevant, nor do I think it's relevant what Ann Richards did as a kid. I just don't think it matters. Did I behave irresponsibly as a kid at times? Sure did. You bet."[77]

There was only one debate in the campaign, and it was scheduled eighteen days before the election. "You can't really win a debate," said Bush. "You can only lose by saying something stupid or looking tired and nervous."[78] Ann Richards was a formidable presence in any debate with a quick tongue capable of devastating sarcasm. For Bush, it was his first public debate and he was understandably nervous. But he had watched Poppy prepare for meeting Dukakis and Clinton, and understood the dangers of being overprepared. A week before the debate he imposed an advice blackout. "I knew the candidate could easily get overwhelmed with last minute suggestions. I ordered that all debate advice be filtered through Karen. If she thought it was essential, she would pass it on. Otherwise, I was keeping my mind clear and focused."[79]

Throughout the debate Bush remained relaxed. When Richards tried to provoke him, he maintained a deferential tone and always referred to his opponent as "Governor." Bush wasn't brilliant or especially impressive, wrote Molly Ivins, "but he was on message and made no mistakes."[80] There were no knockout punches or major bloopers. The only surprise was that Bush had held his own and had not been goaded into losing his self-control. Cousin Elsie Walker, who watched the debate on television, could not believe the transformation Bush had undergone. "He was like a dog with a bone," she told Barbara.[81]

"It wasn't much of a debate," Richards later said to Larry King. "And I don't mean this snidely or unkindly. I think the talent that George Bush has—and I say this with real respect—is that rather than tell you the intricacies of what he knows or what he is going to do, he is rather good at saying things that are all-encompassing. If you say, 'George, what time is it?' he would say, 'We must teach our children to read.'"[82]

In the week following the debate, Bush pulled ahead in the polls. Ross Perot endorsed Richards, but with little noticeable effect. Bush responded by unleashing his mother and Nolan Ryan. In the closing days of the campaign, the two largest newspapers in Texas, the *Houston Chronicle* and *The Dallas Morning News*, endorsed Bush. By 4 p.m. on election day, exit polls showed Bush the clear winner. Bush, Laura, and the twins boarded the campaign plane in Dallas and flew to Austin, where they joined the campaign staff at the Capitol Marriott. At 10 p.m. Governor Richards called and conceded. Final results gave Bush 2,350,944 votes to Richards's 2,016,928—a margin of 334,016, the largest of any Texas gubernatorial candidate in twenty years. *The New York Times* called it "a stunning upset."[83]

Meanwhile in Florida, Jeb was going down to defeat. George W. had waged an almost perfect campaign; Jeb made the errors of a greenhorn. George W. hewed to the middle of the road; Jeb came across as a conservative ideologue. George W. kept Poppy in the background; Jeb flaunted his relationship with the former president. His campaign bus was christened "Dynasty" and he told *The Miami Herald* that he wanted to be able "to look my father in the eye and say, I continued the legacy."[84] And whereas George W. was compassionate and reached out to minority voters,* Jeb took delight in needling them. Asked during

---

* Two Sundays before the election, George W. was invited to speak at the Brentwood Baptist Church in Houston, the city's most prominent African American house of worship. He was

a television debate what he would do to assist the African American population of Florida, he responded, "Probably nothing."[85]

At the personal level, the election had brought George, Laura, and the twins closer together as George dutifully returned home every evening after a hard day on the campaign trail. In Florida, Jeb's candidacy had the opposite effect. Away from home much of the time, his family life was in shambles. Jeb's seventeen-year-old daughter, Noelle, was on drugs, his teenage sons, George and Jebby, were unruly and out of control; and his wife, Columba, felt the family had paid too high a price for Jeb's political ambitions. "You've ruined my life," she was quoted as saying.[86]

For the Bush family the 1994 elections were a turning point. George W., not Jeb, would become the family's standard-bearer. In a sense, he was still a rebel. He had gone against family advice and run for governor when no one thought he could win. And he had achieved something his father had never succeeded in doing: winning a statewide election in Texas. Poppy and Barbara took the change in stride. "The joy is in Texas," the former president told a television interviewer on election night. "My heart is in Florida."[87]

---

preceded by former congresswoman Barbara Jordan, who gave a rousing speech endorsing Richards. George W. was graciousness itself in his response. "I must be doing something right," he told his listeners. "I must have my opponent worried. After all, she has just called on one of the greatest speakers of modern history to make her case. I am humbled to follow the great Barbara Jordan. She is the epitome of a soldier for what is right. I just happen to disagree with her choice for Governor." George W. Bush, *A Charge to Keep* (New York: William Morrow, 1999), 40.

CHAPTER FOUR

Governor

To serve the present age,
My calling to fulfill;
O may it all my powers engage
To do my Master's Will.

"A Charge to Keep"
Charles Wesley, 1762

Since the era of Reconstruction following the Civil War, Texans have subscribed to the doctrine that government is best that governs least. There is no state income tax, the state legislature meets for only 140 days every other year, and the governor's powers, like those of an English monarch, are largely ceremonial. Like the Crown, the governor must give his assent to measures enacted by the legislature, he may call the legislature into special session to deal with a particular issue (few governors have ever done so), and he appoints roughly a thousand members of state boards, commissions, and task forces. Unlike the president of the United States, he is not charged to take care that the laws be faithfully executed, he has no cabinet, and no executive responsibility. Said differently, the governor's office in Texas is perhaps the weakest in the nation.

On the other hand, the functions of the Texas state government are vast. It regulates the production of everything from oil and gas to milk and eggs, oversees fisheries on the Gulf Coast and the production of seed corn in the Panhandle, administers the largest prison system in the Western world and the second largest public education system in

Inauguration as governor, January 18, 1995. The oath was administered by Chief Justice Thomas R. Phillips.

the United States. When Bush took office in 1995, the state budget exceeded $70 billion. But these varied functions are managed for the most part by individuals (such as the secretary of agriculture) elected directly by the voters of Texas. They are independent political figures and are not responsible to the governor. Like the British Crown, the governor of Texas is a head of state. He is a player in the legislative process. His office is a bully pulpit. He can lead public opinion, mobilize it for particular purposes, and symbolize state authority. As Texans might say, the governorship is all hat and no cattle.*

George W. Bush thrived in that setting. The governor's office was, as Bush's most sympathetic biographer has written, the ultimate step for someone who had been the head cheerleader at Ando-

---

* The governor of Texas even lacks the power to grant pardons and reprieves, a traditional prerogative of heads of state. Under the Texas constitution, the governor can grant a stay of execution for thirty days, but the final decision rests with the state Board of Pardons and Paroles. The diminution of the powers of the Texas governor traces to popular rejection of the authoritarian administration of Reconstruction governor Edmund J. Davis, and the desire to prevent a repetition. The powerful Reconstruction constitution was repealed in 1876, and replaced with a document that left the governor with essentially no executive authority. See T. R. Fehrenbach, *Lone Star: A History of Texas and the Texans* (New York: Da Capo, 2000), 435–36.

ver, a fraternity president at Yale, and the public face of a baseball team.[1] Bush developed warm relations with members of the legislature, cultivated the Democratic leaders of the House and Senate, and was not excessively partisan. To most Texans he came across as moderate, caring, and pragmatic—an image he worked hard to establish.

The media in Austin saw Bush in the same light. Drawing on his experience as managing partner of the Texas Rangers, Bush worked the press corps diligently. Like FDR, he remembered the names of journalists and could usually recite a few personal details about each. Bush might inquire about a sick parent or make sure to call on a reporter who brought his or her child to a press conference. And there was a jocular familiarity similar to that in the Rangers' clubhouse. Reporters who saw Bush regularly earned nicknames: Frank Bruni of *The New York Times* became "Pancho"; Candy Crowley of CNN was "Dulce"; David Gregory of NBC was "Stretch." The recipient of the nickname felt flattered, and Bush established his authority.[2]

The Texas capitol is the largest state capitol in the United States, and seven feet taller than the United States Capitol in Washington. It is constructed from hand-cut blocks of pink Texas granite from Marble Falls, and lined with seven miles of oak, walnut, and mahogany paneling. On inauguration day, January 18, 1995, the capitol grounds were packed as Bush took the oath of office as the forty-sixth governor of the Lone Star State and only the second Republican since Reconstruction. The Reverend Billy Graham gave the invocation, and the festivities were highlighted by the Oak Ridge Boys, actor Chuck Norris, Nolan Ryan, and the Dixie Chicks. In his brief inaugural address, Bush took issue with what he saw as the lax morals of the 1960s. "For the last thirty years, our culture has steadily replaced personal responsibility with collective guilt. This must end. The new freedom Texas seeks must be matched with renewed personal responsibility."[3]

Bush resigned as managing partner of the Texas Rangers, sold the house in Dallas, and the family moved into the private quarters on the second floor of the hallowed governor's mansion where Sam Houston once slept.* The twins were again enrolled in private school, this time St. Andrew's Episcopal School in Austin, and Laura became quietly active promoting childhood literacy. Bush later described Laura to *The Dallas Morning News* as "the perfect wife for a governor. There is nothing worse in the political arena than spouses competing for the limelight."[4]

Bush enlarged Ann Richards's office in the capitol to three times its original size, and installed the massive mahogany desk from Brown Brothers Harriman that Prescott Bush had taken to the Senate and Poppy

Sam Houston as Marius.

had used in the White House. He placed his baseball collection in a glass-paneled wooden cabinet at one end of the room, and after considering several possibilities, hung two paintings on his office walls. The first, resurrected from the basement of the capitol, was a full-length portrait of Sam Houston dressed in a Roman toga and standing amidst the ruins of Carthage. Entitled *Sam Houston as Marius*, the painting

---

* The house at 6029 Northwood Road was sold on January 23, 1995, to Paul and Susan Kempe for $348,000. The warranty deed and vendor's lien on file at the Dallas County courthouse suggest that the Bushes made no payments on the mortgage during their occupancy. The entire purchase price was paid to the Compass Bank of Dallas, plus an additional $43,500 paid by the Bushes, a total of $71,500 above the face value of the mortgage, which evidently was for accrued interest. The Bushes paid no money down for the house, made no payments on the mortgage during their occupancy, and paid the accrued interest at the time of sale. This was a sweetheart deal, but it was not illegal.

was done in 1831 by the artist Washington Cooper in Nashville, and depicts Houston as the Roman general Caius Marius.* The painting was done at a time in his life when Houston was drinking heavily, and Bush enjoyed telling visitors that he kept the painting hanging in his office "to remind me that I'm only one bottle away."[5]

The second painting was loaned to Bush by his friends the O'Neills and was entitled *A Charge to Keep*. The painting was a wedding present to the O'Neills, and was done in 1918 by W. H. D. Koerner. Bush was enthralled by the painting. At the church service on the day of his inauguration one of the hymns he selected was the old Methodist favorite "A Charge to Keep," written by movement leader Charles Wesley in the eighteenth century.† *A Charge to Keep* is also the title of Bush's pre-presidential autobiography, which reproduced Koerner's painting on the back of the jacket.

As soon as the painting was hung, Bush sent a memo to his staff. "I thought I would share with you a recent bit of Texas history which epitomizes our mission," he wrote.

> When you come into my office, please take a look at the beautiful painting of a horseman determinedly charging up what appears to be a steep and rough trail. This is us. What adds complete life to the painting for me is the message of Charles Wesley that we serve One greater than ourselves.[6]

---

* The painting is discussed in Marquis James's Pulitzer Prize–winning biography of Houston, *The Raven*, which describes the period as "a painful time for Houston's friends." George W. often called *The Raven* his favorite book. Marquis James, *The Raven: A Biography of Sam Houston* (Austin: University of Texas Press, 1929), 158–59.

† A Charge to Keep
  A Charge to keep, I have
  A God to glorify,
  A never dying soul to save,
  And fit it for the sky.
  To serve the present age,
  My calling to fulfill;
  O may it all my powers engage
  To do my Master's Will!
  Charles Wesley, 1762

Bush saw himself as the rider in the painting, and later hung it in the Oval Office in the White House. The painting was done by Koerner to illustrate a work of fiction by Ben Ames Williams published in *The Country Gentleman*. The story was titled "A Charge to Keep," and tells of a son

A Charge to Keep

who inherits a beautiful forest from his father and is charged to protect it from villainous predators. The scene depicted shows the son in hot pursuit of arsonists.[7] Koerner, a German immigrant, was a regular illustrator for popular magazines, much like Norman Rockwell in later years, and his paintings always hewed closely to the narrative.*

Bush carried his campaign staff over into the governorship. Joe Allbaugh, who had been his campaign manager, became chief of staff. Karen Hughes continued in her capacity as chief spokesperson and communications director, and Karl Rove continued as Bush's primary

---

* In 2007 Sidney Blumenthal published an article on Salon.com asserting that Koerner's painting first appeared in a 1916 *Saturday Evening Post* article by William J. Neidig entitled "The Slipper Tongue," and again the following year in an SEP article by George Pattullo entitled "Ways That Are Dark." Both articles deal with bandits and have nothing to do with a charge to keep. The assertion was repeated by Jacob Weisberg in *The Bush Tragedy* (2008).

Unfortunately, neither Mr. Blumenthal nor Mr. Weisberg appear to have consulted the back issues of the *Saturday Evening Post*. Had they done so, they would have found that Koerner did indeed paint the illustrations for the articles they cite, but the painting "A Charge to Keep" is not among them. Both Blumenthal and Weisberg use the alleged prior publication of the painting as an example of Bush's duplicity. But the facts are entirely on Bush's side. The first appearance of Koerner's painting "A Charge to Keep" was in *The Country Gentleman* article.

See Sidney Blumenthal, "From Norman Rockwell to Abu Ghraib," Salon.com, April 26, 2007; Weisberg, *The Bush Tragedy* (New York: Random House, 2008), 90–91.

The articles they cite are: William Neidig, "The Slipper Tongue," *Saturday Evening Post*, June 3, 1916, and George Pattullo, "Ways That Are Dark," *Saturday Evening Post*, April 4, 1917.

COMPARE, Ben Ames Williams, "A Charge to Keep," *The Country Gentleman*, February 9, 1918.

political adviser. But Rove was not given an office in the capitol nor was
he put on the state payroll. Instead, he remained in his Shoal Creek consulting office about a mile away, was paid a retainer of $7,000 a month
by the Bush election fund, and was linked to the governor's office by a
direct telephone line. Rove was kept at arm's length for several reasons.
First, Harriet Miers, Bush's personal attorney, had counseled Bush that
because of state ethics laws it was advisable to keep Rove—whose duties were entirely political—off the state payroll. Second, by remaining independent, Rove could continue his outside consulting practice,
which was highly lucrative. And third, the relationship between Bush
and Rove was always professional, not personal. Bush needed Rove, and
Rove needed Bush, but they were not intimate friends.

Bush always treated Rove as an employee, and from time to time
publicly humiliated him, calling him "Mr. Big Shot" in front of others
when Rove rambled on too long. Rove, for his part, had other clients,
including tobacco giant Philip Morris, but there was never any question that Bush came first. They made an interesting pair. As one writer
has suggested, Bush had unlimited social confidence but was unsteady
intellectually. Rove was intellectually gifted, but lacked confidence in
social settings. Their relationship was codependent. Rove could not
move ahead without Bush; Bush could not succeed without Rove. But
Bush resented being perceived as dependent on Rove, and always made
a point of treating him as hired help. Bush's nickname for Rove, Turd
Blossom, reminiscent of the little pink flowers that sometimes spring
from cow pies in the pasture, made crystal clear who was in charge.
Rove came to view Bush the way a jockey might view the greatest horse
he would ever ride. He idolized him and feared him at the same time.[8]
Rove was rarely invited to social occasions in the governor's mansion or
later in the White House.

Given the lack of executive responsibility, being governor of Texas
was scarcely a full-time job. According to *Texas Monthly*, Bush arrived
at his capitol office at eight in the morning, left at 11:40 for the track at
the University of Texas where he ran three to five miles, and returned
after lunch at about 1:30. If there were no appointments he would play
video golf or computer solitaire until three, at which time the workday

ended.[9] "There were days when, to be honest with you, he was looking for something to do," said his old Midland friend Dr. Charles Younger. "He would go out and burn some energy. Go jog or do something to kill time."[10]

Bush was a stickler for punctuality and his appointments never ran over. When the allotted time was up an aide would knock at the door. If Bush thought the issue being discussed was sufficiently important, he might wave the staffer away. Exactly five minutes later there would be another knock, Bush would stand up and the visitor would be ushered out. The Bushes often hosted guests for dinner at the governor's mansion, but these always ended promptly at nine. George and Laura retired early, and often read for an hour or two before turning off the lights.

In the office, Bush carried over his style from the Texas Rangers. "He speaks louder with body language than any politician I have ever met," said Austin journalist Paul Burka. "He slouches in a chair to convey utter confidence. He bobs his head when he talks as if to indicate agreement with his own words. And he talks with his eyes. They widen to show sincerity, light up as a prelude to a joke, narrow to show disapproval, and look upward to suggest irony—usually to the accompaniment of a one-syllable guttural chuckle, a 'heh' straight out of *Beavis and Butt-head*."[11]

Bush's primary concern as governor was to secure enactment of his reform agenda: education, juvenile justice, welfare and tort reform. The Democrats had controlled both houses of the Texas legislature since Reconstruction, and the 74th session, which convened the week after Bush took office, was no exception. In the House, Democrats outnumbered Republicans 88–61, with one vacancy. It was somewhat closer in the Senate (17–14), but if Bush was going to get his program adopted, he needed Democratic support.

Texas legislators are paid an annual salary of $7,200, plus a $150 per diem for the 140 days every two years when the legislation is in session. As a consequence, there are no full-time legislators and seniority is a rare commodity. There are two exceptions: the lieutenant governor, who is elected on a statewide basis and presides over the Senate, and the

speaker of the House, whose position is defined by statute. With little
continuity in either chamber, the lieutenant governor and the speaker
enjoy almost unparalleled authority to control the flow of legislation.
In 1995, both were Democrats, both were legendary figures in Texas
politics, and Bush set about to win them over.

The lieutenant governor was sixty-five-year-old Bob Bullock, a
road-hardened professional and the most feared Democrat in the
state. A recovering alcoholic who had been married five times to four
women, he had previously served as state comptroller, secretary of state,
and assistant attorney general. Dubbed a Machiavelli in cowboy boots
by the Austin press corps, he ruled the Senate accordingly. Bullock, like
Lyndon Johnson, loved the game of politics, and was known to package
cattle dung and mail it to offending journalists with a note reading,
"This is bullshit, and so is your column." [12]

The speaker of the House was Pete Laney, a cotton farmer and
used-car dealer from the tiny town of Hale Center (pop. 2,098) in the
Panhandle. Laney was a twenty-five-year veteran of Texas politics, unpretentious, pragmatic, intelligent, and a model of integrity. Four of his
five immediate predecessors as speaker had been indicted for various
criminal acts and the fifth was shot to death by his wife (who was not
indicted).[13] Laney had his hands full every other year explaining House
procedures to newly elected members, and was universally regarded as
an efficient parliamentarian who kept legislation moving. Both Bullock
and Laney had experienced difficulty working with Ann Richards and
were ready to meet Bush halfway. "They were very different Democrats," said Bush. "Bullock would try to dictate a solution; Laney would
finesse one." [14]

Two weeks before the election, Bush had made an unannounced
visit to Bullock, who was recovering from open heart surgery. "I still
am an alcoholic, a recovering alcoholic," Bullock said by way of introduction. Bush responded with stories of his years in Midland, staying
out too late and drinking too much. The two bonded immediately.
What was a courtesy call turned into a four-hour strategy session. Bullock produced lengthy studies on education reform, welfare reform, and
juvenile justice, three of Bush's key issues. "I was very disappointed in

Ann Richards," said Bullock. "If you are going to be that kind of pussy-footing, headline-grabbing governor, forget it."

"I'm going to work with you," Bush replied.[15]

With Laney it was much the same. Laney had watched Bush's campaign unfold and was inwardly pleased that George W. had adopted four issues that were already on the table. "If you find four things that lie fixin' to happen, that you can believe in, then you are politically naïve or dumb not to utilize that," the speaker allowed.[16] The day after the election Bush met with Laney at the Four Seasons Hotel in Austin. "Governor," said Laney, "we're not going to let you fail." [17]

Shortly after Bush took office, he and Bullock and Laney agreed to meet every Wednesday morning for breakfast. At first the meetings were primarily social, but as legislation began to work its way through the system, the breakfasts became vital strategy sessions. "We kept each other's confidence and our commitments, and gradually we built trust and friendship," said Bush.[18]

Perhaps because the Senate was the smaller body, or perhaps because Bullock exerted firmer control, legislation usually made its way through the Senate first and waited for House approval. Soon the breakfast meetings became tense as Bullock pressed Laney for action. At one point Bullock famously boiled over. "Governor," he shouted at Bush, "I am going to fuck you. I am going to make you look like a fool."

Bush rose from his chair, walked over to Bullock, and playfully embraced him. "Okay. If you are going to fuck me, I want a kiss first." [19] Bullock stormed out of the room, but soon came back. Bush had broken the ice. Laney understood that Bullock's tirade was not aimed at Bush, and that it was his way of telling the speaker that it was time to get moving.

Thanks to the cooperation that developed among the three men, the 74th session of the Texas legislature was exceptionally productive. Bush worked hard to learn legislative procedure, and Bullock and Laney proved remarkably good tutors. Bush's people skills served him well. He called on members in their offices, often without an appointment, made himself accessible, and buttonholed relentlessly. "I'm a

listener and a learner," said Bush. "I wanted to hear what was important to each member, what he or she wanted to accomplish during the
session."[20] Legislators in doubt as to how to vote on a particular issue
found themselves invited to lunch or dinner with the governor. Party
lines were ignored. Bush, Bullock, and Laney corralled the votes they
needed, and worked both sides of the aisle.

Education reform proved the most challenging. Bush worked closely
with the chairmen of the relevant House and Senate committees and
eventually a bill emerged that provided for a complete overhaul of the
Texas educational system—the first in almost fifty years. Local school
boards were given greater autonomy, charter schools were established,
minimum standards in core subjects were set (literacy by the end of
grade three became a requirement), schools were granted greater authority to remove disruptive students from the classroom, and the minimum salary for teachers was increased statewide.

Stricter penalties in the juvenile justice system and welfare reform
went hand in hand. Welfare recipients were required to spend at least
thirty hours a week at work or twenty hours in job training; legislation
imposed time limits for welfare assistance and required those on welfare to sign a "responsibility agreement" pledging a drug-free lifestyle.
Thanks partially to the welfare-to-work program, monthly relief rolls
decreased by half (to 474,755) during Bush's first term as governor.[21]

Tort reform was also a major step forward, and Texas became one
of the first states in the union to rein in excessive lawsuits. The new
laws pertaining to civil litigation limited punitive damages, made it
more difficult to sue doctors for malpractice, protected government employees acting in their official capacity, and allowed judges to sanction
lawyers for bringing frivolous lawsuits. The legislation stopped short of
the British and Canadian rule that requires the losing litigant in a civil
action to pay the legal costs of the other party.

When the session ended, Bush had signed 217 bills into law, making
the 74th legislature the most productive in Texas history. "The people
of Texas told us they wanted better schools, tougher juvenile and criminal justice laws, a reformed welfare system, and fairer tort laws," Bush
told *The Dallas Morning News*. "The people of Texas can be proud that

working together we delivered."[22] Bush garnered much of the credit for the success, and his job approval rating climbed from the low 50s to the mid-60s. He jokingly attributed the rise to "a case of low expectations."[23]

Paul Sadler, a prominent Democratic member of the House who chaired the education committee, was impressed with Bush's ability to make crisp decisions. According to Sadler, the governor delegated considerable autonomy to his top aides and gave them wide latitude to evaluate problems and recommend solutions. Bush trusted their advice.

> He had a limited attention span and no stomach for philosophizing endlessly over an issue. I have absolutely no question in his ability to make the right decision if he's presented the facts from all sides. I have watched him do it. Where he gets off track is if he only has one voice in the room.
>
> It's not that he's not smart, not that he's not intelligent, not that he's not a quick study. It's about the need to have different viewpoints in the room. Part of my training as a lawyer is trying to understand what the other side thinks. He comes from an MBA background. He doesn't have that training. To me, that makes it more important to make sure the counselors around him come from different viewpoints.[24]

After the legislature adjourned, Bush marked time in Austin. The twins transferred to public high school for the ninth grade, and in July 1996 Laura threw a surprise birthday party for Bush to celebrate his turning fifty. "I invited his childhood friends, school friends from Andover and Yale, friends from Midland, the familiar and the long lost. We celebrated under the stars with heaps of dripping barbecue and lots of toasts."[25] Toward the end of the evening, Bob Bullock, the Democratic lieutenant governor, made his way to the microphone. "Happy birthday," he told Bush. "You are one helluva governor, and you will be the next president of the United States."[26]

Bush was dumbfounded. "I had been governor for only eighteen months. President Clinton was still in his first term. I had barely thought about my reelection in 1998. Ten years earlier I had been celebrating my fortieth birthday drunk at The Broadmoor. Now I was being toasted on the lawn of the Texas Governor's Mansion as the next president. This had been quite a decade." [27]

The 75th session of the Texas legislature, which convened in January 1997, was anticlimactic. The Republicans captured control of the State Senate, but Bush failed in an effort to achieve a major property tax reform that would have saved Texas homeowners some $4 billion. The saving would be offset by an increase in the state sales tax. The problem, curiously, was with the Republican-controlled Senate, whose members Bush could not convince to go along. "I learned some interesting lessons," Bush wrote later. "First, it's hard to win votes for massive reform unless there is a crisis. Second, Texans appreciate bold leadership. I had earned political capital by spending it. All the dire predictions of damage for trying bold reform were wrong." [28] Bush was planning to run for reelection, and his judgment about the results of the session proved correct when later that fall Bob Bullock, the highest-ranking Democratic officeholder in the state, publicly endorsed him.

"I respect and admire Governor George Bush and feel he deserves reelection for a second term," Bullock told the *Austin American-Statesman*. "During my public career, I've served under seven governors, and Governor Bush is the best I've served under." [29]

Bush announced his candidacy on December 3, 1997, eleven months before election day. Once again he went to the Sam Houston Elementary School in Midland. "Today we face new challenges and new choices," he told a capacity crowd in the school gymnasium. "The times are important. They call for a forward thinking leader who will make the bold call, who will challenge the status quo, who will stand up and say, 'Follow me.' I am that leader." Bush often quoted El Paso artist Tom Lea to say he wanted to live on the side of the mountain that saw the dawn, not the sunset. "I see the day coming when every single child can read, the day when every single Texan who wants a job can find one, the day when every welfare mom finds hope and the help she needs to change her life." [30]

Like Franklin Roosevelt's reelection bid for governor of New York in 1930, the upcoming presidential election loomed in the background.

Already national opinion polls showed Bush running ahead of likely Republican candidates in distant primaries. He had insisted he would not discuss the issue until after the gubernatorial election, and said as much at the news conference following his announcement. "I do not know whether I will run or not run for president of the United States. I intend to get reelected governor." [31]

Bush's Democratic opponent was state land commissioner Garry Mauro. Mauro, a former gridiron star at Texas A&M, had been elected and reelected as land commissioner four times in statewide elections since 1982, was a strong advocate of environmental protection, and had managed President Clinton's reelection campaign in Texas in 1996. But he trailed W by almost 50 percentage points in the polls, had raised little money, and was already under fire from party leaders asking him to drop out lest he bring down the rest of the Democratic ticket. "He's a fine man," Bullock said of Mauro, "but he can't win that race." [32]

With the possibility of another four years in the governor's mansion, Laura and George commenced looking for a country retreat. In February 1998, they found a ranch in the Texas Hill Country, about halfway between Austin and Dallas, and in the spring decided to purchase the property. Roughly 1,600 acres, a full section of prairie grassland, the ranch had been in the hands of the Engelbrecht family, original German settlers in the region, for four generations. Located seven miles northwest of Crawford (pop. 789), it was a working ranch although the cattle and horses had given way to hogs and turkeys. Unlike the arid flatland around Midland, the property was gently rolling, covered with drought-resistant Bermuda grass, and backing onto a series of box canyons with a lengthy frontage on the Middle Bosque River. In August, the Bushes paid the Engelbrechts $1.3 million for the property. Laura immediately began modernizing the six-room ranch house, updating the kitchen, and refurbishing the bedrooms. They called the property Prairie Chapel Ranch, for a tiny chapel nearby, and began to make plans to build a modern dwelling after the election.

The Bushes' purchase of Prairie Chapel Ranch was facilitated by the sale of the Texas Rangers on June 16 to Dallas businessman Tom Hicks. According to *Financial World* magazine, the Rangers, thanks to the Ballpark at Arlington, had become the most profitable franchise in Major League Baseball, and Hicks paid a record $260 million for the team. Bush's share came to $14.9 million: $2.7 million from his original $606,000 investment, plus another $12.2 million contractual bonus for having put together the group of investors in 1989.* "When it is all said and done," Bush told reporters when the deal was announced, "I will have made more money than I ever dreamed I would make."[33] The sale of the Rangers was the proverbial "liberator" for Bush. He was now independently wealthy and had accumulated considerably more money than Poppy had during his years in the oil patch.

The gubernatorial election turned into the rout Bullock had feared. Bush conducted a high-energy statewide campaign and out-spent Mauro twelve to one.† "Got to show them I want the job," he joked. Bush was looser and far more personable on the campaign trail than Poppy or Jeb, and his speeches were funny, self-deprecating, and pleasantly short. Dressed in jeans and cowboy boots, he waded into crowds, clutched arms, patted shoulders, and signed autographs like a rock star. "I'm a political animal," he told reporters. "I don't think campaigns are profound. The issues are profound. The debate should be profound. But campaigning is really just a matter of getting the message out to the voters and getting the voters to the polls. It's not complicated."[34]

Bush courted the Hispanic vote aggressively, beginning with an op-ed in *The New York Times* asking Americans to be less critical of Mexico and its citizens within our borders. "My state shares a 1248-mile border with Mexico," Bush wrote. "The cultural, historical, and

---

* The Bushes' income tax returns, which were made public by the governor's office, showed an income in 1998 of $18.4 million, the bulk of which came from his share of the Rangers' sale. The tax paid totaled $3.77 million. In 1997, the Bushes had reported an income of $258,375 on which they paid $77,084 in taxes. Bush's salary as governor was $88,008.

† Bush raised over $24 million for the campaign, while Mauro made do with less than $2 million. Among Bush's major contributors were the Enron Corporation (Ken and Linda Lay) $312,000; Bass Family Enterprises ($221,000); and Tom Hicks ($153,000). Bush's largest campaign expense, excluding advertising, was for the services of Karl Rove & Co., who were paid $2.8 million from July to December 1998. That figure exceeded the entire cost of Mauro's campaign.

economic ties run deep. Texas is a richer place because of this relationship." [35] Bush spent over a quarter of his well-funded advertising budget
addressing Hispanic voters, visited El Paso, San Antonio, and Latino
communities in the Rio Grande Valley repeatedly, and often appeared
on the stump side by side with the Tejano music star Emilio. The fact
that Bush spoke some Spanish was an added advantage. "I know what
the future is going to look like out here," he told the *Houston Chronicle*, "and we had better make sure Hispanic children are educated, and
that Hispanic entrepreneurs and parents are given encouragement. . . .
Those who say 'English only' poke a stick in the eye of the people of
Hispanic heritage." [36]

On November 3, 1998, Bush won in a landslide, defeating Mauro
68 to 31 percent. Final returns gave Bush 2,550,821 votes to Mauro's
1,165,592. Bush carried 240 of the state's 254 counties, won 49 percent
of the Hispanic vote and 27 percent of the African American. Women
voted for Bush two to one, and his coattails carried every statewide Republican candidate into office.*

"Tonight's victory is a victory of ideas built on a philosophy that is
conservative and compassionate," Bush told cheering supporters in the
Austin Convention Center ballroom. "It says that a leader who is compassionate and conservative can erase the gender gap, open the doors
of the Republican party to new faces and new voices, and win without
sacrificing on principles." [37†]

In Florida, Jeb, who was again seeking the governorship, coasted
to an easy 11-percentage-point victory over Democratic lieutenant governor Ken MacKay. Final results showed Jeb with 2,195,105 votes to
MacKay's 1,773,054. This time Jeb took a leaf from his brother's book,
appeared less cerebral, less ideological, and more willing to accommodate African American voters in the inner cities and Jewish retirees in
South Florida. Unlike 1994, the two gubernatorial campaigns worked

---

* Bullock, in failing health, did not run for reelection as lieutenant governor.

† Throughout the campaign, Bush had described himself as a "conservative with a heart."
Karen Hughes transposed that into "compassionate conservative," an expression Bush used five
times in his victory speech. Karl Rove, *Courage and Consequence* (New York: Threshold, 2010),
122. Also see Karen Hughes, *Ten Minutes from Normal* (New York: Viking, 2004), 110–11.

Prairie Chapel Ranch

closely together, coordinated advertising, and attempted to convey the same message of compassionate conservatism. If W was considering a presidential run, he needed Jeb's support in Florida, and Texas money— well over $1 million by some estimates—began to make its way to Jeb's campaign.[38] The dual victory of George W. and Jeb marked the first time since 1971 that two brothers would serve as governors at the same time.* Poppy called it "the happiest day of my life."[39]

When the election was over, George and Laura turned their attention to Prairie Chapel Ranch. They selected David Heymann of the architecture school at the University of Texas to design the new home, and sited it on a small rise amidst a grove of live oaks and cedar elms. Bush converted a nearby cattle pond into an eleven-acre, man-made lake for fishing, and at the insistence of the twins built a state-of-the-art swimming pool. The house itself was built with native limestone taken from a local quarry, and construction was done by members of a local religious community who sold their services under the trade name Heritage Homestead.

The house itself was of modern design, reminiscent of Mies van

* From 1967 to 1971 Nelson Rockefeller served as governor of New York while his brother Winthrop was governor of Arkansas.

der Rohe's famous Barcelona Pavilion, modified for the Texas Hill
Country. It was a one-story structure, with floor-to-ceiling windows,
high ceilings, cantilevered tin roof, and a wide porch on three sides
that shielded the living quarters from the sun. There was also a central breezeway separating the twins' portion of the house from their
parents—the dogtrot style common in the rural South. As country re-
treats go, it was not large. There were three bedrooms, a living and
dining room combined, a small library, and an additional sitting room
adjacent to the twins' bedrooms. And no stairs or thresholds. "We want
to live at that ranch when we are in our walkers and wheelchairs," said
Laura.[40]

What was unique about the house was the geothermal heating and
cooling system that circulates water three hundred feet deep into the
earth where the temperature is a constant 67 degrees. There is also a
giant 25,000-gallon cistern that collects rainwater from the roof and
recycled household waste for irrigation purposes. Laura worked with
Fort Worth designer Ken Blasingame to furnish the house, and the
result, in Blasingame's words, was "very warm, very comfortable, and
very functional."[41]

Bush's unprecedented two-to-one victory over Mauro catapulted
him to the top of the list of potential Republican nominees for president. Leading party figures from across the country descended on
Austin urging Bush to run and pledging their support. Opinion polls
in December showed Bush leading Al Gore, the Democratic heir apparent, by 12 percentage points. Bush kept his own counsel. "The only
thing I can tell you about all this speculation is that it's just that," he
told *The Dallas Morning News*. "The only future I'm thinking about is
how I will get what I campaigned on into law."[42]

At the personal level, Bush still had doubts. Laura remained close-
mouthed on the subject, and the twins were outright hostile to the idea
of their father running for president. Barbara and Jenna were seventeen
and anxious to pursue their own interests. "Why do you want to ruin
our lives?" they asked.[43] Some of the Bushes' closest friends were also
skeptical. Despite polls showing Bush beating Gore, similar polling revealed that five out of every six Americans believed they were better off

than they had been four years ago. Were they really going to vote for a change, asked W's cousin John Ellis. Bush's youngest brother, Marvin, was more direct. "Are you nuts?" he asked over the Christmas holiday.[44]

Bush's thinking clarified in January. Laura, who always assumed her husband would run—politics was the family business, she often said—gave her approval one evening after dinner. "I'm in," she told George, removing the principal obstacle. "If she had objected, I would not have run," Bush said later.[45] The twins also came around. They accepted the fact that George and Laura had lives to live as well. But the decisive turning point came during the inaugural ceremonies in January 1999. Bush and Laura had scheduled a preliminary church service at the First United Methodist Church in downtown Austin. As the family walked into the church, W turned to his mother and said he was struggling with the decision of whether to run for president.

"George," she said, "get over it. Make up your mind, and move on."

The sermon that day was given by Reverend Mark Craig from Dallas, who spoke of the Lord's summons to Moses to lead the Israelites out of Egypt. The Reverend Craig applied that lesson to the present. The country was starving for moral and ethical leadership, he said. Like Moses, "we have the opportunity, each and every one of us, to do the right thing, and for the right reason."

Barbara Bush looked at George from her seat at the end of the pew. "He is talking to you," she mouthed silently.

"After the service, I felt different," said Bush. "The pressure evaporated. I felt a sense of calm."[46] The decision was made. He called the Reverend James Robison, the outspoken evangelist who hosted the television program *LIFE Today*. "I've heard the call," Bush told him. "I believe God wants me to run for president."[47]

George H. W. Bush was more restrained. "It would be wonderful if George were elected president," Poppy told CBS News. "But it's not—I'm not like Joe Kennedy sitting there: 'Here's a couple of hundred thousand—go out and win the West Virginia primary.' It's not a dynasty. It's not a legacy."[48]

CHAPTER FIVE

The 2000 Election

They worked well together. Whenever Bush could not
think of a fact, Gore would make one up for him.

Jay Leno

Bush may have made the decision to run for president on the day of his inauguration for a second term as governor in January 1999, but he (and his father) were thinking about it as much as eighteen months earlier. The elder Bush was aware that his son had virtually no knowledge of foreign affairs and had scarcely traveled abroad. With that in mind, in the fall of 1997 he arranged for his old and intimate friend Prince Bandar bin Sultan, the longtime Saudi ambassador to the United States, to visit Austin for a private chat with George W.

Bandar in many ways was the Metternich of Washington diplomacy in the 1980s and 1990s, and had personal relationships with world figures such as Mikhail Gorbachev, Margaret Thatcher, and Tony Blair, in addition to leaders in the Middle East and Far East. He was roughly the same age as George W., a seventeen-year veteran fighter pilot in the Saudi air force, and, as George H. W. Bush saw it, someone to whom his son might listen.

Bandar planned his visit to coincide with a trip to Dallas to watch a home game of his favorite NFL team, the Dallas Cowboys. Both he and George W. wanted the meeting to be discreet, and the Cowboys would provide cover. After the game Bandar ordered his private jet to head for Austin. When the plane touched down, Bush was waiting on the tarmac and bounded up the steps of the plane before Bandar could debark.

"Shall we talk here?" asked Bandar. "Yes, I prefer that," said Bush. It was the autumn of 1997, and Bush had not yet announced his intention to seek a second term as governor.

Bush came right to the point. "I'm thinking of running for president," he told Bandar. Bush said he understood domestic politics and had fairly clear ideas of what needed to be done, but "I don't have the foggiest idea about what I think about foreign policy. My dad told me before I make up my mind, go and talk to Bandar. He's our friend, and he knows everyone around the world who counts."[1]

"Governor, I am humbled," said Bandar. "Are you really sure you want to do this?"

Bush replied that he did, at which point Bandar provided a lucid tour d'horizon of international politics, recounting personal assessments of world leaders, their strengths and weaknesses. Diplomacy, he concluded, often made strange bedfellows.

Bush was captivated. He asked Bandar how he should handle those in the United States who were critical of Saudi Arabia and his father—a lightly veiled reference to supporters of Israel and the neocons in the Republican Party who had been critical of George H. W. Bush.

Bandar was frank. "To hell with Saudi Arabia. Anyone who you think hates your dad and who can be important enough to make a difference in winning, swallow your pride and make friends of them."

According to Bandar, Bush seemed troubled by the advice. It wasn't honest, he said. "Never mind," Bandar replied. "This is not a confession booth. If you really want to stick to that and be absolutely honest, just enjoy this term [as governor] and go do something that is fun. In the big boys' game it is cutthroat. It's bloody and it's not pleasant."[2]

In the spring of 1998, while campaigning for reelection as governor, Bush continued to flirt with the possibility of running for president. On

a fundraising trip to San Francisco in late April, he was invited by former secretary of state George Shultz to his home in Palo Alto to meet
with a group of conservative scholars from Stanford's Hoover Institution. Shultz had hosted a similar gathering in 1979 for then California
governor Ronald Reagan, and as Shultz saw it this was another opportunity to bring a potential presidential nominee into contact with the
academic community.* "Same house, same living room, same chairs,
some of the same scholars," said economist Martin Anderson.[3] As with
Reagan, the scholars found Bush appealing. "He is presidential tim-
ber," Shultz told Karl Rove afterward. "He was very relaxed. He had
an inner security which some people have and some people don't."[4]

Three months later, still in the midst of his reelection campaign,
Bush stepped up his pre-presidential preparation. In July, he invited several of the Stanford scholars, including Condoleezza Rice and Shultz,
to a follow-up meeting at the governor's mansion in Austin. They were
joined by former secretary of defense Dick Cheney and his Pentagon
deputy Paul Wolfowitz, who was now dean of the Johns Hopkins
School of Advanced International Studies in Washington. This was a
full six months before Bush made the decision to seek the presidency.
But he told the group he was thinking of running, and asked their help.

The preparations continued in August. George H. W. Bush began
to lay the groundwork for a foreign policy team that W might rely
on during the campaign and later in the White House. Knowing that
George and Laura would be spending two weeks at Kennebunkport,
he invited Condoleezza Rice to join the family for several days. Rice
had already met with George W. twice, and Brent Scowcroft was touting her as a possible national security adviser. "The elder Bush didn't
hide his desire to get me together with his son just so we could get
to know each other better and talk a little about foreign policy," Rice
wrote in her memoirs.[5]

For the next several days Bush and the Stanford provost tested each
other. Over a casual lobster dinner on the back porch at Walker's Point,

---

* In addition to Shultz, those present included Martin Anderson, Michael Boskin, John
Cogan, John Taylor, and Stanford provost Condoleezza Rice.

Bush once again expressed his interest in the presidency and confessed his lack of knowledge about foreign affairs. "This isn't what I do," he told Rice.[6] The two went fishing and worked out together on treadmills, bikes, and rowing machines in the family gym. They touched on foreign policy issues, and found common ground talking about sports. For Bush it was the Texas Rangers, for Rice the Cleveland Browns.

"They bonded at Kennebunkport," said Stanford political science professor Coit Blacker, a close friend of Rice. "She is a sports fanatic and he is too. . . . Condi told me that one of the things she found most endearing about George W. is that he used sports metaphors, and Condi does too."[7]

Rice departed Kennebunkport in the family's good graces. Either at that meeting or shortly afterward Bush decided that Rice should be put in charge of foreign policy if he chose to run. They kept in touch. "We emailed back and forth several times during the fall, mostly friendly chitchat about whatever was in the news," Rice recalled.[8] Later that summer, at the recommendation of Dick Cheney, Bush added a second foreign policy adviser, Wolfowitz, who had worked for both Cheney and Shultz, and who had served on Bob Dole's campaign staff in 1996. Bush was still an empty vessel insofar as foreign policy was concerned, and the fight to color his outlook had begun. The elder Bush and Scowcroft were hoping that Rice could steer him into the realist camp that accepted the world more or less as it was. Cheney and the neocons put their money on Wolfowitz, hoping for a more muscular stance.

On March 2, 1999, Bush announced the formation of a presidential exploratory committee, which, under federal law, would permit him to start raising money for the campaign. In addition to a sprinkling of congressmen and senators, the committee included Shultz, Rice, and former Republican national chairman Haley Barbour of Mississippi. "A good leader surrounds himself with smart, capable people," said Bush. "This will be my hallmark as I explore a national campaign."[9]

By early summer, Bush had raised more than $35 million. That was $7 million more than all of his Republican opponents combined, and twice as much as Vice President Gore, the likely Democratic nominee. When asked by the press to explain his fundraising prowess, Bush said he was always lucky. "I held a press conference [as governor] on the drought, and it rained the next day. Now my mother is calling up for tips on the lottery." [10]

That same summer Bush made several crucial decisions. First, he decided to stick with his Texas team for the coming campaign—the Iron Triangle of Joe Allbaugh, Karl Rove, and Karen Hughes—rather than bring in new blood. None of the three was experienced running a national campaign, but they worked well together, understood the candidate, and had a proven track record. Franklin D. Roosevelt made a similar decision in 1932 when he ran a textbook presidential campaign with his New York team of James Farley, Sam Rosenman, and Louis Howe. Second, Bush decided to run the campaign out of Austin rather than Washington. This was partially dictated by his responsibilities as governor with the legislature in session, but as Rove put it, "that meant that the people who came to work for Bush were likely to be more loyal to him and not treat the campaign as just another job." [11] Finally, having worked in two of his father's presidential campaigns, W resolved to keep expenses low. Raising money did little good if it was spent frivolously, and the Iron Triangle was experienced in making do with less. The Bush campaign had a smaller than normal staff, paid lower salaries, and employed no consultants. Of the ten highest-paid staffers in the Republican primary fight, none worked for Bush. [12]

Bush also resolved to break with Nixon's classic formula of running to the right in the primaries and then moving back to the center for the general election. That put Bush to the left of most of his primary challengers, a compassionate conservative with the emphasis on compassionate. "He is not anti-government," Karen Hughes told Dana Milbank, then with *The New Republic*. "He believes there should be a role for government but it should be limited." [13] Or as Clinton adviser Lanny Davis, a former fraternity brother of Bush at Yale, put it, "Among all of the Republicans running for the nomination, Bush is the closest to the centrist Democratic philosophy. He is as close to Bill Clinton as he possibly could be. George Bush is on the forty-seven-yard line in one direction, Al Gore is on the forty-seven-yard line in the other direction." [14]

As the campaign unfolded, Bush fleshed out his compassionate conservative message. Instead of advocating antiabortion laws, he stressed alternatives such as abstinence and adoption. Instead of lock-'em-up-and-throw-away-the-key, he emphasized rehabilitation programs for prisoners. Instead of a flat tax, he suggested modest cuts for lower income groups. And when asked about the treatment of gays, Bush said, "I believe we should never discriminate against anybody."[15] He also stressed the need for greater education funding as well as equality for new immigrants, especially those of Latino background. "Family values don't stop at the Rio Grande," he famously said.[16] Bush was able to stake out these positions and stick with them because of all the candidates he had the most impressive credentials with the ultraconservative evangelical wing of the party. He had served as his father's liaison with the fundamentalists in the 1988 campaign; he spoke the same language, and no other candidate could claim his legitimacy as a born-again Christian.

By June 1999, Bush was ready to announce his candidacy. In a chartered plane dubbed "Great Expectations" he flew to Iowa, site of the first presidential caucuses. With more than a hundred journalists on board, Bush played flight attendant. "Please stow your expectations securely in the overhead bin," he announced over the public address system. "They might shift during the flight and could fall and hurt someone, especially me."[17]

Speaking to a crowd of more than a thousand supporters in Cedar Rapids, Bush officially threw his hat in the ring. "I am running for president of the United States. There is no turning back. And I intend to be the next president of the United States." After a few generalities about the need for change, he repeated his standard Texas catechism. His goal, said Bush, was to "usher in the responsibility era . . . that stands in sharp contrast to the last few decades, when the culture has clearly said, 'If it feels good, do it.' "[18] A straw poll two months later in Ames, Iowa, gave Bush a commanding lead with 31 percent of the vote. Steve Forbes was second with 21 percent, Elizabeth Dole ran third with 14 percent, and Tennessee governor Lamar Alexander ran fourth with 6 percent. The remainder was divided among eight candidates.

Television debates followed in due course. At a Des Moines debate in December moderated by NBC's Tom Brokaw, the candidates were asked by a local TV anchor to name their favorite philosopher. Bush stunned the audience when he replied, "Christ, because he changed my heart." When asked how, Bush said, "Well, if you don't know, it's going to be hard to explain. When you turn your heart and your life over to Christ, when you accept Christ as the savior, it changes your heart. And that's what happened to me." [19]

After the debate Bush received a congratulatory call from his father and Barbara. "Fine job, son," said the elder Bush. "I don't think your answer will hurt you much."

"Which answer?" asked W.

"You know, that one about Jesus."

Bush was taken aback. He later said he had not calculated his reply but simply said what was in his heart.[20] In any event the younger Bush knew his audience. When the Iowa votes were counted in January, Bush finished well out in front with 41 percent. Forbes trailed with 30 percent, followed by Alan Keyes (14 percent) and Gary Bauer (9 percent). John McCain, who scarcely campaigned in Iowa, polled 5 percent.

The New Hampshire primary followed on the heels of the Iowa caucuses. Bush had concentrated his efforts in Iowa; McCain emphasized New Hampshire. The Arizona senator had spent sixty-five days in the Granite State (compared to Bush's thirty-six), speaking in town hall meetings and crisscrossing the state on his campaign bus, the "Straight Talk Express." New Hampshire voters reciprocated. On February 1, McCain carried the state by 19 percentage points, racking up 49 percent of the votes to Bush's 30 percent. Bush had not been helped by the obvious gap in his knowledge of foreign affairs. Asked by a Boston TV journalist to name the leaders in four world hot spots, Bush drew a blank. Chechnya, Taiwan, India, and Pakistan were terra incognito for the candidate, despite the fact that in Pakistan General Pervez Musharraf had recently led a widely reported military coup ousting Pakistan's longtime prime minister Nawaz Sharif. It was not a good day for the home team. Bush undoubtedly could have named the lineup or pitching rotation for the Texas Rangers but world leaders were beyond his ken.

The unexpected defeat in New Hampshire brought out the best in Bush. When early exit polls indicated the enormity of McCain's victory, he met with his senior staff. Instead of seeking scapegoats, Bush took personal responsibility. "We're a team," he told Allbaugh, Rove, Hughes, and finance chairman Don Evans. "We got here together, and we're going to hold our heads up and go win this together." Bush said he wanted no finger-pointing, no recriminations, no looking back. "We got beat. And now we are going south and we're going to win." [21] Bush did not micromanage. He delegated campaign operations to the Iron Triangle, and when things went wrong he accepted the blame.

It was a character-building moment. "Governor Bush was phenomenal that night," wrote Karen Hughes. "His strength and grace in adversity convinced me that America needed this man to be the next president." [22] Bush took a more modest view. "Voters like to gauge how a candidate responds to adversity. I looked at the defeat as a chance to prove I could take a blow and come back." [23]

In South Carolina the race turned ugly. After McCain's victory in New Hampshire, Bush saw his 19-point lead in the Palmetto State evaporate. Two days after the primary, he trailed the Arizona senator in South Carolina by 5 percentage points. "If we don't win this one, it's over," he told his team in Columbia. Bush had not taken federal campaign funds for the primaries and therefore had no cap on his spending as McCain did. Money poured into the state. The Bush campaign bought up all of the TV time available, and ultimately spent $35 million in South Carolina. Compassionate conservatism went by the boards. Bush, with the vigorous support of Karl Rove and the South Carolina Republican establishment, became the champion of states' rights and the Stars and Bars, with thinly veiled appeals to homophobia, racism, and fundamentalist exclusivity.

The 2000 South Carolina Republican primary was one of the nastiest electoral campaigns on record. Bush kicked off the campaign with a speech to five thousand frenzied undergraduates at Bob Jones University in Greenville, a Christian fundamentalist school that had once been denied its tax exempt status by the IRS because it refused to admit black students. In 2000 the school still banned interracial dating, officially condemned homosexuality, and its president, Bob Jones III, was recently on record referring to Catholicism and Mormonism as "cults which call themselves Christian."[24] After his speech Bush held a press conference in which he dissociated from the university's policies, but his appearance at the school spoke for itself.

For the next sixteen days South Carolinians were bombarded by robo-calls, telephone banks, emails, and anonymous mailings castigating McCain's character. His exemplary Vietnam War record was questioned by fringe veteran groups, it was alleged that he had fathered a black child out of wedlock, and his wife, Cindy, was depicted as a drug addict who stole pharmaceuticals to sustain her habit.* Although the smut was not distributed by the Bush campaign, over the years Bush has been blamed for the descent into the gutter. It was a case of turning a blind eye to the excesses of the campaign's local supporters rather than direct culpability. Karl Rove was in fact deeply troubled by the accusations against the Arizona senator, believing that the McCain campaign, had it been on its toes, could have converted the accusations to their advantage.

> I worried that McCain would stop ranting about negative campaigning and start describing how he and his wife came to adopt their daughter Bridget. It is an extraordinary story of love and compassion. On a trip to Mother Teresa's orphanage in Bangladesh, Cindy McCain was shown an infant who was going to die because the orphanage couldn't provide lifesaving surgery and care. The nuns urged Cindy to take the child home. She did, arriving at the Los Angeles airport to meet her husband with an infant in her arms. It would have been a powerful moment if McCain had chosen to explain it.[25]

On February 19, South Carolina voters turned out in record numbers. Bush swamped McCain 305,998 to 239,984. Steve Forbes and Gary Bauer had dropped out of the race, and Alan Keyes hung on

---

* Not all of the attacks were anonymous. Bob Jones III attacked McCain as a "conniving politician" who dumped his loyal wife for a "rich, attractive, well connected . . . thirty-five-year-old former cheerleader who later became addicted to barbiturates." Bob Jones, "Explaining McCain," *World Magazine*, February 19, 2000.

with 25,999. Three days later in Michigan, McCain rallied and won 51 percent of the vote to Bush's 43. This time it was the Bush campaign that was asleep at the switch. Michigan had recently changed its election laws, and Democrats and Independents were permitted to cross over and vote in the Republican primary—a situation that Rove later confessed he had overlooked.[26] Bush won 67 percent of the registered GOP vote in Michigan, but the heavy turnout of Democrats and Independents in the primary gave the state to McCain.

Nevertheless, the primary race was effectively over. McCain was out of money and the Republican establishment rallied around Bush. McCain continued to do well in New England, but on Super Tuesday, March 7, Bush carried eleven of the fifteen states that went to the polls, including California, New York, and Ohio. The following week six more states, led by Florida and Texas, joined the Bush column, followed by Illinois on March 21, and Pennsylvania and Wisconsin on April 4.

With the nomination secure, Bush confronted the challenge of selecting a running mate. "I knew quite a bit about vice presidents," Bush wrote in his memoirs. "I had followed the selection process closely when Dad was discussed as a possible running mate for Richard Nixon in 1968 and Gerald Ford in 1976. I had watched him serve eight years at President Reagan's side. I had observed his relationship with [his vice president] Dan Quayle."[27] And from the beginning, Bush knew whom he wanted. That was Dick Cheney. Cheney filled the blanks in Bush's résumé. He had been chief of staff to Gerald Ford in the White House and his father's secretary of defense during the Gulf War. In between he had served six terms in Congress, succeeding Trent Lott as the Republican whip in the House.

Cheney knew Washington, was familiar with world politics, and would add gravitas to the ticket. For the last five years he had run Halliburton, the world's largest energy service company, and would be capable of assuming the presidency should that be necessary. He had no higher ambitions. There were downsides. Cheney was also five years older than Bush with a history of heart problems. He had been booted out of Yale not once but twice for academic reasons, and had two

DUI convictions in the early 1960s, including a night in the pokey. But for Bush, who had no love for Yale and had his own DUI problem, these may have made Cheney all the more attractive.

The courtship began in January 2000, two weeks before the Iowa caucuses. Bush dispatched his campaign manager, Joe Allbaugh, to Halliburton headquarters in Dallas to ask Cheney if he was interested in becoming his running mate. Cheney declined. He was happy in the private sector, his oil industry background could be a liability since Bush was also

Dick Cheney

an oil man, and both he and Bush were from Texas, which would raise constitutional issues in the electoral college.* Insofar as Cheney was concerned, the issue was closed. "My message to Joe that day was basically thanks, but no thanks." [28]

Two months later, with the nomination secure, Bush asked Cheney if he would head the search for a running mate. Cheney agreed, and put together a small team including his daughter Liz, who was on maternity leave from her Washington law firm, and David Addington, who had been general counsel in the Pentagon under Cheney. Everything was kept confidential. Prospective candidates were required to

---

* The Twelfth Amendment to the Constitution states that "the Electors shall meet in their respective states, and vote by ballot for President and Vice President, one of whom, at least, shall not be an inhabitant of the same state as themselves." That would preclude the Texas electors from voting for a Bush-Cheney ticket.

answer detailed questionnaires and submit their income tax returns for the last ten years. The documents were kept locked in a file cabinet in the basement of Cheney's daughter's home. By June the list had been narrowed to nine possible candidates.* Notable omissions included Colin Powell and John McCain, both of whom had indicated they were not interested. Cheney put his former mentor Donald Rumsfeld on the list, but Bush struck him off. There was tension between his father and Rumsfeld, said Bush, and a vice presidential slot was not in the cards.[29]

As Bush mulled over the list, he again came to the conclusion that Cheney was far more qualified than any of the candidates they were considering. He called his father for advice, and read the list of names to him. "They are all fine people," his father said.

"What about Dick Cheney," asked W.

"Dick would be a great choice," his father replied. "He would give you solid advice, and you would never have to worry about him going behind your back."[30]

On July 3, Bush and Cheney met at the ranch for a final rundown. They went through the list of candidates, and Bush made it clear he wasn't satisfied. But he was comfortable with Cheney. "You know, Dick, you are the solution to my problem." Cheney recognized that Bush was serious. He also recognized that Bush had a point. "Okay, Governor," he replied, "I will take a look at what I would have to do in order to be a viable candidate. And I have to talk to Lynne."[31] Then Cheney opened up. His daughter Mary was gay. "If you have a problem with this, I'm not your man."

"Take your time, Dick," W replied. "Please talk to Lynne. And I could not care less about Mary's orientation."[32]† By choosing Cheney,

---

* The list included five current or former senators: Jack Danforth of Missouri, Jon Kyl (Arizona), Chuck Hagel (Nebraska), Bill Frist (Tennessee), and Fred Thompson (Tennessee), and four governors: Lamar Alexander (Tennessee), Tom Ridge (Pennsylvania), Frank Keating (Oklahoma), and John Engler (Michigan). George W. Bush, *Decision Points* (New York: Crown, 2010), 67.

† Cheney did not have to complete the lengthy questionnaire required of the other candidates. Had he done so, Bush would have been aware of his five draft deferments during the Vietnam War, the contents of his FBI file, his tax records, and his voting record in the House of Represen-

Bush was looking beyond the election to the White House. Unlike Bush, Cheney was not particularly good on the campaign trail. He had little charisma and in the words of *The New York Times* was "a balding, overweight, middle-aged man who was not especially photogenic."[33] Karl Rove called him "a political Jurassic Park" and "a Beltway retro," and observed that Wyoming's three electoral votes were already safely Republican.[34] But Bush trusted Cheney, and for Bush trust and loyalty trumped all other considerations.

Cheney's doctors, including Denton Cooley, who had performed the world's first heart transplant, gave him the go-ahead, and on July 21 Cheney and Lynne returned to Jackson Hole, Wyoming, to register to vote in the Republican primary. Since the Cheneys had maintained a home in Jackson Hole, there was no problem changing their legal residence from Dallas. And as a Wyoming resident, the Twelfth Amendment requirement would be satisfied. Bush announced his selection of Cheney in Austin on July 25. The following week the Republican convention, meeting in Philadelphia, nominated Bush and Cheney by acclamation.*

On August 17, the Democrats, meeting in Los Angeles, nominated Vice President Al Gore on the first ballot. Unlike Bush, Gore had little primary opposition. House minority leader Dick Gephardt took himself out of the race early, and former New Jersey senator Bill Bradley, the famous "Dollar Bill" who had led the New York Knicks to two NBA titles and Princeton to the NCAA Final Four, waged a lackluster campaign, carried no states, and conceded on March 9, two days after Super Tuesday—the same day that John McCain dropped out of the GOP race.

In some ways Bush and Gore looked remarkably similar. Both were raised in political households (Gore's father, Albert Gore, Sr., was a

---

tatives. Cheney's votes against the Head Start program, school lunches, and the Martin Luther King holiday would become serious campaign issues. Several of the candidates who were considered for the nomination believe that Cheney stacked the deck against them. Their shortcomings were revealed by the questionnaires; Cheney's were not. (Confidential source.)

* All other candidates had withdrawn. On the roll calls, spread over four nights, Bush received 4,328 votes, McCain 1, Alan Keyes 1, and there was one abstention.

three-term United States senator from Tennessee*), went to exclusive all-male prep schools, and had graduated from prestigious Ivy League universities. The similarities were more apparent than real. Bush's early years were spent in the wide-open spaces of a middle-class neighborhood in Midland, Texas. Al Gore grew up in the family's six-room apartment on the eighth floor of Washington's posh Fairfax Hotel, a world of adults, servants, and bellhops. Bush went to Andover and it was a difficult period of adjustment. Gore was a day student at St. Albans, lived at home except for his senior year, when his parents were campaigning in Tennessee, and with hard work finished twenty-fifth in a class of fifty-one. He had "no close friends and no close enemies" a classmate remembered.[35] At Yale, Bush coasted through with a C+ average, distracted by hijinks and the party scene. At Harvard, Gore maintained a C+ average and was not distracted by hijinks and the party scene.[36] Neither took part in the protest demonstrations that were sweeping college campuses in the late 1960s. Bush was Yale '68; Gore, Harvard '69.

After Harvard, Gore volunteered for military service determined—as Bush had been—to avoid damaging his father's political career.[37] Assigned initially to Fort Rucker, Alabama, he married Mary Elizabeth "Tipper" Aitcheson, his longtime girlfriend, in an elaborate ceremony at the Washington Cathedral, May 19, 1970. Gore served five months in Vietnam as an Army journalist assigned to the headquarters of the 20th Engineer Brigade in Bien Hoi. He did not see combat.

After military service, Gore, like many young men, had difficulty finding his footing. Discharged from the Army in 1971, he enrolled in

---

* Albert Gore, Sr., was widely regarded as one of the most liberal of southern Democrats. He was first elected to Congress in Tennessee's fourth congressional district in 1938, and to the Senate in 1952, defeating six-term incumbent Kenneth McKellar. He was one of three senators from the South who refused to sign Strom Thurmond's 1956 Southern Manifesto protesting the Supreme Court's decision in *Brown v. Board of Education* (Estes Kefauver and Lyndon Johnson were the other two); voted for the Voting Rights Act of 1965 ensuring blacks the right to vote in the South, opposed the war in Vietnam, and voted against Senator Everett Dirksen's constitutional amendment that would have permitted school prayer. In 1970 he was defeated for a fourth term by Republican Bill Brock, of the Brock candy fortune. It would be fair to say that the South had grown more conservative by 1970, and Albert Gore, Sr., was one of the casualties.

divinity school at Vanderbilt University in Nashville, but his commitment to the ministry was minimal. Over three semesters he enrolled in eight courses, five of which he failed. Gore later referred to his divinity studies as a period of atonement.[38] From divinity school Gore went to the *Nashville Tennessean*, where he worked as a reporter for two years and then in September 1973 entered Vanderbilt Law School. These were the 1970s and Gore was no stranger to prohibited substances. "He smoked as much as anybody I knew down there," said his friend John Warnecke, "and he loved it."[39]

Law school for Gore was a way station on the road to politics (his grades continued to be in the B– to C+ range), and midway through his second year Joe Evins, the long serving congressman from Gore's home district, announced his retirement. Gore immediately threw his hat in the ring, dropped out of law school, and won the Democratic primary (tantamount to election in Tennessee's fourth congressional district) among a field of nine, defeating his closest rival, the speaker of the Tennessee legislature, 32 to 29 percent. "I think there was a strong sentiment within the Democratic Party that they had let Senator Gore down," said the speaker. "A vote for his son was somewhat of a payback for what they had failed to do for the senator."[40] It was 1974, and Al Gore was twenty-eight. This was four years before George W. challenged Kent Hance for George Mahon's seat in the Texas nineteenth congressional district.

For the next twenty-six years Gore and Tipper lived in Washington. He was elected to the Senate in 1984, taking the seat vacated by Senate minority leader Howard Baker, who chose not to seek reelection, and was reelected over token opposition in 1990. Critics have charged that Gore always had his eyes set on the White House, and in 1988, at the age of forty, he announced his intention to seek the Democratic presidential nomination. He finished last in the Iowa caucuses that year, fifth in New Hampshire, and lost South Carolina to Jesse Jackson, who outpolled him three to one. Gore ultimately finished third behind Michael Dukakis and Jackson with a respectable 13.7 percent of the vote and carried seven states. But his campaign suffered from not having a clear message. As Sidney Blumenthal wrote in *The Washington Post*,

"The premise of Gore's campaign, above all, has been his unironic conviction that he will be president."[41]

Gore also displayed a stiffness on the stump that would become his
hallmark. "How can you tell Al Gore from the Secret Service agents
guarding him," journalists covering the campaign joked. "Gore is the
stiff one."[42] But the most serious flaw was Gore's inability to delegate.
Campaign manager Fred Martin, who had worked on Walter Mondale's run for the presidency in 1984, considered Gore a control freak.
"It was soup to nuts. He was into every large issue and every petty detail
from Tipper's schedule, to car pools, scheduling, hiring, and thank you
notes. He spent an enormous amount of time handling crap."[43]

Gore sat out the presidential primary season in 1992, and with the
nomination in hand, Bill Clinton chose him to be his running mate
from a short list of five.* Gore was by far the most conservative of the
five. "It would be hard for a candidate to get to Gore's right without
looking like an extremist," wrote Louis Menand in *The New Yorker*.[44]
By choosing Gore, Clinton was moving the Democratic Party away
from the Great Society of Lyndon Johnson, George McGovern, and
Walter Mondale into a more conservative mode, a calculated strategy
to win back the "Reagan Democrats" disenchanted with George H. W.
Bush. Clinton's political instincts proved correct, and for the next eight
years Gore had been the Democratic heir apparent.

The election in 2000 was Gore's to lose. The United States was in the
midst of the longest period of prosperity in the nation's history and the
country was at peace. For the last three years the federal budget showed
a surplus, the national debt stood at a generational low of 56 percent of
the gross domestic product, American exports had doubled in the last
eight years, the balance of payments with foreign nations was under
control, the dollar was at an all-time high against the euro, and unemployment levels were the lowest since World War II. Military spend-

---

* Clinton's vice presidential search had been headed by Warren Christopher. After Mario
Cuomo took himself out of consideration, the list included Senators Bob Graham of Florida,
Harris Wofford of Pennsylvania, Bob Kerrey of Nebraska, Congressman Lee Hamilton of In-
diana, and Gore.

ing, which had fallen to 3 percent of GDP, was also at its lowest level since the late 1940s, and not one American had been killed in combat for almost a decade.

Two out of three voters believed Clinton was either "somewhat" or "very" responsible for the nation's prosperity, and the president's job

Joe Lieberman and Al Gore at the Democratic convention.

approval rating stood at 60 percent.[45] The fallout from the Monica Lewinsky affair had largely dissipated, and public opinion increasingly faulted the Republican Congress for bringing impeachment charges for partisan advantage. If Gore could identify with the Clinton record and run on the president's success, he seemed a shoo-in. At the annual meeting of the American Political Science Association in Washington, seven prominent election forecasters unanimously predicted a Gore victory. They disagreed only about the margin, but the consensus was it would be a landslide.[46]

But Gore stumbled on his way to the starting gate. From the beginning he exuded a sense of entitlement. Rather than identify with Clinton, he did his utmost to distance himself. On August 7, one week before the Democratic convention, he announced his selection of Senator Joe Lieberman of Connecticut as his running mate. Lieberman had been one of the most vocal Democratic critics of the president during the Lewinsky affair, and had denounced Clinton's dalliances as "morally reprehensible" and "disgraceful."[47] William F. Buckley, Jr., the custodian of conservative legitimacy, had endorsed Lieberman when he ran for the Senate in 1988 against liberal Republican Lowell Weicker, and Lieberman's voting record in the Senate placed him well on the Democratic right. He supported school vouchers and the privatization of Social Security, and was in the forefront of those who condemned the excesses in the popular culture. Of the Orthodox Jewish faith and deeply religious, Lieberman undoubtedly added moral weight to the ticket. But his "New Democrat" conservatism did little to excite minority voters, and his overall anti-government stance alienated many on the party's left.

In a normal two-party election year that would not have mattered. Gore's choice would have been vindicated as Lieberman enhanced the ticket's appeal to conservative Democrats who might be leaning to Bush. But 2000 was not a normal two-party election year. With Ralph Nader in the race as the candidate of the Green Party, disenchanted liberal Democrats could vote for Nader in protest. And as it turned out, Nader's vote totals eventually helped sink Gore, just as Ross Perot had helped defeat George H. W. Bush in 1992.*

The Democratic convention provided even more striking evidence that Gore was trying to dissociate from Clinton. "I stand here tonight as my own man," said Gore in his acceptance speech. "This election is not an award for past performance. I'm not asking you to vote for me on the basis of the economy we have. Tonight, I ask for your support on the basis of the better, fairer, more prosperous America we can build together." [48] Clinton was not invited to join the candidate on the platform after the speech, and Gore ostentatiously embraced his wife, Tipper, for what seemed the longest kiss ever recorded on television—an implicit rebuke of the president's lifestyle.

Once the campaign began, both Bush and Gore displayed serious flaws on the stump. In Bush's case, it was his seeming unfamiliarity with English grammar and pronunciation. Dwight Eisenhower occasionally played fast and loose with his syntax at press conferences, but it was deliberate on Ike's part to avoid answering a question he wanted to avoid. [49] With Bush, it was a cause for hilarity. He sympathized with

---

* Ralph Nader polled 2,882,738 votes in 2000, roughly 2.8 percent of those cast. But in the pivotal state of Florida, a virtual dead heat between Gore and Bush, Nader received 97,488— a crucial factor contributing to Gore's loss of the state. In New Hampshire, Nader's 22,198 votes would also have given the state to Gore. Richard M. Scammon, Alice V. McGillivray, and Rhodes Cook, *America Votes 24: A Handbook of Contemporary American Election Statistics* (Washington, D.C.: CQ Press, 2001), 9.

Americans trying "to put food on your family," believed the important question pertaining to education was "Is our children learning," and told voters in Des Moines that "We cannot let terrorists and rogue nations hold this nation hostile or hold our allies hostile." He could never pronounce nuclear ("nucular"), tariffs and barriers became "bariffs and terriers," Greeks were "Grecians," and urban pollution was caused by tailpipe "admissions." "Well, I think if you're going to do something and don't do it, that's trustworthiness," said Bush on August 30.[50] Asked about Bush's gobbledygook, his aides said they were the product of an effervescent nature and an agile mind. "His brain works faster than his mouth," said spokeswoman Mindy Tucker.[51]

Gore's problem involved résumé enhancement. He had an irresistible urge to claim credit where no credit was due. He had not created the Internet, he and Tipper were not Erich Segal's models for *Love Story*, he did not discover the chemical disaster on Love Canal, he had not faced enemy fire in Vietnam, nor had he sent criminals to jail as a reporter for the *Nashville Tennessean*. During the first presidential debate Gore claimed to have visited Texas that spring with James Lee Witt, director of the Federal Emergency Management Agency (FEMA), during the wildfires that swept the state, a claim easily disproved since it was Governor George W. Bush who had accompanied Witt. In mid-September, while attacking Bush on the issue of prescription drugs for seniors, Gore claimed his mother-in-law paid three times as much for her arthritis medicine as his dog Shiloh did for the same medicine—which *The Boston Globe* proved was not true.[52] He told a Teamsters rally that he remembered being lulled to sleep as a young boy by his mother singing the garment workers' theme song, "Look for the Union Label"—a song that was not written until 1975 when Gore was twenty-seven. He also claimed credit for taking part in the discussions that led to the creation of the nation's Strategic Oil Reserve. But the oil reserve had been established while Gore was in law school, two years before he was elected to Congress. Bush's verbal guffaws made him appear less intelligent than he was; Gore's exaggerations caused him to look weird and untrustworthy.

The candidates agreed on three debates, and it was widely assumed

On the campaign trail.

that Gore would prevail easily. That did not happen. At the first debate in Boston on October 3, Bush held his own. In a sense, Bush won the debate by not losing it. The perception that Gore was vastly more intelligent was nullified by the vice president's performance. As Frank Bruni of *The New York Times* wrote, "Gore won the debate for Bush."[53] Gore's proclivity to exaggerate his accomplishments played badly, particularly in the press follow-ups of the debate.* But it was Gore's attitude and mannerisms that hurt him most. Viewers found him condescending, arrogant, and petulant. Throughout the debate Gore sighed audibly and rolled his eyes as Bush spoke. Before the debate, Gore led Bush by 11 percentage points in national opinion polls. After the debate, they were even.[54]

The second debate was held at Wake Forest University in Winston-Salem, North Carolina, on October 11. The topic was foreign policy, and again Gore was heavily favored. This time the vice president made an effort to be more agreeable, but to everyone's surprise Bush carried the day. He was warm, relaxed, and thanks to the efforts of Rice and Wolfowitz, reasonably conversant with foreign affairs. And whereas Gore often equivocated, Bush was precise. "I don't think our troops ought to be used for what is called nation building. Our troops ought to be used to fight and win wars."[55] After the debate the Bush team was ecstatic. "I think he won the presidency tonight," Rice

---

* A CNN/*Time* poll immediately after the debate indicated that only 54 percent of the respondents felt Gore was trustworthy enough to be elected president, whereas more than two thirds found Bush trustworthy. Robert V. Friedenberg, "The 2000 Presidential Debates," in *The 2000 Presidential Campaign,* Robert E. Denton, ed. (Westport, Conn.: Praeger, 2002), 155.

told Karen Hughes that evening.[56] Bush now led Gore by 5 percentage points in national polls.

The final debate at Washington University in St. Louis on October 17 was another triumph for Bush. Gore reverted to his aggressive style and at one point, as Bush was speaking, attempted to rattle W by walking up behind him, invading his personal space. Bush glanced toward Gore, nodded his head in a dismissive fashion, and the audience broke out laughing. The incident made Gore look foolish, and was replayed repeatedly on television. After the debate, Bush led Gore in the Gallup poll by 10 percentage points.

It was not just the debates. Throughout the campaign Gore came across as wooden and self-important. Over the years his stiffness had melded into pomposity. When he spoke, he pontificated. "He made everything sound like a university seminar," said one reporter, "so dense with knowledge, so showy with digression."[57] Maureen Dowd of *The New York Times* compared him to the Tin Man in *The Wizard of Oz*: "immobile, rusting, decent, and badly in need of that oil can."[58]

Bush by contrast, appeared likable and approachable—someone you wanted to have a beer with, as the expression went. Bush enjoyed campaigning and was always at ease on the campaign trail. He bantered with the press on his plane, knew most reporters by their first names, and regularly inquired about their families and personal life. By and large, the press reciprocated. As one old-school journalist wrote, "in their political lives the Bushes could be as pitiless as the situation demanded. In their private lives, they seemed truly intent on being as decent and honorable as they could."[59]

Kitty Kelley, no friend of the Bushes, reports an incident at a Washington, D.C., fundraiser at the Willard Hotel. The ticket fee was a thousand dollars and "all the men looked to be lobbyists in expensive suits and huge stomachs." But there was also an old lady in the room, "about eighty-five years old, frail and wearing clothes that looked worn and dated." Bush spoke briefly and started working the crowd. The old lady stepped forward, Bush took her hand, and she asked if he could do something about the price of prescription drugs for the elderly. "I'll try," said Bush. Then he looked at her.

"Did you pay a thousand dollars to come here?" he asked.

"Yes, sir, I did."

"Well, I want you to get your money back." Bush turned to an aide and instructed him to see that she got a check for a thousand dollars.

"No," said the little old lady. "I want you to have it all, Mr. Bush. I want you to win."

"Well," said Bush, "I'll tell you what. I'll keep a hundred dollars and you keep nine hundred dollars and we'll both win."

Observers were touched. "It was such a sweet gesture," said one. "In a crowd of fat-cat lobbyists, that little woman in her tattered coat looked like someone's poor grandmother, and he responded sensitively." [60]

Aside from the different demeanor of the candidates, the Gore campaign was often in disarray. The vice president continued to micro-manage, pollsters came and went with alarming frequency, and midway through the race Gore replaced his campaign chairman, Tony Coelho, a former congressman from California, with William Daley, who was Clinton's secretary of commerce and the son of Chicago's legendary mayor Richard J. Daley. Bush and Gore spent roughly the same amount of money on the race,* but the Gore campaign had a much higher overhead, paid exorbitant salaries, and engaged a bevy of consultants. [61]

By contrast, the Bush campaign kept overhead low and spent its money on advertising and organization at the precinct level. At Karl Rove's insistence, the Bush campaign targeted Arkansas, Tennessee, and West Virginia. The last Republican to carry West Virginia was Herbert Hoover in 1928. Bob Dole had lost the state by 14 points in 1996, and not since Nixon in 1956 had anyone on the GOP presiden-

---

* Both the Bush and Gore campaigns accepted federal funding of $67.6 million. In addition, under federal law, the candidates were permitted to raise private contributions to pay for legal and accounting costs incurred to comply with federal legal requirements, known as General Election Legal and Accounting Compliance funds (GELAC). The Bush campaign raised an additional $6.8 million for this purpose, Gore raised $8.2 million. In sum, the Bush campaign reported total funding of $74.8 million, and the Gore campaign $75.8 million. Federal Election Commission figures, in Anthony Corrado, "Financing the 2000 Elections," *The Election of 2000*, Gerald Pomper, ed. (New York: Chatham House, 2001), 106.

tial ticket campaigned in West Virginia. The Democrats took all three states for granted. But times had changed. Clinton was not on the ticket, which made Arkansas vulnerable; Gore had left his Senate seat eight years earlier and had not cultivated his Tennessee constituency; and West Virginia had succumbed to the "guns, God, and gays" mantra of the fundamentalists, plus a heavy dependence on coal, which made Gore's environmentalism suspect. In November, Bush carried all three states.

But Gore's most serious error was to keep Bill Clinton out of the campaign. At Gore's insistence, the president remained on the sidelines. He was told not to speak in battleground states, and the two never appeared on the same platform together.[62] In 1960, Vice President Richard Nixon had also wanted to demonstrate that he was his own man and kept Dwight Eisenhower out of the campaign. It was bad strategy in 1960, and equally bad in 2000. Bill Clinton could have galvanized low-income voters who traditionally supported the Democratic ticket. But in 2000, low-income voters, evidently turned off by the Gore campaign, voted in considerably smaller numbers than in 1992 or 1996.[63]

As the race entered its final week, Bush continued to lead although his margin had shrunk to 4 points. At the same time, Gallup reported that 64 percent of expected voters had a favorable view of Bush. Only 49 percent felt that way about Gore. But on Thursday, November 2, the Bush campaign received a severe setback when their candidate's credibility was shaken. That evening, Fox News broke the story of Bush's 1976 DUI conviction in Maine. Bush had not revealed the incident. Kent Hance knew of it in the 1978 congressional campaign in Texas but chose not to mention it. And when Bush ran against Ann Richards in 1994, both sides steered clear of past peccadilloes. It also did not come up when Governor Bush ran for reelection in 1998. The Iron Triangle—Rove, Hughes, and Allbaugh—knew of the arrest but assumed it was safely tucked away in the police files of Kennebunkport. Bush later said he didn't reveal it because he didn't want his young daughters to know. "I worried that my disclosing my DUI would undermine the stern lectures I had been giving them about drinking and driving."[64]

Bush's credibility advantage over Gore suddenly evaporated. What had been a 4-point lead shrank to a 2-point margin on November 4, and by election day the candidates were in a dead heat. When the news first broke, Bush was speaking in Milwaukee. He hastily called a press conference and admitted the arrest.

> It's an accurate story. I'm not proud of that. I've often times said that years ago I made some mistakes. I occasionally drank too much. I did on that night. I was pulled over. I admitted to the policeman that I had been drinking. I paid the fine. I regretted that it happened. I learned my lesson.[65]

But the damage had been done. It was not so much that Bush had been arrested, but that he had concealed it.* For many voters, Gore began to look better. "When I went to bed that night in Wisconsin," Bush later wrote, "I realized that I may have just cost myself the presidency."[66]

---

* Dick Cheney's two DUI convictions had long been known and no one seemed to care. In 1996, Bush had the opportunity to disclose his arrest when he had been called for jury duty. As he left the courthouse in Austin, Wayne Slater of *The Dallas Morning News* shouted, "Have you ever been arrested for DUI?" Bush replied somewhat evasively, "I do not have a perfect record as a youth. When I was young I did a lot of foolish things. But I will tell you this, I urge people not to drink and drive." Bush later said he regretted not revealing the arrest that day because it would not have been a problem. He also could have mentioned it in his 1999 campaign biography, *A Charge to Keep*, but did not do so. George W. Bush, *Decision Points* (New York: Crown, 2010), 76.

CHAPTER SIX

The Rule of Law

I was not elected to serve one party, but to serve one nation. Whether you voted for me or not, I will do my best to serve your interests, and I will work to earn your respect.

George W. Bush
December 13, 2000

Bush spent election day in Austin. He and Laura voted early, and then joined the extended Bush family for a celebratory dinner at the Shoreline Grill. But as the returns came in, the mood turned sour. Shortly after 7:30 p.m. Eastern time, the major networks called Florida, Michigan, and Pennsylvania for Gore. If that were the case, the election was lost. Bush and Laura slipped out of the restaurant without touching their food and returned to the governor's mansion. The ride back was quiet. "There isn't much to say when you lose," Bush recalled. "I was deflated, disappointed, and a little stunned. I felt no bitterness. I was ready to accept the people's verdict." [1]

The Bushes had scarcely settled in when Karl Rove called. The networks had it wrong about Florida, he said. The Sunshine State had two time zones, and the polls in the ten counties of the Panhandle were still open. Widely known as the "Redneck Riviera"—that portion of the Gulf coast from Pensacola to Panama City to Apalachicola—the Florida Panhandle was strong Bush country.[2] By ten o'clock, as more votes were counted, the networks reversed themselves and said Florida was too close to call. "Back from the ashes," shouted Jeb Bush as he rushed up the steps of the governor's mansion to convey the news.[3]

The race had come down to Florida. Nationwide, Bush led in twenty-nine states with 246 electoral votes. Gore was ahead in twenty states and the District of Columbia with 266 electors. (One Democratic elector from the District of Columbia abstained.) Neither had the 270 required for election, and Florida, with twenty-five electors, would put either over the top.* The vote was slow coming in. By one o'clock on the East Coast (midnight in Austin), Bush held a slight lead. At 2:15 (EST) the networks called Florida for Bush. Fifteen minutes later Vice President Gore was on the phone conceding the election.

> *Gore:* Congratulations.
> *Bush:* You are a formidable opponent and a good man.
> *Gore:* We sure gave them a cliff-hanger.
> *Bush:* I know it's hard and hard on your family. Give my best to
>   Tipper.[4]

Bush told Gore he was headed out to address his supporters who were gathered at the state capitol. Gore asked Bush if he would wait fif-

---

* Article II, section 1 of the Constitution, dealing with the election of the president, apportions the electors by state: "Each state shall appoint, in such manner as the legislature thereof may direct, a number of electors equal to the whole number of Senators and Representatives to which the State may be entitled to in Congress." The Article further requires that to be elected, a candidate must receive a majority of the electors. In 2000, there were 538 electors, corresponding to the number of senators (100) and members of the House (435), plus three from the District of Columbia added by the Twenty-third Amendment. A majority of electors—one over half—was 270.

Should no candidate receive a majority in the electoral college, the Constitution, as modified by the Twelfth Amendment, provides that the decision shall be made by the House of Representatives from the top three candidates, each state having one vote. This has occurred twice: after the 1800 election when the House elected Thomas Jefferson over Aaron Burr, and after the 1824 election when it chose John Quincy Adams over Andrew Jackson.

teen minutes so that he might speak to his supporters first. Some were taking it very hard, said Gore.[5] Bush agreed, and the family remained glued to the television screen waiting for Gore's concession speech. As the vote totals continued to come in, the race tightened. Fifteen minutes passed, then another fifteen, and no concession speech. At 3:30 a.m. Eastern time, 2:30 in Austin, Bush's campaign chairman, Don Evans, received a call from Bill Daley at Gore's headquarters. They were double-checking some numbers in Florida, said Daley. Then Gore came on the phone. He said he was retracting his concession. "Circumstances have changed dramatically since I first called you," said Gore. "The state of Florida is too close to call."

"Are you saying what I think you're saying?" Bush asked. "Let me make sure that I understand. You're calling back to retract that concession?"

"You don't have to be snippy about it," Gore replied.

"Well, you've got to do what you've got to do," said Bush, ending the conversation.[6]

Bush was steaming. "I'd never heard of a candidate un-conceding. In Texas, it means something when a person gives you his word."[7] Cheney, who had joined the gathering, thought Gore erred in conceding too quickly. In the 1976 election between Gerald Ford and Jimmy Carter, which was also very close, Ford had decided to go to bed and look at the results in the morning before conceding.[8] Several of those in the governor's mansion urged Bush to ignore Gore and speak to the crowd that had gathered in front of the state capitol and declare victory. Bush was tempted to do so. But as he made ready to leave, Jeb pulled him aside. The Florida governor had been huddled over his laptop all evening, logged onto his secretary of state's website. "Don't do it, George," said Jeb. "The count is too close."[9] What had been a sixty-thousand-vote lead when Gore first called had shrunk to less than two thousand. Bush took Jeb's advice. "I'm going to bed," he told the folks in the mansion. "We'll reconvene in the morning."[10]

Before going to bed, Bush learned that the Gore campaign had dispatched a team of lawyers under former secretary of state Warren Christopher to Florida to organize a recount. Campaign manager Don

Evans urged Bush to do the same. "I was confronted with the most bizarre personnel choice of my public life," said Bush. "There was no time to develop a list or conduct interviews." [11] Evans suggested James Baker, who had been George H. W. Bush's secretary of state and was an old friend of the family. W agreed. He called Baker and asked if he would take on the assignment. Baker accepted and flew to Tallahassee on Wednesday. For the next thirty-five days the outcome hung in the balance.

The focus on Florida obscures two vital facts about the 2000 election. First, George Bush and the Republicans waged an extraordinarily successful campaign, capturing ten states that had voted for Clinton in 1996.* Second, the Democrats were correspondingly inept. If Al Gore had carried just one of those states he would have picked up enough electoral votes to put him over the top. Florida would not have mattered. Overall, Gore won a half million more popular votes than Bush: 50,992,335 to 50,455,156. But he lost New Hampshire by 7,000 (Nader had 22,000), Nevada by 21,000, and West Virginia by 40,000. [12] In that sense, the election was not lost in Florida. It was lost by the failure of the Gore campaign to build on Clinton's base.

National exit polls revealed that 80 percent of the electorate believed Bush was honest and trustworthy. Only 15 percent felt that way about Gore. On the other hand, voters gave Gore high marks for experience by roughly the same margin. Fifty-nine percent of those questioned found Bush to be likable, only 38 percent said that about Gore. [13] The likability factor is a sleeping giant in presidential elections. With the exception of Nixon's victory over Hubert Humphrey in 1968, the most likable candidate has been elected in every presidential election since 1932. [14] Among regular churchgoers, Bush trounced Gore 59 to 39 percent. Bush also did well among traditional Democratic constituencies such as low-income voters, Catholics, Hispanics, and the young. Bush took 43 percent of the Hispanic vote in Texas, and in Florida, with its large Cuban population, actually beat Gore 49 to 48 percent. Men

---

* Arizona (8 electoral votes), Arkansas (6), Kentucky (8), Louisiana (9), Missouri (11), Nevada (4), New Hampshire (4), Ohio (21), Tennessee (11), and West Virginia (5).

tended to prefer Bush; women, by a lesser margin, liked Gore. Voters without college degrees, who had voted overwhelmingly for Clinton in 1996, preferred Bush in 2000. More affluent voters, particularly those with advanced degrees, voted heavily for Gore. As Democratic pollster Stan Greenberg put it, "We lost it downscale and gained it upscale." [15]

When it became clear that the recount in Florida would be a lengthy process, Bush and Laura went to the ranch to decompress. "I checked in regularly with Jim Baker to get updates and provide strategic direction," said Bush, "but I decided early on that I would avoid the endless, breathless TV coverage." [16] For a brief period, the Bushes lived a quiet life of watchful waiting. Bush went for long runs and cleared trees; Laura walked, read, and prepared meals for the two. "Like a baseball batter in the ninth inning of game seven of the World Series, we had learned to tune out all the extraneous noise," Laura remembered.[17]

Inauguration day, January 20, 2001, was seventy-four days away, and Bush could not afford to wait for the Florida outcome before moving to assemble his administration. Presidents-elect have adopted various approaches to the problem of transition. Dwight Eisenhower delegated the selection of his cabinet to Lucius Clay and Herbert Brownell and took off for a month to play golf at the Augusta National. George H. W. Bush on the other hand chose each incoming cabinet member personally, and even hectored at least one of the outgoing members of Reagan's cabinet to depart early.* Eisenhower was not familiar with the American domestic scene and relied on the judgment of Clay and Brownell. By contrast, the senior Bush had been in Washington for the previous

---

* When Senator John Tower was nominated by Bush to be secretary of defense, Tower asked Frank Carlucci, Reagan's secretary, to remain in office until he, Tower, was confirmed by the Senate. Carlucci agreed to do so. But shortly thereafter Carlucci received a telephone call from a member of Bush's transition team telling him that the president-elect "wanted everybody out prior to the inauguration." Presumably the other members of Reagan's cabinet received the same call. When Carlucci reminded the staff person that the president and secretary of defense are the National Command Authority statutorily responsible for military action, the staff person simply repeated that the president-elect wanted everyone out prior to the inauguration. At that point, and even though Tower's confirmation now looked doubtful, Carlucci agreed and stepped down. (Confidential source.)

eight years as vice president and knew the political landscape firsthand. As governor of Texas, George W. Bush fell somewhere between the two, but closer to Ike.

With the outcome in Florida in doubt, Bush turned to Cheney to organize the transition—if there was to be one. The recount was under control. What was needed was a slate of potential cabinet and subcabinet appointees ready to take office should Bush win. Cheney volunteered to start assembling the team that would take office on January 20, 2001, and Bush agreed. Politics was involved as well. By acting as winners, Bush and Cheney strengthened the public's perception that they were the winners.

Bush's decision to entrust the formation of the administration to Cheney was unprecedented. No president-elect had ever delegated the organization of his administration to his vice president. It is inconceivable that Franklin Roosevelt would have authorized John Nance Garner to select the key players of the New Deal, or that John Kennedy would have allowed Lyndon Johnson to staff the New Frontier. After the fund exposure and the Checkers speech, Dwight Eisenhower would not have trusted Richard Nixon to sharpen his pencils. It is equally inconceivable that Ronald Reagan would have permitted his primary rival, George H. W. Bush, to pick his cabinet; that Bush would have asked Dan Quayle to do so; or that Bill Clinton would have entrusted the task to Al Gore. Vice presidents do not run transition teams.

But the relationship between Bush and Cheney was different. Secure in the knowledge that Cheney had no higher ambition, Bush had no hesitation in granting him unprecedented authority. Said differently, the Bush administration was staffed largely by Dick Cheney and it was Cheney's people who took office. The problem was that Cheney was light-years to the right of Bush. He could never have been elected president, yet because of Bush's grant of authority it would be the vice president and his people who would set the course for the administration. Bush always reserved the final decision for himself, but the lead-up to that decision and the range of alternatives presented were shaped by Cheney and his appointees.

There were several exceptions. Bush knew whom he wanted close by. Before the election Bush had asked Andrew Card to become White House chief of staff if he were elected. Card had been deputy chief of staff under John Sununu in his father's administration, and Bush wanted a familiar Washington hand in the White House. He liked Card and believed he was temperamentally suited to work with Team Bush from Texas—Rove, Hughes, Alberto Gonzales, and Harriet Miers. "Andy was perceptive, humble, loyal, and hardworking ... along with a caring heart and a good sense of humor." [18]

Bush also chose Colin Powell to be secretary of state without consultation. A year before, Powell had made it clear that he was uninterested in running for vice president, but that he would consider the position at State. Bush was in awe of Powell, and Powell is the only candidate who was considered for the post. "He is a tower of strength and common sense," said Bush when the appointment was announced. "When you find somebody like that, you have to hang on to them. I have found such a man." [19]

For secretary of defense Bush wanted Fred Smith, the founder and chief executive of FedEx. Smith had been two years ahead of Bush at Yale, preceded him as president of DKE, and was also Skull and Bones. Smith fought in Vietnam as a Marine, won a Silver Star, a Bronze Star, and two Purple Hearts, and was a spectacular success in the business world. Smith indicated his willingness to accept the post, but suffered a mild heart attack and had to bow out before the choice was announced. As secretary of commerce, Bush chose his lifelong friend from Midland, Don Evans. Evans had chaired every campaign Bush had waged, and again, no one else was considered for the position.

Bush made two other appointments without consultation. He wanted Condoleezza Rice as his national security adviser, and Larry Lindsey, a resident scholar at the American Enterprise Institute, as his chief economic adviser. Both were carryovers from the campaign trail. Rice had been Bush's primary foreign policy aide during the campaign, and Lindsey had been his senior economics guru. With the key people in place, Bush turned to Cheney and Rove to fill the remaining positions. Cheney became the official chair of the transition team, and Rove added a political litmus test.

After the selection of Powell to be secretary of state, the two principal portfolios to be filled were Defense and Treasury. When Fred Smith stepped aside, Bush initially considered Pennsylvania governor Tom Ridge, and then former Indiana senator Dan Coats for the Pentagon. But Ridge was not acceptable to many in the party because of his pro-choice stand as governor, and Coats, a former member of the Senate Armed Services Committee and a darling of the fundamentalists, flunked his interview with Bush when he said he did not consider a missile defense to be an urgent priority and then went on to deplore the presence of women in combat-related roles. Improved missile defense had been a key element in Bush's election platform, and while the president-elect might be sympathetic to Coats's views on women, their combat-support role was an accomplished fact and there was no need to stir up an unnecessary firestorm. Paul Wolfowitz from the campaign trail was also briefly considered. Bush liked Wolfowitz—called him "Wolfy"—but quickly realized he lacked management experience.

With Ridge, Coats, and Wolfowitz out of the running, Donald Rumsfeld emerged as the leading candidate for the Defense post. Rumsfeld had held the position during the last two years of the Ford administration, had recently chaired a commission established by Congress to assess the ballistic missile threat to the United States,[20] and was currently heading a commission examining problems of security in outer space.[21] He had also chaired Bob Dole's policy committee during his presidential bid in 1996. After leaving government service in 1977 following Gerald Ford's defeat, Rumsfeld had been a success in business, first as CEO of G. D. Searle, the Chicago pharmaceutical firm, then head of General Instrument Corporation, a cable and communications firm, and was currently chairman of Gilead Sciences, a start-up biomedical company in Silicon Valley.[22] His administrative skill had been proven in the marketplace, and his political dexterity was a matter of record. As a young member of Congress in 1965, Rumsfeld played a major role in ousting Charles Halleck as House minority leader and replacing him with Gerald Ford, and later as Ford's chief of staff in the White House figured in the famous "Halloween Massacre" of October

1975 gearing up for the coming election.*

Originally Rumsfeld had been slated to take over the Central Intelligence Agency, but his qualifications for the Defense portfolio were compelling. Con-doleezza Rice urged W to appoint him, George

Donald Rumsfeld

Shultz weighed in heavily on Rumsfeld's behalf, as did Colin Powell.[23] Rumsfeld's greatest supporter was Cheney, who had entered government service as Rumsfeld's protégé, succeeded him as Ford's chief of staff, and had kept in touch over the years. Rumsfeld and his wife, Joyce, had spent election night with the Cheneys in Austin. Many writers have suggested that Cheney saw Rumsfeld as a powerful counterweight to Powell at State. That puts the cart before the horse. The tensions that later developed within the administration were nowhere in sight in December 2000. When Cheney had been secretary of defense, he had recommended Powell to be chairman of the Joint Chiefs, and they shared a mutual respect.[†]

Rumsfeld had two strikes against him. First, there was a noticeable lack of warmth between Rumsfeld and the senior Bush. In the spring

---

* The Halloween Massacre was a major reshuffling of personnel in the Ford administration prior to the 1976 presidential election. Facing a tough primary fight against Ronald Reagan, Ford dropped liberal vice president Nelson Rockefeller as his running mate. Rockefeller agreed to step down, but was not pleased. In addition to dropping Rockefeller, Henry Kissinger agreed to step down as the president's national security adviser (but remained secretary of state); CIA chief William Colby was replaced by George H. W. Bush; James Schlesinger was removed as secretary of defense to be replaced by Rumsfeld; and Dick Cheney succeeded Rumsfeld as White House chief of staff.

† At the time, Powell was the youngest of the fifteen four-star generals and admirals eligible to succeed Admiral William Crowe as chairman of the Joint Chiefs, and Cheney had to overcome the initial opposition of President Bush. See George Bush and Brent Scowcroft, *A World Transformed* (New York: Alfred A. Knopf, 1998), 23.

of 1987, as Reagan's term approached its end, Rumsfeld undertook a bid for the Republican presidential nomination. His campaign never got off the ground, and when he withdrew he threw his support to his old friend from their days in the House, Senator Bob Dole. George H. W. Bush, then vice president, did not take kindly to Rumsfeld's endorsement of Dole, and relations between the two had been strained ever since.* Indeed, when it became clear that Rumsfeld was under consideration for the Defense post, James Baker interceded to warn W. "All I am going to say to you is, you know what he did to your daddy." [24] Andrew Card, who had been deputy White House chief of staff under the elder Bush, also raised the issue, and there is no doubt Rumsfeld and George H. W. Bush did not care for each other.[25] The second strike was delivered by Karl Rove, who reminded Bush that Rumsfeld was a throwback to an earlier era. With Cheney and Powell already on board, did the administration need another retread? And because of their long friendship, would Rumsfeld be seen as a tool of Cheney, detracting from Bush's authority?[26]

Bush decided to see for himself. On December 22 he invited Rumsfeld to Austin. "I was surprised by Governor Bush's request to see me," Rumsfeld remembered. "He had to be aware that I did not have a close relationship with his father. I thought it spoke well of him that he was interested in meeting me himself to draw his own conclusions." [27]

---

*   It has often been suggested that the hostility between George H. W. Bush and Rumsfeld traced to the Halloween Massacre in 1975, Bush believing that his posting to the CIA was a means of removing him from vice presidential consideration in 1976. That is not the case. According to Barbara Bush, her husband was "thrilled" to be able to return from China to head the CIA, and the restriction against his running for vice president in 1976 was imposed by the Senate during his confirmation hearing. Barbara Bush, *Barbara Bush: A Memoir* (New York: Guideposts, 1994), 131.

The idea that Rumsfeld was behind Bush's posting to the CIA as a means of removing him from vice presidential consideration was spawned by Bush's election autobiography, *Looking Forward* (New York: Doubleday, 1987), 157–58. Bush was evidently smarting over Rumsfeld's endorsement of Dole before the New Hampshire primary. The story developed legs and became part of Washington mythology. But when Rumsfeld wrote President Ford asking him to clarify the circumstances of Bush's recall from China to head the CIA, Ford confirmed that it was his sole decision to put Rumsfeld in the Pentagon, and relieve Kissinger of his role as national security adviser. Gerald Ford to Donald Rumsfeld, April 3, 1989, Gerald Ford Presidential Library.

By Bush's standards the meeting was a long one—almost two hours. They discussed both the CIA and the Defense Department. Rumsfeld told Bush that leadership turbulence was a serious problem in the intelligence community. In the past twelve years there had been six directors of central intelligence and seven directors of the Defense Intelligence Agency. "If a corporation changed its management almost every other year it would go broke.[28]*

On defense matters, Rumsfeld was up to speed. The Pentagon was drifting, he told Bush. Senior officials were operating without top-level strategic guidance. The military needed to become more agile and more rapidly deployable. Missile defense required urgent attention. Fixing the problems "would unquestionably require breaking some crockery and bruising more than a few egos." Rumsfeld warned this would carry considerable political risk. "Governor, if I were to serve in your administration I would be leaning forward. If you would be uncomfortable with that, then I would be the wrong man for the job."[29]

Bush was captivated. "Rumsfeld impressed me," he wrote later. "He was knowledgeable, articulate, and confident. As a former secretary of defense, he had the strength and experience to bring major changes to the Pentagon. He would run the bureaucracy and not let it run him."[30] Cheney, who attended the meeting, said, "They clicked and hit it off."[31] Close acquaintances of both Rumsfeld and Bush have noted that they shared a gift for "emotional intelligence."[32] Also like Bush, Rumsfeld brought a rare bounce to public life. Although fourteen years older than the president-elect, Rummy still bubbled with energy and enthusiasm. Like Bush at Yale, Rumsfeld had been a popular member of his class at Princeton. Rumsfeld did not come from a privileged background. But he studied hard, did well academically, and excelled at athletics as captain of the varsity wrestling team, winning the Ivy League wrestling

---

* George H. W. Bush, a former DCI, had made a similar point to his son. Indeed, when Jimmy Carter defeated Ford, the senior Bush had gone to Plains, Georgia, to try to persuade the incoming president to keep him on the job. "Automatically replacing the director in each new administration would tend to politicize what essentially is a career service," GHWB wrote in his memoirs. George Bush and Brent Scowcroft, *A World Transformed* (New York: Alfred A. Knopf, 1998), 21.

championship in his weight class in both his junior and senior years, and captaining the 150-pound (sprint) football team to its best season ever.

With the selection of Rumsfeld for Defense, Bush's national security team was in place. "General Powell is a strong figure, and Dick Cheney is no shrinking violet, but neither is Don Rumsfeld or Condi Rice," said Bush when he announced Rumsfeld's appointment. "I view the four of them as being able to complement one another." [33]

For Treasury, Bush selected Paul O'Neill, the CEO of Alcoa. O'Neill had been deputy director of the Office of Management and Budget under Ford and an outstanding success at Alcoa, making it the world's largest and most profitable aluminum producer. [34] He was a close friend of Cheney as well as George Shultz and Alan Greenspan from the Nixon years, and was vigorously recommended by all three for the cabinet post. "He knew more about the budget and the budget process than just about anyone else and was one of the most capable and competent people I'd ever worked with," said Cheney. [35]

It was Karl Rove who recommended John Ashcroft for attorney general. Ashcroft had just lost his Senate reelection bid in Missouri to deceased governor Mel Carnahan, becoming the only senator in American history to lose his seat to a dead man.* Ashcroft was four years ahead of Bush at Yale, and a devout evangelical. He was also a past client of Rove + Company, Karl Rove's political consulting firm. Another former Rove client was Gale Norton, the attorney general of Colorado, who became the first woman to serve as secretary of the interior. Bush's first choice for Interior was former Wyoming governor Mike Sullivan, a Democrat well versed in conservation issues. But when Sullivan said no, Bush turned to Norton. Bush initially selected Linda Chavez, who had chaired the Civil Right Commission during the Reagan administration, to be secretary of labor, but she was forced to withdraw because of nanny problems. Chavez was replaced by Elaine Chao, wife of

---

* Carnahan was killed in an airplane crash three weeks before the election. Missouri governor Roger B. Wilson announced that if Carnahan defeated Ashcroft, he would appoint Carnahan's widow to the seat, which he did.

Kentucky senator Mitch McConnell and a former director of the Peace Corps.

The remaining members of Bush's cabinet were recommended by Cheney. Norman Yoshio Mineta, secretary of transportation, had served as chairman of the House Committee on Transportation and as Bill Clinton's secretary of commerce for the last six months of the president's term. Of Japanese ancestry, Mineta as a young boy had been interned after Pearl Harbor and spent the war years at a detainment camp in Wyoming, where he became friends with a young Alan Simpson. He was a Democrat and former mayor of San Jose. Ann Veneman, incoming secretary of agriculture, had been deputy secretary under the senior Bush and was currently head of California's Department of Food and Agriculture. Anthony Principi at Veterans Affairs had also headed his department briefly under the elder Bush. All three were seasoned veterans of the Washington scene.

For secretary of education Bush tapped Roderick Paige, the highly regarded superintendent of education in Houston, Texas. Paige was an African American and a native Mississippian. Longtime Wisconsin governor Tommy Thompson became secretary of health and human services. Thompson had worked arduously during the campaign and the ticket owed him. The final two posts were ethnic choices. Spencer Abraham of Michigan, an Arab American who lost his Senate seat to Debbie Stabenow, became secretary of energy, and Mel Martinez, a Cuban American who had co-chaired Bush's campaign in Florida, took over housing and urban affairs.*

The director of central intelligence is not a member of the president's

---

* One of the underreported stories of the 2000 election is the Muslim American vote, which went overwhelmingly for Bush. The U.S. Census does not publish data on Muslims in the United States, and population estimates vary between six and twelve million, with most observers placing the number in 2000 at seven million. The heaviest concentrations are in Michigan, Ohio, and Florida. According to exit polls in Florida conducted by the American Muslim Alliance, 91 percent of Muslims voted for Bush, 8 percent for Ralph Nader, and only 1 percent for the Gore-Lieberman ticket. As Grover Norquist later put it in *The American Spectator*, "George W. Bush was elected President of the United States because of the Muslim vote. That's right, the Muslim vote." The appointment of Spencer Abraham as secretary of energy reflected the GOP's awareness of this often overlooked voting bloc. See Alexander Rose, "How Did the Muslim Vote

cabinet but is nevertheless a major figure in matters of national security. With Rumsfeld going to Defense, Bush chose to stick with his father's recommendation, Clinton's CIA director George Tenet. In the intelligence briefings Bush received before the inauguration he and Tenet hit it off, and Tenet was in especially good standing with the Bush family, having named the CIA headquarters building in Langley, Virginia, for George H. W. Bush the year before. By retaining Tenet, Bush would be sending a message of continuity to the intelligence community.

All presidential cabinets reflect varying degrees of competence and a multitude of political considerations. George Washington's initial cabinet included Alexander Hamilton and Thomas Jefferson. Abraham Lincoln's cabinet was a team of rivals. With Ike it was "eight millionaires and a plumber." George W. Bush's cabinet spanned the spectrum. Colin Powell, Donald Rumsfeld, Paul O'Neill, and Norman Mineta brought enormous expertise to the task. On the other hand, defeated senators in need of a posting—John Ashcroft and Spencer Abraham— added little to the mix. Ethnicity, gender, and social diversity received their due, and there was a symbolic Democrat. As the inauguration approached, Bush's first team was in place. But Florida hung in the balance.

The Florida recount was in some ways a unique experience, but it was not the first time that a state's electoral vote had been questioned. In 1876, in the contest between Democrat Samuel Tilden and Republican Rutherford B. Hayes, the electoral vote of three states—Florida, Louisiana, and South Carolina—was in doubt. Early returns indicated Tilden as good as elected. With 185 electoral votes required, the New York governor had 184 compared to Hayes's 166. To win, Hayes needed the electoral votes of all three disputed states and that seemed unlikely. When the vote count was complete, it appeared that Tilden had carried Florida and Louisiana, while Hayes clung to a narrow lead in South Carolina. This was the era of Reconstruction, and in all three states Republican administrations controlled the returning boards re-

---

in 2000?," *Middle East Quarterly*, Summer 2001, 8; Grover Norquist, "The National Conservatives: Muslims Deliver for the GOP," *American Spectator*, June 2001.

sponsible for certifying the
result. Politically it was a saw
off. The Democrats had used
threats and violence to prevent many African Americans
from voting; the Republicans
used their control of the election machinery to massage the
count.

A special joint commission
composed of five members of
the House of Representatives,
five senators, and five Supreme
Court justices reviewed the results and awarded the electors
in each of the three contested
states to Hayes. Governor Til-

James Baker

den accepted the result with remarkable equanimity. "We have just
emerged from one civil war, and it will not do to engage in another."[36]
His supporters for the most part agreed. In 2000 the outcome of the
election would again be determined in Florida, but the survival of the
Union was not at stake. And by selecting James Baker and Warren
Christopher—both former secretaries of state—to head their respective
efforts in the Sunshine State, Bush and Gore were elevating the level of
discourse. As senior statesmen, both men exuded an unassailable aura
of wisdom and rectitude. "These are two quintessential professionals,"
said a former State Department official who had worked with both
men. "They are the two chief grown-ups."[37]

Warren Christopher, at seventy-five, was the most senior partner
in the Los Angeles law firm of O'Melveny & Myers. As a young man
fresh out of Stanford Law School he had clerked for Supreme Court
justice William O. Douglas, and later served as deputy attorney general during the last two years of Lyndon Johnson's term. Returning
to government as deputy secretary of state in the Carter administration, Christopher led the negotiations that resulted in the release of

the fifty-two Americans held hostage at the U.S. embassy in Tehran. He later conducted the search for a running mate for Bill Clinton, led Clinton's transition team, and served as secretary of state from 1993 to 1997. Gore had tapped Christopher four months earlier to head his own search for a running mate, and his selection to head the Florida recount came as no surprise.

James Baker, at seventy, brought similar credentials to the fight. A senior partner in the Houston law firm of Baker Botts, a firm that had been founded by his great-grandfather, Baker had run five consecutive Republican presidential campaigns between 1976 and 1992. He served as White House chief of staff, then secretary of the treasury under Ronald Reagan, and was secretary of state for most of George H. W. Bush's term as president. He returned to the White House to be the elder Bush's chief of staff and head the 1992 campaign, but according to seasoned observers he rather resented having to leave the realm of diplomacy. In 2000, Baker was serving as the United Nations' negotiator attempting to resolve the conflict in the Western Sahara, and was senior counselor to the Carlyle Group, a global asset management firm in Washington. Despite the obvious similarities, Christopher and Baker were very different men. Warren Christopher was primarily a lawyer with a sideline in politics. Baker was a politician with a sideline in the law. Christopher was cautious and judicious; Baker relentless and partisan. And although both had served as secretary of state and knew many of the same people, they were not friends.[38]

When dawn broke in Florida on Wednesday, November 8, Bush led Gore by 1,784 votes (2,909,135 to 2,907,351), with all sixty-seven counties reporting. Under Florida's election law, that triggered an automatic recount. The secretary of state's office instructed each country to run the ballots through machines again and report the tally by the close of business on Thursday, November 9. The result was that Bush's lead narrowed to 327 out of the almost six million votes that had been cast.* At that point the Gore campaign requested manual recounts in four counties: Broward, Miami-Dade, Palm Beach, and Volusia (Daytona

* The final recount figures were 2,910,198 for Bush and 2,909,871 for Gore.

Beach). All four counties had voted heavily for Gore, and Christopher's team believed that a manual recount would produce enough additional votes to put him over the top.

The Bush campaign responded by seeking an injunction in the United States district court in Miami to prevent a manual recount. "The more often the ballots are recounted, especially by hand, the more likely it is that human errors . . . will be introduced," said Baker. "Let the country step back for a minute and pause and think about what's at stake here. The purpose of our national election is to establish a constitutional government, not unending legal wrangling." Reminding the Democrats of Nixon's refusal to challenge the results from Mayor Richard Daley's Cook County in 1960, Baker suggested it was time for the Gore campaign to accept the results and move on.[39]*

The dispute escalated when Florida's secretary of state, Katherine Harris, who had co-chaired Bush's campaign in the state, issued an advisory opinion to the canvassing boards stating that a manual recount must be limited to ballots that had already been tabulated and could not include any new ballots that might have been overlooked.[40] Democratic attorney general Bob Butterworth, who had co-chaired Gore's campaign, responded the next day with his own advisory opinion saying that Harris had misinterpreted the Florida election statute and that the canvassing boards should proceed with counting all valid ballots.[41] Harris also announced that she would certify the state's vote on November 14, one week after the election, regardless of what recounts might be under way. The Gore campaign answered by filing suit in Florida circuit court to keep Harris from enforcing the November 14 deadline, and back and forth it went.

On Monday, November 13, the Federal district court in Miami heard argument on the Bush motion to stop the manual recount. The case for Bush was presented by Ted Olson of the Washington office of

---

* In the 1960 election, John F. Kennedy carried Illinois by 8,858 votes, thanks to the 318,736-vote margin he received in Chicago. Daley had waited until the downstate vote was in before reporting the Cook County results. Critics have suggested that he waited until he knew how many votes he needed. Final Illinois results gave Kennedy 2,377,846 to Nixon's 2,368,988. In Cook County, Kennedy received 1,378,343 to Nixon's 1,059,607.

Gibson, Dunn & Crutcher. Olson was an icon of the conservative legal community, one of the founders of the Federalist Society, and a veteran of thirteen appearances before the Supreme Court of the United States. He was opposed by Harvard Law School's distinguished constitutional scholar Laurence Tribe. Tribe had argued twenty-nine cases in the Supreme Court, and had been victorious in nineteen. No other attorney came close to that record. After listening to oral argument, Judge Donald M. Middlebrooks dismissed Bush's motion.

> Under the Constitution of the United States, the responsibility for selection of electors for the office of president rests primarily with the people of Florida, its election officials and, if necessary, its courts. The procedures employed by Florida appear to be neutral and, while not yet complete, the process seems to be unfolding as it has on other occasions. . . . I believe that intervention by a federal district court, particularly on a preliminary basis, is inappropriate.
>
> MOTION DISMISSED.[42]

That same afternoon, Leon County circuit court judge Terry Lewis ruled that the statutory seven-day reporting deadline was mandatory, but that the Volusia County canvassing board could amend its returns at a later date. (Presumably the other three counties could do so as well.) Secretary of State Harris was authorized to use her discretion as to whether to accept the amended returns or not. The Bush forces appealed both the federal and state court decisions; the Gore forces appealed that portion of the state court decisions that permitted Harris to exercise her discretion.

Immediately after the court's decision, Harris asked each of the four counties to submit their requests for an extension. The counties complied somewhat haphazardly, at which point Harris rejected all four requests and announced that she intended to certify the results on November 18 following the tally of overseas ballots. The Gore forces appealed, and Judge Lewis ruled that the secretary of state had acted within the scope of her discretionary authority and her decision was final. There would be no extension. When the overseas absentee ballots were added to the count on Friday, November 17, Bush's lead increased to 930.

At this point the Supreme Court of Florida stepped in and issued a stay order prohibiting Harris from certifying the results until it could hear a consolidated appeal of all cases Monday morning, November 20. The court went on to say that "It is NOT the intent of this Order to stop the counting and conveying to the Secretary of State the results of absentee ballots or any other ballots." The Florida Supreme Court had entered the contest with guns blazing. The manual recounts would continue, and Harris was barred from interfering. The fact that all seven members of the Florida Supreme Court had been appointed by Democratic governors was not lost on Baker and his colleagues.

On Tuesday, November 21, the Florida Supreme Court rendered its decision. Harris had been wrong to set a premature deadline, said the justices, and wrong about limiting the scope of a manual recount. The court said the recount should continue, and set a new deadline of Sunday, November 26, which was five days away.[43] This was the high-water mark of the Gore campaign. Scarcely had the ink dried on the court's decision when Ted Olson filed a petition for a writ of certiorari in the Supreme Court of the United States.* The Florida court was changing the rules after the election had taken place, said Olson, and had opened the door to "an electoral catastrophe." The Supreme Court needed to prevent "the ascension of a President of questionable legitimacy, or a constitutional crisis." In a second filing, Olson asked for an expedited hearing of the matter.

Constitutional scholars gave Olson's request for certiorari little chance. As far back as *Marbury v. Madison* in 1803, Chief Justice John Marshall had distinguished between legal issues and political questions. "It is emphatically the province and duty of the judicial department to say what the law is," Marshall wrote, but political questions lay within the sphere of the two political branches—the Congress and the president.[44] And the Florida election was a political question. There

---

* A writ of certiorari, literally a writ of discretion, is the avenue by which the Supreme Court allows a case to come before it. It requires four justices to agree to issuing the writ.

was also the matter of federalism. If there was a touchstone in the judicial philosophy of the William Rehnquist Court, it was the primacy of
states' rights. The Constitution had expressly delegated to the states the
selection of their electors for president, and the Supreme Court of the
state of Florida had spoken. Moreover, the recount was still under way.
Under its normal procedures, the Supreme Court of the United States
insists upon a final judgment before it considers taking a case.

Nevertheless, on Friday, November 24, the Supreme Court granted
certiorari and agreed to hear Bush's appeal. Oral argument was set
for December 1. Specifically, the justices asked whether the action by
the Florida Supreme Court violated federal law,* and also whether
the state court's decision was inconsistent with Article II, section 1
of the U.S. Constitution, which provides that a state's electors shall be
chosen "in such a manner as the legislature thereof may direct."

In Florida the recount continued. Palm Beach County failed to finish by the November 26 deadline, Miami-Dade aborted its effort, and
the final tally showed Bush with 2,912,790 votes to Gore's 2,912,253—
a margin of 537 votes. Katherine Harris signed the official certification at 7:30 on the evening of the 26th in the state capitol, as she had
promised. "I hereby declare Governor George W. Bush the winner of
Florida's twenty-five electoral votes," said Harris. At a press conference
shortly afterward, James Baker claimed victory. "At some point there
must be closure," said Baker. "At some point, the law must prevail and
the lawyers must go home. We have reached that point."[45] In Austin,
Bush met briefly with reporters in the state capitol. "This has been a
hard-fought election, a healthy contest for American democracy. But
now that the votes are counted, it's time for the votes to count." Bush
went on to announce that Dick Cheney would guide the transition,
and listed several of the issues he wanted his administration to address,
including education and prescription drug coverage for elderly Ameri-

---

*   Title 3, section 5, of the United States Code pertaining to presidential elections, which was
enacted after the Hayes-Tilden dispute in 1876, provides that in resolving a dispute about electors, a state's laws enacted "prior to" election day "shall be conclusive, and shall govern the counting of the electoral votes." The issue was whether the Florida Supreme Court's decision changed
the rules after the election had taken place.

cans. It was a low-key appeal for national unity, and Bush stressed that the issues he addressed mattered deeply to Democrats as well.[46]

Meanwhile, the litigation continued. On Friday, December 1, the Supreme Court of the United States, for the first time in American history, heard oral argument on a case involving a disputed presidential election. "If it were purely a matter of state law, I suppose we normally would leave it alone, where the state supreme court found it," Justice Sandra Day O'Connor told Ted Olson. "And so you probably have to persuade us there is some issue of federal law here. Otherwise, why are we acting?"[47] The argument before the Court continued for ninety minutes, Olson speaking for Bush, Tribe for Gore. According to *The New York Times*, the arguments left the courtroom audience totally disoriented. "The Court's jurisdictional challenges to Olson, who argued first, were so tough that it appeared that the lawyers for the Democratic side were about to coast to an easy victory. But Chief Justice Rehnquist and Justice [Antonin] Scalia, who had been quite subdued during the first half of the argument, came alive during the second half, hurling so many questions at Laurence H. Tribe, that a case that had looked almost impregnable suddenly appeared vulnerable."[48]

The justices considered the case over the weekend, and on Monday, December 4, issued a brief unanimous opinion asking the Florida Supreme Court to clarify its ruling instituting a recount. "As a general rule, this Court defers to a state court's interpretation of a state statute," said the justices, but they then went on to note that both the Constitution and federal law also govern presidential elections and asked whether the Florida Supreme Court had taken this into account. The Court's decision gave something to both sides. For Gore, it allowed the Florida court leeway to explain its action; for Bush, it provided a shot across the bow of the State Supreme Court, warning that it was sailing into dangerous waters.[49]

The Florida Supreme Court did not immediately respond. Instead, on Friday, December 8, it reversed a lower state court and ordered an immediate manual recount of thousands of disputed ballots statewide. "There can be no question that there are legal votes within the 9,000 uncounted votes [in Miami-Dade County] sufficient to place the results of this election in doubt." The court went on to order all counties that had not conducted a manual recount "to do so forthwith."[50] This time the decision was 4–3.

The Bush forces immediately filed requests for a stay of the decision from both the Supreme Court of the United States and the U.S. Court of Appeals for the Eleventh Circuit in Atlanta. Shortly after noon the following day, Saturday, December 9, the Court of Appeals declined to stop the recount. Voting 8–4, the full court dismissed Bush's appeal. "Nothing in this order should be construed to prevent, obstruct or impede the continuation of the manual recounts that are currently being conducted," said the court.[51]

Less than two hours later the Supreme Court of the United States issued the stay the Bush forces had requested. The one paragraph order was signed by Chief Justice Rehnquist, and Associate Justices Scalia, Thomas, O'Connor, and Anthony Kennedy.[52] Justices John Paul Stevens, David Souter, Ruth Bader Ginsburg, and Stephen Breyer dissented. Oral argument was set for Monday, December 11, less than forty-eight hours away, and one day before the statutory "safe harbor" deadline for receiving the electoral college returns.* The Court's brief order provided no explanation or justification for granting the stay. In a concurring opinion, Justice Scalia noted that "the issuance of the stay suggests that a majority of the justices, while not deciding the issues presented, believe that the petition has a substantial possibility of success." Justice Stevens, the Court's senior associate justice, wrote a two-page dissent. "Preventing the recount from being completed will inevitably cast a cloud on the legitimacy of the election," said Stevens. "As a more fundamental matter, the Florida court's ruling reflects the basic principle, inherent in our Constitution and our democracy, that every legal vote should be counted."[53]

The Supreme Court's order stopped the Florida manual recount. From Pensacola to Key West the entire enterprise came to a halt. On Sunday, December 10, the Bush and Gore legal teams filed their final

* Under Title 3, section 3 of the United States Code, if the states appoint their electors one week before the electoral college meets, they are in a "safe harbor" immune from congressional inquiry.

briefs with the Court. The Bush lawyers argued that the recount ordered by the Florida Supreme Court was illegal and unconstitutional;
the lawyers for Gore maintained that the only issue in the case was "the
right of voters to have their ballots counted."[54] The case was now styled
Bush v. Gore, and Gore replaced Laurence Tribe with David Boies for
the final argument. Boies had represented Gore in the Florida litigation, and by switching to him Gore believed he would emphasize that
this was a state issue, not a national one. Boies was one of the nation's
leading trial lawyers, but unlike Olson and Tribe he had argued only
one case before the Supreme Court.* That may or may not have been
important. Both sides made competent presentations, but the justices
had voted 5–4 to grant the stay, and nothing in the oral arguments
suggested that any of the justices had changed their minds.[55]

    At 10 p.m. on Tuesday, December 12, thirty-five days after the polls
in Florida had closed and two hours before the statutory "safe harbor"
deadline, the Supreme Court announced its judgment. It was not announced in a court session, as is customary, but was simply distributed
to the parties and the press by the Court clerk's office. The vote again
was 5–4, and the Court's opinion was simply per curium, meaning
none of the justices was identified as its author. The chief justice along
with Justices Scalia, O'Connor, Kennedy, and Thomas were in the
majority. Justices Stevens, Souter, Ginsburg, and Breyer dissented. The
majority opinion stressed that the December 12 "safe harbor" deadline
made it impossible to come up with a way of counting the votes that
could meet "minimal constitutional standards." The Court was concerned by the varying standards used by different counties in counting
the votes.

> We are presented with a situation where a state court with the
> power to assure uniformity has ordered a statewide recount with min-
> imal procedural safeguards. . . . When a state court orders a statewide
> remedy, there must be at least some assurance that the rudimentary re-
> quirements of equal treatment and fundamental fairness are satisfied.[56]

---

* The case was *Pennzoil v. Texaco*, 481 U.S. 1 (1987), in which Boies represented Texaco and
lost to Tribe, who represented Pennzoil.

The majority opinion went on to say that substantial additional work was needed to undertake a constitutional recount, including the adoption of uniform standards from county to county and "orderly judicial review of any disputed matters." There was no way this could be done in time. Finally, in what has become the most notorious sentence in the opinion, the justices restricted the holding to the case of *Bush v. Gore*. It would not become a precedent for future litigation. "Our consideration is limited to the present circumstances, for the problem of equal protection in election processes generally presents many complexities."[57]

The dissenters argued that the December 12 deadline was misplaced, and that Florida had until December 18—the date on which the electoral college was to meet—to remedy the problem. Justices Souter and Breyer wanted to send the case back to the Florida court with instructions to establish uniform standards. "Unlike the majority," wrote Souter, "I see no warrant for this court to assume that Florida could not possibly comply with this requirement before the date set for the meeting of electors."[58] Justice Breyer pointed out that the time problem Florida faced was in large part of the Supreme Court's own making. The recount had been moving along in orderly fashion when "this Court improvidently entered a stay. As a result we will never know whether the recount could have been completed."[59] Justice Ginsburg focused on the question of federalism. "The extraordinary setting of this case has obscured the ordinary principle that dictates its proper resolution: federal courts defer to state high courts' interpretation of their state's own law."[60]

With the Supreme Court's late night decision on December 12, the election ended. George W. Bush would become the nation's forty-third president. In a sense, the Florida recount was a replay of the national election. Gore micromanaged the effort in the Sunshine State; Bush delegated the fight to Baker. "I don't want to be seen with two cell phones and a BlackBerry telling people what to do," Bush told Joe Allbaugh.[61] And just as the Bush team had outthought and outfought the Gore strategists from the get-go during the electoral campaign, Christopher proved no match for Baker. The Democrats focused on making a case for the national media while Baker concentrated on the battle on the ground. Baker's efforts were buttressed by a remarkable group of seasoned litigators and public officials who rallied to Bush's cause. Robert Zoellick, later head of the World Bank, was Baker's deputy in Tallahassee; John G. Roberts, Jr., future chief justice of the United States, was one of sixteen former Supreme Court law clerks who did the grunt work during the litigation.* Gore could not field a comparable team. Republican governors and senators also waded in to support Bush publicly. Most Democrats adopted a stance of watchful waiting. Finally, Gore would have had a better case if, in the beginning, he had requested a manual recount in all sixty-seven counties instead of cherry-picking the four with the largest Democratic majorities.

In the end, Bush was declared victor by the United States Supreme Court. Whether the Court should have stepped in will long be debated. Whether the Court should have turned its back on John Marshall's carefully crafted distinction between legal and political questions is not easily answered. Justice Stevens may have said it best in his dissent in *Bush v. Gore.*

> It is confidence in the men and women who administer the judicial systems that is the true backbone of the rule of law. Time will one day heal the wound to that confidence that will be inflicted by today's decision. One thing, however, is certain. Although we may never know with complete certainty the identity of the winner of this year's Presidential election, the identity of the loser is perfectly clear. It is the nation's confidence in the judge as an impartial guardian of the rule of law.[62]†

---

* Former Supreme Court law clerks working for Baker included, Ted Cruz (Rehnquist), Tim Flanigan (Burger), John Manning (Scalia), Noel Francisco (Scalia), Alex Azar (Scalia), Helgi Walker (Thomas), Rick Garnett (Rehnquist), Bill Kelley (Scalia), Shawn Fagan (Rehnquist), Sean Gallagher (O'Connor), Matt Stowe (O'Connor), Andrew McBride (O'Connor), John G. Roberts, Jr. (Rehnquist), Miguel Estrada (Kennedy), and Tom Hungar (Kennedy). Jeffrey Toobin, *Too Close to Call* (New York: Random House, 2001), 184.

† Subsequent analysis of the Florida presidential vote by the nation's leading newspapers and the research organizations they engaged indicates that if the recount ordered by the Florida Supreme Court had been allowed to proceed, Bush's margin of victory would have increased from 537 votes to 1,665. *New York Times*, April 4, 2001. Also see *Washington Post*, September 7, 2001.

CHAPTER SEVEN

Inauguration

I want to leave the presidency better off than I found it.

George W. Bush

I think he shatters the myth of white supremacy once and for all.

Representative Charles Rangel

Saturday, January 20, 2001, was cold and rainy in Washington. At the invitation of the Clintons, the extended Bush family had spent the last several days at Blair House, the presidential guesthouse across Pennsylvania Avenue from the White House. Bush began the day at 6:30 with coffee with his mother and his brothers Marvin and Jeb. Shortly after nine the family, joined by the Cheneys, attended a prayer service at nearby St. John's Episcopal Church, an inauguration ritual initiated by FDR in 1933. From there Bush and Laura, joined by Cheney and Lynne, drove to the White House, where the president and Hillary were waiting. "Good morning, senator," Laura said to Mrs. Clinton as they entered the executive mansion.[1] Hillary had just taken her seat as the junior senator from New York, and the Clintons appeared buoyant.

Inauguration as the 43rd president of the United States. The oath
was administered by Chief Justice William Rehnquist.

Before the Bushes arrived, Bill and Hillary were observed dancing in
the foyer to the music of a Marine band ensemble.

Earlier that morning Clinton had made his final radio address from
the Oval Office. The inauguration marked "the magic, the mystery, the
miracle of American democracy—the peaceful transfer of power from
one administration to the next."[2] For the president, the bitterness of the
campaign and the Florida recount were forgotten. Clinton flashed a warm
smile when the Bushes entered the White House and Bush reciprocated.
The limousine ride up Pennsylvania Avenue to the Capitol was equally
pleasant. Bush and Clinton chatted like old friends. Each in his own way
was savoring the moment. The election was over. It was time for gestures
of reconciliation, even gallantry. Later, as Bush was about to take the oath
of office, his daughters, Barbara and Jenna, remained in their seats. Clinton rose and escorted them to a position at the podium behind Laura.*

---

*   The behavior of incoming and outgoing presidents toward one another spans the spectrum. On
March 4, 1801, John Adams left Washington early to avoid meeting Thomas Jefferson. John Quincy
Adams refused to attend the inauguration of his successor, Andrew Jackson, and Andrew Johnson
declined to meet Grant. In more recent times, FDR did not get out of the car to call on Herbert
Hoover in the White House, nor did Eisenhower to meet Truman. At the other end of the spectrum is Grover Cleveland, who in 1889 stood holding an umbrella over Benjamin Harrison as Harrison delivered his inaugural address. (Harrison had just defeated Cleveland in his bid for a second
term.) And George H. W. Bush and Bill Clinton became the best of friends after Clinton left office.

Bush spoke for fourteen minutes. Like Clinton before him, he sought the high ground. Rather than offer a partisan program, the new president repeatedly called for civility as he sought to unify the nation. "Civility is not a tactic or a sentiment. It is a determined choice of trust over cynicism, of community over chaos." His remarks were all-inclusive. "Everyone belongs, everyone deserves a chance, no insignificant person was ever born."

> While many of our citizens prosper, others doubt the promise, even the justice of our own country. The ambitions of some Americans are limited by failing schools and hidden prejudice and the circumstances of their birth. And sometimes our differences run so deep, it seems we share a continent but not a country.

"We cannot accept this," said Bush, "we will not allow it." His goals were crisply stated:

- We will reclaim America's schools before ignorance and apathy claim more young lives.
- We will reform Social Security and Medicare.
- We will reduce taxes to recover the momentum of our economy.

Foreign policy and national security were treated minimally. Paraphrasing John F. Kennedy in 1961, Bush said, "The enemies of liberty should make no mistake: America remains engaged in the world, by history and by choice, shaping a balance of power that favors freedom." His emphasis was on caring for those in need. "America at its best is compassionate. In the quiet of American conscience, we know that deep, persistent poverty is unworthy of our Nation's promise. And whatever our views of its cause, we can agree that children at risk are not at fault. . . . When we see that wounded traveler on the road to Jericho, we will not pass to the other side."

Bush employed ten religious references in his speech and concluded with the angel in the whirlwind directing the storm. "Never tiring, never yielding, never finishing, we renew that purpose today, to make our country more just and generous, to affirm the dignity of our lives and every life."[3] It may have been Bush's finest speech, and the absence of partisanship helped launch the administration on a positive note. A middle-of-the-road Democrat like Clinton could have given exactly the same speech without changing a word.

President Bush and Laura walk down Pennsylvania Avenue in the inaugural parade.

At the traditional post-inaugural luncheon with congressional leaders in the Capitol's Statuary Hall, Bush repeated his message of reconciliation. "Expectations in the country is [*sic*] we can't get anything done. People say, 'Well, gosh, the election was so close nothing will happen except for finger-pointing and name-calling and bitterness.' I'm here to tell the country that things will get done, that we're going to rise above expectations, that both Republicans and Democrats will come together and do what's right for America."[4] That evening, Bush and Laura attended eight inaugural balls, danced briefly at each, and were back at the White House well before midnight.

Bush saw himself as the nation's CEO. "A good executive is one that understands how to recruit people and how to delegate. How to align authority and responsibility, how to hold people responsible for results and how to build a team of people."[5] David Gergen, a veteran White House staffer, called Bush "a top-down, no-nonsense, decisive, macho leader who sets his eye on the far horizon and doesn't go wobbly getting there. . . . To lead, in his book, is to decide."[6]*

---

* Bush enjoyed comparing himself as an administrator to Ronald Reagan, with a Reaganesque ability to get to the heart of a matter. But the comparison is more apparent than real. As Professor Hugh Heclo has pointed out, Reagan's "ability to avoid getting lost in details stemmed from a clearly defined long-standing system of ideas, his public philosophy and vision of history. For Bush it is more a matter of decision-making strategy." Reagan was a visionary storyteller; Bush, the CEO of a permanent campaign. Hugh Heclo, "The Political Ethos of George W. Bush," in

Reflecting Bush's style, his White House was far more personalized than previous Republican administrations. Beginning with Dwight Eisenhower in 1953, GOP presidents prided themselves on orderly process that hinged on a powerful chief of staff. With Ike it was Sherman Adams. Nixon had H. R. Haldeman. Ford employed first Rumsfeld and then Cheney. Reagan depended on Donald Regan and James Baker. And Bush 41 had John Sununu and Baker again. Not only did these chiefs of staff keep the trains running on time, they provided a clearly defined focus for presenting alternative viewpoints.*

Bush rejected that model. "All power should not go through an individual to the Oval Office," he told Bob Woodward. "I want a flat structure where my key senior staff members report directly to me."[7] That had been Bush's policy in Austin, and he saw no reason to change. The difference was that in Austin, with its weak governor's office, Bush had no real executive responsibility. It didn't matter who had the last word or was the last person to see him because action was rarely required. In Washington, where orderly procedure is essential to the formulation of sound policy, Bush was asking for trouble. Not since the days of Franklin Roosevelt had White House decision making been so personalized. FDR did not make many gaffes. But when he did—such as his disastrous attempt to pack the Supreme Court in 1937—it was because his decision had not been adequately vetted beforehand.[†]

Bush's staff reflected his personal approach. As chief of staff he in-

---

The George W. Bush Presidency, Fred I. Greenstein, ed. (Baltimore: Johns Hopkins University Press, 2003), 49.

* "Orderly paper flow is the way you protect the president," Cheney told James Baker in 1980. Baker, who was assuming the position of chief of staff to Reagan, had asked Cheney for advice given his experience under Ford. Cheney told Baker it was important to ensure that any proposal presented to the president had been tested against the views of others. Barton Gellman, Angler: The Cheney Vice Presidency (New York: Penguin, 2008), 86.

† It can be argued that the success of the Japanese attack on Pearl Harbor was in no small measure attributable to the lack of coordination between the United States Army and Navy. This was partially due to FDR's determination to deal separately with each service from the Oval Office. The postwar investigation into Pearl Harbor by Congress focused on that lack of coordination, and the creation of the National Security Council under the National Security Act of 1947 was a corrective step to avoid the personalization of policy that had occurred under Roosevelt. U.S. Congress, Pearl Harbor Attack: Hearings Before the Joint Committee on the Investigation of the Pearl Harbor Attack, 39 vols. (Washington, D.C.: Government Printing Office, 1946).

stalled the amiable Andrew Card. Card had been deputy chief of staff under John Sununu in Bush's father's administration and briefly secretary of transportation. He was easy to get along with, perfectly capable of seeing that what needed to be done got done, but scarcely a top-down manager or gatekeeper to the Oval Office.

From Texas Bush brought Karen Hughes, Karl Rove, Alberto Gonzales, Harriet Miers, Margaret LaMontagne, Clay Johnson, deputy press secretary Scott McClellan, and a host of others. All had served with Bush in Austin, all enjoyed a close relationship with the president, and all had direct access to the Oval Office. "Naturally, there's a bond we share because we come from Texas," said McClellan.[8]

FIGURE 1

White House Offices 2001

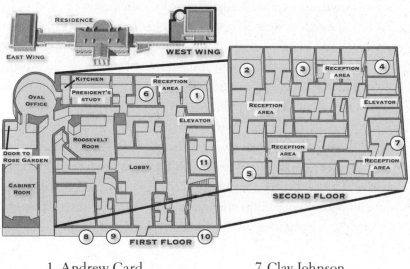

1. Andrew Card	7. Clay Johnson
2. Karen Hughes	8. Ari Fleischer
3. Karl Rove	9. Scott McClellan
4. Alberto Gonzales	10. Condoleezza Rice
5. Margaret LaMontagne	11. Dick Cheney
6. Harriet Miers	

Karen Hughes, who was closest to Bush, was given the title of counselor to the president and the largest office in the West Wing (see figure,

"White House Offices"). Hughes was the White House communications director charged with getting its message out. More importantly, she was the president's confidante and alter ego. "I want you at every meeting where major decisions are made,"[9] Bush told her, and nothing came to his desk that Hughes had not seen. "I've been around a lot of White Houses," said Cheney, "and it's a unique role when the president has total confidence in someone. Karen is the first woman I've seen in that role."[10]

Karl Rove was Bush's political guru. Given the title senior adviser to the president, Rove took over the second-floor West Wing office previously occupied by Hillary Clinton. Rove headed the Office of Strategic Initiatives dealing with Republican strategy, planning, and outreach. Rove saw the presidency as part of a permanent electoral campaign and enjoyed carte blanche to intervene in any issue pertaining to domestic policy—"Anything except baseball," as Rove once put it.[11]

Alberto Gonzales stepped down from the Texas Supreme Court to become White House counsel and occupy another corner office. Margaret LaMontagne, who had been Bush's education adviser in Austin, became director of the Domestic Policy Council and assistant to the president for domestic policy. Harriet Miers, who was W's personal attorney in Austin, became staff secretary—the same post held by General Andrew Goodpaster under Ike, and Missy LeHand under FDR. Clay Johnson, who had been with Bush at Andover and roomed with him at Yale, had been in charge of the governor's appointments in Texas and became personnel director in the White House. Longtime aides Dan Bartlett and Scott McClellan joined the communications office.

"Texas is a state of mind," wrote John Steinbeck,[12] and Bush's team from Texas provided a comfortable cocoon. Bush valued personal loyalty and staff discipline above all else. Team Texas was congenial to a fault. They flattered Bush's whims, did his bidding without question, and worked hard to achieve his goals. But they failed utterly when it came to presenting him with the full range of policy alternatives. They were new to Washington, saw the federal government's career civil service as political opponents, and distrusted professional expertise. "The circle around Bush is the tightest around any president in the modern era," said Christopher DeMuth, former president of the American Enterprise Institute. "It's a too tightly managerial decision-making process. When they make decisions, a very small number of people are in the room, and it constricts the range of alternatives being offered." [13]

John Sununu, chief of staff under the elder Bush, put it best when he told Jeffrey Goldberg of *The New Yorker*, "We always made sure the President was hearing all the possibilities. That's one of the big differences between the first Bush Administration and this Bush Administration." [14] Or as Reagan speechwriter Peggy Noonan put it, "If you put unity over intellectual integrity, you'll lose the second right away, and the first in time." [15]

Condoleezza Rice moved into the office of the national security adviser. Rice was not from Texas but in terms of attitude she could have been. She too sought to provide Bush with what made him most comfortable. As Rice once remarked, what Bush liked least was when she described a foreign policy problem as complex. [16] With Bush it was intuition over intellect, simplicity over detail, a world of right and wrong. Bush had a short attention span, an unnerving level of certitude, and a habit of hiring support staff based on personal loyalty. Once inside the White House charmed circle, people tended to stay there. [17]

"I used to think Condoleezza Rice was a terrible national security adviser," said Richard Armitage, deputy secretary of state under Colin Powell. "But I've changed my mind. I now realize she was doing exactly what Bush wanted her to do." [18]

David Frum, a speechwriter and special assistant to the president, said that the key players in the Bush White House were Karen Hughes, Harriet Miers, and Condoleezza Rice. Bush felt comfortable with them. There was nothing untoward in the relationship, but Bush liked them, trusted them, and relied on them to smooth the way. [19]

The most formidable presence in the West Wing was the vice president. This was a marked departure from precedent. John Nance Garner, a former speaker of the House of Representatives who was FDR's first vice president, said the office of vice president was not worth "a pitcher of warm piss." [20] Alben Barkley, who had been Senate majority leader before becoming Truman's vice president in 1949, often told the story of the woman who had two sons. "One became a sailor and went to sea; the other became vice president of the United States. Neither has been heard from since."[21] Eisenhower held Nixon at arm's length, and as Robert Caro has documented, JFK treated Lyndon Johnson with callous disregard.[22]

Walter Mondale was the first vice president to have an office in the West Wing, but Mondale did not interact with Carter's staff, had no specific areas of responsibility, and confined himself to meeting with the president once a week to offer advice. George H. W. Bush also had an office in the West Wing, but in the words of Reagan's treasury secretary Nicholas Brady, "kept himself out of the White House gear works."[23] Dan Quayle had a similarly limited role. Al Gore was given broader responsibilities than any vice president before him, but was basically restricted to environmental policy and telecommunications.

With Cheney it was different. Having been Gerald Ford's chief of staff, George H. W. Bush's secretary of defense, and a member of Congress for ten years, Cheney not only knew the Washington political scene but was a veteran of White House process and procedure. "From day one George Bush made it clear he wanted me to help govern," wrote Cheney.[24] "I'd have the opportunity to be a major participant in the process, to get involved in whatever issues I wanted to get involved in."[25] The fact that Cheney had no presidential ambition facilitated his rise to field captain of Team Bush in the White House. "The president never had to worry that I was taking a position with an eye toward how it might be perceived by voters in Iowa or New Hampshire."[26]

Cheney's rise to power began with the transition. There were 6,400 political positions in the executive branch to be filled, 1,125 of which required Senate confirmation. Traditionally, each cabinet appointee has been responsible for filling the policy-making posts in his or her department. Nixon began the practice of screening subcabinet nominees in the White House, Ford continued it, and under Reagan each candidate was required to complete a short questionnaire. Cheney and Rove took the process to a new height, carefully vetting all candidates for their political and ideological symmetry. Cheney knew the people,

George W. Bush's first cabinet. From left to right in the front row are Commerce Secretary Don Evans, Interior Secretary Gale Norton, Defense Secretary Donald Rumsfeld, Secretary of State Colin Powell, President Bush, Vice President Dick Cheney, Treasury Secretary Paul O'Neill, Attorney General John Ashcroft, Agriculture Secretary Ann Veneman, and Labor Secretary Elaine Chao; and behind, U.S. trade representative Robert Zoellick, Environmental Protection Agency Administrator Christine Todd Whitman, Secretary of Education Roderick Paige, Transportation Secretary Norman Mineta, Health and Human Services Secretary Tommy Thompson, Secretary of Housing and Urban Development Mel Martinez, Energy Secretary Spencer Abraham, Secretary of Veterans Affairs Anthony Principi, Director of the Office of Management and Budget Mitch Daniels, and White House Chief of Staff Andrew Card.

the issues, and the chemistry. With few exceptions, all of the new appointees in the Bush administration were Cheney loyalists.

To ensure his proximity to the president, Cheney made the vice president's office on the first floor of the West Wing his primary office. The vice president's much larger suite in the Executive Office Building, the traditional workplace for vice presidents, became Cheney's ceremonial office. And his staff was integrated with the White House staff. Scooter Libby, Cheney's chief of staff, became an assistant to the president and sat in on all senior White House meetings. Mary Matalin, who was Cheney's communications director, was also given the title of assistant to the president and worked in tandem with Karen Hughes.

"I view the vice president's staff as part of our team," said Hughes.[27] "We are joined at the hip," said Matalin.[28]

David Addington, Cheney's counsel, worked directly with Gonzales's office, and Cheney's speechwriters with those of Bush. The West Wing became a seamless executive office with the staffs of the president and vice president fully integrated. "In this White House, there aren't 'Cheney people' versus 'Bush people,'" said Cheney. "We are all Bush people."[29] In 2002, the Office of the Vice President was deleted as a line item in the federal budget and consolidated into the larger appropriation for the Executive Office of the President.[30]* The creation of a unified executive office helps explain how Cheney came to play such a large role in the Bush administration. Cheney had no defined area of responsibility. He could choose his issues. "The president made it clear from the outset that the vice president is welcome at every table and at every meeting," said Josh Bolten, Bush's deputy chief of staff. "That's just a standing rule."[31]

Bush was off to a good start. A CBS poll on the eve of the inauguration found only 51 percent of Americans believed Bush had been legitimately elected. Among Democrats, only 19 percent.[32] But the first post-inaugural poll, taken by Gallup in early February, gave him a job approval rating of 58.6 percent. That was seven points ahead of what Ronald Reagan had polled one month into his presidency, and only one point behind Richard Nixon.[33] On the other hand, Bush's disapproval rating stood at 25 percent, the highest of any modern president when he entered office. (George Herbert Walker Bush had a 12 percent disapproval rating; Ronald Reagan had 13 percent.)[34]

Taking a leaf from his first year as governor, Bush kept his legislative agenda simple: tax cuts and education. Tax cuts appealed to the Republican base, education reform resonated among Democrats as well. Bush worked both sides of the aisle. For the first time since Eisenhower took office in 1953, the Republicans controlled both the executive and

---

* Reflecting his constitutional duty as president of the Senate, Cheney's own paycheck came from the Senate. Stephen F. Hayes, *Cheney: The Untold Story of America's Most Powerful and Controversial Vice President* (New York: HarperCollins, 2007), 308.

legislative branches of government. Although the 2000 election had been a squeaker, the GOP retained a 221–212 majority in the House, and while the Senate was evenly divided 50–50, Vice President Cheney held the tie-breaking vote. (In May, Republican senator Jim Jeffords of Vermont split with the party and voted with the Democrats to organize the Senate, but other than a change of committee chairmen, his defection had little effect on the passage of legislation.)*

Tax cuts had been the centerpiece of Bush's election campaign. "This is not only 'no new taxes,' this is, tax cuts, so help me God."[35] As *The New York Times* noted, "there was something almost Oedipal" in Bush's insistence on reducing taxes; as if he were trying to avenge the conservative revolt that upended his father's presidency.[36] The financial climate also appeared favorable. Thanks in part to his father's tax hike, the prudent management of interest rates by Federal Reserve Board chairman Alan Greenspan, and the balanced budget approach of the Clinton administration, the economy was booming. The United States was at peace, and consumers were buying. The federal government, which had run deficits in every year since 1959, recorded surpluses for the previous four years. In 1999, the nonpartisan Congressional Budget Office estimated the accumulated budget surplus would total $2.6 trillion in ten years. In early 2001, that figure was increased to a whopping $5.6 trillion.

The Clinton administration—Clinton, treasury secretaries Robert Rubin and Larry Summers, and to some extent Al Gore—believed the surpluses should be used to reduce the federal debt, which stood at $3.4 trillion. In 1999, Clinton vetoed a Republican-inspired tax cut of $792 billion precisely for that reason. That is not how Bush saw it. As he told the Republican convention in his acceptance speech, "Today,

---

* Jeffords, a moderate Republican, dropped his party affiliation over funding for the Individuals with Disabilities Education Act (IDEA). Jeffords sought to remove $200 billion from Bush's proposed tax cut and direct the money to fund IDEA. When the White House refused, Jeffords left the party and became an Independent. The Democrats rewarded his defection by making him chairman of the Environment and Public Works Committee. For Jeffords's explanation of his shift, see James M. Jeffords, *My Declaration of Independence* (New York: Simon & Schuster, 2001).

our high taxes fund a surplus. The surplus is not the government's money. The surplus is the people's money." [37] That theme was repeated throughout the campaign. As Bush put it in his first debate with Al Gore, "My opponent thinks the surplus is the government's money. That's not what I think. I think it's the hardworking people of America's money." [38]

Bush's tax proposals were fleshed out during the campaign. Overall, he proposed to reduce federal taxes by $1.6 trillion over ten years. The cuts were across the board. The number of tax brackets was reduced from five to four, and the lowest bracket was eliminated, removing five million low-income families from the tax rolls. Bush asked that the top marginal rate be reduced from 39 to 33 percent, that the child tax credit be raised from $500 to $1,000, that the filing penalty for married couples be reduced, and that the federal inheritance tax (the "death tax" to Republican loyalists), which then kicked in at $675,000, be eliminated.

The Bush tax proposals were premised on a booming economy and a rising level of budget surpluses. By February, storm clouds were gathering. The economy was slowing, the stock market had peaked, and unemployment was rising. Treasury Secretary Paul O'Neill, who was increasingly skeptical of the Congressional Budget Office's rosy projections, suggested to Bush that there be triggers in the bill to curtail the tax cuts if the predicted surpluses disappeared. Bush was uninterested. "I won't negotiate with myself," he told O'Neill. "It's that simple. The tax proposal is a closed issue." [39] Or as Karl Rove told *Time* magazine, "the trigger concept was dead on arrival with this president." [40]

O'Neill continued to have doubts and raised the matter with his old friend Cheney. The vice president was equally dismissive. "Reagan proved that deficits don't matter," he told O'Neill. [41] In the months ahead, O'Neill and the economic experts at Treasury would find themselves increasingly frozen out of administration policy. "Administrations are defined by their president," O'Neill said later. "Bush was signing on to strong ideological positions that had not been fully thought through. Of course, that's the nature of ideology. Thinking it through is the last thing an ideologue wants to do." [42]

Fed chairman Alan Greenspan concurred. "The White House

placed little value on rigorous economic policy debate or the weighing of longterm consequences. Much to my disappointment, economic policymaking in the Bush administration remained firmly in the hands of the White House staff." [43]

The lead was taken by Cheney. A tax bill can run hundreds of pages. Bush abhorred the fine print and was delighted to turn the details over to the vice president. Cheney met regularly with an informal group of conservative economists and was fully conversant with the numbing expanse of the Internal Revenue Code. Allen Sinai of Decision Economics, one of the Wall Street gurus whom Cheney consulted, was struck by the fact that the Treasury Department wasn't participating. "It looked to me that these decisions were made by a very small group of people." [44] Economist John Makin, a resident scholar at the American Enterprise Institute who was also a member of Cheney's kitchen cabinet, believed the vice president was playing the role normally taken up by the assistant secretary for economic policy at Treasury. The White House, said Makin, had become the "locus of all major policy initiatives." [45]

Bush sent his tax proposal to Congress March 8. "Today I am sending to Congress my plan to provide relief to all income-tax payers, which I believe will help jump start the American economy. We must give overcharged taxpayers some of their own money back. I urge Congress to help me strengthen our economy by lightening the tax burden on the American people." [46] In the House, the Republican majority pushed the measure through in less than a month. All Republicans voted in favor, all but 10 Democrats opposed. The only change made by the House was that the inheritance tax would be phased out over the next ten years. [47] The bill faced tougher going in the Senate. A combination of Democrats and moderate Republicans, primarily from the Northeast, reduced the overall cut to $1.3 trillion, the rate for the top bracket was pegged at 35 percent, not 33 percent, and the cuts would expire in 2010. The measure passed the Senate on May 23, 50 Republicans and 12 Democrats voting in favor. The final conference report, which was essentially the Senate bill, passed both houses on May 26. In the House of Representatives, all Republicans voted in favor as did 28 Democrats.

In the Senate, 12 Democrats voted in favor and 2 Republicans (Lincoln Chafee of Rhode Island and John McCain) voted against.

President Bush signed the measure into law at a White House ceremony on June 7, 2001. "A year ago tax relief was said to be a political impossibility. Six months ago it was supposed to be a political liability. Today it becomes reality."[48] The tax cuts were made retroactive to January 1, and rebate checks ranging from $300 to $600 were mailed immediately to all taxpayers. Two years later, Congress reduced the tax on capital gains and dividends, and cut taxes on small businesses. The federal government's tax revenue, which stood at 20.9 percent of GDP in 2000, dropped to 16.3 percent in 2004, the lowest percentage since 1950.[49]*

The principal beneficiaries of the Bush tax cuts were those in the higher brackets. Taxes for those earning $10,000 were reduced by $300. For someone earning $100,000, taxes dropped $2,489. For anyone earning $500,000, the decrease amounted to $17,731. Bill Gates, the richest man in America, said the reductions would "widen the gap in economic and political influence between the wealthy and the rest of America."[50] Subsequent estimates suggested that 45 percent of the reductions went to the top one percent of Americans while only 13 percent of the reductions went to the poorest 60 percent.[51]

A more serious problem was that the rosy estimates of the Congressional Budget Office upon which the tax cuts were predicated were flat out wrong. "My regret that the legislation passed without triggers would soon become a lot more intense," wrote Alan Greenspan. "The vaunted surplus, still going strong when Bush signed the tax cut in June, was effectively wiped out overnight. Starting in July, red ink was back to stay."[52] In January 2001, the CBO had estimated total tax re-

---

* American tax rates are among the lowest in the developed world. According to figures prepared by the Organisation for Economic Cooperation and Development, the United States ranks seventeenth in terms of the percentage of gross domestic product collected in taxes. The OECD figures include all forms of taxes: income, sales, value added, state, and local. Sweden leads the list with 50.1 percent, followed by the other Scandinavian countries, France, Italy, Austria, the Netherlands, Britain, Spain, Germany, Portugal, Canada, Turkey, Ireland, and the United States (28.2 percent). Source: Organisation for Economic Cooperation and Development.

ceipts of $2.24 trillion for the coming year. By August 2002, that figure had dropped to $1.86 trillion, a loss of $380 billion.[53] And it would get worse. When Bush took office, the federal government's debt amounted to 56.4 percent of the gross domestic product. In fiscal 2009, the last year for which he was responsible, it amounted to 83.4 percent—a figure not seen since World War II.[54]

If tax cuts were the centerpiece of Bush's election campaign, education reform was the cornerstone of his compassionate conservatism. In his acceptance speech at the Republican convention, Bush stressed the need to upgrade American schools. "Too many children are segregated into schools without standards, shuffled from grade to grade because of their age, regardless of their knowledge. This is discrimination, pure and simple—the soft bigotry of low expectations. And our nation should treat it like other forms of discrimination. We should end it."[55]

The applause was tepid. Bush was moving against the grain of traditional party ideology. Republicans in Congress had voted against Lyndon Johnson's 1965 Elementary and Secondary Education Act designed to promote greater opportunity for poor and minority children, opposed Jimmy Carter's creation of the Department of Education in 1980, and regularly called for its abolition. Both Newt Gingrich's 1994 *Contract with America* and the 1996 Republican platform demanded that the department be disbanded.

Bush was taking the party into new territory. Education reform was an issue in which he genuinely believed. He had achieved significant results in the field as governor of Texas, it was a subject to which Laura was dedicated, and it was good politics. Exit polls in the 1996 presidential election indicated that on matters of education voters preferred Clinton to Bob Dole 78 to 16 percent. In 2000, Bush and Gore initially ran neck and neck, and in the closing weeks of the campaign Bush pulled ahead.[56] According to Republican pollster David Winston, the huge shift in Republican support from Dole to Bush is why Bush was elected. "Education was THE deciding issue in 2000. The groups that were the most interested in education were the key swing voters— independents, Catholics, married women with children."[57] Bush's victory caused many Republicans to rethink their opposition to federal support for education. Ohio's John Boehner, the conservative chairman of the House Education Committee, who had led the fight in 1995 to eliminate the Department of Education, publicly ate crow. "I think we realized that we were sending the wrong signal. The 2000 campaign paved the way for reform, and conservatives must capitalize by implementing the president's plan."[58]

With many Republicans still in doubt, Bush reached out for Democratic support. At the top of the list was Senator Ted Kennedy, the "Lion of the Senate," third in terms of seniority, and the ranking Democrat, later chairman, of the Senate Education Committee.* Unlike tax policy, where Bush allowed Cheney to handle the details, education was Bush's personal domain. Immediately after he and Laura were settled in at the White House they invited Ted and his wife, Vicki, to a private showing of the soon-to-be-released film *Thirteen Days*, depicting John F. Kennedy's handling of the October 1962 Cuban Missile Crisis.[59] "I don't know about you," Bush told Kennedy, "but I like to surprise people. Let's show them Washington can still get things done."

Kennedy, who had struggled unsuccessfully to get a meaningful education bill passed when the Democrats controlled the Senate, was delighted. The following day he wrote Bush:

> *You and Mrs. Bush couldn't have been more gracious and generous to Vicki and me and the members of our family last night. . . . Like you, I have every intention of getting things done, particularly in education and health care. We will have our differences along the way, but I look forward to some important Rose Garden signings.*
>
> *Warm regards,*
> *Ted Kennedy*[60]

With Kennedy on board, the path was open. Bush submitted his legislation—No Child Left Behind—to Congress at the end of Jan-

---

* The Senate's senior senator was Strom Thurmond of South Carolina, who had been elected in 1956, followed by Robert Byrd of West Virginia, elected in 1959. Kennedy had been elected in November 1962 to fill the unexpired term of his brother John.

uary. The bill drew heavily upon his experience in Texas. States were provided more money for education and granted more flexibility in spending it, but were held accountable for student performance. States would test students in math and English every year between third and eighth grade, and once in high school. Each state would compose its own exam, but student scores would be posted publicly, broken down by ethnic groups, income levels, and other subcategories. As in Texas, the posted scores would allow parents to evaluate schools, teachers, and the curriculum. Under Bush's plan, if a particular school consistently underperformed, the federal funds provided to that school could be given to the parents of children as vouchers for tuition in private schools.

Bush lobbied heavily for the bill. His first public appearance outside the White House was at the Merritt Elementary School in a heavily black section of northeast Washington. Laura, Ted Kennedy, John Boehner, and Representative George Miller of California, the ranking Democrat on the House Education Committee, accompanied him. Bush was at his best, joking with students and staff, touting the benefits of accountability. "I know students don't like to take tests, and I'm confident the parents here heard the same thing Laura and I heard when our daughters went to Austin High School. 'We're sick of tests.' And my answer was, 'Well I'm sorry you're sick of it, but we want to know.'" [61] Bush bantered with the assembly for almost two hours. Kennedy and Miller were impressed. "I don't think we need any more hearings," said Kennedy. "We can work together on this." [62]

Congressional action followed quickly. When the Democrats opposed Bush's voucher plan, the White House counted noses and immediately gave way. As undersecretary of education Eugene Hickok explained, "The president had no intention of sacrificing accountability on the altar of school choice." [63] On March 8, the Senate Education Committee approved the bill 20–0, with the voucher provision deleted. The House committee acted similarly on May 7 by a vote of 41–7, the opposition coming from conservative Republicans who objected to dropping the plan for vouchers. The House of Representatives passed the measure on May 23, 384–45, with majority whip Tom DeLay voting against. On June 14 the Senate passed its bill 91–8.

Reconciling the House and Senate versions of No Child Left Behind was delayed in conference committee because of the summer recess. Bush pressed for passage, and was speaking at an elementary school in Sarasota, Florida, on September 11 to apply pressure on the conferees. The events of 9/11 intervened, and final passage was delayed until December. The House voted final approval on December 13, (381–41), followed by the Senate on December 18 (87–10).

With the exception of vouchers, Bush got most of what he wanted. Student accountability was now law, and the measure authorized federal funding of $26.5 billion for fiscal year 2002. Bush signed the act in a special ceremony at Hamilton High School in Hamilton, Ohio, January 8, 2002, flanked by Ted Kennedy and John Boehner. Bush credited Kennedy for bringing Democrats along and Boehner for rallying the Republicans. As Dana Milbank, a longtime observer of George W. Bush, wrote in *The Washington Post*, "the president's victory lap followed a pattern Bush had established as governor of Texas: he would push hard in negotiations, take the best deal he could get, claim victory

President Bush signs into law the No Child Left Behind Act. On hand for the signing are Rep. George Miller of California (far left), Sen. Edward Kennedy of Massachusetts (center, left), Secretary of Education Roderick Paige (center, behind President Bush), and Rep. John Boehner of Ohio.

and share the credit."[64] A *Newsweek* survey after the signing found that 55 percent of the public preferred Bush's policy on education to that of the Democrats. Gallup found the same. For the first time in its sixty years of polling, Americans ranked the GOP above the Democratic party on education.[65] As Bush saw it, No Child Left Behind was not only an educational breakthrough, but "a valuable piece of civil rights legislation."[66]

Bush's program for faith-based initiatives was closely related to his stand on education. Throughout the presidential campaign he had sought a kinder, gentler face for religious involvement in politics. The very term compassionate conservatism avoided the moral absolutism of the fundamentalists and promised a more inclusive approach. "My administration will give taxpayers new incentives to donate to charity, encourage after school programs that build character, and support mentoring groups that shape and save young lives," Bush told the Republican convention in Philadelphia.[67]

The president saw his program for faith-based initiatives cutting across the political spectrum, a reflection of his claim to be a uniter, not a divider. "Church and charity, synagogue and mosque, lend our communities their humanity, and they will have an honored place in our plans and in our laws," he said in his inaugural.[68] On Monday, January 29, immediately after sending his education bill to Congress, Bush issued his first two executive orders establishing the White House Office of Faith-Based and Community Initiatives and ordering a review of community and faith-based programs in five executive departments.[69]* "We will encourage faith-based and community programs without changing their mission," said the president. "We will help all in their work to change hearts while keeping a commitment to pluralism."[70]

To head the White House office, Bush named John J. DiIulio, a political science professor at the University of Pennsylvania and a Demo-

---

* Reviews were ordered in the departments of Education, Health and Human Services, Housing and Urban Development, Justice, and Labor. The offices created were to conduct internal audits, and identify obstacles that prevented community or religious charities from providing social services.

crat. It was an inspired appointment and an ideal way for Bush to stress the ecumenical nature of the office. "Facts, not faith; performance, not politics; results, not religion; and, we pray, humility, not hubris, will guide my office in advising President Bush and in helping the administration put flesh on the bones of compassionate conservatism," said DiIulio upon taking office.[71]

The road ahead was rocky. Liberals and secular Americans believed the Office of Faith-Based Initiatives was little more than an attempt to destroy Jefferson's "wall of separation" between church and state.[72] Fundamentalists objected to the pluralism of the endeavor, and inside the White House, Karl Rove was unwilling to surrender the trump card that religion gave the Republicans.* After establishing the office, Bush took little interest in the details of its operation and in the coming year the opponents of the initiative would scuttle W's nonpartisan vision. DiIulio resigned after eight months, blaming the "Mayberry Machiavellians" on the White House staff.[73]† The Office of Faith-Based Initiatives became little more than an adjunct to Rove's permanent election campaign supporting Republican candidates and funding conservative causes.[74]

Bush led a rigidly structured life in the White House. As David Frum noted, he "was not the easy, genial man he was in public. Close up, one saw a man keeping a tight grip on himself." Frum attributed it to Bush's earlier battle with alcohol. As a friend put it, "Bush wakes up knowing one thing for absolute certain: Today is a day on which he will not have a drink. Everything else falls into place after that."[75]

---

*   In the 2000 election, Bush trounced Gore among regular churchgoers. Sixty-one percent of white Protestants, 57 percent of white Catholics, a whopping 87 percent of regular churchgoers identifying with the Religious Right voted Republican. Mark J. Rozell, "Bush and the Christian Right: The Triumph of Pragmatism," in *Religion and The Bush Presidency*, Mark J. Rozell and Gleaves Whitney, eds. (New York: Palgrave, 2007).

†   As DiIulio saw it, "staff, junior and senior, who consistently talked and acted as if the height of political sophistication consisted in reducing every issue to its simplest, black-and-white terms for public consumption, then steering legislative initiatives or policy proposals as far right as possible." John J. DiIulio, "Afterward: Why Judging Bush Is Never as Easy as It Looks," in *Judging Bush: Studies in the Modern Presidency*, Robert Maranto, Tom Lansford, and Jeremy Johnson, eds. (Stanford: Stanford University Press, 2009), 301.

As in Austin, Bush awoke every morning at 5:45. After dressing and breakfast he was in the Oval Office by 7:30. Some presidents use those early morning hours to read the press. Eisenhower always read the *New York Times, Herald Tribune*, and *Washington Post* before going to work. FDR did the same, adding *The Wall Street Journal* and *Chicago Tribune*. Bush did not read newspapers. That's what his staff was for. When he arrived at his desk, his briefings would begin. Harriet Miers would bring him up to speed on everything that required his attention, then Dick Cheney and chief of staff Andrew Card would file in. At eight o'clock George Tenet would provide an intelligence briefing. These were scheduled for twenty minutes but would often run over. From then until lunch members of the White House staff would come in and out for briefing sessions. Six times a week, Bush would exercise in the White House gym for one to two hours and was not to be disturbed while doing so. Often Condoleezza Rice would join him. The afternoon was more or less a repeat of the morning schedule. Bush would receive visitors and outside appointments, and would finish no later than six, have dinner with Laura in the family quarters at seven, and be in bed by nine.

It was the same schedule he followed as governor. Appointments were timed precisely, and his assistant Logan Walters watched the clock. Since Bush hated long meetings and lengthy presentations, visitors would be ushered out when their time expired. To his aides it seemed that W was perpetually racing the clock. As one biographer put it, "he was restless and he hungered to compete. It seemed a point of pride to him that he could arrive at a finish line—any finish line— faster than the next guy."[76] Reading and reflection were not part of the president's routine.

Bush began every cabinet meeting with a prayer. Not a silent prayer, but a direct appeal for divine guidance. As a born-again Christian, Bush wore his religion on his sleeve. The issue of stem cell research provides the best example. At the first meeting of the White House domestic policy council on January 29, Margaret LaMontagne noted that the Clinton administration had recently promulgated new guidelines that would permit federal funding of embryonic stem cell research despite the "Dickey Amendment," which was designed to prevent it.* Bush was unfamiliar with the issue, and LaMontagne explained. Embryonic stem cells, which are microscopic, have the capacity to yield a variety of cell types that could prove useful for treating ailments ranging from childhood diabetes to Alzheimer's and Parkinson's diseases. But the only way to extract the stem cells is to destroy the embryo from which they come. (An embryo is about the size of the period at the end of this sentence.) The Clinton administration held that despite the Dickey-Wicker Amendment, federal funds could be used for stem cell research if the destruction of the embryo had been privately funded.

For Bush this posed a moral dilemma.

> I had no interest in joining the flat earth society. I empathized with the hopes for new medical cures. I had lost a sister to childhood leukemia.... I believed in the promise of science and technology to alleviate suffering and disease. At the same time, I felt that technology should respect moral boundaries. I worried that sanctioning the destruction of human embryos for research would be a step down the slippery slope from science fiction to medical reality.[77]

Bush wrestled with the issue throughout the spring and early summer of 2001. He consulted widely. Republican heavyweights like Strom Thurmond, Orrin Hatch, and Bill Frist of Tennessee, a distinguished doctor, favored continued research. So did Dick Cheney. Nancy Reagan wrote an impassioned letter urging Bush to support stem cell research and the "miracle possibilities" it offered.[78] Tommy Thompson, secretary of health and human services, also came out strongly in support of continued stem cell research. A *Newsweek* cover story on July 9 cast the issue as a fight between religion and science, "pro-life purists against research." Public opinion polls indicated two thirds of the public favored stem cell research.[79]

---

* In 1996 Congress enacted the Dickey-Wicker Amendment (named for Representatives Jay Dickey of Arkansas and Roger Wicker of Mississippi) to that year's budget act banning the use of federal funds for embryonic research in which human embryos have been destroyed or discarded. The amendment was added to every subsequent budget act.

Those opposed were equally vehement. House majority leader Dick Armey and Republican whip Tom DeLay reminded Bush that "it is not pro-life to rely on an industry of death, even if the intention is to find cures for disease."[80] Speechwriter Michael Gerson believed Bush's presidency should be defined by advocating the "culture of life." Harvesting human embryos could not be part of that.[81] Karl Rove vigorously opposed any stand that would threaten Bush's support from the religious establishment.

In July Bush visited Pope John Paul II at his summer residence, Castel Gandolfo. The Pope suffered from Parkinson's disease but was firm in his view that human life, even in embryonic form, must be protected.

Bush brooded. At a joint press conference with Tony Blair in England on July 19, Bush was asked why he was taking so long deciding. "This is a very serious issue," Bush replied. "I'm going to take my time because I want to hear all sides. This is an issue that speaks to morality and science and the juxtaposition of both. And the American people deserve a president who will listen to people and to make a serious, thoughtful judgment on this complex issue."[82]

When Bush returned from his European trip he met again with his advisers in the White House. Stripped of political connotations, the arguments had crystallized. On the positive side, most of the embryos used to derive stem cells would likely be discarded anyway. The primary source for them was in vitro fertilization clinics. Doctors usually fertilized more eggs than they implanted in the prospective mother. These unused embryos were usually frozen, but were not going to be used to conceive children. Why not use them for research? On the other hand, the embryos—even those long frozen—had a potential for human life. "We are dealing with the seeds of the next generation," said one adviser.[83]

It was in that discussion that Bush worked his way to a decision. He credits Professor Leon Kass, a conservative professor of philosophy at the University of Chicago, with an assist. "The conversation with Leon crystallized my thinking," said Bush. "I decided that the government would fund research on stem cell lines derived from embryos that had already been destroyed. And I would draw a firm moral line: Federal tax dollars would not be used to support the destruction of life [i.e., other embryos] for medical gain."[84]

On August 9, Bush announced his decision in his first nationwide television address after assuming office. It was delivered from the ranch in Crawford. The president reviewed the arguments for stem cell research, then the arguments against, and announced his decision. "My position on these issues is shaped by deeply held beliefs," said the president. "I'm a strong supporter of science and technology, and believe they have the potential for incredible good, to improve lives, to save life, to conquer disease. . . . I also believe human life is a sacred gift from our Creator. I worry about a culture that devalues life and believe as your President I have an important obligation to foster and encourage respect for life in America and throughout the world."

Bush then announced his decision. He would open the door a crack for federal funding. "Embryonic stem cell research offers both great promise and great peril. So I have decided we must proceed with great care." Bush said there were currently sixty different stem cell lines in existence from embryos that had already been destroyed.* "I have concluded that we should allow Federal funds to be used for research on these existing stem cell lines, where the life and death decision has already been made." Bush said he was making $250 million available for further stem cell research, and appointing a presidential council to offer further advice. "I have made this decision with great care, and I pray it is the right one."[85]

Bush followed up with a lengthy op-ed in *The New York Times* of August 12 explaining his decision in further detail. "Stem cell research takes place on a slippery slope of moral concern where much biomedical research is and will be conducted. We must keep our ethical footing. Government has a clear duty to promote scientific discovery—and a duty to define certain boundaries."[86]

The initial response to Bush's decision was one of relief. Americans across the political spectrum appreciated the effort the president had made to square his religious beliefs with the need for scientific progress.

---

* Bush based his statement on figures Hughes received from the National Institutes of Health. Later analysis revealed that there were only twenty-two stem cell lines available. The error is attributable to faulty information initially provided by NIH.

Many in the scientific community were disappointed. The cutbacks in federal aid would slow American research in the field (other countries were moving ahead), but on the positive side at least some research remained possible. "Disappointed Americans who had hoped for a more courageous conclusion may wind up wondering if [Bush's] main concern was a fear of offending the Republican Party's right-wing base," said *The New York Times* editorially.

The *Times*'s argument appeared plausible. The National Right to Life Committee, the nation's largest antiabortion group, said it was "delighted" with Bush's position. So did the Reverend Jerry Falwell and James C. Dobson, president of the conservative Focus on the Family. Pat Robertson, founder of the Christian Coalition, said the president's compromise was "an elegant solution for the thorny issue of stem cell research." The most outspoken opposition came from the Catholic Church. "I seem to be the only man in America who is against the president's policy," said Richard Doerflinger, spokesman for the United States Conference of Catholic Bishops.[87] The extreme right joined in, but for the most part Bush carried the day. The president's deep personal involvement was appreciated, and it was obvious that Bush was speaking from his heart. "With the decision made, I felt a sense of calm," Bush wrote later.[88]*

No Child Left Behind and stem cells were the exception. On those issues, rather than delegate, Bush retained control. And whether they agreed or not, most of the country respected the president's effort. As George Will wrote after the stem cell decision, "Bush's position is so

---

* On March 9, 2009, President Obama reversed Bush's order and issued a new executive order (13505) authorizing renewed federal funding for stem cell research. "For the past eight years, the authority of the Department of Health and Human Services, including the National Institutes of Health (NIH), to fund and conduct human embryonic stem cell research has been limited by Presidential actions. The purpose of this order is to remove those limitations on scientific inquiry, to expand NIH support for the exploration of human stem cell research, and in so doing to enhance the contribution of America's scientists to important new discoveries and new therapies for the benefit of humankind." *Public Papers of the Presidents of the United States, Barack Obama 2009*, Vol. 1, Executive Order 13505, March 9, 2009 (Washington, D.C.: Government Printing Office, 2011).

measured and principled that his critics are in danger of embracing extremism." [89]

But for the most part Bush delegated. That was particularly true for foreign policy and national security. Bush met with the National Security Council for the first time on January 30. "Condi will run these meetings," said the president. "I'll be seeing all of you regularly, but I want you to debate these things out here and then Condi will report to me. She's my national security adviser." [90] There was a brief, scripted discussion about the Middle East. Bush said he was going to tilt back toward Israel, the destabilizing influence of Iraq was laid out by Rice and Tenet, and regime change was touted as the solution. The meeting adjourned in less than an hour. Bush did not meet with the NSC again until after 9/11. Instead, he focused on his domestic agenda. Foreign policy seemed a distraction. With little experience in international affairs, the president was structuring a process that would insulate him from having to deal with conflicting advice.

Bush, who had little executive experience, adopted Harvard Business School's 1975 model of a CEO who let his subordinates thrash out an issue and present him with a solution to which he could say yes or no. Bush saw himself as a decider. He was living in an academic time warp, with business school theory unseasoned by practice. [91] In national security matters, Bush's failure to explore alternatives thoroughly would ultimately prove disastrous.

CHAPTER EIGHT

March of the Hegelians

We create our own reality.

Karl Rove

For the great German philosopher Georg W. F. Hegel, ideas deter-mined reality.[1] And so it was for the Bush White House. Karl Rove's statement in the epigraph epitomized the view of George W. Bush and his immediate associates. Rove's comments were made in an in-terview with a journalist in which he criticized the "reality-based community"—people who believe that solutions to the world's prob-lems emerge from the judicious study of discernible reality. "That's not the way the world really works anymore," said Rove. "We're an empire now, and when we act, we create our own reality. . . . We are history's actors . . . and you, all of you, will be left to just study what we do."[2]

The grandiose view that Rove expounded lies at the root of the in-ternational debacle engineered by the Bush administration. It is attrib-utable to the swashbuckling mind-set of Team Texas, who understood very little of the world beyond America's borders; the chutzpah of the neocons on the White House staff and in the Pentagon who came into office with an imperial ambition to remake the Middle East; the de-termination of the vice president to modify the outcome of the first

Gulf War; the unwillingness of Condoleezza Rice as national security adviser to provide the president with a full range of policy alternatives; and above all to the mental makeup of the president. Unaware of the strictures of international law, unwilling to master the details of complex issues, prone to see the world in black-and-white terms, and convinced he was the instrument of God's will, George W. Bush led the nation into disaster.

Bush's views on foreign policy and national security developed during the presidential campaign under the tutelage of Condoleezza and Wolfowitz, assisted by a group of midlevel officials from the Reagan and Bush 41 administrations. They called themselves the Vulcans, for the Roman god of fire.* Vulcans were also the heroes from outer space in the popular television series *Star Trek* (Spock was of Vulcan heritage), noted for their ability to live by reason and logic. The mythical Vulcans had rescued planet earth after the nuclear holocaust of World War III, and were considered superior to humans in strength and intellect. Whether it was the Roman god of fire or the mythical Vulcans of *Star Trek*, the imagery was smug and condescending.

The Vulcans of the Bush campaign believed in a muscular foreign

---

*   In addition to Rice and Wolfowitz, the Vulcans included Richard Perle, an outspoken hawk who had served on the staff of Senator Henry "Scoop" Jackson, later an assistant secretary of defense under Reagan, and a director of Conrad Black's Hollinger International, which owned the *Jerusalem Post*; Dov Zakheim, former deputy undersecretary of defense for planning and resources under Reagan and an authority on the defense budget; Stephen Hadley, who had served under Wolfowitz in the Defense Department during the George H. W. Bush administration; Robert Blackwill, a career foreign service officer who had served on the NSC with Rice during the Bush years and was currently an associate dean of Harvard's Kennedy School; Robert Zoellick, a close associate of James Baker who had served with Baker in the Treasury Department during the Reagan years, then as counselor of the Department of State when Baker was secretary, and who followed Baker to the White House for the last year of Bush 41's term as deputy chief of staff. Zoellick was currently heading the Center for Strategic and International Studies in Washington but stepped down to assist the Bush campaign. And Richard Armitage, a graduate of the Naval Academy, Vietnam veteran, top aide to Caspar Weinberger at the Defense Department during the Reagan years, who led the negotiations for base rights in the Philippines under Bush 41, and later served as ambassador directing U.S. aid to newly independent states that had been part of the Soviet Union. Armitage was head of Armitage Associates, a lobbying firm in Arlington, Virginia.

policy, military might, and moral clarity. As the most powerful nation on earth, the United States must use its power, unilaterally if necessary, to transform the world and spread democracy. This represented a dramatic break from the realism of the past. Instead of deterrence and containment, instead of accepting the world as it is and working within the structure of international law and diplomacy, the Vulcans would substitute military force and preemption.

Paul Wolfowitz

The intellectual leader of the Vulcans was Wolfowitz, a prototypical Washington defense strategist. His father, Jacob Wolfowitz, had been a mathematics professor at Cornell,* where Paul attended as an undergraduate. There he came under the influence of political science professor Allan Bloom, a disciple of the famous philosopher Leo Strauss, an icon of the conservative movement.[3] Under Bloom's influence, Wolfowitz decided to pursue an academic career in political science. The relationship between Bloom

---

* Personal note. During the campus unrest of the 1960s, Phil Horton, executive editor of *The Reporter* magazine, asked me to go to Cornell and interview a mathematics professor who had new insights into the nature of the student protests. His name was Wolfowitz. I called Professor Wolfowitz, and he was very guarded. "Don't call me again, and do not come to my office," he said. "I am being watched. Meet me on the third bench on the left in the park in front of my office." I did as Professor Wolfowitz requested, and sitting on the bench he told me that the student unrest was a communist plot and the prelude to a full-scale Bolshevik revolution. He was hazy about the details but convinced this was the case. Professor Wolfowitz's family had fled Warsaw in 1920 to escape from a Russian communist occupation, and he worried about a repeat. I wrote the article, but Horton thought it was too far out and did not use it. Shortly after the student protests ended, Professor Wolfowitz left Cornell and went to the University of Illinois. He finished his career at the University of South Florida in Tampa.

and Wolfowitz is treated by Saul Bellow in *Ravelstein*, Bellow's roman a clef portrait of Bloom.[4]*

Wolfowitz did his graduate work at the University of Chicago under Strauss and Albert Wohlstetter, the dean of the anti-détente school of thought in academia. Though Wohlstetter supervised his dissertation, the influence of Strauss and Bloom on Wolfowitz's thinking should not be underestimated. Both believed strongly in moral absolutes, rejected the tolerance of modern liberalism, and saw the world divided between good and evil. Ronald Reagan's denunciation of the Soviet Union as an "evil empire" was a milestone for the Straussians, while international organizations like the United Nations were inherently suspect.[5]

While writing his dissertation, Wolfowitz received an appointment as a lecturer in the political science department at Yale. When the dissertation was completed he was promoted to assistant professor, but for whatever reason the appointment was not renewed.[6] With an academic career closed off, at least at Yale, Wolfowitz went to Washington where, at the recommendation of Wohlstetter, he was hired by the Arms Control and Disarmament Agency.[7] Wolfowitz remained there four years before moving to a midlevel policy position at the Defense Department as deputy assistant secretary for regional programs. In that capacity he prepared the Defense Department's first study of the importance of the Persian Gulf to the United States. In Wolfowitz's mind, the danger arose not only from possible Soviet expansion, but also from Iraq. This was the first instance in which Iraq became the focus of a military planning document. The Carter administration dismissed the idea.[8]

With the election of 1980 looming, Wolfowitz resigned from the Defense Department and assumed a temporary position as a visiting associate professor at the Johns Hopkins School of Advanced International Studies in Washington.[9] When Reagan won, incoming secretary of state Alexander Haig appointed Wolfowitz to head the State

---

* Wolfowitz appears in the novel as Philip Gorman, a former student of Ravelstein [Bloom] who is a senior Defense Department official. At one point, after finishing a telephone conversation with Gorman, Ravelstein tells his guests, "It's only a matter of time before Phil Gorman has cabinet rank, and a damn good thing for the country. He has a powerful mind and a real grasp of great politics, this kid." Saul Bellow, *Ravelstein* (New York: Penguin, 2000), 58–59.

Department's policy planning staff. Haig and Wolfowitz were on the same ideological wavelength, but the chemistry was bad. On March 30, 1982, *The New York Times* carried a story that Haig had notified Wolfowitz he would be replaced. Before Haig could replace Wolfowitz, Reagan replaced Haig with George Shultz, and Shultz became Wolfowitz's guardian angel. Wolfowitz was promoted to assistant secretary of state for East Asia and the Pacific, and in 1986 was made ambassador to Indonesia, a post he held for the next three years and by all accounts performed admirably.

In January 1989, when the George H. W. Bush administration came into office, secretary of defense designate John Tower selected Wolfowitz to be his undersecretary for policy, the senior policy-making position in the Pentagon. But Tower stumbled on his way to Senate confirmation, and Bush chose Dick Cheney, then Republican whip in the House, to replace him. Cheney was initially undecided about Wolfowitz, but after a lengthy conversation found their ideas were compatible and proceeded with his nomination.[10] For the next four years Wolfowitz and Cheney worked hand-in-glove to establish the foundation for a more assertive American foreign policy. The fact that neither Cheney nor Wolfowitz had ever served in the military, much less experienced combat (both received repeated draft deferments while in graduate school), in no way diminished their enthusiasm for using troops abroad. As Dwight Eisenhower could have said, those whose white asses had never been within four thousand miles of a shot fired in anger were always the most eager to send troops into battle.

When the Gulf War came, Cheney argued that Bush had the power to go to war without congressional approval, but Bush decided otherwise and won the vote narrowly.[11] When the war ended, neither Cheney nor Wolfowitz advocated going on to Baghdad, though Wolfowitz regretted the fighting ended so quickly. The reason the United States did not go on to Baghdad was succinctly stated by Colin Powell: "Our practical intention was to leave Baghdad enough power to survive as a threat to an Iran that remained bitterly hostile to the United States."[12] The realist administration of Bush 41 was not interested in remaking the world in America's image, and wanted to use Saddam as a counterweight to the Ayatollah, just as Nixon had cultivated China to check the Soviet Union. To the Vulcans, this was heresy.

In January 1993, just before leaving office, Cheney and Wolfowitz issued a document that became the guiding star for the Vulcans. This was the Defense Planning Guidance report required every two years. Entitled "Defense Strategy for the 1990s," it was distributed over Cheney's signature. The document touted America's strength as the world's only superpower and charted a path for unilateral action. "A future President will need options allowing him to lead and, where international reaction proves sluggish or inadequate, to act independently to protect our critical interests. History suggests that effective multilateral action is most likely to come about in response to U.S. leadership, not as an alternative to it." [13] The senior Bush's White House immediately disavowed the document, as did the Clinton administration, but for the Vulcans in the 2000 campaign it pointed the way to the future.

Wolfowitz spent the next seven years as dean of the Johns Hopkins School of Advanced International Studies in Washington. Given his lack of academic experience—junior lecturer and assistant professor at Yale and one year as a visiting associate professor at SAIS—his appointment came as a surprise, and Wolfowitz's record at SAIS was mixed. He was an effective fundraiser, but his relations with faculty and students were not easy. Like Eisenhower at Columbia, he saw SAIS as a top-down command structure and eschewed the collegiality traditional in academia.

In the late 1990s, while still at SAIS, Wolfowitz became a leading advocate for removing Saddam from power in Iraq. In 1997 he was a founding member of the Project for the New American Century, along with Cheney, Donald Rumsfeld, Fred Iklé, and conservative writer Norman Podhoretz.* The purpose of the Project was "to make the case and rally support for American global leadership." [14] In 1998, Wolfowitz signed an open letter to President Clinton that called for

---

* Signatories to the statement of principles of the Project included Elliott Abrams, William J. Bennett, Jeb Bush, Eliot Cohen, Midge Decter, Steve Forbes, Francis Fukuyama, Donald Kagan, Zalmy Khalilzad, I. Lewis Libby, Dan Quayle, Peter Rodman, Henry Rowen, and Vin Weber.

Saddam's overthrow. "The only acceptable strategy is one that eliminates the possibility that Iraq will be able to use or threaten to use weapons of mass destruction. In the near term, this means a willingness to undertake military action. . . . In the long term, it means removing Saddam Hussein and his regime from power."[15]

After Bush was elected, the Vulcans were given high positions in the administration. Condoleezza Rice became national security adviser and Stephen Hadley was appointed her deputy. Robert Zoellick became U.S. trade representative and given cabinet rank. Armitage became deputy secretary of state under Colin Powell, Wolfowitz was made Rumsfeld's deputy secretary at defense, Dov Zakheim was appointed the Defense Department's comptroller, and Robert Blackwill was sent to India as ambassador. Richard Perle, who was a highly remunerated Washington lobbyist, chose not to accept a position in the administration and was appointed chairman of the Defense Advisory Board under Rumsfeld.* Of all the Vulcans, it would be Wolfowitz who would play the key intellectual role in shaping the foreign policy of the Bush years.[16]

At a Washington cocktail party shortly after Wolfowitz's appointment as deputy secretary of defense was announced, Rumsfeld ran into an old Princeton classmate, George Packard. Packard was Wolfowitz's predecessor as dean at Johns Hopkins, long serving and much beloved.

"Be careful of Wolfowitz," Packard warned Rumsfeld.

"Why?" asked Rumsfeld. "He's very smart."

"That's why," Packard replied.[17]

George W. Bush quickly embraced the concept of American power espoused by Wolfowitz and Cheney. It appealed to his abhorrence of complexity and ambiguity. He agreed that America's status as the world's only superpower should remain unchallenged, that ideas such as collective security and multilateral cooperation were outdated relics of the Cold War, and that American values of democracy and freedom should be projected throughout the world. This required a strong mili

---

* The Defense Advisory Board is a council of thirty former senior officials and scholars who provide advice to the secretary of defense.

tary presence, combined with a willingness to use force when necessary, with or without allies. These were the principles that had been laid out by Wolfowitz and Cheney in the 1992 Defense Planning Guidance document that the senior Bush and Clinton had rejected, but which now became the administration's playbook for asserting American hegemony.

For the first eight months of his presidency, George W. Bush focused on domestic issues. After the initial meeting of the National Security Council on January 30, he did not meet with it again until after 9/11. He also instructed the CIA to reduce the President's Daily Brief from twelve pages to six or seven. This is the first document every president sees each morning when he arrives in the Oval Office. Bush was uninterested in the details of the international situation and wanted broad strokes. "I wish those assholes would put things just point-blank to me," he told Saudi Prince Bandar. "I get half a book telling me about the history of North Korea. I don't do nuance." [18]

Ronald Reagan began his presidency in a similar manner. The administration focused on stimulating the economy, and foreign affairs took a backseat. But as superpower relations deteriorated, Reagan realized such negligence had been a mistake. By 1983 the president had become a diligent student of the international situation. Before the Geneva summit with Mikhail Gorbachev in 1985, NSC staffer Jack Matlock prepared over twenty research papers for Reagan on various aspects of Soviet history and Russian culture, as well as Gorbachev's character and objectives, and the president devoured them.* "They were the most important papers of the last twenty years," said Robert McFarlane, Reagan's national security adviser. "We'd give them to President Reagan once a week. We'd go into a meeting and he'd give me back one of Jack's papers and it would be scribbled all over and he would look at Don Regan [White House chief of staff] and he would

---

* Matlock referred to the papers he prepared as "Soviet Union 101." The papers were 8–10 pages long, single-spaced. The first three dealt with the sources of Soviet behavior, the next nine covered "the Soviet Union from the Inside," ten dealt with assorted foreign policy and national security topics, and the final two evaluated Gorbachev and his political objectives. Jack Matlock, *Reagan and Gorbachev: How the Cold War Ended* (New York: Random House, 2004), 132–135.

say, 'Read this. This is good, this is really worth knowing.'" McFarlane credits Matlock's research papers with much of the success at Geneva. "A year earlier President Reagan would not have had the grasp of the Russian character and as heartfelt an appreciation for Russian history as he did in Geneva. It turned a corner in our relationship with the Soviet Union."[19]

It was not simply a matter of Bush's short attention span. Tax relief, No Child Left Behind, and stem cells required constant care. Bush saw himself as a domestic leader. After education and tax reform he intended to turn to Social Security and prescription drugs for the elderly. Foreign policy was delegated to Rice. As he told the NSC on January 30, "Condi is my national security adviser. She will handle your discussions."[20]

That was a victory for Rice over Cheney, whose staff had suggested that the vice president chair the meetings of the National Security Council in Bush's absence. History was on Cheney's side. Nixon had chaired the NSC when Eisenhower was not there, Humphrey did for Johnson, and Mondale for Carter. The vice president is a statutory member of the NSC and the national security adviser is not. But in later years, beginning in Reagan's second term, meetings without the president have been chaired by the national security adviser.* Supposedly, this gives the president greater control. The irony is that the National Security Council was established after World War II (and patterned on the British war cabinet) precisely to ensure that there would never again be such a concentration of power in the hands of the president as had occurred during the war under FDR.

When Cheney's staff recommended that the vice president chair the meetings, Rice "threw a fit" according to White House colleagues, cited recent precedent, and Bush acquiesced.[21] The decision reflected W's personal style. He was comfortable with Rice. But the choice was

---

* After the Iran-contra scandal, Reagan replaced Admiral John Poindexter with Frank Carlucci as his national security adviser. Carlucci insisted that he chair the meetings of the NSC in Reagan's absence, and the president agreed. George Shultz, as secretary of state, objected, but in June of 1987 Reagan issued an executive order adopting Carlucci's request.

not without drawbacks. Rice had little experience at that level of policy making and initially assumed she was Bush's surrogate. "Rice's first months in office were a learning experience," wrote Rumsfeld in his memoirs. "She and her staff did not seem to understand they were not in the chain of command." [22]

Bush was structuring a White House similar to the governor's mansion in Austin. In Texas, given the requirements of the state constitution, Bush did not deal with the heads of departments and had no executive responsibility. Except for the leaders of the legislature, his contacts were almost exclusively with the governor's staff. Accordingly, it is not surprising that in Washington he interposed his White House staff between himself and the members of his cabinet.* Paul O'Neill and the Treasury Department were largely excluded from the formulation of tax policy; Colin Powell and the State Department would soon find themselves excluded from major foreign policy decisions; and Donald Rumsfeld and the Joint Chiefs would find that the White House staff wanted to issue orders and provide guidance to combat commanders. Powell, O'Neill, and Rumsfeld were heavy hitters and seasoned executives with decades of experience in the ways of Washington. Rather than rely on them, Bush preferred inexperienced, in-house talent. As one scholar of the period observed, "the palace guard eclipsed the King's ministers." [23]

Another difficulty is that the White House staff, like the governor's staff in Austin, told Bush what he wanted to hear. Rather than bringing the institutional expertise of cabinet departments to bear, often

---

* The growth of the White House staff, and particularly the NSC, has been exponential. Under Reagan, the NSC staff was three times as large as under Kennedy and Johnson, and under Clinton it doubled again. Bush retained that structure and Cheney added another fourteen national security specialists to his staff. In addition there are approximately one hundred professional staffers seconded from State, Defense, and the CIA. The organization of the NSC parallels that of the State Department, with over two hundred professionals dealing with essentially the same issues. The NSC has its own legal adviser, press officer, congressional liaison, and intelligence division. The growth of the NSC staff reflects the personalization of national security policy in the White House. See David J. Rothkopf, *Running the World: The Inside Story of the National Security Council and the Architects of American Power* (New York: PublicAffairs, 2005); Amy B. Zegart, *Flawed by Design: The Evolution of the CIA, JCS, and NSC* (Stanford: Stanford University Press, 1999).

with conflicting viewpoints, the White House staff simplified issues to the point of obfuscation. This was particularly true of Rice and the staff of the NSC. Rice defined her job as Bush's enabler and enforcer, a translator of his instincts and intuition into policy. That was not what Bush needed, but it appears to have been what he wanted.[24]

Colin Powell, who had been national security adviser under Reagan, and chairman of the Joint Chiefs under the elder Bush and Clinton, lamented the change. There were no longer formal papers in which departments laid out their positions as under Reagan, no intense Oval Office discussions as under Bush's father, and no endless debates in the formal meetings of the NSC as under Clinton. "Under George W. Bush," said Powell, "decisions seemed to come out of the ether."[25]

An even harsher critic of the Bush administration's national security style was Rumsfeld. In particular, Rumsfeld believed that by delegating primary responsibility to Rice, Bush was not exposed to the full ramifications of many issues. His decisions therefore were not based on a full understanding of what was involved, but on the perspective that Rice applied. Even worse, Rice had a desire to present Bush with a consensus, even when differences remained unresolved. "The most notable feature of Rice's management of the interagency policy process," wrote Rumsfeld,

> was her commitment . . . to "bridging" differences between agencies, rather than bringing these differences to the president for decision. . . . While disharmony is a word that can have a negative connotation, the fact is that a vigorous debate about policy options can be healthy.[26]
>
> Rice was a regular presence at Camp David and in Crawford, and was almost always the last person the president talked to on any given national security issue. She used that proximity and authority to press for action in the president's name. But it was not always clear to me when she had been directed by the president to do something or when she simply believed she was acting in the president's best interest—one could not check every question with the president himself.[27]

Richard Armitage, who as Powell's deputy secretary differed from Rumsfeld on a number of things, saw eye to eye with him on Rice. Armitage called her an "acceleratron," meaning that she reinforced Bush's wrong impulses when she should have been applying the brakes.[28]

In Washington usage, when the members of the National Security Council meet without the president, it is called a meeting of the principals. Between the inauguration and 9/11, the principals met twenty-two times. Six of the meetings dealt with Iraq, five with Russia, four with the Balkans, and two with China.* Bush did not attend these meetings, and the difficulty of attempting to frame policy without the president soon became apparent.

On March 1, the principals met to consider American policy toward North Korea. This was in anticipation of a state visit by South Korean president Kim Dae-jung later that week. In 1994 the Clinton administration had reached a tentative agreement with communist North Korea in which the United States promised significant economic assistance and eventual diplomatic recognition in return for North Korea's pledge to freeze and ultimately dismantle its nuclear weapons program. Negotiations continued fitfully, and in October 2000, Secretary of State Madeleine Albright made a historic visit to Pyongyang during which the North Koreans offered to terminate the production, testing, and deployment of their mid- and long-range missiles in return for a presidential visit and help in launching three satellites a year. Clinton attempted to schedule a visit to Pyongyang but his term ended before that could be done.[29]

Parallel to Washington's efforts to normalize relations with North Korea, the South Korean government of Kim Dae-jung had launched a "sunshine policy" consisting of economic and social incentives to nudge the North toward national reconciliation. The policies of Washington and Seoul were complementary, and this double-barreled approach seemed ready to bear fruit.

At the meeting of the principals on March 1, Powell laid out the situation and indicated that an agreement that would eliminate North Korea's nuclear threat was in the offing. On March 6, the day before Kim Dae-jung's arrival in Washington, Powell hosted a press confer-

* The other meetings were devoted to North Korea, Sudan, Europe, Turkey, and the biological weapons convention.

ence with Swedish foreign minister Anna Lindh and was asked by a reporter about President Bush's plans for the two Koreas. Powell replied that the administration supported South Korea's efforts to reach an accommodation with the North and would work closely with Seoul and Pyongyang. "We do plan to engage with North Korea and to pick up where President Clinton and his administration left off."[30] The next morning *The Washington Post* printed Powell's remarks under the headline, "Bush to Pick Up Clinton Talks on N. Korean Missiles."[31]

The *Post* article set off alarm bells in the White House. Bush had not attended the meeting of the principals on March 1 when Powell laid out the situation, Cheney had been represented by Scooter Libby, and Rice evidently had not passed on to the president what Powell had said. At a hastily convened meeting in the Oval Office attended by Cheney, Rice, Powell, Karen Hughes, and chief of staff Andy Card, Powell was told the *Washington Post* story had to be corrected before Bush and Kim met the press later that day. Powell dutifully stepped out of the meeting and reversed course. The administration, he told White House reporters, was undertaking "a full review of our relationship with North Korea. When our review is finished, we'll determine at what pace and when we will engage with the North Koreans." Powell said that if there had been "some suggestion that imminent negotiations are about to begin, that is not the case."[32]*

Shortly afterward, Bush and South Korean president Kim Daejung held a joint press conference at which Bush made it clear that he was in no hurry to resume discussions with the North Korean leadership. In an obvious rebuke to Kim (and Powell), Bush told reporters, "I was forthright in describing . . . my skepticism about whether or not we can verify an agreement with a country that doesn't enjoy the freedoms that our two countries understand—and have a free press like we have here in America."[33]

Initial press reports emphasized that Powell had erred by tying the

---

* Several weeks later newsmen asked Powell if the administration was sending mixed messages on Korea. Powell laughed and said, "Yeah, and I delivered both of them. Sometimes you get a little too far forward on your skis." William Douglas, "Powell Acknowledges Some Miscues," *Newsday*, May 5, 2001.

administration to the policies of Clinton. But the problem was more fundamental. Powell and the State Department hoped an agreement with North Korea would be a positive step reducing the threat of nuclear war. Bush, Cheney, and the Vulcans, wedded to a view of the world as a Manichaean contest between good and evil, rejected the idea of negotiating with a state they deemed immoral. If the United States had brought the evil empire of the Soviet Union to its knees, why deal with a state vastly smaller, weaker, and more repressive?

Bush's response to Kim Dae-jung's visit set the tone for the administration. The United States would not enter into an agreement that kept a brutal regime in power. For Bush, foreign policy was an exercise in morality. That appealed to his religious fervor, and greatly simplified dealing with the world beyond America's borders. "I loathe [North Korea's leader] Kim Jong Il," Bush told Bob Woodward. "I've got a visceral reaction to this guy. . . . Maybe it's my religion, but I feel passionate about this."[34] Bush's personalization of foreign policy and his refusal to deal with North Korea was the first of a multitude of errors that came to haunt his presidency. Instead of bringing a denuclearized North Korea peacefully into the family of nations, as seemed within reach in 2001, the Bush administration isolated the government in Pyongyang hoping for its collapse. In the years following, North Korea continued to be an intractable problem for the administration. By the end of Bush's presidency, North Korea had tested a nuclear device and was believed to have tripled its stock of plutonium, accumulating enough for at least six nuclear weapons.[35]

Aside from their attachment to the idea of American hegemony, the worldview of Bush, Cheney, and the Vulcans was predicated on a false reading of history. A keystone of belief was that Ronald Reagan's harsh rhetoric and policy of firmness had forced the collapse of the Soviet Union and ended the Cold War. In actuality, Ronald Reagan's harsh rhetoric during his first three years in office actually intensified the Cold War and heightened Soviet resistance. Not until Reagan changed course, replaced Alexander Haig with George Shultz, and held out an olive branch to the Soviets did the Cold War begin to thaw. Beginning with the Geneva summit in 1985, Reagan would meet with Gorbachev five times in the next three years, including a precedent-shattering visit to the Kremlin and Red Square. What about the "evil empire"? the president was asked. "I was talking about another time, another era," said Reagan.[36] President Reagan deserves full credit for ending the Cold War. But it ended because of his willingness to negotiate with Gorbachev and establish a relationship of mutual trust.* For Bush, Cheney, and the Vulcans this was a lesson they had not learned.

When Kim Dae-jung left Washington, Bush was standing tall. He had reversed the Clinton policy of accommodation with North Korea, put the world on notice that the United States would not negotiate with regimes it deemed immoral, and diminished the luster of Colin Powell. As a senior White House official said, "It was an early signal that the president was not going to allow the secretary of state to say whatever he wanted. It was a useful signal to other cabinet members too."[37]

On the heels of the about-face on Korea came Kyoto and global warming. In the case of North Korea, Bush reversed almost ten years of preparatory negotiations, overruled the South Korean government, and dismissed the judgment of Secretary Powell and the State Department. On global warming, Bush also reversed course, rejected the views of Christie Todd Whitman and the Environmental Protection Agency that she headed, the efforts of Powell and the State Department to find a long-term formula, and the concerns of Paul O'Neill and the Treasury. Once again, the president decided the issue without consulting the agencies involved.

The Kyoto Protocol, named for the Japanese city in which it was negotiated in 1997, was an international agreement that committed thirty-seven highly industrialized nations to curtail the emission of greenhouse gases in order to reduce global warming. The Clinton ad-

---

*   In his memoirs, Soviet Ambassador Anatoly Dobrynin states it succinctly. "It may sound like an historical paradox, but if the President [Reagan] had not abandoned his hostile stance toward the Soviet Union for a more constructive one . . . Gorbachev would not have been able to launch his reforms and his new thinking. Quite the contrary. Gorbachev would have been forced to continue the conservative foreign and defense policies of his predecessors." Anatoly Dobrynin, *In Confidence: Moscow's Ambassador to Six Cold War Presidents* (New York: Random House, 1995), 611.

ministration had signed the protocol, but had never submitted it to the Senate for ratification. Among other flaws, the protocol did not apply to China and India, and the Senate of its own accord voted 95–0 to reject its provisions in 1997. On the campaign trail in 2000, George W. Bush noted his opposition to the protocol, but repeatedly reaffirmed his belief that the United States should work with other nations to reduce harmful emissions. Speaking in Michigan, Bush specifically called for legislation to require the mandatory reduction of greenhouse gases from power plants, including carbon dioxide. A mandatory cap on carbon dioxide emissions was also listed in "Transition 2000," a compendium of Bush's campaign promises compiled by his transition team. When Bush nominated New Jersey governor Christie Todd Whitman to head the Environmental Protection Agency, environmentalists were reassured that the administration took global warming seriously. Whitman's national reputation was in many respects second only to Colin Powell's, and she had a proven track record fighting for environmental causes.

Whitman, who as a Republican governor had often shared thoughts with Bush while he was governor of Texas, believed she and the president saw the problem of global warming similarly. She intended to reassure America's allies at an upcoming meeting of environmental ministers from the G-8 countries (Britain, Canada, France, Germany, Italy, Japan, and Russia) in Trieste that the United States would move quickly to cap carbon dioxide emissions. Before leaving for Trieste, Whitman met with Condoleezza Rice and confirmed that she would be repeating the president's campaign pledge to limit CO_2 emissions. Rice thought that was a sound approach. Whitman also checked with White House chief of staff Andy Card and got a green light as well.[38]

At Trieste on March 2, Whitman laid out what she assumed was the administration's position. "The president has said global climate change is the greatest environmental challenge we face and we must recognize that and take steps to move forward." Whitman said the United States was preparing to list carbon dioxide as a toxic substance, a step that would permit the EPA to cap its emissions. America's G-8 partners were initially skeptical, but Whitman assured them Bush's commitment was genuine. When the two-day conference adjourned, press reports were glowing. The *Financial Times* noted the delegates were "pleasantly surprised" and "impressed by the stance taken by Christie Whitman."[39] Reuters said environmental activists were encouraged and that "Christie Todd Whitman, head of the U.S. Environmental Protection Agency, had provided a clear welcome signal to G-8 partners that the White House was serious about global warming."[40]

Press reports from Trieste ignited a firestorm in Washington. Cheney, who was heading Bush's energy task force, immediately protested that a ban on CO_2 emissions would exacerbate the nation's energy crisis; Rove feared its impact on the Republican base; and industry leaders, labor and management alike, cautioned regarding its negative effect on the economy. Four Republican senators led by Chuck Hagel of Nebraska wrote Bush asking for "a clarification of your administration's policy on climate change"—a clear invitation for the president to reverse course. Whitman and Treasury Secretary Paul O'Neill believed the White House had inspired the letter, and that Cheney was behind it. "I bet they didn't dream up the idea of writing this letter on their own," O'Neill told Whitman. "This is the kind of thing where somebody on the White House staff would have maybe called up Hagel and said, 'Chuck, why don't you ask us for a letter of clarification.' I wouldn't be surprised if you found out that the White House requested this letter of clarification and that the Vice President was preparing the response."[41]

Whitman requested an immediate appointment with the president. The meeting was set for 10 a.m. on March 13. Whitman assumed Bush had read the reports from the EPA and the Treasury stressing the need for action.[42] Seated in the Oval Office, Whitman began her presentation. Bush cut her off. "Christie, I've already made my decision." The president said he had changed his mind. He not only opposed the Kyoto Protocol, but no longer favored a cap on carbon dioxide emissions. Bush said he had prepared a reply to Hagel, and read portions of it to her. "I do not believe . . . that the government should impose on power plants mandatory emission reductions for carbon dioxide, which is not a pollutant under the Clean Air Act."[43] Bush had pivoted 180 degrees. Neither the EPA, nor the Treasury, nor the State Department had been consulted or informed beforehand.

As a stunned Whitman left the Oval Office she met Cheney rushing past. "He muttered a brief hello to me as he asked an aide who had come up behind me, 'Do you have it?' The aide handed him a letter, which he tucked into his pocket as he rushed out."[44] It was Bush's letter to Hagel, and Cheney was on his way to Capitol Hill to deliver it.

The global fallout was immediate. The *Times* of London wrote,

> At a single stroke, the United States has condemned the planet to a more polluted, less certain future. Mr. Bush has made it clear he has concerns far more pressing than the global environment. The country that emits 25 percent of the world's carbon dioxide with less than four percent of its population is not going to slow down.[45]

Colin Powell and the State Department were blindsided. "They all got together . . . and said to hell with everybody else and they just signed it with no reference to our allies, no reference to 'Let's work with them and find a way forward on carbon emissions or whatever,'" said Powell. "Cheney was anxious to get it up there, so he just walked it up."[46]

Condoleezza Rice was dumbfounded. She also had not been consulted. "I said, 'Mr. President, this is going to color your foreign policy from the outset, and that's a problem.' I also said that I was appalled that the Vice President had been allowed to take a letter to Capitol Hill on a matter of international importance without any clearance from me or, more important, that of the secretary of state."[47]

Christie Todd Whitman remained in the administration another two years, a lonely moderate surrounded by hawkish ideologues. Shortly after leaving office she wrote, "The administration's insistence on playing strictly to the base in explaining the president's opposition to ratifying the Kyoto Protocol, coupled with his reversal on the regulation of carbon dioxide, was an early expression of the go-it-alone attitude that so offended our allies in the lead-up to the Iraq war."[48]

Paul O'Neill was equally pessimistic. "What became clear to me [after Bush reversed course] is that the presence of me and Colin and Christie helped convince people that this would be an administration that would look hard to find the best solutions, without regard for which party had claimed the idea first or some passing political calculation. Thinking back on how all three of us started to be banged up early on, from the inside, it now seems like we inadvertently may have been there in large part as cover."[49]*

After rejecting the Kyoto Protocol and declining to place a cap on carbon dioxide emissions, Bush announced his intent to unilaterally "move beyond the constraints" of the 1972 Anti-Ballistic Missile Treaty with the Soviet Union and develop a missile defense system for the United States. In June, reflecting the concerns of the National Rifle Association, he pulled the United States out of a proposed international agreement to control cross-border trafficking in small arms. This was followed in quick succession by rejection of a new international convention on biological weapons, the Comprehensive Test Ban Treaty, and the International Criminal Court. Within six months, the administration announced its intention to reject six international agreements. Bush's opposition to these agreements was heavy-handed: as the world's only superpower, there was no reason for the United States to accept restrictions imposed by others. Bush's opposition to membership in the International Criminal Court, which Clinton had agreed to, was especially sharp. Not only did Bush make it clear that he would not submit the treaty to the Senate, he also sought to persuade the other signatories to agree they would not hand over Americans to the tribunal for trial.

Bush let domestic politics color his view of international affairs, and did not recognize the need for allies and mutual support. Team Texas in the White House was calling the shots based on electoral appeal. Powell and the State Department were ignored. For whatever reason, Bush held the State Department in low regard. Andy Card later told Powell that he was the only person at the State Department the president trusted. Richard Haass, who headed the State Department's Pol-

---

* Cheney does not discuss the Kyoto Protocol or the letter to Hagel in his autobiography, *In My Time* (New York: Threshold, 2011).

icy Planning Staff, was not sure Bush trusted Powell all that much. "Whatever the reason or reasons, the bottom line is that George W. Bush and Colin Powell never forged the sort of close relationship that is essential if a secretary of state is to succeed."[50]

If Korea and the treaty rejections were stepping-stones on the imperial road to American hegemony, an incident on Sunday, April 1, 2001, pulled Bush up short. A Chinese J-8 fighter jet and a Navy EP-3 reconnaissance plane collided over the South China Sea, some seventy miles from the island of Hainan. The Chinese plane and its pilot, Lieutenant Commander Wang Wei, crashed into the sea; the damaged American plane with its supersensitive monitoring equipment made an emergency landing at Lingshui military airfield on Hainan. The Chinese impounded the plane, detained the crew of twenty-four (twenty-one men and three women), and demanded an apology.

The issue was complicated. The People's Republic of China claimed the area of the overflight as part of the PRC's exclusive economic zone under the United Nations Convention on the Law of the Sea, to which it was a signatory. China contended it had the right to prevent military flights in the area. The United States, which is not a party to the convention, maintained that the convention permits free navigation within a country's economic zone even for military ships and aircraft. Reconnaissance flights by the lumbering, propeller-driven EP-3s had been going on for years, and the Chinese had routinely buzzed the planes with interceptor jets. This time they got too close. Whether the Chinese jet bumped the wing of the U.S. plane, or whether the EP-3 turned into the path of the jet remains in dispute. What was not in dispute was that the Chinese had the plane and the crew, and the United States wanted them back.

Congressional hawks, media pundits, and hardliners on the White House staff urged Bush to retaliate. Economic sanctions, opposition to China's bid to host the 2008 Olympics, cancellation of Bush's scheduled visit to Beijing, and the suspension of military contacts were suggested as possible responses. The Defense Department even considered plans to destroy the plane on the ground to protect the highly classified equipment on board. Powell and Rice urged restraint, as did Cheney. China was America's fourth largest trading partner (after Canada, Mexico, and Japan), the collision was an accident, and there was no reason to create another hostage crisis like the one Carter confronted in Tehran. Apologize and get the crew and the plane home.

Initially Bush took a hard line. Meeting with reporters on April 2, the president said "the Chinese must promptly allow us to have contact with the 24 air men and women that are there and return our plane to us without further tampering. I sent a very clear message and I expect them to heed the message."[51] But the Chinese held firm. In a public statement, Chinese president Jiang Zemin replied that the United States "bears full responsibility" for the accident and repeated his demand for an apology.[52] At that point Bush rethought his position.* There was no reason to escalate the crisis. On April 3, the president authorized Powell to negotiate a solution. Speaking to the American Society of Newspaper Editors two days later, Bush backed down. "I regret that a Chinese pilot is missing, and I regret one of their airplanes is lost. And our prayers go out to the pilot and his family.... We should not let this incident destabilize relations. Our relationship with China is very important, but they need to realize that it's time for our people to be home. We're working all diplomatic channels to effect that. My mission is to bring the people home. And as to whether we have good relations, my intention is to make sure we have good relations with China."[53]

Following the president's statement, negotiations progressed rapidly. The crew of the EP-3 was moved from the military barracks at Ling-shui airfield to more comfortable quarters in Haikou, the provincial capital, and on April 11, Vice Admiral (ret.) Joseph Prueher, the American ambassador in Beijing, delivered a formal letter to Chinese foreign minister Tang Jiaxuan, the text of which had been mutually agreed. Known as the "letter of the two sorrys," the letter said the United States was "very sorry" for the death of Chinese pilot Wang Wei, and "We are very sorry the entering of China's airspace and the landing did not have

---

* Tangential evidence suggests Bush changed his mind following an unscheduled visit to the White House by Henry Kissinger. Kissinger first spoke with Cheney, then at some length with Bush, after which the president reversed course. (Confidential source.)

verbal clearance."[54] The Chinese called it a letter of apology; the U.S. embassy said it was an expression of sorrow and regret. The distinction is in the eye of the beholder. Wang Wei was posthumously honored by China as a "Guardian of Territorial Airspace and Waters," and President Bush wrote a personal letter of condolence to his widow.[55] The aircrew was released on the morning of April 11 and returned to a heroes' welcome in Hawaii. Bush briefly considered going to Hawaii to meet them, but ultimately decided against it. "The spotlight should be on them, it's their reunion with their families. We can have them here later."[56]

The incident was an important benchmark in American relations with China. The reconnaissance flights of the EP-3s continued, the Chinese continued to scramble their jets to monitor them, but kept a respectable distance. The letter of the two sorrys allowed China to save face, and except for the sensitive surveillance equipment that fell into Chinese hands, the United States did not surrender anything of value. When it was called to Bush's attention that the Chinese held the high cards, he cut his losses. Public opinion in the United States hailed the return of the aircrew, and careful diplomacy had prevailed.*

Rumsfeld, who did not initially agree with the president's decision, nevertheless praised Bush's leadership.

> The vice president, the secretary of state, the secretary of defense, the chairman of the Joint Chiefs of Staff, the director of the CIA, and the national security adviser all had an opportunity to offer their views to President Bush at the height of the crisis. Having considered the options, and the advice we recommended, he decided the course he thought was best. Even though Bush chose a course somewhat different from my recommendations, he made the decision. I thought that was exactly how the NSC should have functioned. Regrettably, that would not always be the case.[57]

---

* The disassembled EP-3 was returned to the United States aboard a Russian airline Antonov An-124 on July 3, 2001. The United States paid for the dismantling and shipping of the plane, as well as $34,000 for food and lodging for the EP-3 crew.

The return of the EP-3 flight crew was a victory for the voices of moderation within the administration. Bush recognized that good relations with the People's Republic were too important to be sacrificed on the altar of moral clarity and American jingoism. When the United States announced the sale of eight older diesel-powered submarines to Taiwan later in April, administration spokesmen made it clear that in deference to Beijing, the White House had refused to sell state-of-the-art destroyers equipped with Aegis radar systems to Taipei.[58] Bush stumbled briefly during an interview with ABC's Charles Gibson celebrating his first hundred days in office, but quickly corrected himself. Asked by Gibson what the United States would do if Taiwan were attacked, Bush said the United States would respond with "whatever it took to help Taiwan defend herself." At first blush it looked as though he was reversing the policy of ambiguity first enunciated by Eisenhower in 1955, but when Rice and Powell called his attention to the gaffe he immediately issued a statement that he was not changing long-standing American policy concerning the defense of Taiwan.[59]

To the dismay of the Vulcans, Bush was now convinced of the importance of maintaining good relations with China. On June 1, the president extended normal trade relations with Beijing for another year. "The United States has a huge stake in the emergence of an economically open, politically stable, and secure China," Bush told Congress. "Recent events have shown not only that we need to speak frankly and directly about our differences, but that we also need to maintain dialogue and cooperate with one another on those areas where we have common interests. An important area where the interests of our two countries converge is in maintaining a healthy trading relationship." [60]

In June, Bush flew to Europe to attend summit meetings of NATO and the European Union. This was his first trip across the ocean as president (he had previously visited Mexico City and Ottawa), and Bush anticipated being quizzed about his rejection of the Kyoto Protocol and missile defense. Before leaving Washington he made a damage control speech in the Rose Garden. "America's unwillingness to embrace a flawed treaty should not be read by our friends and allies as an abdication of responsibility. To the contrary, my administration is committed to a leadership role on the issue of climate change." Bush went on to list a number of principles that would guide the administration, but did not explicitly pledge to cap carbon dioxide emissions.[61]

Bush and Laura stopped first in Madrid. Looking back on the trip to Europe, Laura recalled, "The flights were invariably overnight, and the expectation was that we would arrive looking perfectly rested and impeccably groomed."[62] After a courtesy call on King Juan Carlos and Queen Sofía at the Palacio Real de Madrid, Bush met with Spain's president José María Aznar for most of the day. At a joint press conference late in the afternoon, Bush and Aznar noted their disagreement on Kyoto (Spain had ratified the protocol) but agreed to work together to combat global warming. Aznar supported Bush's effort to develop a workable missile defense system, and Bush was circumspect in his response:

> The ABM Treaty is a relic of the past. It prevents freedom loving people from exploring the future. And that's why we've got to lay it aside. And that's why we've got to have the discussion necessary to explain to our friends and Allies, as well as Russia, that our intent is to make the world more peaceful, not more dangerous.[63]

The decision to launch Bush's European visit in Spain was well thought out. The president was able to get off a few words in Spanish—"a language we hear the President speaking better and better every day," Aznar joked—and the policy differences were minimal.[64] From Madrid, Bush went to Brussels for a NATO summit. He and Laura paid the customary visit to Albert, King of the Belgians, and Queen Paola at the Laeken Palace, Bush met with NATO leaders for a working lunch, and Laura dined with their spouses. This time the questioning was more intense. It was Bush's first opportunity to meet many of the NATO heads of government, and he emerged from the lunch reassured. "It's very rare that the prime minister, presidents, and the chancellor have an opportunity to discuss privately among themselves the broader issues before the Alliance," said Lord Robertson, NATO's secretary general, "but that's what we've been able to do today. And personally I believe it was an exceptionally useful meeting." Asked about American unilateralism, Bush said, "Unilateralists don't come around the table to listen to others and to share opinions. I count on the advice of our friends and allies. Sometimes we don't agree, and I readily concede that. But there's a lot more that we agree upon than we disagree about."[65]

After Brussels, Bush attended a meeting with the leaders of the European Union in Göteborg, Sweden. Bush and Laura paid the obligatory formal call on King Carl Gustaf and Queen Silvia, and Laura spent the day touring the botanical garden and a children's center. The meeting with EU heads of government was to some extent a rerun of the meeting in Brussels except with a larger cast. "The European Union will stick to the Kyoto Protocol and go for a ratification process," said Swedish prime minister Göran Persson. "The United States has chosen another policy. But we have the same targets, and we have to meet the same problems."

"We didn't feel like the Kyoto treaty was well-balanced," said Bush in reply. "It didn't include developing nations. The goals were not realistic. However, that doesn't mean we cannot continue to work together and will work together on reducing greenhouse gases."[66]

Warsaw was the fourth city in four days that Bush and Laura visited. After attending a commemorative ceremony at the Warsaw Ghetto Memorial, Laura visited the Lauder Kindergarten, founded by cosmetic magnate Ronald Lauder for children of the few Jewish families who had survived the Holocaust. Laura was struck by the fact that all of the children were blond. "That's why their families escaped," Lauder told her. "They were the ones who were able to blend in."[67] Bush held a day of conferences with Poland's leaders, and spoke at Warsaw University that evening.[68]

Warsaw was a prelude to the high point of Bush's five-day whirlwind visit to Europe, a meeting with Russian president Vladimir Putin in Slovenia on June 16. Bush placed a high value on personal relationships, and establishing a bond with Putin was particularly important. Eisenhower at the height of the Cold War had established rapport with Soviet premier Nikita Khrushchev at Camp David and on the farm in Gettysburg; Reagan and Gorbachev hit it off at Geneva and Reykjavik, and Clinton and Russian president Boris Yeltsin had become bosom buddies.

"This will be the first of what I hope will be many meetings be-

Bush and Russian president Vladimir
Putin at Brdo pri Kranju, June 2001.

tween Mr. Putin and me," Bush said at his final press conference in Warsaw. "And first and foremost is to develop a trust between us. The definition of the relationship will evolve over time, but first and foremost, it's got to start with the simple word 'friend.' " [69]

The site of the meeting was the sixteenth-century castle of Brdo, just outside of Ljubljana, which had been Marshal Tito's summer residence. Like Geneva and Reykjavik, it was neutral ground. Bush arrived early. He stood waiting for Putin with Donald Ensenat, who had just been sworn in as the State Department's chief of protocol. Ensenat and Bush were old friends, classmates at Yale, members of the same fraternity, and later roommates in Houston during Bush's nomadic years. "It's amazing, isn't it, Enzo?" said Bush.

"Yes, Mr. President."

"It's a long way from Deke House and Yale."

"Yes, Mr. President." [70]

Putin arrived and the two men, accompanied by Rice and Russian national security adviser Vladimir Rushailo retreated to a small sitting room for an intimate discussion. They began with small talk. Both had daughters named for their mothers-in-law. Bush suggested that was proof of their skill at diplomacy. Putin noted that Bush's father, like himself, had worked for an intelligence agency.* They spoke about

---

* Putin, following his graduation from Leningrad State University in 1975, served in the KGB for sixteen years, rising to the rank of lieutenant colonel. From 1985 to 1990, he headed the KGB unit in Dresden, East Germany, and was fluent in German.

NATO, China, and Chechnya. Bush said he intended to withdraw from the ABM treaty and would like to do so by mutual agreement. Putin said he could not agree to that, but he understood Bush's position. There was no saber rattling. Putin raised the question of Pakistan and the ties between the Musharraf government and the Taliban and al Qaeda. Those extremist organizations were being funded by Saudi Arabia, said Putin, and it was only a matter of time before a major catastrophe occurred. Bush and Rice were surprised at Putin's vehemence, and attributed it to the Soviet Union's recent war in Afghanistan.[71] They took no action on his warning.

The discussion continued. Both men seemed to appreciate the opportunity to speak face-to-face. "Is it true your mother gave you a cross that you had blessed in Jerusalem?" asked Bush. "I was touched by the fact that your mother gave you a cross." Putin relaxed. He explained that he had hung the cross in his dacha, but the dacha caught fire. When the firefighters arrived, he told them he was primarily concerned about the cross. According to Bush, Putin dramatically re-created the moment when one of the firemen unfolded his hand and revealed the cross, "as if it was meant to be."

"Vladimir," Bush replied, "that is the story of the cross. Things are meant to be." According to Bush, "I felt the tension drain from the room."[72]

The meeting, which had been originally scheduled for one hour, continued for two. At one point Bush told Putin, "I have to know whom you trust. Who is the person we should turn to if there are sensitive matters between us?"

Putin named his minister of defense, Sergei Ivanov, who later also became Russia's deputy prime minister.

Bush replied that for him it would be Condi.[73] The asymmetry was striking. Bush chose a member of his White House staff who had no ministerial responsibility. Not since Franklin Roosevelt and Harry Hopkins had executive power been so personalized.

When the meeting concluded, Bush invited Putin to his ranch in Crawford. "Let's not get stuck in history," said Bush. "Let's not be Brezhnev and Nixon. Let's be Bush and Putin. Let's make history together."[74]

At the press conference that followed, both men were optimistic. "My meeting with President Putin today is an important step in building a constructive, respectful relationship with Russia," said Bush. "I said in Poland, and I'll say it again, Russia is not the enemy of the United States. As a matter of fact, after our meeting today, I'm convinced it can be a strong partner and friend, more so than people could imagine."[75]

Putin was equally upbeat. "First of all, I want to confirm everything that has been said by President Bush about our meeting. I was counting on an open, frank dialogue. But in this regard reality was a lot bigger than expectations. And it was very interesting and positive. I think we found a good basis to start building on our cooperation. We compared our approaches in key areas, and once again we established our common ground."[76]

Asked by a reporter whether Putin was a man Americans could trust, Bush could not have been more explicit:

I found him to be very straightforward and trustworthy. I was able to get a sense of his soul, and I appreciated so very much the frank dialogue. There was no diplomatic chitchat, trying to throw each other off balance. There was a straightforward dialogue. And that's the beginning of a very constructive relationship. I wouldn't have invited him to my ranch if I didn't trust him.[77]

For Bush, the meeting with Putin was the high point of his trip to Europe. "I just feel that this is the start of something really historic," he told Rice on the flight home.[78] Moral clarity had its limits. Russia's military strength made her a formidable presence on the world scene, and China was on its way to becoming America's second largest trading partner. Bush understood that pragmatism, not principle, must govern relations with those two countries. A more troubling issue involved the personalization of executive power. Bush relied on the White House staff rather than his cabinet. This was particularly true in foreign affairs. Contact Rice if there is a problem, Bush told Putin. Not Powell or the State Department. Rice assumed her duty was to translate Bush's instincts and intuition into policy. Instincts and intuition are a poor substitute for reasoned analysis. Vice President Cheney offered the most optimistic assessment of Bush's discharge of his foreign relations responsibilities before 9/11. "He was feeling his way," said Cheney.[79]

CHAPTER NINE

Asleep at the Switch

*The threat from global terrorism is real, it is immedi-
ate, and it is evolving. . . . Osama bin Laden and his
global network remain the most immediate and serious
threat. He is capable of planning multiple attacks with
little or no warning.*

George Tenet
February 2001

Bush and Laura returned to Washington June 17. It was a slack time.
The tax bill had been signed into law, No Child Left Behind had
passed both the House and the Senate and was in conference committee, and the appropriation measures were making their way through
the legislative process. The administration was settling in. Laura and
Bush took time off. A five-day weekend on the ranch in Crawford, the
next weekend at Camp David, and then to Kennebunkport for the annual Bush family retreat. The visit to Kennebunkport turned out to be
less relaxing than Bush anticipated. His tilt toward Israel was creating
serious problems in the Middle East, particularly with the Saudis, and
his father and Brent Scowcroft pressed for a course correction.

Following the collapse of the Clinton administration's diplomatic effort to resolve the Israeli-Palestinian conflict, a new cycle of violence had broken out in the Middle East, marked by Arab suicide bombings and harsh Israeli reprisals. When Bush entered office, the "Al Aqsa" intifada had been going on for four months. Bush publicly deplored the violence but did not want to repeat what he regarded as Clinton's mediation folly.* At the initial meeting of the NSC on January 30, Bush announced his decision to withdraw from the peace process and throw American support to Israel, contending that Israel had a right to defend itself against terrorism.

In February, the hawkish Ariel Sharon was elected to replace Ehud Barak as prime minister, Israeli policy hardened, and the violence escalated. Satellite TV carried pictures throughout the Arab world of Israeli soldiers attacking Palestinians day after day. When queried, the Bush administration attributed the violence to Yasser Arafat.[1]

This infuriated the Saudis, particularly Crown Prince Abdullah, the de facto ruler of Saudi Arabia. So much so that in May, Abdullah declined an invitation to visit the White House. "We want them [the United States] to consider their own conscience," the crown prince told the *Financial Times*. "Don't they see what is happening to the Palestinian children, women, the elderly—the humiliation, the hunger?"[2] Abdullah's comments alarmed the senior Bush and Scowcroft. W, it appeared, was jeopardizing America's relationship with its oil-rich ally at a time when the United States was increasingly dependent on foreign oil. Scowcroft, speaking at the Council on Foreign Relations, observed that moderate Arab countries "were deeply disappointed with this administration and its failure to do something to moderate the attitude of Israel."[3] Since Scowcroft had been George H. W. Bush's national security adviser and the coauthor of his presidential memoirs, it could be assumed he was speaking with the senior Bush's approval.

At Kennebunkport that July weekend, George W. met with his fa-

---

* Former president Clinton vividly described his pre-inaugural transition meeting with Bush to journalist Fareed Zakaria. "I'll never forget what he said to me," said Clinton. "He told me, 'You know the names of every street in the old city and look what it got you. I'm not going to fool around with this now.'"

ther and Scowcroft, who had flown in especially for the occasion. They explained the problem. W, who was taken aback, assured them he had not intended to provoke the Saudis and regretted it if he had done so. At that point, George H. W. Bush called Crown Prince Abdullah. With W sitting in the room, the senior Bush assured Abdullah that his son's "heart is in the right place" and he was "going to do the right thing." The tone of the conversation was said to be warm and familiar.[4]

The intervention of former president Bush temporarily assuaged Saudi concerns, but did little to improve family relations. In mid-July, when *The New York Times* printed the story of the senior Bush's intervention, the president was particularly unhappy. "Both were upset about it," said a former adviser to Bush 41. "It looked like Poppy was helping out his son." Both Bushes agreed that henceforth their conversations would be kept confidential.[5] The problem was that W was unfamiliar with foreign affairs. As Cheney said, he was feeling his way. Three months earlier Henry Kissinger had smoothed American relations with China, and now Bush 41 was doing the same with respect to Saudi Arabia.

Ten days later the president and Mrs. Bush departed Washington for a meeting with the British royal family and Tony Blair in London, followed by a G-8 summit in Genoa, and a meeting with Pope John Paul II at his summer residence. Just before their departure, the British ambassador, Christopher Meyer, presented the president with a bust of Sir Winston Churchill for the Oval Office. Asked by a reporter why put a bust of an Englishman in the Oval Office, Bush said that Churchill was one of the great leaders of the twentieth century. "He was an enormous personality. He stood on principle. He was a man of great courage. He knew what he believed, and he really kind of went after it in a way that seemed like a Texan to me."[6]

In London, Bush and Laura had lunch with Queen Elizabeth and Prince Philip at Buckingham Palace, and then went by helicopter to Chequers, the country estate of British prime ministers, where they spent the night with Tony and Cherie Blair. The brief sojourn at Chequers provided an informal respite. The Blair children were present, as was daughter Barbara and a classmate from Yale, and according to Laura the kids peppered everyone with questions on whatever came to mind, including missile defense and capital punishment. Cherie Blair said later that no one could say Bush did not have a very good sense of humor.[7]

From London, Bush flew to Genoa and the summit meeting of the G-8. The president was accompanied by Condoleezza Rice, who remained at his side throughout the conference. Afterward, she flew to Moscow to continue discussions with President Putin about the ABM treaty. Rice, not Secretary of State Colin Powell, had become the principal foreign policy adviser and negotiator, and Powell's absence at the summit was duly noted. As a senior European diplomat told *The New York Times*, "We trust him; he is easy to deal with. But we are not clear on his place in the alignment."[8]

In truth, Colin Powell found himself increasingly marginalized. His relationship with Bush remained stiff and formal. Karl Rove said he thought Powell had lost a step and was not living up to his advance billing.[9] *USA Today* carried a lead article in July—evidently leaked by the White House—headlined "Powell Finds Steep Learning Curve in New Job." *The Philadelphia Inquirer* called Powell "the invisible man," "nothing more than a silent symbol or messenger boy."[10] *Time* magazine followed with a cover story, "Odd Man Out." Powell had yet to put a "distinctive mark" on foreign policy, said *Time*, and was leaving "shallow footprints." "I've been struck by how not struck I am by him," an unnamed White House official was quoted as saying. *Time* thought Powell was "chum in the water" for the conservative sharks in the administration.[11] Powell later acknowledged that the summer of 2001 "was a really bad time." There were "strong ideological differences," and the cards he held—national popularity, experience, and ability— were not necessarily a winning hand in the Bush administration.[12]

The Genoa summit was another opportunity for Bush and Putin to renew their relationship. "I was struck by how easy it is to talk to President Putin," Bush told reporters afterward. "We're young leaders who are interested in forging a more peaceful world."[13]

Putin agreed. "I can confirm that we've not only maintained but in many ways strengthened the spirit of Ljubljana." After their press conference, Bush told Karen Hughes, "The chemistry is great. He gets it. Very few leaders have had the chance to refashion how the world thinks about security."[14]

From Genoa, Bush and Laura went to visit John Paul II at Castel Gandolfo. As Bush recalled, "the Holy Father's vigor and energy had given way to frailty, yet his eyes sparkled. He was filled with an unmistakable spirit. He gingerly walked Laura, our daughter Barbara, and me to a balcony, where we marveled at gorgeous Lake Albano below."[15] The president and John Paul then withdrew to a small conference room where they discussed a number of issues, including stem cell research. Four years later, when the Pope died, Bush and Laura attended his funeral in the Vatican, along with Bush 41 and former president Clinton—three presidents paying their respects, a benchmark in American relations with the Catholic Church.

After seeing the Pope, Bush and Laura paid a whirlwind visit to the seven thousand American troops deployed in Kosovo as part of the NATO peacekeeping force. They were joined by Rice, Andy Card, Karl Rove, and Karen Hughes. Rice and Card flew in a small plane with the president and Laura; Hughes and Rove in an identical plane. The plane with Hughes and Rove went first. "As we approached Kosovo, our plane did a long series of elaborate circles and maneuvers that made our stomachs churn," said Hughes. "Karl and I looked at each other. No one admitted it, but we knew we were a decoy. If anyone wanted to shoot at the president's plane, our aircraft would have drawn fire first."[16]

Back in Washington, the Bushes found themselves suddenly beset with family issues. The twins, like most college freshmen, were partying too much. Unlike other freshmen, when the Bush daughters did it, it made national headlines. In May, Jenna and Barbara had been arrested at a popular Tex-Mex restaurant in Austin. Barbara was charged with underage drinking; Jenna for trying to buy liquor using a friend's driver's license. Jenna was fined $600 and had her driver's license suspended for thirty days, Barbara was fined $100 and sentenced to three months probation and eight hours of community service. Other incidents followed. The Secret Service agents assigned to the girls did not feel that it was their responsibility to protect the president's daughters from themselves, and late night TV hosts had a field day.

Laura and Bush were concerned, particularly in the case of Jenna, since a third conviction in one year for underage drinking carried a mandatory jail sentence in Texas—a statute that Bush had signed into law as governor. Laura, who worried about genetic predisposition, believed the twins would benefit from professional help. Bush resisted the idea. Instead, the girls were summoned to Camp David and given a stern talking-to. "I'm sorry there are things other kids can get away with and you can't," said the president. "But what you do reflects on this office and on your family, and that's just the way it is." [17] Called to account, the girls promised they would stay away from bars until they were twenty-one and would not use false IDs. Barbara Bush, the president's mother, later joked about her granddaughters' antics to reporters. "George," she said, "was getting back some of his own." [18]

In Washington, the summer doldrums had set in. Bush was surrounded by his White House staff, his daily routine varied little, and there were no crises on the horizon. "I don't feel any of the so-called loneliness of the job," he told Karen Hughes. "Andy Card understands the chief of staff role as well as anyone conceivably could. Information gets to me in an efficient way and he does not feel threatened that I have close friends as part of my inner circle." Bush said that despite his unfamiliarity with many of the issues, he enjoyed dealing with foreign policy. "Europe is anxious for our help, yet at the same time they want to tie our hands. They are trying to bind us to international treaties that restrict our capacity to act, and I'm not going to let them do that." [19] For Bush, belief in American exceptionalism came naturally.

At the beginning of August, Bush and Laura went to Crawford to spend the month at the ranch—the longest presidential vacation since Lyndon Johnson went to his Texas ranch in the summer of 1968. That was Johnson's last year in office, he was not seeking reelection, and his health was failing. In Johnson's case, it was a long overdue vacation after thirty years at the center of action in Washington. For Bush, it was the normal course of things. "The president is in a bubble," he told reporters. "I like to expand the diameter of the bubble. The ranch is a good place to do so." [20]

At the ranch, Bush awoke every day at 5:45 without the aid of an alarm clock, and shuffled off to the kitchen to make coffee. As the coffee was brewing he took his dogs Barney and Spot outside to relieve themselves. When the coffee was ready, the president carried two cups back to the bedroom, where he and Laura briefly perused the morning newspapers before getting up. Bush would then go for a four-mile run, walk another mile to cool down, and return to the house shortly before eight. A shower, a change of clothes, and then his daily intelligence briefing from the CIA.

At nine or so Bush would begin to work the telephone, speaking with Rice and Card in the White House, Cheney, Rove, and others. That would consume roughly an hour, sometimes two. The president would then head out, chainsaw in hand, to clear brush in a remote corner of the ranch. The heat did not seem to affect him. Returning to the house shortly past noon, he and Laura would have a light lunch, followed by several hours of quiet time. By three o'clock, Bush was out again, fly-fishing for bass in his pond or driving Laura around the ranch in their pickup. An early dinner, almost always with friends, and in bed by 9:15. Laura would read herself to sleep, and W usually watched baseball on television. Lights out at ten.

The president's daily briefing by the CIA was the one fixed item on his schedule. In Washington, these briefings were often presented by George Tenet himself. In Crawford, a briefer from the agency was in residence. The briefing on August 6 carried the ominous title "Bin Laden Determined to Strike in U.S.," and represented an attempt by the CIA to bring Bush up to date on the danger of a terrorist attack. This was one of forty-four morning intelligence reports from the agency mentioning the al Qaeda threat that Bush received before 9/11, and was by far the most alarming. [21] The report noted that after the unsuccessful U.S. missile strike on his base in Afghanistan in 1998, Osama bin Laden planned to retaliate and "bring the fighting to America." According to the report, "Al-Qa'ida members—including some who are U.S. citizens—have resided in or traveled to the U.S.

for years, and the group apparently maintains a support structure that could aid attacks."

The CIA said that in 1998 bin Laden was reported to have announced he wanted to hijack U.S. aircraft, and while they could not confirm that, "FBI information since that time indicates patterns of suspicious activity in this country consistent with preparations for hijackings or other types of attacks." The report concluded by noting that the FBI was "conducting approximately 70 full field investigations throughout the US that it considers bin Laden-related."[22] Bush made no response. According to *The New York Times*, "reports at the time show that Mr. Bush broke off from work early and spent most of the day fishing."[23]

Until 9/11, the Bush White House showed little interest in al Qaeda or bin Laden, even though during the transition Sandy Berger, Clinton's national security adviser, had stressed the danger of terrorism. "You're going to spend more time during your four years on terrorism generally and al Qaeda specifically than any other issue,"[24] he told Condoleezza Rice. Rice did not reply. Richard Clarke, the career civil servant who headed the NSC's Counterterrorism and Security Group (CSG), briefed Rice on al Qaeda in January and also found her unreceptive. "Her facial expression gave me the impression she had never heard the term before." According to Clarke, Rice and her deputy Steve Hadley "were still operating within the old Cold War paradigm from when they had worked on the NSC. Rice viewed the NSC as a 'foreign policy' coordinating mechanism and not some place where issues such as terrorism in the U.S. or domestic preparedness ... should be addressed."[25] Clarke's position was downgraded, and the issue of terrorism and al Qaeda was passed off to the deputies, who did not consider the matter until April.

At the meeting of the deputies, when Clarke pressed for action against bin Laden, Wolfowitz objected. "I don't understand why we are beginning by talking about this one man bin Laden." When Clarke replied that it was only bin Laden and al Qaeda that posed an immediate threat to the United States, Wolfowitz maintained the Iraqi terrorist threat was even greater. Clarke pointed out that there had been no Iraqi threat to the United States since 1993, and was supported by the deputy director of the CIA. Wolfowitz continued to focus on Iraq. "You give bin Laden too much credit. He could not do all these things . . . without state sponsorship. Just because FBI and CIA have failed to find linkages does not mean they don't exist."[26]

The Bush administration turned a deaf ear to Clarke's urgings. Similarly, George Tenet's warnings were dismissed. In February, Tenet told the Senate, "The threat from global terrorism is real, it is immediate, and it is evolving. . . . Osama bin Laden and his global network remain the most immediate and serious threat."[27] On May 30, Tenet, Cofer Black, the CIA's counterterrorism chief, and Clarke told Rice "The mounting warning signs of a coming attack are truly frightening." On June 28, Tenet and Black presented Rice with ten specific pieces of intelligence about impending attacks. On July 10, Tenet and Black again met with Rice to present CIA intercepts of al Qaeda communications. "There will be a significant terrorist attack in the coming weeks or months. Multiple and simultaneous attacks are possible, and they will occur with little or no warning." Clarke agreed, but Rice brushed off the warning. Black said later they wanted to shake Rice. "The only thing we didn't do was pull the trigger of the gun we were holding to her head."[28]

The Rice NSC staff also dismissed the warnings of outgoing deputy national security adviser Lieutenant General Don Kerrick. Just after the inauguration Kerrick sent a blunt memo to Rice: "We are going to be struck again." They never responded, said Kerrick. "Terrorism was not high on their priority list."[29]

Bush remained at the ranch until Labor Day, clearing brush, taking nature walks, fishing for bass, and enjoying the solitude. There were no subsequent meetings to discuss terrorism. Bush appeared to be in his element on the ranch and seemed to enjoy the anguish of journalists assigned to cover him. Crawford (pop. 789) was not Kennebunkport or Martha's Vineyard, where Bush 41 and Clinton vacationed, and the temperature was certain to rise above 100 degrees during the day, and rarely fell below eighty at night. "I love to go walking out there, seeing the cows," Bush told reporters. "Occasionally, they talk to me, being the good listener that I am."[30]

On August 23, he visited Crawford Elementary School to meet with the youngsters. Bush liked children and communicated easily with them. "Do any of you read more than you watch TV?," Bush asked the kids. Almost all shouted yes. "Well, that's important," said the president. "It's so easy to watch TV, and it's hard to read. You need to read more than you watch TV, because when you get to be a good reader it makes learning so much easier. And then when you learn a lot of things it helps you realize your dreams."

Bush took questions from the children. "Is it hard to make decisions?" one asked.

"Not really," said the president.

If you know what you believe, decisions come pretty easy. If you are one of these types of people that are always trying to figure out which way the wind is blowing, decision making can be difficult. But I know who I am. I know what I believe in, and I know where I want to lead the country. And most decisions come pretty easily for me.[31]

Bush held one press conference during his vacation, and that was on August 24. Asked about the increasing violence in Israel, Bush replied that "the Israelis will not negotiate under terrorist threat, simple as that. And if the Palestinians are interested in a dialog, then I strongly urge Mr. Arafat to put a 100-percent effort into stopping the terrorist activity. And I believe he can do a better job of doing that."[32] Crown Prince Abdullah, who was watching the president's news conference on television from the royal palace in Riyadh, "just went bananas," according to Saudi sources. Abdullah had just seen television images of Israeli tanks penetrating deeper into Palestinian territory on the West Bank, and found Bush's statement incomprehensible.[33] The senior Bush's earlier assurances about his son's heart being in the right place seemed wishful thinking.

Abdullah immediately called Prince Bandar, the Saudi ambassador to the United States, who was at his mountain retreat in Aspen, Colorado. "This is it," Abdullah shouted at Bandar. "Those bastards [meaning the Israelis]. Even women—they are stepping all over them."[34] The ambassador was instructed to see Bush immediately and call him to task. The crown prince then dispatched a blistering twenty-five-page message to the Saudi embassy for Bandar to deliver. "We believe there has been a strategic decision by the United States that its national interest in the Middle East is 100 percent based on Israeli prime minister Ariel Sharon." This was America's right, said Abdullah, but Saudi Arabia could not accept that decision. "Starting from today, you're from Uruguay, as they say. You Americans, go your way, I, Saudi Arabia, go my way. From now on, we will protect our national interests, regardless of where America's interests lie in the region."

Abdullah went on to say that he rejected the bias "whereby the blood of an Israeli child is more expensive and holy than the blood of a Palestinian child. I reject people who say when you kill a Palestinian, it is defense; when a Palestinian kills an Israeli, it's a terrorist act." [35] The message made clear that Abdullah was writing off Bush. General Salih Ali bin Muhayya, the Saudi chief of staff, who had just arrived in Washington for consultations, was ordered home, and a delegation of forty senior Saudi officers who were about to leave for Washington was told to stand down.

On August 27, with Bush still on the ranch, Prince Bandar delivered Abdullah's message to Rice in the White House. "This is the hardest message I've had to deliver between our two countries since I started working here in 1983," said Bandar. "In light of the president's decision to adopt Sharon's policy as American policy," Bandar told Rice, "the crown prince feels that he cannot continue dealing with the United States." [36]

Rice replied she was totally shocked by the message, and assured Bandar there had been no change in U.S. policy. She immediately flew to Crawford to inform Bush of the crisis. For the next day, Bush and Rice worked feverishly to prepare a reply to Abdullah. When it was complete, Condoleezza returned to Washington and gave the message to Prince Bandar. It was thirty-six hours from the time Bandar had first called, and Bush had surrendered on all points. "Nothing should ever break relations between our two countries," said the president. "I am troubled and feel deeply the suffering of ordinary Palestinians in their day to day life and I want such tragedies and sufferings to end. I firmly believe that the Palestinian people have a right to self-determination and to live peacefully and securely in their own state in their own homeland, just as Israelis have the right to live peacefully and safely in their own state."[37]

For the first time, Bush placed himself on record supporting a Palestinian state. Bandar immediately took the letter to Riyadh. The president had shot from the hip at his press conference, and Abdullah had called him on it. Bush recognized his error and made amends. "Where he stood was not that much different from where Clinton stood when he left office," said Adel Jubeir, Abdullah's foreign policy adviser.[38] Before the letter, Bush was considered "goofy." After the letter, "he was strong, judicious, deliberate. His reputation [among the Saudis] went from rock bottom to sky high."[39]

When Bush returned to Washington on Labor Day, he had spent a total of fifty-four days at his ranch since inauguration. "That's almost a quarter of his presidency," said *The Washington Post*. "Throw in four days last month at his parents' seaside estate in Kennebunkport, Maine, and 38 full or partial days at the presidential retreat at Camp David, and Bush will have spent 42 percent of his presidency at vacation spots or en route."[40]

Back in Washington, events moved quickly. On Thursday, September 6, the Bushes hosted their first state dinner at the White House, to honor visiting Mexican president Vicente Fox. The decision to honor Fox with full White House formality was a reflection of Bush's continuing concern with U.S.-Mexican relations and immigration reform. Bush favored a guest worker program; Fox pressed for "regularization"—granting legal status to all Mexicans currently in the United States. "I made clear that would not happen," said Bush, but the discussions were cordial and highly symbolic.[41]

"I was not nervous before my own wedding," Laura remembered, "but I was anxious now. A state dinner is far more intricate, an elaborate display of hundreds of moving parts."[42] Laura's dinner partner that evening was Clint Eastwood, and Bush wore cowboy boots with his tuxedo. After dinner there was an elaborate fireworks display, which the Bushes and Foxes watched from the White House balcony. "The sky was so bright you could barely look at it," said Karen Hughes. "We are testing our new missile defense system," quipped Condoleezza Rice.[43]

On Friday evening, Laura and the president attended a gala at the Library of Congress to launch the National Book Festival—a project Laura had designed similar to her book fair in Austin. "I felt this was my debut as first lady," said Laura afterward. "I was doing what I loved."[44] The National Book Festival was a three-day affair bringing authors of recent books to a glorious setting on the Mall in Washington. The festival has proved a resounding success, and has become one of the high points of the summer season in Washington.

Friday, September 7, was also the date on which Saudi Prince Bandar returned from Riyadh with a reply from Crown Prince Abdullah. A meeting was hastily arranged in the family quarters of the White House, where Bush and Bandar were joined by Cheney, Powell, and Rice. Bandar read from Abdullah's letter. "Mr. President, I was particularly pleased with your commitment to the right of the Palestinians to self-determination as well as the right to peace without humiliation, within their independent state."[45] The crown prince said he had shown Bush's letter to the leaders of Egypt, Jordan, Syria, Lebanon, and Yemen, and had extracted a promise from Arafat "to exert a hundred percent effort as you have requested."

> Today, we face a turning point that leads either to disaster, God forbid, or to peace. This historic turning point requires a historic leader who will prevent this disaster. I have great hope in you, Mr. President, that you will be that leader.[46]

Abdullah said it was crucial for Bush to publicly announce his support for an independent Palestinian state. "Such a declaration will eliminate the common impression prevailing in the region of the U.S. bias to Israel."[47] The atmosphere at the meeting was euphoric. Bush agreed to make his commitment public, and plans were set in motion for a big announcement the week of September 10. There was also discussion of a Bush-Arafat meeting at the United Nations later in September, and the president indicated his willingness to do so.[48] For those at the meeting it appeared a genuine breakthrough had been made. Prince Bandar said later he was "the happiest man in the world. I felt we really were going to have a major initiative that could save all of us."[49]

President Bush reads *The Pet Goat* to students at Emma E. Booker
Elementary School in Sarasota, Florida, on September 11, 2001.

On Monday, September 10, Bush flew to Florida to continue his
campaign for No Child Left Behind, which was stalled on Capitol Hill
in conference committee. The president stayed that night at the Colony
Beach & Tennis Resort on Longboat Key, had a quiet dinner with his
brother Jeb and a few select Republican donors, and went for his usual
morning run at a nearby golf course. September 11's schedule included a
photo-op with second-graders at Sarasota's Emma E. Booker Elementary School, followed by a major speech on education funding. After
his intelligence briefing, Bush left the resort at 8:35 and arrived at the
school about twenty minutes later. As he greeted the staff and teachers outside the building, Karl Rove told him that a plane of some sort
had crashed into the north tower of the World Trade Center in New
York. An assistant in Washington had informed Rove via cell phone
and had no further details. Rove assumed it was pilot error. "Keep me
informed," said Bush. Shortly afterward, Rice called the president with
the same message. Again, there were no details.[50]

Bush entered the classroom, seated himself on a small red stool, and
the reading lesson began. As the teacher led the children through the
pages of *The Pet Goat*, the president nodded his approval. Seven minutes into the lesson, Andy Card stepped into the room, leaned over to
Bush, and whispered into his ear. "A second plane hit the second tower.
America is under attack."[51]

The president was stunned. Blood drained from his face. He remained in the classroom another five minutes, and then took his leave.
"Very impressive. Thank you all so much for showing me your reading
skills." [52] Bush said later that he did not want to leave abruptly because
it might "scare the children and send ripples of panic throughout the
country." [53] Outside the classroom, Bush paused before a hastily set
up television screen and saw a replay of the second plane hitting the
south tower. Details were trickling in. American Airlines flight 11 had
taken off from Logan Airport in Boston at 7:59 a.m. and crashed into
the north tower of the World Trade Center at 8:46. United Airlines
flight 175 had left Boston at 8:14 and crashed into the south tower at
9:03. A third plane, American 77, had taken off from Dulles International Airport in Washington at 8:20, and was lost to air traffic control-
lers. All three flights had been bound for Los Angeles.

Bush moved quickly to the school auditorium, where the audience
was expecting a major speech on education. He spoke briefly and extemporaneously. He looked drawn. "Ladies and Gentlemen, this is a
difficult moment for America. Two airplanes have crashed into the
World Trade Center in an apparent terrorist attack on our country."
Bush promised that the full resources of the federal government would
be employed to assist the victims and their families and "to find those
folks who committed this act. Terrorism against our nation will not
stand." [54] The president then asked the audience to join him in a moment of silence. At 9:30 Bush was racing to the airport to board Air
Force One and return to Washington.

As the presidential motorcade sped toward Sarasota-Bradenton
International Airport, Bush called Rice from the secure phone in his
limousine. Rice told him that the third plane, American flight 77 from
Dulles, had just crashed into the Pentagon.

"Mr. President, you cannot come back here. Washington is under
attack." [55]

Bush bounded up the stairway of Air Force One and into his private
cabin. "Be sure to get the first lady and my daughters protected," he
instructed the Secret Service agents on board.[56] Laura was on Capitol
Hill in Senator Ted Kennedy's office waiting to testify before the Sen-

ate Education Committee when flight 77 struck the Pentagon, and had been quickly whisked away by an Emergency Response Team to Secret Service headquarters in downtown Washington. Barbara at Yale (code name Turquoise) was taken to the Secret Service office in New Haven, and in Austin, Jenna (code name Twinkle) was relocated to the Driskill Hotel under Secret Service protection.

As the president's plane climbed swiftly to 45,000 feet, well above its normal cruising altitude, Bush called Cheney, who was now in the Presidential Emergency Operations Center (PEOC), the concrete bunker under the White House grounds that had been constructed for FDR in World War II. "We're at war," the president said.[57] He told Cheney that he would make whatever decisions were required from Air Force One and that the vice president should implement them on the ground. Constitutional scholars have noted that the vice president is not in the military chain of command, but that seemed of little consequence as events unfolded on September 11.

Within minutes Cheney was on the phone again. A fourth plane, United flight 93 from Newark bound for San Francisco, appeared to have been hijacked and was headed toward Washington. The military asked permission to engage the aircraft. Bush agreed. "You have my authorization," he told Cheney.[58] The vice president passed the order along, and at 10:03 United 93 plowed into an open field near Shanksville, Pennsylvania.* "Did we shoot it down, or did it crash," Bush asked Cheney. At that moment no one knew for certain.

Bush was determined to return to Washington and take control. Air Force One headed out northeast over Florida and when it reached the Atlantic turned north. At that point, Cheney called once more and urged Bush not to return to the capital. "There is still a threat," said the

---

* It is unclear whether Cheney ordered the military to engage the aircraft and then got Bush's approval, or whether the president authorized the shoot-down first. The telephone logs are imprecise, and the 9/11 Commission confessed they did not know. The point is moot since the passengers on flight 93 overpowered the hijackers and no action was required. For a detailed summary of the issue, see Barton Gellman, *Angler: The Cheney Vice Presidency* (New York: Penguin, 2008), 118–28. Also see *The 9/11 Commission Report* (New York: W. W. Norton, 2004), 40–41.

Bush on Air Force One leaving Offutt Air Force Base, speaking with Vice President Cheney, September 11, 2001.

vice president. The Federal Aviation Administration (FAA) believed six planes had been hijacked, and two were still airborne. The Secret Service and Andy Card immediately added their voices to those urging Bush not to return. Conditions in Washington were too volatile.

Bush held firm. "I told them I was not going to let terrorists scare me away. I'm the president. And we're going to Washington." [59]

But Card and the Secret Service remained adamant, and Bush yielded. He was not happy about it. "He expressed his anger bluntly and forcefully at me," said Karl Rove, "telling me how important it was for him to get back to Washington and how fears about his security were overblown." [60] At the recommendation of the Secret Service, Air Force One was diverted to Barksdale Air Force Base in Shreveport, Louisiana, headquarters of the Eighth Air Force. By coincidence, Barksdale was conducting a nuclear training exercise and was already on the highest alert. "Landing at Barksdale felt like dropping into a movie set," Bush wrote later. "F-16s from my old unit at Ellington Air Force Base in Houston had escorted us in. The taxi way was lined with bombers. It made for a striking scene." [61]

The presidential party was rushed to base headquarters, where Bush set up in the office of the Eighth Air Force commander, General Tom Keck. He made a quick phone call to Laura, who assured him that she and the twins were safe, and then to Rumsfeld. The secretary of defense had been unreachable for the last hour or so assisting relief efforts at the Pentagon, and was now back at the command center in the building's basement. "The ball will soon be in your court," said the

president." [62] Bush then
recorded a brief mes-
sage, which was tele-
vised at 2:30 p.m. It
was not reassuring.
The president spoke
haltingly and mispro-
nounced several words.
"The United States
will hunt down and
punish those responsi-

View of the destruction of the Pentagon on September 11.

ble for these cowardly acts," said Bush. "The resolve of our great nation
is being tested. But make no mistake. We will show the world that we
will pass this test." [63] Bush did not mention war in his address from
Barksdale. "To declare war you have to know who your enemy is," he
told Karl Rove, and at that point it was unclear. [64]

Bush was eager to return to Washington, but Cheney and Card
insisted it was unsafe. "The right thing is to let the dust settle," said
Card. [65] Once again Bush agreed, and at 1:30 Air Force One took off
for Offutt Air Force Base in Bellevue, Nebraska, headquarters of the
Strategic Air Command, where communications facilities were better. Upon arrival, the president convened a videoconference with the
National Security Council. "We are at war against terror," said Bush.
"From this day forward, this is the new priority of our administration." [66] Bush was changing the rules. Hitherto, acts of terrorism were
considered crimes punishable through the legal process. Calling it an
act of war escalated the issue and brought an entirely new set of rules
into play. The implications would be profound. Whether Bush was
aware of the consequences is open to doubt. The president then said he
was coming back to Washington as soon as his plane was refueled. "No
discussion. I'm coming back." [67]

Still on the video screen, Bush asked Richard Clarke, the NSC's
counterterrorism chief, for a briefing of what had taken place, and afterward turned to George Tenet. "Who did this?" the president asked.
Tenet replied with two words, "al Qaeda." The CIA director said it

was manifestly clear that bin Laden was behind the attacks. Al Qaeda was the only terrorist organization capable of mounting such an assault. Intelligence-monitoring devices had already picked up a number of known bin Laden associates congratulating each other on the attacks. Tenet said all of the attacks had taken place before 10 a.m.; it was now three o'clock, and there was little chance of more attacks that day.[68]

Rumsfeld then briefed the president on the status of forces. The Pentagon would reopen the next day, forces worldwide were on full combat alert, fighter planes were patrolling the skies above major metropolitan areas, and the Atlantic Fleet had departed Norfolk heading for New York. Richard Armitage, representing the State Department (Colin Powell was en route back to Washington from Peru), said all U.S. embassies had been placed on alert. FEMA head Joe Allbaugh reported on relief efforts in New York, and Norman Mineta, secretary of transportation, said that all civilian air traffic had been grounded indefinitely. The FAA had managed to land over four thousand planes within an hour, and all flights bound for the United States from overseas had been diverted to Canada.

Bush was concerned about halting air traffic. It was the very chaos al Qaeda was seeking to foment. He wanted to get the airlines flying as soon as possible. "We won't be held hostage."[69] With that the president terminated the conference and departed for Washington.

Air Force One touched down at Andrews Air Force Base outside the capital at 6:44 p.m. Bush deplaned and immediately boarded Marine One for the twelve-minute helicopter flight to the White House. Normally, Marine One flies at a respectable height and opens up a vista of Washington. Not that night. The pilot, accompanied by two look-alike decoy helicopters, flew an evasive pattern at treetop level. As the helicopter approached the Potomac, a black plume of smoke rising from the Pentagon dominated the horizon. "You are looking at the face of war in the twenty-first century," Bush told Karl Rove.[70]

Bush landed on the South Lawn of the White House shortly before seven and went directly to the Oval Office and then to the PEOC bunker, where Laura was waiting. "We didn't have a lot of time to talk," said the president, "but we didn't need to. Her hug was more powerful than any words."[71]

The Secret Service told Bush that he and Laura would be sleeping underground that night in a small room off the PEOC conference room. The bed was a foldout couch that had been installed for FDR in 1943. Bush rejected it. "We're not going to sleep down here," said the president. "We're going to go upstairs and you can get us if something happens."[72]

Bush was scheduled to address the nation from the Oval Office at 8:30. Karen Hughes and chief speechwriter Michael Gerson had prepared a draft reflecting Bush's thoughts as conveyed from Air Force One. There was roughly an hour before the speech was due, and the three huddled in the small study off the Oval Office. They were soon joined by Andy Card, chief White House spokesperson Ari Fleischer, and Rice. Gerson had included a sentence about the terrorist attack being an act of war. Bush instructed him to delete it. "Our mission tonight is reassurance," said the president.[73] When the draft was finished, Bush rehearsed it. The delivery time was eight minutes. "Today our Nation saw evil, the very worst of human nature. And we responded with the best of America." Bush then personalized the issue. Reciting the 23rd Psalm, the president said, "Even though I walk through the valley of the shadow of death, I fear no evil, for You are with me."[74]

It was Bush's first speech from the Oval Office, and his delivery was dreadful. He was much better before a live audience, and he was clearly ill at ease. His facial expression was vapid, he tried a half smile at the camera, and there was something weak and tentative about the set of his jaw. When Bush was nervous he often chewed the inside of his lips, and it caused his mouth to shift about when it should have been firm.[75] For the television audience it was apparent that the president had been shaken by the events that day.

The most important sentence in the speech that evening was written by Bush himself just minutes before airtime. "We will make no distinction between the terrorists who committed these acts and those who harbor them." This was the first prong of what later became known as the Bush Doctrine. With that sentence, the president was placing the United States on a permanent war footing. The United States would attack the terrorists, and also those countries that harbored the terrorists. It was an extreme example of executive overreach and a prime illustration of Bush's view of presidential power.

Once again, the president was acting on his instincts. The sentence had been crafted moments before delivery, the White House staff, including Condoleezza Rice, nodded their approval, but the principal agencies of government had not been consulted. Bush was taking the country to war with a rhetorical flourish. Cheney, Powell, Rumsfeld, and Attorney General John Ashcroft were not asked to comment.* The Department of State and the Justice Department were ignored. And the Defense Department would be left to pick up the pieces. Bush's single sentence, scrawled by him on the spur of the moment, represented the first step on the road to war. As Bob Woodward observed, "The president, Rice, Hughes, and the speechwriters had made one of the most significant foreign policy decisions in years, and the secretary of state had not been involved." [76]

Following the speech, Bush met with the national security council for almost two hours—his first meeting with them since January 30. The meeting was held in the cramped quarters of the PEOC. Unlike his television appearance, Bush appeared confident and in control. "What I remember more than anything else was the president's manner," wrote George Tenet. "He was absolutely in charge, determined, and directed." [77]

"I want all of you to understand that we are at war and will stay at war until this is done," said the president. "Nothing else matters. Everything is available for the pursuit of this war. Any barriers in your way, they're gone. Any money you need, you'll have it. This is our only agenda." [78]

Colin Powell, who had arrived just moments before from Peru, said that the United States must make clear to Pakistan and Afghanistan that the time to act was now. The Taliban was giving shelter to bin Laden, and Pakistan had the closest relations with them. "We have to make clear to Pakistan and Afghanistan that this is show time." [79]

---

* In her memoirs, Rice asserts that she consulted Cheney, Powell, and Rumsfeld and that they agreed. But there was insufficient time between when Bush penned the sentence and the speech's delivery for her to have done that. Compare, Condoleezza Rice, *No Higher Honor* (New York: Crown, 2011), 77, and Bob Woodward, *Bush at War* (New York: Simon & Schuster, 2002), 30.

Bush said the foreign policy implications were far broader. "This is an opportunity beyond Afghanistan. We have to shake terror loose in places like Syria, and Iran, and Iraq."[80] Bush was escalating the issue.

Rumsfeld raised a number of practical questions. "I told the president and the NSC that, for the moment at least, the American military was not prepared to take on terrorists. A major military effort would take several months to assemble." Then there was the question of targets. "Should we be planning to strike terrorist targets in nations with whom we had friendly relations?" Rumsfeld suggested they think of the problem more broadly and employ every tool in the national arsenal, not just the military, but financial, legal, and diplomatic. "If we put enough pressure on those states they might feel compelled to rein in the terrorist groups they supported."[81]

According to Richard Clarke, when Rumsfeld noted that international law allowed the use of force only to prevent future attacks, not for retribution, Bush exploded. "No," the president shouted. "I don't care what the international lawyers say, we are going to kick some ass."[82]

With that bellicose flourish, Bush launched the United States on the path to two major wars. On the evening of September 11, the United States enjoyed the sympathy of the world. Rather than capitalize on that and move through the normal channels of law and diplomacy, Bush chose to act unilaterally. Within a month, the United States had lost world sympathy. Flouting the rules of international behavior, Bush would "kick ass." Powell and Rumsfeld saluted and fell into line. Rice, Cheney, Tenet, and the others present did not question the president's decision. Should they have objected that evening? Should they have challenged Bush's misplaced trust in the irresistibility of American power? Hindsight clearly says yes. Bush was reacting viscerally to the events of 9/11 and needed to be guided and advised forcefully. Again, the personalization of presidential power swept away reasoned analysis.

After dismissing Rumsfeld's questions, Bush turned to economic issues. "I want the economy back, open for business, banks, the stock market, everything tomorrow." Kenneth Dam, deputy secretary of the treasury (Paul O'Neill was rushing back from a financial conference in Tokyo), pointed out that there was significant physical damage to the

Wall Street infrastructure. Bush said that as soon as the rescue operations were completed, every effort should be made to repair that damage as soon as possible. The president then pressed Norman Mineta
for a date when air travel could be resumed. Mineta said the FAA was
trying for noon the next day. With that the meeting adjourned.[83]

Bush returned to the family quarters in the White House shortly
after ten. "Sleep did not come easily," said the president. "My mind
replayed the images of the day: the planes hitting the buildings, the
towers crumbling, the Pentagon in flames. I thought of the grief so
many families must be feeling."[84]

At 11:08 Bush and Laura were awakened by a Secret Service agent
at the door. "Mr. President, Mr. President, you've got to get up. The
White House is under attack."[85] An unidentified plane was heading
toward the executive mansion. Bush and Laura jumped out of bed and
headed down the corridor. The president was barefoot, wearing his
running shorts and a T-shirt. Mrs. Bush wore a robe and slippers, but
forgot her contact lenses. Bush wanted to take the elevator down to the
bunker but the agent said it was not safe. They would have to use the
stairs. "My head was pounding," said Laura. "All I could do was count
stairwell landings, trying to count off in my mind how many more
floors we had to go."[86]

Eventually they reached the tunnel leading to the bunker. "I heard
the slam of a heavy door and the sound of a pressurized lock," said
Bush. "The agents rushed us through another door. *Bang. Hiss.*"[87] In
the bunker the Bushes were joined by Card, Rice, and Stephen Hadley,
who were working late. Shortly an enlisted man walked in. "Mr. President," he said matter-of-factly, "it was one of ours." False alarm. The
plane was an Air Force F-16 fighter flying down the Potomac emit-
ting the wrong transponder signal. Bush and Laura returned to their
bedroom. Before turning in, the president dictated a message into his
recording machine by the bed. "The Pearl Harbor of the 21st century
took place today."[88]

For George W. Bush, 9/11 was the second major watershed of his
life. "This is what I was put on earth for," he said early on. "I'm here
for a reason."[89] Just as his coming to Christ in his late thirties gave

meaning to what had been an aimless and dissolute life, so the war on terror became his sacred mission.[90] "Our responsibility to history is clear," said the president at the National Cathedral on September 14. "To answer these attacks and rid the world of evil."[91] Believing he was the agent of God's will, and acting with divine guidance, George W. Bush would lead the nation into two disastrous wars of aggression. It is no surprise that he initially referred to America's effort as a crusade, a messianic image evoking Christian knights battling infidels for control of the holy land.

Not since Woodrow Wilson has a president so firmly believed that he was the instrument of God's will. After coming from behind to win the Democratic nomination at the Baltimore convention in 1912, Wilson told his campaign manager it was God's decision. "I am a Presbyterian and believe in predestination," said Wilson. "It was Providence that did the work in Baltimore."[92]* And like George W. Bush, Wilson carried that view of divine purpose into foreign policy. As Margaret MacMillan observed in her prize-winning study of the Paris Peace Conference in 1919, Wilson's strength lay in his ability "to frame his decisions so that they became not merely necessary, but morally right. Those who opposed him were not just wrong but wicked."[93] Or as British prime minister David Lloyd George put it, "Wilson came to the Peace Conference like a missionary to rescue the heathen Europeans."[94]

Just as Wilson's religious certitude led him into disaster at Versailles, so George W. Bush's messianic conviction distorted his leadership in the days following 9/11.

---

*   William F. McCombs, Wilson's hardworking campaign manager who had engineered the victory in Baltimore, was understandably taken aback. "I must confess I felt a chill because I thought that if he attempted to apply that Predestination doctrine to the extreme, the Democratic [presidential] campaign might find itself very much in the muck." William F. McCombs, *Making Woodrow Wilson President* (New York: Fairview Publishing Co., 1921), 180–81.

CHAPTER TEN

Toppling the Taliban

Onward, Christian soldiers,
Marching as to war,
With the cross of Jesus
Going on before.

Sabine Baring-Gould, 1865

George W. Bush was in over his head. Confronted by the tragic events of 9/11, he responded by leading a shocked and grieving nation into an ill-defined "war on terror." He did so impulsively. There was little reflection. Rather than measured retaliatory action against al Qaeda, rather than working through the comity of nations and the rule of law, Bush escalated the issue into a global war against terror. In the process, he squandered much of the sympathy for Americans that the 9/11 attacks aroused almost everywhere in the world. Even worse, rather than classify the attackers as a band of barbarian fanatics, he chose to define them as the manifestation of evil, investing the military campaign and himself as its leader with religious sanctification.

The loyal White House advisers rallied around, the secretary of state and the secretary of defense knuckled under, and reasoned analysis fell by the wayside. The initial reluctance of Powell and Rumsfeld to question Bush's war against terror parallels the unwillingness of Dean Rusk and Robert McNamara to question Lyndon Johnson's decision to deploy American ground troops in Vietnam. As a regretful McNamara wrote in retrospect, "We failed to ask the most basic questions. Was it true that the fall of South Vietnam would trigger the fall of the rest of Southeast Asia? Would that constitute a threat to the West's security? It seems beyond all understanding, incredible, that we did not force ourselves to confront such issues head on."[1] Had Bush's more experienced advisers been more forceful or more willing to restrain the president, the resulting fiascos in Afghanistan and Iraq might have been avoided.

Like Lyndon Johnson, Bush had little experience in foreign affairs and national security. Like Johnson, he was comfortable with domestic issues, thought he understood the electorate, and had staked out a plausible program as a compassionate conservative. Nine months into office, his record of domestic accomplishment compared favorably with that of Clinton and his father. But the world beyond America's borders was alien domain. During the election campaign Bush had asked Paul Wolfowitz if Germany was a member of NATO.[2] Now he was leading the United States on a global crusade, inspired by God, to rid the world of evil. It was a blunder of historic proportions. Bush's arrogance, ignorance, and certitude set the tone for an administration dedicated to the projection of American hegemony. With a deficit of introspection and an absence of reflection, the president resorted to a terminology with which he was familiar. The nation was at war.

Terminology is important. The word "war" carries enormous implications. From 1861 to 1865 Congress never declared war on the Confederacy. Neither was there a war between the states. President Lincoln was suppressing a rebellion in the southern states, which according to the Supreme Court in *Texas v. White*, remained part of the Union.[3] After the Japanese attack on Pearl Harbor, President Roosevelt asked Congress for a declaration of war against Japan, but refrained from adding Japan's Axis partners, Germany and Italy, to the request until after they declared war on the United States. During the Korean conflict the administration studiously avoided use of the term war. President Truman was repelling North Korean aggression pursuant to a United Nations mandate. In Vietnam, John Kennedy and LBJ never considered asking Congress for a declaration of war against Hanoi. The same holds true for George H. W. Bush's intervention against Saddam Hussein in 1991. Neither the United Nations resolution authorizing the use of force nor the subsequent congressional joint resolution mentioned war.[4]

"War" is a word responsible statesmen try to avoid. Dwight Eisenhower never called himself a war president. "I hate war as only a soldier who has lived it can," Eisenhower once said.[5]*

On the morning of September 12 Bush pressed ahead, heedless of the consequences. He had spoken to the nation three times the day before—from Florida, from Barksdale Air Force Base, and from the Oval Office—and had failed to reassure the nation that he could handle the crisis. When he awoke on the 12th, he was determined to take charge. Cheney, who was aware of Bush's limitations, met with the president early that morning. He volunteered to chair a special executive committee to frame policy options and present the possible choices to Bush for final decision. It would streamline decision making and free the president from excessive detail. Cheney made the offer in good faith. It was not a power grab but a reflection of the president's unfamiliarity with the issues. And as a former secretary of defense, Cheney was eminently qualified to assume such responsibility.

Bush rejected the offer. "No," said the president. "I'm going to do that. I will run the meetings. This is the job of the commander in chief and cannot be delegated."[6] Bush said he wanted to signal that he was in

---

*   Of all of Bush's senior advisers, only Rumsfeld questioned the terminology of the war on terror. "I became increasingly uncomfortable with labeling the campaign against Islamist extremists a 'war on terrorism' or a 'war on terror'," said Rumsfeld. "To me, the word 'war' focused people's attention on military action. . . . I was also concerned about the other word in the phrases: terrorism or terror. Terror is not the enemy, but rather a feeling. Terrorism was also not the enemy but a tactic. . . .

"As I developed these thoughts over the weeks and months following 9/11, I periodically raised them with the president, and with members of the National Security Council. I urged that we find ways to avoid the phrase war on terror and consider other alternatives. . . . Ultimately, President Bush settled the issue and decided against my suggestions by reaffirming that we were fighting a global war on terror. I was not able to come up with a perfect alternative." Donald Rumsfeld, *Known and Unknown* (New York: Sentinel, 2011), 352–53.

charge and calling the shots. Henceforth, he would chair the meetings of the National Security Council and Rice would continue to chair the meetings of the principals when he was not present.

"The focus of my presidency had changed," Bush wrote later. "I had expected it to be domestic policy. Now it was war."[7] Bush was fascinated with the idea of war. "My West Texas optimism helped me project confidence. I also drew strength from my faith. I found solace in reading the Bible."[8] Meeting the press later on the morning of September 12, Bush made it explicit that insofar as he was concerned the nation was at war. "The deliberate and deadly attacks which were carried out yesterday against our country were more than acts of terror. They were acts of war. This will be a monumental struggle of good versus evil, but good will prevail."[9]

Rather than attempting to calm the nation, Bush exacerbated the crisis. Rather than reassuring the country that everyone was safe, Bush blustered about war. The events of 9/11 were tragic, but scarcely catastrophic. This was not Pearl Harbor. Foreign armies were not on the march through the Philippines, Malaya, and the Dutch East Indies. America's military forces had not been crippled. The National Center for Health Statistics recorded a 44 percent jump in the expected death rate on September 11 followed by a return to normal the following day. The center's annual summary indicated 2,922 lives lost to "terrorism involving the destruction of aircraft," a figure comparable to the 3,209 pedestrians killed by trucks and automobiles that year. Over 17,000 Americans lost their lives in homicides in 2001, and 101,537 in accidents.[10] The economic damage at the World Trade Center was enormous, but scarcely comparable to losses sustained in Hurricane Katrina or the subprime mortgage meltdown in Bush's second term.[11]

Meeting later that morning with congressional leaders, Bush again talked about war. "The president looked drained, both mentally and physically," one senator remembered.[12] Bush said that as elected leaders they had to stay focused and fight the war until they prevailed. The enemy fostered hate. "They hate Christianity. They hate Judaism. They hate everything that is not them. Other nations will have to choose."[13] The word "war" was used repeatedly. Eventually Tom Daschle, the

Senate majority leader, objected. "I expressed my concern about the un-intended consequences of employing the term 'war' in this context." War is a powerful word, said Daschle. There was a war on poverty and a war on drugs. "This kind of wholesale and indiscriminate use of the term 'war' can minimize its meaning. We risked the possibility as we now considered a 'war on terror.'" [14] Terror is a tactic, like blitzkrieg. You don't declare war against blitzkrieg. The distinction eluded Bush. He cut Daschle off. The president was adamant. This was war. The American way of life was under attack, and he was in command.

With the exception of Daschle, Bush's view that the United States was at war was rarely questioned. Neither the House nor the Senate disputed the administration's interpretation. The Washington press corps, normally quick to challenge presidential policy, appeared frozen in the White House headlights. Journalists who had established reputations for objective analysis were drawn inexorably into the frontier atmosphere that surrounded Bush. Chris Matthews of MSNBC—scarcely an administration supporter—waxed eloquent about Bush's "amazing display of leadership" and macho swagger. "I think we like having a hero as our president." [15] Laura Ingraham on Fox described Bush as a "real man" for leading the country to war. [16]

The academic community was equally complicit. Scholars in a variety of disciplines have traditionally provided perspective on government policies, yet it was not until the fall of 2003 that the first articles appeared in major academic journals questioning Bush's war on terror. [17] The shock of 9/11, rather than the reality, dominated public discourse. John le Carré, an astute English observer of the United States, was not far off the mark when he wrote in *The Times* of London that the American public was not just misled, it was being ushered into a state of ignorance and fear. [18]

Was this deliberate on Bush's part? Or were his actions a reflection of his inexperience and lack of perspective? Or perhaps of his initial failure to understand the full implications of his rhetoric? Bush could have said that war has been declared upon us by nineteen young men, or by a group of terrorists, or by Osama bin Laden. [19] He could have isolated the terrorists and treated them as criminals to be dealt with as such. Instead, he launched the nation on a global war against terror and elevated the terrorists to the status of belligerents. The arrogance of asserting that the United States was undertaking a struggle to rid the world of evil is breathtaking. It provided an umbrella for two costly and futile wars and a wholesale assault on American civil liberty.

Bush met with the National Security Council at 9:30 a.m. on September 12 and again at four o'clock. In addition to the statutory members, the president added the attorney general, the White House counsel, and the director of the FBI. Each member brought his deputy. Cheney brought two: Scooter Libby and Eric Edelman. Powell brought Armitage, Rumsfeld took Wolfowitz, Rice brought Hadley, and down the line. Twenty-three persons crowded into the White House Cabinet Room.[20] This became Bush's expanded war council.

Bush began both meetings with a prayer. Not a silent prayer as Eisenhower had done,* but a vocal request for the Lord's help. Bush considered himself the agent of God placed on earth to combat evil. He was invoking the Lord's help, and by so doing authenticating his leadership. But he was playing with fire. By recruiting Christianity as his ally and mainstreaming religious invocations into official business he was structuring another Crusade against the evildoers of the Muslim world.

Bush stressed that he not only wanted to punish those who were behind the attacks but those who harbored them as well. Rice remembers being struck by the president's clarity. "He wanted an option for boots on the ground."[21] Bush, who had avoided service in Vietnam, was sending men into combat. He had no second thoughts. Would he have done so if America still had a draft? If national service was mandatory?

---

* At the recommendation of Ezra Taft Benson, his secretary of agriculture and an elder in the Church of Jesus Christ of Latter Day Saints, Eisenhower agreed to commence cabinet meetings with a silent prayer. One day he forgot. Max Rabb, who was cabinet secretary, passed him a note. "Mr. President, you have forgotten the silent prayer." Ike read the note and blurted out, "Goddamnit, we've forgotten the silent prayer." In 1953 Eisenhower also proclaimed the Fourth of July a national day of prayer. On that day he fished in the morning, golfed in the afternoon, and played bridge in the evening. As columnist George Will asked, "Were the prayers in the interstices of these recreations? Maybe when the president faced a particularly demanding putt." George Will, "Religion in the American Republic," *National Affairs* (Summer 2013), 110. Also see Jean Edward Smith, *Eisenhower in War and Peace* (New York: Random House, 2012), 566.

But the United States had a professional military, and the president was eager to unleash it.

"What could the military do immediately?" Bush asked Rumsfeld.

"Very little, effectively," the secretary of defense replied. Rumsfeld said he was pressing the services, but it would take time to devise plans and get troops in place. Afghanistan was a landlocked country very far away.

Bush was impatient. "I want to get moving." Later, the president told Bob Woodward that the Pentagon had to be pushed. "They had to be challenged to think on how to fight a guerrilla war using conventional means."[22] The parallel to LBJ's decision to put ground troops into Vietnam, striking though it was, did not seem to register with Bush.

The discussion about boots on the ground gave Wolfowitz an opening. What about Iraq? he asked. Al Qaeda might have mounted the attacks, but the operation was too sophisticated for a terrorist organization to have pulled it off without state support. "Iraq must have been helping them."[23]

Cheney provided oblique support. "To the extent we define our task broadly, including those who support terrorism, then we get at states. And it is easier to find them than it is to find bin Laden."

The secretary of state pushed back. The focus should be al Qaeda, Powell insisted. "We should go after the organization that acted yesterday." Bush agreed. "Start with bin Laden, which Americans expect." But the president was already hedging his bets. "If we succeed we've struck a huge blow and can move forward."[24] Iraq was not ruled out. Bush said he would prefer to have allies with us but if we were at war, and if America had to stand alone, we would.[25]

After the meeting, Richard Clarke, the NSC counterterrorism chief, approached Powell. "I thought I was missing something here," said Clarke. "Having been attacked by al Qaeda, for us to go bombing Iraq would be like invading Mexico after the Japanese attacked Pearl Harbor."

"It's not over yet," Powell replied.[26]

Powell was right. Later that evening, Bush encountered Clarke in the White House Situation Room. "Look," said the president, "I know you have a lot to do, but I want you, as soon as you can, to go back over everything. See if Saddam did this. See if he's linked in any way."

Clarke was stunned. "But Mr. President, al Qaeda did this."

"I know, I know, but . . . see if Saddam was involved. Just look. I want to know any shred. . . ."

"Absolutely," Clarke replied. "But we have looked several times for state sponsorship of al Qaeda and have not found any real linkage to Iraq. Iran plays a little, as does Pakistan, and Saudi Arabia, Yemen."

Bush was visibly annoyed. "Look into Iraq, Saddam." With that the president turned abruptly and walked away.[27]

Bush visited the Pentagon twice on September 12. Once in the early afternoon to inspect the damage, then again at six o'clock to meet with Rumsfeld and the Joint Chiefs of Staff. The meeting was brief. Bush wanted to assert personal control and bring the chiefs on board. "I noticed the president had already adopted the tone and attitude of a wartime commander in chief," said undersecretary of defense Douglas Feith. Bush spoke crisply. "We believe we are at war and we'll fight it as such. I want us to have the mindset of fighting and winning a war."[28] With smoke still billowing from the Pentagon, the president said he wanted the Joint Chiefs to present military options designed to achieve important results. "We won't just pound sand." Bush warned that the war would mean casualties, but he would see to it that the services had whatever they needed to fight. At 6:30 the meeting adjourned. The president had made his point. He was in command.

At 9:30 the following day, September 13, Bush met once more with his extended war council in the White House Situation Room. Secretary of the Treasury Paul O'Neill, back from Japan, announced that the stock markets would reopen on Monday, September 17. "We only get one chance at this. It has to be done right."[29] Then George Tenet briefed the president on the CIA's plans to fund and strengthen Afghanistan's Northern Alliance to oust the Taliban and ferret out al Qaeda. With the infusion of weapons and CIA paramilitary personnel, said Tenet, the Alliance could become a cohesive force that could be augmented by U.S. Special Forces. Tenet was followed by Cofer Black, the CIA's counterterrorism chief, who gave a PowerPoint presentation outlining the agency's strategy. Black said they would not only go after al Qaeda but also the Taliban because the two were inseparable. "When we are through with them, they will have flies walking across their eyeballs." [30] Black's lumping of the Taliban and al Qaeda together was not questioned.

"How quickly can we deploy the CIA teams?" the president asked.

"In short order," Black replied.

"How quickly, then, could we defeat the Taliban and al Qaeda?"

"A matter of weeks," said Black. [31]

Black cautioned there would be American casualties. "There could be a lot."

"All right," said Bush. "Let's go. That's war. That's what we're here to win." [32]

The president then turned to Iraq. Was the CIA looking into possible Iraqi involvement in the events of 9/11? Tenet dodged the question. The agency was making "a worldwide effort," he told Bush. [33]

The president inquired about military preparations. Army General Hugh Shelton, chairman of the Joint Chiefs, said the military had plans to attack bin Laden with unmanned Tomahawk cruise missiles, but had been constrained by policy directives that instructed them to focus only on bin Laden rather than the Taliban and to use cruise missiles exclusively. Bush told Shelton to "take all constraints off your planning." Rumsfeld interjected that it was difficult to locate terrorist targets in Afghanistan. "We need to figure out how to fight bin Laden's entire network globally."

The secretary of defense turned to Iraq and Saddam Hussein. Iraq, he said, was a country that supported terrorism and might someday offer terrorists weapons of mass destruction to use against us. And unlike Afghanistan, Iraq had an abundance of military targets. "In Iraq we could inflict the kind of costly damage that could cause terrorist-supporting regimes around the world to rethink their policies."

Bush followed up. If the United States attacked Iraq, we would have to do more than just make a statement, said the president. "It would have to bring about a new government. I want a plan on what it would take and what it would cost," Bush told Rumsfeld and Shelton.

"Can we do the Afghanistan and Iraq missions at the same time?" the president asked Shelton.

"Yes," the chairman replied.

George Bush's father congratulates him after his address
at the National Cathedral, September 14, 2001.

Bush ended the meeting by directing those present to devise a proper mission, "not a photo-op war. Get something with a consequence done soon."[34] The die was cast. The president was leading the country to war. More than that, he was opening two fronts in this war.

Bush declared Friday, September 14, a National Day of Prayer and Remembrance—a memorial to those who perished on 9/11. At 1 p.m. the president mounted the rostrum at the National Cathedral in Washington to deliver what may have been the most moving address of his presidency. His voice no longer had that high, tentative tone of forced optimism that the country had heard on September 11. The setting was impressive. The audience at the cathedral included former presidents Ford, Carter, Bush, and Clinton, as well as defeated Democratic candidate Al Gore, and their wives. Virtually every member of Congress was there, the justices of the Supreme Court, the cabinet, the Joint Chiefs of Staff, the diplomatic corps, and families of the victims. It was a solemn occasion, made even more somber by the understated grandeur of the cathedral.

As Bush climbed the steps to the lectern he recited a silent prayer, "Lord, let your light shine through me."[35] The speech itself was replete with religious imagery, as was befitting a service at the cathedral. "God's signs are not always the ones we look for," said the president.

We learn in tragedy that his purposes are not always our own. . . . This world He created is of moral design. Grief and tragedy and hatred are only for a time. Goodness, remembrance, and love have no end. . . . As we have been assured, neither death nor life . . . can separate us from God's love. May He bless the souls of the departed. May He comfort our own, and may He always guide our country.[36]

But the speech was not simply a religious invocation. It was also a call to war. "Our responsibility to history is already clear," said Bush.

To answer these attacks and rid the world of evil. War has been waged against us by stealth and deceit and murder. This nation is peaceful, but fierce when stirred to anger. This conflict was begun on the timing and terms of others. It will end in a way and at an hour of our choosing.[37]

Bush was throwing down the gauntlet. The audience was hushed. When Bush took his seat, his father reached over and gently squeezed his arm. It was a symbolic gesture—the passing of the torch from father to son.

George W. Bush's religious certitude gave him an inner strength. "I'm in the Lord's hands," he told the president of the American Red Cross on September 12.[38] At his meeting with the congressional leadership that same day, Robert Byrd of West Virginia, the senior member of the Senate, closed the meeting telling Bush, "Mighty forces will come to your aid."[39] And when the president invited a small group of evangelical leaders to the White House for spiritual guidance concerning 9/11 he received the same message.

"Mr. President, you and I are fellow believers in Jesus Christ," said James Merritt, former president of the Southern Baptist Convention. "We both believe there is a sovereign God in control of this universe. Since God knew that those planes would hit those towers before you and I were ever born, since God knew that you would be sitting in that chair before this world was ever created, I can only draw the conclusion that you are God's man for this hour."[40]

At that point, the president reportedly lowered his head and cried.

Whether Bush was the victim of pious simplification will long be debated. A useful contrast is the response of Abraham Lincoln when visited by a delegation of Protestant clergymen in the late summer of 1861, shortly after the battle of Bull Run. The spokesman for the group told Lincoln that he had experienced a vision from heaven the night before, and the Lord said He was on the president's side. Lincoln is reported to have replied, "I hope to have God on my side, Reverend, but what I must have is Kentucky."[41]

Immediately after the service at the cathedral, Bush boarded Air Force One to fly to New York and inspect the damage at the World Trade Center. The plane landed at McGuire Air Force Base in New Jersey shortly after 3 p.m. The president was greeted by New York governor George Pataki and Mayor Rudolph Giuliani, and the three climbed aboard Marine One for the short flight to Ground Zero. As Bush recalled, both men looked exhausted, having spent the last three days dealing directly with the tragedy. When he arrived at the site, Bush was stunned by the damage. "The Pentagon had been wounded, but not destroyed," he recalled. "That was not the case with the twin towers. They were gone. There was nothing left but a pile of rubble. The devastation was shocking and total."[42]

Bush walked among the rescue workers and shook their hands. It was an emotional mo-

Bush speaking in the rubble of the World
Trade Center, September 14, 2001.

ment. A soot-covered fireman looked the president in the eye. "George, find the bastards who did this and kill them." It is not often that someone calls the president by his first name, but the setting seemed to demand it.[43] The rescue workers wanted the president to speak. Bush climbed atop a charred fire truck that had been pulled from the rubble. An aide placed a bullhorn in his hand, and the president began to speak extemporaneously.

"We can't hear you," people shouted.

"I can hear you," Bush replied. "The rest of the world hears you. And the people who knocked these buildings down will hear all of us soon."[44] The crowd of workers exploded with shouts of U-S-A, U-S-A, U-S-A. "It was a release of energy I have never felt before," Bush recalled.[45]

After visiting Ground Zero, Bush and Giuliani drove three miles north on the West Side Highway to the Jacob K. Javits Convention Center, which had been converted into a holding area for the families of missing first responders. "I was amazed by the number of people on the West Side Highway waving flags and cheering," said Bush.

"I hate to break it to you, Mr. President, but none of these people voted for you," Giuliani joked.

At the Javits Center, Bush spent two hours speaking individually with family members of missing workers. He spoke with every family. It was a personal touch that came from the heart, the type of one-on-one encounter at which Bush excelled. Toward the end of his visit the president met Arlene Howard, whose son, a Port Authority police officer, had last been seen rushing into the dust and smoke to save others. "This is my son's badge," Mrs. Howard told Bush. "His name is George Howard. Please take it to remember him." Bush accepted the badge with tears in his eyes, and carried it with him for the remainder of his presidency.[46]

It was also on September 14 that Congress adopted a joint resolution authorizing the president to use "all necessary and appropriate force" to respond to the attacks on 9/11. The measure passed the Senate 98–0 and the House 420–1.* There was no debate. According to the text:

---

* Republican senators Larry Craig of Idaho and Jesse Helms of North Carolina abstained. In the House, the single dissenting vote was cast by Barbara Lee, a Democrat from Califor-

The President is authorized to use all necessary and appropriate force against those nations, organizations, or persons he determines planned, authorized, committed, or aided the terrorist attack that occurred on September 11, 2001, or harbored such organizations or persons, in order to prevent any future acts of international terrorism against the United States by such nations, organizations, or persons.[47]

The resolution was far-reaching, and entrusted Bush with vast powers not given to a chief executive since the Gulf of Tonkin Resolution of 1964, which led to the escalation of the war in Vietnam. But it was not as far-reaching as Bush had requested. The original White House

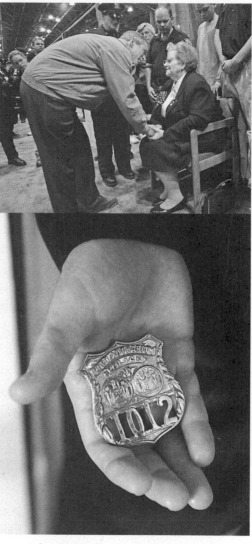

Arlene Howard presenting Bush with her son's Port Authority policeman's badge at New York's Javits Center, September 14, 2001.

nia. Congresswoman Lee was reelected in 2002 with 81.5 percent of the vote. Lee said the Act "was a blank check to the president to attack anyone . . . anywhere, in any country, without regard to our nation's longterm foreign policy." Barbara Lee, "Why I Opposed the Resolution to Use Force," *SF Gate*, September 23, 2001.

draft would have given the president the power "*to deter and preempt any related future acts of terrorism or aggression against the United States.*"[48] The blank check for preemption was too much for Congress to swallow, even after 9/11.

The speech at the National Cathedral, followed by the visit to Ground Zero and passage of the joint congressional resolution, made September 14 one of the most significant days of George W. Bush's presidency. His cathedral address energized the nation, the visit to Ground Zero was awe-inspiring, and the action by Congress entrusted him with vast powers. There was no longer any question about Bush's ability to take charge. And the president himself was on an emotional high. He departed that evening for Camp David and a weekend conference with his war cabinet that would lay the plans for the coming conflict. The president's confidence—which had seemed lacking on September 11—was now boundless.

Camp David, nestled in the Catoctin Mountains of Maryland some sixty-five miles northwest of Washington, has been the rustic retreat of presidents since Franklin Roosevelt. It was originally built by the WPA in the 1930s as a vacation spot for federal employees. FDR began using the facility during World War II and christened it "Shangri-la"—the fictional Himalayan utopia depicted in James Hilton's popular 1933 novel *Lost Horizon*. In 1953, the Eisenhower administration slated the site to be closed as an economy measure, but Mamie intervened, redecorated the main lodge, and when it was finished Ike renamed the facility "Camp David" in honor of his five-year-old grandson. The name stuck, and every president since Eisenhower has enjoyed the retreat. By 2001 it resembled a five-star resort hotel more than a rustic retreat.

Bush awoke at Camp David on the morning of September 15 with his spirits buoyed beyond recognition. This was war, he was in command, and the pieces were falling into place. Victory appeared in the offing. Or so it seemed that crisp September morning.

Before meeting with his war council, Bush spoke briefly to the press. He was itching for a fight. "We will find those who did it. We will smoke them out of their holes. We will get them running, and we will bring them to justice. We will not only deal with those who dare attack America; we will deal with those who harbor them and feed them and house them. . . . We are at war," the president said, "and we will respond accordingly." [49]

Bush carried that optimism into the meeting with his advisers. Colin Powell spoke first about the coalition being assembled. Most importantly, President Musharraf of Pakistan had agreed to go along. Bush was impressed. During a break in the proceedings he called Musharraf directly and thanked him for his support. "The stakes are high," said Musharraf. "We are with you." [50]

Powell was followed by Paul O'Neill, who briefly reported on Treasury's efforts to track the financial transactions of the terrorists. After O'Neill came George Tenet, who laid out at length the CIA's plan to defeat al Qaeda and the Taliban with paramilitary teams deployed with the Northern Alliance, U.S. military Special Forces, and anti-Taliban tribes in southern Afghanistan. It was an organized, optimistic presentation and Bush was impressed. "Great job," he told Tenet. [51]

The CIA director then presented a draft directive granting the agency virtual carte blanche to go after terrorists worldwide without having to seek the president's case-by-case approval (as was currently required). The order authorized the agency to conduct renditions, cyber attacks, and "kill, capture, and detain members of al Qaeda anywhere in the world." [52] It was a global plan for a secret war fought not by the military but by the CIA, invisibly and without public accountability. In effect, it would convert the CIA from being an intelligence-gathering agency into an action arm of government. As Tenet put it, "the CIA needed new, robust authority to act without restraint." [53] Bush immediately agreed. Though apparently made on the spur of the moment, this would become one of the most far-reaching decisions made by the president pertaining to the war on terror.*

After Tenet, General Hugh Shelton presented the military options.

---

* On September 17, 2001, Bush signed the formal "Memorandum of Notification" that Tenet requested. It had been written by Cofer Black, the CIA's counterterrorism chief, and was not reviewed by the State Department, the Defense Department, the Department of Justice, or the National Security Council. As one former administration official stated, "America was at war, but instead of the Department of Defense running it, the CIA was, so Tenet was for all intents and purposes the Secretary of Defense. Cofer was his top general, who grabbed it with both hands. They were the most powerful people in the bureaucracy." Jane Mayer, *The Dark Side:*

This was a snap back to reality. The CIA director had provided a rosy scenario. The chairman of the Joint Chiefs was more cautious. There were three options, said Shelton. Option one called for cruise missile strikes on al Qaeda camps in Afghanistan. Option two involved cruise missile strikes plus the use of manned bombers. The third option added troops on the ground. Shelton, a highly decorated Special Forces veteran who had commanded the U.S. intervention in Haiti in 1997, noted that the third option would take time to prepare. There were no plans on the shelf, no base rights, and no overflight permissions, all of which would be required to intervene in Afghanistan. Shelton's term as chairman was about to expire; his successor, Air Force General Richard Myers, had been named, and Shelton had no reason to curry favor. His presentation was scarcely what the Bush team wanted to hear.

Rice asked if there was a danger of getting bogged down in Afghanistan. Were there other military targets to consider? Once again, Wolfowitz picked up the thread. Why not Iraq? The enemy in Afghanistan was elusive, whereas Iraq offered an abundance of targets. Its regime was brittle and ripe for toppling. Iraq was doable. If the war on terror was to be taken seriously, the United States would have to go after Saddam sooner or later. Why not now?[54]

Rumsfeld agreed. "Dealing with Iraq would show a major commitment to antiterrorism."[55]

Powell intervened sharply. We would lose coalition support if we attacked Iraq at this time, said the secretary of state. "Going after Iraq now would be viewed as bait and switch. It's not what they signed up to do."[56]

Bush became impatient. He cut Powell off. The president said he didn't want other countries dictating the terms and conditions for the war on terror. "At some point," said Bush, "we may be the only ones left. That's O.K. with me. We are America."[57]

The discussion was rambling and at that point Bush decided to break for lunch. When they reconvened later in the afternoon, the

The Inside Story of How the War on Terror Turned into a War on American Ideals (New York: Doubleday, 2008), 40.

president asked for final recommendations. Powell restated his position, adding that military action against both Afghanistan and Iraq would fall under the jurisdiction of the Defense Department's Central Command (CENTCOM). It was Powell's ace in the hole. To everyone present it was obvious that CENTCOM could not fight two wars at the same time. Powell said they should adopt Tenet's plan, issue a warning to the Taliban with a deadline for ejecting al Qaeda, and if they did not comply, launch a sustained air assault.[58]

George Tenet felt much the same. "To hit Iraq now would be a mistake. The first target needs to be al Qaeda."[59] Rumsfeld said, "This is a marathon, not a sprint. It will be years, not months before it is over." He did not mention Iraq.[60] Vice President Cheney spoke last. He said he understood the threat Saddam Hussein posed, and believed it would have to be addressed. "But now is not a good time to do it. We would lose momentum."[61] In the final round, all four of Bush's most senior advisers had voted against attacking Iraq. The president thanked everyone and adjourned the meeting. "I'm going to think about it, and I'll let you know what I decide."[62]

Bush returned to Washington by helicopter Sunday afternoon. He was still on an emotional high. As he strutted across the South Lawn he stopped to speak with reporters. This was contrary to his usual practice, but the president was energized and wanted to speak out. He also took questions. Within a period of five minutes, Bush referred to "evil" and "evildoers" seven times. And he got into trouble. Carried away by his enthusiasm, the president said, "This crusade, this war on terrorism, is going to take a while." The characterization of the war on terror as a crusade was a major blunder. Bush undoubtedly said what he meant, but it was a word he should not have used. Muslims across the world pounced on it as proof that the United States was continuing the crusades launched against Islam by Christian Europe centuries earlier.

Even worse in some respects was his flippant reference to the war on terror as "the first war of the 21st century." This war was something we had to win decisively.[63] The trivialization of war by the president is astounding, but speaks volumes about his mind-set. "The first war of the 21st century." Rather than an undertaking of the utmost seriousness, war appeared to be the equivalent of an athletic contest—something we have to win today before the game next week—in the president's eyes. It also betrayed Bush's utter ignorance of history and the real world. At that very moment there were ongoing real wars in Colombia, Kashmir, Congo, Angola, and Sudan, of which the president was evidently unaware.

On Monday morning, September 17, Bush met again with his war council. "The purpose of this meeting," said the president, "is to assign tasks for the first wave of the war on terrorism. It starts today."[64] Bush said he was approving all of Tenet's requests. "I want the CIA to be the first on the ground."* He then ordered Attorney General Ashcroft to develop a legislative package that would expand the powers of federal law enforcement authorities to combat terrorism at home. Powell was told to prepare an immediate ultimatum to the Taliban "warning them to turn over bin Laden and his al Qaeda or they will suffer the consequences. If they don't comply, we'll attack them." Treasury Secretary O'Neill was instructed to launch an immediate assault on terrorist financial networks, and General Shelton was told to prepare option three. "We'll attack with missiles, bombers, and boots on the ground. Let's hit them hard. We want to signal this is a change from the past. We want to cause other countries like Syria and Iran to change their views. We want to hit as soon as possible."[65]

Bush said he thought Iraq was involved, "but I am not going to strike them now. I don't have the evidence at this point. There will be plenty of time to do that." Exactly thirty minutes after he began, Bush closed the meeting. "Start now," the president instructed his war cabinet. "It's very important to move fast. This is the new way."[66] Bush was in command and asserting his authority.

At eleven o'clock the president went to the Pentagon for a briefing on Special Forces and a limited Reserve call-up. As he left the building he was mobbed by reporters. "Do you want bin Laden dead?" asked one.

"I want justice," Bush replied. "There's an old poster out West, as

---

* The following day Bush signed a secret executive order, the first of many, allocating $900 million to the CIA for overseas operations. Ron Suskind, *The One Percent Doctrine: Deep Inside America's Pursuit of Its Enemies Since 9/11* (New York: Simon & Schuster, 2006), 20.

I recall, that said, 'Wanted: Dead or Alive.'"[67] It was a reckless remark that he soon regretted. "It was a little bit of bravado," he told Bob Woodward. "Tone it down, darling," said Laura.[68]

On Tuesday, September 18, French president Jacques Chirac visited Washington, the first foreign head of state to come to the White House since 9/11. It was a symbolic gesture underscoring French support for the United States. At a joint press conference in the Oval Office, Chirac was asked whether he agreed "that we are in a war, and is France in it? Will you fight side by side with U.S. troops?"

"I don't know whether I would use the word 'war,'" said Chirac, "but what I can say is that we are faced with a conflict of a completely new nature." The French president then pledged to work "in complete solidarity with the United States" to eliminate terrorism.[69] Chirac was distancing himself from the "war" metaphor that Bush found so attractive.

Bush carried his message to the country with a speech before a joint session of Congress on September 20. The House chamber was packed, and 82 million Americans watched on television—the largest audience ever to watch a presidential address. "On September 11th," said the president, "the enemies of freedom committed an act of war against our country." It was an emotional speech designed to engender a war spirit, and was crafted for mass consumption. The Godfather imagery spoke for itself. "Al Qaeda is to terror what the mafia is to crime," said the president, in one of the more colorful passages. He gave the Taliban an ultimatum to surrender bin Laden and al Qaeda. "These demands are not open to negotiation or discussion. They will hand over the terrorists or they will share their fate." The president also announced the creation of an Office of Homeland Security and announced that Governor Tom Ridge of Pennsylvania would head it.

The most significant passage was the drawing of battle lines, in retrospect a serious overstatement.

> Every nation, in every region, now has a decision to make: Either you are with us, or you are with the terrorists. From this day forward; any nation that continues to harbor or support terrorism will be regarded by the United States as a hostile regime.

Like Big Brother in George Orwell's *1984*, the president launched the nation on a never-ending struggle. "Our war on terror begins with al Qaeda, but it does not end there. It will not end until every terrorist group of global reach has been found, stopped, and defeated."

Bush closed on a personal note. "I will not forget this wound to our country and those who inflicted it. I will not yield; I will not rest; I will not relent in waging this struggle for freedom and security for the American people."[70] Bush's words mark a climax of the personalization of presidential power and the macho pursuit of American unilateralism.

British prime minister Tony Blair came to Washington to attend Bush's speech, and was seated in the House gallery next to Laura. Blair's reasons for coming were twofold: to demonstrate British support for the United States, and to rein Bush in. Like Chirac, Blair was concerned that Bush was determined to go it alone rather than working through the G-8, NATO, and the United Nations. As Jonathan Powell, Blair's chief of staff, put it, former prime minister Margaret Thatcher had gone to see the senior Bush to say, "This is no time to wobble" while Tony Blair was visiting the junior Bush to say "This IS the time to wobble."[71]

On September 21, the President's Daily Briefing provided by the CIA stated unequivocally there was "no evidence" linking the Iraqi government to the attacks of 9/11 and no reason to assume Saddam Hussein had any ties to al Qaeda. To the contrary, Saddam viewed al Qaeda and other radical Islamic groups as a threat to his secular regime. "What the president was told on September 21st," said a former high-level official, "was consistent with everything he has been told since—the evidence was just not there."[72] The information was also passed along to Cheney, Powell, Rumsfeld, and Rice. It was as definitive as a CIA briefing can be.

The following day, Bush called Putin from Camp David. They spoke for forty-two minutes. Bush asked for Russian support for the upcoming Afghanistan campaign. Putin agreed. "We can't put any Russian troops on the ground," he said. "That makes no sense for you or for us." But Putin agreed to open Russian airspace for U.S. military flights and to use his influence with the former Soviet republics bordering Afghanistan to secure base rights for American troops. "We have no objection to a U.S. role in Central Asia so long as it has the object of fighting the war on terror and is temporary and not permanent." Putin also said he would provide search and rescue teams for any downed American planes in northern Afghanistan and would have his generals brief their U.S. counterparts on their experience in Afghanistan. Putin had his own terrorist problem with Muslim fundamentalists and was eager to help. As he told Bush, Russia would be doing more for the United States in Afghanistan than its traditional allies.[73]

Meanwhile, planning for the attack on al Qaeda and the Taliban moved ahead. On September 21, Rumsfeld took General Tommy Franks, the commander of Central Command, to the White House to brief the president. To maintain utmost secrecy, the meeting was held in the family quarters. Powell, Rice, and Tenet were not there, just the military. Bush and Franks hit it off from the start. Tommy Franks was a combat commander, not a desk officer. He spoke in simple sentences, often laced with profanity, and thought clearly. He was also from Midland, Texas, and shared Bush's frontier perspective. He had graduated from Midland High School the year before Laura, enlisted in the Army, went to Officer Candidate School not West Point, was commissioned in the field artillery, fought in Vietnam and the first Gulf war, and was appointed to head CENTCOM by President Clinton in early 2000. He had been on the job for eighteen months, knew the territory, and was familiar with the history of Afghanistan.

The meeting was scheduled for two hours but lasted over three. "I asked Tommy a lot of questions," said Bush. "How many troops would we need? What kind of basing was available? How long would it take to move everyone? I did not try to manage the logistics or the tactical decisions. My instinct was to trust the judgment of the military leadership. I remembered the Vietnam era photos of Lyndon Johnson and Defense Secretary Robert McNamara poring over maps to pick bombing targets for routine missions."[74]

The plan Franks laid out had four phases. Phase one, which was already under way, involved a buildup of forces and the insertion of

General Tommy Franks

CIA and Special Forces advance teams to link up with the Northern Alliance. Phase two called for a massive air campaign to take out Taliban and al Qaeda targets. The third phase involved the introduction of U.S. ground troops to seek out and eliminate the final pockets of resistance. This would flow seamlessly from phase two. "I estimated we would need no more than ten to twelve thousand troops for this phase," said Franks. "We wanted to avoid a cumbersome Soviet-style occupation by armored divisions. It hadn't worked for the Soviets, and it wouldn't work for us." * The final phase would be to stabilize the country to prevent the reemergence of terrorism and provide humanitarian relief. According to Franks, this would take three to five years. "I was certain that surviving Taliban and al Qaeda units would resort to guerrilla combat once their large formations had been destroyed." [75]

When the briefing concluded Bush asked Franks when he could launch the air assault. "What is your ideal timing?"

"Two weeks," Franks replied.

---

* The decision to keep U.S. ground forces at a minimum has often been criticized, but Rumsfeld provides a convincing rationale. "My willingness for our forces to work with the Northern Alliance was based on my conviction that we would be making a mistake if our military effort appeared to the Afghans as an American invasion aimed at taking control of their country."

In addition, "If we were going to employ overwhelming force at the outset, we would have needed many months to build a large occupation army. . . . We would have risked additional terrorist attacks in the interim, and made it easier for our enemies to portray us as imperialist invaders and occupiers." Donald Rumsfeld, *Known and Unknown* (New York: Sentinel, 2011), 372–73, 377.

"I understand," said the president. "Two weeks."[76]

On Saturday, October 6, Franks's forces were in place. "We need a 'go' for operation," Rumsfeld told the president. "Go," said Bush. "It's well thought through. It's the right thing to do."[77] Operation Enduring Freedom kicked off the next day.* The attack began at 12:30 p.m. Eastern Time (9:30 p.m. in Kabul). Bombers and cruise missiles struck al Qaeda training camps, Taliban air defense systems, military installations, and command-and-control centers. At 1 p.m. President Bush addressed the nation on television.

> More than two weeks ago, I gave Taliban leaders a series of clear and specific demands. None of these demands were met. And now the Taliban will pay a price.
>
> Today, we focus on Afghanistan, but the battle is broader. Every nation has a choice to make. In this conflict, there is no neutral ground. If any government sponsors the outlaws and killers of innocents, they have become outlaws and murderers themselves.[78]

The air bombardment lasted twelve days. On October 19 the first U.S. Special Forces teams landed and the Northern Alliance took the offensive. Bush's presidential approval rating soared to between 88 and 92 percent in various opinion polls—the highest rating ever attained by a sitting president. The administration had wrapped itself in the flag. To question the president's actions was unpatriotic.

On October 30, Bush went to New York to throw out the ceremonial first pitch in the third game of the World Series between the Yankees and the Arizona Diamondbacks. Yankee Stadium was jammed to capacity. "Are you going to throw it from the mound?" asked Derek Jeter.

"What do you think?" Bush replied.

"Yeah. Be a man. Throw it from the mound."

"Okay, I will," said the president.

"Just don't bounce it. If you do, they'll boo you."[79]

---

* CENTCOM had originally selected the name Operation Infinite Justice for the Afghanistan campaign, only to learn that Muslims considered infinite justice reserved for God alone. In late September the name was changed to Operation Enduring Freedom.

Throwing out the first pitch in the 2001 World Series at Yankee Stadium.

Bush took the mound wearing a New York Fire Department windbreaker and threw a perfect strike. The crowd roared its approval and spontaneously broke into the chant U-S-A, U-S-A, U-S-A. Sitting in owner George Steinbrenner's box, Karl Rove felt a twinge of uneasiness: "It's like being at a Nazi party rally."[80]

In Afghanistan, the Northern Alliance, supported by U.S. airpower and stiffened by U.S. Special Forces, continued to move forward. On November 9, it captured the key northern city of Mazar-e-Sharif. Kabul fell on November 13, and on December 7 the southern city of Kandahar, spiritual capital of the Taliban, surrendered to the Northern Alliance. American casualties were light, eleven dead and thirty-five wounded. The Taliban and al Qaeda lost an estimated eight to twelve thousand fighters.[81] The downside was that the al Qaeda and Taliban leadership, including Osama bin Laden and Mullah Omar, escaped with their followers to the mountain redoubt of Tora Bora on the Pakistan border. Two weeks later, leaders of Afghanistan's various ethnic and political groups meeting in Bonn, Germany, named Hamid Karzai to head an interim government.

For George W. Bush it appeared to be a total victory. The smell of success was overpowering. On November 27, fourteen days after the fall of Kabul, General Tommy Franks received a telephone call from Rumsfeld. "General Franks," said the secretary of defense, "the president wants you to look at options for Iraq. What is the status of your planning?"[82] The global war on terror was just beginning.

CHAPTER ELEVEN

L'État, c'est moi

I'm the commander. I don't need to explain. That's the interesting thing about being president. I don't feel like I owe anybody an explanation.

George W. Bush

The war on terror carried the United States beyond the bounds of legally acceptable international behavior. The domestic impact was equally extreme. Once again, George W. Bush was in command. And once again, cabinet officers saluted and fell into line. Whether it was government snooping or shoes off at airports, the president set the pace.* And just as Bush was unfamiliar with the rules and norms of the world beyond America's borders, he seemed equally unaware of the constitutional guarantees of individual liberty. What was important, as Bush saw it, was to prevent another terrorist attack, and in his mind

---

* The United States is the only country in the world in which airline passengers must remove their shoes for the pre-flight security check. Recent changes exempt persons seventy-five or over, which illustrates the arbitrariness of the requirement. Is a person seventy-five or over less likely to be a shoe bomber? The requirement makes no sense, except to keep the public on edge, another Orwellian twist.

that required the rapid and seemingly boundless expansion of presidential power.

By defining the issue as a struggle between good and evil, Bush exempted himself from examining the causes of the conflict or the reasons behind al Qaeda's quarrel with the West. Evil is evil, and there can be no compromise. Americans rallied around the president. The tragic events of 9/11 momentarily united the country in a global crusade to rid the world of evil. As Professor Chester Crocker, who had been assistant secretary of state for Ronald Reagan, observed, support for the war on terror was sustained by a toxic mix of nationalism and gullibility. The public was ill-prepared to interpret what was happening and simply followed the president's lead. The same can be said for Congress and the media.[1]

The Bush White House managed the news to an exceptional degree. The president would hold only one third as many press conferences as Bill Clinton, and only one fifth as many as his father. Access by the media to Bush was strictly limited. The effect was to shield the president from impromptu exchanges with informed questioners, which was not his strong suit. The White House also severely limited opportunities for staff and even cabinet members to speak to the press. Under rules imposed before 9/11, no member of the White House staff could talk to reporters without prior approval from Karen Hughes's communications office. After 9/11, it became next to impossible to get such approval. The Bush administration also classified documents at twice the rate of previous administrations.[2]

It was not just the White House. On September 21, the Department of Justice issued a blanket directive closing all deportation hearings to the public, press, and family members.[3] Then, on October 12, Attorney General John Ashcroft severely restricted the scope of the Freedom of Information Act (FOIA). Under the Clinton administration, Attorney General Janet Reno had instructed government officials to operate under a "presumption of disclosure" unless it was "reasonably foreseeable that disclosure would be harmful." Ashcroft ordered those same officials to reject FOIA requests if it was at all possible to do so, even if the information sought was harmless.[4]

Bush added to the restrictions. On November 1, he signed an executive order imposing new limits on access to presidential documents. Under the Presidential Records Act passed by Congress in 1978 after Watergate, all White House files were declared public property, including "confidential communications between the president and his advisers." These documents were to be made available to the public twelve years after an administration left office. In spite of the law, Bush declared that all presidential records would remain sealed if the current president or the past president wanted them withheld as "privileged."[5]*

For George W. Bush, the war on terror was a global undertaking, not only against enemies abroad, but domestically as well. "Putting America on a war footing was one of the most important decisions of my presidency," he stated in his memoirs.[6] In his request to Congress for authorization to use force, the authorization the House of Representatives and the Senate enacted on September 14, Bush had asked that the measure empower the president "to use all necessary and appropriate force *in the United States and* against those nations, organizations, and persons" linked to 9/11 (emphasis added). Bush sought full military powers against domestic terrorists. That would strip suspects of constitutional and statutory protections and make them enemy combatants. They could be shot on sight, held without trial, denied legal rights, and there would be few limits on government surveillance. The Congress refused to go along, and the resolution as adopted omitted any reference to a domestic state of war.

The protections Americans enjoy against arbitrary power are substantial. The Fourth Amendment to the Constitution prohibits unreasonable searches and seizures, the Fifth ensures the right of a defendant not to incriminate himself, and the Sixth ensures a fair public trial, including the right to counsel. The case law interpreting these amendments is extensive, and the rights of a defendant are carefully protected. The Posse Comitatus Act of 1878, passed after Reconstruction, prohibits the use of federal military force domestically.[7] The Foreign Intelligence

---

* On his first full day in office, January 21, 2009, President Obama revoked Bush's order. See Executive Order 13489, 74 *Federal Register* 4669.

Surveillance Act, adopted after Watergate, requires the government to obtain a warrant from a special FISA federal court whenever it wants to monitor communications on U.S. soil. To get permission to tap a telephone or eavesdrop on email, the government must produce evidence that there is probable cause to believe that the targeted person is a terrorist or spy. The statute explicitly states that the warrant procedure is the "exclusive" legal means for the government to monitor communications that reach U.S. soil, and that any violation is a criminal offense.[8]

FISA was one of the key reforms Congress enacted after Watergate. Prior to its enactment, presidents were free to employ the CIA and the National Security Agency to spy on enemies and undertake a variety of warlike acts, including assassination, in secret and without oversight. Nixon and LBJ used government operatives to eavesdrop on their domestic political opponents. These practices were brought to light during the 1975 investigations by the Frank Church and Otis Pike committees, and corrective legislation was adopted. As Senator Church said, there was a "tremendous potential for abuse" if the National Security Agency "were to turn its awesome technology against domestic communications." It would mean the end of privacy, said Church, and could be a tool of political suppression.[9]* The FISA Act was signed into law by President Carter in 1978, and its requirements were observed by every succeeding administration.

Bush was aware of these restrictions but chose not to comply. He also decided against asking Congress to amend the FISA act on behalf of NSA. "We considered going to Congress to get legislation," said Bush, "but key members from both parties . . . agreed that the surveillance

---

* As early as 1975 the potential for abuse by NSA was recognized. Church said the agency had the technological capacity to monitor every telephone conversation and telegram. That would effectively destroy the right to privacy. If a dictatorship were ever to arise in America, Church said, the government could use NSA to ensure that security forces knew of any attempt to resist. "I don't want to see this country ever go across the bridge," said Church. "I know the capacity that is there to make tyranny total in America, and we must see to it that this agency and all agencies that possess this technology operate within the law and under proper supervision, so that we never cross over that abyss. That is the abyss from which there is no return." *Meet the Press*, October 29, 1975, quoted in James Bamford, *The Puzzle Palace* (Boston: Houghton Mifflin, 1982), 477.

was necessary and that a legislative debate was not possible without exposing our methods to the enemy."[10] Instead, Bush chose to proceed in secrecy. He was encouraged to do so by a series of memoranda prepared by the Office of Legal Counsel (OLC) of the Department of Justice— the official advisory counsel to the federal government. *Newsweek* once called the OLC "the most important government office you've never heard of," and its opinions are definitive.[11]*

Beginning with two secret memorandums on September 25, 2001, the Office of Legal Counsel told the White House that the president was not bound by certain existing laws. The first memorandum dealt with the president's power to use military force and concluded that "the President has the plenary constitutional power to take such military actions as he deems necessary."

> Military actions need not be limited to those individuals, groups, or states that participated in the attacks on the World Trade Center and the Pentagon: The Constitution vests the President with the power to strike terrorist groups and organizations that cannot be demonstrably linked to the September 11 incidents, but that, nonetheless, pose a similar threat to the security of the United States and the lives of its people *whether at home or overseas.* (Emphasis added.)

Not only was the president free to use military force on U.S. soil, but according to the OLC, Congress was powerless to "place any limits on the President's determination as to any terrorist threat, the amount of military force to be used in response, or the method, timing, and nature of the response. *These decisions, under our Constitution, are for the president alone to make.*"[12] (Emphasis added.)

The second memorandum dealt with the Foreign Intelligence Surveillance Act and noted that the president, as commander in chief, "must be able to use whatever means necessary to prevent attacks upon

---

* Among the former members of the Office of Legal Counsel are Chief Justice William Rehnquist and Justice Antonin Scalia, former attorney generals Nicholas Katzenbach and William Barr, and former solicitor generals Theodore Olson and Walter Dellinger.

the United States: this power, by implication, includes the authority to collect information for its effective exercise."

> This Office has maintained, across different administrations and different political parties, that the President's constitutional responsibility to defend the nation may justify reasonable, but warrantless, counter-intelligence searches.[13]*

Armed with these memoranda, Bush proceeded to unleash the full array of government snooping against those suspected of being domestic terrorists. This was done in secret and without warrants. And the OLC provided the necessary support. A memorandum from the OLC is binding on the entire executive branch of government. If the OLC says it is legal to tap telephones without a warrant, it is virtually impossible to prosecute U.S. officials who do so pursuant to that advice. As Jack Goldsmith, who headed the OLC in 2003, put it, the office wields "one of the most momentous, and dangerous powers in the government: the power to dispense get-out-of-jail-free cards."[14] During Bush's first

---

* Both memorandums were written by Deputy Assistant Attorney General John C. Yoo, who had joined the Office of Legal Counsel on leave from the law school at the University of California, where he was a professor of constitutional law. Yoo graduated from Yale Law School in 1992, clerked for Supreme Court justice Clarence Thomas, and had spent a year in Washington as counsel to Senate Judiciary Committee chairman Orrin Hatch of Utah. In 1996 he established his reputation as a controversial constitutional scholar with an article in the *California Law Review* arguing that the president enjoyed the authority to launch wars without congressional permission. "The Continuation of Politics by Other Means," 84 *Cal. L. Rev.* (1996): 167–241.

Yoo's scholarship has often been criticized. Whether he was acting as an impartial lawyer or as an advocate for presidential power has been questioned. Yale law school dean Harold Koh, who had been Yoo's mentor at Yale, testified in January 2005 before the Senate Judiciary Committee that Yoo's memos raised profound ethical questions. "If a client asks a lawyer how to break the law and escape liability, the lawyer's ethical duty is to say no. A lawyer has no obligation to aid, support, or justify the commission of an illegal act."

Yoo responded to the attacks in his 2006 memoir *War by Other Means: An Insider's Account of the War on Terror* (New York: Atlantic Monthly Press, 2006). "The law does not give us all the answers," wrote Yoo. "The law requires our elected leaders to make policy judgments" (p. 202). Also see Yoo, *The Powers of War and Peace: The Constitution and Foreign Affairs After 9/11* (Chicago: University of Chicago Press, 2005).

term, the Office of Legal Counsel provided the White House with eleven memoranda justifying and explaining a domestic surveillance program outside the reach of the Federal Intelligence Surveillance Act. Ten of these eleven memoranda remain classified.[15]

John Yoo

Bush's decision to circumvent FISA was taken early. As the president put it, "After September 11th, I spoke to a variety of folks on the front line protecting us, and I said, is there anything more we could be doing, and General Mike Hayden of the NSA said there is."[16] Lieutenant General Michael Hayden, the director general of the National Security Agency, had long pressed to expand NSA's surveillance role, and had proposed in a transition report to the incoming Bush administration in January 2001 that the organization establish a "powerful, permanent presence on the commercial communication networks." Hayden often said he was "troubled if he was not using the full authority allowed by the law," and that he was "going to live on the edge," where "his spikes will have chalk on them." Bush's response to 9/11 gave Hayden the opportunity.[17]*

---

* Michael Hayden was appointed by President Clinton to head the National Security Agency in March 1999. In that capacity Hayden undertook a public campaign to demystify NSA. "Despite what you see on television, our agency does not do alien autopsies, track the location of your automobile by satellite, nor do we have a squad of assassins," he said in a speech at American University in 2000. At the same time, Hayden was one of the principal advocates for expanding the domestic role of NSA. Hayden was rewarded by Bush, who promoted him to the four-star rank in April 2005 and made him director of national intelligence. In May 2006 Hayden became director of the CIA, a post he held until the Obama administration took office in 2009. Dana Priest, "Covert CIA Program Withstands New Furor," *Washington Post,* December 30, 2005; James Risen, *State of War: The Secret History of the CIA and the Bush Administration* (New York: Free Press, 2006), 39–44; Jane Mayer, *The Dark Side* (New York: Doubleday, 2008), 69.

The National Security Agency is an extremely high-tech intelligence-gathering organization headquartered at Fort Meade, Maryland, about twenty miles northeast of Washington. It was established in 1952 by President Truman to obtain "signal intelligence" on the Soviet Union and was given authority to analyze intercepted phone calls and other communications to learn what America's enemies were saying to one another. Before 9/11 the agency was limited to spying on non-U.S. citizens abroad, where neither domestic legislation such as FISA nor the constitutional guarantees of the Fourth Amendment applied. Hayden suggested that NSA use its powerful surveillance technology to hunt for possible terrorist communications on U.S. soil.

Bush agreed. "Why should it be tougher to monitor al Qaeda communications with terrorists inside the United States than with their associates overseas? If al Qaeda operatives were calling into or out of the United States, we damn sure needed to know who they were calling and what they were saying. And given the urgency of the threats, we could not allow ourselves to get bogged down in the court approval process." [18]

With the opinion from the Office of Legal Counsel in hand, Bush convened a meeting with Hayden, Tenet, and Cheney in the Oval Office on the morning of October 4, at which he approved the Terrorist Surveillance Program. "I know this is a big deal," the president said. "We are undertaking something that may be unprecedented." [19] As Bush wrote later, "The purpose of the program was to monitor so-called dirty numbers, which intelligence professionals had reason to believe belonged to al Qaeda operatives." [20]

The Terrorist Surveillance Program employs NSA in a domestic eavesdropping capacity without the use of warrants. This is contrary to the Federal Intelligence Surveillance Act. But Bush was convinced American soil was a battlefield, and the OLC had informed him that Congress lacked the power to restrict the commander in chief's tactics confronting an enemy on the battlefield. If the president decided it was necessary for NSA to collect battlefield intelligence within the United States, no statute enacted by Congress could regulate how he did that. Bush said the appropriate members of Congress would be notified, "as soon as I judge that it can be done consistent with the national defense needs."[21]

Bush's adoption of the warrantless surveillance program by NSA after 9/11 was the first of a series of steps that loosened the constitutional and statutory provisions that bound the president's hands. Bush secretly adopted the power to ignore the Foreign Intelligence Surveillance Act, and then acted on that power. The president's decisions set a new and dangerous precedent. As conservative legal analyst Bruce Fein later told Congress, "The theory invoked by the president to justify eavesdropping by the NSA in contradiction to FISA would equally justify mail openings, burglaries, torture or internment camps, all in the name of gathering foreign intelligence." It was, as Fein noted, "a defining moment in the constitutional history of the United States."[22]

The crisis atmosphere that engulfed the White House was intensified by an anthrax scare shortly after 9/11. On October 5, Robert Stevens, a photo editor for the *National Enquirer* in Florida, succumbed to what was later determined to have been inhalation anthrax—the first such death in the United States in twenty-five years. The following week several employees who handled the mail at the headquarters of ABC, CBS, and NBC in New York came down with a milder form of the illness transmitted through the skin. One of the contaminated letters was addressed to NBC's Tom Brokaw, and media coverage was extensive. Vice President Cheney appeared on *PBS NewsHour with Jim Lehrer* and suggested that bin Laden might well be behind the attacks. "We know that he's trained people in his camps in Afghanistan. We have copies of the manuals that they've actually used to train people with respect to how to deploy and use these kinds of substances. I think the only responsible thing for us to do is proceed on the basis that the September 11 and the anthrax attacks could be linked."[23]

The crisis was heightened on October 15 when Senate majority leader Tom Daschle received a letter through the mail laced with a lethally potent powder that on testing proved to be anthrax. The anthrax spores in the letter Daschle received were so professionally refined that the CIA believed the powder must have been sent by experienced terrorists, quite possibly al Qaeda. The envelope to Daschle contained a single sheet of paper with a terse message. It was dated 9/11:

> YOU CANNOT STOP US.
>
> WE HAVE THIS ANTHRAX.
>
> YOU DIE NOW.
>
> ARE YOU AFRAID?
>
> DEATH TO AMERICA.
>
> DEATH TO ISRAEL.
>
> ALLAH IS GREAT.

The Hart Senate Office Building, where Daschle's office was located, was immediately evacuated. Capitol Hill shut down for a week, and all mail to federal offices was placed under quarantine. The Hart Building and the massive Brentwood postal facility in northeast Washington that handled the mail were sealed and chlorine gas pumped through to kill any lingering anthrax bacteria. Two postal employees at the Brentwood facility would later die from inhaled anthrax.

An hour or so after the contaminated letter to Daschle was discovered, Bush held a joint press conference with visiting Italian prime minister Silvio Berlusconi at the White House. Bush was asked about the anthrax attacks. Was there a link to bin Laden and al Qaeda?

> *President Bush:* There may be some possible link. We have no hard
> data yet, but it's clear Mr. bin Laden is a man who is an evil man.
> He and his spokesmen are openly bragging about how they hope
> to inflict more pain on our country. So we are watching every
> piece of evidence. I wouldn't put it past him, but we have no hard
> evidence yet.[24]

White House staffers said that the anthrax letters had a far greater impact on the president than anyone ever imagined. "It was the seminal event," said one. "It was the thing that changed everything. The president's resolve grew unshakable. No more Americans would be killed, he swore, by the murderous plotting of evildoers."[25]

The anthrax letters created a momentary panic throughout the country. Many were afraid to open their mailboxes. White House speechwriter David Frum said that for the next month he opened his mail wearing rubber gloves. "My wife packed a suitcase and a box full of emergency supplies and put them in the basement," said Frum. "We designated a place of rendezvous a hundred miles away in case we were separated."[26]

Laura Bush was equally affected. "The White House was now literally cut off," she wrote. "Any letter or package being sent was entombed in an off-site facility. Letters could not reach us, not even ones from fourth-grade girls. It was impossible to send any kind of envelope to the White House grounds. For years, the mail sat in sacks, unopened and waiting to be irradiated."[27]

The anthrax scare lasted well into November. Ultimately a total of eighteen people would be infected and five died.[28] For the president, this was another manifestation of the evildoers at work. After an extensive investigation, the Department of Justice and the FBI concluded that all of the anthrax letters had been mailed by Dr. Bruce Ivins, a mentally disturbed microbiologist working at the Army's Medical Research Institute for Infectious Diseases at Fort Detrick in Frederick, Maryland.* Informed of his pending indictment, Dr. Ivins committed suicide by taking an overdose of Tylenol. He died on July 29, 2008.

The anthrax scare of October–November played out before the backdrop of Bush's overriding fear of a biological attack. In the sum-

---

* When the Senate mailroom was closed down after the Daschle letter was discovered, a second letter was found addressed to Senator Patrick Leahy of Vermont that was also laced with anthrax spores. Both senators had been involved in the nation's anthrax policy. Several months before receiving his letter, Daschle had written to the Pentagon expressing concern over the safety of the anthrax vaccines administered to soldiers. Shortly afterward, the Defense Department announced it was curtailing the program, threatening the careers of scientists like Dr. Ivins at Fort Detrick.

Senator Leahy, the second ranking Democrat on the Senate Agriculture Committee, chaired the subcommittee on Research and Nutrition, which oversaw the funding for biosafety animal research facilities, including the anthrax laboratory at Fort Detrick. He had approved the cutback. See Kurt Eichenwald, *500 Days: Secrets and Lies in the Terror Wars* (New York: Simon & Schuster, 2012), 115.

mer of 2001, well before 9/11, the Johns Hopkins Center for Civilian Biodefense Strategies conducted a war game called Dark Winter simulating a bio-terrorist attack on the United States using smallpox.* The exercise was staged June 22–23, 2001, at Andrews Air Force Base outside Washington. In the scenario, the National Security Council wrestled with the problem of smallpox infestation following a major crisis in the Taiwan Strait. The response of various government agencies was challenged, and the purpose of the exercise was to increase awareness of the scope and character of the threat posed by biological weapons. Former Georgia senator Sam Nunn acted as the president, David Gergen was his national security adviser, James Woolsey was head of the CIA (a post he had formerly held), Margaret Hamburg, later commissioner of the Food and Drug Administration, served as secretary of Health and Human Services, William Sessions played the role of director of the FBI (a position he formerly held), and Frank Keating played himself as the governor of Oklahoma. As part of the war game, scripted TV news clips were made and can be seen on YouTube.

Smallpox had taken the lives of an estimated 300 million people in the twentieth century, including two million in 1967. The World Health Organization began a massive campaign to eradicate the disease that year, and by 1977 the disease had been wiped out. Only the United States and Russia were permitted to retain research samples of the virus under secure and closely monitored conditions, although American intelligence sources believed North Korea and Iraq could possess undeclared stocks.[29]

The Dark Winter exercise depicted an imaginary attack on the United States in which shopping malls in Oklahoma City, Atlanta, and Philadelphia were infected with smallpox. The incubation period for smallpox can be up to fourteen days, and after the second week 2,000 cases were reported in fifteen states. After three weeks the number of

---

* The exercise has been criticized repeatedly for taking worst-case scenarios, but it is chilling to watch the TV clips. See Tara O'Toole, Mair Michael, and Thomas V. Inglesby, "Shining Light on 'Dark Winter,' " 34 *Journals for the Royal Society of Topical Medicine and Hygiene, Clinical Infectious Diseases* (2002): 972–83.

victims approached 300,000 and supplies of the smallpox vaccine were exhausted. Using worst-case projections, the exercise predicted that ultimately there would be as many as three million cases of smallpox in the United States and up to a million deaths. Shortly after 9/11, Vice President Cheney insisted the president and members of the National Security Council receive a briefing on Dark Winter. This was arranged for September 20, and the conclusion was that the United States was virtually defenseless against smallpox or any other biological attack. "The anthrax business didn't worry me very much," said Rumsfeld, "but the *Dark Winter* scenario really caught my attention." [30]

After the anthrax scare, Cheney pressed Bush to introduce a universal, mandatory smallpox vaccination program in the United States to guard against the possibility of a smallpox attack by Saddam Hussein. Health service professionals, including Dr. Donald Henderson of Johns Hopkins, who had led the fight to eradicate smallpox, resisted the effort. They did not accept the view that Iraq was working with smallpox, and in any event believed the techniques they had used to eradicate smallpox would be sufficient if there was an attack. Bush listened to the professionals. Mandatory vaccinations were ordered for 500,000 military personnel, and an equivalent number of health care workers were provided the vaccine on a voluntary basis, but no general order was given. Bush himself was vaccinated, but Laura and the girls were not, nor was Cheney.[31] On the other hand, the president and first lady, and almost everyone on the White House staff, commenced taking the antibiotic Cipro as a precaution against bio-terrorism.

The fear in the White House of another terrorist attack was heightened further by a new security-reporting technique Bush ordered. Concerned by his failure to grasp the warnings of a terrorist attack on 9/11, the president demanded to see the raw intelligence reports concerning possible terrorist threats on a daily basis. This became known as the "threat matrix," and was presented to Bush every morning at 8:30 by FBI director Robert Mueller. The reports were not screened and there was no filter. In effect, George W. Bush became an intelligence case officer poring over dozens of pages of uncorroborated reports about impending terrorist attacks. "You could drive yourself crazy reading even half of what was in the threat matrix," said Jim Baker, head of the Justice Department's Office of Intelligence Policy and Review.[32]

"Most of the threat matrix was garbage," said one high-level official. Bush had no intelligence background and was not trained to put the raw material in context. After a while "you suffer from sensory overload," said Baker. "Reading the threat matrix every day is like being stuck in a room listening to loud Led Zeppelin music." Deputy attorney general James Comey believed that the cumulative effect of a daily exposure to the threat matrix turned national security concerns into "an obsession" in the White House.[33] Fear of another terrorist attack, justified or not, came to dominate White House thinking. As Bush saw it, after 9/11 it was "better to be safe than sorry."

The contrast to Franklin D. Roosevelt is striking. In 1933, facing the greatest economic crisis in the nation's history, FDR reassured Americans by reminding them they had nothing to fear but fear itself. George W. Bush on the other hand repeatedly reminded Americans of the dangers they faced. The war on terror was a neverending struggle. Roosevelt banished the nation's fears; Bush reinforced them.[34]

The centerpiece of Bush's domestic war on terror was the Patriot Act, which amended the Foreign Intelligence Surveillance Act and greatly expanded the investigative powers of the CIA, the FBI, and the Secret Service.* The 342-page act was rushed through Congress with no hearings and little debate, and was the product of the atmosphere of fear that 9/11 engendered and the Bush administration abetted.† "The Government will enforce this law with all the urgency of a nation at war," said Bush as he signed the measure at the White House on October 26.[35]

The Patriot Act was a direct assault on the civil liberties Americans enjoy, particularly the right to privacy, and may be the most ill-

---

* The USA Patriot Act, Public Law 107–56, 115 Stat. 272, is the acronym for the Uniting and Strengthening America by Providing Appropriate Tools Required to Intercept and Obstruct Terrorism Act of 2001.

† The Patriot Act passed the House on October 24 by a vote of 357–66. Representative Ron Paul (R., Texas) told *The Washington Times* that members were not permitted to read the bill before voting. It passed the Senate the next day 98–1. Senator Russ Feingold of Wisconsin voted against.

conceived piece of domestic legislation since the Alien and Sedition Acts of 1798. It has been castigated by both the Democratic left and the libertarian right, and three provisions of the act have been struck down by the courts as unconstitutional.* The act was drafted under the direction of Attorney General John Ashcroft, who prepared it according to Bush's instructions. "Don't let this ever happen again," Bush had told Ashcroft on the day after 9/11, and Ashcroft considered that an order from the commander in chief.[36] Like Powell and Rumsfeld, Ashcroft voiced no objection.

Although the Patriot Act amended FISA to provide greater leeway for the FBI and CIA to monitor domestic communications, it made no reference to the National Security Agency or the intelligence gathering Bush had authorized. The White House could have easily included NSA in the revision, but chose to keep the agency's activities secret. NSA's domestic surveillance program would become far greater and more extensive than those of the FBI and CIA combined, yet when offered the opportunity to legalize the program and conduct it aboveboard, Bush declined.

---

* In 2004, pursuant to a suit brought by the American Civil Liberties Union, a United States district court in New York declared that portion of Title V of the act that provided for National Security Letters to be in violation of the First and Fourth Amendments to the Constitution. A National Security Letter is a form of executive subpoena requiring the recipient to turn over various records and data pertaining to individuals. National Security Letters require no probable cause, were not subject to judicial oversight, and contained a gag order preventing the recipient from disclosing that the letter was ever issued. The case was *Doe v. Ashcroft*, 334F. Supp. 2d 471 (S.D.N.Y. 2004).

Also in 2004, a federal court in Los Angeles found that portion of Title VIII of the act prohibiting "expert advice and assistance to terrorist groups" to be in violation of both the First and Fifth Amendments. The terminology was so vague that it "could be construed to include unequivocally pure free speech and advocacy protected by the First Amendment," said the court. *Humanitarian Law Project v. Ashcroft*, 309 F. Supp. 2d 322 (C.D. Cal. 2004).

In 2007, in the highly publicized case of lawyer Brandon Mayfield related to the train bombing in Madrid, a federal district court in Oregon struck down the "Sneak and Peek" provisions of the act, holding they were an end run around the Fourth Amendment. The decision of the trial judge was vacated on narrow grounds by the Ninth Circuit, Court of Appeals which held that the Mayfield family did not have standing to raise a constitutional claim. *Mayfield v. Gonzales*, 504 F. Supp. 2d 1023, *rev'd*, 599 F. 3d 964 (9th Cir.).

The most egregious example of executive overreach by the Bush administration was the Domestic Security Enhancement Act (Patriot II), a draft proposal sent to Congress by the Justice Department in January 2003.[37] Under Patriot II, the attorney general would have been able to strip an American of his or her citizenship and deport him "if he becomes a member, or provides support to, a group that the United States has designated as a 'terrorist organization.'" This flies in the face of Supreme Court decisions for the last fifty years. "Citizenship is not a license that expires on misbehavior," said Chief Justice Earl Warren speaking for the court in 1958.* Or as Justice Hugo Black put it in the leading case of *Afroyim v. Rusk*, 387 U.S. 253 (1967):

> Citizenship in the nation is a cooperative affair. Its citizenry is the country and the country its citizenry. The very nature of our free government makes it completely incongruous to have a rule of law under which a group of citizens temporarily in office can deprive another group of citizens of their citizenship. *We hold that the Fourteenth Amendment was designed to, and does, protect every citizen of the nation against a congressional forcible destruction of his citizenship.* (Emphasis added.)[38]

It is inconceivable that the Justice Department was not aware of the Supreme Court's holdings, yet in Bush's war against terror, well-grounded constitutional precedent seemed irrelevant.

George W. Bush was consumed by the war. After his daily Bible meditation and breakfast, he arrived in the Oval Office for the daily

---

* The case was *Trop v. Dulles*, 356 U.S. 86 (1958), overturning legislation that deprived a soldier of his citizenship for desertion from the Army in wartime. This was followed by *Nishikawa v. Dulles*, 356 U.S. 129 (1968), in which the Court held that Congress could not deprive someone of his citizenship for serving in the Japanese army in wartime. Five years later in the companion cases of *Kennedy v. Mendoza-Martinez*, 372 U.S. 144 (1963), and *Rusk v. Cort*, 369 U.S. 367 (1962), the Court overturned legislation that would strip citizenship from someone who sought to evade the draft by fleeing to a foreign country (*Mendoza-Martinez*) or remaining in a foreign country (*Cort*). And in *Schneider v. Rusk* 377 U.S. 163 (1964), the Court held that a naturalized American could not be deprived of his or her citizenship by returning to live in the country of their birth.

intelligence briefing from George Tenet. This was scheduled for thirty minutes, but often went on for an hour. Then the threat matrix with Robert Mueller and the FBI took up another half hour and sometimes more. For Bush it was chain of command. He was commander in chief, and frequently spoke of himself as such in the third person.[39] Unlike his father and Bill Clinton, Bush did not discuss the nuances of policy with his cabinet secretaries at great length. It was up or down, yes or no, and he made the decisions.

This lack of concern for complexities led to mistakes. Among the most serious was his decision on November 13 to try those captured in the war on terror by military commissions rather than in a court of law. Bush signed a hastily written executive order to that effect prepared by the White House staff just before boarding Marine One on the first leg of a flight to Texas where he was planning to host Vladimir Putin at the ranch.[40] The Criminal Division of the Department of Justice was not consulted, Powell and Rice were blindsided, and America's allies were appalled. Bush, in his single-minded approach to the war against terror, made the decision with little reflection and had no second thoughts. As he told reporters shortly afterward, "It's the absolute right thing to do. We're fighting a war against the most evil kind of people. And I need to have that extraordinary option at my fingertips. It's in our national security interest we have a military tribunal available."[41]

Bush's executive order on the trial of detainees is important not only for the legal and constitutional issues involved, but for what it said about the president's decision-making style. Under the order, the president assumed the authority to designate any person who was not an American citizen as an enemy combatant who could be tried by military authority. The accused would have no right to remain silent, classified information could be withheld from the defendant, and the traditional rules of evidence would not apply. As the order put it, "It is not practicable to apply in military commissions under this order the principles of law and rules of evidence generally recognized in the trial of criminal cases in the United States district courts."[42] Proceedings would be closed, coerced testimony was admissible, conviction required only a two-thirds vote of the members of the commission, and defendants could be sentenced to death. There was no appeal to the federal courts.

The public outcry was immediate—and not only from the libertarian fringe. William Safire, writing in *The New York Times*, castigated what he called Bush's seizure of dictatorial power.

> Intimidated by terrorists and inflamed by a passion for rough justice, we are letting George W. Bush get away with the replacement of the American rule of law with military kangaroo courts.
>
> No longer does the judicial branch and an independent jury stand between the government and the accused. In lieu of those checks and balances central to our legal system, non-citizens now face an executive that is now investigator, prosecutor, judge, jury, and jailer or executioner.[43]

The International Committee of the Red Cross observed that if the United States was making "war," then the prisoners it takes should be considered prisoners of war "until the individual can be shown by a competent judicial tribunal to be a terrorist."[44] The professional military were aghast. Rear Admiral Donald Guter, the Navy's judge advocate general, said, "We were marginalized. We were warning them we had this long tradition of military justice, and we didn't want to tarnish it. They didn't want to hear it." Major General Thomas Romig, the Army's judge advocate general, was equally critical. "The United States was going to be perceived as unfair," he warned, "because it [the military commissions] were unnecessarily archaic."[45]*

The decision to try suspected terrorists by military commission rather than in a court of law or by court-martial under the Uniform

---

* Perhaps the most severe criticism was provided by Marine Major Dan Mori, who defended one of the first detainees at Guantánamo. "I hope we are not confusing military justice with these 'military commissions,'" said Mori. "This is a political process set up by the civilian leadership. It's inept, incompetent, and improper. The administration clearly didn't know anything about military law or the laws of war. . . . The fundamental problem is that the rules were constructed by people with a vested interest in conviction." Jane Mayer, *The Dark Side: The Inside Story of How the War on Terror Turned into a War on American Ideals* (New York: Doubleday, 2008), 89.

Code of Military Justice (UCMJ) was one of the most serious errors Bush made, and reflected his impulsive style of decision making. This was a command decision, everyone fell into line, and the nuances and ramifications were largely ignored.

The idea of trying captured enemy combatants and suspected terrorists by military commission originated with Vice President Cheney and his staff. In mid-October, when it became obvious that provisions needed to be made for handling captured fighters from al Qaeda and the Taliban, Secretary of State Powell formed an interagency working group under Pierre-Richard Prosper, the State Department's ambassador-at-large for war crimes. Prosper had won the world's first conviction for genocide before the International Criminal Tribunal for actions in Rwanda, and was well acquainted with the issue. The group he assembled included lawyers from the Justice Department, the military, and the NSC, and was slowly working its way through a host of complicated issues. The lawyers from Justice pressed for trying terrorist suspects in the regular criminal courts as was done in Europe and as the United States had done after the 1993 World Trade Center bombing. The military lawyers argued for courts-martial under the Uniform Code of Military Justice, and a third option involved multinational tribunals patterned on the Nuremberg war crimes trials. Each of these options brought a raft of problems, and Prosper's task force was wrestling with them.

Cheney and his legal staff became impatient with Prosper's approach. "The interagency task force was constipated," said one Cheney aide.[46] Rather than contribute to the interagency task force, Cheney decided to preempt the process. He instructed his staff to prepare an executive order for the president to sign that would provide for the trial of suspected terrorists by military commissions. This would avoid the constitutional and legal problems that civilian trials would entail, as well as the procedural guarantees of the UCMJ and the Geneva Conventions. Prosper and the interagency task force were not informed. As another of Cheney's aides said, it would be constructive to show the bureaucrats that the president could act "without their blessing—and without the interminable process that goes along with getting their blessing."[47]

The military commissions established in Cheney's proposal were patterned after the seven-man military commission Franklin Roosevelt had convened in 1942 to try eight Nazi saboteurs who had been landed on American shores by a German submarine. The eight were convicted, sentenced to death, and the Supreme Court, meeting in the dark days of World War II, upheld their convictions. The case was *ex parte Quirin*, the Court was unanimous, and its decision had never been reversed.[48] Cheney and his legal staff believed they had the answer.

On Tuesday, November 6, Cheney and Bush were having their regular weekly lunch in the president's private dining room down the corridor from the Oval Office. Midway through the meal Cheney gave Bush the draft order for military commissions. "This is something my people have been working on," said the vice president. "I think it deserves serious consideration."

Bush read the brief document and returned it to Cheney. "This is good," he said. "Let's keep going on this." The president asked no questions.

"Do you want to bring it to the NSC?" asked Cheney.

Bush said no. "Let's just keep this thing moving." Referring the matter to the National Security Council would simply delay things.[49]

Later that day John Yoo provided the White House with a thirty-five-page opinion from the Office of Legal Counsel confirming that the president had "inherent authority" as commander in chief to establish military commissions and that it was not necessary to consult Congress or the federal courts. Yoo also dismissed international law, suggesting that the president was not bound by it. "The President may choose to enforce these standards as a matter of policy, but they are not 'law' that limits the President as Commander in Chief." Most tellingly, Yoo concluded that terror suspects were not automatically entitled to "receive the protections of the Geneva Conventions or the rights that the laws of war accord to lawful combatants."[50] The Office of Legal Counsel had provided the White House with what it wanted to hear.

A slight problem arose when Attorney General Ashcroft found out about the draft order. Ashcroft was incensed that as the nation's chief law enforcement officer he had not been consulted. Ashcroft met with

Cheney in the White House on Saturday morning, November 10, and according to those present it devolved into a shouting match. Ashcroft was primarily concerned that the order gave the Defense Department, not the Department of Justice, the authority to decide which terrorists would be tried by military commissions. It was a turf battle. The attorney general did not raise issues of constitutionality, the applicability of the Geneva Conventions, or how the commissions would operate.

After the meeting, Andrew Card reported Ashcroft's outburst to Bush. The issue was whether the Pentagon or the Justice Department would decide which detainee could be tried. The president thought about it for a moment and then resolved the issue. He was the commander in chief. He would decide who would be tried before the commissions. "I'll do it," Bush told Card.[51] Cheney was advised and the order was rewritten to give the president the authority to decide which terrorists were to be brought before the commissions.

At lunch on Tuesday, November 13, Cheney presented the revised four-page order to Bush. The State Department, the NSC, and the Defense Department had not been consulted, and the Department of Justice's contribution was limited to Ashcroft's turf battle on Saturday. Bush read the document quickly and told Cheney, "That's it. Ready to go."

Bush was leaving shortly for the ranch, and Cheney rushed to put the order in final form for the president's signature. When the formal order was completed, deputy White House counsel Bradford Berenson and deputy staff director Stuart Bowen rushed it to the Oval Office. Marine One was idling on the South Lawn.

"Mr. President, here's a document that requires your signature before you leave," said Bowen. "It's the military order authorizing the secretary of defense to establish military commissions."[52]

Bush scanned the order briefly, took a Sharpie from his coat pocket, and signed it. He then walked toward the door and the waiting helicopter. Less than one hour after the luncheon with Cheney, the military commissions order became the law of the land.

Colin Powell learned of the decision watching CNN that evening. "What the hell happened?" he asked.[53] Condoleezza Rice was equally incensed. "The interagency process exists so that the President gets a comprehensive look at the potential impact of his decisions," said Rice. Cheney had short-circuited the process, but in so doing he had Bush's approval every step of the way. "When I learned what had happened," Rice wrote in her memoirs, "I went to see the President. 'If this happens again . . . I will have to resign.'"[54] According to Rice, Bush apologized, but the damage had been done.

The president and Laura departed the White House at 3:05 that afternoon en route to Crawford. It would be Bush's first visit to the ranch since 9/11, and he was looking forward to hosting Vladimir Putin. "We're going to be riding John Deere Gators," Bush told reporters upon his arrival in Waco. "They are a little more compassionate than some horses."[55]* That morning before leaving, Bush and Putin had met for two hours in the Oval Office. It was Putin's first visit to the White House, and the fourth meeting between the two heads of state. "It's a new day in the relationship," said Bush. "When we were both growing up it was one based upon hostility, mistrust, and anger. And now it's the exact opposite. We're finding ways to find areas to work together for the benefit of both countries."[56]

One of those areas was the reduction of nuclear weapons. "I told President Putin that our Government was going to reduce our nuclear arsenal to between 1,700 and 2,000 warheads over the next decade. He is going to make a similar declaration." This was a major breakthrough. Under the Strategic Arms Reduction Treaty (START) negotiated by the first President Bush and Mikhail Gorbachev in 1991, each nation was allowed six thousand warheads. Bush was announcing what amounted to a two-thirds reduction. He said they were also working to reduce nuclear proliferation. "This is an incredibly important issue, to make sure that arms and potential weapons of mass destruction do not end up in the hands of people who will be totally irresponsible."[57]

Putin, who flew first to Houston, arrived at the ranch the next afternoon. It was raining heavily. "Any time it rains in Texas, it enhances the dinner,"[58] Bush joked with reporters. Laura had arranged the decora-

---

* A John Deere Gator is an open, four-wheel-drive, crossover vehicle.

tions for the evening and strung lights through the branches of the live oaks. The dinner had a western theme with tables set up in the house dogtrot—the open hallway between the two wings. The guests ate catfish and cornbread, followed by mesquite-grilled beef tenderloin. "I've never been to the home of another world leader," said Putin toasting his host, "but it's hugely symbolic to me and my country that it's the home of the president of the United States. The United States is fortunate at such a critical time to have a man of such character at its helm."[59]

The following morning, Bush invited Putin to attend his daily briefing from the CIA, and then escorted him to Crawford High School, where they answered students' questions. The mood was jovial. "I told President Putin he was welcome to come back next August," said Bush. "He said, 'Fine, maybe you would like to go to Siberia in the winter.'"*

The students had been primed, and their questions were good. One asked Bush whether he had come to any conclusion about deploying a national missile defense system.

"Are you with the national press corps," quipped the president. He then went on to answer:

> This is an area we've had a lot of discussions about. As you might re-
> member, in the presidential campaign I said I felt the ABM Treaty
> signed in 1972 is outdated. . . . And I made this very clear to the Pres-
> ident [Putin]. He understands our position that it is in our Nation's
> interest and, I think, in his nation's interest, to determine whether or
> not we can be able to deploy defensive systems to prevent people who
> might have weapons of mass destruction from hurting us or holding us
> hostage. He'll be glad to give you his position. We have a difference of
> opinion. But the great thing about our relationship is, our relationship

---

* At the end of the meeting with the students, Putin gave his version of the conversation. "On our way here, the President invited me to come here when it's plus-40 Celsius, more than 110, and he invited me to join the plus-40 club who jog when it is 110 and more. In our country, there are regions where people live where the temperatures were minus-50 Celsius for two weeks running. My promise is I will not terrorize your President with such low temperatures." *Public Papers of the Presidents, 2 George W. Bush, 2001,* "Question and Answer Session at Crawford High School," November 15, 2001, 1418.

is strong enough to endure this difference of opinion. And that's the positive development.[60]

Putin's visit offered a brief respite from the war on terror. But Bush's mind was set, and he had Saddam Hussein fixed in his sights. When he returned to the ranch for the Christmas holidays, he invited General Tommy Franks to come to Crawford on December 28 to provide an update on plans to invade Iraq. The president sent Air Force One to fetch Franks, who arrived at the ranch shortly after eight in the morning. They went immediately to a double-wide trailer that had been converted into a secure communications center. Bush sat at the head of an oak table and Franks at his right, facing a large plasma television screen at the end of the room. Bush flicked it on and the screen opened to a series of rectangles showing the members of the NSC. Cheney was at his home in Jackson Hole, Wyoming; Rumsfeld was at his home in Taos; while Powell, Rice, Tenet, Andy Card, and General Richard Myers were in the White House Situation Room.

After a brief report from Franks on the situation in Afghanistan, the president turned to Iraq. Franks briefly sketched the military's current plan, which was basically Desert Storm II and had not been updated since 1998. This involved an assault force of 400,000 men assembled over a six-month period. Franks pointed out that the Iraqi armed forces had shrunk from one million men to about 350,000 since the first Gulf War, with significantly less armor and artillery.

Cheney was first off the mark. "Does that mean the Iraqi army is only half as effective?" he asked Franks.

"Sir, smaller does not necessarily mean weaker," Franks replied. "The Republican Guard has dropped from ten divisions to six, but those units are well manned and well armed. Four of them are heavy divisions equipped with upgraded T-72 tanks."

"What do you think of the existing plan, Tommy?" Bush asked.

"Mr. President, it's outdated. Aside from the long buildup required, American weaponry is enormously more effective than it was a decade ago." Franks then went on to present what he called a new Commander's Concept. "Please note that regime change and WMD removal are the working assumptions of this concept." According to Franks, "there was a murmur of approval around the loop." He then laid out a four-phase operation, the fourth phase of which—post-hostility operations—would last years, not months. And there were three options: Robust, Reduced, and Unilateral. These depended on the degree of cooperation from the countries in the region. "We could begin ground operations with as few as one hundred thousand troops, and continue to build our force levels as long as necessary to ensure success."

"Tommy," said Bush when Franks finished, "heck of a job. Keep working on this concept. It's headed in the right direction." The president paused for a moment, and then concluded the meeting. "Protecting the security of the United States is my responsibility. We cannot allow weapons of mass destruction to fall into the hands of terrorists. I will not allow that to happen."[61] To those attending, it was clear that Bush was focused on Iraq.

Bush's public saber rattling began with his State of the Union message to Congress on January 29, 2002. The Taliban had been subdued, there had been no further terrorist incidents, and the president's public approval rating stood at a whopping 84 percent. Bush told his staff the public had to be readied for the next phase of the war on terror.[62] And the staff complied. "Provide a justification for a war," chief White House speechwriter Michael Gerson instructed David Frum.[63] As Frum wrote later, "Bush needed something to assert, something that made clear that September 11 and Saddam Hussein were linked after all and that for the safety of the world, Saddam Hussein must be defeated rather than deterred."[64]

Bush's 2002 State of the Union address may be the most memorable speech of his presidency. The House chamber was packed, newly chosen Afghan leader Hamid Karzai was in the gallery, and Bush pulled out all the stops. "Our war against terror is only beginning," said the president.

> North Korea is a regime arming with missiles and weapons of mass destruction. . . . Iran aggressively pursues these weapons and exports terror. . . . Iraq continues to flaunt its hostility toward America and

support terror. . . . States like these, and their terrorist allies, constitute
an axis of evil, arming to threaten the peace of the world.* By seeking
weapons of mass destruction, these regimes pose a grave and continuing danger. . . . The price of indifference would be catastrophic.

It was clear, or should have been clear, to all listening that Bush was
raising the ante.

Time is not on our side. I will not wait on events while dangers gather.
I will not stand by as peril draws closer and closer. The United States
of America will not permit the world's most dangerous regimes to
threaten us with the world's most destructive weapons. Our war on terror is well begun, but it is only begun. . . . We can't stop short. History
has called America and our allies to action, and it is both our responsibility and our privilege to fight freedom's fight.[65]

For better or worse, George W. Bush was leading the nation to war
against Iraq. In the hothouse climate of the president's certitude, doubt
withered away.[66]

---

* Frum's original draft referred to an axis of hatred. Gerson, an evangelical Christian, substi-
tuted evil for hatred to better comply with Bush's theological orientation.

CHAPTER TWELVE

The Torture Trail

Who authorized putting him on pain medication?

George W. Bush

April 2002

George W. Bush was regarded by many of his classmates at Harvard Business School as "dynamically ignorant." He was energetic, but ill-informed, untutored, and unread. And he flaunted it. Little had changed. His 2002 State of the Union and the phrase "axis of evil" reeked of arrogance and obtuseness. Once again, Bush had spoken without weighing the consequences.

French foreign minister Hubert Védrine called the speech "simplistic." Bush, he said, "had reduced all the world's problems to the struggle against terror."[1] German foreign minister Joschka Fischer, a longtime friend of the United States, warned that alliance partners were not satellites—a telling Cold War metaphor. In a long interview with the influential German daily *Die Welt*, Fischer said that "all the European foreign ministers felt that way."[2] Christopher Patten, Great Britain's delegate to the European Union and former head of the Conservative Party, quoted Winston Churchill, a secular deity in the Bush White House: "In working with Allies, it sometimes happens they have ideas of their own."[3] Even Condoleezza Rice, who had seen the phrase "axis of evil" in earlier speech drafts and had not objected, later recognized the error. In her memoirs she wrote, "The phrase helped brand the Bush administration as radical and bellicose, given to hot rhetoric and a preference for military force."[4]

Bush was unrepentant. "No backing off," he told White House spokesman Ari Fleischer. Speaking three days afterward to reporters, Bush said, "All three countries I mentioned are now on notice that we intend to take their development of weapons of mass destruction very seriously."[5] For many Americans, Bush's certitude was comforting. For much of the world, it was another example of the president's unthinking ignorance.

Bush's decision to imprison al Qaeda and Taliban detainees at Guantánamo Naval Base in Cuba, his order to deny them prisoner of war status and the protection of the Geneva Conventions, as well as the use of "enhanced interrogation techniques"—a euphemism for torture—also reflected the president's mind-set. In a war of good versus evil, no holds were barred. These were not decisions made by Cheney, Tenet, Rumsfeld, or the military. They were direct decisions of the president. Bush often talked about what he called the five levels of government. He was level one, Cheney was level two, the cabinet level three, and then there were levels four and five—the subcabinet figures who liked to talk to reporters and take credit or spread blame for the actions of their superiors.[6] For Bush, efficient government was all about the chain of command. As America's commander in chief, he made the decisions and expected his subordinates to fall into line. No conference committees, no "process decisions," as Bush derisively called them. It was straight up or down and he was calling the shots.

Bush's decision to imprison al Qaeda and Taliban detainees at Guantánamo followed his presidential order of November 13 to try terrorist suspects by military commissions. Under that order, the prisoners were to be "detained at an appropriate location designated by the Secretary of Defense outside or within the United States."[7] The official designation would be made by Rumsfeld. But the final decision where to hold the detainees would be made by the president. And indeed, Rumsfeld was not enthusiastic about becoming the jailer for the president's war on terror. "I questioned whether our military was the appropriate institution to hold captured enemy combatants." This was an unconventional conflict against an amorphous enemy with no finite duration. "Our armed forces did not have experience or established procedures for dealing with captured terrorists. . . . I preferred to hand over major detention responsibilities to another department or agency. Suffice it to say that there were no departments of the government eagerly coming forward to assist." [8]

The criteria Bush specified narrowed the choices. The site should be safe from terrorist attacks, controlled by the United States but not on U.S. soil so as to minimize possible legal challenges, and with a suitable infrastructure to support the prisoners. After reviewing the options, Rumsfeld recommended Guantánamo, located at the southeastern tip of Cuba. It was, in his phraseology, "the least worse place." [9] But as he told the senior military leadership in the Pentagon, the facility "would probably be the source of more trouble and more criticism than any of us can foresee." [10] In late December, Rice transmitted Rumsfeld's recommendation to Bush. "Mr. President," she said, "Don recommends that we put the detainees in Guantánamo Bay, and we support that." [11] Bush agreed. His decision was announced by the Pentagon on December 27.

The U.S. naval station at Guantánamo was in some respects an idyllic tropical setting. In 1903, following the Spanish-American War, the United States secured a lease from the new Cuban government on forty-five square miles of land and water to establish a naval base. In 1934, Washington and Havana agreed by treaty that the lease, for which the United States paid Cuba $4,085 a year, could be terminated only by mutual consent. The Castro government had repeatedly called the 1934 treaty invalid and had sought to close the base, but since the United States did not recognize the Castro regime, Washington ignored those efforts.* Today, the seventeen-mile perimeter of the base adjacent to Cuba is a fortified no-man's-land often referred to as the "Cactus Cur-

---

* The Cuban government has not cashed a lease check from the United States since 1959.

Detainees at their arrival at Guantánamo Bay Naval Base.

tain." The Clinton administration temporarily housed some forty thousand Cuban and Haitian "boat people" there to preclude them from claiming political asylum on U.S. soil. But the prison facilities were minimal, and when the decision to place the detainees there was announced, Navy engineers worked around the clock to build temporary barbed wire stockades.

The first twenty detainees arrived from Afghanistan on January 11, 2002. Dressed in orange jumpsuits and wearing blacked-out goggles and heavy ear muffs, the prisoners were chained at the wrists and ankles. Photographs released by the Defense Department's public affairs office showed them kneeling on the gravel of their cages while Marine guards patrolled nearby. Ultimately some six hundred detainees would be housed at the base. New facilities were constructed and living conditions were improved, but the legal status of those imprisoned there became a major issue. Amnesty International called Guantánamo "the gulag of our times." [12]

Once again George W. Bush bears personal responsibility. By defining the struggle against terrorism as an unlimited war between good and evil, he stacked the deck. Fighters in the cause of evil deserved no wartime recognition. The detainees were placed at Guantánamo so as to deny them access to the American judicial system and the rule of law. Then, on January 18, Bush decided they were also not entitled to prisoner of war status or the protections of the Geneva Conventions.* They were "unlawful combatants who do not have any rights under the Geneva Conventions."[13]

Bush's decision was supported by the Office of Legal Counsel. Once again, the OLC provided the president with what he wanted to hear. According to the OLC, al Qaeda was a stateless entity with no rights under international law, and the Taliban represented a "failed state" whose treaty rights Bush could suspend pending the restoration of a legitimate government. "To the extent that the Taliban militia was more akin to a non-governmental organization that used military force to pursue its religious and political ideology than a functioning government, its members would be on the same legal footing as al Qaeda." As had become habit for the Office of Legal Counsel, the president's status as commander in chief placed him above the law, whether that law was constitutional, statutory, or a treaty to which the country was a party.

> We conclude that customary international law, whatever its source and
> content, does not bind the President, or restrict the actions of the United

---

* The Geneva Conventions, drafted in Geneva in 1949 and ratified by 195 countries—including the United States and Afghanistan—are four separate conventions providing detailed rules governing different classes of protected persons. Geneva I protects the sick and wounded on land; Geneva II protects the sick, wounded, and shipwrecked at sea; Geneva III protects prisoners of war; and Geneva IV protects civilians. There is no gap between Conventions III and IV. According to the International Committee of the Red Cross, "Every person in enemy hands must have some status in international law: he is either prisoner of war and, as such, is covered by the Third Convention, or a civilian covered by the Fourth Convention. . . . There is no intermediate status; nobody in enemy hands can fall outside the law."

In addition, all persons detained during an armed conflict are protected by Common Article 3 (in all four conventions). This article bans all "violence to life and persons," "cruel treatment and torture," "outrages to personal dignity," and "humiliating and degrading treatment."

Article 5 of the POW convention requires that "any doubt" concerning a person's status be resolved by a "competent tribunal" and that all "detainees enjoy POW status until a tribunal determines otherwise."

All four Geneva Conventions were ratified unanimously by the United States Senate, July 6, 1955. See 6 *United States Treaties and Other International Acts Series* 3115 (Convention I); 3219 (Convention II); 3517 (Convention III); and 3317 (Convention IV).

States Military, because it does not constitute federal law recognized under the Supremacy Clause of the Constitution.[14]

Rumsfeld immediately transmitted the president's decision to General Myers for distribution to all military commanders. According to the text, "The United States has determined that Al Qaeda and Taliban individuals under the control of the Department of Defense are not entitled to prisoner of war status for purposes of the Geneva Conventions of 1949."[15] The military and the State Department objected immediately. Bush had made his decision as commander in chief without consulting those most directly involved. The issue was never discussed by the National Security Council. The secretary of state and the chairman of the Joint Chiefs of Staff were not asked for their opinion. Bush had been given advisory opinions by the White House counsel and the OLC, and he saw no reason to consult further. It was another unfortunate example of the personalization of presidential power under George W. Bush.

The military were particularly upset. The Geneva Conventions were an everyday aspect of a soldier's life. As General Myers noted, "The Geneva Conventions were a fundamental part of our military culture and every military member was trained on them. In addition, our military personnel were trained to treat detainees and prisoners humanely. Objectively applying the conventions was important to our self-image. It would continue to make the U.S. armed forces the 'gold standard' of the world's militaries and would increase our ability to get other countries to work with us."[16]* In Afghanistan, General Tommy Franks specifically ordered his troops to comply with the Geneva Conventions, and all captured al Qaeda and Taliban prisoners were

---

* The official directive on the law of war issued by the chairman of the Joint Chiefs of Staff states, "The Armed Forces of the United States will comply with the law of war during all armed conflicts, however such conflicts are characterized." The Geneva Conventions are an integral component of the law of war. Department of Defense Directive 5100.77, DoD Law of War Program, Chairman of the Joint Chiefs Instruction, in "The Schlesinger Report: Final Report of the Independent Panel to Review DoD Detention Operations," reprinted in *The Torture Papers: The Road to Abu Ghraib*, Karen J. Greenberg and Joshua L. Dratel, eds. (New York: Cambridge University Press, 2005), 908–75.

accorded POW status until an individual hearing could be held to determine their status.[17]

Franks's order was fully consistent with America's military heritage. In the Revolutionary War, George Washington insisted that the Continental Army treat prisoners "with humanity, and let them have no reason to complain of us copying the brutal manner of the British Army." Washington's orders bolstered the morale of his troops and encouraged desertion among British and Hessian soldiers. As David Hackett Fischer observed in his Pulitzer Prize–winning history, *Washington's Crossing*, Washington's orders "reversed the momentum of the war. They improvised a new way of war that grew into an American tradition."[18]

During the Civil War, Professor Francis Lieber of Columbia University prepared General Orders 100 for the United States Army, the first comprehensive attempt to codify the rules of land warfare, including the treatment of prisoners. Known universally as the Lieber Code, and subsequently adopted in principle by all European nations, General Orders 100 made it clear that fighting for a cause was not a crime, and that captured combatants must be spared "intentional suffering or indignity," "cruel imprisonment, want of food, mutilation, death, or any other barbarity." And most importantly, "Military necessity does not admit of cruelty . . . nor of torture to extort confessions."[19]

After World War I, the United States played a prominent role in drafting the predecessor to the current Geneva Conventions, the 1929 Geneva Convention Relative to the Treatment of Prisoners of War. During World War II, the United States complied explicitly with the 1929 Convention. According to Army Field Manual 30–15 (1943):

> In accordance with the Geneva Convention of 1929, no coercion may be used on prisoners or other personnel to obtain information relative to the state of their army or country; and prisoners or others who refuse to answer may not be threatened, insulted, or exposed to unpleasant or disadvantageous treatment of any kind.[20]

This was true for all prisoners in American captivity, despite the fact that Japan was not a signatory to the 1929 Convention, and its treatment of Allied prisoners often entailed heartless brutality.

Similarly in Korea, General Douglas MacArthur ordered the United Nations forces under his command "to abide by the humanitarian principles of the 1949 Geneva Conventions, particularly the Common Article Three [which prohibits "cruel treatment, torture, outrages to human dignity, and humiliating and degrading treatments"]." [21] In 1955, the Eisenhower administration pressed the Senate to ratify the 1949 Geneva Conventions. "Our nation has everything to gain and nothing to lose by being a party to the Conventions now before the Senate and by encouraging their most widespread adoption," said Secretary of State John Foster Dulles.[22] On July 6, 1955, the Senate ratified the Geneva Conventions by a vote of 77–0.

In Vietnam, the United States adhered rigorously to the Geneva Conventions even though the Vietcong often wore civilian clothes and Hanoi routinely tortured and mistreated captured American pilots.* The same was true in the Gulf War, and the interventions in Grenada, Panama, Somalia, Bosnia, Haiti, and Kosovo.[23] Even more pertinent perhaps was the War Crimes Act that Congress enacted in 1996, which made grave breaches of the Geneva Conventions a federal crime punishable by life imprisonment or death. (Grave breaches include "willful killing, torture or inhuman treatment, including biological experiments, willfully causing great suffering or serious injury to body or health.") The act was supported strongly by the military, who argued that it "would set a high standard for others to follow." [24]

---

* Upon arrival in Vietnam, American troops were given small indoctrination cards entitled, "The Enemy in Your Hands," and containing the following instructions:

AS A MEMBER OF THE US MILITARY FORCES, YOU WILL COMPLY WITH THE GENEVA CONVENTIONS OF 1949 TO WHICH YOUR COUNTRY ADHERES.
YOU CANNOT AND MUST NOT
MISTREAT YOUR PRISONER
HUMILIATE OR DEGRADE HIM
TAKE ANY OF HIS PERSONAL EFFECTS WHICH DO NOT HAVE SIGNIFICANT MILITARY VALUE
REFUSE HIM MEDICAL TREATMENT IF REQUIRED AND AVAILABLE
ALWAYS TREAT YOUR PRISONER HUMANELY

Major General George S. Prugh, *Law of War: Vietnam, 1964–1973* (Washington, D.C.: Department of the Army, 1975), 143.

Given this history, it is not surprising that General Myers opposed Bush's decision. He immediately made his objections known to Rumsfeld, and called for a meeting of the NSC to review the issue. As he told undersecretary of defense Douglas Feith, "I want you to know I feel very strongly about this. And if Rumsfeld doesn't defend the Geneva Conventions, I'll contradict him in front of the president." [25]

Secretary of State Colin Powell was equally flabbergasted. Like General Myers, he was appalled that the United States would reject the Geneva Conventions. And like Myers, he had had no advance notice despite the fact that the Conventions are formal U.S. treaty obligations clearly under the purview of the State Department. Powell was on a diplomatic mission to South Asia when he learned of the decision, and assumed the White House had taken advantage of his absence from Washington to make the change. "Bush has these cowboy characteristics," Powell later told his deputy Richard Armitage, "and these swaggering bits of his self-image often lead to decisions like this." [26]

Powell, who was shuttling between New Delhi and Islamabad, immediately called Condoleezza Rice. Powell was hot under the collar. "You'd better hold on," he warned Rice. "I think we are making some mistakes here." [27] Powell told Rice that he wanted to meet with the president as soon as he returned to Washington. He rarely went to the Oval Office to argue about policy differences and strongly believed such matters should be discussed in meetings of the principals. That was the system he was accustomed to under Reagan, the elder Bush, and Clinton. But the president's decision to scuttle the Geneva Conventions without consulting the State Department was too much to accept quietly.

Powell met with Bush in the Oval Office on the morning of January 21. He urged the president to rethink the issue. The meeting was tense. None of Bush's closest advisers could ever remember the president changing a decision once he made it. [28] And Bush made it clear to Powell that he did not like being second-guessed. But this time Powell persisted. American soldiers were at risk, he told the president. The military depended on the Geneva Conventions for their own safety, and a unilateral rejection by the United States would have grave implications for future conflicts. "I said I wanted everybody covered, whether

Taliban, al Qaeda, or whatever," Powell recalled, "and I think the case was there for that." [29]

Powell said he understood the need to gather intelligence, and pointed out that the Geneva Conventions permitted the interrogation of detainees. They just could not be treated in an inhumane or degrading manner. Wearing his diplomatic hat, Powell told Bush his decision would provoke widespread condemnation among America's allies, discourage other nations from cooperating in the war against terror, and encourage some countries to avoid compliance with the Conventions by looking for "technical loopholes." [30] If any detainees were excluded from the protection of the Geneva Conventions it should be "on a case by case basis following individual hearings as provided for in Article 5 of the POW [Third] Convention." [31]

Powell was strongly supported by the State Department. William Howard Taft IV, the department's chief legal officer and great-grandson of the twenty-seventh president, filed a forty-page rebuttal to the Office of Legal Counsel's finding. The OLC's factual assumptions and legal analysis were both "seriously flawed," said Taft. The concept of a failed state, which was central to the OLC finding, "had no legal basis," and the Geneva Conventions did not permit one signatory to unilaterally suspend the rights of another. Taft pointed out that under the Supremacy Clause of the Constitution, "Treaties to which the United States is a party are the law of the land," and the president had no authority to suspend them.* After an analysis of the conflict in Afghanistan, Taft concluded that the Taliban had a legitimate claim to POW status until individual hearings could be held to determine otherwise, and the members of al Qaeda, while not entitled to POW status, were clearly covered by the Fourth Geneva Convention. Finally, to emphasize the seriousness of the issue, Taft noted that a repudia-

---

* The second paragraph of Article Six of the Constitution, often referred to as the Supremacy Clause, reads as follows:

> This Constitution, and all the Laws of the United States which shall be made in Pursuance thereof; *and all Treaties made, or which shall be made, under the Authority of the United States*, shall be the Supreme Law of the Land, and the Judges of every State shall be bound thereby, anything in the Constitution or Laws of any State to the Contrary notwithstanding. (Emphasis added.)

tion of the Geneva Conventions could constitute a "grave breach" that "raises a risk of future criminal prosecution for U.S. civilian and military leadership and their advisers." [32]

Bush now recognized that he had a problem. Confronted with General Myers's request and Colin Powell's persistence, the president scheduled a National Security Council meeting to review the issue the following Monday, January 28. But he was visibly annoyed. As commander in chief he had decided the issue and that should have been sufficient.

To prepare Bush for the NSC discussion, Alberto Gonzales, the White House counsel, wrote a brief four-page memorandum.* "The arguments for reconsideration and reversal are unpersuasive," said Gonzales.[33] "The Office of Legal Counsel has ruled that as a matter of international and domestic law the Geneva Convention does not apply to the conflict with al Qaeda, and it has also held that you have the authority to determine that it does not apply to the Taliban. *The OLC's interpretation of this legal issue is definitive.*" (Emphasis added.)

> As you have said, the war against terrorism is a new kind of war. . . .
> This new paradigm renders obsolete Geneva's strict limitation on questioning of enemy prisoners and renders quaint some of its provisions requiring that captured enemy be afforded such things as commissary privileges, athletic uniforms, and scientific instruments.[34]

Gonzales's memorandum was written on Friday, January 25. The following morning *The Washington Times*, a reliable champion of the administration published by South Korean Reverend Sun Myung Moon, carried a lengthy front-page article restating Gonzales's arguments and mocking Colin Powell. According to the paper, "Administration sources last night expressed anger at Mr. Powell, whom they accused of bowing to pressure from the political left." [35] When he read

---

* There is considerable tangential evidence to suggest that the memorandum was drafted by members of Vice President Cheney's staff. See Karen DeYoung, *Soldier: The Life of Colin Powell* (New York: Alfred A. Knopf, 2006), 370; Jane Mayer, *The Dark Side: The Inside Story of How the War on Terror Turned into a War on American Ideals* (New York: Doubleday, 2008), 124; Kurt Eichenwald, *500 Days: Secrets and Lies in the Terror Wars* (New York: Touchstone, 2012), 224–25.

the article, Powell erupted. The article was not "put in *The Washington Times* to have a balanced view of the issues," he later told Karen DeYoung. "It was in *The Washington Times* in order to try to screw me." Whoever leaked it "wanted to blow me out of the water."[36] Bush did not leak the article and later that day he called Powell in an effort to calm him down. But it is clear that the article was inspired by a leak from the Bush White House, and, despite the call, Bush was not particularly upset by the development.

The NSC meeting on Monday was a formal ritual—a staged setting to allow Powell and Myers to vent their dissatisfaction, with the outcome preordained. Powell argued that to reject the Geneva Conventions was not only legally indefensible, but would "reverse over a century of U.S. policy and practice." Why refuse to invoke the Conventions? Powell asked. Even if the detainees are not deemed to be prisoners of war under the definition of Geneva III, they were entitled to an individual hearing. "We have an image to uphold around the world," said the secretary of state. "If we don't do this, it will make it much more difficult for us to try and encourage other countries to treat people humanely."[37]

General Myers followed. "Colin Powell and I were on the same page," Myers wrote in his memoirs, "but not everyone in the Situation Room was convinced." Myers argued that it was a moral and military question. The United States must apply the Geneva Conventions to the Taliban, said Myers. "This was consistent with our military culture and training; and we wanted our own people to receive fair treatment, should they fall into enemy hands. But the basic issue was respect for the Geneva Conventions."[38]

When Myers finished, Rumsfeld spoke. He agreed with Myers and said it would be "highly dangerous if countries make application of the Geneva Conventions hinge on subjective or moral judgments as to the quality or decency of the enemy's government."[39]

Attorney General Ashcroft restated the Justice Department position. The Geneva Conventions did not apply. Afghanistan was a failed state and the Taliban prisoners had fought for an illegitimate government. In Ashcroft's view, the Taliban and al Qaeda were a "coalition of pirates."[40]

Cheney spoke last. "This is a matter of law," said the vice president. The Taliban and al Qaeda were not lawful combatants. "We all agree that they should be treated humanely, but we don't want to tie our hands. We need to preserve flexibility. And under the law we can do that." [41]

After forty-five minutes, Bush terminated the discussion. He had heard enough. He said he would consider what had been said and announce his decision shortly. Speaking to reporters later that afternoon in the Rose Garden, Bush said he was reconsidering his decision whether al Qaeda and Taliban prisoners held at Guantánamo should be protected under the Geneva Conventions, but he quickly added they were "killers who would not be granted the status of prisoners of war." [42]

Bush announced his decision on February 7. There was a veneer of compliance with the Geneva Conventions, but the holding remained the same. Indeed, in some respects, Bush's order of February 7 was much more far reaching. "I didn't agree with it," said Powell. "The president knows I didn't agree with it. And it's been causing us problems ever since." [43]

Entitled "Humane Treatment of al Qaeda and Taliban Detainees," Bush's order stripped them of Geneva coverage. "The war against terror ushers in a new paradigm," said the president (repeating the phraseology of Gonzales's memo) and "this new paradigm requires new thinking in the law of war." [44] Bush said that under his authority as the nation's commander in chief and chief executive, he had determined that none of the provisions of the Geneva Conventions applied to al Qaeda "because, among other reasons, al Qaeda is not a High Contracting Party to Geneva." He said that Geneva applied to the Taliban, but "based on the facts supplied by the Department of Defense and the recommendation of the Department of Justice, *I determine that the Taliban detainees are unlawful combatants and, therefore, do not qualify as prisoners of war under Article 4 of Geneva.*" (Emphasis added.) Said more simply, there would be no change. None of the detainees would be covered by Geneva.

Most tellingly, Bush went on to explicitly exclude protection under Common Article 3 of all Geneva Conventions, "because, among other reasons, the relevant conflicts are international in scope and Common Article 3 applies only to 'armed conflicts not of an international character.'" The exclusion of Article 3 was intended to shield members of his administration from prosecution under the War Crimes Act, which explicitly defined the term "war crime" to include "a violation of Common Article 3."[45]

To soften the impact of his order, Bush said that the detainees should "be treated humanely, and *to the extent appropriate and consistent with military necessity*, in a manner consistent with the principles of Geneva." (Emphasis added.) The concept of "military necessity" had been rejected by the United States ever since the Lieber Code in 1863. It was a loophole large enough to encompass virtually any abuse. Bush's order of February 7 was not only eyewash, it was a permit to use whatever tools the military (or the CIA) felt necessary to extract information—a broad presidential directive for humane treatment combined with an unrestrained authority to make exceptions. It was a giant step on the torture trail, and George W. Bush bears personal responsibility for ordering it.

Bush's February 7 decision was greeted abroad with consternation and concern. Post-9/11 sympathy for the United States eroded further. In Europe, the criticism was harsh. It seemed another example of Bush's disregard for the rule of law. Denying the detainees POW status and trying them by military commissions without the normal procedural safeguards seemed akin to the administration's withdrawal from the International Criminal Court treaty, the abrogation of the Anti-Ballistic Missile Treaty with the Russians, and its rejection of the Kyoto Protocol aimed at lowering greenhouse gas emissions. While Colin Powell attributed the decision to Bush's cowboy instinct, numerous writers have suggested that the president, who was notorious for not reading much or paying attention to details, was led to these decisions by his staff. The evidence suggests that Powell was correct. George W. Bush saw himself as the nation's commander in chief, and he reveled in making decisions like this.

Bush's decision to override Common Article 3 remained in effect for four years. But on June 29, 2006, the United States Supreme Court, in a sweeping decision, ruled that the president, even in war, was bound by American laws and treaties, including the Geneva Conventions.* The Court held that the administration could not move forward with military commissions without specific congressional authorization, and more ominously held that Common Article 3 of the Geneva Conventions applied to all al Qaeda and Taliban detainees. Said Justice John Paul Stevens for the Court, "the scope and application of the Article must be as wide as possible."[46] This meant that the 1996 War Crimes Act would be applicable to the administration's treatment of detainees, and sent chills through the White House, the Defense Department, and the CIA. The decision was a stunning rebuke to George W. Bush and his extreme theory of executive power.

Bush's personalization of the war on terror combined with his macho assertiveness as the nation's commander in chief were a recipe for disaster. Rather than adhere to constitutional values, treaty obligations, and the rule of law, he chose to rule by presidential prerogative. The president's command of the military and intelligence agencies, his ability to act in secret, and his power to self-interpret the legal limits on his authority thanks to a compliant Office of Legal Counsel, created extraordinary opportunities for abuse. This was particularly true in the military and in the intelligence agencies, where questioning a presidential decision could be interpreted as insubordination.

Closely related to Bush's decision to evade the requirements of the Geneva Conventions was his decision to authorize "extraordinary renditions"—the transfer of prisoners for further interrogation to the custody of security services in countries like Egypt, Jordan, Morocco, and Syria with well-deserved reputations for torture. "We don't kick the shit out of them," a CIA official involved in the process told Dana Priest of *The Washington Post*. "We send them to other countries so they can kick the shit out of them."[47] Like Bush's decision on the Geneva Conventions, this decision was in direct violation of American treaty

---

* *Hamdan v. Rumsfeld*, 548 U.S. 577 (2006). The decision was 5–3, with Chief Justice Roberts not participating.

obligations. Article 3 of the Convention Against Torture, to which the United States is a party, states unequivocally:

> No Party shall expel, return or extradite a person to another state where there are substantial grounds for believing that he would be in danger of being subjected to torture.[48]*

Historically, the United States had been in the forefront of those nations seeking to rid the world of torture. In 1948, Eleanor Roosevelt, as the first head of the United Nations Commission on Human Rights, took the lead in drafting the Universal Declaration of Human Rights, Article 5 of which proclaimed, "No one shall be subjected to torture or to cruel, inhumane or degrading treatment or punishment."[49] Thirty years later, the International Covenant on Civil and Political Rights, which the United States played a major role in developing, made it equally explicit that "No one shall be subjected to torture or to cruel, inhumane, or degrading punishment."[50] But the most compelling prohibition is that contained in the Convention Against Torture, which President Reagan signed in April 1988. "The United States participated actively and effectively in the negotiation of the Convention," said Reagan when he sent the Convention to the Senate for ratification. "It makes a significant step in the development during this century of international measures against torture and other inhumane treatment or punishment. Ratification of the Convention by the United States will clearly express United States opposition to torture, an abhorrent practice unfortunately still prevalent in the world today."[51]

The Senate approved the Convention on October 27, 1990, by unanimous vote. There was little debate. Senator Claiborne Pell (D., R.I.), chairman of the Senate Foreign Relations Committee, called the Convention "a major step forward in the international community's cam-

---

* Article 4 of the Convention Against Torture is equally compelling: "Each State Party shall ensure that all acts of torture are offenses under its criminal law. The same apply to any attempt to commit torture *and to an act by any person which constitutes complicity or participation in torture.* (Emphasis added.)

paign to combat terror because it makes torture a criminally punishable offense."[52] Senator Jesse Helms (R., N.C.), the ranking Republican on the committee, called the Convention "the expression of the revulsion of civilized nations against torture."[53] Senator Patrick Moynihan (D., N.Y.) said, "Our diplomats labored to make this Convention more than just words on paper. They made its obligations concrete, meaningful, and as never before, enforceable. I believe that this is an important step in the continuing battle to end man's inhumanity to man."[54]

Formal ratification of the Convention came on October 21, 1994, following the passage of the necessary implementing legislation to make the treaty enforceable as domestic law in the United States. That enforceability was further strengthened in 1998 with the passage of the Foreign Affairs Reform and Restructuring Act, which announced that as a matter of policy the United States would not "expel, extradite, or otherwise effect the involuntary removal of any person to a country where there are substantial grounds for believing that the person would be in danger of being subjected to torture, *regardless of whether the person is physically present in the United States.*" (Emphasis added.)[55]

George W. Bush not only turned his back on the long heritage of American opposition to torture, he actually ordered and approved the violation of explicit statutory and treaty commitments. Once again he was aided by the Office of Legal Counsel, which on March 13, 2002, provided a memorandum upholding the president's action. Said the OLC, despite treaty requirements and congressional legislation, "we conclude that the President has plenary constitutional authority, as the Commander in Chief, to transfer such individuals who are captured and held outside the United States to the control of another country."[56] The opinion of the OLC was definitive. Bush believed he was home free. He could authorize the "extraordinary rendition" of detainees without being concerned about the statutory and treaty commitments to the contrary.

Once again, the president's decision failed to pass the test of time. Just as the Supreme Court had overruled his decision to bypass Common Article 3 of the Geneva Conventions, the Office of Legal Counsel would overrule its earlier holding pertaining to extraordinary renditions. On January 15, 2009, as Bush's presidency was winding down, the OLC issued a memorandum for the files explicitly rejecting the holding of the March 13, 2002, memorandum as well as those in eight other memoranda that were issued during the period 2001–2003. "Mindful of this extraordinary historical context, we nevertheless believe it appropriate and necessary to confirm that the following propositions contained in the opinions identified below do not currently reflect, and have not for some years reflected, the views of the OLC."

The March 13, 2002, memorandum was the first one cited, and the OLC specifically took issue with the assertion that "the power to dispose of the liberty of individuals captured and brought under the control of the United States armed forces during military operations remains in the hands of the President alone."*

Bush's decision on extraordinary rendition pales beside his support for torture itself—"enhanced interrogation techniques," as the White House called it. The president's overriding concern was to prevent another terrorist attack like 9/11. The eight o'clock briefing by George Tenet followed by the threat matrix with Robert Mueller shaped his day. "First comes offense, then defense," Bush joked one morning as the two made their switch-off.[57] As Bush saw it, obtaining information was essential. How that information was obtained was unimportant. "My most solemn responsibility as president was to protect the country," Bush wrote in his memoirs. "I approved the use of the interrogation techniques."[58]

The issue arose in April 2002 following the capture of Abu Zubaydah, a trusted lieutenant of Osama bin Laden and the first "high-value detainee" to fall into American hands. Zubaydah had been badly wounded during his capture and was under heavy sedation. When Bush asked Tenet what information they were getting from Zubaydah, Tenet replied that he was still too groggy from painkillers to talk coherently.

---

* Department of Justice, Office of Legal Counsel, "Memorandum for the Files," January 15, 2009. The memorandum was signed by Steven G. Bradbury, principal deputy assistant attorney general.

"Who authorized putting him on pain medication?" the president asked.[59]

As Zubaydah recovered, he began answering questions but the CIA believed he was holding back. "George Tenet told me interrogators believed Zubaydah had more information to reveal," said Bush. "If he was hiding something more, what could it be? Zubaydah was our best lead to avoid another catastrophic attack."[60]

Tenet asked the president's permission to use more aggressive techniques, including waterboarding. Bush agreed. As the president saw it, "Had I not authorized waterboarding on senior al Qaeda leaders, I would have had to accept a greater risk that the country would be attacked."[61]* Once again, Bush was moving in direct violation of America's commitment under the Convention Against Torture, Article 2 of which states:

> No exceptional circumstances whatever, whether a state of war or a threat of war, internal political instability or any other public emergency, may be invoked as a justification of torture.

Ultimately, Zubaydah would be waterboarded eighty-three times. Whether any information of value was derived will long be debated. What is clear is that Bush's decision was another giant step on the torture trail in total disregard for treaty and statutory restrictions to the contrary. And it was not just waterboarding. The interrogation practices Bush approved including stripping detainees of their clothing, forcing them to stand for long hours, sleep deprivation, rectal feeding,

---

* During the Philippine Insurrection in 1900, the United States Army court-martialed Major Edwin F. Glenn for using waterboarding (the water cure) on captured Philippine fighters. Glenn defended his approach as an urgent military necessity and said that desperate times called for desperate measures. The court rejected that argument. "The necessity defense fails completely, inasmuch as it is attempted to establish the principle that a belligerent who is at war with a savage or semi-civilized enemy may conduct his operations in violation of the rules of civilized war. This no modern state will admit for an instant." Since that date, the Army has always considered waterboarding a form of torture that is clearly prohibited. Court-Martial of Major Edwin F. Glenn, April 1902, reprinted in *The Laws of War: A Documentary History*, Leon Friedman, ed. (New York: Random House, 1972), 814–19.

cramped confinement, slapping them in the face and elsewhere, requiring them to assume stress positions for extended periods, and mock executions such as making a prisoner believe he is being buried alive.*

Once again the Office of Legal Counsel provided Bush with what he needed. "At my direction, Department of Justice and CIA lawyers conducted a careful legal review," said Bush. "They concluded that the enhanced interrogation program complied with the Constitution and all applicable laws, including those that ban torture." [62] The August 1, 2002, Interrogation Memorandum provided by the Office of Legal Counsel may be the most egregious example on record of bending the law to suit the president's purpose.† In the words of former *New York Times* legal affairs columnist Anthony Lewis, the memo reads "like the advice of a mob lawyer to a mafia don on how to skirt the law and stay out of prison." [63]

The memorandum redefined torture so as to make it all but impossible to commit. Interrogators could inflict pain up to a level just shy of that "associated with serious physical injury so severe that death, organ failure, or serious impairment of bodily functions will likely result." Mental suffering, to be considered torture, must "result in significant psychological harm of significant duration, *e.g.*, lasting months or years." In addition, the memo was studded with loopholes. Even if an act fell under the definition of torture, the interrogator would be guilty only if torture had been his "precise objective. If causing such harm is not the objective, he lacks the requisite specific intent" to be found guilty of torture. Finally and perhaps most important, the president, as commander in chief, could order any interrogation technique he deemed necessary.

---

* For a discussion of the enhanced interrogation techniques approved and the justification presented by the Office of Legal Counsel, see the Memorandum on Interrogation of al Qaeda Operative [Zubaydah] the OLC sent to John Rizzo, chief legal officer at the CIA, August 1, 2002. Reprinted in David Cole, *The Torture Memos: Rationalizing the Unthinkable* (New York: New Press, 2009), 106–27. Also see *The CIA Torture Report: Unclassified*, issued by the Senate Select Committee on Intelligence, December 3, 2014.

† Entitled "Standards of Conduct for Interrogation under 18 U.S.C. § 2340–2340A," the memorandum is reprinted in *The Torture Papers: The Road to Abu Ghraib,* Karen J. Greenberg and Joshua L. Dratel, eds. (New York: Cambridge University Press, 2005), 172–222.

Any effort by Congress to regulate the interrogation of battle-field combatants would violate the Constitution's sole vesting of the Commander-in-Chief authority in the president. There can be little doubt that intelligence operations, such as the detention and interrogation of enemy combatants and leaders, are both necessary and proper for the effective conduct of military campaigns. Indeed such operations may be of more importance in a war with an international terrorist organization. . . . Just as statutes that order the president to conduct warfare in a certain manner or for specific goals would be unconstitutional, *so too are laws that seek to prevent the President from gaining the intelligence he believes necessary to prevent attacks upon the United States.*[64]* (Emphasis added.)

Bush was now proceeding without restraint along the torture trail. The brutal treatment of detainees, the fiasco that would happen at Abu Ghraib, and the further destruction of America's international reputation for fairness and justice were in no small measure attributable to the president's decisions to jettison the Geneva Conventions, the Convention Against Torture, and the legislation implementing them. In the summer of 2002, at a prison whose location has never been disclosed, Abu Zubaydah became the first person ever to be waterboarded at the command of the president of the United States.[65] The full extent of the CIA's torture program would eventually be detailed in the final report of the Senate Select Committee on Intelligence released by Senator Dianne Feinstein in January 2015.[66]

---

* Following the debacle at Abu Ghraib in 2004, the memorandum was officially withdrawn by the Office of Legal Counsel. See Memorandum for James B. Comey, Deputy Attorney General, "re: Legal Standards Applicable Under 18 U.S.C. § 2340–2340A," December 30, 2004. Both the August 1, 2002, and the December 30, 2004, memoranda are reprinted in David Cole, *The Torture Memos: Rationalizing the Unthinkable* (New York: New Press, 2009), 41–100, 128–51.

CHAPTER THIRTEEN

Waging Aggressive War: The Prelude

We cannot wait for the final proof, the smoking gun
that could come in the form of a mushroom cloud.

George W. Bush

October 7, 2002

Bush remained focused on Iraq. And the planning for the invasion continued. "The lesson of 9/11 was that if we waited for a danger to fully materialize, we would have waited too long," said the president. "I reached a decision; we would confront the threat from Iraq, one way or another."[1] Two days after his State of the Union address, Bush hosted German chancellor Gerhard Schroeder in the White House. He informed Schroeder he was deadly serious about dealing with Iraq. "I told the German chancellor, the military option was my last choice, but I would use it if necessary."[2]

Public opinion was overwhelmingly behind Bush. Shortly before his speech to Congress, a CNN/*USA Today*/Gallup poll showed 77 percent of Americans favored military action against Iraq. Only 17 percent opposed. Another poll found 72 percent believed Saddam Hussein was "personally involved in the September 11 attacks."[3]

The day after the president's discussion with Schroeder, Rumsfeld met with Tommy Franks at the Pentagon to review plans for the attack. CENTCOM had christened the invasion Generated Start, an allusion to the belief that the United States would rapidly generate the forces required to topple Saddam. Under the plan, the president would give CENTCOM thirty days advance notice that he had decided to attack, then Franks would require an additional sixty days to deploy the necessary forces. The attack would be launched with three divisions, and ultimately build to six, or roughly 275,000 troops. Unlike Desert Storm, the attack would begin while troops were still streaming into Kuwait, and the air and ground attacks could begin simultaneously. As Franks saw it, that would catch the Iraqis off balance. Rumsfeld pressed Franks to reduce the timeline, but was otherwise satisfied.

"Remember, there is a fine balance between thorough preparation and triggering a war," the secretary cautioned Franks. "And the president has not decided to go to war."

"I understand, Mr. Secretary," Franks replied.[4]

Technically, Rumsfeld was correct. The order had not been given. But it was clear that it was coming. Earlier in the week, Rumsfeld had asked Franks by videoconference whether the campaign could begin in April 2002. Franks believed the secretary was reflecting White House pressure, and warned that because of the summer heat he did not want to start fighting on the ground in Iraq after April 1. Given the necessary time for preparation, that would put off an attack until autumn at the earliest.[5]

Secretary of State Powell, who normally avoided harsh rhetoric, joined in the public attack on Iraq. As Powell saw it, there was always the possibility that Saddam would become sufficiently rattled to agree to new U.N. weapons inspections.[6] Speaking to the House International Relations Committee on February 6, Powell said the president was examining the full range of options of how to deal with Iraq. "We still have a policy of regime change . . . and regime change is something the United States might have to do alone. How to do it? I would not like to go into any of the details of the options that are being looked at, but it is the most serious assessment of options that one might imagine."[7]

The day after Powell spoke, Bush met with Franks at the White

House. This time it was a briefing for the full National Security Council. After discussing the situation in Afghanistan, Franks laid out the plan for Generated Start he had discussed with Rumsfeld. The principal problem was timing. Franks said that because of their training cycle, the combat readiness of the Iraqi military fluctuated throughout the year. From May through late September the Iraqi army was at full strength and most formidable. In October and November, the units were winding down, and from December through February combat strength was at its lowest. Weather was also a problem. In midsummer, heat could reach 130 degrees. Sandstorms in early spring posed another obstacle. "Therefore, Mr. President, optimum operational timing would be from December to mid-March."

"Would CENTCOM have to wait until December to initiate action?" asked Rumsfeld.

"Mr. Secretary," Franks replied, "we can deploy and execute at any time the President orders us to do so."

"Could we go earlier, if necessary," Bush asked.

"We could, Mr. President, but it would be ugly. A longer, sequential operation with higher casualties on both sides. And probably with considerably more destruction of Iraqi infrastructure than if we conduct the kind of operation I have described."

Bush seemed satisfied. After an hour and ten minutes he adjourned the meeting. "Great job, Tommy. Keep it up. We will do what we have to do to protect America."[8]

Bush met with Franks again on March 3. CENTCOM had moved ahead with the planning for Generated Start, but there were a number of issues on which Franks needed help. A "coalition of the willing" depended on allied support. Franks required access to foreign bases and overflight permission from various nations in the Middle East. After listening to Franks's presentation, Bush decided to dispatch Cheney to the region to organize support. "I was scheduled to visit twelve countries in ten days," said Cheney. "I planned to discuss the next phases in the War on Terror, which meant talking about the threat posed by Saddam Hussein."[9]

Bush's selection of Cheney for the mission was understandable.

As former secretary of defense and later head of Halliburton, Cheney knew the region and had contact with various heads of state. In addition, those who met with him understood that in talking to the vice president, they would be speaking directly to the White House. Three days later, Franks met with Cheney to explain what he needed to execute Generated Start. The list had been worked out with Rumsfeld, and varied from country to country. Cheney would not engage in detailed negotiations but would simply establish a basis for Franks's people to work from later on.

Cheney departed Washington on March 10, and stopped briefly in London to consult with Prime Minister Tony Blair. "I told Blair that the president had not decided about military action against Saddam Hussein and he wanted to consult with our allies as the process unfolded. I also told the prime minister, as I did other leaders on the trip, that if war came, there should be no doubt about the outcome. The president wanted it to be absolutely clear that if he decided to go to war, we would finish the job." [10]

From London, Cheney went to Jordan, where his reception was chilly. "Iraq's neighbors were keenly aware of the threat Saddam posed," said Cheney, "but they were apprehensive about the consequences of military action." [11] In Egypt, President Hosni Mubarak was more supportive, as were the Gulf States, and Kuwait. Saudi Arabia, however, proved complicated. Crown Prince Abdullah was skeptical of Bush's plan and Cheney extended to him an invitation from the president to visit the ranch in Crawford, where Rumsfeld and General Franks would provide a briefing about U.S. plans for military action. Abdullah accepted, and a visit was arranged for April 25. Turkey was even more difficult. The country was a member of NATO and the Turks had supported the Afghan operation wholeheartedly. But Iraq was different. Turkish public opinion was overwhelmingly against another war with Iraq, and the government feared the possible breakup of Iraq and the establishment of an independent Kurdish state, which would encourage secessionist tendencies among Turkish Kurds. Cheney also riled the government when he sought a private meeting with the chief of the Turkish general staff. Later he wrote, "I think we failed to understand the magnitude of the shift that was taking place in Turkey. The sense of an Islamic government taking power in one of America's most important NATO allies was in a sense obscured because of all the other challenges we faced."[12]

Cheney returned to Washington late on March 20, and had an early breakfast with the president the next morning. Shortly after eight they took questions from reporters in the Oval Office. When asked about Iraq, Cheney said he had gone to the Middle East to consult, and to report back to the president. "And that's exactly what I have done."

Bush followed up. "This is an administration that when we say we are going to do something we mean it; that we are resolved to fight the war on terror; that this isn't a short term strategy for us; that we understand history has called us into action; and we are not going to miss this opportunity to make the world more peaceful and more free. And the vice president delivered that message."[13]

Franks and his CENTCOM staff continued to plan for the invasion. "This is fucking serious," Franks told his subordinate commanders. "You know, if you guys think this is not going to happen, you're wrong."[14] Franks, as CENTCOM commander, did not report to the Joint Chiefs of Staff but directly to the secretary of defense. The chain of command went from Bush to Rumsfeld to Franks. The Joint Chiefs were charged by statute with the responsibility to recruit, train, and equip their particular service. But under the Goldwater-Nichols Defense Reorganization Act, which Congress enacted in 1986, they were no longer in the chain of command.[15]* The chairman of the Joint Chiefs was designated as the senior military adviser to the president, but was not given any command responsibility. The intent of the act was to reinforce the power of theater commanders, improve interservice cooperation, and emphasize civilian control. Bush to Rumsfeld to Franks. That greatly simplified planning for the attack on Iraq. It also provided

---

*   Relations between Franks and the Joint Chiefs were often testy. In an earlier meeting on Afghanistan, he called them "Title Ten Motherfuckers," only partly in jest. The reference is to Title 10 of the United States Code, which lays out the Chiefs' military responsibilities. Tommy Franks, with Malcolm McConnell, *American Soldier* (New York: HarperCollins, 2004), 277.

Rumsfeld's key aides—Paul Wolfowitz, Douglas Feith, and Stephen Cambone—considerably more authority than they would have enjoyed if the invasion had been run by the Joint Chiefs.

The command arrangement specified in Goldwater-Nichols stood in direct contrast to the American command structure in World War II, Korea, and Vietnam. In the Second World War, General George Marshall, as Army chief of staff, commanded Eisenhower in Europe and MacArthur in the Pacific. During the Korean War, General Omar Bradley as chairman of the Joint Chiefs commanded the generals in Korea, and during the Vietnam conflict the Joint Chiefs were in command as well. That was no longer the case. The most senior officers in each service were shunted to the sidelines.

In early April, Bush and Laura hosted Tony and Cherie Blair at the ranch in Crawford. A British reporter accompanying Blair interviewed Bush for a program that would be aired in the United Kingdom but not in the United States. "Have you made up your mind that Iraq must be attacked?" the reporter asked.

"I've made up my mind that Saddam needs to go," said Bush. "That's about all I'm willing to share with you."

"And you would take action to make sure that happens?"

"That's what I just said. The policy of my Government is that he goes."

"So you're going to go after him?"

"As I told you, the policy of my Government is that Saddam Hussein not be in power."

"And how are you going to achieve this, Mr. President?"

"Wait and see," Bush replied.[16]

Two days later, meeting the press with Tony Blair at the conclusion of Blair's visit, Bush repeated the message. "I explained to the Prime Minister that the policy of my government is the removal of Saddam Hussein, and that all options are on the table. . . . Obviously, the Prime Minister is somebody who understands this clearly, and that's why I appreciate dealing with him on the issue."[17]

And the planning continued. Franks met with the president at Camp David on Saturday, April 20, and again on May 11. At the

Bush and Putin signing the Strategic Arms Reduction Treaty, May 2002.

May 11 meeting, Bush stressed that it was important to portray the invasion as the liberation of Iraq. The president told Franks that messages should be prepared stressing that American forces were moving to free the Iraqis from Saddam's tyranny and were not interested in becoming occupiers.[18] Franks, for his part, produced an alternative war plan that he called Running Start. Unlike Generated Start, the plan could be activated almost immediately with an extended air war followed by an invasion with as little as a two-thousand-man Marine expeditionary unit and two Army brigades. Franks left both plans on the table, and Bush did not commit himself. The president said he was worried that Saddam might turn the defense of Baghdad into a Mesopotamian Stalingrad, but Franks assured him that would not be a problem.[19]

In late May the president headed to Moscow to sign the treaty he had negotiated with Vladimir Putin to reduce each country's arsenal of nuclear warheads. On the way to Moscow he stopped briefly in Berlin to meet once more with Chancellor Gerhard Schroeder. At a joint press conference, Bush was asked about Iraq. "I told the chancellor that *I have no war plans on my desk,* which is the truth."[20] On his return from Moscow, the president stopped in Paris to confer with Jacques Chirac. Again he was asked about Iraq, and he used the same formulation. "The stated policy of my Government is that we have a regime change.

And as I told President Chirac, *I have no war plans on my desk.* And I will continue to consult closely with him. We do view Saddam Hussein as a serious threat to stability and peace." [21] In a literal sense, Bush was correct. Franks had not put the invasion plans on his desk. But that was true only in the literal sense.

In Moscow, Bush and Putin signed the Strategic Arms Reduction Treaty, dramatically reducing the number of nuclear warheads each country maintained to between 1,700 and 2,200. "President Putin and I today ended a long chapter of confrontation and opened up an entirely new relationship between our two countries," said the president. "This treaty liquidates the Cold War legacy of nuclear hostility between our countries." [22] Bush's visit to Russia was a return engagement following Putin's visit to the ranch in Crawford. "Our relations with Russia were calm, even warm," Condoleezza Rice remembered.[23] Putin and his wife, Lyudmila, hosted the president and Laura at their home in St. Petersburg, and then escorted the presidential party on a "white night" excursion on the Neva River at midnight, the setting brightly lit by the long northern sunlight.

Back in the United States, the president went to West Point on June 1 to deliver the commencement address. Bush's speech at West Point, together with his axis of evil State of the Union address, made it abundantly clear he was leading the nation to war. The purpose of the speech, according to chief speechwriter Michael Gerson, was to change the country's mind-set, and Gerson believed it was the most important speech he had ever worked on.[24] Addressing the almost one thousand graduating cadets and their families, Bush said, "The war on terror will not be won on the defensive. We must take the battle to the enemy, disrupt his plans and confront the worst threats before they emerge. In the world we have entered, the only path to safety is the path of action."

The president was explicit. "If we wait for threats to fully materialize, we will have waited too long.

> Our security will require all Americans to be forward looking and resolute, *to be ready for preemptive action* when necessary to defend our liberty and to defend our lives.

"We are in a conflict between good and evil," said Bush, "and America will call evil by its name. By confronting evil and lawless regimes, we do not create a problem; we reveal a problem. And we will lead the world in opposing it." [25]

Writing in *The New York Times*, Elisabeth Bumiller said the president's West Point address was "a toughly worded speech that seemed aimed at preparing Americans for a potential war with Iraq." [26] White House deputy press secretary Scott McClellan agreed. "Just as we'd sought to shape and manipulate sources of public opinion to our advantage to pass tax cuts and education reform, we were setting the conditions for selling military confrontation with Iraq." [27]

The doctrine of preemption became the hallmark of Bush's policy. He met with Franks again on June 19 to review plans for both Generated Start and Running Start. Franks now had two Army brigades on the ground in Kuwait and planned to add two more by early July. That, plus a Marine expeditionary unit nearby, gave him a force of fifty thousand men—enough to commence the attack if the president wished to do so. Franks said he could move another two divisions into Kuwait within two or three weeks. Bush expressed his appreciation. He urged Franks and Rumsfeld to insure the necessary logistical support was available to support an attack. Franks perceived a sense of urgency. Meeting with his subordinate commanders at Ramstein in Germany on June 27 and 28, he instructed them to focus on Running Start. [28]

Colin Powell and the State Department were left out of the initial planning. In early July, Richard Haass, the director of policy planning at the State Department and an old friend of Condoleezza Rice from the George H. W. Bush NSC, raised the question of Iraq with her during one of their regular White House meetings. "I told her I worried Iraq would come to dominate the administration's foreign policy and that it would prove far more difficult to do and yield far less in the way of dividends than its advocates advertised.

"She brushed away my concerns, saying the president had made up his mind." According to Haass, he emerged from the meeting "quite taken aback." It was clear that war was in the offing. [29]

The British government came to the same conclusion. In a secret Downing Street memo recording a July 23 meeting between Tony Blair, the chief of British intelligence ("C"), foreign secretary Jack Straw, the minister of defense Geoff Hoon, and attorney general Lord Peter Goldsmith, "C" reported on his recent visit to Washington.* "C," later identified as Sir Richard Dearlove, said "there was a perceptible shift in the attitude," within the Bush administration. "Military action was now seen as inevitable. Bush wanted to remove Saddam through military action, justified by the conjunction of terrorism and WMD. But the intelligence and facts were being fixed around the policy," said Sir Richard. "The NSC had no patience with the UN route, and no enthusiasm for publishing material on the Iraqi regime's record." And according to Dearlove, "There was little discussion of the aftermath of military action."

Jack Straw, the British foreign secretary, said, "It seemed clear that Bush had made up his mind to take military action, even if the timing was not yet decided. But the case was thin. Saddam was not threatening his neighbors, and his WMD capability was less than that of Libya, North Korea or Iran. We should work up a plan for an ultimatum to Saddam to allow back the UN weapons inspectors. This would also help with the legal justification for the use of force." [30]

Tony Blair added his own opinion. "It's worse than you think," he told his colleagues. "I actually believe in doing this." [31]

Franks briefed Bush and the members of the NSC again on August 5. This time he added a third possibility his planners had developed. Franks called it Hybrid, a combination of Running Start and Generated Start that would provide greater flexibility.† Time would be

---

* "This record is extremely sensitive," said the memo. "No further copies should be made." Nevertheless, the memorandum was leaked to British journalist Michael Smith, who published it in *The Sunday Times*, May 1, 2005. Its authenticity has never been seriously questioned.

† The Hybrid plan had four phases. Phase One consisted of a sixteen-day period to establish an air bridge and transport the necessary forces to the region. Phase Two consisted of sixteen days of air attacks and Special Forces operations. Phase Three involved 125 days of combat operations, followed by Phase Four, stability operations of an unknown duration. Tommy Franks, with Malcolm McConnell, *American Soldier* (New York: HarperCollins, 2004), 389–93.

optimized, said Franks, and "a rapid force deployment enhances our military capability on Iraq's borders, and also assists in placing diplomatic pressure on Saddam's regime." All three plans anticipated a maximum of 250,000 troops. "At some point we can begin drawing down our force, [but] our exit strategy will be tied to effective governance by Iraqis, not a timeline."[32]

"We will want to get Iraqis in charge of Iraq as soon as possible," said Rumsfeld.[33]

"I like the concept," said Bush. The president then turned to postwar planning. "How would Iraqis react to an overthrow of Saddam Hussein by the American military?" he asked George Tenet. "Most Iraqis will rejoice when Saddam is gone," Tenet replied.[34] On that note the meeting ended. "President Bush thanked me warmly," said Franks. " 'See you soon' he said."[35]

Colin Powell said little at the meeting. He was increasingly uneasy with the planning for military action and requested a private session with the president. Bush invited Powell and Rice for dinner that evening in the White House family quarters. Afterward they adjourned to the Treaty Room for further discussion. It was Powell's longest meeting with the president since the inauguration. Bush listened attentively as Powell expressed his concerns. To invade Iraq would sap the energy from the larger war on terror and every other foreign policy priority. It risked destabilization in the Middle East, a possible spike in oil prices, and would dominate the remainder of the president's term.

"When you hit this thing," said Powell, "it's like a crystal glass. It's going to shatter. There will be no government. There will be civil disorder. You break it, you own it. . . . You'll have twenty-five million Iraqis standing around looking at each other."[36]

"Colin was more passionate than I had seen him at any NSC meeting," Bush recalled.[37] The president asked Powell what he would recommend. "We should take the problem to the United Nations," said the secretary of state. "Iraq is in violation of multiple UN resolutions. The UN is the legally aggrieved party. Even if the UN doesn't solve it, making the effort . . . gives you the ability to ask for allies or ask for help."[38]

After two hours the meeting broke up. Powell had been trying to warn the president of what could go wrong, but Bush showed little interest. Later he said, "My job is to secure America. And I believe that freedom is something people long for." Bush considered himself a strategist. Powell was talking tactics.[39]

Powell was not alone. Speaking on the CBS Sunday program *Face the Nation* on August 4, Senator Chuck Hagel, a distinguished Vietnam veteran who had helped the administration torpedo the Kyoto Protocol, questioned the wisdom of attacking Iraq preemptively. Hagel noted it was the thirty-eighth anniversary of the Gulf of Tonkin Resolution, which had given Lyndon Johnson open-ended authority to wage war in Vietnam. "We didn't ask any questions before we got into Vietnam," said Hagel. "That's why it is important to do so now."[40]

Hagel was followed on the program by Brent Scowcroft. Scowcroft warned that an invasion of Iraq "could turn the whole region into a cauldron. The president has announced that terrorism is our number one focus. Saddam's a problem, but he's not a problem because of terrorism." The only link between al Qaeda and Saddam, said Scowcroft, was that they shared "an intense dislike of the United States."[41]

Scowcroft followed up on August 15 with an op-ed in *The Wall Street Journal*. Entitled "Don't Attack Saddam," it buttressed the case against military action.

> The United States could certainly defeat the Iraqi military and destroy Saddam's regime. But it would not be a cakewalk. On the contrary, it undoubtedly would be very expensive—with serious consequences for the U.S. and global economy and could as well be bloody.
>
> Worse, there is a virtual consensus in the world against an attack on Iraq at this time. So long as that sentiment persists, it would require the U.S. to pursue a virtual go-it-alone strategy against Iraq, making any military operations correspondingly more difficult and expensive.[42]

Before publishing the article, Scowcroft had sent a copy to George H. W. Bush. He received no reply. To Scowcroft, that meant the former president had no objections and that it was all right to publish the article. Silence means consent.[43]

When Scowcroft's article appeared, George W. was at the ranch in Crawford. The president was furious. "He was pissed off and let everyone within shouting distance know it," said Dan Bartlett, who had replaced Karen Hughes as White House communications director.[44] The president made an immediate call to his father. "Son," the elder Bush replied, "Brent is a friend."[45] The point was that the former president was not going to reprimand his former NSC director. Dick Cheney, an old friend of Scowcroft, read the article as well and thought Brent was living in the past. "I found myself thinking that it reflected a pre-9/11 mindset, the worldview of a time before we had seen the devastation that terrorists armed with hijacked airplanes could cause."[46]

Scowcroft was unrepentant. The op-ed in *The Wall Street Journal* was no different from what he had said on television two weeks before. He didn't want to break with the administration, but as Rice wrote afterward, "the level of trust between the president and Brent plummeted until there was nothing left."[47]

The fact that the senior Bush was not in sympathy with his son's policy toward Iraq became abundantly clear ten days later when former secretary of state James Baker published an article on the op-ed page of *The New York Times* urging the administration to seek United Nations support. James Baker lived near the former president in Houston, saw him frequently, and had been a close friend for many years. His message to the younger Bush was clear. "Although the United States could certainly succeed, we should try our best not to have to do it alone, and the president should reject the advice of those who counsel doing so." In some respects, Baker was even more critical than Scowcroft had been. "The president should do his best to stop his advisers and their surrogates from playing out their differences publicly and try to get everyone on the same page."[48]

The United Nations now seemed key. For many months, Bush had been scheduled to address the opening session of the U.N. General Assembly in New York on September 12. Should he discuss Iraq? On August 16, from the ranch in Crawford, he convened a meeting of the National Security Council by teleconference to discuss the issue. Colin Powell repeated the arguments in favor, and to Powell's surprise everyone, including Cheney, agreed.[49] "Fine," said the president, "I'll do it." Later that day Bush called speechwriter Gerson at the White House. "We are going to do something a little different," said the president. "We're going to tell the UN that it's going to confront this problem or it's going to condemn itself to irrelevance."[50]

The administration was also shifting its rationale for attacking from regime change to removing weapons of mass destruction. On August 26, and with Bush's approval, Cheney delivered a fire-and-brimstone speech to the annual convention of the Veterans of Foreign Wars at the Opryland Hotel in Nashville. Regime change was not mentioned. Instead, Cheney focused on WMD.

> Simply stated, there is no doubt that Saddam Hussein now has weapons of mass destruction. There is no doubt he is amassing them to use against our friends, our allies, and against us.
>
> As President Bush has said, time is not on our side. Deliverable weapons of mass destruction in the hands of a terror network, or a murderous dictator, or the two working together, constitutes as grave a threat as can be imagined. The risks of inaction are far greater than the risk of action.

Just to be certain his message was clear, Cheney said "wars are never won on the defensive. We must take the battle to the enemy. We will take every step necessary to make sure our country is secure, and we will prevail."[51] As Bush had done at West Point, Cheney was advocating preemption.

Retired Marine General Anthony Zinni, who had been Franks's predecessor as commander of CENTCOM, was sitting beside Cheney on the rostrum that day in Nashville and almost fell off his chair. "In my time at CENTCOM, I watched the intelligence and never—not once—did it say 'He had WMD,'" said Zinni. Since retiring, General Zinni had retained all of his security clearances, was a regular consultant with the CIA on Iraq, had reviewed all the current intelligence, and had seen nothing to support Cheney's contention. "It was never, never, there," he said later. Zinni thought the administration was going to war without the evidence and that they did not realize what they were getting into.[52]*

George Tenet was equally surprised at Cheney's claim. "The speech went well beyond what our evidence would support," said the CIA director. Tenet wrote later that he thought the emphasis on WMD was an attempt by Cheney "to regain the momentum toward action against Iraq that had been stalled eleven days earlier by Scowcroft's op-ed piece."[53]

Tenet was correct. The momentum had stalled. A CNN/*USA Today*/Gallup poll published shortly after Scowcroft's article indicated that 58 percent of Americans thought Bush had not "done enough to explain why he might take action in Iraq."[54] Bush was concerned. On September 3, at the president's direction, chief of staff Andy Card formed what became known as the White House Iraq Group (WHIG), whose purpose was to promote the war. Composed of Card, Rice, Karl Rove, Stephen Hadley, Scooter Libby, communications chief Dan Bartlett, and Michael Gerson, the group met regularly in the Situation Room "to make clear what lies ahead"—in the words of Karl Rove.[55] WHIG was an exclusive White House operation. Bush was leading the country to war, and his senior staff helped pave the way. Neither the Defense Department nor the State Department was informed or consulted. Soon after WHIG was set up, the White House began stretching the case. Smoking guns became mushroom clouds. It was a sales campaign, Card told *The New York Times*. Why establish it now? "From a marketing point of view, you don't introduce new products in August."[56]

On September 4, Bush invited eighteen senior members of the House and Senate to the White House to consider action against Iraq. The president commenced the discussion by distributing a letter he had just written to House speaker Dennis Hastert. "Doing nothing in the face of a grave threat to the world is not an option," the president had written. "At an appropriate time and after consultations with the lead-

---

* At a meeting of senior defense officials from the United States, Britain, France, and Germany in Berlin on September 4 and 5, 2002, undersecretary of defense Douglas Feith told his counterparts that "war is not optional. At stake is the survival of the United States as an open and free society. So with regard to Iraq, the question of whether one can prove a connection between Iraq and the September 11th attack is not (repeat not) of the essence." George Tenet, *At the Center of the Storm: My Years at the CIA* (New York: HarperCollins, 2007), 310–11.

ership, I will seek congressional support for U.S. action to do whatever is necessary to deal with the threat posed by Saddam Hussein's regime."

"I am in the process of deciding how to proceed," the president wrote Hastert. No sentence better captures the personalization of presidential power that had taken place under Bush. "I am in the process of deciding how to proceed."[57] The commander in chief would decide, and he expected the country to follow. A mid-twentieth-century European dictator could have said the same. "I am in the process of deciding how to proceed *against Ethiopia*." Or "I am in the process of deciding how to proceed *against Finland*." Or perhaps, "I am in the process of deciding how to proceed *against Poland*." Bush was intent on launching an aggressive war against Iraq, and wanted Congress on board.

The reaction of the eighteen members was generally supportive, although most were surprised the president was moving so quickly. Senate majority leader Tom Daschle questioned why Bush was acting before the November election. House majority leader Dick Armey, a conservative Republican from Texas, was more critical. Armey remembered Lyndon Johnson, another president from Texas, and what a reckless war had done to the Great Society. "Mr. President," he said, "if you go in there, you're likely to be stuck in a quagmire that will endanger your domestic agenda for the rest of your presidency." Armey said later, "I was the skunk at the garden party."[58]

Cheney said it would be a good idea if Armey did not dissent from the president's position in public. Armey said he didn't realize the president had established a position. Bush then asked Armey if he would withhold any comment until he had the intelligence briefings and could understand how important it was to take action. Out of deference to the president, Armey agreed. "I won't speak publicly about this again until I am fully briefed," said the House majority leader. Later, Armey told Michael Isikoff of *Newsweek* he thought Bush and Cheney were gripped by a "he-man macho psychosis where they felt the need to go out and shoot somebody to show they were the tough guy on the block."[59]

When the meeting concluded, Bush called in the press. "We spent most of our time talking about a serious threat to the United States, a serious threat to the world, and that's Saddam Hussein," said the president. "One of the things I made very clear to the Members here is that doing nothing is not an option. . . . At the appropriate time, this administration will go to the Congress to seek approval for—necessary to deal with the threat."[60]

The administration's publicity campaign for the invasion of Iraq moved into high gear. On Sunday, September 8, *The New York Times* carried a lead front-page article, "U.S. Says Hussein Intensifies Quest for A-Bomb Parts." The story was studded with alarming details provided by the White House of Saddam's efforts to acquire aluminum tubes that could be used for centrifuges to enrich uranium. Unidentified "senior Bush officials" were quoted at length. One quote stands out. The administration was worried that "the first sign of a smoking gun might be a mushroom cloud." The phrase had been crafted by speechwriter Michael Gerson at the WHIG meeting three days before, and would become the battle cry of the administration.[61]

Cheney and Rice followed up on the Sunday morning talk shows. Appearing on NBC's *Meet the Press* with Tim Russert, Cheney pointed to the *Times* article as proof. "It's now public," said the vice president, "that Saddam has been seeking to acquire, and we have been able to intercept and prevent him from acquiring through this particular channel, the kinds of tubes that are necessary to build a centrifuge." Cheney told Russert that while "no decision has been made yet to launch a military operation, clearly we are contemplating that possibility."[62] Condoleezza Rice followed on CNN's *Late Edition*. She said there was "increasing evidence that Saddam continues his march toward weapons of mass destruction." Repeating Gerson's memorable phrase, Rice said "We don't want the smoking gun to be a mushroom cloud."[63]

As the first anniversary of 9/11 approached, the administration intensified its message. On September 10, Attorney General Ashcroft declared an orange terror alert, a chilling reminder of the dangers the country faced.* Then, on the anniversary of 9/11, Bush spoke to the

---

* The color-coded terrorism threat alert was established in Homeland Security Presidential Directive 3, issued by the White House on March 11, 2002. The threat potential was depicted in five colors: Red—severe; Orange—high; Yellow—elevated; Blue—guarded; and Green—low. Responsibility for managing the system was entrusted to the attorney general.

Bush speaking to United Nations General Assembly, September 12, 2002.

nation from Ellis Island, with the Statue of Liberty as a dramatic backdrop. "We will not allow any terrorist or tyrant to threaten civilization
with weapons of mass destruction," said the president.[64]

The high point of the campaign was Bush's speech to the United
Nations General Assembly the following day. The president spoke for
twenty-six minutes. He began by announcing that the United States
would resume membership in UNESCO—the United Nations Educational, Scientific, and Cultural Organization—and would "participate fully in its mission to advance human rights and tolerance and
learning." The president received a warm round of applause. He then
launched into an attack on Saddam Hussein and continued for the next
twenty-five minutes. The members of the General Assembly looked on
in silence. Not once during those twenty-five minutes was Bush interrupted for applause. It was abundantly clear that the General Assembly
was not in tune with the president's message. Bush said afterward, "It
was like speaking to a wax museum. No one moves."[65]

Bush was surprised. "For a guy who is used to clapping and cheering, dead silence is interesting."[66] He and Gerson had worked hard on
the speech, and there were numerous places where members could have
demonstrated their approval. They did not. It was a chilling reminder
that the United States was isolated when it came to dealing with Saddam.

Bush carefully laid out the White House message. Iraq was expanding its nuclear program, withholding information, and attempting to buy high-strength aluminum tubes to enrich uranium. "The conduct of the Iraqi regime is a threat to the authority of the United Nations and a threat to peace." Total silence.

"My nation will work with the UN Security Council to meet our common challenge. If Iraq's regime defies us again, the world must move deliberately, decisively to hold Iraq to account." Total silence.

"We will work with the UN Security Council for the necessary resolutions. But the purpose of the United States should not be doubted." Total silence.

"We cannot stand by and do nothing while dangers gather. We must stand up for our security and for the permanent rights and hopes of mankind. By heritage and by choice, the United States will make that stand."[67] Total silence.

The other nations of the world clearly were not ready to support an American attack on Iraq. On the one hand, the president was stunned. On the other, it confirmed his belief that the United Nations could not be relied on. "I'm a patient man," Bush told Karen DeYoung of *The Washington Post*. "I made the decision to go to the UN and therefore we are willing to work with the UN. But if they cannot bring themselves together to disarm Saddam Hussein, then we will lead a coalition to do just that."[68]

The president remained on the offensive. In the next five days he spoke publicly five times, and each time called on the U.N. to take action or face irrelevance. In his weekly radio address to the nation on September 14, Bush said, "Saddam Hussein's defiance has confronted the United Nations with a difficult and defining moment. . . . Will the United Nations serve the purposes of its founding or will it be irrelevant?"[69]

At a joint press conference with visiting Italian prime minister Silvio Berlusconi later that day:

> The UN will either be able to function as a peacekeeping body as we head into the 21st Century, or it will be irrelevant. And that's what we're about to find out.[70]

Two days later at a Sears manufacturing plant in Davenport, Iowa:

I told the United Nations it can show us whether or not it's going to serve its purpose to help keep the peace, or whether it's going to be irrelevant. . . . If Iraq continues to defy us and the world, we will move deliberately and decisively to hold Iraq to account.[71]

At a Republican fundraiser in Davenport that afternoon:

I went to the United Nations and said, "Either you can be relevant in the world or not, your pick."[72]

And at a fundraiser for senatorial candidate Lamar Alexander in Nashville on September 17:

I gave a speech at the United Nations. I said for the sake of peace, for the sake of security, after 11 years of not doing what he said he would do, it is time for us to deal with Saddam Hussein. The United Nations must act. It's time for them to determine whether or not they'll be the United Nations or the League of Nations. It's time for them to determine whether they'll be a force for good and peace or an ineffective debating society.[73]

The president seemed to delight in mocking the United Nations. His swagger had returned. Once again Bush was strutting like a West Texas cowboy. If the U.N. didn't act, the United States would. The next day, September 18, he asked Congress for authorization to attack Iraq. The request was open-ended. It gave the president absolute discretion. No checks, no balances. Whether America went to war would be decided by the president alone. According to the text:

The president is authorized to use all means that he determines to be appropriate, including force, in order to enforce United Nations Security Council resolutions, defend the national security interests of the United States against the threat posed by Iraq, and restore international peace in the region.[74]

Asked afterward by reporters if he would be willing to negotiate with Iraq, Bush said, "They have nothing to negotiate. The negotiations are over."[75]

That evening the president played host to Republican governors at a dinner in the White House. He repeated the message. Saddam Hussein was a "brutal, ugly, repugnant man who needs to go. He is also paranoid. I would like to see him gone peacefully. But if I unleash the military, I promise you it will be swift and decisive." Again, Bush spoke in singular terms. "If *I* unleash the military."

Bush told the governors he was going to make a prediction. "Write this down. Afghanistan and Iraq will lead that part of the world to democracy. They are going to be the catalyst to change the Middle East and the world."

One governor asked Bush about the timing for military action. "If we are going to go in militarily," said the president, "it will be as soon as possible. . . . If Saddam Hussein gets his hands on nuclear weapons, it will change the world. If he does it during my term, I will have failed."[76]

The following day the White House issued a formal document entitled *The National Security Strategy of the United States of America.* This is a document required of the president every two years as a statement of administration policy, and Bush took advantage of the fact to officially proclaim the doctrine of preemption. "We cannot let our enemies strike first. . . . The overlap between states that sponsor terror and those that pursue WMD compels us to action. . . . To forestall or prevent such hostile acts by our adversaries, the United States will, if necessary, act preemptively. . . . The United States cannot remain idle while dangers gather."[77] The *National Security Strategy* document is the formal statement of American policy. What Bush had said at West Point was now official. "We must deter and defend against the threat before it is unleashed."[78]*

---

* In his covering letter, Bush stated, "As a matter of common sense and self-defense, America will act against such emerging threats before they are fully formed. We cannot defend America and our friends by hoping for the best. So we must be prepared to defeat our enemy's plans, using

Once again Bush was walking a fine line. The doctrine of preemption is legally suspect. It is considered appropriate if an enemy is massing troops at the border for an attack, but dubious if the threat is more remote. Attacking without an imminent threat is universally regarded as preventive war and is in direct violation of the U.N. Charter's ban on unprovoked war. The Japanese claimed they were threatened by the United States when they attacked Pearl Harbor.[79]

Bush's request to Congress for authorization to attack Iraq was much too broad to win approval. With the president's reluctant acquiescence, it was rewritten by the House leadership to make it less sweeping. The president's authority to use military force against Iraq was retained, but the power to "restore international peace in the region" was deleted. The president was also required to report to Congress within forty-eight hours of launching military action why diplomatic means were no longer feasible, to continue reporting to Congress every sixty days so long as hostilities continued, and to fill Congress in on peacekeeping efforts after the fighting ended. "Nothing in this resolution supersedes any requirement of the War Powers Resolution," said the revised measure.[80]

On October 2, Bush hosted the congressional leaders at the White House. "I want to thank in particular Speaker Hastert, [House minority] Leader [Dick] Gephardt [D., Mo.] and [Senate minority] Leader [Trent] Lott [R., Miss.] for the tremendous support in building bipartisan support for this vital issue. . . . None of us here today desires to see military conflict, [but] Saddam must disarm period. If he chooses to do otherwise the use of force may become unavoidable."[81]

To buttress the president's case for action, the CIA rushed a National Intelligence Estimate (NIE) to Congress on October 1 emphasizing Iraq's WMD capability. The ninety-two-page NIE stated authoritatively that:

---

the best intelligence and proceeding with deliberation. History will judge harshly those who saw this coming danger but failed to act. In the new world we have entered, the only path to peace and security is the path of action." Presidential letter of transmission, *National Security Strategy of the United States of America*, The White House, September 20, 2002.

- Baghdad is reconstituting its nuclear weapons program.
- If Baghdad acquires sufficient fissile material from abroad, it could make a nuclear weapon within several months or a year.
- All key aspects of Iraq's offensive Biological Weapons program are active and most elements are larger and more advanced than they were before the Gulf War.
- Baghdad has renewed production of mustard gas, sarin, GF (cyclosaria) and VX nerve gas.
- Iraq maintains a small missile force and several development programs, including one for a U[nmanned] A[erial] V[ehicle] probably intended to deliver biological warfare agents.
- Baghdad's UAVs could threaten Iraq's neighbors, US forces in the Persian Gulf *and if brought close to, or into, the United States, the US Homeland.*
- Iraq is developing medium-range ballistic missile capabilities . . . more powerful than those in its current missile force.[82]

The NIE was written hastily, exaggerated the dangers, minimized doubts and dissents, and had a powerful impact on the members of Congress who read it. Two years later the Senate Select Committee on Intelligence would issue a blistering report castigating the major findings of the NIE as unsubstantiated by the agency's own research.[83] George Tenet in his memoirs called it "flawed analysis,"* and Senator Pat Roberts, a conservative Republican from Kansas who chaired the Intelligence Committee, told *The New York Times* that he was "not sure that Congress would have authorized the war had they known of the flimsiness on which the prewar intelligence assessments were based."[84]

The Central Intelligence Agency had turned its back on an intel-

---

* In his memoirs, Tenet wrote, "The press of business and the shortened time available to produce the document meant we were headed uphill from the beginning. Had we started the process sooner, I am confident we would have done a better job highlighting what we did and didn't know about Saddam's WMD programs. . . . The flawed analysis compiled in the NIE provided some of the material for Colin Powell's February 5, 2003 UN speech, which helped galvanize public support for the war." George Tenet, *At the Center of the Storm: My Years at the CIA* (New York: HarperCollins, 2007), 323.

ligence community tradition of objective analysis. Just as the Office of Legal Counsel had provided the president with a legal platform for wiretapping and torture, the CIA tailored its analysis to conform to Bush's determination to lead the country to war. As Paul Pillar, the CIA's national intelligence officer who was responsible for the Middle East, said later, "It was clear that the Bush administration would frown on or ignore analysis that called into question a decision to go to war and welcome analysis that supported such a decision. Intelligence analysts . . . felt a strong wind consistently blowing in one direction. The desire to bend with such a wind is natural and strong, even if unconscious." [85]

On October 7, with the revised authorization measure awaiting action on Capitol Hill, Bush went to Cincinnati to deliver a prime-time television address to the nation. The most recent CNN/USA Today/Gallup poll indicated that while 53 percent of Americans would support invading Iraq, only 46 percent believed the administration had done all it could to solve the crisis diplomatically. And if the United States had to invade Iraq alone, support dropped to 38 percent. The poll also indicated that if Congress opposed the invasion, support dropped even further. [86]

Bush saw the Cincinnati speech as an opportunity to rally support on the eve of the congressional vote. "Tonight I want to take a few minutes to discuss a grave threat to peace and America's determination to lead the world in confronting that threat," said the president. "The threat comes from Iraq." Bush proceeded to lay out almost verbatim the case the CIA had provided in their National Intelligence Estimate. In effect, the president was attempting to convince the nation using the exaggerated information the Central Intelligence Agency had provided.*

---

* As Paul Pillar observed later in an article in *Foreign Affairs*, "The Bush Administration deviated from the professional standard not only in using policy to drive intelligence, but also in aggressively using intelligence to win public support for its decision to go to war. . . . In the upside-down relationship between intelligence and policy that prevailed in the case of Iraq, the administration selected pieces of raw intelligence to use in its public case for war, leaving the intelligence community to register varying degrees of private protest." Paul R. Pillar, "Intelligence, Policy, and the War in Iraq," *Foreign Affairs*, March/April 2006.

We know the regime has produced thousands of tons of chemical
agents, including mustard gas, sarin nerve gas, VX nerve gas. . . . Iraq
possesses ballistic missiles with a likely range of hundreds of miles. . . .
The evidence indicates that Iraq is reconstituting its nuclear weapons program. . . . If the Iraq regime is able to produce, buy, or steal an
amount of highly enriched uranium a little larger than a single softball,
it could have a nuclear weapon in less than a year.

The CIA had been leery of tying Saddam to al Qaeda, but Bush
had no qualms. "We know that Iraq and al Qaeda have had high level
contacts that go back a decade. . . . Iraq could decide on any given day
to provide a biological or chemical weapon to a terrorist group or individual terrorists. Alliance with terrorists could allow the Iraqi regime
to attack America without leaving any fingerprints."* In conclusion,
there was Gerson's smoking gun. "Facing clear evidence of peril, we
cannot wait for the final proof, the smoking gun that could come in the
form of a mushroom cloud."

For Bush, it was a call to action.

The time for denying, deceiving has come to an end. Saddam Hussein
must disarm himself, or for the sake of peace we will lead a coalition
to disarm him. If we have to act, we will take every precaution that is
possible. We will plan carefully. We will act with the full power of the
United States military . . . and we will prevail.[87]

Bush's confidence had a galvanizing effect. On October 10 the
House of Representatives voted 296–133 to authorize the president to
use force in Iraq. All but six Republicans voted for the measure; the

---

* In 2004, the 9/11 Commission said there had been prewar contacts between Iraq and al
Qaeda but no "collaborate operational relationship. Nor have we seen evidence that Iraq co-
operated with al Qaeda in developing or carrying out any attacks against the United States."
A Pentagon report declassified in 2007 said essentially the same. *The 9/11 Commission Report:
Final Report of the National Commission on Terrorist Attacks on the United States* (New York:
W. W. Norton, 2004), 66; "Review of the Pre-Iraq War Activities of the Office of the Under-
secretary of Defense for Policy," Inspector General, United States Department of Defense.

Democrats split 81 in favor, 126 against, with minority leader Dick Gephardt voting in favor. Dick Armey held his breath and voted yes. The Senate voted shortly after midnight. Twenty-nine Democrats joined forty-eight Republicans to pass the measure. Twenty-one Democrats, one Republican (Lincoln Chafee of Rhode Island), and one Independent (Jim Jeffords of Vermont) opposed. Among the Democrats, Joe Biden, Tom Daschle, Hillary Clinton, and John Kerry voted in favor. Ted Kennedy, who had voted against the first Gulf War, voted against the second as well. "The administration has not made a convincing case that we face such an imminent threat to our national security that a unilateral, preemptive American strike and an immediate war are necessary," said Kennedy. "Nor has the administration laid out the cost in blood and treasure for this operation." [88]

Republican Chuck Hagel of Nebraska was equally skeptical but voted in favor. "We should not be seduced by the expectations of 'dancing in the streets' after Saddam's regime has fallen," said Hagel. "How many of us really know and understand much about Iraq, the country, the people, its role in the Arab world? Imposing democracy through force in Iraq is a roll of the dice." [89]

When he was informed of the Senate's action, Bush was overjoyed. "Today's vote sends a clear message to the Iraqi regime. It must disarm and comply with all existing UN resolutions, or it will be forced to comply. There are no other options for the Iraqi regime. There can be no negotiation. The days of Iraq acting as an outlaw state are coming to an end." [90]

Congress's vote to authorize the president to use military force gave Bush a free hand. "Right now we have accomplished what we had to do to take the action we need to take, and we don't need the Security Council," a senior White House official told *The New York Times.* "So if the Security Council wants to stay relevant, then it has to give us similar authority." [91] Rarely in American history has the voice of unilateralism spoken so forcefully.

CHAPTER FOURTEEN

Invasion

After Vietnam we had a whole cottage industry de-
velop, centered in Washington, D.C., that consisted of
a bunch of military fairies that had never been shot at
in anger.

General H. Norman Schwarzkopf
May 15, 1991

The congressional vote authorizing the president to use military force in Iraq coincided with an uptick in popular support for the war. When informed of the shift by Karl Rove, Bush responded sharply. "If it were 20–80 against the use of force, I'd still go after the guy," said the president. "That's what you need to know about me. Is he a threat to the country, and do we need to deal with him now instead of five years from now?" Ari Fleischer, who witnessed the exchange, said "the president wasn't asking Karl, or anyone else on the domestic staff, for an opinion." Bush was "the Decider." He had made up his mind. It was simply a question of when.[1]

Planning for the invasion continued. In mid-October 2002, the Joint Staff in the Pentagon alerted senior U.S. military commanders around the world. "We are preparing to order that a war with Iraq be considered part of the war on terror."[2] It was a warning. Be ready. Franks met with Bush twice in October, and the invasion plan now had an official designation: OPLAN 1003 Victory. The plan called for 150,000 troops to be deployed immediately, with another 300,000 in the pipeline. Air and naval support were additional. So too was whatever support the United States might receive from coalition partners.[3]

In late October, Bush brought the Joint Chiefs into the picture. Thus far the planning for the invasion had been strictly chain of command— Bush to Rumsfeld to Franks. The Chiefs had been briefed on Plan 1003V a week earlier. What did they think? Could each service do what was asked? The president wanted to know. Once more the contrast to World War II, Korea, and Vietnam was evident. The invasion of Iraq was being planned by the president, the secretary of defense, and the area commander. The most senior officers in the military were relegated to the sidelines.

Air Force chief of staff General John P. Jumper believed the air plan in 1003V was supportable and that Iraq's air defenses could be overcome. The air transport system that would be required to get troops and equipment to the region would be stretched, but Jumper believed it could be done. Admiral Vern Clark, the chief of naval operations, was slightly concerned that Iraq would be a second front for Navy aircraft carriers with operations still ongoing in Afghanistan, but said it could be done. Army chief of staff General Eric Shinseki pointed out that the supply lines were long and the initial assault force might be too small, but supported the plan. The Marine commandant, General James L. Jones, said he worried about fighting in a contaminated environment if the Iraqis employed chemical or biological weapons and was concerned about possibly fighting in the city of Baghdad.

"What do you think about the plan for Baghdad?" Bush asked.

"I haven't seen the details," Jones replied, "but I understand they are being worked out."[4]

None of the Chiefs wanted to question the commander in chief. General Franks said later it was a "very, very positive session." As for Shinseki's concern about the long supply lines, "I took it, and I think everyone else in the room took it, to mean this isn't going to be a cakewalk."[5]

It was also in October that Rumsfeld introduced his "Parade of Horribles" to the National Security Council. It was well enough to anticipate victory, but what could go wrong? Rumsfeld had written out by hand a list of possible setbacks. "I went through the items one by one," said the secretary of defense. "The list was meant to generate serious, early thinking about the potential risks and what might be done to assess and reduce them." That did not happen. As Rumsfeld notes, "the discussion was brief." [6] Two days later he prepared a typewritten memo for the president listing twenty-nine possible things that could go wrong, and according to Bob Woodward, "walked him through it." [7] Among the problems cited by Rumsfeld were:

- If the US seeks UN approval, it could fail; and without a UN mandate, potential coalition partners may be unwilling to participate.
- US could fail to find WMD on the ground in Iraq and be unpersuasive to the world.
- There could be higher than expected collateral damage—Iraqi civilian deaths.
- US could fail to manage post-Saddam Hussein Iraq successfully. . . .
- The dollar cost of the effort could prove greater than expected and contributions from other nations minimal.
- Rather than having the post-Saddam effort require 2 to 4 years, it could take 8 to 10 years, thereby absorbing US leadership, military and financial resources.
- World reaction against "pre-emption" or "anticipatory self-defense" could inhibit US ability to engage in the future.
- Recruiting and financing for terrorist networks could take a dramatic upward turn from successful information operations by our enemies, positioning the US as anti-Muslim.
- Iraq could experience ethnic strife among Sunni, Shia, and Kurds. [8]

Rumsfeld's list provides a precise compendium of what went wrong in Iraq. Why did he write it? * "I wrote the memo because I was un-

---

*   In her memoirs, Condoleezza Rice says, "I suspected that the Defense Department's motive was really to issue a documented warning just in case the whole endeavor failed." *No Higher Honor* (New York: Crown, 2011), 192.

easy that, as a government, we had not fully examined a broad enough spectrum of possibilities. Unfortunately, although the Department of Defense prepared for those contingencies in our area of responsibility, there was never a systematic review of my list." [9]

With congressional midterm elections approaching, Bush hit the campaign trail. In the final week of the campaign, he spoke in twenty cities. Each speech was a Republican stem-winder, and in each, as he approached his conclusion, he turned to Iraq. The words were virtually identical from speech to speech, and the president was repeatedly interrupted by cheers of U-S-A, U-S-A from the audience. Saddam Hussein was an evil man who hated America.

> We not only know he's got chemical weapons, but incredibly enough he's used chemical weapons. He's used them on his own people. This is a man who has got terrorist connections, who would like nothing more than to provide the arsenal and the training grounds for these coldblooded killers. And they could attack us, and he would leave no fingerprints behind. He's a threat.

After lambasting Saddam, Bush went on to taunt the United Nations.

> It's a historic moment, as far as I am concerned, for the UN. They can show the world whether or not they can work together to keep the peace, whether they will be the United Nations or whether they'll be the League of Nations, an ineffective debating society. And the choice is theirs.
>
> And the choice is Saddam Hussein's as well. For the sake of peace he must disarm. But if he doesn't disarm, and if the United Nations cannot find the backbone necessary to assume its responsibilities . . . the United States, for the sake of peace, will lead a coalition of nations to disarm Saddam Hussein. [10]

Bush was beating the drum for war and the country responded. For the first time since Franklin Roosevelt's historic triumph in 1934, the party in power gained seats in both Houses of Congress in a mid-term election. The Republicans regained control of the Senate (51–49), and added eight seats to their majority in the House. For Bush, it was a remarkable vindication after the cliffhanger in 2000, and a vote of confidence for what might lie ahead.

On November 8, three days after the congressional elections, the United Nations Security Council voted unanimously (15–0) to find Iraq in "material breach" of previous resolutions concerning weapons of mass destruction. The Security Council resolution (1441) gave Iraq "a final opportunity to comply with its disarmament obligations." Saddam was required to cooperate with "an enhanced inspection regime" and to submit within thirty days a complete accounting of his weapons programs. Failure to do so would result in "serious consequences."[11] Unanimous passage of the resolution represented a remarkable triumph for Colin Powell, who had worked for the past eight weeks—since Bush's U.N. speech—to cobble it together. The resolution was not as strong as the administration hoped for: "serious consequences" was purposely vague, and the Security Council had not signed off on the issue. Said differently, it was not a self-executing ultimatum that would authorize military action. Nevertheless, it was a diplomatic triumph. The fact that France, Russia, and China supported the resolution was remarkable, and at the last moment Syria, the only Arab country on the Security Council, agreed to go along.

Powell immediately called the president. "Hey, Boss, we got it done."[12] Bush was pleased. Within the hour the president was standing in the Rose Garden before dozens of reporters, photographers, and television cameras. He thanked Powell profusely. "With the resolution just passed, the United Nations Security Council has met important responsibilities, upheld its principles, and given clear and fair notice that Saddam Hussein must fully disclose and destroy his weapons of mass destruction." But war was still very much in the president's mind. And it was obvious he was prepared to take action:

America will be making only one determination. Is Iraq meeting the terms of the Security Council resolutions or not? The United States has agreed to discuss any material breach with the Security Council, but without jeopardizing our freedom of action to defend our country. If Iraq fails to fully comply, the United States and other nations will disarm Saddam Hussein.[13]

Planning for the invasion continued. On November 26, two days before Thanksgiving, Franks presented Rumsfeld with the initial deployment order for troops to the Persian Gulf. Franks called it the "mother of all deployment orders." It would have authorized the immediate deployment of 300,000 troops to the Gulf. Rumsfeld hesitated. Moving 300,000 troops would not go unnoticed. The United Nations weapons inspectors were just reentering Iraq for a new round of inspections, and it would look as if the United States had written them off. After consulting with the president, Rumsfeld broke the deployment into increments. "We're going to dribble this and slowly so as not to discredit diplomacy," said Rumsfeld.[14] The troops would move in two-week intervals, beginning in December.

"Are you satisfied with this force structure?" Rumsfeld asked Franks.

"I'd go to war with this force structure," Franks replied.

"You may have to," said Rumsfeld.[15]

Under the Goldwater-Nichols Defense Reorganization Act, planning for the invasion of Iraq was the responsibility of Rumsfeld and Franks, with an assist from General Myers, who as chairman of the Joint Chiefs was the senior military adviser to the president and secretary of defense. "Among Myers, Franks, and me, there was no conflict whatever regarding force levels," wrote Rumsfeld in his memoirs.[16] But among the uniformed military, that was not the case. Shortly after the deployment order was issued, *The Washington Post* carried a front-page article stating that General James Jones, the Marine Corps commandant, and Army chief of staff General Eric Shinseki, thought the plan devised by Franks and Rumsfeld was excessively risky. "With war possible soon in Iraq, the chiefs of the two U.S. ground forces are challenging the belief of some senior Pentagon civilians that Iraqi president Saddam Hussein will fall almost immediately upon being attacked and are calling for more attention to planning for worst-case scenarios." [17]

Retired General H. Norman Schwarzkopf, "Stormin' Norman" of Desert Storm, added his concerns. In a lengthy interview with journalist Thomas Ricks, Schwarzkopf questioned the wisdom of attacking Iraq. "I think it is very important for us to wait and see what the inspectors come up with," said Schwarzkopf. "Whatever path we take, we have to take it with a bit of prudence."

Schwarzkopf, who was a hunting companion of George H. W. Bush and who had campaigned in Florida with Dick Cheney during the 2000 election, was particularly critical of the Defense Department's civilian leadership. "It's scary," he told Ricks. Schwarzkopf thought Rumsfeld "seems to be enjoying it. He gives the perception that he's the guy driving the train and everybody else better fall in line behind him."* Even worse, Rumsfeld and his principal assistants, Paul Wolfowitz and Douglas Feith, lacked the combat experience that Schwarzkopf thought necessary to make sound military decisions. "Let's face it: There are guys at the Pentagon who have been involved in operational planning their entire lives. And for this wisdom, acquired during many operations, wars, and schools to be ignored, and in its place have somebody who doesn't have that training, is a concern." Schwarzkopf also worried what would happen after Saddam was toppled. "What is postwar Iraq going to look like, with the Kurds and the Sunnis and the Shiites? I would hope that we have in place the adequate resources to become an army of occupation, because you are going to walk into chaos." [18] Schwarzkopf was America's most distinguished combat com-

---

* During the first Gulf War, which was also fought under the Goldwater-Nichols Defense Reorganization Act, Dick Cheney, as secretary of defense, kept Colin Powell (who was chairman of the Joint Chiefs) in the chain of command. The orders transmitted to Schwarzkopf in the field all came from Powell. Cheney said he did that because when he became secretary of defense in 1989 the military, all of whom had served in Vietnam, blamed the Defense Department's civilian leadership, specifically Robert McNamara, for the quagmire there. As a consequence, Cheney wanted to keep the Joint Chiefs, and especially Powell, involved.

When Cheney took office in 1989, he invited all but one of his predecessors as secretary of defense to a formal lunch at the Pentagon. McNamara was not invited. That was a message Cheney was sending to the military. Personal interview, January 29, 2014.

mander. He was speaking with the voice of experience. And he was ignored.

On December 7, Iraq submitted a twelve-thousand-page weapons report to the United Nations as required under Resolution 1441. This was twenty-four hours ahead of schedule, and according to Iraqi officials confirmed that Baghdad had no weapons of mass destruction and no current program to develop them. "When we say we have no weapons of mass destruction, we are speaking the truth," said Major General Hassam Muhammad Amis, the senior Iraqi official in charge of the document's preparation.[19]

Washington held its fire. "We will judge the declaration's honesty and completeness only after we have thoroughly examined it, and that will take some time," said the president in his weekly radio address. Bush added a veiled threat. "Americans seek peace in the world. War is the last option for confronting threats, yet the temporary peace of denial and looking away from danger would only be a prelude to a broader war and greater horror. America will confront gathering dangers early." [20]

The administration's official response to the Iraqi document was provided by Secretary of State Colin Powell at a press conference on December 19. "Our experts have found it to be anything but currently accurate, full, or complete," said Powell. "The Iraqi declaration may use the language of Resolution 1441, but it totally fails to meet the resolution's requirements." [21]

Bush's determination as commander in chief to remove Saddam Hussein charted the course for the United States. Cheney believed that the president came into office intent on taking action, and that after 9/11 he was doubly determined.[22] George Tenet agreed. Tenet was unsure of the exact date, but certainly after 9/11 there was no question of the president's focus.[23] By Christmas 2002, Bush was clearing the decks for action. On Saturday, December 21, he called on the CIA to lay out the public case for attacking Iraq—the case that could be presented to America and the world concerning Saddam's possession and possible use of WMD.

The presentation was made in the Oval Office. Bush was joined by

Cheney, Andy Card, Condoleezza Rice, and Scooter Libby. For almost an hour, John McLaughlin, the deputy CIA director, went through an illustrated lecture presenting photos and voice recordings of the evidence on hand. "I was very careful in the presentation," McLaughlin said later. "I wasn't trying to sell anything. I was basically saying, this is what we think we can confidently say."[24]

Bush was disappointed. He needed a convincing case, and McLaughlin had fallen short. "Nice try," said the president. "It's not something that Joe Public would understand or would gain a lot of confidence from."[25] Bush suggested that the CIA could add punch to the presentation if they brought in some lawyers who were accustomed to arguing cases before juries. According to Tenet, "At no time did he or anyone else in the room suggest we collect more intelligence to find out if the WMD were there or not. . . . The focus was simply on sharpening the arguments."[26]

Writing in his memoirs five years later, Tenet said, "Some might criticize us for participating in what was essentially a marketing meeting," but at the time he was caught up in the bellicose atmosphere that engulfed the White House. Asked by Bush, "Is this the best we've got?" Tenet replied, "It's a slam dunk." A longtime basketball fan of the Georgetown Hoyas, Tenet repeated the phrase. "Don't worry," he told the president. "It's a slam dunk."[27] Tenet was referring to the public presentation the CIA could make, not to the evidence itself. Afterward, Bush told Card and Rice, "This needs a lot of work." He too was referring to the public presentation.[28]

Bush and his family spent Christmas at Camp David. While there, the president spoke privately with his father. "For the most part, I didn't seek Dad's advice on major issues, but Iraq was one issue where I wanted to know what he thought." George W. walked his father through the diplomatic strategy. "I told Dad I was praying we could deal with Saddam peacefully but were preparing for the alternative." The senior Bush told his son he hoped diplomacy would succeed. "You know how tough war is, son, and you've got to try everything you can to avoid war." According to the president, his father then said, "But if the man won't comply, you don't have any other choice."[29] Bush reports this conversation in his memoirs, invoking his father's support for what had already been decided.

Toward the end of the Christmas holidays, Bush and Laura returned to the ranch in Crawford. Smitten with his role as commander in chief, Bush went to Fort Hood on January 3 to speak to the troops, in this case, the 1st Cavalry Division. "Laura and I are honored to kick off the new year with the soldiers and families of Fort Hood," said the president. Bush spoke extensively about Iraq, and the troops responded frequently with a military "Hooah." When the president turned to the possibility of war, there was silence. Said Bush:

> In crucial hours, the success of our cause will depend on you. As members of our military, you serve this nation's ideals. As commander in chief, I have come to know the men and women who wear America's uniform. I have seen your love of country and your devotion to a cause larger than yourself. I know that every order I give can bring a cost. I also know without a doubt that every order I give will be carried out with skill and unselfish courage.
>
> Some crucial hours lie ahead. We know the challenges and dangers we face. If this generation of Americans is ready, we accept the burden of leadership. We act in the cause of peace and freedom, and in that cause we will prevail.[30]

Like a football coach before a big game, Bush was giving the troops a pep talk. This time, when he finished, there was no "Hooah" from the audience.

Back at the White House, the president met with the bipartisan leadership of the House and Senate on January 8. "Sometimes it takes a little muscle to secure good diplomacy," said Bush. "Before I make a decision, I will make the reason known to Congress and everyone in America." According to Ari Fleischer, none of the congressional leaders objected. "If they had misgivings, they kept them to themselves."[31]

Later that day, Bush entertained congressional Republicans in the family quarters of the White House and was more candid. "There's a chance, a good chance, I'll have to address the nation and commit troops to war," said the president. "It's clear Saddam Hussein is not disarming." [32]

On January 9, Bush met with Rumsfeld and Franks to review once more the plans for the attack. Franks was concerned that Turkey was hedging on whether to allow American forces to assemble on Turkish soil. Franks said that meant there would be no northern front. The president queried Franks on what would happen if Saddam decided to attack before American forces were fully assembled. Franks said the four hundred aircraft already in the region would be sufficient to repel any Iraqi attack. They also discussed timing. "What's my last decision point?" asked Bush. "When have I finally made a commitment?"

Franks said that once Special Forces were deployed inside Iraq, war would begin. The general said he would be ready in about three weeks. "I'll be ready in early February, but I'd really like the 1st of March." [33]

It was also on January 9 that U.N. weapons inspector Hans Blix delivered a preliminary report to the Security Council. Blix said the U.N. inspectors could not say with certainty that Iraq had weapons of mass destruction, but also could not say that there were none. So far, they had found no "smoking gun." Blix said the inspections were continuing and Baghdad seemed to be cooperating. But it was going to require more time to give a definitive answer. [34]

It was clear that war was coming. On Saturday, January 11, at Bush's direction, Vice President Cheney met with Saudi ambassador Prince Bandar to inform him of the impending attack. Saudi Arabia had a six-hundred-mile border with Iraq, and the United States needed Saudi support. The invasion would be launched from Kuwait, but the Saudi border had to be secured and it would be helpful if Franks could utilize nearby Saudi airbases. Cheney had met with Bandar before Desert Storm in 1991, and in some respects this was a repeat. Rumsfeld and General Myers presented Bandar with a complete briefing of the American attack plan. Bandar, who was an experienced fighter pilot, understood the strategy, but had one concern. "Is Saddam going to survive this time?" he asked Cheney.

"Bandar," Cheney said, "once we start this, Saddam is toast." [35]

Bandar said he was convinced, but before he could inform Crown Prince Abdullah, he had to hear it directly from the president. Bush met with Bandar the following Monday. The Saudis needed the president's personal assurance that Saddam would be toast, said Bandar.

"You got the briefing from Dick, Rummy, and General Myers?" asked Bush.

"Yes."

"Any questions for me?"

"No, Mr. President."

"That is the message I want you to carry for me to the crown prince. The message you are taking is mine," said the president.[36]

With war looming, Bush needed the administration to be in step. Cheney, Rumsfeld, and Tenet were ready, but what about Powell? On Monday, January 13, just after meeting with Bandar, the president sat down with Powell in the Oval Office.

"I really think I'm going to have to take this guy out," said Bush as they settled into wing chairs facing the fireplace.

"Okay," Powell replied. "We'll continue to see if we can find a diplomatic way out of this. But you realize what you are getting into? You realize the consequences of this?"[37]

"Yes, I do. Are you with me on this? I think I have to do this. I want you with me."

"I'll do the best I can," said the secretary of state. "Yes, sir. I will support you. I'm with you Mr. President."

"Time to put your war uniform on," said Bush, ending the conversation.[38]

For Powell, it was chain of command. Bush was not asking his opinion. The president as commander in chief had made the decision to go to war and wanted to know if his secretary of state was on board. The closest parallel was in 1948 when President Truman recognized the state of Israel. General Marshall, who was secretary of state, was strongly opposed, as was the State Department. After Truman's decision, Marshall's aides asked why he did not resign on principle. "No," Marshall replied. "You don't take a post of this sort and then resign when the man who has the constitutional responsibility to make decisions makes one you don't like."[39] In later years, Powell would often cite Marshall's example as "a heck of a note of inspiration."[40]

Bush had decided to go to war, but at the United Nations the coalition Powell had assembled to pass Security Council Resolution 1441 was crumbling. At a meeting of the Security Council on January 20, German foreign minister Joschka Fischer said, "We are greatly concerned that a military strike against the regime in Baghdad would involve considerable and unpredictable risks for the global fight against terrorism. . . . Iraq has complied fully with all relevant resolutions and military action would have disastrous consequences." Fischer said that Germany rejected the very idea of war.[41]

Russian foreign minister Igor Ivanov joined in. "We must be careful not to take unilateral steps that might threaten the unity of the anti-terrorist coalition," he warned. Russia favored "a political settlement of the situation concerning Iraq." Chinese foreign minister Tang Jiaxuan agreed. But the most devastating blow was delivered by French foreign minister Dominique de Villepin. Speaking at a press conference after the meeting, de Villepin said, "We believe that nothing today justifies envisaging military action." If Washington should decide to act unilaterally without Security Council approval, it "would be perceived as a victory for the law of the strongest, an attack on the rule of law and on international morality."[42]

Confronted with the obvious reluctance of Germany, France, Russia, and China to authorize military action, Bush decided to appeal directly to President Chirac. In a phone call to the French president the day after the Security Council meeting, Bush implored Chirac to take action. "Jacques," said the president, "Saddam is digging in. He's lying to the world and he is lying to Blix. We can't let him think the UN is a paper tiger that won't enforce its own resolutions."

"I understand your concerns, George, but the inspectors need more time. War should be the last option, and it will be our admission of failure. I am not convinced that the situation is urgent or even that the weapons are there. Before we take an irreversible step, we need to be certain."

After several more exchanges, Bush changed course. "Jacques," he said, "you and I share a common faith. You're Roman Catholic, I'm Methodist, but we are both Christians committed to the teachings of the Bible. We share one common Lord."

Chirac did not reply, and the president continued. "Gog and Magog are at work in the Middle East. Biblical prophesies are being fulfilled. This confrontation is willed by God, who wants to use this conflict to erase His people's enemies before a new age begins."[43]

Chirac had no idea what Bush was talking about. Gog and Magog are Old Testament images that evangelicals employ as the personification of evil in an apocalyptic conflict in the time of the Messiah. In the New Testament's Book of Revelation the names Gog and Magog are applied to the evil forces that will join Satan in the great struggle at the end of times. According to that rendition, God will send fire from heaven to destroy them and then preside over the last judgment.[44] The Book of Revelation is the favorite book in the Bible for many evangelicals, and is often regarded even more highly than the gospels themselves. For George W. Bush, it was the epicenter of the universe.

When Chirac's staff eventually untangled the Gog and Magog reference, it confirmed the French president's worst fears. Biblical writings were determining Bush's decision about war in the Middle East. Weapons inspections would never be sufficient if the president believed a war with Iraq was God's will. For Chirac the answer was clear. France was not going to fight a war based on George Bush's interpretation of the Bible.[45]

Bush's religious certitude and his invocation of Gog and Magog scuttled the possibility of French support for military action. Two days after his conversation with Bush, Chirac hosted a formal celebration in the Hall of Mirrors at Versailles marking the fortieth anniversary of the Treaty of Reconciliation between France and West Germany negotiated by Charles de Gaulle and Konrad Adenauer. Speaking to over a thousand legislators from the Bundestag and the Chamber of Deputies, Chirac hailed the cooperation that had grown between the two countries, and in his conclusion turned to Iraq. "War is not inevitable," said the French president. "For us, war is always proof of failure and the worst of solutions, so everything must be done to avoid it." Germany and France, he said, were working for a peaceful solution. German chancellor Gerhard Schroeder followed Chirac and was explicit. "Don't expect Germany to approve a Security Council resolution legitimizing war," said Schroeder. "Don't expect it."[46]

Bush was livid. "Surely our friends have learned lessons from the past," the president told reporters gathered in the Roosevelt Room of the White House. "Surely we have learned how this man deceives and delays." Whether the French and Germans supported a Security Council resolution was immaterial. "Time is running out," said Bush. "I believe in the name of peace, Saddam must disarm. And we lead a coalition of willing nations to disarm him. Make no mistake about that, he will be disarmed."[47]

Donald Rumsfeld unwittingly exacerbated the tension with France and Germany. Several hours after Chirac and Schroeder spoke, Rumsfeld visited the Pentagon's foreign press center for a scheduled briefing. Charles Groenhuijsen, a Dutch journalist, asked about the European leaders' comments. "These are U.S. allies. What do you make of that?"

"What do I think about it? Well, there isn't anyone alive who wouldn't prefer unanimity," said Rumsfeld.

> But you're thinking of Europe as Germany and France. I don't. I think that's the old Europe. If you look at the entire NATO Europe today, the center of gravity is shifting to the east. Germany has been a problem, and France has been a problem. But if you look at the vast number of other countries in Europe, they're not with France and Germany on this. They're with the United States.[48]

On Monday, January 27, Hans Blix delivered his second interim report to the Security Council. Blix's team of 250 inspectors had visited 230 sites in the last sixty days and still had not found a smoking gun. Blix said Iraq was cooperating with the inspections process—granting unfettered access to all sites—but not the substance. "It is not enough to open doors. Inspection is not a game of 'catch as catch can.'" The inspections were continuing, said Blix, and they would be able to verify Iraqi disarmament "in a reasonable period of time."[49]

Blix was followed by Mohamed ElBaradei, the director general of the International Atomic Energy Agency, whose team of inspectors had visited 109 locations during the past two months. "We have to date found no evidence that Iraq has revived its

United Nations weapons inspectors
Hans Blix and Mohamed ElBaradei.

nuclear weapons program since its elimination of the program in the 1990s," said ElBaradei. He was not prepared to give Iraq a clean bill of health, but told the Security Council, "We should be able within the next few months to provide credible assurance that Iraq has no nuclear weapons programs. These few months would be a valuable investment in peace, because they could help us avoid war."[50]

The administration was appalled. Bush immediately told Colin Powell that he wanted him to appear before the Security Council and present the evidence against Saddam. "We've really got to make the case," Bush told Powell, "and you've got to make it. You have the credibility to do this. Maybe they'll believe you."[51]

The next day Bush delivered his third State of the Union address to Congress. Sixty-two million Americans watched as the president laid out the case for war. To some extent, the speech was a rerun of Bush's speech in Cincinnati on the eve of congressional elections. Contrary to what Blix and ElBaradei had just reported, the president once again depicted Saddam as a WMD menace who was sitting on a huge stockpile of chemical and biological weapons and who was again on the trail of nuclear weapons. There were not only the disputed aluminum tubes, but "the British government has learned that Saddam Hussein recently bought significant quantities of uranium from Africa." *

---

* This was a reference to the alleged yellowcake deal with Niger, which George Tenet had deleted from earlier speeches. Tenet was given a copy of Bush's State of the Union speech the day

"Today, the gravest danger in the war on terror, the greatest danger facing America and the world, is outlaw regimes that seek and possess nuclear, chemical and biological weapons." Bush said the United States would consult with other nations, "but let there be no misunderstanding. If Saddam Hussein does not fully disarm, we will lead a coalition to disarm him."

The president made clear what was coming. "Sending Americans into battle is the most profound decision a President can make. . . . If war is forced upon us we will fight with the full force and might of the United States military, and we will prevail." Bush closed by invoking God's help.

> We Americans have faith in ourselves, but not in ourselves alone. We do not know—we do not claim to know all the ways of Providence, yet we can trust in them, placing our confidence in the loving God behind all of life and all of history.[52]

Two days later Bush met with Rumsfeld, Franks, and the Joint Chiefs of Staff in the Cabinet Room of the White House to review OPLAN 1003V. "Do any of you have any concerns about the war plan?" the president asked.[53] As Rumsfeld notes, "This was one more chance for the most senior officers of the United States military to express any reservations they might have to the President."[54] Only Army chief of staff Eric Shinseki voiced concerns. Shinseki was still worried about the size of the attacking force, the long supply lines, and the refusal of Turkey to allow American troops to enter Turkish soil to mount an attack from the north. According to witnesses, Shinseki's critique was delivered in a mild-mannered way, but totally undercut the strategy Rumsfeld and Franks had devised. "It's the only time in my life where I felt like you could hear the hinge of history turn," said NSC staffer

---

before its delivery but passed it off to his staff and did not read it. As Michael Isikoff and David Corn point out, CIA officials and White House speechwriters "were eager to go as far as they could to depict Saddam as a danger. Nobody insisted on rigorous fact checking, which might end up diluting the power of the president's message." *Hubris: The Inside Story of Spin, Scandal, and the Selling of the Iraq War* (New York: Crown, 2006), 171–72.

Kori Schake. "The president didn't know what to do. So he thanked Shinseki and moved on."[55]

The following day, January 31, Bush met with Tony Blair in the Oval Office. Blair had come to Washington to urge the president to seek a second Security Council resolution explicitly authorizing war. Britain's attorney general Lord Peter Goldsmith had told Blair he did not think Resolution 1441 was sufficient, and the British public was dead set against military action. A recently released poll in London's *Mirror* indicated only 2 percent of the respondents thought a war with Iraq would make the world a safer place. Blair doubted whether he could survive as prime minister if they did not make the effort to win U.N. support. "Our balls are really in a vice," said Alastair Campbell, Blair's spokesman and confidant.[56]

Bush was sympathetic to Blair's plight. He did not want to leave his principal ally in the lurch. The president told Blair the United States would work hard to get a new resolution. "We'll twist some arms and even threaten if we have to. But if we fail, we are going to take military action anyway."[57]

The president then brought Blair up to date on the military planning. "The start date for the military campaign is penciled in for March 10. That's when we're planning to get going with the bombing." Bush said the air campaign would probably last four days. "We are going to be very careful to avoid killing innocent civilians. But I don't think there is going to be much danger for them for too long. The bombing is going to ensure a quick collapse of Saddam's regime. It's going to destroy his 'command and control' very quickly. The army's going to fold." Bush, who was totally unaware of Sunni and Shiite hostility, or the nationalist aspirations of the Kurds, said he "thought it was unlikely that there would be internecine warfare between different religions and ethnic groups." But the military timetable was tight, and so there was not much time to get the second U.N. resolution that Blair needed.[58]

Colin Powell presented the administration's case to the Security Council on February 5. Powell hoped he could duplicate Adlai Stevenson's historic speech to the Security Council during the Cuban Mis-

Colin Powell holding a model vial of anthrax at a presentation to the United Nations Security Council.

sile Crisis of 1962, when Stevenson convincingly documented the presence of Soviet missiles in Cuba. With CIA director George Tenet sitting behind his right shoulder, Powell spoke for an hour and fifteen minutes. He and his staff had worked diligently for the past week to sift through the intelligence reports and strip out the most egregious errors, but the fact is there was no evidence that Saddam was rearming with WMD and it was difficult to make a case that he was.

Powell's presence was imposing, he appeared sincere, and most Americans were convinced by his presentation. A *Newsweek* poll taken just after the speech found that half of all Americans polled were ready to go to war, versus only a third a month before.[59] *The Washington Post* called the evidence Powell presented "irrefutable," and *The New York Times* said that Powell had made "the most powerful case to date that Saddam Hussein stands in defiance of Security Council resolutions and has no intention of revealing or surrendering whatever unconventional weapons he may have."[60]

But the rest of the world was unimpressed. Chinese foreign minister Tang Jiaxuan said he hoped that any country with hard evidence would turn it over to the U.N. inspectors. Russian foreign minister Igor Ivanov said he thought Powell's information provided more, not less, reason to continue the inspections, and France's de Villepin noted there were good reasons to increase the number of U.N. inspectors in Iraq. No speaker who followed Powell thought he had presented a casus belli.[61]

On February 10, Putin, Schroeder, and Chirac added their concerns. At a joint press conference in Paris, the three leaders disputed the case Powell presented and called for continued inspections. "Nothing today justifies war," they said. "Russia, Germany, and France are in favor of pursuing inspections with a substantial strengthening of human and technical capabilities by all possible means, within the limits of resolution 1441."[62] The graphic news coverage of the three European leaders standing together was a chilling reminder that George W. Bush had lost the battle for world opinion. In his desire to fulfill what he believed to be God's will, in his determination to defeat Gog and Magog and rid the world of evil, the president was leading the United States into what was clearly a war of aggression.

On February 14, Hans Blix and Mohamed ElBaradei delivered their third interim report to the Security Council. Their remarks stood in sharp contrast to what Powell had presented nine days earlier. Blix told the council his investigators had visited over three hundred sites and had found no evidence of WMD. "All inspections were performed without notice, and access was almost always provided promptly." Blix said Powell had presented evidence of continuing Iraqi arms programs, but his inspectors had found none. "The inspectors, for their part, must base their reports only on the evidence which they can themselves examine and present publicly." Blix concluded by saying that if Iraq were to cooperate even more fully, "the period of disarmament through inspections could be short."[63]

ElBaradei spoke next and was even more explicit. He reminded the Security Council that his Vienna agency had neutralized Iraq's nuclear program by 1998, "hence our focus has been on verifying whether Iraq revived its program in the intervening years. We have to date found no evidence of ongoing prohibited nuclear or nuclear-related activities in Iraq."[64]

The day after Blix and ElBaradei reported to the Security Council, protests against the coming war broke out across the world. Over a million demonstrators turned out in Rome, London, and Paris. But in the United States, the country rallied behind Bush. The French were denounced as "cheese-eating surrender monkeys," some restaurants relabeled French fries as "freedom fries," and Rush Limbaugh called foreign protesters "anti-American, anti-capitalist, pro-Marxist and communists."[65] In the United States Senate, only Robert Byrd of West Virginia, the longest-serving Democrat on Capitol Hill, spoke out and criticized his colleagues' silence. "We stand passively mute in the United States Senate, seemingly stunned by the sheer turmoil of events," said Byrd.

> This nation is about to embark upon the first test of a revolutionary doctrine—the doctrine of preemption—the idea that the United States or any other nation can legitimately attack a nation that is not immi-nently threatening but may be threatening in the future—a radical new twist on the traditional idea of self-defense. It appears to be in contra-vention of international law and the UN Charter.[66]

The buildup for the invasion continued. Thirty-nine thousand mil-itary reservists were called to active duty, and by mid-February there were more than 100,000 U.S. troops in the Persian Gulf region, includ-ing three aircraft carrier task forces, with a fourth, the USS *Theodore Roosevelt*, on the way, and a fifth, the USS *Kitty Hawk*, scheduled to be deployed shortly. But within the Pentagon, many professional soldiers, including Shinseki, continued to question the administration's assump-tions about a cakewalk in Iraq. Shinseki made his doubts public at a hearing of the Senate Armed Services Committee on February 25. He was asked by Senator Carl Levin of Michigan, the senior Democrat on the committee, for an estimate of how many troops would be re-quired to occupy Iraq "following a successful completion of the war?" Shinseki had carefully prepared for his testimony and had asked the Army's Center of Military History for projections based on the postwar occupation of Germany and Japan. Researchers told him the number should be roughly 260,000. That was the figure Shinseki had in mind when Levin asked the question.

As customary, Shinseki followed protocol. He was not in the chain of command, and told Levin he would have to rely on the estimates of the combatant commander, General Franks. "How about a range?" asked Levin.

"I would say that what's been mobilized to this point, something on the order of several hundred thousand soldiers are probably a figure that would be required." Shinseki said Iraq was a large country with

ethnic tensions, "so it takes significant ground force pressure to maintain a safe and secure environment to ensure that people are fed, that
water is distributed, and all the normal responsibilities that go along
with administering a situation like this."[67] The Bush administration
was aghast. At Rumsfeld's direction, Paul Wolfowitz, deputy secretary
of defense, told the secretary of the army that Shinseki had spoken out
of turn and was off base.[68]

Two days after the Army chief of staff testified, Wolfowitz was
on Capitol Hill presenting the administration's case. Speaking to the
House Budget Committee, the deputy secretary said, "There has been
a good deal of comment—some of it quite outlandish—about what our
postwar requirements might be in Iraq. Some of the higher end predic-
tions that we have been hearing recently, such as the notion that it will
take several hundred thousand U.S. troops to provide stability in post-
Saddam Iraq are wildly off the mark." Wolfowitz told the congressmen
he was reasonably certain that the Iraqis "will greet us as liberators, and
that will help keep requirements down. . . . The notion that hundreds
of thousands of American troops are needed is way off the mark."[69]

As Andrew Bacevich has pointed out, the debate between Shinseki
and Wolfowitz involved more than simply questioning occupation
strategy.

> Given that the requisite additional troops simply did not exist, Shinseki
> was implicitly arguing that the U.S. armed services were inadequate
> for the enterprise. Further, he was implying that invasion was likely to
> produce something other than a crisp, tidy decision. Unexpected and
> costly complications would abound. In effect, Shinseki was offering a
> last-ditch defense of a military tradition that Wolfowitz was intent on
> destroying, a tradition that saw armies as fragile, that sought to harness
> military power, and that classified force as an option of last resort. The
> risks of action, Shinseki was suggesting, were far, far greater than the
> advocates for war let on.[70]

On March 5, Bush met with Franks and Rumsfeld for a final review of plans for the attack. Franks had now assembled a force of some

200,000 troops with another 60,000 en route. By March 20, he anticipated coalition forces in Kuwait would number 292,000, of whom 170,000 would be ground combat troops. "Mr. President," said Franks, "all key infrastructure improvements have been completed, and the required force is now in place in the theater."

Bush asked about Turkey. On March 1 the Turkish parliament had rejected U.S. requests to move troops through their country. Where did that leave us? the president asked. Franks said the 4th Infantry Division—some 15,000 men—was still loaded on thirty-seven ships in the eastern Mediterranean. "If the Turks change their minds, we will offload and be on Iraq's northern border within ten days. If not, we will transit the Suez and offload the division in Kuwait—probably after the commencement of hostilities."[71]

Franks explained the phasing of combat operations and then raised the question of collateral damage. His planners had identified twenty-four high-collateral-damage targets where civilian casualties could be high. "I'm not picking targets," said Bush. "I want you to tell us about targets you think you have to hit to secure victory and to protect our troops."[72]

Franks told the president he would like forty-eight hours notice before any attack. "That will give me time to get the special operations teams into western Iraq to take down border observation posts, stop any Scud attacks, and secure the oil wells."

"Forty-eight hours," the president replied. "Two days. All right, Tommy, you'll have the warning if it comes to that."[73]

Shortly after lunch on March 5, Bush met with Cardinal Pio Laghi, a personal envoy sent by Pope John Paul II to dissuade the president from attacking Iraq. Laghi had previously served as the Vatican's ambassador to the United States and was an old friend of the Bush family. Laghi said there would be civilian casualties and an attack would deepen the gulf between Christians and Muslims. It would not be a just war, it would be illegal, and it would not make things better. Bush corrected the cardinal. "It will make things better," said the president.[74]

That same day the foreign ministers of France, Germany, and Russia emerged from a meeting in Paris and issued a joint statement that the weapons inspections conducted by Blix and ElBaradei were "producing increasingly encouraging results" and should be expedited. "We will not let a proposed resolution pass that would authorize the use of force. *Russia and France, as permanent members of the Security Council, will assume all their responsibilities at this point.*" (Emphasis added.) The foreign ministers did not say veto explicitly but there could be no doubt what they meant. In an oral statement accompanying the declaration, Russian foreign minister Igor Ivanov added that China shared the European approach.[75]

On the evening of March 6, Bush held a televised news conference in the East Room of the White House. Asked repeatedly about Iraq, the president made it clear that military action was near. "Inspection teams do not need more time or more personnel," said Bush. If Saddam doesn't voluntarily disarm, "we will disarm him." Asked if he worried that the United States "might be viewed as defiant of the United Nations if you went ahead with military actions without specific and explicit authorization from the UN," the president replied he was confident the American people understood that "when it comes to our security, if we need to act, we will act, and we really don't need United Nations approval to do so."

Bush answered reporters' questions for almost an hour. The most telling exchange came toward the end. "I've not made up my mind about military action," said the president in response to a question from Ann Compton of ABC News. After that exchange, Bob Deans of Cox Newspapers put the issue in context.

> *Q:* Mr. President, millions of Americans can recall a time when
> leaders from both parties set this country on a mission of regime
> change in Vietnam. Fifty thousand Americans died. The regime
> is still there in Hanoi, and it hasn't harmed or threatened a single
> American in the 30 years since the war ended. What can you say
> tonight sir, to the sons and daughters of the Americans who served
> in Vietnam, to assure them that you will not lead the country
> down a similar path in Iraq?

The President: That's a great question. Our mission is clear in Iraq.
Should we have to go in, our mission is clear: disarmament. In
order to disarm, it will mean regime change. I'm confident we'll
be able to achieve that objective in a way that minimizes the loss
of life. No doubt there's risk in any military operation. I know that.
But it is very clear what we intend to do. And our mission won't
change. We have got a plan that will achieve that mission, should
we need to send forces in.

Lyndon Johnson, Dean Rusk, and Robert McNamara would have
answered in very much the same way at the time of the Gulf of Tonkin
Resolution. Perhaps what differentiated Bush was his faith in God. "My
faith sustains me because I pray daily," said the president. "I pray for
guidance and wisdom and strength. If we were to commit our troops,
I would pray for their safety, and I would pray for the safety of innocent
Iraqi lives as well."[76]

The following day, March 7, 2003, the United States, Great Britain,
and Spain introduced a resolution in the Security Council demanding
that Iraq surrender all weapons of mass destruction by March 17 or face
military action.[77] Given the announced opposition of France, China,
and Russia, three of the five permanent members of the Security Council, each with a veto, the resolution had little chance. But Tony Blair
believed he needed to make the effort, and Bush supported him.

That same day, Blix and ElBaradei gave their fourth and what would
be their final inspection report to the Security Council. Once again the
inspectors could find nothing to substantiate American charges. Blix
said there was no evidence that Iraq was operating mobile weapon labs.
There was also no evidence of underground armament facilities. Blix
said the Iraqis were being more cooperative, but the inspectors needed
more time. "It will not take years, nor weeks, but months."[78]

Blix was followed by ElBaradei, who said that after three months
of intensive inspections the IAEA had "found no evidence or plausible
indication of the revival of a nuclear weapons program in Iraq." El-
Baradei then delivered two body blows to administration arguments.
First, the much publicized aluminum tubes that Iraq had attempted
to import were not related to the manufacture of centrifuges for the

enrichment of uranium.
Second, the contract al-
leged to have been made
between Iraq and Niger
for the importation of
uranium—the yellow-
cake deal Bush had re-
ferred to in his State of
the Union—was a for-
gery.[79]

British prime minister Tony Blair with Bush.

Despite the reports of
the weapons inspectors,
the American buildup
in Kuwait continued. As the troops moved into battle formation, Bush
consulted once more with Tony Blair by telephone. Bush told Blair that
French opposition to a second Security Council resolution made it unlikely to be adopted. He said that upon withdrawal of the resolution he
planned to give a speech saying the diplomatic phase is over and giving
Saddam a forty-eight-hour ultimatum. Blair said he thought that with
Tory support he could survive a hostile motion in Parliament on the
war, but the opposition might sense an opportunity to get rid of him
and vote for a no confidence motion. On the positive side, Blair's attorney general, Lord Peter Goldsmith, had reversed himself and now
thought Britain did not need a new U.N. resolution to go to war. "I've
decided to come down on one side," Goldsmith told foreign minister
Jack Straw on March 13. "1441 is sufficient." [80]

For Bush the coming attack would mark the beginning of the final
battle to rid the world of evil. He may or may not have believed it would
be a cakewalk, but he was certain it was God's will. Senior administration officials, who, with the exception of Powell, had never seen
combat, also anticipated an early and complete victory. Some in the
military were equally giddy. On March 14, Tommy Franks summoned
subordinate commanders to his headquarters in Qatar for a final briefing. As the officers entered the CENTCOM command center, the
lights dimmed and they were treated to opening clips from the film
Gladiator. Russell Crowe, the favorite general of the emperor Marcus

Aurelius, was preparing to smash a rebellious German tribe resisting the expansion of the Roman Empire. The Romans gave the barbarians a final chance to surrender, but their offer was refused. As the Roman legions readied themselves for battle, the clip ended with Crowe exhorting his men, "On my signal, unleash hell."[81]

With the attack imminent, Bush decided it would be useful to meet once more with Tony Blair. Without Britain's support, the United States would be virtually alone, and the president wanted to assist Blair all he could. Shortly after noon on March 14, White House spokesman Ari Fleischer announced that Bush and Blair would meet two days later in the Azores, some eight hundred miles off the coast of Portugal. They would be joined by Spanish president José María Aznar. Portugal's prime minister, José Manuel Durão Barroso, who also supported the war, would serve as host. The purpose, said Fleischer, was "to review this diplomacy as it is brought to a conclusion."[82] Bush had originally suggested they meet in Bermuda, where President Eisenhower had met Churchill and later Harold Macmillan, but the British believed Bermuda was geographically too close to the United States and thus symbolically suspect.

Air Force One touched down at Loujes Field in the Azores in the early afternoon, Sunday, March 16. Blair and Aznar were waiting. José Barroso gave a short welcoming address, and the four headed off to the American portion of the airbase, where a conference room had been prepared. After briefly reviewing the diplomatic maneuvering, the four agreed that the chances of the Security Council adopting their proposed second resolution were virtually nil. If there was no breakthrough within the next twenty-four hours, they would formally withdraw it at ten the next morning. "This is our last effort," said Bush. "Everyone has to be able to say we did everything we could to avoid war. But this is the final moment, the moment of truth."[83]

The president then told Blair and the other leaders that he was going to deliver a speech the next day giving Saddam a forty-eight-hour ultimatum to leave Iraq or face war. "That's what I'm going to do, okay?" Bush was not consulting. He was telling Blair, Aznar, and Barroso what was coming. War would commence forty-eight hours after he spoke. "So everybody knows," said the president.[84]

The meeting was brief. Afterward, the four leaders met with the press. "We've had a really good discussion," Bush told the assembled reporters. "And we concluded tomorrow is the moment of truth for the world." The president said the logic of U.N. Resolution 1441 was inescapable. "The Iraqi regime will disarm itself, or the Iraqi regime will be disarmed by force. And the Iraqi regime has not disarmed itself."[85] After a quick dinner in the Azores, the four leaders departed. Bush asked Blair about the upcoming vote in Parliament and expressed confidence that he would survive.

At 9:45 the next morning Bush instructed Ari Fleischer to announce that the United States, Britain, and Spain had withdrawn their Security Council resolution. There would be no U.N. vote. Fleischer appeared in the press room shortly afterward for his regular morning session with White House reporters and dispensed with his usual reading of the daily schedule. His statement was brief. "The United Nations has failed to enforce its demands that Iraq immediately disarm. As a result, the diplomatic window has now been closed. The president will address the nation tonight at 8 p.m. He will say that to avoid military conflict, Saddam Hussein must leave the country." Reporters ran from the briefing room. "It was like the old days in the movies," Fleischer recalled, "when men with hats would sprint to phones to file their stories."[86]

Bush alerted Tommy Franks. "I'm not giving you the order yet, but you have to be ready. Do all the last minute things you need to do."[87]

That evening, before speaking to the nation, Bush met with the congressional leadership. "We did everything we could in the UN," said the president, "but it was impossible because of the French. We will now remove Saddam Hussein from power." Bush said that if Saddam left, which was unlikely, "we'll go in anyway. That way we can avoid ethnic cleansing. We'll go in a peaceful way, and there will be a list of country after country after country all who are solidly with us in this coalition."[88]

At eight o'clock, Bush addressed the nation. He spoke for fifteen minutes. Dismissing the findings of Hans Blix and Mohamed ElBaradei, the president said

> Intelligence gathered by this and other governments leaves no doubt that the Iraq regime continues to possess and conceal some of the most lethal weapons ever devised. . . . The United States and other nations

did nothing to deserve or invite this threat. But we will do everything to defeat it.

Saddam Hussein and his sons must leave Iraq within 48 hours. Their refusal to do so will result in military conflict, commenced at a time of our choosing. For their own safety, all foreign nationals, including journalists and inspectors, should leave Iraq immediately.[89]

The United States was going to war. The following day, Bush formally advised Congress that diplomatic efforts to avoid war had failed, and that pursuant to recent congressional legislation the United States would take the appropriate action.[90]* Blair went before the House of Commons that same day and put his government on the line. "This is a tough choice," said Blair. "To stand British troops down now and turn back or to hold firm to the course that we have set. I believe passionately that we must hold firm to that course."[91] The debate in the Commons went on well into the night. Finally, at 10:15 p.m. London time (5:15 p.m. in Washington) the Commons divided. Blair won 396–217. He lost 139 members of his own Labour Party, but the Tories voted with him. Britain would be joining the United States to invade Iraq.

The next morning, Wednesday, March 19, Bush met with his advisers in the White House for a final review. "Do you have any last comments," the president asked. None did. At that point a bank of television screens lit up showing Franks and nine of his senior commanders. "Tommy," said Bush, "I would like to address your team." The president then asked each commander, "Do you have everything you need? Everything to accomplish your mission?" "My command and control is all up," said Lieutenant General Michael Moseley, Franks's Air Force commander. "I am in place and ready. I have everything we need to win."

Lieutenant General David McKiernan, the Army ground commander, said the same. "We are moving forward into attack positions. Our logistics are in place. We have everything we need to win." Vice Admiral Timothy Keating said he had ninety American ships and fifty-nine from coalition partners. "Green across the board."[92] The

---

* Bush's reference is to House Joint Resolution 114, enacted October 10, 2002. *Public Law* 107–243. See Chapter 13.

President Bush after making the decision to invade Iraq, March 19, 2003.

president repeated the question to each of the other commanders and all replied affirmatively.

"Mr. President," said Franks, "this force is ready. D-Day, H-Hour is 2100 hours tonight Iraq time, 1800 hours Greenwich mean, 1300 hours East Coast time."

Bush nodded and turned to Rumsfeld. "Mr. Secretary, for the peace of the world and the benefit and freedom of the Iraqi people, I hereby give the order to execute Operation Iraqi Freedom. May God bless the troops."

"Mr. President," Franks replied, "may God bless America."[93]

Franks saluted, and Bush returned his salute. The president was overcome with emotion. Tears welled up in his eyes. The nation was at war. He stood and moved rapidly out of the room without speaking. With his dog Spot he went for a walk on the South Lawn to collect himself.

"It was an emotional moment for me," Bush later recalled.

I prayed as I walked around the circle. I prayed that our troops would be safe, be protected by the Almighty, that there would be minimal loss of life. Going into this period, I was praying for strength to do God's will. . . . I pray that I be as good a messenger of His will as possible. And then, of course, I pray for personal strength and forgiveness.[94]

CHAPTER FIFTEEN

"Mission Accomplished"

Major combat operations in Iraq have ended. In the battle of Iraq, the United States and our allies have prevailed. And now our coalition is engaged in securing and reconstructing that country.

George W. Bush
May 1, 2003

At 10:16 on the evening of March 19, Bush addressed the nation from the Oval Office. "At this hour," said the president, "American and coalition forces are in the early stages of military operations to disarm Iraq. . . . On my orders, coalition forces have begun striking selected targets of military importance to undermine Saddam Hussein's ability to wage war." Bush spoke four minutes. He said that by removing Saddam Hussein, he was lessening the threat of another terrorist attack on American soil. "Now that the conflict has come, the only way to limit its duration is to apply decisive force. And I assure you this will not be a campaign of half measures, and we will accept no outcome but victory." [1]

As Bush spoke, the forces of Central Command launched their attack. Unlike the 1991 Gulf War, or recent operations in Afghanistan,

General Franks ordered the air and ground offensives to begin simultaneously. By so doing he hoped to achieve tactical surprise. Allied aircraft flew over 1,500 sorties the first day, the command launched more than 600 cruise missiles at preselected Iraqi military installations, and the ground attack—some 145,000 troops with 500 tanks and armored vehicles—moved out in three separate thrusts. The British 1st Armoured Division headed for the southern city of Basra, the 1st Marine Expeditionary Force moved to capture the Rumilyah oil fields, and the 3rd Infantry Division, followed by the 82nd and 101st Airborne, moved in the direction of Baghdad. The attack was titled Operation Iraqi Freedom, and according to Franks, the name had been chosen by Bush himself. "The goal was not conquest, not oil, but freedom for twenty-six million Iraqis," said Franks.[2] Or as Rumsfeld put it, "Bush often expressed his belief that freedom was a gift of the Almighty. He seemed to feel almost duty bound to help expand the frontiers of freedom in the Middle East."[3]

On the eve of the attack, Franks told Wolfowitz he did not want to be bothered by the Joint Chiefs of Staff. "Operation Enduring Freedom in Afghanistan had been nitpicked by the Service Chiefs and the Joint Staff and I did not intend to see a recurrence in Iraq," said Franks. He told Wolfowitz he did not want the Joint Chiefs present during his daily videoconferences with Rumsfeld. "They do not have sufficient Joint background or understanding to be operationally useful." Franks said he did not want to be "treed by Chihuahuas" while trying to orchestrate the attack.[4] The CENTCOM commander had reason to be concerned. In the first Gulf War, Powell and Cheney did not interfere with Schwarzkopf's day-to-day control. Modern advances in communications technology had complicated the issue of command, and Franks was calling it to Rumsfeld's (and Bush's) attention.*

The American media called the attack "Shock and Awe," and the

---

* The contrast to World War II is striking. During the early morning hours of D-Day, June 6, 1944, General Marshall was awakened in his quarters by a phone call from the Pentagon telling him the troops had landed on the French coast. He thanked the caller and hung up. He then passed the news to Mrs. Marshall. She asked how they were doing. Marshall replied he didn't inquire. "That's Eisenhower's business," said the chief of staff.

public was fascinated by the television coverage as Franks's blitzkrieg moved north. But for most of the world, this was a war of American aggression. At the United Nations, French foreign minister Dominique de Villepin portrayed the choice between war and peace as between two diametrically opposed visions of the world. "To those who choose to use force and think they can resolve the world's complexity through swift and preventive action, we offer in contrast determined action over time. . . . The outbreak of force in this area which is so unstable can only exacerbate the tensions and fractures on which the terrorists feed."[5] German foreign minister Joschka Fischer noted that the world had experienced the horrors of war all too often. "War is a terrible thing. It is a great tragedy for those affected and for all of us. . . . There is no basis in the UN Charter for a regime change by military means."[6] The Chinese foreign ministry issued a statement on March 20 expressing its "serious concern" that the United States had resorted to war.[7] Vladimir Putin stressed the importance of international law and the United Nations in resolving such disputes,[8] and Kofi Annan, the U.N. secretary-general, in a subsequent interview with Australian television, called the American invasion of Iraq "illegal" and a violation of the United Nations charter.[9]

Like most Americans, Bush remained glued to the television set and talked of little else. "He was just totally immersed," said his old Yale friend (and Texas Rangers investor) Roland Betts.[10] On March 27, Bush hosted Tony Blair at Camp David. The war was going exceptionally well. "Thousands are just taking off their uniforms and going home," said the president. "Yes, they are just melting away," Blair replied.[11] Alastair Campbell, Blair's aide and confidant, thought Bush looked very fit. "He did casual gear a lot better than T[ony] B[lair] but I guess the White House logo on everything helped a fair bit." Campbell provided a thumbnail sketch of Bush for his diary:

He was a real early to bed early to rise man. He was obsessed with punctuality. He liked to read a brief, then discuss, then decide. He was open to ideas. He was very religious. He was loyal to friends but once you fell out with him, that was that.[12]

In Iraq, Franks's forces advanced 251 miles in six days. As Bush told Blair, Iraqi forces were offering light resistance. There were no mass surrenders. Conscript troops were simply taking off their uniforms and walking away, just as Bush said. The most serious opposition came from irregular forces known as the "Saddam Fedayeen" (literally "those who sacrifice themselves"), originally organized by Saddam's son Uday in 1995, and named to evoke memories of guerrilla attackers of Israel in the 1950s. CENTCOM had not prepared for an irregular war, and this would become a serious problem, but they pressed ahead.* No WMD had been discovered and a three-day sandstorm caused only a temporary delay in Franks's advance.

Bush relished his role as commander in chief. On March 26, six days after the ground war began, he visited Central Command headquarters at MacDill Air Force Base in Tampa, and gave a rousing pep talk to the assembled servicemen. "The liberty we prize is not America's gift to the world," said the president, "it is God's gift to humanity." [13] On the 31st he spoke to the Coast Guard in Philadelphia, and then on April 3, as Franks's forces approached Baghdad, he and Laura flew to Camp Lejeune in North Carolina to visit the Marines. Camp Lejeune was the home of the 1st Marine Expeditionary Force and had sent over seventeen thousand troops to Iraq. "This is a time of hardship for many military families," said Bush. "Some of you have been separated from your loved ones for quite a while. All of America is grateful to you for your sacrifice, and Laura and I are here to thank each of you."

---

* Lieutenant General William Scott Wallace, commanding V Corps, created a brief firestorm when, on March 26, he told Rick Atkinson of *The Washington Post* and Jim Dwyer of *The New York Times* that "The enemy we're fighting is a bit different from the one we war gamed against, because of these paramilitary forces. We knew they were here but we did not know how they would fight." Wallace said, "We're dealing with a country in which everybody has a weapon, and when they all fire them in the air at the same time, it's tough." Wallace's remarks caused consternation at the Pentagon, and Rumsfeld pressed Franks about Wallace's trustworthiness.

Wallace of course was correct, and Franks to his credit backed his corps commander. Rick Atkinson, "General: A War Likely; Logistics, Enemy Force Reevaluation," *Washington Post*, March 27, 2003; Jim Dwyer, "A Gulf Commander Sees a Longer Road," *New York Times*, March 28, 2003; Tommy Franks, with Malcolm McConnell, *American Soldier* (New York: HarperCollins, 2004), 508–9.

The president spoke to the twelve thousand Marines remaining at Lejeune from a makeshift stage on a giant drill field ringed by tanks and howitzers. "Overcoming evil is the noblest cause and the hardest work. And the liberation of millions is the fulfillment of America's founding promise."[14] Bush and Laura joined the troops for lunch in the mess hall, and then went to the chapel to meet with the families of five Marines killed in Iraq. Two of the Marines left behind children they had never met, babies who were born after their deployment. The president and Laura spoke with each family. Bush was deeply moved and teary-eyed by the time he left the chapel to board Marine One. According to Ari Fleischer, the president sat in utter silence on the twenty-five-minute flight back to Air Force One. "He looked out the window, alone with his thoughts."[15]

In a private moment, Stephen Hadley, Condoleezza Rice's deputy, asked the president how he was holding up. "I made the decision," Bush said. "I sleep well at night."[16]

In Iraq, Franks's blitzkrieg continued. Armored columns from the 3rd Infantry division reached Baghdad International Airport at midday on April 4. Fearing the determined defense of Fortress Baghdad, Franks ordered his armored commanders to make a "thunder run" through the city. A thunder run is an American military maneuver dating to the Vietnam War. As Franks explained, "it is a unit of armor and mechanized infantry moving at high speed through a built-up area like a city. The purpose was to either catch the enemy off guard or overwhelm him with force."[17] At dawn on April 5, an armored column of fifty tanks and armored vehicles roared into Baghdad at speeds up to forty-five miles an hour. Iraqi defenders were stunned. The American vehicles were virtually impervious to Iraqi small arms fire, supporting aircraft and helicopter gunships neutralized enemy armor, and the tanks drove to the center of the city and then back to the airport. The battle lasted eight hours, only one tank was lost, and Iraqi casualties were put at two thousand. More important, the morale of the Iraqi military was shattered.

A second thunder run on April 7 comprised 130 tanks and armored vehicles, and this time they remained in the city. The American military had taken Baghdad. The thunder runs exhibited the U.S. Army at its best. The maneuver was boldly conceived and superbly executed. Organized resistance ended. Two days later, Saddam's statue on Firdos Square in downtown Baghdad was toppled, and the Iraqi dictator went into hiding. "For twenty days I had been filled with anxiety," wrote Bush in his memoirs. "Now I was overwhelmed with pride."[18]

The statue of Saddam Hussein is toppled in Firdos Square, April 9, 2003.

The toppling of Saddam's statue was the high-water mark of the invasion. CNN replayed the incident every 7.5 minutes on April 9, and Fox News every 4.4 minutes.[19] Rumsfeld compared the toppling of the statue with the fall of the Berlin Wall in 1989 and the collapse of the Iron Curtain, and Bush's public approval rating surged from 57 to 77 percent.[20]

The following day, Bush spoke to the Iraqi people in a televised address. "At this moment," said the president, "the regime of Saddam Hussein is being removed from power, and a long era of fear and cruelty is ending." Bush told the Iraqis, "You are a good and gifted people, the heirs of a great civilization that contributes to all humanity."[21] As Bush was speaking, Iraqi mobs were looting the National Museum in Baghdad of its art treasures, its literary artifacts, and records. "You'd have to go back centuries, to the Mongol invasion of Baghdad in 1258, to find looting on this scale," said Eleanor Robson, a noted archaeologist at All Souls College, Oxford. Coalition forces did not intervene. "I don't think that anyone anticipated that the riches of Iraq would be looted by the Iraqi people," said CENTCOM spokesman Brigadier General Vincent Brooks.[22]*

---

* Brooks was blowing smoke. On March 26, the Pentagon's Office of Reconstruction and Humanitarian Assistance (ORHA), the agency in charge of postwar Iraq, sent a memo to

In Washington, the Bush administration minimized the looting. "What you are seeing is a reaction to oppression," said White House spokesman Ari Fleischer. For Fleischer, the looting was "a way station on the road to liberty and freedom." Or as Rumsfeld put it at a Pentagon briefing, "Stuff happens!" The secretary of defense was aglow with victory. Saddam had been ousted, Baghdad captured, and coalition casualties had been exceptionally light. When asked about the looting, Rumsfeld said,

> In terms of what's going on in that country, it is a fundamental misunderstanding to see these images over, and over, and over again of some boy walking out with a vase and say, "Oh, my goodness, you didn't have a plan!" That's nonsense. They [coalition forces] have a plan, and they're doing a terrific job. And it's untidy, and freedom's untidy, and free people are free to make mistakes and commit crimes and do bad things. They're also free to live their lives and do wonderful things, and that's what's going to happen here.[23]

The looting of the National Museum and the administration's failure to respond was the beginning of the erosion of American authority in Iraq. The glib comments of Fleischer and Rumsfeld not only betrayed a fundamental misunderstanding of what was at stake, but severely damaged the credibility of the United States. As Fred Iklé, one of the chief hawks of the Reagan administration, noted, "America lost most of its prestige and respect in that episode. To pacify a conquered country, the victor's prestige and dignity is absolutely critical."[24] The message sent to the Iraqis was that the United States did not care. The

CENTCOM instructing military commanders to protect the Iraq National Museum and other historic sites. "Coalition forces must secure these facilities in order to prevent looting and the resulting irreparable loss of cultural treasures," said the memo. The National Museum ranked second on the list of sixteen sites to be protected. "Its collections cover over 5,000 years of recorded history and represents the fruits of 200 years of scientific investigation by both Western and Iraqi archeologists." ORHA, Guidance for CFLCC [Central Command] Priorities for Securing Key Baghdad Institutions; Paul Martin, "Troops Were Told to Guard Treasures," *Washington Times*, April 20, 2003.

failure to respond effectively to the looting undercut the legitimacy of
the occupation from the very beginning. As a prominent Iraqi archaeologist put it, "A country's identity, its value and civilization resides in
its history. If a country's civilization is looted, as ours has been here, its
history ends. Please tell this to President Bush. Please remind him that
he promised to liberate the Iraqi people, but this is not liberation, this
is humiliation." [25]

On April 15, as Iraqi mobs continued the looting of museums and
government ministries, Bush met with the National Security Council
to review plans for withdrawing American troops from Iraq. The president believed coalition forces enjoyed the respect and admiration of the
Iraqi people for liberating them from Saddam. A large post-hostilities
force should not be necessary. During the 2000 election campaign,
Bush had sharply criticized the open-ended peacekeeping efforts of the
Clinton administration in Kosovo, and Rumsfeld had recently restated
that view in a major public speech entitled "Beyond Nation Building."
"If the United States were to lead an international coalition in Iraq,"
said the secretary, "it would be guided by two constraints. Stay as long
as necessary, and to leave as soon as possible." [26] In Iraq, Tommy Franks
shared that assessment. The Iraq War should be considered a thun-
derstorm: short, violent, and decisive, but without a burdensome, long-
term troop commitment.

At Franks's recommendation, Bush approved the quick drawdown of American forces. The combat units should pull out within
sixty days. New units would arrive to help stabilize the country,
but would stay only 120 days. By August, less than thirty thousand
troops would be in Iraq. CENTCOM anticipated that there would
be a functioning Iraqi government within thirty to sixty days, and as
Franks put it, commanders should take as much risk coming out of
Iraq as they had taken going in. [27] Most importantly, Franks pressed
the president to declare victory and pave the way for the American
withdrawal.

Bush was eager to oblige. Saddam had been ousted and the fighting
was all but over. Why not declare victory? The White House staff was
enthusiastic. Stephen Hadley called Richard Armitage to find out how

victory parades were organized after the first Gulf War.* Bush wanted a setting that would galvanize the country and display American military might at its zenith. White House deputy chief of staff Joe Hagin told the president that the USS *Abraham Lincoln*, a nuclear-powered aircraft carrier, was returning to port in San Diego after a nine-month stint in the Persian Gulf, the longest deployment of any vessel since the Vietnam War. The *Lincoln* had played a prominent role in Operation Iraqi Freedom where its high-performance F-14 and F-18 fighter jets had dropped a total of six hundred tons of bombs on enemy targets. Why not declare victory from the flight deck of the carrier? Bush could fly to the *Lincoln* as it approached the coast, land on the flight deck, and deliver his address. Hollywood could scarcely have suggested a more impressive setting.

Bush was enthralled with the idea. A former National Guard pilot, he loved the idea of suiting up and strutting before the cameras as a combat pilot. The details were put in place. The president would take the copilot's seat in one of the *Abraham Lincoln*'s S-3B Vikings, a four-person antisubmarine jet. Andy Card would accompany the president in a second S-3B Viking. At the Navy's insistence, the president and Card undertook water-survival training in the White House swimming pool. They donned aviator's flight suits, put on harnesses, and practiced jumping into the deep end and removing the gear before they hit bottom. Bush "did not want to cheat the system," said Card. "So what everybody else had to go through, he wanted to have to go through."[28]

The victory ceremony was set for May 1. Bush arrived at the Naval Air Station on North Island in San Diego Bay in the early afternoon and met his pilot, Commander John Lussier, the senior aviator of the *Abraham Lincoln*'s Viking squadron. After explaining the cockpit ejection procedures to the president, Lussier said, "There is always some danger inherent in carrier naval aviation. Ninety-nine point nine percent of the time everything goes smoothly. But there

---

* In 1991, General Schwarzkopf and his troops rode in a ticker tape parade through lower Manhattan and then marched down Pennsylvania Avenue in Washington.

is always that one-tenth of one percent chance that something could happen."

"Luce, you don't need to worry about that. We've got a great vice president."[29]

Bush sat in the right front seat next to Lussier. The copilot sat behind Bush, joined by a Secret Service agent. After the plane (dubbed Navy One) reached cruising altitude, Lussier asked the president if he wanted to take the controls. "I do," said Bush, and for the next fifteen minutes the president flew the jet at a speed of four hundred miles an hour, the first sitting president to pilot an aircraft. Card, who had served briefly in the Merchant Marine, also briefly took the controls of his plane. As the planes approached the *Abraham Lincoln*, the pilots retook control. Lussier lowered the plane's tailhook and aimed for the third of four retaining wires stretched across the flight deck. The plane came in a little too flat, missed the third wire but snagged the fourth. The wire held and the plane came to a lurching stop as Lussier cut the engine.

Bush climbed out of the cockpit grinning from ear to ear. Wearing his combat gear he plunged into a crowd of Navy flight crews, shaking hands and slapping backs like a veteran from *Top Gun*. Bush was scheduled to spend five minutes on deck but stayed for thirty. "It was a joyous moment," he said later. "They were just so pleased to see the president. These were sailors who were coming back from a battle. They had been deployed for months. They were anxious to get home, and here comes the commander in chief flying in one of their fighters to greet them, and they were thrilled."[30]

Bush went below, ate with the enlisted personnel, changed into a business suit and tie, and returned to the flight deck to speak. The president stood in the middle of a vast open space, five thousand members of the crew arranged around him, with a giant banner proclaiming "Mission Accomplished" hanging behind him. It was dusk, and the lighting had that special glow that comes when the sun is just above the horizon. Both the setting and the timing had been arranged by Karl Rove and White House communications aide Scott Sforza—the dramatic first step of a yet-to-be-announced 2004 presidential campaign.[31]

"Mission Accomplished," May 1, 2003.

"Major combat operations in Iraq have ended," said the president. "In the battle of Iraq, the United States and our allies have prevailed. And now our coalition is engaged in securing and reconstructing that country." Bush spoke for twenty minutes. He praised the military repeatedly. "Operation Iraqi Freedom was carried out with a combination of precision and speed and boldness the enemy did not expect and the world had not seen before. . . . You have shown the world the skill and might of the American Armed Forces."

It was a victory lap without end. "In the images of fallen statues, we have witnessed the arrival of a new era. . . . Today, we have the greater power to free a nation by breaking a dangerous and aggressive regime. . . . All can know, friend and foe alike, that our Nation has a mission: We will answer threats to our security, and we will defend the peace."

In the most controversial portion of the speech, Bush conflated al Qaeda and Saddam Hussein, advancing a claim that was dubious at best. "The liberation of Iraq is a crucial advance in the campaign against terror. We've removed an ally of Al Qaeda and cut off a source of terrorist funding. And this much is certain. No terrorist network will gain weapons of mass destruction from the Iraqi regime because the regime is no more." Not only was the tie between Saddam and al Qaeda nonexistent, but no weapons of mass destruction had been found anywhere in Iraq.

As was his habit, Bush concluded on a biblical note.

> All of you—all of this generation of our military—have taken up the highest calling of history. You are defending your country and protecting the innocent from harm. And wherever you go, you carry a message of hope, a message that is ancient and ever new. In the words of the prophet Isaiah, "To the captives, 'come out,' and to those in darkness, 'be free.'"[32]

It was a triumphant moment for Bush. But as Thomas Ricks of *The Washington Post* noted, the president's victory celebration was like tearing the goalposts down at halftime.[33] The insurgency in Iraq was just beginning, the six largely Sunni provinces west of Baghdad had mutinied, no weapons of mass destruction had been found, and the coalition military was winding down.

The president remained on the *Abraham Lincoln* overnight, and then flew to California's Silicon Valley, where he gave a major speech on the economy. Bush was always aware of his father's stunning victory in the first Gulf War and how quickly his domestic support had eroded. With the 2004 presidential election just eighteen months away, he was determined to avoid a repeat. By addressing domestic issues early, the president was sending a message that he was in touch with voters' concerns.

The Department of Labor had just announced that the nation's unemployment rate had risen to 6 percent. For Bush, the remedy was a massive $550 billion tax cut and an end to the tax on dividends. "I urge the United States Congress to look at the unemployment numbers that came out today and pass a tax relief plan that will matter, a tax relief plan robust enough so that the people of this country who are looking for work can find a job."[34] It was an impressive performance. The president was in a flight suit one day celebrating victory, and the next day he was wearing a business suit standing on a platform in Silicon Valley addressing the economy.

Bush's 2004 presidential campaign had informally begun on New Year's Day 2003 in the living room at the ranch in Crawford when Karl Rove and the president laid the groundwork. Bush made it clear that until Saddam was toppled and his regime destroyed, he would not be involved in the campaign. Rove would be in charge, and all White House input would be channeled through him. On January 27, 2003, Ken Mehlman, then the director of the White House Political Affairs Office, was named campaign manager, and a strategy board of Rove, Mehlman, Mark McKinnon, and Matthew Dowd began to frame the campaign. Bush said he would not campaign actively in 2003, except to attend official fundraisers. The speech in Silicon Valley on May 2 was not a campaign speech as such, but clearly depicted the president's interest in domestic matters. Two weeks later, on May 16, the campaign committee headed by Rove filed notice of Bush's candidacy with the Federal Election Commission.[35]

Bush's announcement of the end of combat operations in Iraq from the flight deck of the *Abraham Lincoln* marked the end of Phase III of Operation Iraqi Freedom and the beginning of Phase IV— post-hostilities stabilization and reconstruction. On January 20, 2003, Bush had issued a presidential directive entrusting the Defense Department with postwar planning and reconstruction.[36] Rumsfeld established the Office of Reconstruction and Humanitarian Assistance (ORHA) to handle the task, and recruited retired Lieutenant General Jay Garner to head the office. Garner was supremely qualified. He had served in the first Gulf War, was on good terms with Colin Powell and the State Department, and had commanded Operation Provide Comfort at the end of the Gulf War, assisting Iraqi Kurds to secure an autonomous enclave in northern Iraq. He was highly regarded both by the Iraqis and the military, and as Rumsfeld put it, "believed, as I did, in empowering local populations to do things for themselves. Once the military had toppled Saddam's regime, I thought it was strategically important to put the United States in a supporting role to the Iraqis as soon as possible. This was the Pentagon's and—at least as I understood it—the president's vision."[37]

For Rumsfeld and Garner (and Franks, for that matter), the goals were straightforward. Iraq should remain united as a single country, it should not be a threat to its neighbors, the rights of minorities should be respected, and it should not be hospitable to terrorists. But otherwise, the future of the nation should be determined by the Iraqis.[38] On April 2, Rumsfeld instructed the military to support Garner "as required." Garner's mission, said the secretary, was "to help create the conditions for transition to Iraqi self-rule and the withdrawal of coalition forces upon completion of their military objectives."[39]

But Garner soon ran into difficulty. He had no use for Ahmed Chalabi, the candidate of Washington neocons to head an Iraqi government ("I thought he was a thug, very sleazy"); declined to remove experienced Baathists from senior leadership positions in government and industry; and was planning to reorganize the Iraqi army into three reliable divisions to "maintain order, suppress various militias, put an Iraqi face on security, and relieve the burden on Coalition military."[40] Garner was determined to get Iraq running again with as little disruption as possible.

Suddenly, that was no longer White House policy. Rather than sticking with the rapid drawdown and allowing the Iraqis to determine their future, Bush became entranced with the idea of bringing Western-style democracy to Iraq. His victory speech on the *Abraham Lincoln* announced the shift. "The transition from dictatorship to democracy will take time," said the president, "but is worth every effort. Our coalition will stay until our work is done. And then we will leave, and we will leave behind a free Iraq."[41] Bush was unilaterally changing the plan. Rather than a quick transition, rather than in and out, the United States would remain in Iraq until democracy had been established.

In his memoirs, Rumsfeld took issue with the change. "This was not the way I understood our plan," wrote the secretary. "A nation that had suffered under decades of dictatorial rule was unlikely to quickly reorganize itself into a stable, modern, democratic state. I hoped Iraq would turn toward some form of representative government, but I thought we needed to be clear-eyed about democracy's prospects in the country."[42]

Once again Bush had made the decision on his own. There was no National Security Council meeting to discuss the shift, and neither

L. Paul Bremer

Rumsfeld nor Powell was consulted. Once again, it was the personalization of presidential power. Bush, aided by Condoleezza Rice and the White House staff, had changed course.*

To speed the process of democratization, Bush decided to supersede Garner and Rumsfeld's Office of Reconstruction and Humanitarian Assistance with an all-powerful presidential envoy. The White House would take control. Paul Wolfowitz asked to be considered for the post but was turned down, partly because he was considered a thinker rather than a doer, and also because a Jewish viceroy in the Arab world would be difficult.[43] Rumsfeld became concerned that the new presidential envoy would supersede the Defense Department's control of the occupation, and so to preserve his department's authority, he devoted himself to finding the right person for the job. Rather than support Garner and the ORHA, Rumsfeld led the search to find his replacement. In retrospect, that was a mistake. The first person on Rumsfeld's list was L. Paul Bremer, who had been initially recommended by George Shultz and whom Rumsfeld considered "an action-oriented executive able to get things done."[44]

At sixty-one, Bremer appeared to be the personification of the

---

* "It is hard to know exactly where the president's far-reaching language about democracy originated," wrote Rumsfeld in his memoirs. "It was not a large part of his original calculus in toppling Saddam's regime, at least from what I gleaned from private conversations and NSC meetings. I didn't hear rhetoric about democracy from Colin Powell or State Department officials. I know it did not come from us in the Department of Defense. Condoleezza Rice seems to be the one top adviser who spoke that way, but it was not clear to me whether she was encouraging the president to use rhetoric about democracy or whether it was originating with the president." *Known and Unknown* (New York: Sentinel, 2011), 499.

American establishment. The son of the president of Christian Dior Perfumes, Bremer had graduated from Andover and Yale, took an MBA from Harvard, and continued his studies at the Institut d'études Politiques in Paris. He then served twenty-three years in the State Department. In 1981 he became Secretary of State Alexander Haig's executive assistant, was appointed ambassador to the Netherlands by Ronald Reagan in 1983, and ambassador-at-large for counterterrorism in 1986. After retiring from the foreign service in 1989, Bremer became managing director of Henry Kissinger's consulting firm, and then in 2000 joined Marsh & McLennan as chairman and CEO of Marsh Crisis Consulting, a risk-management subsidiary. He had no experience in the Middle East, did not speak Arabic, and had never run anything larger than an embassy. But he exuded what State Department colleagues called a Kissingerian confidence, and seemed to relish making decisions.

Rumsfeld met with Bremer in late April, and then wrote Andy Card. "You will recall we discussed him with the president. I have had a good talk with him. I like him. I think he is the man."[45] Bush accepted Rumsfeld's recommendation. He met with Bremer, who preferred to be called Jerry, in the White House on May 6, and over lunch in the small dining room off the Oval Office quizzed him about Iraq. Bush liked what he heard. Bremer was ardent about creating a democratic Iraq, and told the president it would take longer than currently estimated. "We'll stay until the job is done," said Bush. "You can count on my support irrespective of the political calendar or what the media might say."[46]*

Following lunch, Bush took Bremer to meet with reporters. "Today, it is my honor to announce that Jerry Bremer has agreed to become

* As Bremer expressed it, "The president's instructions to me . . . when I had lunch with him alone on May 6, were that we're going to take our time to get it right. . . . The president had effectively, though perhaps not formally, changed his position on the question of a short or long occupation, having before the war been in favor of a short occupation. By the time I came in, that was gone." Special Inspector General for Iraq Reconstruction, interview with Ambassador L. Paul Bremer III, March 18, 2008, cited in *Hard Lessons: The Iraq Reconstruction Experience* (Washington, D.C.: U.S. Independent Agencies and Commissions, 2009), 69.

the Presidential Envoy to Iraq. He is a man of enormous experience, a person who knows how to get things done. He's a can-do type person," said the president. "The ambassador goes with the full blessings of this administration and the full confidence of all of us in this administration that he can get the job done." [47]

After the press filed out of the Oval Office, Bush and Bremer met with Cheney, Powell, Rumsfeld, Rice, and Card. "I don't know whether we need this meeting at all," said Bush. "Jerry and I just had it." The president's message was clear. As commander in chief, he was taking control. Or as Bremer expressed it, "I was neither Rumsfeld's nor Powell's man, I was the president's man." [48] Rumsfeld was stunned by the president's remarks. After the meeting he made a note to himself. "POTUS had lunch with him alone—should not have done so. POTUS linked him to the White House instead of DoD or DoS [State]." [49] The seeds of the coming debacle had been sowed. As Rumsfeld wrote later, Bremer "assumed he had direct access to President Bush from the start. The president and Rice both not only accepted but facilitated Bremer's unfiltered contact with them. . . . The muddled lines of authority meant there was no single individual in control or responsible for Bremer's work. There were far too many hands on the steering wheel, which, in my view, was a formula for running the truck into the ditch." [50]

Bremer arrived in Iraq on May 11. He considered himself the president's viceroy, and wrote that his assignment combined the vice-regal responsibilities of Douglas MacArthur in Japan and Lucius D. Clay in Germany. Bremer was no MacArthur and certainly no Lucius D. Clay.* He established himself in one of Saddam Hussein's grand pal-

---

* Lucius D. Clay headed the American occupation of Germany from the end of World War II to the establishment of the Federal Republic in 1949. He literally brought a defeated Germany back into the family of nations. He saw to it that the Germans were fed, that they were housed, and that they had work. He preserved Germany's art treasures and prevented their pillage as restitution, conducted a major currency reform, and established the deutschemark. When the Soviets blockaded Berlin in 1948, Clay organized the airlift that kept the city supplied with food and fuel for almost a year. I asked the general if he cleared the airlift with Washington. "No," said Clay. "If Washington didn't like it, they could have relieved me." When Clay died in 1978,

aces, titled his operation the Coalition Provisional Authority, and sent Garner and presidential representative Zalmay Khalilzad, an experienced authority on the Middle East with extensive contacts in Iraq, packing. Four days after arriving, Bremer issued CPA Order Number 1 outlawing the Baath Party and removing tens of thousands of Iraqis from government service. Implementation of the ban was entrusted to Ahmed Chalabi. Under Saddam, Iraq was a one-party state and had been for twenty-five years. People joined the party as a career move, and it was these people who were holding the country's fragile infrastructure together. Garner recognized that and, except for the very top level, was ready to work with them. Bremer, with Bush's approval, wanted to start over. Not only did that reduce the infrastructure to shambles, it inflamed Iraq's Sunni minority (many of whom were Baathists), who quickly became embittered at the American presence in the country.

One week later Bremer issued CPA Order Number 2 disbanding the Iraqi army. This too was contrary to what Garner had planned and took CENTCOM by surprise. "We were working with the army when we were told to disband them," said Marine Major General James Mattis.[51] Overnight some 385,000 soldiers, plus another 285,000 employees of the Ministry of Interior—the home of police and domestic security services—were without jobs. Abruptly terminating the livelihood of these men created a vast pool of humiliated, antagonized, politicized men, many of whom were armed. It also represented a major setback in restoring order. As Colonel John Agoglia, the deputy chief of planning at Central Command said, "That was the day we snatched defeat from the jaws of victory and created an insurgency."[52]

Bremer's third game-changing decision was to reverse Garner's plan to set up an interim Iraqi government as quickly as possible.* Meeting

---

the Berliners placed a monument at the foot of his grave: "Wir danken dem Bewahrer unserer Freiheit." (We thank the defender of our freedom.) See Jean Edward Smith, *Lucius D. Clay: An American Life* (New York: Henry Holt, 1990.)

* On April 28, Garner, assisted by ambassadors Khalilzad and Crocker, had met with the Senior Leadership Council, a well-chosen group of Iraqi leaders that included all the major players, and it was resolved that they would create an interim government at their next meeting in four

with the Senior Leadership Council, the Iraqi advisory group Garner had created, Bremer told them, "You are not the government. The CPA is in charge."[53] According to Bremer, a power-sharing arrangement between coalition authorities and the Iraqis would not work. The advisory group never met again.*

On May 22, Bremer wrote Bush that he had made clear to the Iraqis that the country could have only one government at a time. An Iraqi government could come only after free elections, and that would take time. Bush gave his approval the following day, making it clear that he had dropped the idea of a quick handover of authority to the Iraqis and was prepared for a longer occupation. "You have my full support and confidence," the president wrote Bremer. "You also have the backing of our Administration that knows our work will take time. We will fend off the impatient."[54] Neither Rumsfeld nor Powell was informed beforehand.

Meanwhile, the drawdown of forces continued. Franks retired, and Lieutenant General David McKiernan, who had commanded coalition ground forces, withdrew his command unit from Iraq and was replaced by Lieutenant General Ricardo Sanchez, who had recently succeeded Lieutenant General Scott Williams as commander of V Corps. A corps commander heading the remnant of coalition forces as the drawdown continued was a standard decision by the military. What was not anticipated was that the drawdown would soon be reversed. Bush's determination to convert Iraq into a Western-style democracy, his belief that he was executing God's will, the replacement of Garner with Bremer, and the establishment of the Coalition Provisional Authority converted

---

weeks. Special Inspector General for Iraq Reconstruction, *Hard Lessons: The Iraq Reconstruction Experience* (Washington, D.C.: U.S. Independent Agencies and Commissions, 2009), 63, 64.

* Ali Allawi, a senior Iraqi figure who later served as minister of trade, defense, and finance in successive Iraqi governments, said he was "completely flabbergasted" by Bremer's decision. "Within the space of a few days, the entire process that was to lead to a provincial Iraqi government had been abruptly stopped, and then upended. The change raised suspicions among Iraq's indiginous tribal, political, and religious leadership, who chafed at the idea of an occupation by foreigners, after suffering under Saddam's dictatorship for decades." Special Inspector General for Iraq Reconstruction, *Hard Lessons*, 73.

coalition forces from liberators into occupiers. Instead of becoming a free people with the toppling of Saddam's regime, the Iraqis were now a conquered people.*

The results were immediate. Virtually everything in Iraq shut down. Instead of continuing life as usual, the Iraqis were confronted with chaos. The banks closed and commerce was virtually nonexistent. With Bremer's de-Baathification order, the judicial system disappeared. Local law enforcement became a thing of the past. Schools, universities, and most hospitals were closed. The distribution of fuel and electricity became sporadic. Food was in short supply. The Iraqis responded as a conquered people might. For many, the American army became the enemy. By the end of June, seventy-eight U.S. soldiers had been killed by insurgents since Bush had declared combat operations over from the flight deck of the *Abraham Lincoln*, and another 202 wounded. There were no formal battles, just a string of bombings and snipings that were killing soldiers in ones and twos.

Washington was oblivious to the problem. Rumsfeld initially called the insurgents "dead-enders." Wolfowitz, testifying on Capitol Hill, said, "I think these people are the last remnants of a dying cause."[55] Bush was also in denial. Meeting with reporters in the Roosevelt Room of the White House on July 2, the president was asked about the growing insurgency in Iraq.

"There are some who feel that the conditions are such that they can attack us there," Bush replied. "My answer is: Bring them on. We've got the force necessary to deal with the security situation."[56]

Bush's braggadocio made headlines around the world. The cocky Texas swagger may have appealed to those who listen to Rush Lim-

---

* As former undersecretary of defense Douglas Feith notes, "Had U.S. officials promptly put Iraqis in charge of Iraq, the United States might have maintained the image of liberator in Iraq. No one can say that Iraq would have glided smoothly to democracy if only the United States had seized that moment. But whatever problems were inherent in Iraq's emergence from decades of tyrannical stability, the United States aggravated the situation by setting itself up in the Green Zone—in Saddam's own palaces—as an occupying power. . . . The occupation was a barrier to cooperation. In fact, it encouraged active opposition." Douglas J. Feith, *War and Decision: Inside the Pentagon at the Dawn of the War on Terrorism* (New York: HarperCollins, 2008), 498.

baugh regularly but most were appalled. Ari Fleischer, speaking privately to Bush after the reporters departed, asked the president if he realized how his remarks "would sound to a mother who had just lost her son in Iraq?"

"I hadn't thought of that," said Bush. "I was just trying to express my confidence in the military."[57] Bush later acknowledged his error. "The firestorm of criticism showed that I had left a wrong impression. I learned from the experience and paid close attention to how I communicated . . . in the years ahead."[58]

But the damage was done. Bush's bravado became a rallying cry for insurgents in Iraq. Attacks increased in magnitude, sophistication, and frequency. They were organized mostly by former Baathists, disaffected ex-soldiers, and foreign jihadists. Hundreds of Iraqis were also murdered. Assassinations of policemen, civil authorities, and ordinary citizens employed by the American occupation authority became commonplace. On July 11, General John Abizaid, who had succeeded Franks as CENTCOM commander, reversed Franks's drawdown order. "In light of the current situation," said Abizaid, the forces in Iraq would remain in place. The troops would deploy for "one year boots on the ground."[59] Instead of shrinking to 30,000 as Franks had programmed, U.S. forces would remain at 138,000, plus 20,000 coalition troops. The administration was shocked. Rumsfeld had approved Abizaid's decision, but as General Sanchez noted, "the Secretary really had no choice by then. It was either that or total chaos in a couple of months."[60]*

At the same time, the search for WMD was going nowhere. Since Cheney's speech to the Veterans of Foreign Wars in Nashville in August 2002, the administration had made Iraq's possession of WMD the centerpiece of its campaign to invade. "That is what this war was about,"

---

*   In his memoirs, Rumsfeld credits Abizaid with firmly insisting on the reversal. "Abizaid didn't back down. In response to my queries, he gave reasons why he believed it was guerilla war. . . . He had done what I expected of all those who served in the military: when questioned by the Secretary of Defense, he marshalled the facts and arguments to support his position. He convinced me that we were indeed facing an insurgency." *Known and Unknown* (New York: Sentinel, 2011), 522.

said Ari Fleischer midway through Operation Iraqi Freedom.[61] The negative findings of Hans Blix and Mohamed ElBaradei had been rejected; Colin Powell had placed his reputation on the line in his speech to the United Nations Security Council, and the CIA had provided the White House what it wanted to hear. Bush believed Saddam possessed WMD, and everyone fell into line. "It was the one issue that everyone could agree upon," said Paul Wolfowitz.[62]

After several false starts, Bush entrusted the search to George Tenet and the CIA. "The size of the WMD hunt would prove mammoth," Tenet later wrote. "Iraq had 130 known ammunition depot sites, two of them roughly equal to the square mileage of Manhattan."[63] To head the search, Tenet turned to David Kay, who had been the chief U.N. nuclear weapons inspector in Iraq after the 1991 Gulf War and had successfully uncovered Saddam's nuclear program. Kay assumed control of a 1,400-man team known as the Iraq Survey Group (ISG). "Don't fuck up," said Tenet as Kay departed for Iraq.[64]

Kay initially assumed that finding Saddam's stockpile of WMD would not be difficult. But he quickly discovered that was not the case. "There was nothing to back up the idea that there had been stockpiles of chemical and biological weapons," and the "whole story was falling apart."[65] On July 26, Kay returned to Washington to brief Tenet on his initial findings. The next morning, Tenet took Kay to the White House to inform the president.

"We have not found large stockpiles," Kay told Bush, "but you can't rule them out. We haven't come to the conclusion that they're not there, but they're sure not any place obvious. We've got a lot more to search for and to look at."

"Keep at it," said the president. "You understand you're to find the truth about the program. What do you need that we can do for you?"

"Sir, the only thing we need right now is time and patience."

"You have the time," said Bush. "I have the patience."[66]

Kay and his team continued the search but to no avail. In October he testified before Congress. The Iraq Survey Group had discovered evidence of a clandestine network of laboratories for research purposes, but no "smoking gun." Kay remained in Iraq until January 2004, at which point he resigned. After a six-month search, no WMD had been found. "I don't think they existed," Kay told Reuters correspondent Toby Zakaria. "What everyone was talking about is a stockpile produced after the last Gulf War, and I don't think there was a large-scale production program in the '90s." [67]

On January 28, Kay testified before the Senate Armed Services Committee. "Let me begin by saying we were almost all wrong, and I certainly include myself here." Kay noted that his inspectors had found "hundreds of cases" of prohibited activities involving weapons research by Iraqis, but those activities fell short of actually creating or storing weapons. [68]

Bush invited Kay for lunch the next day. They were joined by Cheney, Rice, and Andy Card in the small dining room off the Oval Office. "How did you reach your conclusions," asked the president, "and how did U.S. intelligence miss this?"

"We missed it because the Iraqis behaved as if they had the weapons." According to Kay, Saddam didn't have WMD but wanted to appear as if he did. His purpose was deception. He did not think the United States would invade, and was using the mythical WMD to keep the Kurds and Shiites in line. Kay also pointed out that one reason the intelligence community had fallen short was that Bush had made Tenet part of the political process. "You're paying a price for having the director of the CIA essentially a cabinet officer and being too close. George comes here every day for the briefing. And inevitably that communicates a sense of the political process to the people at the agency." [69]

On February 2, Secretary of State Colin Powell noted his discomfiture. In an interview with *The Washington Post*, Powell acknowledged that he might not have supported the invasion if he had known there were no weapons of mass destruction. "I don't know," said Powell. "It was the stockpile that presented the final little piece that made it more of a real and present danger and threat to the region and to the world. The absence of a stockpile changes the political calculus and changes the answer you get." [70]

The weekend after Powell spoke, Bush appeared on Tim Russert's *Meet the Press*.

Russert: The night you took the country to war, March seventeenth [2003], you said this: "Intelligence gathered by this and other governments leaves no doubt that the Iraqi regime continues to possess and conceal some of the most lethal weapons ever devised."

President Bush: Right.

Russert: That apparently is not the case.

President Bush: Correct.

Russert: How do you respond to critics who say that you brought the nation to war under false pretenses?

President Bush: First of all, I expected to find the weapons. Sitting behind this desk making a very difficult decision of war and peace, and I based my decision on the best intelligence possible. . . . And I made a decision based upon that intelligence in the context of the war against terror. In other words, we were attacked, and therefore every threat had to be reanalyzed. Every threat had to be looked at. Every potential harm to America had to be judged in the context of the war on terror. . . . And we remembered the fact that [Saddam] had used weapons, which meant he had weapons. We knew he was paying for suicide bombers. We knew he was funding terrorist groups. In other words, he was a dangerous man. . . . I don't think America can stand by and hope for the best from a madman, and I believe it is essential that when we see a threat, we deal with those threats before they become imminent. It's too late if they become imminent. It's too late in this new kind of war, and so that's why I made the decision I made.[71]

In October 2004, Charles Duelfer, who succeeded Kay as head of the Iraq Study Group, issued the group's final report confirming that Saddam Hussein had no weapons of mass destruction.[72] Bush had taken the nation to war. His justification was the flimsy notion that he was removing a potential threat to the United States. It was preventive war. The precedent is devastating. And the cost has been horrendous.

When George W. Bush declared combat operations in Iraq to be over from the flight deck of the *Abraham Lincoln* on May 1, 2003,

172 Americans had been killed in action and another 552 wounded. By the end of 2003, American casualties totaled 580 dead and 2,420 wounded. When Bush left office in January 2009, 4,539 U.S. servicemen and women had lost their lives in Iraq. Another 30,740 had been wounded.[73] These tragic figures pale beside the number of Iraqi casualties.* Saddam had been overthrown. But no weapons of mass destruction had been found, and the United States had sullied its image as the world's standard-bearer of democracy.

Worse perhaps, the decision to move from liberator to occupier in Iraq was the president's alone. Bush consulted neither the State Department nor the Pentagon, and he bears personal responsibility for the disaster. It was an instinctive decision. Bush did not examine the possible consequences beforehand, and he made no effort to consider what might go wrong. It was strictly chain of command. The commander in chief had decided the United States would bring democracy to Iraq, and everyone fell into line. Once again the president was aided by a White House staff that was more interested in accommodating Bush's instincts and intuition rather than questioning them or advising him of the possible consequences.

---

*   According to figures compiled by Iraq Body Count, 106,362 Iraqi civilians had been killed by acts of violence between March 2003 and January 2009, https://www.iraqbodycount.org /database/.

CHAPTER SIXTEEN

Four More Years

The other party's nomination battle is still playing out.
The candidates are an interesting group, with diverse
opinions: for tax cuts and against them; for NAFTA
and against NAFTA; for the Patriot Act and against
the Patriot Act; in favor of liberating Iraq and opposed
to it. And that's just one senator from Massachusetts.

George W. Bush
February 23, 2004

As the 2004 presidential election approached, Bush faced crucial decisions involving three key figures in his administration: Colin Powell, Dick Cheney, and Donald Rumsfeld. And he faced a growing body of evidence that the war in Iraq was going badly, and getting worse by the day.

Powell's doubts about Bush's decision to invade Iraq underlined once again his differences with the administration. When his comments were published in *The Washington Post*, Bush was furious, and Rice called Powell to demand a clarification. Powell was not surprised. In his view, there was "a persistent White House machismo that took aim at anything that suggests any weakness in the administration's position, regardless of common sense." [1]

"There are people who would like to take me down," Powell told Karen DeYoung. "It's been that way since I was appointed. By take down, I mean keep him in his place." Powell said that even if he had more time to consider the question asked by the *Post* reporter, he would have answered the same way. "The answer is so right. . . . I don't *know* what I would have recommended if somebody had said, 'There ain't no weapons of mass destruction.' How could you *not* reconsider? If the CIA, after saying for *a year and a half,* suddenly said, 'Whoops.' "[2]*

Powell recognized he was out of step, but did not plan to resign before the election. That would embarrass the president and Powell did not wish to do so. He had great respect for the office of the president, and perhaps an exaggerated sense of duty. Powell was always fond of quoting General George Marshall. "I never haggled with the president," Marshall said of his relationship with FDR. "I swallowed the little things so I could go to bat on the big ones. I never handled a matter apologetically and I was never contentious."[3] Powell had been used by the Bush administration, and he knew it. George Bush and his advisers had continually benefited from Powell's reputation and prestige—witness his U.N. speech—even as they disregarded his advice. His deputy and friend Richard Armitage had often urged Powell to resign because the Bush team exploited his credibility whenever they got into a jam. Powell's wife Alma agreed. She thought her husband had been used to promote a war that should have never happened. "They needed him to do it because they knew people would believe him."[4]

In the early spring of 2004, Powell met privately with Bush to tell the president that he planned to step down at the end of the first term.

---

* Powell's views were more than vindicated in October 2004, when Charles Duelfer, who had succeeded David Kay as head of the Iraq Study Group, submitted a final report on the hunt for Iraq's WMDs. Like Kay, Duelfer concluded that Saddam Hussein had no such weapons and was making no effort to develop them. His WMD stockpiles and production capacity had been effectively destroyed in the first Gulf War and by U.N. inspectors in the 1990s. There was no evidence that Saddam had made "concerted efforts to restart" a nuclear weapons program, and although the Iraqi dictator dreamed of reconstituting his arsenal of chemical and biological weapons, there was no indication that he had taken steps to do so. Paraphrasing Kay, Duelfer concluded, "We were almost all wrong." Report of the Iraq Study Group, October 6, 2004. Also see Dana Priest and Walter Pincus, "US. 'Almost All Wrong'," *Washington Post*, October 7, 2004.

"As I said at the beginning, I only wanted to serve one term, and so after the election I should go."[5] Bush was not surprised, nor was he especially disappointed. "The early notification gave me plenty of time to think about a successor. I admired Colin, but it sometimes seemed like the State Department he led wasn't fully on board with my philosophy and policies. It was important to me that there be no daylight between the president and the secretary of state."[6]

Powell thought the issue was more fundamental. The president's system was not working. "We are of too many different philosophical views and we are not reconciling them," he told Bush. "You need to reconcile this for your second term, and I think you should get a whole new team. And it begins with my departure because I am so different from the rest of your team. But I really think you need a new team."[7]

At about the same time, Dick Cheney also offered to step down. "Three times before the 2004 campaign got under way I offered to the president to take myself off the Republican ticket," Cheney recalled. "I had become a lightning rod for attacks from the administration's critics. If President Bush felt he had a better chance to win with someone else as his running mate, I wanted to make sure he felt free to make the change."[8]

Switching vice presidential nominees is scarcely unprecedented. In 1940, FDR dropped John Nance Garner for Henry Wallace, and four years later jettisoned Wallace for Harry Truman. Eisenhower considered dumping Nixon in 1956 (Thomas Dewey and Lucius Clay urged him to do so), and in 1992 George W. suggested his father replace Dan Quayle with Cheney, who was then secretary of defense. Cheney himself had been instrumental in helping Gerald Ford push vice president Nelson Rockefeller off the ticket in 1976 so that Ford could win the Republican nomination against Ronald Reagan. "I always saw the vice president as expendable," said Cheney. "I still do."[9]

The first two times Cheney made the offer, Bush brushed him off. So Cheney raised it a third time. "I emphasized the seriousness with which he should consider the matter. So he went away and thought about it."[10]

Bush was impressed with Cheney's offer. "It was so atypical in power-hungry Washington." Cheney said he did not make the offer lightly. "All the president had to say was 'Dick, I am ready to make a change,' and I was out of there." [11] And Bush briefly considered possible replacements. At the top of the list was Bill Frist, the Senate majority leader from Tennessee. Bush liked Frist, he was a staunch believer in compassionate conservatism, and he was working with the White House to expand Medicare to include prescription drugs for seniors. He also represented a generational change. And Cheney had faults. In Bush's words, "he was seen as dark and heartless—the Darth Vader of the administration." There was also the widespread perception that Cheney was running the White House. "Accepting Dick's offer would be one way to demonstrate that I was in charge." [12]

But the more Bush thought about it, the more he felt Cheney should remain on the ticket. "I hadn't picked him to be a political asset," said the president. "I had chosen him to help me do the job. That was exactly what he had done. He accepted any assignment I asked. He gave me his unvarnished opinions. He understood that I made the final decisions. When we disagreed, he kept our differences private. Most important, I trusted Dick." [13]

After several weeks, the president informed Cheney of his decision. He wanted him to stay. Cheney accepted. The issue was off the table. Bush rarely revisited a decision, and the 2004 GOP ticket was now set well in advance of the convention.

A third major personnel change also offered itself in early 2004. At ten o'clock on the morning of May 5, Secretary of Defense Donald Rumsfeld walked into the Oval Office and gave Bush a handwritten note:

Mr. President,

    I want you to know that you have my resignation as Secretary of Defense anytime you feel it would be helpful to you.

                                      Don Rumsfeld

The precipitating issue was Abu Ghraib. On April 28, the CBS program *60 Minutes II* televised grotesque photos of obscene prisoner abuse by American soldiers at the infamous Abu Ghraib prison on the western outskirts of Baghdad. World reaction was swift. The Vatican called the abuse "a more serious blow to the United States than September 11," and said it would gravely affect American relations with Islam.[14] Colin Powell, appearing on the Larry King show, compared it to My Lai during the Vietnam War, and Senator Ted Kennedy, speaking on the Senate floor,

Abu Ghraib

said that Saddam's torture chambers at Abu Ghraib had been reopened under U.S. management.[15]

Rumsfeld took personal responsibility. "I believed my resignation as secretary might demonstrate accountability on the part of the U.S. government. I also thought my resignation might allow the administration and the Iraqi people to move beyond the scandal."

Bush was deeply affected by the photos. "I felt sick, really sick. I considered it a low point of my presidency." Bush told Rumsfeld that "someone's head has to roll on this one."

"You have my resignation, and I think you should accept it," Rumsfeld replied.

Bush said he would think about it. That evening the president called Rumsfeld at the Pentagon. "Your leaving would be a terrible idea," said Bush. "I don't accept your resignation."[16] Later, the president said he didn't blame Rumsfeld for the problem at Abu Ghraib, and "I didn't want to turn him into a scapegoat. I wanted the problem fixed, and I wanted him to fix it."[17]

Two days later Rumsfeld testified for seven hours on Capitol Hill. "These events occurred on my watch," said Rumsfeld. "As Secretary of Defense, I am accountable for them. I take full responsibility." On May 9, Rumsfeld wrote a second letter of resignation. "By this letter I am resigning as Secretary of Defense. During recent days I have given a good deal of thought to the situation, testified before Congress, and considered your views. . . . I have concluded that the damage from the acts of abuse that happened on my watch, by individuals for whose conduct I am responsible, can best be responded to by my resignation."[18]

Again, Bush declined to accept Rumsfeld's offer.

> I respected Don for repeating his offer. . . . It was a testament to his character and his understanding of the damage Abu Ghraib was causing. I seriously considered accepting his advice. I knew it would send a powerful signal to replace the leader of the Pentagon after such a grave mistake. But a big factor held me back: There was no obvious replacement for Don, and I couldn't afford to create a vacuum at the top of Defense.[19]

The following day, Bush sent Cheney to the Pentagon to talk Rumsfeld out of resigning. "Don," said Cheney, "thirty-five years ago this week, I went to work for you, and on this one you're wrong."[20] Rumsfeld acquiesced and stayed on. But he always regretted it. "Abu Ghraib and its follow-on effects . . . became a damaging distraction. More than anything else I have failed to do . . . I regret that I did not leave at that point."[21]*

Abu Ghraib may have been the low point of his presidency for Bush, but to some extent it was a self-inflicted wound. The incidents depicted in the photos shown on *60 Minutes II* occurred in November and December 2003. They were reported to the Army's Criminal Investigation

---

* When I discussed his resignation with Rumsfeld on April 15, 2014, he was still of the opinion that he had made a mistake in not leaving. "There was no one else in the chain of command who was responsible. I had replaced some of the senior people, others were new to their job and were not there when the offenses were committed. Someone had to take the fall, and I was the obvious candidate. It would have cleaned the slate and that would have been useful."

Division in Iraq on January 13, 2004, when a disgusted Army sergeant provided a computer disc containing over two hundred explicit images of the abuse. General Sanchez, the commander in Iraq, was informed immediately. Sanchez informed General Abizaid at Central Command, and Abizaid promptly notified Rumsfeld, who told President Bush. By January 15, 2004, the entire chain of command was aware of the problem. The Army appointed Major General Antonio Taguba to investigate what had happened, and the administration assumed everything was under control. The abuses were committed by members of the 372nd Military Police Company, recycled hillbillies from Cumberland, Maryland, and the military would deal with it.[22]

That was the administration's position: it was a routine military matter caused by unqualified reservists. The facts differed considerably. General Taguba quickly discovered that the incidents had occurred because members of Military Intelligence and other government agencies (OGA)—a euphemism for the CIA—had encouraged the MPs to harass the prisoners to prepare them for interrogation. All of the incidents occurred in that wing of the prison where "high-value" detainees were held, and all occurred prior to the questioning conducted by Military Intelligence and the CIA. The purpose was to break the will of the prisoners and force them to cooperate. As Taguba said in his report, "I find that contrary to the provision of AR190-8, Military Intelligence and Other U.S. Government Agency's (OGA) interrogators actively requested that MP guards set physical and mental conditions for favorable interrogation of witnesses."[23]* In effect, the administration was bringing to Iraq the same techniques of torture and intimidation used in Afghanistan and at Guantánamo despite the fact that Iraq was a war zone explicitly covered by the Geneva Conventions.

Taguba listed the measures employed, ranging from "forcing naked male prisoners to wear women's underwear," to "forcing detainees to

---

* Taguba quotes a number of MPs reporting the guidance given to them by Military Intelligence and the CIA. "Loosen this guy up for us." "Make sure he has a bad night." "Good job, they are breaking down real fast. They answer every question." "The Taguba Report," in Karen J. Greenberg and Joshua L. Dratel, *The Torture Papers: The Road to Abu Ghraib* (New York: Cambridge University Press, 2005), 418.

remove their clothing and keeping them naked for several days at a time," to "using military working dogs (without muzzles) to intimidate and frighten detainees," a total of thirteen measures contrary to Army regulations.[24] What he did not say was that the measures used were within the guidelines that had been approved by Bush for CIA renditions.

Taguba completed his report in early March 2004 and sent it forward. The Pentagon was informed but no corrective action was taken. (General Taguba was ordered to retire the following year. "They always shoot the messenger," he told Seymour Hersh.)[25] Instead, a second investigation was launched under Major General George R. Fay. In his report, Fay said essentially what Taguba had said but in more restrained language.

> This investigation identified forty-four (44) alleged instances or events of detainee abuse committed by MP and MI Soldiers, as well as civilian contractors. On sixteen (16) of these occasions, abuse by MP Soldiers was, or was alleged to have been, requested, encouraged, condoned, or solicited by MI personnel. . . . MI solicitation of MP abuse included the use of isolation with sensory deprivation, removal of clothing and humiliation, the use of dogs as an interrogation tool to induce fear, and physical abuse.[26]

A follow-on military investigation by Lieutenant General Anthony R. Jones said more or less the same. General Jones noted the difference between the procedures permitted at Guantánamo and Afghanistan as compared to Iraq, and suggested the soldiers at Abu Ghraib were not adequately informed. He also noted the role played by the CIA. "Interaction with OGA and other agency interrogators who did not follow the same rules as U.S. Forces" was a definite factor contributing to the fiasco at Abu Ghraib. "There was at least the perception, and perhaps the reality, that non-DOD agencies had different rules regarding interrogation and detention operations. Such perceptions encouraged Soldiers to deviate from prescribed techniques."[27]

The Schlesinger Report, reflecting the findings of a four-person commission headed by former secretary of defense James Schlesinger, appointed by Rumsfeld to investigate the matter, was in some respects even more damning. "The abuses were not just the failure of some individuals to follow known standards, and they were more than the failure of a few leaders to enforce proper discipline. There is both institutional and personal responsibility at higher levels." [28]

In the end, eleven soldiers were convicted by courts-martial for violations of Army regulations. Brigadier General Janis Karpinski, who had been commanding officer at the prison, was relieved of command and demoted to colonel. And Colonel Thomas Pappas, the head of Military Intelligence at Abu Ghraib, was relieved of command and given a Memorandum of Reprimand, which effectively ended his military career. The contributing role of President Bush was glossed over. But as General Taguba later wrote, Abu Ghraib was the direct result of the fact that "the Commander-in-Chief and those under him authorized a systematic regime of torture." [29] Said differently, the Abu Ghraib scandal was simply payback for the administration's decision to embark along the torture trail.

In addition to resolving the future for Powell, Cheney, and Rumsfeld, Bush did make two major changes in his administration during the first term, both in the economic sphere. In December 2002, Treasury Secretary Paul O'Neill and chief White House economic adviser Larry Lindsey were tossed overboard. O'Neill was an outspoken deficit hawk and skeptical of launching a preventive war against Iraq. He also disapproved of Bush's command style of governance and believed the president was living in an echo chamber, surrounded by praetorian guards and uninterested in factual analysis. [30] "He and I met regularly, but never clicked," said Bush. [31] Lindsey had committed the unpardonable sin of going off message and telling *The Wall Street Journal* that the war in Iraq might cost $200 billion, a figure that left the White House speechless. [32] Bush did not speak to either O'Neill or Lindsey, and delegated both dismissals to Dick Cheney.

George Tenet also departed. After Bob Woodward's *Plan of Attack* was published and the "slam dunk" reference appeared, Tenet realized his days were numbered. "Woodward's books, dependent as they are on insider access, have long been used in just this way—to deflect blame and set up fall guys. Now it had happened to me."[33] Tenet submitted his resignation to the president the evening of June 2. It was immediately accepted. Bush announced it the following day. "He's been a strong leader in the war on terror, and I will miss him," said the president.[34] Unlike with Rumsfeld, Bush made no effort to dissuade Tenet from leaving.

Throughout 2003, Bush continued to embrace the ideals of compassionate conservatism. In 2001 he had engineered enactment of No Child Left Behind, a significant educational reform that greatly benefited children from less affluent families. By requiring states to set common standards and test students regularly in reading, writing, and arithmetic, NCLB ended the practice of promoting all students at the end of the school year whether they were qualified or not. The act also required schools and school districts to focus on the academic achievement of traditionally underserved groups of children, such as those from low-income families, students with disabilities, and those from racial and ethnic subgroups.

In 2003 the issue was prescription drugs for seniors, and Bush was relentless in pressing for its passage. Since the adoption of Medicare in 1965, the price of prescription drugs for seniors had skyrocketed, and the plan Bush was pushing would be the most far-reaching expansion of the Medicare program since its inception. Democrats opposed the plan, calling it a sop to the pharmaceutical industry,* and conservative Republicans also opposed it as an unnecessary expansion of the

---

* The Democrats wanted the bill to allow the Medicare administrators to negotiate prices with pharmaceutical companies, as the Veterans Administration does. A report released by Democratic staff on the House Government Reform Committee showed that under the new plan, prices for ten commonly prescribed drugs were 80 percent higher than those negotiated by the Veterans Department, 60 percent above that paid by Canadian consumers, and still 3 percent higher than volume pharmacies such as Costco and Drugstore.com. The report concluded that "The prices offered by the Medicare drug plans are higher than all four benchmarks, in some cases significantly so. This increases costs to seniors and federal taxpayers and makes it doubtful that the complicated design of Medicare Part D provides any tangible benefit to anyone but drug manufacturers and insurers." Because of this objection, only 19 House Democrats voted for the bill.

federal government's involvement in everyday life. "I didn't come to Washington to increase the size of government," a balky conservative congressman told Bush.[35]

After months of logrolling and arm-twisting, House Speaker Dennis Hastert brought the measure to a vote in the early morning hours of November 22, 2003. When the roll call concluded, Bush was down 15 votes. Hastert kept the vote open as the Republican leadership implored dissenters to switch. At 4:45 a.m. Bush was awakened in the White House and told he had to speak personally with wavering congressmen. For the next hour Bush cajoled and pleaded with individual members. The tipping point came about 5:30 a.m. when the president spoke with a group of conservatives led by Representative Trent Franks of Arizona. Franks wanted a quid pro quo. "If we could get the president of the United States to give his word of honor tonight that he would only appoint Supreme Court justices that he knew would overturn *Roe v. Wade*, would uphold the personhood of the unborn in the Constitution and be strict constructionists, we could get this done right now."

"Congressman, I think I'm going to make that commitment. You know I am a man of my word."

"I know you are a man of your word," Franks replied. "Do I have your word?"

"Yes, congressman, you have my word."[36]

Franks and a few other members switched their votes, and at 5:53 a.m. Hastert announced that the prescription drug bill had passed, 216–215. The roll call vote lasted two hours and fifty-one minutes. That was twice as long as the longest roll call in the history of the House of Representatives.

The following day the Senate took up the measure and majority leader Bill Frist needed 60 votes to close off debate. He had 59. Frist convinced Trent Lott, the man he replaced as majority leader, to vote for cloture, and the following day, November 25, the Senate passed the prescription drug bill 54–44, Lott voting against.

Bush's move to appease House members on the extreme right in order to secure passage of prescription drugs for seniors was not a step backward for the president. The 2004 presidential election was coming, and Bush's team had concluded that a more conservative stance by the president would be beneficial.

Traditionally presidential candidates, after winning their party's nomination, move to the center of the political spectrum to compete for the undecided voter in the middle. Republican candidates go left, Democrats go right. The exceptions were Barry Goldwater in 1964 and George McGovern in 1972, and both got clobbered. But Matthew Dowd, Bush's pollster, convinced Rove, and then Bush, that this was a mistake. After an extensive analysis of the presidential election results between 1976 and 2000, Dowd found that the percentage of swing voters had declined steadily from 22 percent in 1976 to 7 percent in 2000. Partisanship and polarization had replaced the uncommitted voter. According to Dowd, there was no longer any point in moving toward the center. "It's about *motivation* rather than *persuasion*," he told Rove. "We maximize the number of Republicans on election day and we win." [37] The midterm elections in 2002 had validated Dowd's thesis. Even though Republicans lost the undecided vote, they gained overall by 4 percentage points by focusing on getting out the vote.

Bush began his appeal to the conservative base in his 2004 State of the Union address. The issue he chose was same-sex marriage. "A strong America must also value the institution of marriage," said the president.

> Activist judges, however, have begun redefining marriage by court order, without regard to the will of the people. . . . If judges insist on forcing their arbitrary will upon the people, the only alternative left to the people would be the constitutional process. Our nation must defend the sanctity of marriage. [38]

Bush did not explicitly advocate a constitutional amendment, and Laura had urged him not to make gay marriage an issue in the campaign. "We have, I reminded him, a number of close friends who are gay or whose children are gay." [39] Cheney, whose daughter Mary was gay, also opposed making it an issue. But Bush pressed ahead. On February 24, the president formally endorsed a constitutional amendment banning same-sex marriage. Speaking before reporters in the Roosevelt Room of the White House, Bush said, "The union of a man and woman is the most enduring human institution, honored and encouraged by all cultures and by every religious faith." Bush said he thought states should be allowed to enact alternative arrangements such as civil unions, and he discouraged harsh rhetoric. "We should conduct this difficult debate in a matter worthy of our country without bitterness and anger."[40] Privately, Bush had always deplored gay bashing, but the politics of the issue were clear. A Gallup poll taken a week before the president spoke indicated that 64 percent of Americans opposed same-sex marriage while only 32 percent were in favor. Among conservative voters, the margin was even more lopsided.[41] And eleven states were planning to put the question on the November ballot, mobilizing even more conservative Republican voters. The president chose to play to his base.

As the election campaign got under way, Bush cast himself as the war president: the man Americans could trust to keep them free from terrorist attack. But difficulties soon became apparent. Domestically, the Terrorist Surveillance Program (TSP), authorizing the National Security Agency to conduct warrantless searches, was in trouble. The program, which needed regular renewal, was about to expire. John Yoo was no longer in the Office of Legal Counsel, having returned in 2003 to his teaching position at Berkeley, and a new set of lawyers at the Department of Justice concluded that the program was illegal. Led by Jack Goldsmith, a conservative law professor from the University of Chicago who was now head of the Office of Legal Counsel, and James Comey, a former federal prosecutor who was now deputy attorney general, the Justice Department lawyers convinced Attorney General Ashcroft that the program should not be reauthorized when it expired on March 11. Shortly after that meeting, Ashcroft was rushed to the hospital suffering from pancreatitis. Comey became acting attorney general, and he informed the White House of the Justice Department's decision.

A firestorm ensued. "How can you possibly be reversing course on something this important after all this time," asked Dick Cheney. Comey replied that the program's importance did not change the legal issues. John Yoo's opinion authorizing the program, said Comey, was fatally flawed. "No lawyer reading it could reasonably rely on it."

"Well, I'm a lawyer and I found it thoroughly convincing," said one of Cheney's aides.

"No *good* lawyer," Comey replied.[42]

The following morning, March 10, Cheney informed Bush that because of the Justice Department objections, the Terrorist Surveillance Program would expire at the end of the day. "How can it possibly end?" asked the president. "It's vital to protecting the country." Bush was flying to Cleveland that day to deliver a speech on trade policy, and instructed Andy Card to work it out with the Justice Department. When he returned to Washington that evening, Card informed him that no progress had been made. The Justice Department was holding firm.

"Where the hell is Ashcroft," asked Bush.

"He's in the hospital," Card replied.[43]

Bush immediately called Ashcroft in the hospital. The attorney general was recovering from emergency gall bladder surgery and was still groggy. Bush informed him that he was sending Card and White House counsel Alberto Gonzales over to the hospital with the TSP reauthorization order for him to sign. The commander in chief had decided that the Terrorist Surveillance Program must continue, and he expected the Justice Department to fall into line.

Ashcroft hung up and relayed the conversation to his wife, Janet. She called Ashcroft's chief of staff at the Justice Department, who in turn called Comey, who was in his car driving home. Comey recognized that the White House was attempting an end run around the department's legal objections by taking advantage of Ashcroft's enfeebled condition. He rushed to the hospital and urged FBI director Robert Mueller and Goldsmith to do the same. Speeding through Washington traffic, Comey arrived at Ashcroft's bedside shortly before Card and Gonzales. They walked in at 7:35 p.m., did not greet Comey, and told Ashcroft they had a document the president wanted him to sign.

Ashcroft lifted his head from his pillow and told Gonzales he shared Comey's concerns. "But that doesn't matter, because I'm not the attorney general." Pointing to Comey, Ashcroft said, "There's the attorney general." And with that Ashcroft returned his head to his pillow.

Card and Gonzales, who still had not acknowledged Comey's presence in the room, turned abruptly and left. "Be well," said Card on the way out. As they left, Mrs. Ashcroft stuck her tongue out at them. According to Comey, "It was just despicable. I thought I had just witnessed an effort to take advantage of a very sick man."[44]

Later that evening, Card summoned Comey to the White House. Before going, Comey met with the senior leadership in the Justice Department. All agreed that they would resign if the White House overruled their judgment. When Comey arrived at the White House at 11 p.m., the battle lines had been drawn. Comey refused to back down.

The following day, March 11, Bush on his own authority signed the order renewing the surveillance program. Gonzales countersigned the order in place of Ashcroft. Comey, Goldsmith, and Mueller drafted letters of resignation. "Should the president order the continuation of the FBI's participation in the program, and in the absence of further advice from the AG, I would be constrained to resign as Director of the FBI," wrote Mueller in longhand.[45]

The next morning, when Bush arrived in the Oval Office, Card broke the news. "Mr. President, we've got a major problem. Jim Comey is going to resign because you extended the TSP and so are a bunch of other Justice Department officials."

"I was stunned," Bush wrote in his memoirs. Later that morning, following the FBI briefing, Bush spoke with Comey alone. "I just don't understand why you are raising this at the last minute," said the president.

Comey was equally surprised. "Mr. President, your staff has known about this for weeks." Comey said he wasn't the only one planning to resign. So were Robert Mueller and a host of others. "I was about to witness the largest mass resignation in modern presidential history, and we were in the midst of a war," Bush remembered. After Comey, the president spoke with Mueller, who confirmed he planned to resign. Bush faced a choice. "I was willing to defend the powers of the presidency, but not at any cost. I thought about the Saturday Night Massacre in October 1973 when President Richard Nixon's firing of Watergate prosecutor Archibald Cox led his attorney general and deputy attorney general to resign. That was not a historical crisis I was eager to replicate."[46] Over the objections of Cheney and other hardliners on the White House staff, Bush agreed to modify the Terrorist Surveillance Program to conform with Justice Department objections.

Bush's staff had not informed him of the Justice Department's objections beforehand. "I was relieved to have the crisis over," said Bush, "but I was disturbed it had happened at all. I made clear to my advisers that I never wanted to be blindsided like that again."[47]

Meanwhile in Iraq, Saddam Hussein had been captured in December, but the situation continued to deteriorate. Attacks on U.S. servicemen increased from twenty-five a day in January 2004 to roughly twice that number in early spring. As one analyst in Baghdad noted, Iraqis had come to see the U.S. military as part of the problem, "a liability whose presence makes things more dangerous." Or as Colonel Alan King, commander of the 442nd Civil Affairs Battalion, put it, "we began to smell like losers."[48] Support for Bremer's Coalition Provisional Authority fell even more sharply. By March 2004, less than 14 percent of Iraqis expressed confidence in the CPA. Colonel Ralph Hollenbeck, a retired Army officer who worked for the CPA, noted the turn in Iraqi sentiment. "I remember watching that turn," said Hollenbeck. "Iraqis were saying, 'Not only do I not like these guys, they can't do anything for me, and they step on my dignity.'"[49]

The situation erupted in late March in two separate and unrelated incidents that inflamed both the Shiite and Sunni communities. On March 27, Bremer ordered the closing of the newspaper *al-Hawza*, a weekly journal run by Moqtada al-Sadr, a radical Shiite cleric and the son of the late Grand Ayatollah Mohammed Sadiq al-Sadr. *Al-Hawza* had been highly critical of Bremer and the American occupation, and unlike Lucius Clay in Germany—who encouraged the German press to criticize Allied policy—Bremer ordered the paper closed.* When

---

*   "The best way for the Germans to comprehend the advantages of a free press is to have one," Clay told E. J. Kahn of *The New Yorker*. When writing Clay's biography, I asked the general

the U.S. military chained and locked the doors of *al-Hawza*, it touched off a violent reaction from Sadr and his supporters that swept through the Shiite community.

At virtually the same moment, a two-vehicle convoy from the Blackwater security firm was ambushed while traveling through the Sunni city of Fallujah in Anbar province west of Baghdad. The four American occupants were killed, and their bodies mutilated, burned, and dragged through the streets. The four burned and mutilated corpses were hung from a bridge that spanned the Euphrates River. The incident was widely covered by the media, and the photos of the corpses hanging from the bridge launched a swift demand for retaliation.

Once again the White House took charge. The Marines who were stationed in Fallujah advocated a measured approach, but Bush insisted on a major assault. "This is what the enemy wants," protested Major General James Mattis, commanding the 1st Marine Division. Or as Lieutenant General James Conway, the senior Marine commander in Iraq, put it, "we ought to probably let the situation settle before we appeared to be attacking out of revenge."[50] The military made their argument for restraint in a videoconference with the president and the NCS on April 3. General Abizaid, the CENTCOM commander, said the Marines favored a "kid glove" approach with the Sunnis, and he supported that. Bush replied that he appreciated the caution, but was ordering an attack. Abizaid and General Sanchez acknowledged the president's decision, but again pointed out that it "was going to be a pretty ugly operation, with a lot of collateral damage." They also noted that the Arabic television network Al Jazeera was certain to broadcast live coverage of the battle, which would compound the problem.

"We know it's going to be ugly," the president replied, "but we are committed."[51]

---

about it. "That's right," he said. "My information bureau sent out an order curtailing the issue of this newspaper because it had an article quite critical of me, and I remember it very well, because I said, 'I think this is wonderful.' It was. So I revoked the order, and I think it helped the Germans understand what a free press meant." Jean Edward Smith, *Lucius D. Clay: An American Life* (New York: Henry Holt, 1990), 245; E. J. Kahn, Jr., "Soldier in Mufti," *The New Yorker*, January 13, 1951.

The Marines began their attack on April 4. At the same time, the Army was moving against the Shiite forces of Sadr. "The fighting was intense and bloody," Sanchez reported.[52] On April 7, the command in Baghdad gave Bush an update in another teleconference. The president was in a fighting mood. "Al-Sadr's Mahdi Army is a hostile force," said Bush. "It is absolutely vital that we have robust offensive operations. . . . It is essential he be wiped out."

According to Sanchez, Bush then launched into an impassioned pep talk. "Kick ass," said the president. "If someone tries to stop the march to democracy, we will seek them out and kill them. We must be tougher than hell. . . . Our will is being tested, but we are resolute. Stay the course! Kill them! Be confident! Prevail! We are going to wipe them out! We are not blinking!"[53]

The fighting in Fallujah was fierce. And the reaction among Iraqis to the American offensive was uniformly hostile. Members of Bremer's Governing Council threatened to resign if the attack continued, imperiling the handover of authority to Iraqis now scheduled for June 30. At this point Bremer blinked, then Rice blinked, and then Bush blinked. Late on April 8, just one day after his blistering pep talk, the president instructed Abizaid and Sanchez to halt the offensive in Fallujah. The following day, the troops were ordered to stand down. The Marines were furious. Thirty-nine Marines and U.S. soldiers had been killed in four days of fighting, and combat commanders believed they were relatively close to seizing their final objectives. "If you are going to take Vienna, take fucking Vienna," General Mattis snarled at Abizaid, updating a famous comment made by Napoleon.[54]

Bush had scarcely provided the robust leadership he advertised. One minute he was tough, the next he knuckled under. General Sanchez called it a strategic disaster for the United States.

By stopping the attacks in Fallujah, and by not taking out Muqtada al-Sadr, we set the stage for increased violence ignited by the insurgency, a new civil war, and a major surge in al Qaeda terrorist activity. The highest levels of the executive branch of the U.S. government gave us the order to attack in Fallujah. But when the hard fighting was shown on Al Jazeera and CNN, and pressure began to build on all sides, the Bush administration immediately backed away. Essentially, they ordered us to cut and run.[55]

On April 13, Bush met with the press in the East Room of the White House. This was his third prime-time press conference since assuming office. His father had held twelve by that point in his administration, and Clinton eight. Bush disliked press conferences at any time, but especially in prime time, when he thought reporters were attempting to make him look foolish. As Bill Sammon, the pro-Bush White House correspondent for *The Washington Times*, observed, the April 13 session was "unequivocally, a low point of his presidency."[56]

Bush was stunned by the reversals in Iraq. Not only the thirty-nine casualties in the aborted Fallujah offensive, but the fact that he had been forced to call it off. "Good evening," said the president. "Before I take your questions, let me speak with the American people about the situation in Iraq. This has been tough weeks in that country." That is not a misprint. *"This has been tough weeks in that country."*[57] From there the press conference went downhill.

The most devastating exchange was with John Dickerson of *Time* magazine. Dickerson had a habit of asking probing questions. At previous press conferences he had asked Bush whether he thought Muslims worshipped the same God as Christians, and whether he agreed with many of his supporters that homosexuality was immoral.* This time he asked the president about his mistakes after 9/11.

> *Dickerson:* Mr. President. In the last campaign, you were asked a question about the biggest mistake you made in your life, and you used to like to joke that it was trading Sammy Sosa. . . . After 9/11,

---

* When the president replied that he thought Muslims and Christians worshipped the same God, many evangelicals were appalled, and when he answered the questions about homosexuality by asking for tolerance—"we are all sinners"—critics attacked Bush for implying homosexuality was sinful.

what would your biggest mistake be, would you say, and what
lessons have you learned from it?

Bush was stunned. He had not anticipated being asked so directly.
He began with a quip. "I wish you would have given me this written
question ahead of time, so I could plan for it." The president paused,
evidently collecting his thoughts. A full ten seconds elapsed. "John, I'm
sure historians will look back and say, 'Gosh, he would have done it
better this way or that way.'" Another embarrassing pause. "You know,
I just, —." Another pause. The president was flummoxed.

"Have you ever experienced seconds that felt like minutes?" asked
White House press secretary Scott McClellan. "I found myself thinking, 'Come on, sir, this one is not difficult. Just say something like "I'm
sure I've made plenty of mistakes, and history will judge them."'"[58]
Bush stumbled on. "I'm sure something will pop into my head here
in the midst of this press conference, with all the pressure of trying to
come up with an answer, but it hasn't yet." Another awkward silence.
The president then launched into a muddled, rambling, rather incoher-
ent response that spoke volumes about his thought process as to why he
went into Iraq.

> I would have gone into Afghanistan the way we went into Afghanistan.
> Even knowing what I know today about the stockpiles of weapons,
> I still would have called upon the world to deal with Saddam Hussein.
> See, I happen to believe that we'll find out the truth on the weapons.
> That's why we've sent up the independent commission. I look forward
> to hearing the truth, exactly where they are. They could still be there.
> They could be hidden, like the 50 tons of mustard gas in a turkey farm.
>
> One of the things that Charlie Duelfer talked about was that he
> was surprised at the level of intimidation he found amongst people who
> should know about weapons, and their fear of talking about them be-
> cause they don't want to be killed. There's a terror still in the soul of
> some of the people in Iraq; they're worried about getting killed, and,
> therefore, they're not going to talk.
>
> But it will all settle out, John. We'll find out the truth about the

weapons at some point in time. However, the fact that he had the capacity to make them bothers me today, just like it would have bothered
me then. He's a dangerous man. He's a man who actually—not only
had weapons of mass destruction—the reason I can say that with certainty is because he used them. And I have no doubt in my mind that
he would like to have inflicted harm, or paid people to inflict harm, or
trained people to inflict harm on America, because he hated us.[59]

Bush was aware he had blown the answer to Dickerson's question.
"I hope I—I don't want to sound like I've made no mistakes. I'm confident I have. I just haven't—you just put me under the spot here, and
maybe I'm not as quick on my feet as I should be in coming up with
one."[60] Far more important than the inarticulateness of the president's
answer to Dickerson is the flimsiness of his justification for invading
Iraq. Like Captain Queeg in his rambling courtroom testimony in *The
Caine Mutiny*, George W. Bush was in a state of denial. His refusal to
face up to the fact that an exhaustive effort by his own investigators to
find an Iraqi WMD program had found none suggests a willfulness
that borders on psychosis. It also reveals that he had ordered a major
and costly war for no good reason.

Public reaction was overwhelmingly negative. By May, the president's approval rating was down to 47 percent, the lowest of his presidency thus far.[61] The upcoming 2004 election was in the offing, and
Bush was clearly in trouble. But one factor worked to his advantage.
The 2000 census had reshuffled the electoral vote. Four states that Bush
carried against Al Gore (Arizona, Florida, Georgia, and Texas) gained
two electoral votes. Three others (Colorado, North Carolina, and Nevada) gained one. Major Democratic states like New York and Pennsylvania lost two. Altogether, when gains were matched against losses,
states carried by the Republicans showed a net gain of seven electoral
votes.[62]

Initially ten candidates entered the race for the Democratic nomination. But by the time of the Iowa caucuses in January 2004, the effective field had dwindled to six. The front-runner was former governor
Howard Dean of Vermont, a physician who had pioneered the way for

civil unions in Vermont and was widely regarded as the most liberal of
the candidates. Second was former House minority leader Dick Gephardt of Missouri, followed by Senator John Kerry of Massachusetts,
a Vietnam War hero turned critic, and North Carolina senator John
Edwards, a photogenic trial lawyer serving his first term in the Senate. Connecticut senator Joe Lieberman, Gore's running mate in 2000,
and retired General Wesley Clark, the NATO commander in Kosovo,
completed the field. Lieberman, Gephardt, Kerry, and Edwards had all
voted in favor of war with Iraq, while Dean and Clark were vigorously
opposed. A Zogby poll on the eve of the Iowa caucuses showed Dean in
the lead with 25 percent, Gephardt 23, Kerry 15, Edwards 14, Clark 3,
and Lieberman 3.[63]

The Iowa caucuses provided an upset. Front-runners Dean and
Gephardt ran negative campaigns attacking each other, allowing Kerry
and Edwards to break through. Final results gave Kerry 38 percent
of the vote, Edwards 32, Dean 18, and Gephardt 11. Gephardt immediately dropped out of the race, and Howard Dean's widely televised post-election rant effectively doomed his candidacy. Two weeks
later in New Hampshire, Kerry again finished first, with 38 percent.
With that, his support snowballed, and Kerry won the next ten primaries. Lieberman, Clark, and Dean withdrew, and on Super Tuesday,
March 2, Kerry clinched the nomination with decisive victories in every
state except Vermont, which voted for former governor Dean although
he had already withdrawn from the race. In the end, Kerry carried
every state except Vermont; South Carolina, which went to Edwards;
and Oklahoma, which voted for Clark. The evening of Super Tuesday,
Bush called Kerry to congratulate him as the presumptive Democratic
nominee.

Bush considered Kerry a formidable opponent: a four-term United
States senator, a polished debater, and a tough campaigner. Laura believed Edwards would have been more formidable. He was young and
charming, while Kerry came across as cold and austere. And for the
twins, Barbara and Jenna, the election was a wake-up. Neither had
participated in the 2000 election and had made it clear to their parents
that they wanted nothing to do with politics.[64] But shortly after Kerry

clinched the Democratic nomination, Jenna wrote a deeply moving
letter to her father. "I had a dream
last night," she wrote, "a dream so
vivid I woke up in tears." Jenna,
who was a senior at the University
of Texas in Austin, said she would
like to work full-time in the campaign after she graduated. "In my
dream, I didn't help you. And
I watched somebody win who isn't
supposed to. And I cried. I cried
for you, for our country, and for
my guilt. I don't want my dream
to become a reality, so if I can help
in any way please let me. I love
you and am so proud of you." [65]

John Kerry

Bush was deeply moved by Jenna's letter. He was also moved when
Barbara at Yale said she wanted to help in the election as well. "I was
thrilled they wanted to join the campaign," said Bush. "My last campaign would be their first." [66]

As Bush recognized, John Kerry had an Achilles' heel. Speaking
at Marshall University in Huntington, West Virginia, on March 16,
Kerry committed a gaffe that would haunt him throughout the campaign. Prior to his arrival at Marshall, the Bush team had aired an
ad on West Virginia television showing Kerry voting "No" on the
Senate floor to the $87 billion supplementary military appropriations
bill to cover expenses in Iraq. Kerry decided to answer the attack ad.
Addressing the audience at Marshall with a microphone in his hand,
the senator explained that Iraq expenses should have been funded
with the help of other nations, or by repealing the Bush tax cuts for
upper-income Americans, which Kerry had proposed in an amendment. And then the blooper, "I actually did vote for the $87 billion
before I voted against it." [67]

For the Bush campaign, Kerry's flip-flop was solid gold. Within hours the senator's words were running in television ads throughout the country. Bush was ecstatic when he heard the sound bite. "There's our opening," he told Karl Rove. "We grabbed the 'flip-flop' theme and ran with it for the rest of the campaign." [68] Rove said the television ad showing Kerry's comment "was our most powerful and persuasive TV message, and it helped close the deal with voters up for grabs." [69] Speaking with ABC's Diane Sawyer several months later, Kerry confessed "I had one of those inarticulate moments when I was dead tired, and I didn't say something very clearly." [70]

With his nomination secure, Kerry courted John McCain for the next three months to be his running mate. He and McCain were old friends, fellow Vietnam veterans, and shared a mutual dislike for George W. Bush. Appearing on ABC's *Good Morning America* on March 10, McCain was asked about the possibility of a Kerry-McCain ticket by host Charles Gibson.

"A lot of Democrats say a dream ticket would be if John Kerry would reach across the aisle and take you as a vice presidential candidate. Are you going to say no?"

"Charlie, it's impossible to imagine the Democratic Party seeking a pro-life, non-protectionist deficit hawk," McCain replied.

"But let me, let me imagine it," said Gibson. "If he asked you, if he came across the aisle and asked you, would you even entertain the idea, or would you rule it out?"

"John Kerry is a very close friend of mine. We've been friends for years. Obviously, I would entertain it." [71]

McCain's reply to Gibson set off a flurry of speculation. Many Democrats relished the idea of a national unity ticket. "Senator McCain would not have to leave his party," former senator Bob Kerrey of Nebraska told *The New York Times.* "He could remain a Republican, would be given some authority over the selection of cabinet people. The only thing he would have to do is say, 'I'm not going to appoint any judges who would overturn *Roe v. Wade.*'" [72]

For Bush and his campaign team, the possibility that McCain might accept Kerry's offer was a nightmare. Not only would McCain draw Republican votes that were essential, but a Kerry-McCain ticket would field two genuine Vietnam War heroes against a National Guard drop-out president and a vice president who had avoided military service with five college deferments. Kerry met repeatedly with McCain that spring to entice the senator into joining the ticket. The courtship dragged on until late May when McCain said no definitively. As McCain saw it, the 2008 GOP nomination was open, and the Arizona senator decided he had a better shot at it if he supported the president's reelection. He buried his dislike for Bush, and joined the campaign.

On June 18, McCain accompanied Bush to a Republican rally at Fort Lewis, Washington, the first of twenty-four appearances he would make on behalf of the Bush campaign. The lingering bitterness of the 2000 primary campaign was evident (it was their first appearance together in four years), but they made the best of it. Bush's reference in his speech to McCain's presence on the platform was at best perfunctory, and McCain's subsequent physical embrace of Bush looked as if he was hugging a porcupine.[73]

In July, on the eve of the Democratic convention, and with McCain no longer a possibility, Kerry chose North Carolina senator John Edwards to be his running mate. As *Tonight Show* host Jay Leno put it that evening, "John Kerry said, 'I can't tell you how proud I am to have John Edwards on my team, especially after John McCain turned us down.'"[74]

The Democratic convention convened in Boston the last week in July. The keynote address was given by Barack Obama, who was then a candidate for the United States Senate from Illinois. In contrast to the Bush strategy of divide and conquer, Obama famously said, "There is not a liberal America and a conservative America—there is the United States of America."[75] Other speakers included former presidents Clinton and Carter, Al Gore, Hillary Clinton, Ted Kennedy, and Ronald Reagan's son Ron. All followed the same script. Rather than appeal to the liberal Democratic base, rather than bash the Bush administration for its shortcomings, the speakers at the Democratic convention emphasized patriotism and national unity.

John Kerry began his acceptance speech with a crisp military salute and the phrase "I'm John Kerry, and I'm reporting for duty." Unlike the state-of-the-art Bush campaign, which focused on motivating Republicans to go to the polls and vote, the Kerry campaign was mired in the conventional wisdom of the past fifty years. A successful presidential campaign must appeal to independents and the uncommitted. The problem was, as Matthew Dowd and Karl Rove understood, there were no longer that many undecided voters. According to the *USA Today*/CNN/Gallup poll, Kerry enjoyed the support of 47 percent of the nation's registered voters when the Democratic convention convened. When it adjourned, he enjoyed the support of 47 percent of the registered voters.[76] There was no convention bounce.

The Republican convention met in New York City on August 30, the first Republican convention ever held in New York, and less than two weeks before the third anniversary of 9/11. In contrast to the Democratic gathering, it was a partisan extravaganza. And the staging in Madison Square Garden was superb. "We are turning this convention into a TV show," said Russ Schriefer, the GOP program director. "Shorter segments, more graphics, faster pacing."[77] Lead-off speakers the first evening included McCain and former New York mayor Rudolph Giuliani. "President Bush deserves not only our support, but our admiration," said McCain. Giuliani, who epitomized heroism on 9/11 and the war on terror, said, "From the first Republican president, Abraham Lincoln, to President George W. Bush, our party's great contribution is to expand freedom in our own land and all over the world." But it was California governor Arnold Schwarzenegger who stole the show the following evening when he accused the Democrats of being economic girlie-men. "If you believe we must be fierce and relentless and terminate terrorism, then you are a Republican."[78]

The next evening, Wednesday, September 1, Bush was renominated 2,508 to zero, with one delegate abstaining. The principal speaker was Dick Cheney. "Senator Kerry's liveliest disagreement is with himself," said Cheney. "His back-and-forth reflects a habit of indecision and sends a message of confusion. And it is all part of a pattern. He has, in the last several years, been for the No Child Left Behind Act—and against it. He has spoken in favor of the North American Free Trade Agreement—and against it. He is for the Patriot Act—and against it.

Senator Kerry says he sees two Americas. He makes the whole thing mutual—America sees two John Kerrys."[79]

Bush gave his acceptance speech the following evening. Like Cheney, he took on Kerry with a frontal assault, arguing that the Democratic nominee was on the wrong side of core American values. "Because a caring society will value its weakest members, we must make a place for the unborn child." Bush then reaffirmed his support for a constitutional amendment defining marriage as between a man and a woman. After reciting Kerry's parade of flip-flops, he quoted the Massachusetts senator calling the coalition of the willing the "coalition of the coerced and bribed." As Bush put it, "That would be nations like Great Britain, Poland, Italy, the Netherlands, Denmark, El Salvador, Australia, and others—allies that deserve the respect of all Americans, not the scorn of politicians."

"You may have noticed, I have a few flaws too," said the president as he approached his conclusion. "People sometimes have to correct my English. I knew I had a problem when Arnold Schwarzenegger started doing it. Some people look at me and see a certain swagger, which in Texas is called 'walking.' . . . One thing I have learned about the presidency is that whatever shortcomings you have, people are going to notice them. And whatever strengths you have, you're going to need them."

Bush concluded by invoking God's will. "Like generations before us, we have a calling from beyond the stars to stand for freedom. This is the everlasting dream of America—and tonight, in this place, that dream is renewed."[80]

The delegates were on their feet cheering madly. Bush was joined on the stage by Laura and the Cheneys. Before the convention, the *USA Today*/CNN/Gallup poll showed Bush and Kerry tied at 46 percent. When it adjourned, Bush led 50 to 42, a whopping 8-point advantage.[81]

Aside from the effectiveness of the Republican convention, Kerry faced a more serious problem pertaining to his service in Vietnam. His crisp salute at the Democratic convention was intended to evoke memories of his heroic role in combat. But it galvanized a Republican group of veterans—who styled themselves Swift Boat Veterans for Truth—

into mounting television ads challenging Kerry's service record. Led by retired Rear Admiral Roy Hoffmann, who had commanded swift boat forces in Vietnam, the group was tightly organized, well funded, and determined to tarnish Kerry's combat record. In many respects it was similar to the attack mounted by Bush supporters in South Carolina in the 2000 Republican primary against John McCain, and McCain was outspoken in his condemnation. "The ad is dishonest and dishonorable," the Arizona senator told the Associated Press. "John Kerry served honorably in Vietnam." [82] But the damage continued throughout the campaign. Kerry was slow in responding just as McCain had been in South Carolina and never fully recovered. As Karl Rove put it, "the ad raised disturbing questions about Kerry's character that would not go away. . . . They were easily the most effective independent ads of 2004." [83]

Once again there were three presidential debates. In 2000, Bush more than held his own against Al Gore, but the debates in 2004 were a disaster. Bush had been commander in chief for three and a half years. He was surrounded by the White House echo chamber, saluted by obedient men and women, and accustomed to being "the Decider." As the nation's maximum leader, he found it irksome to be on a level playing field with a mere senator. [84] And like Al Gore in 2000, his condescending attitude was painfully apparent.

The first debate was held at the University of Miami on September 30, and Bush held a commanding 8-point lead in the Gallup poll going in. The television audience exceeded 62 million—about a third more than tuned in for the first Bush-Gore debate in 2000. Moderator Jim Lehrer began by asking Kerry if he thought he could do a better job than President Bush in preventing another 9/11-type terrorist attack on the United States. "Yes, I do," Kerry replied, and went on to castigate Bush's record item by item. Throughout the debate, Kerry's answers were succinct and focused. A champion debater since high school, he systematically laid out Bush's "colossal error in judgment" in invading Iraq without a plan to win the peace, and outsourcing the hunt for Osama bin Laden to Afghanistan. Television networks covering the debate used split screen images. As Kerry spoke, the audience saw Bush glower and grimace. Just as Gore's sighs were off-putting in 2000, Bush's facial expressions turned the audience against him. Brett O'Donnell, the debate coach at Liberty University who had helped prepare Bush for the debate, believed he was watching the most comprehensive beating ever to occur in a presidential debate.[85]

Returning to Washington that evening in Air Force One, campaign adviser Karen Hughes broke the news to Bush. "They are going to say you lost the debate," she told him.

"Why?"

"Because you looked mad."

"I wasn't mad. Tell them that."

"I can't. Because you *did* look mad."[86]

Karl Rove agreed. "Bush looked annoyed and irritated. I told him that his dislike for Kerry was making him come across as unlikeable."[87] Former Republican chairman Haley Barbour, an old friend of the Bush family who watched the debate from his home in Yazoo City, Mississippi, said "the president looked like he didn't want to be there."[88] Laura Bush agreed. "I don't know what happened," she told her husband. "You've got to be yourself and you weren't."[89] The 8-point lead that Bush had going into the debate evaporated overnight. The next USA *Today*/CNN/Gallup poll showed Bush and Kerry tied at 49 percent. "We came out of that debate and it was a whole new ball game," said Bush campaign aide Matthew Dowd. "The performance was a disaster."[90]

Up next was the vice presidential debate between Cheney and John Edwards. "You've got to stop the bleeding," Dowd told Cheney.[91] The debate took place at Case Western Reserve University in Cleveland on October 5. For the first forty minutes the debate was more or less even as Cheney and Edwards traded barbs. Then Gwen Ifill of PBS, who was moderating, asked Cheney about his disagreement with Bush over same-sex marriage. "People ought to be able to choose any arrangement they want," Cheney replied. "It's really no one else's business. That's a separate question from the issue of whether or not the government should sanction or approve or give some sort of authorization to those relationships." Cheney said he thought that should be left to the states, but the president set the policy for the administration and he supported the president.

When Ifill called on Edwards to respond, the senator blew it. "Let me say first that I think the vice president and his wife love their daughter. I think they love her very much. And you can't have anything but respect for the fact that they're willing to talk about the fact that they have a gay daughter, the fact that they embrace her. It's a wonderful thing. And there are millions of parents like that who love their children." Edwards, who was conducting an extramarital affair during the campaign, was outing Cheney's daughter Mary before a national television audience of 42 million.

Cheney, who was furious, kept his composure. When Ifill asked him to respond—"Mr. Vice President, you have ninety seconds."—Cheney said, "Well, Gwen, let me simply thank the senator for the kind words he said about my family and our daughter. I appreciate that very much."

"That's it?" Ifill asked.

"That's it," Cheney replied.[92]

Edwards had taken a cheap shot, and Cheney, to his credit ignored it. The bleeding stopped. The next *USA Today*/CNN/Gallup poll showed that the Republican decline had been arrested.[93]

Three days later Bush met Kerry for their second debate, this time at Washington University in St. Louis. The format was town hall style, with members of the audience posing questions. Bush was better prepared, and stifled any sense of annoyance he may have had, but Kerry won once again. A focus group organized by the Bush campaign in Orlando, Florida, found that "John Kerry exceeded voters' expectations in the two debates" and was seen as "more likeable, knowledgeable and charismatic than expected."[94]

The third and final debate was held on October 13 at Arizona State University in Tempe. The format was similar to the first debate, and was moderated by Bob Schieffer of CBS News. This time the issue was domestic affairs, and again Kerry came across as the more polished debater. But like Edwards the week before, he made a monumental error that redounded to Bush's advantage. Midway through the debate, Schieffer asked both candidates about same-sex marriage. "Do you believe homosexuality is a choice?"

Bush replied cautiously. "I just don't know," said the president. "I do know that we have a choice to make in America, and that is to treat people with tolerance and respect and dignity." Bush went on to say that he believed marriage was between a man and a woman and that the law should reflect that.

Kerry, like Edwards, raised the matter of Mary Cheney. "We're all God's children, Bob, and I think if you were to talk to Dick Cheney's daughter, who is a lesbian, she would tell you that she's being who she was, she's being who she was born as."[95] It was a mistake. For Kerry and Edwards to raise the matter of Mary Cheney's sexuality backfired badly. Kerry said that he agreed with the president that marriage is between a man and a woman, but for the titular head of the Democratic Party to use the word "lesbian" sent shock waves through the country. The liberal Democratic base was appalled, and Bush-Cheney supporters offended. Mary Cheney became the unsung hero of the hour. The Bush campaign got an immediate 3-point bump in the polls and now led Kerry 49 to 46 percent. Cheney called it the "Mary Cheney bounce."[96]

As the candidates entered the home stretch three weeks before the election, the advantage had shifted to Bush. "I felt relaxed," said Bush afterward. "I didn't force myself to be relaxed, but I was relaxed. It was my last campaign. Plus, I was energized by enormous crowds. These crowds were big and they were loud and they were very enthusiastic. There was no question in my mind that coming down the stretch we were going to win, and the reason why is because I hadn't seen such large crowds that were full of such universally enthusiastic people. These weren't people coming to get a sense of 'who is this guy?' They were absolute advocates ready to go to work and turn out the vote."[97]

During the last three weeks of the campaign, Bush delivered fifty-eight stump speeches across the country, concentrating on swing states Republicans hoped to carry. Fourteen of the speeches were in Florida, nine in Ohio, and seven each in Iowa and Wisconsin. "In some ways, the 2004 campaign was easier than 2000," said Bush. "I benefitted from the trappings of the presidency, especially Air Force One and Marine One."[98]

In the 2000 election, the Bush campaign had been jolted by an October Surprise—the revelation by Fox News of Bush's DUI conviction in Maine. In 2004, the October Surprise was provided by Osama bin Laden, who on October 29 released an audiotape to Al Jazeera implicitly calling for Bush's defeat. "People of America, this talk of mine is for you and concerns the ideal way to prevent another Manhattan. Even though we are in the fourth year after the events of September 11, Bush is still engaged in distortion, deception, and hiding from you the real causes. And thus, the reasons are still there for a repeat of what occurred."

Bin Laden went on to mock Bush's reading of *The Pet Goat* while the twin towers smoldered, and dismissed his claim that al Qaeda attacked the United States because it had freedom. If that were the case, he asked, "Why did we not attack Sweden?" The tape continued for fifteen minutes, concluding with the accusation that Bush went to war with Iraq for the oil revenue. "The darkness of the black gold blurred his vision. So the war went ahead, the death toll rose, the American economy bled, and Bush became embroiled in the swamps of Iraq that threaten his future." [99]

This time the October Surprise worked to Bush's advantage. Bin Laden's reminding Americans of 9/11 and the war on terror caused the president to profit. Bush overruled Ashcroft, who wanted to raise the nation's threat level, and declined to make an issue of bin Laden's intervention. "But I thought it was going to help. I thought it would help remind people that if bin Laden doesn't want Bush to be president, something must be right with Bush." [100] Opinion polls on the eve of the election gave the Bush-Cheney ticket a 49–47 point lead among likely voters. [101]

On Monday, November 1, the day before the election, Bush spoke in Ohio, Pennsylvania, Wisconsin, Iowa (twice), New Mexico, and Texas. He finished in Dallas just before midnight. "My opponent has been talking about the day that is gone," said the president. "I'm talking about the day that is coming. I'm talking about a better day for every American. I see a day where prosperity reaches every corner of our country, and a day where every child can read and write. And I see a day that this world becomes more peaceful." [102]

Bush, Laura, and the twins spent the night at the ranch in Crawford, were up early, and went to the Crawford firehouse to vote as soon
as the polls opened. Speaking briefly to reporters afterward, Bush was
asked about Senator Kerry. "I wish him the best," said the president.
"He and I are in the exact same position. We've given our all, and I'm
sure he is happy like I am that the campaign has come to a conclusion." [103]

Bush boarded Air Force One to return to Washington, and stopped
briefly in Columbus, Ohio, for a final rally. As the plane approached
Andrews Air Force Base, Rove received the first exit poll results. They
were not good. The ticket was behind by 17 points in Pennsylvania, 3
in Florida, 4 in Ohio, and 1 in South Carolina and Virginia. Alabama
and Mississippi were even. "The exit polls are dreadful," Rove told the
president. "If they're accurate, we're not going to win." [104]

"I don't believe it," said Bush. "If this is what they've decided, fine.
But I don't believe it." [105]

The mood on the plane was grim. When they landed, Bush and
his aides put on smiling faces and made their way to the White House.
It seemed like 2000 all over again. Voting ended at 7 p.m. in several
eastern states, and by 7:30 it was obvious that the exit polls were wrong.
Bush jumped into big early leads in Kentucky and Indiana, and was
ahead by 13 points in West Virginia. Pennsylvania went for Kerry, but
at 11:39 ABC called Florida for Bush. An hour later, Fox News called
Ohio for Bush. With Ohio, Bush's electoral vote count stood at 269 with
Iowa, Nevada, and New Mexico still up in the air. Bush was one vote
away from the required 270. If Bush carried any one of the outstanding
states, he would be over the top. He would ultimately carry all three.
At 4 a.m. the networks called Nevada for Bush. Karl Rove, Andy Card,
and speechwriter Michael Gerson urged the president to declare victory. Bush hesitated. Laura told him to wait. Give Kerry time to concede. "George, you can't go out there. Wait until you've been declared
the winner." [106] Bush agreed. He went to bed. At eleven the next morning, John Kerry called to concede.

"Congratulations, Mr. President."

"You were an admirable, worthy opponent," Bush replied. "You waged one tough campaign." The president and Kerry chatted graciously for almost five minutes and they agreed to try to unite the nation now that the election was over. "I hope you are proud of the effort you put in. You should be,"[107] said Bush.

The 2004 presidential election was in some ways unique. Total voter turnout increased by 16 percent—a historic record. When Bush ran against Gore in 2000, 105 million people voted; in 2004, 123 million did. Even more impressive, the 2004 turnout represented 61 percent of the eligible voters. In 2000, only 51 percent voted. Bush received 50.7 percent of the popular vote and became the first president since his father in 1988 to win a majority. Kerry received 48.3, and the remaining one percent went to third party candidates. In the electoral college, Bush won 286 votes to Kerry's 251. Bush carried all of the states he won in 2000 except New Hampshire, and picked up Iowa and New Mexico—a net gain of 8 electoral college votes. But the margins were slim. In Iowa, with a million and a half votes cast, Bush won by 10,059. In New Mexico, with 750,000 votes cast, Bush carried the state by 5,988.

Bush's strongest support was among white men, where he received almost two thirds of the vote. Overall, men voted for Bush 55–44 percent, while women preferred Kerry 51–48. By race, white voters gave Bush a 58–41 edge. Eighty-eight percent of African Americans voted for Kerry, as did 55 percent of Asians and 53 percent of Latinos. Bush also did best among voters over thirty, and especially among those over sixty. Young people voted overwhelmingly for Kerry. Married people voted for Bush 57 to 42 percent. Unmarrieds voted for Kerry by a similar margin.

The key to Bush's victory lay in the religious breakdown. Sixty-one percent of regular churchgoers voted for Bush. Among evangelicals and born-again Christians the figure rose to 78 percent. Catholics also preferred Bush 52 to 47 percent, even though Kerry was Catholic. On the other hand, three quarters of Jewish voters and those of other religions voted for Kerry, as did those who did not claim to belong to a church. Gun owners voted for Bush two to one; gays, lesbians, and bisexuals voted for Kerry by an even greater margin, despite his cheap shot at the Cheneys in the third debate.

If issues are considered, those who felt the Iraq War was a mistake voted for Kerry 73 to 26 percent. If terrorism was most important, Bush carried the day 86 to 14 percent. Bush also won hands down among those who believed moral values were of primary importance and those eager for tax cuts.[108]

Overall, there is no question but that Bush and Karl Rove ran a superb campaign. They appealed to their base and concentrated on turning out the vote. Under Rove's direction, the Bush campaign built an organization of 1.4 million active volunteers to insure people got to the polls. The Democrats made do with 233,000. Bush's concentration on core Republican values clearly enhanced his appeal to the party's base. It also exacerbated the political polarization of the nation.

CHAPTER SEVENTEEN

Katrina

Brownie, you're doing a heck of a job.

George W. Bush
September 2, 2005

Bush had scored a historic victory. "America has spoken," the president told a belated victory rally at the Ronald Reagan Building on Pennsylvania Avenue. "I am humbled by the trust and confidence of my fellow citizens. With that trust comes a duty to serve all Americans, and I will do my best to fulfill that duty every day as your President." Bush paid a special tribute to Karl Rove, whom he described as the architect of victory, and briefly restated his campaign promises. "Reaching these goals will require the broad support of Americans. So today I want to speak to every person who voted for my opponent. To make this Nation stronger and better, I will need your support and I will work to earn it. . . . We have one country, one Constitution, and one future that binds us. And when we come together and work together, there is no limit to the greatness of America."[1] It was a masterful performance. Having waged a successful campaign by emphasizing the differences that set Americans apart, the president was now attempting to put the pieces back together.

The next morning, Thursday, November 4, Bush met with his cabinet and thanked them for their support. And he signaled there would be shifts in the lineup. "I expect there will be lots of rumors and speculation about changes in the cabinet for our second term. Well, a few changes are likely, but I haven't had time to think about them yet."[2] The president briefly laid out his domestic agenda: Social Security reform, revising the tax code, immigration reform, and limiting excessive litigation. He then turned to Iraq and Afghanistan. Achieving results can sometimes be "ugly," said Bush, but he believed progress had been made. "You've got to have faith people want to be free, even in impoverished areas. Iraq will change the world."[3]

As press secretary Scott McClellan put it, the victory speech at the Reagan Building and the cabinet meeting made Bush's state of mind clear to anyone who knew him. "He was dead set on pushing ahead aggressively, selling his big ideas, and leaving his mark on history."[4] Bush said as much in his first post-election news conference later that day. "I earned capital in this campaign," the president told reporters. "Political capital. And now I intend to spend it. It's my style."[5]

Bush's first task was to revamp his cabinet. After his news conference Thursday, Bush and Laura departed for Camp David. With them were Condoleezza Rice and White House chief of staff Andrew Card. Card had offered to step down, but the president asked him to remain. Bush depended on familiar faces in his immediate circle, and he liked and trusted Card. The State Department was a different matter. Powell was evidently reconsidering his decision to leave at the end of the first term. Yasser Arafat was in a French hospital reportedly at death's door, opening the possibility for a settlement of the Palestinian-Israeli issue, and Powell wanted to pursue the opportunity. Bush was uninterested.[6] Under Powell's leadership, the State Department had become a thorn in the president's side. As Cheney put it, Powell and Armitage "were essentially mounting an insurgency against the rest of the national security team."[7] It was time for a change.

The obvious choice as Powell's successor was Condoleezza Rice. Bush had previously told Rice on several occasions that Powell was leaving and he wanted her to take his place. At Camp David that Fri-

Secretary of State Condoleezza Rice

day morning he made the offer explicit. "I want you to be secretary of state," the president told her. Rice, who assumed the offer was coming, said she wanted to think about it. That evening at dinner she accepted. "I would be honored to become the sixty-sixth secretary of state," she told the president.[8]

Rice's relationship with Bush was unique. She worked out with him in the White House gym almost daily, often had dinner with the president and Laura in the White House family quarters, and was a regular at Camp David and the ranch in Crawford. Bush trusted her completely. They were so close that at a Washington dinner party she once spoke of the president as "my husb-" before catching herself.[9] There was nothing improper in the relationship. As Rice later said, "I'm simply internalizing his world."[10]

Rice was also adept at avoiding blame for administration failures and her own bad judgment. "I was struck by how deft she is at protecting her reputation," said Scott McClellan. "No matter what went wrong, she was somehow able to keep her hands clean, even when the problems related to matters under her direct purview, including the WMD rationale for war in Iraq, the decision to invade Iraq, the sixteen words in the State of the Union address,* and postwar planning and implementation of the strategy in Iraq." McClellan added that when she and the president were alone, Rice "complemented and reinforced Bush's instincts rather than challenging or questioning them. . . . She

---

* McClellan is referring to Bush's 2003 State of the Union address in which he said: "The British Government has learned that Saddam Hussein recently sought significant quantities of uranium from Africa." *Public Papers of the Presidents of the United States, George W. Bush, 2003*, Vol. 1, State of the Union Address, January 28, 2003 (Washington, D.C.: Government Printing Office, 2006), 82–90.

knew how to read him and how to translate his ideas, feelings, and proclivities into concrete policies." [11]

As had been the case when Treasury Secretary Paul O'Neill was tossed overboard, Bush declined to speak with Powell directly. Instead, he instructed Card to call Powell on Wednesday, November 10, and ask for his resignation by Friday. Powell was surprised by the suddenness. "I thought we were going to talk about it," he told Card. Card said the plan was to include Powell's resignation with other cabinet changes "so they can be announced at the same time." Powell said fine. That evening at his home, Colin Powell typed out his resignation. Rather than place the onus on Bush, Powell took responsibility for his leaving. "As we have discussed in recent months, I believe that now the election is over the time has come for me to step down as Secretary of State and return to private life." Powell signed the letter "Very respectfully," the phrase used within the military when writing to a superior.[12] Once again, the call of duty took precedence for Powell. The letter was delivered as requested on Friday, November 12.

On the following Monday, the White House announced Powell's resignation, along with those of Roderick Paige as secretary of education, Spencer Abraham as secretary of energy, Ann Veneman as secretary of agriculture, and Edward Gillespie as chairman of the Republican National Committee. Bush made no public appearance to discuss Powell's departure, or those of the other cabinet officers. But the next day, Tuesday, November 16, the president appeared in the Roosevelt Room of the White House to announce the appointment of Condoleezza Rice to succeed Powell, and Stephen Hadley to take Rice's place as national security adviser. Powell was not present. On Wednesday, Bush announced the appointment of his aide Margaret Spellings to succeed Paige as secretary of education. Like Powell, Paige did not attend. With two strokes, Bush had elevated two of his closest White House associates to cabinet portfolios. And a third was in the offing.

If Colin Powell had become a thorn in the president's side, John Ashcroft was a pain in the posterior. A darling of the evangelicals and fundamentalists—Ashcroft had ordered the nude bosom of the statue of justice in his department's auditorium draped with cloth—the attorney general had a disconcerting habit of appearing on Sunday talk shows and announcing policy that was not for him to unveil. With John Yoo no longer in the department, he had defied Bush on the renewal of NSA's surveillance program and was opposed to holding detainees indefinitely at Guantánamo. He also sought to provide some form of legal due process for those tried by military commissions. No doubt realizing that his days were numbered, Ashcroft wrote out in longhand a lengthy letter of resignation on election day and personally delivered it to Bush. Ashcroft's letter documented his achievements as attorney general, and was written with an eye to its public release.[13]

Bush immediately accepted it. To replace the attorney general, he named White House counsel Alberto Gonzales—the third member of Bush's immediate White House entourage to join the cabinet. In 1961, John Kennedy had named his brother Robert to be attorney general, not because of Robert's superior legal ability but largely to keep an eye on J. Edgar Hoover and insure that the FBI director did not stray from the reservation. Bush named Gonzales to insure that the administration's expansive reading of its constitutional authority would not be challenged by its own Department of Justice. And with Rice, Spellings, and Gonzales in the cabinet, Bush took another step toward the personalization of presidential power. These were people who knew the president, had worked closely with him, and were prepared to do his bidding.

Bush continued his cabinet shakeup. Of his original fourteen appointees in 2001, only Rumsfeld at Defense, Norman Mineta at Transportation, Gale Norton (Interior), and Elaine Chao (Labor) would continue into the second term. Carlos Gutierrez, a Cuban émigré who headed the Kellogg Company, replaced Don Evans as secretary of commerce; Governor Mike Johanns of Nebraska replaced Ann Veneman at Agriculture; James Nicholson, a career soldier who had served as Bush's ambassador at the Vatican for the last three years, replaced Anthony Principi at Veterans Affairs; Samuel Bodman, who had been deputy secretary of the treasury, became secretary of energy, replacing former senator Spencer Abraham; and Michael Leavitt, the head of the Environmental Protection Agency, became secretary of health and human services, replacing former Wisconsin governor Tommy Thompson.

The most difficult replacement was that of Tom Ridge, who was stepping down as secretary of homeland security. The Department of Homeland Security was in its infancy trying to absorb and integrate twenty-two previously independent federal agencies with over 750,000 employees. It required a skilled leader with compelling administrative ability. Former mayor Rudolph Giuliani called Bush and recommended his close friend former New York City police commissioner Bernard Kerik. The president was enthusiastic. He knew Kerik, had first met him in the rubble of the World Trade Center, and had been extremely impressed. Kerik came from a hardscrabble background, had worked his way up through the New York police department, became Giuliani's corrections commissioner, then police commissioner, and had gone to Baghdad briefly as interim minister of the interior under Paul Bremer to train Iraqi security forces. He had also spoken at the Republican convention in New York in support of Bush.

The president believed Kerik would make an ideal secretary of Homeland Security, and instructed Gonzales to run a background check. This was a departure from standard practice, since background checks are normally conducted by the FBI. But Bush wanted to expedite Kerik's appointment. Gonzales did as instructed and discovered that Kerik had a somewhat complicated past, including various sexual improprieties and perhaps more seriously, had accepted a series of gifts from a New Jersey construction firm with alleged Mafia connections that was seeking a major New York City contract. Bush dismissed Gonzales's findings, and on December 3 nominated Kerik in a public ceremony at the White House. "Bernard Kerik is one of the most accomplished and effective leaders of law enforcement in America," said the president. "His broad, practical, hands-on experience makes Bernie superbly qualified to lead the Department of Homeland Security."[14]

Press coverage of the nomination was extensive, and under public scrutiny Kerik's past proved to be even more checkered than Gonzales had discovered. When it was revealed that Kerik had not paid Social

Security taxes for a nanny who was an illegal immigrant, he reluctantly stepped down. Bush had been aware of most of the problems in Kerik's past and because of his resounding electoral victory thought he could force the nomination through. He was tripped up on what was essentially a technicality.*

Replacing Kerik was not easy. The position was offered to Richard Armitage, who said no. So did Senator Joe Lieberman. Eventually, Bush settled on Michael Chertoff, a former Justice Department official who had been appointed to the United States Court of Appeals for the Third Circuit in 2003. Chertoff had helped draft the Patriot Act and was a known figure within the administration, but his qualifications for managing a vast government agency were unproved.

Like Franklin Roosevelt following his landslide victory over Alf Landon in 1936, George Bush believed his triumph over Kerry empowered him to act. Once again, hubris prevailed. In 1937, FDR moved immediately after his inauguration to expand the size of the Supreme Court from nine justices to fifteen. The proposal was hatched secretly in the White House with no congressional input, and split the Democratic Party down the middle. Roosevelt's plan was eventually defeated, and the president never recovered his domestic clout.

In George Bush's case, the initial overreach came with his inaugural address on January 20. Encouraged by conservative scholars,† Bush

---

* In 2001, Linda Chavez had to step back as Bush's nominee for secretary of labor for not paying Social Security for a domestic, as had Zoe Baird and Kimba Wood, whom Clinton had nominated to be attorney general in 1993. On November 5, 2009, after an investigation that lasted four years and involved numerous issues, Kerik pled guilty to eight felony charges involving tax evasion in a plea deal with federal authorities. He was sentenced to four years imprisonment at the minimum security U.S. prison in Cumberland, Maryland, and was released on October 15, 2013.

† Bush was especially enchanted with the writings of Natan Sharansky, whom he invited to the Oval Office after reading Sharansky's *The Case for Democracy*, just after the election. Bush later wrote that he appreciated Sharansky's "moral clarity." Yale Cold War historian John Lewis Gaddis also provided the president with a three-page memo urging Bush to call for an ending of "tyranny in our time." Gaddis later expanded this into an article, "Grand Strategy for the Second Term," that appeared in the January-February 2005 issue of *Foreign Affairs*. Also see George W. Bush, *Decision Points* (New York: Crown, 2010), 398.

pledged American support for the spread of democracy "in every nation and culture, with the ultimate goal of ending tyranny in our world." Rather than promote peace and international stability, the United States would seek to transform the world by exporting democracy. It was the Bush Doctrine in spades. Or as one pro-administration reporter called it, the inaugural address was "George W. Bush on steroids." [15]

Bush saw his second inaugural address as a benchmark redefining his presidency. Two days after the election, he told chief speechwriter Michael Gerson, "the future of America and the security of America depends on the spread of liberty." [16] As the president saw it, democracy throughout the world was not just a moral aspiration, but was intrinsically tied to American security. And by spreading democracy, Bush hoped to secure his place in history.

On inauguration day, Thursday, January 20, Washington was covered with a light blanket of snow. The crowd on the west front of the Capitol watched solemnly as Dick Cheney took the oath of office, sworn in by House Speaker Dennis Hastert. Then, at five minutes before noon, Bush stood at the rostrum, his left hand on the family Bible, his right arm raised, and faced Chief Justice William Rehnquist. Rehnquist was suffering from thyroid cancer and looked frail. He walked with a cane and spoke haltingly. With the oath completed, the United States Marine Band saluted the president with a stirring rendition of "Hail to the Chief."

Bush then delivered his address. At twenty-one minutes, it was brief by presidential standards, but six minutes longer than his first inaugural. And it was an unmistakable call for action. "After the shipwreck of communism came years of relative quiet, years of repose, years of sabbatical, and then there came a day of fire." For the president, the nation's future was at stake. "The survival of liberty in our land increasingly depends on the success of liberty in other lands. The best hope of peace in our world is the expansion of freedom in all the world."

Bush was explicit. There was little reflection and little effort to weigh the consequences. "So it is the policy of the United States to seek and support the growth of the democratic movements and institutions in every nation and culture, with the ultimate goal of ending tyranny in our world." The policy of the United States? Was this unilaterally determined by the president? Bush evidently assumed so.

> We will persistently clarify the choice before every ruler and every na-
> tion, the moral choice between oppression, which is always wrong, and
> freedom, which is eternally right.
>
> All who live in tyranny and hopelessness can know: The United
> States will not ignore your oppression or excuse your oppressors. When
> you stand for your liberty, we will stand with you.

Bush buttressed his case by invoking the Maker of Heaven and Earth, and concluded on a religious note. "History has an ebb and flow of justice, but history also has visible direction, set by liberty and the Author of liberty. . . . Renewed in our strength, tested but not weary, we are ready for the greatest achievements in the history of freedom." [17]

Bush's second inaugural was intended to set the course for his next four years in office. The United States would spread freedom throughout the world. The president was explicitly rejecting what had been the basis of American policy since World War II—namely, the pursuit of international stability—and was embarking on a quest to export democracy. Democrats were astounded. Former Republican secretaries of state like Henry Kissinger and James Baker were appalled. Conservative columnist Pat Buchanan prophetically noted, "These words will be thrown back at Bush and will haunt him as long as he lives." [18] But it was Colin Powell who put it best. "Oh boy! We've got a lot of friends who are going to be saying: Who do you think you are? You're telling me, the King of Saudi Arabia, who's had a very successful run for two hundred years with this royal family, that the Americans actually think we'd be better off with an election in Saudi Arabia?" [19]

Without consultation, without considering the future implications or consequences, Bush was attempting to embark on a global policy of spreading democracy. Having won the election, he assumed the world was his to remake. Not since FDR in 1937 has presidential hubris been so evident, or so misguided. And Buchanan was right. Bush's second

Bush taking the oath of office at his second inaugural, January 20, 2005.

inaugural address must rank as one of the most ill-considered of all time.

Bush made no more than passing reference to domestic affairs in his inaugural address. In his State of the Union, delivered on February 2, 2005, he continued to focus on spreading democracy throughout the world, but also launched his drive to reform Social Security. "Thirteen years from now, in 2018, Social Security will be paying out more than it takes in. And every year afterward will bring a new shortfall, bigger than the year before. . . . By the year 2042, the entire system would be exhausted and bankrupt. If steps are not taken to avert that outcome, the only solution would be dramatically higher taxes, massive new borrowing, or sudden and severe cuts in Social Security benefits or other government programs."[20] Congressional audiences for a president's State of the Union address are usually polite and receptive, but Bush's attack on the existing formula for Social Security caused the Democrats to erupt in a crescendo of boos and catcalls. The president was biting off more than he could chew, and his domestic agenda was imperiled from the very beginning of his second term.

Bush's decision to press for changes in Social Security reflected his own deeply held feelings. Ever since his unsuccessful run for Congress in 1978, he had talked about restructuring Social Security so that citizens could invest some of their payroll taxes in the markets, giving them greater control over their own futures. Just as No Child Left Behind and prescription drugs for seniors marked the domestic achievements of his first term, Bush believed that Social Security reform would be the defining domestic legacy of his second.[21] This was the president's personal decision. There was little discussion by the White House staff, and no interagency consultation. Bush was somehow convinced that his reelection gave him a mandate to revise Social Security.

Numerous advisers, including Grover Norquist, president of Americans for Tax Reform, and Kentucky's Mitch McConnell, the Republican whip in the Senate, warned Bush that he did not have the votes. The president dismissed their warnings. Bush was confident he could assert his will. As the president saw it, this was his opportunity to refashion Roosevelt's New Deal and Lyndon Johnson's Great Society into his conservative "Ownership Society." As White House aide Peter Wehner wrote, "For the first time in six decades, the Social Security battle is one we can win—and in doing so, we can help transform the political and philosophical landscape of the country."[22] Bush was reaching for the stars. His foreign policy aim was to spread democracy throughout the world, his domestic goal was to enshrine individual choice. The common denominator was personal liberty.

In addition to replacing Colin Powell with Condoleezza Rice, Bush made two additional appointments early in his second term to advance his agenda of promoting democracy abroad. In March he convinced Karen Hughes to return from Texas to become undersecretary of state for public diplomacy, hoping she could breathe life into the State Department's moribund program to promote American values overseas. At the same time he nominated deputy secretary of defense Paul Wolfowitz to be president of the World Bank. The Wolfowitz appointment was criticized by a number of economists, and was not greeted with enthusiasm at the World Bank, but Bush was confident that Wolfowitz would provide vital support for promoting democracy abroad.

At the inauguration, it had been apparent that Chief Justice Rehnquist's health was failing and that he would soon be forced to step down.

The last Republican appointee to the Supreme Court was Clarence Thomas, who had been named by George H. W. Bush in 1991. That was fourteen years ago. Bush wanted to be ready when the vacancy occurred, and delegated the search for a replacement to Cheney, assisted by Harriet Miers, who had succeeded Alberto Gonzales as White House counsel. It speaks volumes about the current role of the Supreme Court in the United States that the search for a replacement for the chief justice should be entrusted to a nonlawyer. Cheney immediately assembled a team to review possible candidates, and decided that he wanted to interview each of the top contenders personally. One by one the leading candidates were covertly brought to the vice president's residence at the Naval Observatory. Cheney was joined at these sessions by Attorney General Gonzales, Miers, Karl Rove, and Andy Card. Only Gonzales and Miers were lawyers.

The leading candidates to emerge from the process were John Roberts, a fifty-year-old judge on the Court of Appeals for the District of Columbia whom Bush had appointed in 2003, and Michael Luttig, a judge on the Fourth Circuit in Richmond, who had been appointed by Bush's father in 1991. Both had sterling conservative credentials. Roberts had worked as a volunteer on James Baker's staff in the 2000 Florida recount, had clerked for Chief Justice Rehnquist, and had argued thirty-nine cases before the Supreme Court, prevailing in twenty-five of them. Luttig had clerked for Chief Justice Warren Burger, was a close friend of Justice Antonin Scalia, for whom he also clerked while Scalia was on the Court of Appeals, and as a young lawyer in the Justice Department had helped prepare Sandra Day O'Connor, Clarence Thomas, and David Souter for their confirmation hearings. When he was appointed to the appeals court in 1991 he was thirty-seven years old and became the youngest judge on the court. Lawyers appearing before the Fourth Circuit held Luttig in great respect, and his scholarship was impeccable.

The long expected vacancy on the Supreme Court occurred on June 30, but it was not Rehnquist who was stepping down. To everyone's surprise, Sandra Day O'Connor submitted her resignation to the president. O'Connor was leaving the Court to care for her ailing husband. She had been appointed by Ronald Reagan in 1981, and was confirmed unanimously by the Senate, one of the few justices of the modern era to enjoy that distinction. On the Court she hewed to a middle course, and was often the swing vote on crucial issues. She voted with the majority in *Bush v. Gore*,[23] but consistently refused to overturn Justice Harry Blackmun's abortion decision in *Roe v. Wade*.[24] In 2003 she wrote a concurring opinion in *Lawrence v. Texas*,[25] holding that state laws that prohibited homosexual sodomy were a violation of the Equal Protection Clause of the Fourteenth Amendment, and the following year wrote the Court's opinion in *Hamdi v. Rumsfeld*,[26] rejecting the government's authority to hold U.S. citizens in custody without due process. "A state of war is not a blank check for the President," said O'Connor.[27]

To replace O'Connor required a somewhat different calculus than replacing Rehnquist. Laura pressed for a woman, but Bush ultimately settled on Roberts. Luttig was second. Altogether, Bush personally interviewed five candidates,* but it was John Roberts and his easy charm that Bush found most appealing. All five candidates whom Bush interviewed were judges on the United States Court of Appeals with established track records and were fully qualified for the appointment. Bush chose Roberts because of his personality. The president believed he would be a consensus builder and a true leader on the Court.† On July 19, the president made it official. At a televised White House ceremony, Bush announced Roberts's appointment to succeed O'Connor. "In meetings with Judge Roberts, I have been deeply impressed," said the president. "He is a man of extraordinary

---

* In addition to Roberts and Luttig, the president interviewed Samuel Alito of the Third Circuit in Philadelphia, J. Harvie Wilkinson III of the Fourth Circuit in Richmond, and Edith Brown Clement of the Fifth Circuit in New Orleans.

† Bush's stress on personality was not misplaced. It was John Marshall's personality that solidified his position as chief justice. Marshall led the Court for thirty-five years, establishing its role in American government. His intellect was outstanding. But it was Marshall's charm and easy manner among his colleagues that won their respect. In nominating John Roberts, albeit for O'Connor's seat, Bush was opting for the same characteristic. See my biography *John Marshall: Definer of a Nation* (New York: Henry Holt, 1996).

accomplishment and ability. He has a good heart. He has the qualities Americans expect in a judge: experience, wisdom, fairness, and civility." [28]

Bush began his vacation at the ranch in Crawford on August 2. It was his forty-ninth visit to the ranch as president, and he planned to remain for five weeks—his longest vacation since assuming office. Ronald Reagan held the record for presidential vacations, spending 335 days at his ranch in California over eight years. Bush, in just four and a half years, had already spent 318 days in

Cindy Sheehan

Crawford and would easily surpass Reagan on this trip. Bush relished his vacations, loved the seclusion, and appreciated the distance from Washington. Driving his Ford F-250 pickup truck, riding his mountain bike, and clearing brush in the 100-degree heat gave him a noticeable lift. But there were costs. Critics noted that Bush had spent a leisurely month at the ranch in 2001 before 9/11 and had ignored CIA warnings of an impending al Qaeda attack.

Bush's 2005 vacation was marred by the arrival on August 5 of Cindy Sheehan, the mother of a soldier killed in Iraq. Sheehan came in a bus painted red, white, and blue bearing the banner "Impeachment Tour." She was stopped by the Secret Service at the ranch entrance, and then encamped on the side of the dusty, unpaved road, vowing to remain there until the president saw her. Sheehan was one of the mothers Bush had met with during his campaign appearance at Fort Lewis, Washington, the year before. She had become an ardent critic of the war, and blamed the president for her son's death. Her presence on the roadside outside the ranch was covered extensively by the media and did little to improve Bush's image. He declined to meet with her, but was clearly troubled by her presence. Eventually, Bush sent his na-

tional security adviser, Stephen Hadley, and deputy White House chief
of staff Joe Hagin to meet with her. "Don't let the president say that he
needs to send more troops to get killed in order to honor the sacrifice of
my son," she told them.[29]

At his press conference on August 11, Bush spoke to reporters about
Sheehan, and it was obvious she had made an impression. "I sympa-
thize with Mrs. Sheehan," said the president.

> She feels strongly about her position. And she has every right in the
> world to say what she believes. This is America. She has a right to her
> position. And I've thought long and hard about her position. I've heard
> her position from others, which is, "Get out of Iraq now." And it would
> be a mistake for the security of this country and the ability to lay the
> foundation for peace in the long run, if we were to do so.[30]

Except for Cindy Sheehan, Bush's vacation had been quiet and
uneventful. But as August wound down, that would change abruptly.
Hurricane Katrina, the costliest natural disaster in American history,
began as a tropical depression over the Bahamas on Tuesday, August
23, 2005. By Wednesday it had become a tropical storm, and by Thursday a Category 1 hurricane headed toward South Florida. At 6:30 p.m.
on Thursday the storm came ashore between Hallandale Beach and
Aventura with 110-mile-an-hour winds, ripping roofs off buildings,
toppling trees, dropping eighteen inches of rain, and leaving 500,000
people without power. Fourteen persons were killed in Florida and
Governor Jeb Bush declared a state of emergency.

Friday afternoon, as the storm moved north, it pivoted ominously
to the northwest over the Gulf of Mexico, heading toward the coast of
Mississippi and Louisiana. By Saturday, August 27, in the warm waters
of the Gulf, Katrina had strengthened to a Category 3 hurricane and
was headed directly toward New Orleans. On Sunday, still offshore,
the storm became a Category 4 and then a Category 5 hurricane with
winds reaching 175 miles an hour. It had also grown dangerously in
size, with hurricane-force winds extending 120 miles outward from the
storm's center.

Bush was at the ranch in Crawford, with one week remaining in his vacation. Other members of the administration were scattered. Cheney was at his home in Wyoming, Andy Card was in Maine, and much of the White House staff was traveling to Greece to attend the wedding of two Bush aides, Nicolle Devenish and Mark Wallace. Initially, no one took the impending disaster very seriously. As Scott McClellan put it, the White House staff had dealt with so many crises "we were probably a little numb and a little complacent. 'What, another tragedy? We've been through this before.' . . . We allowed our response to go on autopilot. . . . It was a costly blunder."[31]

Bush was informed at the ranch of the hurricane's growing strength, but did not see the warning as a cause for action on his part. At the request of Mississippi governor Haley Barbour and Louisiana governor Kathleen Blanco, the president declared coastal Mississippi and Louisiana disaster areas on Saturday, but that was largely pro forma to allow the costs of state emergency preparations to be reimbursed by the federal government. He also urged New Orleans mayor Ray Nagin to order a mandatory evacuation of the city prior to Katrina's arrival. But Bush accepted that state and local authorities were the first responders and could handle the hurricane, just as Jeb had done in Florida.

Instead of thinking about Katrina, Bush remained focused on Iraq. At noon on Sunday, he sat in briefly on a videoconference that Federal Emergency Management Agency (FEMA) director Mike Brown had convened with officials on the Gulf coast. The purpose was to insure that everyone was ready as Katrina neared landfall. The principal presentation was made by Max Mayfield, director of the National Hurricane Center in Miami. "I don't have any good news here at all today. This is a very dangerous hurricane, and the center is about 225 miles south-southeast of the mouth of the Mississippi River." Mayfield emphasized the size of Katrina and the danger that entailed. "When you have a large diameter eye like this, and as strong as this one is, I really don't expect to see any weakening. So I think the wisest thing to do here is plan on a Category Five hurricane." The storm surge would be at least twelve feet. Mayfield said it was unclear whether that would top the levees. "The current track suggests that there will be at minimum flooding in the city of New Orleans itself, but we've always said that the storm surge model is only accurate within about twenty percent. If that track were to deviate just a little for the west, it would make all the difference in the world." [32] Mayfield was followed by two researchers from the National Hurricane Center who spoke briefly about problems of rainfall that could reach fifteen inches.

At that point Brown introduced Bush to the teleconference. "I'd like to go to Crawford, Texas. Ladies and gentlemen, I'd like to introduce the President of the United States." Bush spoke briefly, much like a football coach giving a pregame pep talk.

Mike, thank you very much. I appreciate so very much the warnings that Max and his team have given to the good folks in Louisiana and Mississippi and Alabama. . . . I do want to thank the good folks in the offices of Louisiana, Alabama, and Mississippi for listening to these warnings and preparing your citizens for this—this huge storm. I want to assure the folks at the state level that we are fully prepared to not only help you during the storm, but we will move in whatever resources and assets we have at our disposal after the storm to help you deal with the loss of property. And we pray for no loss of life. Unfortunately, we've had experience at this in recent years, and I—the FEMA folks have done great work in the past. And I'm confident, Mike, that you and your team will do all you can to help these good folks in the affected states.

Again, I want to thank Governor Blanco, Governor [Bob] Riley [of Alabama] and Governor Barbour, Governor Bush of Florida for heeding these warnings and doing all you possibly can with your state folks and local folks to prepare the citizens for this storm.

In the meantime, I know the nation will be praying for the good folks in the affected areas, and we just hope for the very best.

Mike, thanks for letting me speak to the people I know who are working long hours. Again, I want to thank everybody involved in this effort. I appreciate the long hours you are keeping. I expect you to keep more long hours until we've done everything we can in our power to help—to help folks in the affected areas. Thank you, sir. [33]

That was it. Bush asked no questions of Mayfield or Brown, and departed immediately after speaking to make a national television address dealing with Iraq. The meeting continued for thirty-five additional minutes. Bush assumed the situation was in hand, and was eager to announce the completion of work by Iraqi political leaders on drafting a new constitution. He prefaced his television remarks with a brief comment on Katrina, but it was perfunctory. "Hurricane Katrina is now designated a Category Five hurricane. We cannot stress enough the danger this hurricane poses to

Hurricane Katrina.

Gulf coast communities. I urge all citizens to put their own safety and the safety of their families first by moving to safe ground. Please listen carefully to instructions provided by State and local officials."[34] Bush then turned to Iraq and discussed the new constitution for fifteen minutes. It was clear that the president was pleased with the progress that had been made in Baghdad. When he completed his remarks, he had the rest of the day to himself. He did not consider what action the federal government might take concerning Katrina, or order any special preparations. It was vacation time in Texas.

On Monday, August 29, Katrina made landfall in the early morning hours near the Louisiana-Mississippi border, about forty miles east of New Orleans. Winds of 135 mph lashed the coastline, bringing eight to ten inches of rain, and a storm surge of thirty-four feet: roughly three times what Max Mayfield had predicted. The Mississippi coastline was devastated. Downtown Gulfport was under ten feet of water, but initial reports suggested New Orleans might have dodged the bullet. The levees appeared to be holding.

At nine o'clock that morning Bush and Laura left Crawford aboard Air Force One to take part in a Presidential Conversation on Medicare with seniors in El Mirage, Arizona. It was an off-year campaign event. In his introductory remarks, the president briefly mentioned Katrina. "I know my fellow citizens here in Arizona and across the country are saying our prayers for those affected by Hurricane Katrina. Our Gulf coast is getting hit and hit hard. I want the folks there on the Gulf coast to know that the federal government is prepared to help you when the storm passes. I want to thank the governors of the affected regions for mobilizing assets prior to the arrival of the storm to help citizens avoid this devastating storm."[35] As Bush saw it, the situation was under control, and it was essentially a problem for state and local government. The federal government would help after the storm passed.

From El Mirage, Bush flew to Rancho Cucamonga, California, where he spoke that afternoon to another group of seniors about Medicare and prescription drugs at the James L. Brulte Senior Center. Again, Bush made a passing reference to Katrina, but it was little more than an aside. The president was unaware of the damage that was taking place in New Orleans, and continued to believe state and local officials could manage things. After a reception in Cucamonga, Bush and the presidential party flew to San Diego, where they spent the night at the historic Hotel del Coronado. The president was scheduled to speak Tuesday at the North Island Naval Air Station to a military audience commemorating the sixtieth anniversary of V-J Day and the end of the war in the Pacific. Bush went to bed that evening unaware that a catastrophe was unfolding in New Orleans, although it had been accurately reported on the nation's television networks for the past several hours.

At 5 a.m. Tuesday (eight o'clock Washington time), Bush was awakened in his hotel room and told the situation in New Orleans had become far more serious than originally anticipated. The levees had failed, water from Lake Pontchartrain was pouring into the city, and it was getting worse by the hour. For an update, Bush joined a videoconference along with Cheney, Andy Card, Mike Brown, and Michael Chertoff, secretary of homeland security. "What's the situation?" the president asked Brown.

"Bad," said Brown. "This is the Big One. Ninety percent of the people in New Orleans have been displaced from their homes by the hurricane."

"Ninety percent?" asked Bush. "Are you sure?"[36] The president was stunned. Bush decided to cut short his vacation and return to Washington, but not immediately. He would complete the day's schedule in San Diego, spend the night at the ranch in Crawford, and then fly to Washington on Wednesday, August 31. That would give his staff time to return from their own vacations, and as Bush saw it, would look more deliberate rather than returning in a panic.[37] In retrospect, given the speed with which the crisis was unfolding, that was a serious error.

After breakfast, Bush traveled by motorcade to the North Island Naval Air Station, gave an interview to Armed Forces Radio, and then spoke to the assembled military audience about victory over Japan in World War II. Bush tied the war in the Pacific to the struggle in Iraq, and much of the speech was devoted to defending his policy there. "Our goal is clear. We will defeat the terrorists. We will build a free Iraq that will fight terrorists instead of giving them aid and sanctuary. . . . A free Iraq will show that when America gives its word, America keeps its word."[38]

Hurricane Katrina was mentioned in passing, but it was obvious that the president was not yet involved in handling the crisis. The day was highlighted when Mark Wills, a country music singer, presented Bush with a guitar bearing the presidential seal. Bush strummed it briefly, unaware that Martha Raddatz of ABC News was filming him. On television that evening, the photos of Bush strumming the guitar in San Diego were juxtaposed with pictures of the incredible suffering along the Gulf coast. It seemed a disconnect from reality, and the president was hammered accordingly.

Bush was not the only member of the administration disconnected that Tuesday. Michael Chertoff, the cabinet officer responsible for homeland security, was in Atlanta at the Centers for Disease Control listening to lectures about avian flu, apparently unconcerned about the

Bush surveys Hurricane Katrina damage
in New Orleans, August 31, 2005.

flooding in New Orleans despite warnings of its seriousness that he had received from FEMA officials on the scene.[39] The White House also seemed disconnected. Mike Brown's calls from New Orleans asking for assistance were ignored. "Guys," he recalled saying, "this is bigger than what we can handle. This is bigger than what FEMA can do. I am asking for help."[40] Similarly, Governor Blanco's attempt to reach Bush by telephone Wednesday morning failed. The White House would not put her through, nor was she allowed to speak with Andy Card. Blanco assumed it was because she was a Democrat. "They were trying to blame Louisiana for all the problems," Blanco told historian Douglas Brinkley. "The White House just flat out made up stuff."[41]

Bush spent Wednesday morning at the ranch and boarded Air Force One shortly after lunch to return to Washington. Karl Rove suggested they fly over the devastated area. As Rove put it, it was a political opportunity. "We should have him looking out and surveying the damage in New Orleans and along the coast of Mississippi and Alabama." It would demonstrate the president's concern. McClellan and White House counselor Dan Bartlett strongly disagreed. He'll be high up in the air looking at people being rescued off rooftops, said McClellan. "He'll look out of touch and detached. If he goes, he needs to be on the ground visiting with those affected and seeing the damage close up."[42] McClellan was right and Rove was wrong, but in the end Bush chose to follow Rove's advice. Air Force One diverted from its normal flight path, and at 1:45 p.m. on Wednesday descended gently from its cruising altitude of 37,000 feet to 2,500 feet so that the president could inspect the damage. As the plane descended, Bush moved from his private cabin to the left side of the plane to get a better view. He was joined by Rove, McClellan, and deputy national security adviser J. D. Crouch.

The destruction was staggering. "It's devastating," said the president. "It's got to be doubly devastating on the ground." [43] New Orleans was awash with floodwater and Bush could see desperate people still waiting on rooftops to be rescued. The hurricane had come through two days earlier, and waters from Lake Pontchartrain still swirled through the city. The levee system had been breached in fifty-three places, and 80 percent of New Orleans was flooded. The damage along the Mississippi coast was if anything even greater. Battered by a twenty-six-foot storm surge, beachfront neighborhoods had been completely leveled. Ninety percent of the structures within a half mile of the coastline were totally destroyed. Looking at Pass Christian, Mississippi, Bush said, "It's totally wiped out." [44] The mood on the plane was somber. Everyone was struck by how devastating the storm had been. [45]

Midway through the thirty-five-minute flyover, Karl Rove invited the photographers riding in the rear of the plane forward to take pictures of Bush surveying the damage. Rove intended it as a photo op depicting the president's compassion. It backfired badly. Television coverage that evening was brutal. Rather than depicting Bush's compassion, the photos of the president gazing out the window of Air Force One showed Bush the tourist—detached, powerless, and marveling at the damage. The flyover was bad enough. But to have photos of the president merely watching the scene below was disastrous.

Bush would have been well advised to have followed the example set by Lyndon Johnson. In September 1965, forty years earlier, during the height of the war in Vietnam, New Orleans was hit by Hurricane Betsy.* Despite his concern for the war, the next evening President Johnson was on the scene, visiting shelters for the homeless. With no electricity available, Johnson held a flashlight to his face so the people could see him. "This is the president of the United States and I am here

---

* Hurricane Betsy hit the Florida Keys early on September 8, 1965, with winds of 125 mph. Like Katrina, it turned northwest and hit the Louisiana coastline the evening of September 9 with winds of 130 mph. Levees in the Lower Ninth Ward failed, flooding the city and driving residents from their homes. One hundred sixty-four thousand homes were flooded, and it was ten days before the water receded.

to help you."[46] Instead of providing immediate leadership as Johnson had done, Bush had remained at the ranch and then in California for three days as the storm struck.

Bush arrived back at the White House shortly after 4 p.m. Wednesday. He met briefly with cabinet officers concerned with Katrina, and then went to the Rose Garden to address the country on live television about the situation on the Gulf coast. Fully rested from a month at the ranch and brimming with energy, Bush once again seemed out of touch with conditions on the ground. In an editorial the next day, *The New York Times* said "Nothing about the president's demeanor yesterday—which seemed casual to the point of carelessness—suggested that he understood the depth of the current crisis." According to the *Times*:

> George W. Bush gave one of the worst speeches of his life yesterday, especially given the level of national distress and the need for words of consolation and wisdom. In what seems to be a ritual in this administration, the president appeared a day later than he was needed. He then read an address of a quality more appropriate for an Arbor Day celebration: a long laundry list of pounds of ice, generators and blankets delivered to the stricken Gulf Coast. He advised the public that anybody who wanted to help should send cash, grinned, and promised that everything would work out in the end.[47]

Bush was in denial about the administration's responsibility for the Katrina disaster. As one White House aide put it, "Throughout that first week, we focused on how poorly prepared and overwhelmed state and local officials had been, but we largely ignored the fact that the federal government was the vital backup, the fail-safe mechanism supposed to compensate for breakdowns at lower levels."[48] Mike Brown, the director of FEMA, who was in Louisiana, had repeatedly contacted both his superior, Michael Chertoff, the secretary of homeland security, and the White House to report the catastrophe unfolding in New Orleans, and to ask for help, but had been largely ignored. As Brown later told Congress, the problem was that Hurricane Katrina was a natural disaster, rather than terrorist attack. "If there had been a report that

said, yes, we've confirmed that a terrorist has blown up the 17th Street
Canal Levee, then everybody would have jumped all over that and
been trying to do everything they could. But because this was a natural
disaster, it became the stepchild within the Department of Homeland
Security."[49]

On Friday, September 2, Bush returned to the Gulf coast to inspect
the damage close up. It was another public relations disaster. Landing in Mobile, Alabama, shortly after 10 a.m., the president made two
bloopers that signaled how out of touch he was. Speaking to reporters
at Mobile Regional Airport, a buoyant Bush gave another congratulatory pep talk. "The good news is—and it is hard for some to see it
now—that out of this chaos is going to come a fantastic Gulf coast, like
it was before. Out of the rubble of Trent Lott's house—he's lost his entire house—there's going to be a fantastic house. And I'm looking forward to sitting on the porch."[50] It was a callous remark that illustrated
Bush's lack of compassion. Surrounded by death and devastation, the
president lamented the misfortune of a millionaire senator who had
lost his vacation home. For poor people struggling to survive—many
of whom had lost their homes and could scarcely afford to rebuild—it
was a monumental error.

Bush's second clinker came a few minutes later. After congratulating everyone for the work they were doing, Bush turned to Michael
Brown. "Again, I want to thank you all for—and Brownie, you're doing
a heck of a job. The FEMA Director is working 24—they're working
24 hours a day."[51] Clearly, Bush did not yet recognize how bad things
were on the Gulf coast, or how much Brown was in over his head. As
Peter Baker of *The New York Times* has noted, Bush "cemented an impression of disconnect with a gaffe that would harden into one of the
worst moments of his presidency."[52]

After a brief stop in Biloxi, Mississippi, Bush went on to New Orleans, where he met with Governor Blanco, Mayor Ray Nagin, and
members of the Louisiana congressional delegation aboard Air Force
One parked on the runway at the airport. The principal issue discussed was law enforcement. Bush wanted to federalize the Louisiana
National Guard and assume command. Blanco did not see how that

would help. There were two statutes involved. The 1878 Posse Comitatus Act, which prohibits federal troops from exercising police powers on American soil, and the Insurrection Act of 1807, which gives the president the authority to deploy federal troops with full law enforcement power. As Blanco saw it, if the Guard was federalized, the Posse Comitatus Act would apply and the Louisiana troops would be unable to suppress the lawlessness that had broken out in the city. The option was for Bush to invoke the Insurrection Act, but for political reasons he did not wish to do so without a request from the governor.

Eisenhower had invoked the Insurrection Act over the head of Arkansas governor Orval Faubus when he sent the 101st Airborne to Little Rock in 1957, and John Kennedy had defied Mississippi governor Ross Barnett when he sent troops to the University of Mississippi to insure the admission of James Meredith in 1962. These were highly charged racial issues, and given the white Republican base in the South, doubtful precedents for Bush to follow. Far better was his father's invocation of the Insurrection Act in 1992 during the Rodney King race riots in Los Angeles when he did so at the request of Governor Pete Wilson. Bush wanted to send federal troops to New Orleans to maintain order. But for political reasons felt he needed a request from Governor Blanco to do so.[53]

Blanco was unreceptive. She saw no reason to step aside and allow Bush to become the hero. There were already 34,000 National Guard troops in New Orleans, and another 10,000 en route. In Blanco's view, the White House had been trying to put the blame on her for the problems in New Orleans and was now trying to swoop in and claim credit when the situation was being brought under control. Blanco was also disturbed by the origin of the plan. She had first heard the proposal from Louisiana Republican senator David Vitter, who told her the plan originated with Karl Rove. The fact that it originated with Rove set off alarm bells. It had politics written all over it. The White House had not asked Mississippi's Republican governor Haley Barbour to relinquish control of the Guard, why Louisiana? In Blanco's view, if there was a problem it was primarily attributable to Bush's failure to provide prompt backup support, the seeming lack of interest or ineffectiveness of the new secretary of homeland security, Michael Chertoff, and the failings of Michael Brown and FEMA.[54]

When he returned to Washington that evening, Bush continued to press Blanco to surrender control. At 11:20 p.m., the White House dispatched a memorandum to the Louisiana governor outlining a plan in which the governor would request the federal government to take charge of the situation, but the military commander, Lieutenant General Russel Honoré, who commanded the First Army, would report to her in matters concerning the Louisiana National Guard as well as to the Pentagon.* The memorandum was faxed to Blanco by General Steven Blum, chief of the National Guard Bureau.

"I want you to sign it and send it back to me in five minutes," said Blum.

"I'll read your letter, but I'm not signing anything until my lawyers look at it," the governor replied.

"It needs to be signed tonight," said Blum.

"Why does it need to be signed tonight?"

"The president wants it signed tonight." At that point, Card got on the phone and told Blanco that Bush planned to announce the move first thing in the morning.

"I'm not signing anything," the governor told him. "You guys are now coming in and trying to save face. I've got thousands of people here in the trenches while you play politics. You go ahead and declare the Insurrection Act and you take over that way. I'm going to go and say you all care more about politics than saving lives."[55]

Blanco prevailed. Confronted with the governor's refusal to relinquish control, Bush threw in the towel. Rather than invoke the Insurrection Act, the president would send federal troops to New Orleans without law enforcement powers. "I was anxious about the situation," said Bush. "If they [the troops] got caught in a crossfire, it would be my fault. But I decided that sending troops with diminished authority was better than not sending them at all."[56] At Bush's order, 7,200 troops

---

* "Memorandum of Agreement Concerning Authorization, Consent and Use of Dual Status Commander for JTF [Joint Task Force] Katrina." The document had been prepared in the White House by Andy Card and Harriet Miers.

from the 82nd Airborne and 1st Cavalry Division reported to New Orleans and did a commendable job going from house to house looking
for survivors. That freed the Louisiana National Guard to handle law
enforcement.

Saturday morning, Bush spoke to the nation as scheduled. He did
not take command. The president said he was ordering additional
troops to the region and let it go at that. "Our priorities are clear. We
will complete the evacuation as quickly and safely as possible. We will
not let criminals prey on the vulnerable, and we will not allow bureaucracy to get in the way of saving lives." [57]

Eighteen hundred thirty-six people died in Hurricane Katrina and
the subsequent flooding: 1,577 in Louisiana, 238 in Mississippi, and 14
in Florida.* Property damage exceeded $108 billion, 300,000 homes
were destroyed, and 1.7 million people temporarily displaced, the largest diaspora in American history. The devastated area exceeded the size
of Great Britain, and the environmental effects were profound. Wild-
life was decimated, and over a million acres of forest land destroyed. [58]
Ultimately, Bush would make seventeen trips to the Gulf coast, and
Laura twenty-four. But politically he could never recover.

"As the leader of the federal government, I should have recognized
the deficiencies sooner and intervened faster," the president wrote in
his memoirs. "I prided myself on my ability to make crisp and effective
decisions. Yet in the days after Katrina, that didn't happen. The problem was not that I made the wrong decisions. It was that I took too
long to decide." [59] After the second week Michael Brown was relieved
as the director of FEMA and replaced by Vice Admiral Thad Allen of
the Coast Guard, one of the few federal officials who had performed
effectively during the hurricane. Chertoff remained as secretary of
homeland security for the remainder of Bush's term, but his clout was
severely diminished.

Hurricane Katrina was a decisive turning point in George W.

---

* In addition, there were two fatalities in Alabama, two in Georgia, one in Kentucky, and two
in Ohio. A total of 1,836. John L. Beven II, et al., "Annual Summary: Atlantic Hurricane Season
of 2005," 136 *Monthly Weather Review* (March 2008), 1131–41.

Bush's presidency. He had won reelection with more votes than any candidate in history. At his inauguration in January 2005, his approval rating stood at 52.3 percent. After Katrina, it fell to 38.3 percent and never recovered.[60] Bush's political capital was spent. "This is the end of the presidency," Steve Schmidt, a White House staffer, emailed a colleague.[61] And it was not just carelessness on Bush's part. Throughout the crisis the president's consuming interest had been Iraq. "We spent most of the first week in a state of denial," wrote press secretary Scott McClellan. "When the storm hit and the damage proved worse than anyone expected, our inability to adjust bespoke a failure of responsibility."[62]

Bush was overwhelmed, much as Herbert Hoover had been facing the Great Depression. Surrounded by a White House staff too eager to do his bidding, he lived in a world of make-believe. An additional deficiency was Bush's demeanor. Throughout the crisis he appeared jovial bordering on flippant. His bouncy exuberance and the associated swagger helped do him in.

CHAPTER EIGHTEEN

Perils of a Second Term

The executive branch shall construe [the new statutory torture ban] in a manner consistent with the constitutional authority of the president . . . as Commander in Chief.

George W. Bush
December 30, 2005

Since Grover Cleveland stepped down as president on March 4, 1897, eight presidents (nine including Obama) have been reelected to a second term. In each case, with the exception of Dwight Eisenhower, the second term has been perilous, and in some cases disastrous. William McKinley was assassinated. Woodrow Wilson lost the Senate vote on the Versailles Treaty, and then suffered a massive stroke from which he never recovered. FDR was plagued by his Court-packing fiasco and then an economic downturn that continued until the Second World War. Nixon had Watergate and resignation. For Reagan it was Iran-contra. And with Clinton, Monica Lewinsky and impeachment. For George W. Bush, Hurricane Katrina was a warning.

The news initially was not all bad, however. The nomination of John Roberts to succeed Sandra Day O'Connor was moving ahead rapidly with confirmation hearings set to begin on September 6. The nomination appeared in good shape. Roberts had done a superb job of presenting his case informally on Capitol Hill, deftly charming the senators he called on with an encyclopedic knowledge of constitutional law combined with an open, self-deprecating personality that was difficult to dislike. "A good judge is like an umpire," Roberts was fond of saying, "and no umpire thinks he is the most important person on the field."[1]

Three days before Roberts's confirmation hearings were scheduled to convene, the situation changed abruptly. On Saturday evening, September 3, after the president and Laura had gone to bed, Bush was awakened by a phone call from Karl Rove. Chief Justice Rehnquist had died. It was not unexpected. Rehnquist had been battling thyroid cancer for a year, and had missed the last term of the Court while undergoing treatment. Suddenly there was a second vacancy on the Court, and as Bush saw it another opportunity to reshape the judicial branch.

Cheney and Karl Rove suggested that Bush elevate Justice Antonin Scalia, a darling of the conservative base, to the chief justiceship. Bush hesitated. In 1968, when Chief Justice Earl Warren stepped down, Lyndon Johnson attempted to promote his close friend Justice Abe Fortas to the position. Fortas's nomination created an uproar in the Senate, and critics of Johnson and the Warren Court had a field day. With his approval rating hovering at 38 percent, Bush saw no reason to give the Democrats additional ammunition. Scalia's confirmation would be difficult. Why go through the motions?

Late on Sunday afternoon, September 4, Bush called Roberts to ask if he would be willing to serve as chief justice. Roberts agreed, and at eight o'clock Monday morning joined the president in the Oval Office where Bush announced his nomination. The next term of the Supreme Court would begin on October 3. That gave the Senate only four weeks to confirm Roberts, but the road ahead looked clear.* Said Bush,

---

* Chief Justice Earl Warren presided over the Supreme Court for one term in 1953 without Senate confirmation. Warren was appointed by President Eisenhower on September 30, 1953, but Congress was not in session. It was a recess appointment. Warren took the oath of office on October 5, 1953, and presided over the fall term of the Court, but was not confirmed by the Senate until March 1, 1954.

For the past two months, members of the United States Senate and the American people have learned about the career and character of Judge Roberts. They like what they see. He's a gentleman. He's a man of integrity and fairness. And throughout his life he has inspired the respect and loyalty of others. . . . Judge Roberts has earned the nation's confidence, and I'm pleased to announce that I will nominate him to serve as the 17th Chief Justice of the Supreme Court.[2]

Bush's decision was vindicated. Roberts performed brilliantly before the Senate Judiciary Committee, answering the most detailed questions without ever referring to his notes. Roberts said he would endeavor to bring "a greater degree of coherence and consensus to the opinions of the Court," cited the Court's unanimous decision in the desegregation case of *Brown v. Board of Education* as an example, and rephrased his baseball metaphor. "It's my job to call balls and strikes, and not to pitch or bat."[3] He was approved by the committee (13–5) on September 23, and confirmed by the Senate 78–22 on September 29. Twenty-two Democrats voted in favor; 22 against.

John Roberts's political sagacity quickly became apparent. William Rehnquist had redesigned the gown worn by the chief justice by adding gold stripes to the sleeves, much like a costume in a Gilbert and Sullivan operetta. His colleagues were aghast, but said nothing. Roberts was aware of the embarrassment they felt.* Before taking office, Roberts visited the home of John Marshall in Richmond, inspected Marshall's black gown, and chose to follow Marshall's example. When the Supreme Court convened on the first Monday in October, Roberts led his colleagues into the chamber wearing the traditional black robe of a Supreme Court justice.

Bush's nomination of John Roberts was an inspired choice. Finding a

---

* On September 12, *The New York Times* ran several op-eds advising Roberts what he should do upon confirmation. One contained the following paragraph: "One of John Marshall's first actions upon becoming chief justice was to take his colleagues out of their multicolored robes and put them in simple black. Do you intend to revert to that tradition, and retire that Gilbert and Sullivan chief justice costume that William Rehnquist designed?" Roberts evidently read the op-ed.

replacement for Sandra Day O'Connor proved more difficult. Laura, who normally did not involve herself in policy matters, pressed strongly for a woman, and Bush leaned that way as well. The White House had drawn up a list of potential women nominees for judicial positions, and the vet-

John G. Roberts is sworn in as the 17th chief justice of the United States by Associate Supreme Court Justice John Paul Stevens. Roberts's wife, Jane, holds the Bible.

ting began as soon as Roberts withdrew. But the search proved unproductive. Some of those considered were not interested, others had financial disclosure problems, sometimes their husbands did, and others were not considered sufficiently conservative. At that point Bush turned to Harriet Miers, his White House counsel. Three of Bush's White House aides had been elevated to cabinet positions, why not name Miers to the Court? Laura agreed wholeheartedly. Harriet Miers had a flawless record serving Bush, was exceedingly competent, and well liked by her colleagues. As a White House veteran, she could be counted upon to embrace Bush's expansive view of presidential power. Equally important, Bush believed she would bring a unique perspective to the Court, that of someone outside the judicial fraternity of Ivy League appellate judges.

To Bush, Miers's credentials looked good. In many respects she was a legal pioneer. The first woman president of the Texas Bar Association, the first woman managing partner of a major Texas law firm, and a first-rate litigator, she had served as Bush's private attorney when he was governor. In 2001, she became the president's staff secretary in the White House—a position established by Dwight Eisenhower and initially held by General Andrew Goodpaster—and was the last person to see any document before it went into the Oval Office. When Alberto Gonzales was appointed attorney general, she

Bush nominates White House Counsel Harriet Miers
as a Supreme Court justice, Monday, October 4, 2005.

became White House counsel.

Miers had no judicial experience, but Bush did not think that was important. Many of the greatest Supreme Court justices had no judicial experience when they were appointed. Rehnquist had been an assistant attorney general in charge of the Office of Legal Counsel in the Department of Justice. Earl Warren was governor of California, and before that state attorney general and a district attorney. The great justices of the Franklin Roosevelt era, Hugo Black, William O. Douglas, Felix Frankfurter, and Robert Jackson had never sat on the bench before they were appointed. Jackson did not even attend law school. Louis Brandeis had no judicial experience when he joined the Court, nor did Charles Evans Hughes when he was appointed by President Taft in 1910. The same was true of Roger Brooke Taney and John Marshall. Experience as an appellate judge might be useful, but it was surely not a prerequisite.

Bush announced Miers's nomination in the Oval Office at eight o'clock on the morning of October 4. "This morning, I'm proud to announce that I am nominating Harriet Ellan Miers to serve as Associate Justice of the Supreme Court," said the president. "I've known Harriet for more than a decade. I know her heart. I know her character.... I believe that Senators of both parties will find that Harriet Miers's talent, experience, and judicial philosophy make her a superb choice to safeguard the constitutional liberties and equality of all Americans."[4]

A firestorm ensued. Many of Bush's supporters on the right were appalled. Within minutes of the president's announcement, the airwaves were crackling with hostile criticism. William Kristol, editor of *The Weekly Standard*, said he was "disappointed, depressed, and demoralized" by the nomination.[5] Charles Krauthammer observed that, "If Harriet Miers were not a crony of the president of the United States, her nomination to the Supreme Court would be a joke, as it would have occurred to no one else to nominate her."[6] George Will was especially harsh. "The president's 'argument' for her amounted to: Trust me. There is no reason to. He has neither the inclination nor the ability to make sophisticated judgments about competing approaches to construing the Constitution. Few presidents acquire such abilities in the course of their pre-presidential careers, and this president particularly is not disposed to such reflections."[7]

For rock-ribbed conservatives, a vacancy on the Supreme Court was the opportunity of a lifetime—a chance to move decisively toward restoring God in the classroom and ending a woman's right to abortion. Previous Republican presidents did not seem aware of that. With the exception of Antonin Scalia and Clarence Thomas, recent Republican appointees to the Court had proved unreliable. Sandra Day O'Connor, though named by Ronald Reagan, was a moderate. John Paul Stevens, Gerald Ford's only appointee to the Court, now anchored the liberal wing. Anthony Kennedy, appointed by Reagan after the Robert Bork confirmation fiasco, could not be counted on, and David Souter, named to the Court by George H. W. Bush, was a definite disappointment. With Sandra Day O'Connor's seat now vacant, the Republican Party's conservative wing was determined to move the Court to the right, and Harriet Miers did not measure up.

Bush was taken by surprise. He had enjoyed conservative support throughout his first term. Despite occasional misgivings, Republican members of Congress had supported No Child Left Behind and prescription drugs for seniors, why would they not take his word for Harriet Miers's conservative credentials? The president fought back. His radio address on October 8 was devoted entirely to defending his nomination of Miers. "When she goes before the Senate, I am confident that all Americans will see what I see every day: Harriet Miers is a woman of intelligence, strength, and conviction. And when she is confirmed by the Senate, I am confident she will leave a lasting mark on the Supreme Court and will be a justice who makes Americans proud."[8]

Appearing with Laura on the *Today* show three days later, Bush went all out. Asked by host Matt Lauer whether he was surprised by the conservative reaction to the nomination, Bush replied that he had made a decision "to put someone on the Court who hadn't been a part of what they call the judicial monastery." The president said he was aware that people would ask whether it made sense to bring someone in from the outside, but he was convinced Miers was the best person for the job. "Just because she hasn't served on the bench doesn't mean she can't be a great Supreme Court justice."

Laura agreed. "I know Harriet well," said the first lady. "I know how accomplished she is. I know how many times she's broken the glass ceiling. She's a role model for young women around our country. Not only that, she's deliberate and thoughtful, and will bring dignity to wherever she goes; certainly to the Supreme Court. She will really be excellent."

> *Lauer:* So you are convinced she will be confirmed?
> *The President:* Absolutely. Not only am I convinced she will be confirmed; I'm convinced that she'll be a fine, great judge.[9]

Bush was wrong. Unlike John Roberts, Miers was underwhelming when she paid courtesy calls on Republican senators and her support crumbled. Not having been a member of the Federalist Society she was unfamiliar with the packaged answers many conservatives expected, and her humanity seemed all too frail. The decisive blow came on October 19 when Republican senator Arlen Specter of Pennsylvania, chairman of the Judiciary Committee and normally a supporter of the president, returned the traditional questionnaire she had filled out for the committee because her responses were inadequate. It was a public humiliation from which Miers could not recover. On October 26, Senate majority leader Bill Frist told Bush they did not have the votes. That evening, Miers called the president and asked him to withdraw her nomination. Bush agreed. "I was sad," he later told journalist Bill Sammon. "I thought Harriet didn't get a fair shake, that people jumped to conclusions about Harriet before she had a chance to make her case."[10]

To replace Miers, Bush turned to Judge Samuel Alito of the Court of Appeals Third Circuit in Philadelphia. Alito, along with Michael Luttig, had been at the head of the list the White House staff had prepared earlier and had previously been interviewed by Bush. A graduate of Princeton and Yale Law School (Miers had gone to Southern Methodist), Alito had been on the appellate bench since 1990 and had an established record of judicial decisions. Conservatives were delighted. The only hitch came during the confirmation hearings when it was revealed that Alito had belonged to an organization called Concerned Alumni of Princeton. Founded by Shelby Cullom Davis '30 in 1972, Concerned Alumni of Princeton opposed the admission of women, sought to reduce the number of minority and Jewish students on campus and increase the number of legacies. Bill Bradley '65 was on the advisory board of the organization briefly.*

Alito never took part in any of the organization's activities. He had simply listed it on his résumé to certify his conservative credentials when seeking a political appointment in the Justice Department during the Reagan administration. Asked about his membership at the hearing, Alito said, "I disavow them. I deplore them. They represent things I have always stood against and I can't express that too strongly."[11] Alito's denial was convincing. The Judiciary Committee approved his appointment in a party-line vote (10–8) on January 24, and he was confirmed by the Senate 58–42 on January 31, 2006. Senators John Kerry and Ted Kennedy briefly attempted a filibuster, but the Senate easily voted cloture (72–25). With the appointment of Alito to replace O'Connor, the Supreme Court shifted noticeably to the right. Roberts for Rehnquist was at best a wash. But Alito proved far more conservative than O'Connor. Bush had lost the fight to put his friend Harriet Miers on the bench, but ultimately won the day with the appointment of Alito.

On October 28, two days after Harriet Miers stepped down, Bush

---

* For an analysis of the origins of Concerned Alumni of Princeton, see E. J. Kahn, "A Tiger by the Tail," *The New Yorker,* May 23, 1977, 88–108. The organization petered out and ceased operations in 1985.

received another blow when Scooter Libby, Vice President Cheney's chief of staff and national security adviser, was indicted by a federal grand jury on multiple charges of perjury and obstruction of justice. Under the unified White House staff that Bush had created, Libby was a major player in presidential decision making and a hawk in foreign policy. His indictment was shattering for both Bush and Cheney, and did much to increase the tension that was slowly building between the two. The issue involved the disclosure of the identity of Valerie Plame, a covert CIA officer peripherally involved in the Niger yellowcake uranium affair.* Libby was not charged with disclosing her identity, but

---

*   In February 2002, the American intelligence community was apprised of a British report alleging that Iraq had sought to purchase five hundred tons of yellowcake uranium from Niger. Initial analysis suggested the report was baseless, but to be sure the Counterproliferation Division of the CIA dispatched former Ambassador Joseph Wilson to Niger to investigate. Wilson was an old Africa hand with numerous contacts in Niger and in the African mining industry. Wilson spent a week in Niamey, the capital of Niger, in March 2002, and confirmed that there was nothing to the story. His findings were well known within the intelligence community. Nevertheless, in his 2003 State of the Union, George W. Bush had included the famous sixteen words alleging that according to British intelligence Iraq had attempted to buy yellowcake uranium in Niger. On March 7, 2003, the International Atomic Energy Agency definitively declared that the documents on which Bush had relied were "obvious forgeries."

It was in this context that Ambassador Joseph Wilson published an article on the op-ed page of *The New York Times* on July 6, 2003, entitled "What I Didn't Find in Africa." Rather than acknowledge its error at that point, the White House undertook a campaign to discredit Wilson, during the course of which it was leaked to journalists that Wilson's wife, Valerie Plame, worked for the CIA and by implication had been instrumental in selecting Wilson for the assignment. Under the Intelligence Identities Protection Act of 1982, it is a criminal offense to disclose the identity of a covert CIA employee. The CIA requested the Justice Department to investigate, and on December 30, 2003, acting attorney general James Comey appointed Patrick J. Fitzgerald special counsel to investigate the disclosure.

After twenty-two months of investigation, Fitzgerald indicted Libby for obstruction of justice, and for lying to FBI agents and to the grand jury concerning his conversations with journalists Tim Russert of NBC News and Matthew Cooper of *Time*. According to the indictment, the obstruction of justice count stated that Libby, while testifying before the grand jury on March 5 and March 24, 2004, "knowingly and corruptly endeavored to influence, obstruct, and impede the grand jury's investigation by misleading and deceiving the grand jury as to when, and the manner and means by which, he acquired, and subsequently disclosed to the media, information concerning the employment of Valerie [Plame] Wilson by the CIA." The two perjury counts pertained to his testimony before the grand jury on March 5 and March 24, and the two false statement charges derived from his interviews with the FBI on October 14 and November 26,

with lying to FBI agents and the grand jury investigating the disclosure.

Bush was devastated by Scooter Libby's indictment. "It was the lowest point of his presidency," said Peter Wehner, White House director of strategic initiatives.[12] Memories of Iran-contra and Watergate put the indictment in perspective. In Iran-contra, the trials of national security adviser John Poindexter and Oliver North tarnished the image of Reagan in the final days of his term, and the Watergate trials had brought Nixon down. Bush was determined to avoid a repeat. The wound caused

I. Lewis "Scooter" Libby

by Libby had to be cauterized. At the president's direction, Harriet Miers, who was back at her post as counsel, issued a memo to White House staff that essentially disowned Libby. "All White House staffers," wrote Miers, "should not have any contact with Scooter Libby about any aspect of the investigation."[13] Bush also recognized that Libby's trial would once again raise questions pertaining to the veracity of the administration's case for invading Iraq. It would reflect on Cheney, and could involve other White House staffers including Karl Rove. In that sense, Libby's indictment became a source of friction between Bush and Cheney. Bush sought to distance himself from Libby; Cheney believed that Libby was an administration hero who should be defended.

Speaking to reporters on the White House lawn immediately after

2004. Indictment, *United States of America v. I. Lewis Libby*, United States District Court for the District of Columbia, October 28, 2005. Also see George Tenet, *At the Center of the Storm* (New York: HarperCollins, 2007), 452–75; Ambassador Joseph Wilson, *The Politics of Truth* (New York: Carroll & Graf, 2004), 1–30, 325–98.

the indictment came down, Bush said, "While we're saddened by to-day's news, we remain wholly focused on the many issues and opportu-nities facing this country. I've got a job to do and so do the people who work in the White House. We've got a job to protect the American people, and that's what we'll continue working hard to do." [14]

Libby went on trial January 16, 2007. The basic issue was how he learned that the CIA's Valerie Plame was married to Ambassador Jo-seph Wilson, whom the CIA had sent to Niger in 2002 to investigate the alleged yellowcake uranium purchase. The White House wanted to diminish Wilson's credibility, and his marriage to Plame was seen as a means of doing so. In his testimony before the grand jury and in his interviews with the FBI, Libby maintained that he learned of the tie between Plame and Wilson in conversations with journalists who had interviewed him. The government proved that Libby had been told of the marriage by Dick Cheney before he met with the reporters, and that he had lied to the grand jury presumably to con-ceal Cheney's role in the affair. As special counsel Patrick Fitzgerald noted in his summation at the trial, "There is a cloud over the vice president, and that cloud remains because this defendant obstructed justice." [15]

On March 6, 2007, Libby was convicted on four of the five counts in the indictment—two counts of perjury, one of obstructing justice, and one of the two counts of making false statements to FBI investiga-tors. He was sentenced to thirty months' imprisonment, fined $250,000, and required to perform four hundred hours of community service fol-lowing his release from prison. Cheney immediately pressed Bush to issue a pardon for Libby, but the president declined to do so. Speak-ing to reporters in Heiligendamm, Germany, after the sentence was announced, Bush said, "I will not intervene until Libby's legal team has exhausted all of its avenues of appeal. . . . It wouldn't be appropriate for me to discuss the case until after the legal remedies have run their course." [16]

At a hearing on June 14, Judge Reggie Walton, who had presided over the trial, ordered Libby to report to prison pending his appeal of the jury's verdict. That meant Libby would go to jail immediately.

Libby's lawyers appealed Judge Walton's order to the United States Court of Appeals for the District of Columbia Circuit, and on July 2, a three-judge panel of the appeals court (two of whom had been appointed by Republican presidents) unanimously rejected it. In a brief decision, the appeals court said Libby "has not shown that the appeal raises a substantial question under federal law that would merit letting him remain free." [17]

Bush was in Kennebunkport with Vladimir Putin when the appeals court decision came down. As the president saw it, he had three choices. "I could let Scooter go to jail. I could use my power under the Constitution and grant him a pardon. Or I could commute his sentence, meaning his conviction would stand but his prison sentence would not." [18] Once again, Cheney and his supporters pressed Bush to grant Libby a pardon and exonerate him for any transgression. Bush declined. "I decided it would send a bad message to pardon a former staff member convicted of obstructing justice, especially after I had instructed the staff to cooperate with the investigation." [19] *

Bush decided on option three. Returning to Washington on Air Force One, he issued a statement that was remarkably balanced. After praising special counsel Patrick Fitzgerald as "a highly qualified professional prosecutor who carried out his responsibilities as charged," the president noted that critics of the investigation had pointed out that Libby was a first-time offender with years of exceptional public service and was handed a harsh sentence based in part on allegations never presented to the jury. On the other hand, said Bush, "our entire system of justice relies on people telling the truth. And if a person does not tell

---

* When the investigation into the Plame affair began in September 2003, Bush was asked by reporters whether he thought it could be conducted fairly. "Yes," said the president. "There are too many leaks of classified information in Washington. . . . And if there is a leak out of my administration, I want to know who it is. And if the person has violated the law, the person will be taken care of. . . . I have told our administration—people in my administration—to be fully cooperative. I want to know the truth." *Public Papers of the Presidents of the United States, George W. Bush 2003*, Vol. 2, Remarks Following a Meeting with Business Leaders and an Exchange with Reporters in Chicago, September 30, 2003 (Washington, D.C.: Government Printing Office, 2006), 1215.

the truth, particularly if he serves in government and holds a public trust, he must be held accountable.

> I respect the jury's verdict. But I have concluded that the prison sentence given to Mr. Libby is excessive. Therefore, I am commuting the portion of Mr. Libby's sentence that required him to spend 30 months in prison.
>
> My decision to commute his prison sentence leaves in place a harsh punishment for Mr. Libby. . . . He will remain on probation. The significant fines imposed by the judge will remain in effect. The consequences of his felony conviction on his former life as a lawyer, public servant, and private citizen will be long lasting.
>
> The Constitution gives the President the power of clemency to be used when he deems it to be warranted. It is my judgment that a commutation of the prison term in Mr. Libby's case is an appropriate exercise of this power.[20]

Bush's decision weighed heavily upon him. What Libby had done was wrong, but he believed he was acting in support of the administration, perhaps shielding Cheney from the special prosecutor. Few were happy with Bush's compromise. On the left, Bush was criticized for abetting Libby's crime. On the right, Cheney and others continued to agitate for a full presidential pardon. As Bush was leaving office in January 2009, Cheney continued to appeal on Libby's behalf. Bush wrestled with the decision his last weekend at Camp David, and came to the same conclusion. The decision of the jury should be respected. When he informed Cheney, the vice president was dumbfounded. "I can't believe you are going to leave a soldier on the battlefield," he told Bush. For Cheney, the fight against terrorism was never-ending and there were no boundaries. "I had never seen Dick like this, or even close to this," the president wrote in his memoirs. "I worried that the friendship was about to be severely strained, at best."[21]

The Scooter Libby affair diminished Bush's confidence in Cheney. When the investigation into the disclosure of Valerie Plame's identity began in late 2003, Scott McClellan, the White House spokesman, had been asked by reporters whether Libby was involved. McClellan said he was "not going to go down a list of every single member of the staff in the White House ... from this podium,"[22] and believed the issue had been settled. But both Libby and Cheney wanted McClellan to issue a specific denial absolving Libby. Cheney spoke to Bush about it, Bush told Andy Card to have McClellan issue the denial, and McClellan did as instructed. "It was clear to me Scooter had enlisted the vice president to personally appeal to the president to have me publicly deny his involvement," said McClellan.[23] Given the fact that Cheney had enlisted the president in Libby's defense, and given that Libby was concealing Cheney's role in the leak, it is unlikely that Bush failed to remember that when Libby was convicted. That not only eroded Cheney's credibility with the president, but may also help explain why Bush declined to pardon Libby.

The year was turning sour for Bush. His belated and lackadaisical response to Katrina had been a catastrophe. His nomination of Harriet Miers to the Supreme Court had aborted. Top White House aide Scooter Libby was indicted for obstruction of justice, and his legislative program was going nowhere. Bush had campaigned vigorously to alter the Social Security system but his efforts had been unsuccessful. Congressional Democrats remained opposed to any change in the present system, and House Republicans had not included the item in their wish list of priority legislation.[24] Even worse, the situation in Iraq showed no signs of improving. Already more than two thousand American troops had been killed in the fighting there and another fifteen thousand wounded.[25] A *Washington Post*/ABC News poll published on November 4 found that two thirds of those polled disapproved of the way Bush was handling the war. Seventy-three percent said the casualty level was unacceptable, and 55 percent believed the administration had deliberately misled the country in making its case for war.[26] "Bush lied, people died," said critics on the left.

Bush was embattled on other fronts as well. Once again, the issues of torturing prisoners in American captivity and government snooping attracted the nation's attention. On July 24, Senator John McCain, who had supported Bush in the 2004 election against his friend John

Kerry, introduced an amendment to the defense budget authorization bill banning the use of torture and strictly regulating the interrogation techniques that could be used on terror suspects. Under McCain's amendment, military interrogators were forbidden to exceed the limits specified in the *Army Field Manual on Intelligence Interrogation*—essentially the Geneva Conventions—when questioning detainees no matter what their superiors might authorize. The amendment also prohibited all U.S. personnel, including the CIA, from engaging in torture and all other forms of "cruel, inhuman, or degrading treatment" on anyone in their custody anywhere in the world.[27] In effect, McCain was blowing the whistle on what the Bush administration had condoned since 9/11. The amendment was co-sponsored by Lindsey Graham (R., S.C.), Chuck Hagel (R., Nebr.), Susan Collins (R., Maine), and John Warner (R., Va.), chairman of the Senate Armed Services Committee.

Bush was appalled. At his direction, Cheney went to Capitol Hill to lobby against the measure. He met with McCain three times, and the meetings became increasingly testy. "Basically, he told me that if our legislation passes, I am going to have planes flying into buildings," McCain told his staff afterward.[28] Unable to convince McCain, Cheney asked Senate majority leader Bill Frist to withdraw the defense authorization bill rather than risk passage of the legislation with McCain's amendment attached. It was an ill-considered maneuver. At some point a military appropriations bill would have to be voted on, and in the meantime support for McCain intensified. More than two dozen retired generals and admirals, led by General John Shalikashvili, a former chairman of the Joint Chiefs of Staff, sent an open letter to McCain urging passage of the amendment. "The abuse of prisoners hurts America's cause in the war on terror, endangers U.S. service members who might be captured by the enemy, and is anathema to the values Americans have held dear for generations," said the officers.[29]*

---

* The flag officers continued with a blast at Bush's policy:
  It is now apparent that the abuse of prisoners at Abu Ghraib, Guantánamo and elsewhere took place in part because our men and women in uniform were given ambiguous instructions which in some cases authorized treatment that went beyond what was allowed by the *Army Field Manual.* Administration officials confused matters further by declar-

Colin Powell also waded in to support the amendment. "I align myself with the letter written to you by General Shalikashvili and a distinguished group of senior officers," Powell wrote McCain. "Our troops need to hear from Congress," said Powell. "I also believe the world will note that America is making a clear statement with respect to the expected future behavior of our soldiers. Such a reaction will help deal with the terrible public diplomacy crisis created by Abu Ghraib." [30] Later, on *Larry King Live*, Powell hit out at the administration. "I have no idea why they would be against it," he told King. "But the president is against it and the administration is against it because they think it will constrain them in some ways with respect to interrogation of detainees." [31]

Bush's hope to avoid a vote on McCain's amendment lasted until October, when it became necessary to pass a defense spending bill. As soon as Frist introduced the measure, McCain again offered his amendment. "I hold no brief for the prisoners," said McCain, but "I do hold a brief for the reputation of the United States of America." [32]

The White House continued to resist. Meeting with reporters on October 5, press secretary Scott McClellan said that Bush had decided to use the first veto of his presidency if the McCain amendment was adopted. The torture ban, said McClellan, "would limit the president's ability as commander in chief to effectively carry out the war on terrorism." [33]

McClellan's threat convinced no one. Later that evening, the Senate voted on McCain's amendment. As the vote approached, McCain made one of his most eloquent appeals, invoking his experience in Vietnam.

---

ing that U.S. personnel are not bound by longstanding prohibitions of cruel treatment when interrogating non-U.S. citizens on foreign soil. As a result, we suddenly had one set of rules for interrogating prisoners of war, and another for "enemy combatants"; one set for Guantánamo, and another for Iraq; one set for our military, and another for the CIA. Our service members were denied clear guidance, and left to take the blame when things went wrong. They deserve better than that.

The letter from the retired generals and admirals was posted on Senator McCain's website on October 3, 2005, and published in *Executive Intelligence Review*, October 14, 2005.

Where did the brave men I was privileged to serve with in Vietnam draw the strength to resist the cruelties inflicted upon them by our enemies? Well, they drew strength from our faith in each other, from our faith in God, and from our faith in our country. Our enemies didn't adhere to the Geneva Convention. Many of my comrades were subjected to very cruel, very inhumane and degrading treatments, a few of them even unto death. But every one of us—every single one of us—knew and took great strength from the belief that we were different from our enemies, that we were better than them, that we, if the roles were reversed, would not disgrace ourselves by committing or countenancing such mistreatment of them.[34]

A packed Senate chamber listened with rapt attention. The clerk called the roll. When the roll call concluded, McCain had carried the day 90–9. Forty-six of the Senate's 55 Republicans had voted in favor of the amendment as well as every Democrat who voted.*

Despite the Senate's overwhelming support for McCain's antitorture amendment, Bush continued to fight it. The rules of procedure are far more restrictive in the House of Representatives, and at White House urging the House Republican leadership did not permit the amendment to be introduced. Ultimately a conference committee that reconciled the House and Senate versions of the defense appropriations bill would deal with the matter, but for the moment it was off the table. It was in this context that in late October Bush sent Cheney and CIA director Porter Goss (who had succeeded George Tenet) back to Capitol Hill to urge McCain to exempt CIA interrogators from the torture ban when they were questioning foreign prisoners abroad.[35] By specifically exempting the CIA interrogators, Congress in effect would be authorizing the abusive treatment of detainees held abroad. McCain was outraged and in no mood to compromise. "I don't see how you could possibly agree to legitimizing an agent of the government engaging in torture. No amendment at all would be better than that."[36]

Bush received another blow the following week when Dana Priest of

---

*   Jon Corzine (D., N.J.) was absent and did not vote.

The Washington Post published a stunning exposé describing the CIA's use of secret "black site" prisons in foreign countries where detainees could be held indefinitely and interrogated without restraint. The sites were located in eight countries, three of which were in Eastern Europe. As Priest observed, "It is illegal for the government to hold prisoners in such isolation in secret prisons in the United States, which is why the CIA placed them overseas."[37] According to Priest, more than a hundred suspected terrorists had been sent to the black sites, where they were subjected to the enhanced interrogation techniques—including waterboarding—that Bush had approved in 2002. Priest's article set off an international furor questioning American behavior. The Bush administration responded by launching an investigation into how Priest got the story.[38]

Bush was in Latin America when the story broke, and was asked about it at a news conference in Panama City. Would the president allow the Red Cross to have access to the prisoners held at the black sites, and should the CIA be exempt from legislation banning torture?, asked Toby Zakaria of Reuters.

Bush avoided a direct answer. "Our country is at war," he replied, "and our government has the obligation to protect the American people. . . . And we are aggressively doing that. We are finding terrorists and bringing them to justice. We are gathering information about where the terrorists may be hiding. We are trying to disrupt their plots and plans. Anything we do to that effect, to that end, in this effort, any activity we conduct is within the law. We do not torture."[39]

Bush was whistling in the dark. Not only did he not answer Zakaria's questions, but his claim of legality hinged upon his prior authorization of enhanced interrogation techniques—an authorization that the Supreme Court would strike down the following year in *Hamdan v. Rumsfeld* when it held that the Geneva Conventions applied to all detainees.[40] The president was not above the law. Bush had difficulty accepting that.

On November 17, the president received another setback when Congressman Jack Murtha of Pennsylvania, the ranking Democrat on the House defense appropriations subcommittee, and until now a staunch supporter of the war in Iraq, came out in bitter opposition. Murtha was a decorated veteran of the Vietnam War, a former Marine Corps officer who had been elected to Congress in 1974—the first Vietnam veteran to be elected to Congress—and a decided hawk in military matters. He was one of the most experienced Democrats dealing with defense policy, and his public statements often reflected the thinking of senior military officers at the Pentagon. Out of the blue, as it were, Murtha lambasted the war in Iraq as "a flawed policy wrapped in illusion," and called for the immediate withdrawal of American forces. U.S. troops, he said, "have become the enemy in Iraq," which deserved to be "free from United States occupation." And he was especially critical of Cheney. "I like guys who got five deferments and never been there, and send people to war, and then don't like to hear suggestions of what needs to be done."[41]

Murtha's outburst meant that mainstream House Democrats were beginning to question the war in Iraq. Minority Leader Nancy Pelosi said she supported Murtha, and that in her opinion a majority of the caucus did as well.[42] Taken by surprise, the White House fought back. Bush was in the Far East at the time, and at Cheney's direction Scott McClellan issued a statement accusing Murtha of "endorsing the policy positions of Michael Moore [an ultraliberal documentary filmmaker] and the extreme liberal wing of the Democratic party." McClellan's comments aroused indignation on Capitol Hill, particularly given Murtha's established reputation as a friend of the military. Sensing that a full-scale revolt was looming, Bush decided to calm the waters. On November 20, in between meetings with Chinese leaders, Bush summoned reporters to his suite in Beijing's St. Regis Hotel.

Implicitly rejecting the stance taken by Cheney and McClellan, the president told reporters,

> There's an important debate underway back in Washington. I particu-
> larly want to discuss the position that Democrat[ic] congressman John
> Murtha announced this past week. Let me start off by saying that Con-
> gressman Murtha is a fine man, a good man, who served our country
> with honor and distinction as a Marine in Vietnam and as a United

States congressman. He is a strong supporter of the United States military. And I know the decision to call for an immediate withdrawal of our troops by Congressman Murtha was done in a careful and thoughtful way. I disagree with his position.

Bush went on to describe his own position on Iraq, but explicitly recognized the right of others to disagree. Where Cheney and McClellan had been harsh, Bush was conciliatory. "This is a debate worthy of our country," said the president. "It is an important issue. It does not have to be a partisan issue. . . . Those elected leaders in Washington who do not support our policies in Iraq have every right to voice their dissent. They also have a responsibility to provide a credible alternative. The stakes are too high and the national interest too important for anything otherwise." [43]

Bush had elected to take the high road. Asked by Suzanne Malveaux of CNN about Murtha's criticism of Cheney for not having served in Vietnam, the president simply dismissed it. "I don't think the vice president's service is relevant in this debate. And I would hope all of us in this debate talk about policy and have an honest, open debate about whether or not it makes sense to immediately withdraw our troops." [44]

The rift between Bush and Cheney was growing. Bush recognized that public support for the Iraq War was fading and that he had to restore it; Cheney was more militant and unwilling to yield to the changing winds of public opinion. This difference led to a subtle change in the White House. Rather than being a formulator of policy, Cheney increasingly became someone Bush used to implement it. Just as Eisenhower kept John Foster Dulles around to walk through minefields for him,* Bush increasingly used Cheney in that same capacity. Or as

---

* Immediately after World War II, Eisenhower and Marshal Georgy Zhukov struck up a warm relationship. At one point Ike asked Zhukov how he had penetrated German minefields with his armored forces without losing any tanks. Zhukov told him it was easy. He sent the infantry through first. As Murray Kempton has pointed out, Eisenhower used John Foster Dulles as his infantry. Ike would not have trusted Dulles "with a stick of dynamite to blow up a duck pond," wrote Kempton, but he found him very useful in clearing minefields. Murray Kempton, "The Underestimation of Dwight D. Eisenhower," *The New Yorker*, September 1967.

one State Department official put it, the Cheney camp had become a "shrinking island" in the White House.[45]

After returning from China, Bush launched a public relations campaign with five major speeches within three weeks defending his Iraq policy. Speaking to the assembled midshipmen at Annapolis on November 30, Bush held forth for forty-three minutes and used the word "victory" fifteen times. But he was careful not to bad-mouth those who dissented. "We should not fear the debate in Washington," he told the midshipmen. "It's one of the great strengths of our democracy that we can discuss our differences openly and honestly, even in times of war. . . . Some are calling for a deadline for withdrawal. Many advocating an artificial timetable for withdrawing our troops are sincere, but I believe they are sincerely wrong. Pulling our troops out before they have achieved their purpose is not a plan for victory."[46]

Bush said much the same speaking at the Council on Foreign Relations in New York on December 7. It was the sixty-fourth anniversary of Pearl Harbor, and Bush drew the parallel. "Like generations before us, we've faced setbacks on the road to victory, yet we will fight this fight without wavering. And like the generations before us, we will prevail." Once again Bush acknowledged the debate in Washington. But he did so with restraint. "Withdrawing on an artificial deadline would endanger the American people, would harm our military, and make the Middle East less stable. It would give the terrorists exactly what they want."[47]

In Philadelphia on December 12, Bush spoke to the World Affairs Council describing the progress that had been made in Iraq,[48] and then on the 14th addressed scholars at the Woodrow Wilson Center in Washington. For the first time, Bush publicly accepted blame for past mistakes. "As president, I'm responsible for the decision to go into Iraq, and I'm also responsible for fixing what's wrong by reforming our intelligence capabilities." He acknowledged the debate about an immediate withdrawal of U.S. forces from Iraq, and responded with remarkable civility. "I've listened carefully to all the arguments, and there are four reasons why I believe setting an artificial deadline would be a recipe for disaster.

First, setting an artificial deadline would send the wrong message to the Iraqis. . . .

Second, setting an artificial deadline would send the wrong message to the enemy. . . .

Third, setting an artificial deadline would send the wrong message to the region and the world. . . .

Finally, setting an artificial deadline would send the wrong message to the most important audience, our troops on the frontline.

One of the blessings of our free society is that we can debate these issues openly, even in time of war. . . . Whatever our differences in Washington, our men and women in uniform deserve to know that once our politicians vote to send them into harm's way, our support will be with them in good days and in bad, and we will settle for nothing less than complete victory.[49]

At the same time Bush was speaking to the scholars at the Woodrow Wilson Center, the McCain anti-torture amendment was working its way through the House of Representatives. It was time to reconcile the House and Senate versions of the defense appropriations bill, and the House was moving to appoint its negotiators to the conference committee. As the senior Democrat on the House defense appropriations subcommittee, Jack Murtha would lead the Democrats on the conference committee, and he had the floor. At that point Murtha moved that the House negotiators be instructed to accept the Senate position on the McCain amendment. "Torture does not help us win the hearts and minds of the people it is used against," said Murtha. "Congress is obliged to speak out."[50] Procedurally, the Democrats had won the day. The amendment would be voted on. When the roll call was complete, the House had voted 308–122 to accept the McCain amendment. One hundred and seven Republicans joined 200 Democrats and one Independent to put the measure across.* Cheney urged Bush to continue fighting, but Bush recognized McCain had the votes to override his veto.

---

* One Democrat, James Marshall of Georgia, a Vietnam veteran, voted against.

The following day, Bush invited McCain and Senator John Warner to the White House. If he was going to lose, Bush wanted to do it with style. It was a page from his playbook as governor of Texas. The president recognized that McCain would be an important ally in later confrontations over Iraq, and it was best to smooth over their differences. When the two senators arrived, Bush invited reporters and camera crews into the Oval Office to record his shaking hands with them. The president tried to minimize his defeat by embracing McCain's ideas as his own. "It's my honor to welcome two good friends here to the Oval Office," he said. "We share a common goal and that is to protect the American people and win the war on terror.

> Senator McCain has been a leader to make sure the United States of America upholds the values of America and we fight and win the war on terror. And we've been happy to work with him to achieve a common objective, and that is to make it clear to the world that this government does not torture and we adhere to the international convention of torture, whether it be here at home or abroad.

McCain was delighted with his reception by the president, and also did his best to minimize their differences. "I want to take this opportunity to thank you for the effort that you made to resolve this very difficult issue," he told Bush. "I'm very pleased we reached this agreement, and now can move forward and make sure the whole world knows that, as the president has stated many times, that we do not practice cruel, inhuman treatment or torture."[51]

The message was clear. Bush would sign the bill, and the law banning torture would be absolute, with no exceptions for the CIA or for black sites overseas. The New York Times ran the story with banner headlines on its front page. "President Backs McCain Measure on Inmate Abuse." According to the Times, while the outcome was "a stinging defeat" for the president, who had threatened to veto the bill, it was "a particularly significant setback for Vice President Cheney, who since July has led the administration's fight to defeat the amendment or at least exempt the Central Intelligence Agency from its provisions."[52]*

Bush's difficulties were not over, however. On December 16, the day after Bush received McCain and Warner at the White House, *The New York Times* published its own sweeping exposé of the warrantless surveillance program that the National Security Agency had been conducting pursuant to presidential order. Written by James Risen and Eric Lichtblau, who like Dana Priest would win a Pulitzer Prize for their article, the *Times* revealed that shortly after 9/11 Bush had authorized NSA to monitor the international telephone calls and email messages of thousands of Americans without seeking a warrant.[53] The existence of the program was so secret that few in the administration were aware of it. Risen and Lichtblau had learned of NSA's activities in late 2004 and had written about it then, but at the urging of the White House the *Times* had not published the story. But by late 2005 the situation had changed. Risen was writing a book about the program that would soon be published,[54] and the *Times* editors were increasingly concerned about the legality of NSA's activities given the president's stance on interrogation and rendition. "As time passed," said Bill Keller, the *Times* senior editor, "they demonstrated that they are entitled to somewhat less benefit of the doubt."[55]

In early December, the *Times* editors advised the White House they were planning to run the article, and were invited to the White House, where they met with Stephen Hadley, Condoleezza Rice, John Negroponte, the director of national intelligence, and CIA director General Michael Hayden. Once again, the White House made the case that NSA's activities were essential, and that if the *Times* published the article they would share the blame for the next attack that terrorists might

---

* Cheney was unrepentant. Speaking to ABC News during a surprise visit to Iraq on December 18, Cheney said, "You can get into a debate about what shocks the conscience and what is cruel and inhuman. And to some extent, I suppose that's in the eye of the beholder. But I believe, and we think, it's important to remember that we are in a war against a group of individuals, a terrorist organization that did, in fact, slaughter 3,000 innocent Americans on 9/11, that it's important for us to be able to have effective interrogation of these people when we capture them." Cheney interview with Terry Moran of ABC News, December 18, 2005.

make on the United States.[56] The *Times* editors were not convinced. When apprised of the standoff, Bush intervened. The president said he wanted to meet personally with Arthur Sulzberger, Jr., the owner and publisher of the *Times*.

The meeting was arranged for December 5. Bush was joined by Hayden and Hadley. Sulzberger brought Keller and Phil Taubman, chief of the Washington bureau. According to Keller, they received a fire-and-brimstone lecture from the president. If there is another attack, "there'll be blood on your hands," said Bush.[57] After the meeting, Keller told Sulzberger, "Nothing I heard in there changed my mind."[58] Sulzberger agreed.

The *Times* had decided to publish, but it was not clear when. It was the White House that precipitated publication. The *Times* learned that the administration was considering a Pentagon Papers–type injunction to prevent the paper from publishing the NSA story. "This was a bombshell," according to Lichtblau. "Few episodes in the history of the *Times*, or for that matter in all of journalism, had left as indelible a mark as the courtroom battle over the Pentagon Papers."[59] Sulzberger's father had been publisher of the *Times* when the Nixon administration sought its injunction.

Once the *Times* editors learned that the administration might seek an injunction, they moved quickly. Rather than chance a last-minute intervention, the story was posted on the *Times* website the night before its publication in the print version of the paper. The *Times* editors were worried that once they notified the White House that they were running the story, a last-minute injunction could shut down the presses before the paper was printed. By contrast, posting the story on the Internet was instantaneous.

Bush was furious. The *Times* had promised to give the White House notice if they were going to publish, and Keller did call Hadley, but it was just minutes before the article appeared on the website. The cat was out of the bag. In his radio address the following day, Bush took full responsibility for the NSA program. "This is a highly classified program that is vital to our national security. Yesterday, the existence of this secret program was revealed in media reports, after being improperly provided to news organizations. As a result, our en-emies have learned information they should not have, and the un-authorized disclosure of this effort damages our national security and puts our citizens at risk." Bush was certain the *Times* was wrong to disclose the information, and he was not going to yield. "The Amer-ican people expect me to do everything in my power under our laws and Constitution to protect them and their civil liberties. And that is exactly what I will continue to do, so long as I am president of the United States." [60]

The following evening, Bush spoke to the nation on television from the Oval Office. He did not mention the *Times* article. It was his first address from his desk since launching the Iraq War thirty-three months earlier, and the fifth speech in his effort to regain public sup-port. In many respects, it was one of Bush's best. "As your president," he said, "I am responsible for the decision to go into Iraq. Yet it was right to remove Saddam Hussein from power."

Bush acknowledged that the war had been costly, and "has brought danger and suffering and loss. This loss has caused sorrow for our whole nation, and has led some to ask if we are creating more problems than we are solving." He admitted mistakes. "The work in Iraq has been especially difficult—more difficult than we expected. Reconstruc-tion efforts and the training of Iraq security forces started more slowly than we hoped. We continue to see violence and suffering, caused by an enemy that is determined and brutal, unconstrained by conscience or the rules of war."

And he was conciliatory. "We will continue to listen to honest crit-icism and make every change that will help us complete the mission." Indeed, the president went far beyond his normal rhetoric to extend an olive branch to those who disagreed.

> I also want to speak to those of you who did not support my decision to
> send troops to Iraq. I have heard your disagreement, and I know how
> deeply it is felt. . . . I don't expect you to support everything I do, but
> tonight I have a request: Do not give in to despair, and do not give up
> on this fight for freedom.[61]

As the year headed to a close, Bush appeared to have regained the initiative. With the exception of the exposé articles by Priest and by Risen and Lichtblau, he was managing to live with the reversals. His willingness to assume responsibility, his admission of mistakes, and his acceptance of criticism caused many to rethink their dismissal of the president as a stubborn autocrat. His ungrudging acceptance of the McCain amendment on torture was in some respects a watershed. Almost overnight his approval rating zoomed from 38 to 47 percent—a 9 percent bounce in the *Washington Post*/ABC News poll.[62]

As was their habit, the Bushes spent Christmas at Camp David and then departed for the ranch in Crawford. After a difficult year, it was a welcome respite. On Friday afternoon, December 30, with Bush at the ranch, the White House issued a presidential statement concerning the Defense Department appropriations act and the McCain amendment. It was straightforward and praised the bill for what it would accomplish.

> The administration is committed to treating all detainees held by the United States in a manner consistent with our Constitution, laws, and treaty obligations, which reflect values we hold dear. U.S. law and policy already prohibit torture. Our policy has also been not to use cruel, inhuman or degrading treatment, at home or abroad. This legislation now makes that a matter of statute for practices abroad. . . . These provisions reaffirm the values we share as a Nation, and our commitment to the rule of law.[63]

Bush, it appeared, was sticking to the course he charted out after McCain's victory. But at eight that Friday evening, everything changed. The White House issued a signing statement that reneged on what had been previously agreed to. Bush would interpret the new anti-torture law as he saw fit.

> The executive branch shall construe [the new torture ban] in a manner consistent with the constitutional authority of the president to supervise the unitary executive branch and as Commander in Chief and consis-

tent with the constitutional limitations on the judicial power, which will assist in achieving the shared objective of the Congress and the president . . . of protecting the American people from further terrorist attacks.[64]

In a word, the president would continue to do what he wanted, amendment or not.

With that signing statement, Bush was officially advising CIA interrogators that despite the new law, he still had the power as commander in chief to waive the torture ban when he saw fit. Said differently, he was telling interrogators that if they received authorization to inflict suffering on a detainee, they should not worry about the torture ban because it was an unconstitutional intrusion into his power as commander in chief.[65] McCain and Warner were incensed, Congress up in arms, and the public dismayed. Senator Lindsey Graham said Bush's action endangered American troops by setting a precedent that any head of state could set aside the Geneva Conventions if he believed torture necessary to protect national security.[66] Bush's approval rating began a downhill slide that would continue for the remainder of his presidency. With his signing statement on the evening of December 30, 2005, the president snatched defeat from the jaws of victory.

CHAPTER NINETEEN

The Mess in Mesopotamia

A great country can have no such thing as a little war.

The Duke of Wellington
British Prime Minister, 1828–1830

George W. Bush's signing statement on December 30 blocking the McCain anti-torture amendment was part of a pattern. In office for five years, Bush had yet to veto a single piece of legislation passed by Congress. Instead, he would issue a signing statement specifying how the executive branch would interpret the measure and identifying those sections he thought were unconstitutional. Those sections would not be enforced. It was the equivalent of a line-item veto. And line-item vetoes are not available to the president under the Constitution.[1]

By the end of 2005, Bush had attached signing statements to 123 bills passed by Congress, challenging the constitutionality of well over eight hundred separate sections.[2] By contrast, all of Bush's predecessors combined, from George Washington to Bill Clinton, had used signing statements to challenge the constitutionality of less than six hundred sections of the tens of thousands of bills they had signed.[3]* And there

* There are two types of presidential signing statements: rhetorical and constitutional. Rhetorical statements have been used by presidents since Washington to claim credit, reward sup-

was a further distinction. Bush's predecessors used their signing statements simply to describe their interpretation of the laws. Bush used his to explicitly override those provisions he felt intruded upon his authority.[4]

Bush's failure to use his veto power also stood in direct contrast to all modern presidents. Harry Truman vetoed 250 bills passed by Congress, Eisenhower vetoed 181, Reagan 78, and Clinton 37. Bush's father during his four years in office had vetoed 44. Not since the early nineteenth century had a president made so little use of his veto power as did Bush. That did not mean George W. Bush was acquiescing in the will of Congress. To the contrary. A signing statement offered two distinct advantages over a presidential veto. It could not be overridden by Congress and therefore gave the president the last word, and it allowed the president to focus on a particular section of a statute rather than having to overturn the entire measure.

Bush's most egregious use of signing statements came when Congress attempted to curtail his tendency to intrude upon the internationally recognized rules of war or the guarantees Americans enjoy against unreasonable searches and seizures under the Fourth Amendment. Three months after he eviscerated the McCain anti-torture amendment, Bush repeated the maneuver when he signed the extension of the Patriot Act. Renewal of the Patriot Act had not been easy. Revelations about the FBI's use of their expanded powers to secretly conduct searches without warrants and seize banking and Internet records had fueled a Senate filibuster to prevent passage of the extension. With the act scheduled to expire, the administration reluctantly agreed to accept additional oversight restrictions on the FBI in order to bring the bill to

---

porters, and chastise opponents. Constitutional signing statements are of more recent origin, and are designed to shape policy by imposing the president's view as to the constitutionality of the measure. It is a form of presidential prerogative that is unilateral. While scholars can point to scattered historical examples dating to James Monroe, the real use of constitutional signing statements commenced with Ronald Reagan, who during his eight years in office issued ninety-five. The process expanded under George H. W. Bush, who issued signing statements challenging the constitutionality of 232 sections of bills he signed. Clinton used signing statements to challenge 140 sections over eight years.

a vote. The White House was not happy with the changes, but as with the McCain amendment, put on a good face.

An elaborate signing ceremony for the Patriot Act extension was set for the East Room of the White House the afternoon of March 9. Speaking before some four dozen members of the House and Senate, and a vast assemblage of reporters and cameramen, Bush gave no hint of what was in store. "This is a really important piece of legislation," said the president. "It is a piece of legislation that's vital to win the war on terror and to protect the American people. . . . It will improve our nation's security, while we safeguard the civil liberties of our people."[5]

To all present, it seemed the compromise that had been agreed upon would become the law of the land. But later that afternoon, after the crowd in the East Room departed, Bush issued an official signing statement declaring he did not consider himself bound by the new oversight requirements.

> The executive branch shall construe the provisions of H.R. 3199 [the Patriot Act renewal] that call for furnishing information to entities outside the executive branch [i.e., Congress], in a manner consistent with the President's constitutional authority to supervise the unitary executive branch and to withhold information the disclosure of which could impact foreign relations, national security, the deliberative processes of the Executive, or the performance of the Executive's constitutional duties.[6]

Bush was nullifying those provisions of the bill that required the FBI to report to Congress and reneging on the compromise that had ended the Senate filibuster.

The signing statements Bush issued on the McCain anti-torture amendment and the renewal of the Patriot Act were the tip of the iceberg. Four times Congress passed legislation forbidding American troops from engaging in combat in Colombia, where the U.S. military was providing support for the Colombian government in its battle against Marxist rebels. Each time Bush issued a signing statement stating that he was the commander in chief and that Congress's injunction was simply "advisory in nature."[7] Twice Congress enacted legislation forbidding the military from using information that was not "lawfully collected." Both times Bush issued signing statements telling the military that only the commander in chief could make decisions pertaining to the use of intelligence data.[8] Similarly when appropriation bills were passed that required the president to notify Congress before spending money for black sites overseas, or that contained new rules for military prisons, Bush signed the measures but added signing statements telling the military that as commander in chief he was not bound to obey the requirements.

After Abu Ghraib, Congress established an inspector general for Iraq. Bush issued a signing statement that effectively gutted the law. Likewise when Congress imposed reporting requirements on the Department of Justice pertaining to its use of wiretaps, Bush signed the legislation but told the executive branch he could withhold the information. And so it went. Whether it was homeland security, scientific information, or the transfer of nuclear technology, whenever Congress passed legislation requiring reports, Bush signed the bills but then issued signing statements that nullified the requirements.[9]

This was also true concerning domestic matters. When Congress passed legislation designed to ensure that minorities were included among the recipients of government jobs, a requirement that was generally included in appropriations bills, Bush took exception on nine separate occasions. Similarly, he repeatedly nullified whistle-blower job protection provisions for federal employees in which Congress had assured government workers they could not be fired for telling members of Congress about possible government wrongdoing.[10]

The Constitution in Article I gives Congress the exclusive authority to legislate. It also bestows on Congress the power "to make rules for the government and regulation of the land and naval forces." The president is charged in Article II to "take care that the laws be faithfully executed." What Bush was doing in his signing statements was indicating those portions of a piece of legislation he didn't like, and then refusing to enforce them based on his "reading" of the Constitution. Not only was he intruding on the power of Congress to legislate, but he was usurping the authority of the Supreme Court to interpret the Constitution.

For the most part, Bush's signing statements went unnoticed until he overturned the McCain anti-torture amendment and scrapped the compromise leading to the Patriot Act renewal. Charlie Savage of *The Boston Globe* wrote a series of articles laying out the history of Bush's earlier signing statements, and the public outcry was enormous. "The president's constitutional duty is to faithfully execute the laws as written by Congress, not to cherry-pick the laws he decides he wants to follow," said Senator Patrick Leahy of Vermont, the ranking Democrat on the Senate Judiciary Committee.[11] "We are a government of laws, not men," said Senate minority leader Harry Reid (D., Nev.). "It is not for George W. Bush to disregard the Constitution and decide that he is above the law."[12]

Savage, like Dana Priest, James Risen, and Eric Lichtblau, would win the Pulitzer Prize for his articles.[13] And with public opinion running so heavily against him, Bush changed course during his last two years in office. He vetoed twelve pieces of legislation (four of which were overridden), and issued only fourteen signing statements.[14] The American Bar Association established a blue-ribbon panel to look into Bush's use of signing statements. Their final report says it all. "The president's constitutional duty is to enforce laws he has signed into being, unless and until they are held unconstitutional by the Supreme Court. The Constitution is not what the president says it is."[15]

Meanwhile, the situation in Iraq was not improving. The U.S. military was not happy with its role as occupier. General John Abizaid, who had been deputy to Tommy Franks during the invasion of Iraq and then succeeded him as CENTCOM commander, was in Washington on March 16, 2006, to testify before the Senate Armed Services Committee. Afterward he went to see his old friend Congressman Jack Murtha in the Rayburn Office Building. Sitting in an armchair in the congressman's private office, Abizaid told Murtha he wanted to speak frankly. He then raised his hand and held his thumb and forefinger a quarter of an inch apart. "We're that far apart," he told Murtha.[16] Abizaid's meaning was clear. He thought Murtha was correct. It was time to withdraw. The military had relished its role as liberator and had done an outstanding job. But they had not anticipated that they would be required to occupy postwar Iraq.*

The uniformed military and the civilian leadership at the Pentagon had both assumed the Iraqi invasion would be short. General Franks planned to have the troops out in ninety days, and Rumsfeld shared that view.† He appointed Jay Garner to establish an interim government and turn over control to the Iraqis as soon as possible. Neither Rumsfeld nor Garner was concerned about how democratic that government would be. The purpose of the invasion was to remove Saddam Hussein from power. The Army would then withdraw and let the Iraqis put their house in order. The agreed goal was to leave an Iraq that was whole, was respectful of its minorities, and that would not support terrorism or attack its neighbors. That was what Bush had approved as well.

But on May 1, 2003, the goal had changed. Instead of an early withdrawal, George Bush altered his strategy. Speaking from the flight deck of the *Abraham Lincoln*—under a banner reading "Mission Accomplished"—Bush announced that the United States was going to bring democracy to Iraq.[17] This was a unilateral decision made by the president. Bush was supported by Rice, Cheney, and the White House staff. But the principal departments of the government and the military services had not been consulted.‡ Nor had Congress. By Bush's order,

---

* In his prepared statement to the Armed Services Committee, Abizaid hinted at what he revealed to Murtha, while toeing the administration line. "Our long-term strategy in the region will not likely be furthered by the continuing presence of a large U.S. military footprint in the Middle East. But our current strategy would be undermined by a precipitous withdrawal of U.S. forces from Iraq." Statement of General John P. Abizaid before the Senate Armed Services Committee on the 2006 Posture of Central Command, March 16, 2006, page 22.

† In his memoirs, Rumsfeld wrote, "Our Arab friends had consistently urged us to leave Iraq as soon as possible if war came. Riots and demonstrations might break out . . . especially if we were seen as occupiers. That argument seemed reasonable to me. I know it also registered with Abizaid, Franks, and I believe, with President Bush." *Known and Unknown* (New York: Sentinel, 2011), 663.

‡ It seems obvious that neither Bush, nor Cheney, nor Rice had fully recognized or understood the distinction between being liberators and being occupiers. I spent an hour with Cheney at his home in McLean, Virginia, on April 23, 2014, probing that distinction and came away with the impression that it had not been fully discussed or seriously considered.

the United States military moved from being liberators to being occupiers. It was downhill from there. When the invasion ended successfully in April 2003, the United States had lost 172 men killed in battle. Three years later, by May 2006, American casualties totaled 2,701 with another 18,369 wounded.[18] Iraqi casualties were much greater. According to figures compiled by Iraqbodycount.org, at the end of April 2003, 7,417 Iraqi civilians had perished through violence. By May 2006, that figure stood at 49,266.[19]

George W. Bush's decision to invade Iraq will likely go down in history as the worst foreign policy decision ever made by an American president. That error was compounded when he unilaterally decided to bring democracy to Iraq. Bush had little familiarity with the politics of the Middle East, was unaware of the burden this would place on the American military, and was oblivious to how the Iraqis and the rest of the world would view his decision.

To appreciate the distinction between a liberated country and an occupied one, particularly in military terms, consider General Eisenhower's treatment of France and Germany in World War II. Eisenhower did not want his armies bogged down governing captured French territory as they moved eastward across France. At Ike's insistence, General Charles de Gaulle was flown from Algiers to London on June 4—two days before D-Day—and entrusted with the government of what would become liberated France. President Roosevelt and the State Department were strongly opposed, but Eisenhower prevailed.* On June 14, when the first French town was liberated, de Gaulle went across the channel and was greeted by an outpouring of affection. Vichy officeholders switched their allegiance from Vichy to the Free French, and de Gaulle overnight became the de facto head of a sovereign French state. And because of de Gaulle's vigorous leadership, liberated France was spared the long anticipated civil war between the communist left and Vichyite right, and a possible repeat of the Paris

---

* For the details of how General Eisenhower outmaneuvered FDR and the State Department, see Jean Edward Smith, *Eisenhower in War and Peace* (New York: Random House, 2012), 338–39, 369–71.

Commune of 1871. Even more important from a military standpoint, Eisenhower did not have to concern himself with governing France. De Gaulle was in many respects a difficult ally, but he could be relied upon to provide stability.

In Germany by contrast, as soon as Allied troops set foot on German soil they began to govern. Germany was occupied militarily by Ike's forces, German officeholders were discharged, and the government at all levels became Eisenhower's responsibility. The military did not have to concern itself with governing France. Governing Germany, on the other hand, became their constant concern. That is the distinction between being liberated and being occupied. And in Iraq, the military had originally assumed they would be liberators.

Bush's decision to occupy Iraq and bring Western-style democracy to the country was personified by L. Paul Bremer, who became the president's personal envoy directing the newly established Coalition Provisional Authority. By presidential directive, Bremer enjoyed full authority over every aspect of Iraqi government. The interim governing body that Garner had established was dismissed, the Iraqi army and various police forces were disbanded, and the Baath Party outlawed. Overnight what order there had been in Iraq disappeared. Bremer ensconced himself in the militarily protected Green Zone, brought numerous young Americans over to Baghdad to assist in governing, and attempted to take charge. The American military, which had been planning to leave Iraq, was required to remain, and the maintenance of law and order became their responsibility. The scheme was wrongheaded from the beginning, and Bremer made it worse. Not only did he err in not continuing the interim authority Garner had organized, and in dissolving the Iraqi army, but his decision to outlaw the Baath Party not only deprived Iraq of its administrative core, but exacerbated the sectarian strife that followed. The Baath Party was a strongly secular force in Iraq, and by removing it, Shiite and Sunni were free to go at each other.

Bremer lasted for a year, but the damage was done. On June 28, 2004, he returned to the United States, surreptitiously flying out of Baghdad in a camouflaged National Guard C-130, and sovereignty was officially transferred to an interim Iraqi government headed by Ayad Allawi, a London expatriate who had been on the CIA payroll for the past decade.[20] To some degree it was simply a front, and the United States continued to call the shots. Bremer was replaced by veteran diplomat John Negroponte, who became American ambassador to the new Iraqi government, and on the military side, General George Casey came from the Pentagon to replace Ricardo Sanchez.

The change of American leadership and the superficial transfer of sovereignty did little to stop the violence. In the summer of 2004, the number of insurgency-inspired attacks rose to over three thousand monthly, roughly a hundred a day. The Iraq insurgency, which began primarily as a Sunni effort to reclaim supremacy, had by 2004 mushroomed into an Islamic nationalist catch-all combining secular Baathists with Muslim fundamentalists (both Sunni and Shiite) determined to drive the United States from Iraq. By October 2004 the violence in Iraq was ten times greater than when Bush had declared "Mission Accomplished" from the deck of the *Abraham Lincoln* in May 2003. One incident suffices to illustrate the intensity of the conflict. On October 23, insurgents dressed as Iraqi police commandeered a bus loaded with forty-nine newly trained Iraqi soldiers, forced them to lie flat on the ground, and executed them. At that point it became clear that the Iraqi army could not be counted on.[21]

In November 2004, United States forces launched a set piece assault on the insurgent stronghold of Fallujah. Set piece assaults were something that U.S. forces did well, and after some of the toughest fighting to date, Marines successfully cleansed the city of insurgents. Casualties were high. Ninety-five Americans were killed in combat and another five hundred wounded, making November 2004 the bloodiest month of the occupation.[22] Insurgent losses exceeded one thousand dead.

The second battle of Fallujah demonstrated that when it came to fighting set piece battles, the heavily armed U.S. military was unbeatable.* Guerrilla warfare was something else. Not surprisingly, the Iraqi

---

* At the same time U.S. forces were retaking Fallujah, Iraqi insurgents were capturing the city of Mosul, the third largest in Iraq. The Iraqi police and army deserted their barracks, and

insurgency responded accordingly. Rather than hold real estate and confront U.S. forces in conventional warfare, the insurgency melted into the population. There was also a serious downside to the second battle of Fallujah. It turned Iraq's Sunni population overwhelmingly against the United States. An opinion poll conducted by WorldPublic-Opinion.org shortly after the battle indicated that 88 percent of Sunni Arabs approved of attacks on U.S. troops.[23] The United States had subdued Fallujah, but in doing so lost the battle for public support.

Bush had difficulty understanding the internal Iraqi situation. He was determined to bring democracy to Iraq, and unwilling to listen to the problems that entailed. As he once said, "A president has got to be the calcium in the backbone. If I weaken, the whole team weakens. . . . It's essential that we be confident and determined and united. I don't need people around me who are not steady. . . . And if there's kind of a hand-wringing attitude going on when times are tough, I don't like it."[24]

Bush's certitude made it difficult for many in the administration to tell him the truth, or to acquaint him with the possibility of failure in Iraq. As Senator Carl Levin put it, "I've never thought that Bush was dumb at all. But I think he is intellectually lazy and I think he wants people around him who will not challenge him but will give him the ammunition which he needs or wants in order to achieve some more general goal."[25]

Deputy Secretary of State Richard Armitage was willing to speak frankly. Returning to Washington after a visit to Iraq in December 2004, Armitage met with Bush in the White House. "What did you find?" asked Bush. "We're not winning," said Armitage. "We're not losing. But not winning over a long period of time works for the insurgents." Armitage told Bush that the campaign of intimidation conducted by the insurgents was incredibly successful.[26] Bush heard Armitage, but

---

the insurgents remained in Mosul for a week before withdrawing, having decided not to stand and fight. The capture of Mosul by the insurgents was scarcely reported by the Western news media. See Patrick Cockburn, *The Occupation: War and Resistance in Iraq* (London: Verso, 2006), 164–65.

made no comment. Whether it registered is not clear. Elections in Iraq were on tap and the president was hoping for a successful outcome that would put Iraq on the road to democracy.

On January 30, 2005, Iraqis went to the polls to elect a national assembly, which among other things, would draft a constitution. The Sunnis for the most part boycotted the election, but otherwise the turnout was heavy. The principal Shiite party, the United Iraqi Alliance, won 48 percent of the vote and together with Moqtada al-Sadr's radical Shiite bloc captured a slim majority in the legislature. The Kurdish Alliance was second with 27 percent, followed by Prime Minister Ayad Allawi's Iraqiyya party with 14 percent. The Iraqiyya was the only secular party in the contest and had been favored by U.S. authorities in Baghdad, but would not be part of the new government.

Despite the overwhelming victory of the religious parties, Bush believed the high turnout validated his democracy agenda for Iraq. To celebrate the occasion, Bush gave a brief televised address to the nation from the White House. "The world is hearing the voice of freedom from the center of the Middle East," said the president. "In great numbers and under great risk, Iraqis have shown their commitment to democracy." [27]

That turned out to be wishful thinking. A new government was not formed until April, when the Shiite Ibrahim al-Jaafari was named prime minister. This was not a secular government, but strongly Shiite, backed by both Grand Ayatollah Ali Sistani and Moqtada al-Sadr. It was also supported by Iran, which complicated things further. And most tellingly, the violence did not subside. January 2005 was the second deadliest month for the United States military in Iraq when the Army and Marines suffered 127 casualties. Another 497 were wounded. Altogether, American losses for the year 2005 totaled 897 killed and 5,942 wounded. Iraqi casualties soared as well. Civilian deaths attributed to terrorist violence totaled 16,388 in 2005, as opposed to 11,650 in 2004. [28]

The White House continued its refusal to accept reality. On May 30, 2005, Memorial Day, Cheney appeared for an hour interview on CNN's *Larry King Live*. Asked by King about the insurgency in

Iraq, Cheney said, "I think they are in the last throes, if you will, of the insurgency." [29] There was little to support Cheney's assertion. American and Iraqi casualties in May were significantly higher than the month before.[30] Cheney said later he thought the increased violence amounted to "final acts of desperation, last efforts to terrorize and destroy." [31]

Bush was equally in denial. On June 21, 2005, the president invited Senate Republicans to have their weekly policy lunch at the White House. Bush spoke for about twenty-five minutes but did not mention Iraq. When he finished, John Warner, chairman of the Armed Services Committee, raised the issue. Warner had been secretary of the navy in the Nixon administration while James Schlesinger was secretary of defense. Warner said he recently had dinner with Schlesinger. "My former boss is very concerned about Iraq because he sees some very eerie parallels developing with Vietnam." [32] Bush responded with his standard 9/11, Saddam, WMD refrain. Nothing about the current situation.

At that point, Ted Stevens (R., Alaska), chairman of the Appropriations Committee, repeated the inquiry. "I want to echo part of what John Warner has just said. I think there are some serious issues here." [33] Again, Bush gave his standard answer. It was the right thing to do, said the president, and they had to stick it out.

After the lunch, Chuck Hagel spoke with Bush privately. "I believe you are getting really bubbled in here in the White House on Iraq," said Hagel. "Do you ever reach outside your inner circle of people, outside your national security council? Are you getting other viewpoints?"

"Well, I kind of leave that to Hadley," Bush replied.

"I know your national security adviser talks to people," said Hagel, "but do you talk to people? . . . When a nation is at war, the president is under tremendous pressure. You go deeper into that bunker, and I don't think it's good for you." [34]

Bush agreed that was good advice, but nothing changed. Hadley invited Hagel to come to the White House for a chat, but Hagel remained convinced that Bush was out of touch. Speaking afterward to reporters from *U.S. News & World Report*, Hagel said, "Things aren't getting better; they are getting worse. The White House is completely disconnected from reality. It's like they're just making it up as they go along. The reality is that we're losing in Iraq."[35]

Hagel was correct. And the military was bearing the burden. Unlike Vietnam, this was a professional Army. There were no draftees. Many were on their second tour in Iraq, and some on their third. At the end of September 2005, the Army announced that it had fallen short of its recruiting quota by the widest margin in twenty-five years.[36] Rumsfeld instituted a stop-loss program that extended enlistments, and the services began offering bonuses up to $40,000 for new recruits. Immigrants were offered a fast track to citizenship for enlisting, and the Pentagon greatly increased the number of "moral waivers" so that those convicted of serious misdemeanors and even felonies could enlist. Add to that a sharp spike in the number of desertions, suicides, and divorces within the military and the problem becomes manifest. As General Casey put it, "People aren't designed to be exposed to the horrors of combat repeatedly, and it wears on them."[37]

At the presidential level, and from a distance, Bush was familiar with the suffering the war entailed for the military. He visited the wounded in hospitals several times monthly, and his visits were not always pleasant. Once at the Naval Medical Center in Bethesda, Maryland, Bush encountered a terminally wounded young man originally from Trinidad who lay in critical condition. His mother was with him, and Bush held her hand for a moment. "How could you do this?" she shouted at the president. "This is not your daughter."[38] Bush understood her resentment. It was a moving experience for the president, but little changed.

On October 15, 2005, Iraqis went to the polls for a second time to vote on the new constitution that had been drafted by the transitional government. The constitution was ratified by a vote of 79 to 21 percent, with the Sunni population largely voting against. Bush hailed the constitution's ratification as an important step on the road to democracy. "On behalf of the American people, I'd like to congratulate the people of Iraq for the successful completion of a vote on their draft constitution," said the president. "This is a very positive day for the Iraqis and as well for world peace. Democracies are peaceful countries. . . . Iraq is a country that will serve as an example for others who aspire to live in freedom. So, again, I congratulate the Iraqi people. . . . Thank you for doing what is right." [39]

Once again, Bush was whistling in the dark. The Iraqi constitution had been drafted in sixty days under intense American pressure. The Iraqis who voted on October 15 had not seen, read, studied or debated the document they voted on.[40] U.S. State Department officials who supervised the drafting seem to have ignored Iraqi constitutional and legal history and reduced the Iraqi state to a collection of Shiites, Sunnis, and Kurds. Instead of focusing on those elements that united Iraqis, the document emphasized religious differences and divisiveness. Iraq became a decentralized federal structure with a weak central government entrusted only with authority over foreign, fiscal, and defense policy. Primary power resided with sectarian regional authorities. The result was a tragic failure. According to a recent study published by the London School of Economics: "The hasty way the Constitution was drafted, the many external interventions, the absence of real Iraqi constitutional experts, the weakness of the central government and the sharp divisions undermining the country have all contributed to the precarious situation in Iraq in 2013." [41]

The contrast to postwar Germany is striking. In Germany, the drafting of a new constitution (Basic Law) did not commence until three years after the war ended, and American authorities kept hands off. When the State Department suggested a presidential form of government, General Lucius Clay rebuked them. The Germans were wedded to a parliamentary tradition, said Clay, and the United States must honor that. As military governor, Clay insisted that drawing up the Basic Law was a German responsibility. He brought Professor Carl Friedrich from Harvard, a recognized constitutional scholar, to Germany to advise him, but left drafting the law to the Germans. "I think that indirectly we influenced the Basic Law," said Clay. "If we had tried to dictate it, the drafting convention would have adjourned. There wouldn't have been any constitution." [42]

The continued deployment of American troops in Iraq increased the tension between the Pentagon and the State Department, particularly between Rumsfeld and Rice. Rumsfeld believed the Iraqis should be cut loose and allowed to shape their own destiny. He likened the situation to teaching a young child to ride a bicycle. "After you run down the street steadying the bicycle by holding the seat, you eventually have to take your hand off the seat. The person may fall once or twice, but it's the way he learns. If you're not willing to take your hand off the bicycle seat, the person will never learn to ride."[43] Rice demurred. "If you take your hand off the bicycle and it goes over a ravine, that's not a very good thing either."[44]

The issue came to a head on Veterans Day 2005, when Bush was scheduled to deliver a speech at the Tobyhanna Army Depot in Pennsylvania. Bush's draft, which was circulated to the principals beforehand, endorsed Rice's position. "Our strategy [in Iraq] is to clear, hold, and build. We're working to clear areas from terrorist control, to hold those areas securely, and to build lasting, democratic Iraqi institutions through an increasingly inclusive political process."[45] Rumsfeld objected. "We need to avoid the dependency syndrome," said the secretary of defense.[46] He urged the White House to delete the phrase. Rumsfeld thought the president's reference to clear, hold, and build would come back to haunt them. It was bumper sticker jargon that bore little relation to reality. Rumsfeld lost the argument. Bush used the phrase in his speech, and the United States became more deeply involved.

The following month, on December 15, Iraqis went to the polls for a third time to elect a new parliament. The results further solidified Iraq's sectarian division. The principal Shiite party, the United Iraqi Alliance, once again came in first, the Kurds were second, and the Sunnis, who participated in the election, came in a distant third. Turnout was high—close to 70 percent.[47] Bush celebrated the election by posing in the White House for photos with six young Iraqis who had just voted. "I've assured these good Iraqi citizens that the United States will stay with them and complete this job.

> This is a major step forward in achieving our objective, which is having a democratic Iraq, a country able to sustain itself and defend itself, a country that will be an ally in the war on terror, and a country that will send such a powerful example to others in the region.[48]

| **Feb. 2, 2004** | **Feb. 22, 2006** |

The Golden Mosque of Samarra, Iraq. Before and after.

It would take the Iraqis until April 2006 to choose a new prime minister, when under heavy State Department pressure, Prime Minister Jaafari stepped aside and was succeeded by Nouri al-Maliki. And it took Maliki until May 20 to form a government.* In the meantime, the violence intensified. On February 22, 2006, Sunni insurgents blew up one of the holiest Shiite shrines in Iraq, the Golden Mosque of Samarra, containing the tombs of the revered tenth and eleventh Shiite imams, Ali al-Hadi, who died in 868, and his son Hassan Ali al-Askari, who died in 874.

The destruction of the Golden Mosque launched what amounted to a civil war in Iraq. Shiite militias swarmed into the streets of major cities and in retaliation destroyed twenty-seven Sunni mosques, killing three imams and kidnapping a fourth. Over 1,300 Iraqis were killed that day as Shiite and Sunni death squads marauded in the streets.[49] Sectarian hatred had reached a boiling point.

---

* Under the Iraqi constitution, it required a two-thirds vote of parliament to install a new government. In this case, as after the previous election, the Shiites and Kurds formed a coalition with the major departments divided between the two. "We pretend there is a national government," said Anthony Cordesman, a keen observer of the Iraqi situation at the Center for Strategic and International Studies in Washington, "but it's a coalition in which ministries have been divided among the political parties. Ministries have been the spoils, and since there is no civil service they barely run at all." *Washington Post*, November 24, 2006. Also see, Cordesman, "Iraqi Election Results Uncertain for Months," *New York Times*, December 18, 2005.

Bush appealed for calm. "I ask all Iraqis to exercise restraint," said the president. "Violence will only contribute to what the terrorists sought to achieve by this act. The United States stands ready to do all in its power to assist the government of Iraq to identify and bring to justice those responsible for this act."[50]

There was little the United States could do. The streets of Baghdad and other Iraqi cities became death traps. Iraqis responded by fleeing, especially the professional classes. According to reports filed by the United Nations High Commissioner for Refugees, some two thousand Iraqis were going to Syria daily, and another thousand to Jordan. Even more people were leaving major cities for the countryside. Overall, the High Commissioner estimated that since March 2003, 1.6 million Iraqis had been displaced internally, and up to 1.8 million had gone abroad.[51]

The free fall in Iraq was reflected in Bush's plunging approval ratings, which by March 2006 were down to 36 percent. Two thirds of Americans polled felt the war was a mistake, less than a third approved Bush's handling of the conflict, and just 20 percent believed that the United States could win.[52] At a White House news conference on March 21, Hearst columnist Helen Thomas, the eighty-five-year-old dean of the White House press corps, put Bush on the spot. Thomas began her career as a White House correspondent under Eisenhower, and George Bush was the tenth president she had covered. She was not impressed.

> *Thomas:* I'd like to ask you, Mr. President, your decision to invade Iraq has caused the death of thousands of Americans and Iraqis, wounds of American and Iraqis for a lifetime. Every reason given, publicly at least, has turned out not to be true. My question is, why did you really want to go to war? . . . What was your real reason?

Bush was caught flatfooted. Living in the president's White House cocoon and surrounded by a largely unquestioning staff, Bush was flummoxed by Thomas's directness. He rambled a lengthy nonresponsive reply, citing the events of 9/11 as his motivation. Thomas corrected him. The Iraqis had nothing to do with 9/11, she pointed out. "They did," said Bush, "the Taliban provided safe haven for Al Qaeda." Again Thomas interrupted. "I'm talking about Iraq," she told him. Bush corrected himself. "Afghanistan provided safe haven for Al Qaeda. That's where they trained. That's where they plotted. That's where they planned the attacks that killed thousands of innocent Americans." Bush went on to say he saw a threat in Iraq. "I was hoping to solve this problem diplomatically. That's why I went to the Security Council. . . . We worked with the world. We worked to make sure that Saddam Hussein heard the message of the world. And when he chose to deny inspectors, when he chose not to disclose [neither of which was true], then I had the difficult decision to make to remove him. And we did, and the world is safer for it."[53] It was a dismal performance. Bush was testy and evasive, and his poll numbers continued to plummet.

Aside from the acceleration of violence, the situation in Iraq was further complicated by the pervasive corruption that had crept in after Bremer's dismissal of indigenous law enforcement authority. As Dr. Mahmoud Othman, a respected Kurdish political leader said, "Iraq is being destroyed by the occupation, terrorism and corruption—and all are doing equal damage."[54] Stuart Bowen, the inspector general for Iraq reconstruction (SIGIR), disclosed that $8.8 billion allocated to Paul Bremer's CPA was unaccounted for because oversight was nonexistent. Frank Willis, who was second in command of the transport ministry under the CPA, confirmed to *60 Minutes* that not only was there no accounting of how the money was spent, but that the funds were always kept in cash. "Fresh, new, crisp, unspent, just printed $100 bills. It was the Wild West."[55]

Within the Iraqi government, corruption had become pervasive. High-ranking officials in the defense ministry made off with approximately $2 billion from the arms procurement budget before they fled to other countries. "It was possibly the largest robbery in the world," said Judge Radhi al-Radhi, head of the Iraqi Integrity Commission.[56] Corruption in the oil industry was equally out of control. U.S. officials noted that about 10 percent of refined fuels were diverted to the black market and about 30 percent of imported fuels smuggled out of Iraq and sold for a profit. "It's the money pit of the insurgency," said one American official.[57] In September 2006, the government of Nouri al-Maliki issued eighty-eight arrest warrants for former government officials charging them with fraud, only to find that over sixty had departed Iraq and were living in other countries.[58]

For Iraqis, 2006 was the most deadly year of the occupation, with civilian casualties estimated at 30,000 and 100,000 wounded. U.S. military losses totaled 873 killed and another 6,412 wounded.[59] As General Casey phrased it, "In the aftermath of the Samarra bombing, the fundamental nature of the conflict had changed from an insurgency against the coalition to a struggle among Iraq's ethnic and sectarian groups for political and economic power in Iraq."[60] Said differently, Iraq was fighting a civil war. For Bush, the setback was unnerving. "I don't think anything disturbed him more than the sectarian violence that occurred in the wake of the Samarra mosque bombing," said John Negroponte, who had left Iraq and was now serving as the first director of national intelligence. "I think he went through a period for several weeks—I don't know if he went into a state of depression, but I think he was visibly discouraged by the situation in Iraq, almost to the point of despondence, because I think it looked to him like the whole game was going down the drain. He was really bothered by that. It was almost as if he was pleading with us not to give him any more bad news."[61]

Many on the White House staff sought to make Rumsfeld the culprit, despite the fact that the secretary of defense had consistently pointed out the mishaps that could occur during an occupation. Meeting informally with his closest advisers in the family quarters of the White House late in April, Bush asked directly how many thought Rumsfeld should go. Card, Rice, Michael Gerson, Karen Hughes, Josh Bolten, Ken Mehlman, Ed Gillespie, and Margaret Spellings all said yes. Karl Rove, Stephen Hadley, and Dan Bartlett thought not, as did Dick Cheney.[62] Bush agreed with the second group. As he told reporters in the Rose Garden, "I'm the decider, and I decide what is best. And what's best is for Don Rumsfeld to remain as secretary of defense."[63]

Despite Bush's noble intentions to bring democracy to Iraq, the hostility to the United States was increasing daily. As one former CIA official noted, "The sad truth is Sunnis and Shiites have come to vie with each other in pushing to get rid of the Americans."[64] Or as a Shiite cleric put it, "There is anger. You can hear it in the slogans at Friday prayers: 'Death to America.' They're burning American flags. They're saying 'The Americans won't leave except by the funerals of their sons.'"[65] A U.S. intelligence report found that "The Iraq conflict has become a 'cause celebre' for jihadists, breeding a deep resentment of U.S. involvement in the Muslim world and cultivating supporters of the global jihadist movement."[66] The National Intelligence Estimate issued by the CIA agreed. The war in Iraq had actually increased the threat of terrorism by "shaping a new generation of terrorist leaders and operatives."[67] That assessment was more than borne out in 2014. According to *The New York Times*, the leadership of the Islamic State of Iraq and Syria (ISIS), almost to a man, augmented their military skill "with terrorist techniques refined through years of fighting American troops. . . . ISIS is in effect a hybrid of terrorists and an army."[68]

Where did Bush err? Former diplomat Peter Galbraith, whose book *The End of Iraq* is one of the most perceptive treatments of the debacle, states it succinctly. "In my recent trips to Iraq," wrote Galbraith in 2006, "I have asked its elected political leaders where they thought the United States went wrong. All gave the same answer: when the United States became an occupier instead of a liberator. In short, when the Bush Administration decided it was more capable of determining Iraq's future than the people of the country itself."[69]

As the situation in Iraq deteriorated, Bush became increasingly single-minded. At his desk in the Oval Office at 7:30 each morning, the president began his day studying casualty reports from Iraq. White House staffers who came in to discuss other issues found him mesmerized just as Lyndon Johnson had been about Vietnam by messages detailing assassinations, bombings, ethnic cleansing, and sectarian strife. "It's Iraq, Iraq, Iraq," Andy Card told Josh Bolten, who succeeded Card as White House chief of staff on March 28, 2006.[70]*

---

* Andrew Card resigned as chief of staff under his own volition. Having been in that position for more than five years, he was exhausted. Bush initially attempted to dissuade him, but eventu-

Bush took the reversals personally. It was "the worst period of my presidency," he wrote in his memoirs. "I thought about the war constantly. . . . For the first time, I worried we might not succeed. If Iraq split along sectarian lines, our mission would be doomed. We could be looking at a repeat of Vietnam—a humiliating loss for the country, a shattering blow to the military, and a dramatic setback for our interests."[71]

Like most chief executives, Bush did his utmost to conceal his distress. He was acutely aware he was under constant scrutiny, and was determined not to appear overwhelmed as Lyndon Johnson had been by Vietnam. "Can you imagine the signal I would have sent?" said Bush after leaving office.[72] Laura did her best to relieve the pressure her husband felt. "It was painful to see the man I loved, the man I knew, so misrepresented by his opponents." Laura took it upon herself to invite George's younger brother Marvin, who lived in nearby northern Virginia, to the White House or Camp David on weekends to join the president in front of the television set watching baseball or football. "The two of them could lose themselves in sports for an hour or two, in that easy way that brothers have, the unspoken language of friendship that would pass between them." Bush's sister, Doro, and her family were also frequent visitors. As Laura put it, "The richness of their friendship and their love for me and George was of great solace as we waited for improvement in Iraq. The Bush children had seen their father lead the nation during the Gulf War; now it was their brother, in a longer, more difficult fight."[73]

Old friends from Texas came by. Joe O'Neill, who had introduced George to Laura, was a sometimes visitor to the White House. "He did get kind of down," O'Neill later told journalists.[74] Bush turned increasingly to religion. "I get guidance from God in prayers," he told Saudi Arabia's Prince Bandar.[75] He also consulted regularly with or-

---

ally acquiesced. To replace Card, the president chose Bolten, who had formerly been vice chief of staff, and since 2003 director of the Office of Management and Budget. A hard charger, Bolten immediately set about reorganizing the White House staff, replaced Scott McClellan as press secretary with Tony Snow, and demoted Karl Rove from his position as deputy chief of staff for policy, a post Rove had been given after the 2004 election.

dained ministers. Kirbyjon Caldwell, the eloquent African American pastor of a Methodist mega-church in Houston, Texas, who had given the benediction at both of Bush's inaugurals and spoke at the National Cathedral memorial service for 9/11, was a special friend whom Bush relied on. Bush had spoken over the telephone to Pastor Caldwell before his first presidential debate with Al Gore in 2000. "His voice gave me such comfort and calm that I made the telephone prayer with Kirbyjon a tradition before major events for the rest of the campaign and during my presidency," said Bush.[76] Caldwell consoled Bush about the loss of life in Iraq. He would later officiate at Jenna's marriage to Henry Hager in May 2008. Another pastor on whom Bush relied was Lieutenant Commander Stan Fornea, the chaplain at Camp David. The president found inspiration in Fornea's upbeat sermons. As Fornea put it, "The Scriptures put great premiums on faithfulness, perseverance, and overcoming. We do not quit or give up. We always believe there is no such thing as a hopeless situation."[77]

Clearly, Bush was troubled. He could not comprehend Iraq's sectarian division or understand why it had become such an impediment on the road to democracy. He also had trouble accepting the possibility that Western-style democracy might not fit Iraq. And he was fascinated looking at the daily body counts he received each morning. To the military, this brought back memories of Vietnam. As General Casey remarked to a friend, he believed Bush reflected "the radical wing of the Republican party that kept saying, 'Kill the bastards! Kill the bastards! And you'll succeed.'"[78] For Casey, it seemed that Bush believed in an attrition strategy of simply killing the bad guys. Had he learned nothing from Vietnam? Regardless of how many insurgents they killed, more would follow. In the three years they had been in Iraq, the United States had killed tens of thousands of Iraqis, roughly a thousand a month. But the situation was not getting better.

Like Rumsfeld, both Casey and Abizaid believed the conflict was one the Iraqis had to win for themselves. In their weekly videoconferences with Bush, Casey and Abizaid tried to emphasize that the Iraqis had to carry the burden. And they repeatedly advised the president to reduce the number of American forces. The Iraqis "are never going to like us," said Casey. "And I don't believe we will ever succeed in Iraq by doing it for them." Both Abizaid and Casey believed that the American military presence in Iraq on such a large scale and for so many years was doing more harm than good. Abizaid was blunt. "We need to get the fuck out," he told a friend in private.[79]

Good news from Iraq was fleeting, but in early June 2006, Bush received a dollop when U.S. Special Forces located the headquarters of Abu Musab al-Zarqawi, the chief of al Qaeda in Iraq, at a suburban house in Baqubah, some thirty kilometers north of Baghdad. On June 7, two Air Force F-16s dropped a number of five-hundred-pound bombs on the house, leveling the structure and killing most inside, including Zarqawi. When Zarqawi's body was positively identified, Bush was immediately notified. The president took the news calmly. "I'm not sure how to take good news anymore," he told a White House aide.[80] The following day, June 8, Bush announced Zarqawi's death to the nation. "We have tough days ahead of us in Iraq that will require the continued patience of the American people. Yet the developments of the last 24 hours give us renewed confidence in the final outcome of this struggle, the defeat of terrorist threats, and a more peaceful world for our children and grandchildren."[81] The death of Zarqawi was a symbolic victory. But his death had little effect on the violence that continued to rage in Iraq.

By late spring 2006, Bush recognized that the situation in Iraq was not improving. "This is not working," he told national security adviser Stephen Hadley. "We need to take another look at the whole strategy. I need to see some new options."[82] At Hadley's suggestion, Bush scheduled a two-day retreat at Camp David beginning June 12, where the president and his top advisers could take a fresh look at the situation. They were joined by General Abizaid from CENTCOM headquarters in Qatar, and General Casey and Ambassador Zalmay Khalilzad in Baghdad, who were piped in by secure video. The meeting began with a briefing on the present situation by Casey and Abizaid. Both argued that strategic success ultimately depended upon the Iraqis. The destruction of the Golden Mosque had been a setback, but Casey believed that by mid-2007 the situation could be stabilized. By 2009, he believed the Iraqis could stand alone. In the meantime, the drawdown of U.S. forces should continue. "For us to be successful," said Casey, "we ultimately have to leave Iraq." [83]

Casey and Abizaid were followed by Rice, who argued that the situation in Iraq was not improving, and that the administration should "prepare the U.S. public for a long struggle." Changing the governing culture of Iraq, said Rice, would "require a generation." [84] Rice was clearly in favor of a continued American presence in Iraq, as were most members of the NSC staff in the White House. At that point the conference broke for lunch.

After lunch, Bush and his colleagues were treated to four scholarly presentations that had been arranged by Hadley. Three of the four speakers were prominent Washington neoconservatives who had advocated regime change in Iraq for a decade. All had vigorously supported the invasion, and all were now urging the president to step up American efforts. The most aggressive presentation was made by Frederick Kagan, a resident scholar at the American Enterprise Institute, who urged Bush to beef up the U.S. military presence in Iraq and wage a full-scale war to defeat the insurgents. Eliot Cohen, a professor at the Johns Hopkins School of Advanced International Studies, supported Kagan and told Bush he needed to hold the military commanders accountable for producing results. Robert Kaplan, national correspondent for *The Atlantic*, likewise urged a more robust counterinsurgency strategy.

The sole argument for a drawdown of U.S. forces was made by Michael Vickers, a senior vice president at Washington's Center for Strategic and Budgetary Assessments. Vickers, a former Army Special Forces officer, had been the architect of the CIA's successful effort to arm the Afghan resistance against the Soviet Union in the 1980s and 1990s, a role popularized in the film *Charlie Wilson's War*. He argued that additional U.S. forces in Iraq would be counterproductive. "One of the many paradoxes of modern counterinsurgency is that less is often more," said Vickers. [85] Instead, he suggested the United States shift to an indirect approach, continue the drawdown, and provide increasing support for Iraqi security forces.

Bush and Iraqi prime minister
Nouri al-Maliki, June 13, 2006.

The battle lines were drawn. The generals in the Middle East, Rumsfeld and the leadership at the Pentagon, and Vickers preferred to continue the withdrawal of U.S. forces and the placing of responsibility on the Iraqis.* Rice, Hadley, the White House NSC staff, and three of the guest speakers preferred the United States to step out in front, increase its military commitment, and take the fight to the enemy. So did Dick Cheney.

The battle lines were drawn, but the issue was not joined. Bush retired early that evening, and the assumption was the showdown would come the next day. But instead of going to bed, the president slipped into a car to go to the Camp David helipad. There he boarded Marine One for the flight to Andrews Air Force Base, where he climbed aboard Air Force One for an overnight flight to Baghdad. Bush wanted to meet with Maliki, and he wanted to do so in secret. With so much at stake in Iraq, he wanted to take the new prime minister's measure. None of the president's senior advisers were aware of his plans, and that too was deliberate. The ongoing meeting at Camp David provided perfect cover for

---

* Several weeks after his presentation at Camp David, Rumsfeld appointed Vickers assistant secretary of defense for special operations and low-intensity conflict. He remained in that post until 2009, when Obama appointed him undersecretary of defense for intelligence—a post he still holds. Robert Kaplan later reversed his position, and in 2008 published an article in *The Atlantic* acknowledging his error. "When I and others supported a war to liberate Iraq, we never fully or accurately contemplated the price that would have to be paid." "Iraq: The Counterfactual Game," *The Atlantic*, October 24, 2008.

Bush's trip to Baghdad. It was "a brilliant fake-out," said White House chief of staff Josh Bolten.[86]

Bush arrived in Baghdad at midday on Tuesday, June 13. On his previous trip at Thanksgiving in 2003, he had not left the airport. This time he flew by Army helicopter to the U.S. embassy in the Green Zone. The helicopter, one of several, flew fast and low, shooting off the occasional flare as protection against heat-seeking missiles. Maliki was waiting when he arrived.

"Your decisions and actions will determine success," said the president. "It will not be easy, but no matter how hard it is, we will help you."

Maliki replied as Bush had hoped. "We will achieve victory over terror, which is a victory for democracy." The president was pleased with Maliki's manner. The prime minister had a gentle exterior, but Bush sensed an inner toughness. "His personal courage was a seed that I hoped to nurture, so he could grow into the strong leader the Iraqis needed."[87]

After meeting with Maliki and his cabinet, Bush conferred with General Casey. It was early evening in Baghdad, and the two men stood on the veranda of the embassy watching the sunset.

"We have to win," said the president.

"I'm with you," Casey replied. "I understand that. But to win, we have to draw down. We have to bring our force levels down to ones that are sustainable both for them and for us."[88] The real battle, as Casey saw it, was to prepare the Iraqis to protect themselves. He was fond of quoting British Lieutenant Colonel T. E. Lawrence, Lawrence of Arabia, who had played a pivotal role in the founding of Iraq after the First World War. "Better they do it imperfectly with their own hands than you do it perfectly with your own," said Lawrence, "for it is their war and their country, and your time here is limited."[89]

Casey could see that Bush was not satisfied with his explanation. "I know I've got work to do to convince you of that," said the general. "I need to do a better job explaining why winning means getting out."

"You do," Bush replied.[90] The president was not convinced that Casey was wrong, but he was less and less sure that he was right. The upshot was there would be no decision. Bush did not want to overrule the military, but he was increasingly doubtful that the Iraqis could handle the problems themselves.

Bush returned to Washington energized by the trip. The meeting with Maliki had gone well, and the president was not yet ready to alter the strategy in Iraq. At a news conference in the White House the day after his return, Bush shared his newfound optimism with the press. Responding to a question posed by Bret Baier of Fox News, the president said, "I know there is a lot of discussion about troop levels. Those troop levels will be decided upon by General Casey. He will make the recommendation in consultation with an Iraqi government. But whatever decision General Casey makes, the message is going to be: 'We will stand with you.'"[91] For the moment, Rumsfeld and the generals had prevailed. Or so it appeared. Bush was not yet ready to unroll his new strategy.

CHAPTER TWENTY

Rummy Walks the Plank

Common Article 3 [of the Geneva Conventions] is applicable here and . . . requires that Hamdan be tried by a "regularly constituted court affording all the judicial guarantees which are recognized as indispensable by civilized peoples."

Opinion of the Court
Hamdan v. Rumsfeld

The summer of 2006 offered Bush little respite. In addition to the deteriorating situation in Iraq, his approval rating in opinion polls sagged to 32 percent. With congressional elections looming in November, Republican lawmakers became wary of the president's embrace. The Supreme Court added to Bush's discomfiture on June 29 when in a historic decision it overturned his 2001 order to try detainees by military tribunals rather than in courts of law or by courts-martial. The Court also held that all detainees, regardless of where they were held, were entitled to the protection of the Geneva Conventions.

The significance of the Supreme Court's decision can scarcely be overstated. In constitutional terms, it ranks alongside the Court's holding in the 1952 case of *Youngstown Sheet & Tube v. Sawyer*[1] when it rejected President Truman's seizure of the steel mills during the Korean War, and its 1974 decision in *United States v. Nixon*[2] ordering President Nixon to turn over the Watergate tapes to federal authorities. Yale Law School dean Harold Koh called the decision "a stunning rebuke to the extreme theory of executive power that has been put forward for the past five years. It is a reminder that checks and balances continue to be a necessary and vibrant principle, even in the war on terror."[3]

The case was *Hamdan v. Rumsfeld*,[4] and involved Salim Ahmed Hamdan, a citizen of Yemen who was taken prisoner during the fighting in Afghanistan in November 2001, and taken to Guantánamo in June 2002. Hamdan was a driver and bodyguard for Osama bin Laden. After being incarcerated at Guantánamo for two years, he was indicted for conspiracy "to commit . . . offenses triable by military commissions."[5] Other than serving as bin Laden's chauffeur, no specific act was cited. His military attorney filed for a writ of habeas corpus in United States District Court for the District of Columbia challenging the constitutionality of the military commissions. On November 8, 2004, the District Court granted the writ, holding that the commissions were an illegal extension of presidential power.[6] The United States Court of Appeals for the District of Columbia circuit reversed.[7] Chief Justice Roberts was one of the judges who sat on the case in the Court of Appeals and therefore recused himself when the Supreme Court granted certiorari.

The Supreme Court's decision in *Hamdan* was written by Justice John Paul Stevens, the senior justice on the Court, who had been appointed by Gerald Ford in 1975. Stevens held that the president had exceeded his authority when he established the commissions without congressional approval; that the procedures adopted by the commissions violated both the Uniform Code of Military Justice and the Geneva Conventions; and most importantly, that regardless of the president's opinion as commander in chief, the United States was bound by the Geneva Conventions.

Common Article 3 [of the Geneva Conventions] obviously tolerates a great degree of flexibility in trying individuals captured during armed conflict; its requirements are general ones, crafted to accommodate a wide variety of legal systems. But *requirements* they are nonetheless. The commission that the president has convened to try Hamdan does not meet those requirements.[8]*

Equally important, Common Article 3 of the Geneva Conventions not only guarantees fair trials to all people captured in an armed conflict, but specifically outlaws "cruel treatment, torture [and] outrages upon personal dignity, in particular, humiliating and degrading treatment."[9] If the United States was bound by Common Article 3, then the "enhanced interrogation" techniques Bush had authorized were potentially war crimes punishable under the War Crimes Act of 1996.[10]

Bush was stunned by the Supreme Court's decision. Cheney was incensed. Rumsfeld and the Defense Department did their best to comply. The secretary immediately issued a directive to all military personnel that incorporated Common Article 3 of the Geneva Conventions verbatim, and the Army Field Manual on Interrogations was rewritten to incorporate the protections provided.[11] The military services had taken this position from the beginning of the war on terror. Their stand was now vindicated. The CIA was less responsive. If "enhanced interrogation" was a war crime, the agency needed ex-post-facto protection.

An equally serious problem raised by the decision was the status of the military tribunals. In their present form, the Court had overturned them. Cheney urged Bush to take a hard line. Rather than comply with the Court's ruling, the vice president advocated seeking immediate leg-

---

* The Court also held that "None of the overt acts that Hamdan is alleged to have committed [i.e., driving for bin Laden], violates the law of war. . . . At a minimum, the Government must make a substantial showing that the crime for which it seeks to try a defendant by military commission is acknowledged to be an offense against the law of war. That burden is far from satisfied here . . . conspiracy is not a violation of the law of war." *Hamdan v. Rumsfeld*, 548 U.S. 577, 613, 616–17, 620.

After passage of the Military Commissions Act by Congress in September 2006, Hamdan was retried and convicted. He was sentenced to six years imprisonment, reduced by time served. He was transferred to Yemen and released in December 2008. In October 2012, the United States Court of Appeals overturned his conviction and he was acquitted of all charges. *Hamdan v. U.S.* 696 F. 3d 1238 (D.C. Cir. 2012).

islation to annul the decision. At Cheney's direction, his staff drafted a one-page bill that would strip the Supreme Court of jurisdiction and affirm the president's authority to try detainees by military commissions. Republicans could ram it through Congress, and no one in the intelligence agencies would need to worry about war crimes prosecution. Attorney General Alberto Gonzales and Harriet Miers, back in her post as White House counsel, supported Cheney's plan. The president should not surrender his authority, they urged.

Josh Bolten, Stephen Hadley, and others on the White House staff were appalled at Cheney's idea, as was Condoleezza Rice. Rice believed adherence to the Geneva Conventions would enhance America's image abroad, which had been badly tarnished by Bush's earlier disavowal. Rumsfeld and the Joint Chiefs believed adherence would better protect U.S. military personnel abroad. Karen Hughes also urged Bush not to undo the *Hamdan* decision. The issue came to a head at a tense meeting in the Oval Office immediately after the decision came down. "Mr. President," said Rice, "you cannot reverse the Supreme Court." [12]

Bush was torn. "I disagreed strongly with the Court's decision, which I considered an example of judicial activism. But I accepted the role of the Supreme Court in our constitutional democracy. . . . Whether presidents like them or not, the Court's decisions are the law of the land." [13] Instead of asking Congress to overrule the Court, Bush elected to seek legislation that would authorize him to establish military tribunals, a step he should have taken back in 2001.

The president announced his decision at a news conference in Chicago on July 7. Asked by Kelly O'Donnell of NBC News about the Court's decision in *Hamdan*, Bush replied:

> I am willing to abide by the ruling of the Supreme Court. And the Supreme Court said that in this particular case . . . that we should work with the United States Congress to develop a way forward. . . . And we will work with Congress. . . . I have been waiting for this decision in order to figure out how to go forward. . . . So this is new ground. This is different than any president has been through before in terms of how to deal with these kind of people. . . . And so in working with

the Supreme . . . in listening to the Supreme Court, we'll work with Congress to achieve that objective.[14]

Congress had just adjourned for its annual summer recess, and would not return to Washington until after Labor Day. That gave the White House time to draft the necessary legislation. In the meantime, Bush turned to the problem of the black sites overseas. The Supreme Court had ruled that all detainees were covered by the Geneva Conventions regardless of where they were held. Should the prisoners incarcerated in the black sites be transferred to Guantánamo? Michael Hayden, the former NSA head who was now director of the Central Intelligence Agency, urged the president to do so. So did Rice. It was now five years after 9/11 and time to recalibrate. NSC adviser Hadley agreed. The Supreme Court's decision made the black sites untenable. What had been acceptable at the outset of the war on terror was no longer defensible. In Hadley's view, the sites had served their purpose.[15] Once again, Cheney was strongly opposed, as was Gonzales, who feared top administration officials could be prosecuted for war crimes if the existence of the black sites was admitted. "Gonzales was scaring everyone," said one White House official.[16]

The issue was discussed at a meeting of the National Security Council in the Roosevelt Room of the White House in late August. Rice argued that Bush should publicly acknowledge the CIA's role in incarcerating detainees abroad and announce the transfer of all remaining prisoners to Guantánamo, where they would face trial. "Now is the time. Democracies don't disappear people." Hayden agreed. "We are not the nation's jailers," said the CIA director.[17]

Again, Cheney objected. "I oppose this, Mr. President. I think this is a bad idea. They [the prisoners] might have intelligence value." Cheney also believed disclosing the overseas prisons would embarrass the countries in which they were located. And he worried about "what would come to light," meaning what else might be revealed about the methods the CIA had used.[18]

Rice and Cheney went back and forth for several minutes. "It was the most intense confrontation of my time in Washington," said Rice afterward. The other members of the NSC watched silently. Finally, Rice concluded the discussion. "Mr. President, don't let this be your legacy." [19]

Bush thanked everyone, but did not announce his decision. He wanted to think about it. In her memoirs, Rice said it was one of the few times she could not read the president. "When he said he needed to think about it, I prayed that he understood the consequences fully." [20]

Bush thought about the question overnight. The following morning he told Hadley to inform everyone that he had decided to close the overseas prisons, and that he would announce it in a speech to the nation. Having made the decision, Bush was buoyant. As he saw it, this was an opportunity to push back against his critics and explain what he had done. "He was very animated," White House lawyer William Burck recalled. "All this information was stuff he had known . . . for three years and he couldn't tell anybody about it. . . . And now he was going to share it and tell the people. 'Here is what we have been doing, here is what we have been doing to protect you.'" [21]

Bush's exuberance got the better of him. By the time he delivered his address to the nation on September 6, his decision to acknowledge and close down the black sites overseas had morphed into a ringing defense of what the CIA had done. Misreading the mood of the country, Bush touted the program as "one of the most vital tools in our war against terror," and insisted that everything that had been done was legal. The president believed he could turn the CIA's inquisition into a winning issue in the upcoming congressional elections.

To emphasize the patriotic aspect of the program, Bush spoke from a podium in the East Room of the White House, a row of American flags behind him, and flanked by Vice President Cheney, Attorney General Gonzales, and CIA director Hayden. The audience included the Republican leadership in Congress and family members of those killed in the 9/11 attacks. Bush spoke for thirty-seven minutes. He revealed that the CIA had been running secret overseas prisons for some high-value detainees for whom the normal rules did not apply.

> These are dangerous men with unparalleled knowledge about terrorist networks and their plans for new attacks. The security of our nation

and the lives of our citizens depend on our ability to learn what these terrorists know.

Many specifics of this program, including where these detainees have been held and the details of their confinement cannot be divulged. Doing so would provide our enemies with information they could use to take retribution against our allies and harm our country. I can say that questioning the detainees in this program has given us information that has saved innocent lives by helping us stop new attacks, here in the United States and across the world.[22]

Bush said the detainees at the black sites had been subjected to what he called "an alternative set of procedures." The president said he "could not describe the specific methods used. . . . But I can say they were tough, and they were safe and lawful and necessary." Khalid Sheikh Mohammed had been waterboarded 183 times. Abu Zubaydah had been waterboarded eighty-three times. Bush did not acknowledge the fact. He also did not disclose the other techniques he had approved, including forced nudity, keeping prisoners awake for extended periods, placing them in dark, cramped boxes with insects, or slamming them into walls.[23]

"I want to be absolutely clear with our people and the world: The United States does not torture. It's against our laws, and it's against our values. I have not authorized it and I will not authorize it."[24] What the president was saying was that so long as the Office of Legal Counsel determined that a tactic was not torture, then he could say he was not authorizing torture, the Geneva Conventions notwithstanding.[25]*

Bush had turned 180 degrees. Rather than apologize for the program, he touted it. The president believed he was holding a winning

---

* As Bush was speaking, the Army released its new manual on interrogation practices incorporating the Geneva Conventions. Said Lieutenant General John Kimmons, "No good intelligence is going to come from abusive practices. I think history tells us that. I think the empirical evidence of the past five hard years tells us that . . . any piece of intelligence that is obtained under duress through the use of abusive techniques would be of questionable credibility . . . nothing good will come from them." Jane Mayer, *The Dark Side: The Inside Story of How the War on Terror Turned into a War on American Ideals* (New York: Doubleday, 2008), 326.

hand. Fourteen prisoners held in the black sites would be moved to Guantánamo, but the sites would not be closed. "The current transfers mean that there are now no terrorists in the CIA program. But as more high-ranking terrorists are captured, the need to obtain intelligence from them will remain critical. And having a CIA program for questioning terrorists will continue to be critical to getting lifesaving information."[26] Rice and her State Department colleagues were profoundly disappointed. "We wanted this [the president's speech] to be about change," said one. "But instead of turning the page, the president laminated it." "Yuck! Alternative procedures?" said Karen Hughes. "It sounds scary."[27] Or as John Bellinger, the State Department's chief lawyer, put it, what looked like victory for those who wanted the black sites closed had turned into defeat.[28]

The second half of Bush's speech was devoted to the proposed Military Commissions Act that he was sending to Congress that day. The act was necessary, said the president, because of the recent Supreme Court decision. "So today I'm sending Congress legislation to specifically authorize the creation of military commissions to try terrorists for war crimes." Bush also said he was asking Congress to "make it clear that captured terrorists cannot use the Geneva Conventions as a basis to sue our personnel in U.S. Courts." The president was contemptuous of Common Article 3, which he said was vague and undefined. "Some believe our military and intelligence personnel involved in capturing and questioning terrorists could now be at risk of prosecution under the War Crimes Act simply for doing their jobs in a thorough and professional way. This is unacceptable. . . . So today I am also asking Congress to pass legislation that will clarify the rules for our personnel fighting the war on terror."[29]

Bush concluded his remarks by asking Congress to act quickly. "Time is of the essence. Congress is just in session for a few more weeks, and passing this legislation ought to be a top priority."[30] In retrospect, it seems clear that Cheney had won on all counts. The black sites were emptied but not closed, Congress was being asked to authorize the military commissions, and Common Article 3 of the Geneva Conventions would be weakened significantly.

The Republican leadership on Capitol Hill considered the Military Commissions Act a godsend. If the Democrats opposed, they could be painted as soft on terrorism in the upcoming election. But the road was not open. Once again the military establishment made clear their opposition to any diminution in the protections afforded by the Geneva Conventions. Two dozen retired generals and admirals, led by General Joseph Hoar (USMC) and Admiral Stansfield Turner, wrote a lengthy letter of protest to Senators John Warner and Carl Levin, the chairman and ranking member of the Senate Armed Services Committee. "Now that the Supreme Court has made clear that treatment of al Qaeda prisoners is governed by the Geneva Conventions standards, the Administration is seeking to redefine Common Article 3, so as to downgrade those standards. We urge you to reject this effort." [31]

General John W. Vessey, former chairman of the Joint Chiefs under Ronald Reagan, wrote Senator John McCain and invoked General George C. Marshall on the importance of observing internationally accepted rules of war.* Vessey, who had served in the military for forty-six years, reminded McCain of the sufferings American soldiers had experienced in Japanese prison camps during World War II, in North Korea, and in Vietnam. "Through those years we held to our own values. We should continue to do so." [32]

Colin Powell joined the attack. Writing to McCain on September 13, Powell said, "I have read the powerful and eloquent letter sent to you by one of my distinguished predecessors as Chairman of the Joint Chiefs of Staff, General Jack Vessey. I fully endorse his powerful argument. The world is beginning to doubt the moral basis of our fight against terrorism. To redefine Common Article 3 would add to those doubts. Furthermore, it would put our troops at risk." [33]

---

* Under General Marshall's direction while he was secretary of defense, the Defense Department issued a small book entitled *The Armed Services Officer*. The last chapter is entitled "Americans in Combat" and lists twenty-nine principles that govern the conduct of Americans in war. Number XXV states, "The United States abides by the laws of war. Its Armed Forces, in their dealing with other peoples, are expected to comply with the laws of war, in spirit and in letter. . . . Wanton killing, torture, cruelty or the working of unusual hardship on enemy prisoners or populations is not justified under any circumstances."

Despite the military's objections, the president's bill passed quickly. Debate was minimal. Introduced in the Senate by majority whip Mitch McConnell on September 22, the Senate voted its approval on September 28. The vote was 65–34, with one abstention.* Every Republican except Lincoln Chafee of Rhode Island voted in favor. The Democrats split, 12 in favor, 32 against. The Senate's only Independent, Jim Jeffords of Vermont, also voted against. Of the twelve Democrats who voted in favor, six were up for reelection. The House of Representatives passed the bill the following day, 250–170, after which it adjourned *sine die*. All of the House was up for reelection. Nevertheless, the Democratic leadership pressed its opposition to the measure. Minority leader Nancy Pelosi voted against, as did whip Steny Hoyer and 160 of their colleagues. If Bush and the Republicans wanted to make it an issue in the coming election, the Democrats in the House were ready to meet the challenge.

The Military Commissions Act of 2006 effectively overturned the Supreme Court's decision in *Hamdan v. Rumsfeld*. In addition to authorizing the trial of detainees by military commissions, the act denied defendants the right to file petitions for habeas corpus. It also emasculated Common Article 3 of the Geneva Conventions by granting the president exclusive authority to determine what constituted torture. That eliminated the possibility that anyone in the CIA could be prosecuted for war crimes. The act also permitted coerced evidence to be admitted in trials if a judge believed it to be reliable. And perhaps most serious, the president was given the authority to label anyone an enemy combatant, including United States citizens. The government was authorized to imprison without trial not only those who were "engaged in hostilities" against the United States, but those who "materially supported" terrorist groups. That could include those who donated to charities linked to terrorist groups. *The New York Times* called the act "our generation's version of the Alien and Sedition Acts."[34]

Bush signed the bill into law in a White House ceremony on October 17, 2006. "This bill will allow the Central Intelligence Agency

---

* Senator Olympia Snowe (R., Maine), who was up for reelection, abstained.

to continue its program for questioning key terrorist leaders," said the president. "This program has been one of the most successful intelligence efforts in American history. It has helped prevent attacks on our country. And the bill I sign today will ensure that we can continue using this vital tool to protect the American people for years to come."[35]

Bush was partially right. The Military Commissions Act remained in place until June 12, 2008, when the Supreme Court once again overturned that portion of the act that denied detainees the right to file for habeas corpus. "To hold that the political branches have the power to switch the Constitution on or off at will . . . would lead to a regime in which Congress and the President, not this Court, 'say what the law is,'" said Justice Anthony Kennedy speaking for the Supreme Court (and invoking the words of Chief Justice John Marshall in *Marbury v. Madison*).[36]*

Bush's hard line against detainees was a reflection of his growing determination to resume the offensive in Iraq. After a month at the ranch, the president returned to Washington at the end of the summer energized and ready for action. All presidents profit from their time away from the capital, but no president has made more of his vacations than George W. Bush.

Bush was in excellent physical condition, probably the best of any occupant of the White House. On July 6, he celebrated his sixtieth birthday at the ranch, and shortly afterward the White House released the results of his annual physical at the Naval Medical Center in Bethesda. "The president remains in the 'superior' fitness category for men his age (greater than the ninety-ninth percentile for 60–64 year-old men)," said the report. "The president exercises six times per week. Workouts include bicycling (15–20 miles, 15–18 mph), treadmill (low impact 'hill

* The case was *Boumediene v. Bush*, 533 U.S. 733 (2008). The case involved Lakhdar Boumediene, a citizen of Bosnia and Herzegovina imprisoned at Guantánamo. The Court held that the United States had de facto sovereignty over Guantánamo and that the detainees could not be denied the protections provided in Article I, section 9 of the Constitution. On October 28, 2009, President Obama signed into law the Military Commissions Act of 2009, which provided new rules for the commissions and restored the protections of Common Article 3 of the Geneva Conventions.

work'), elliptical trainer, free weight resistance training, and stretching. The president has not missed work due to illness since his last physical exam." Specifically, the report noted:

Height:	71.5 inches
Temperature:	97.5 degrees F.
Weight:	196.0 lbs.
Body Composition:	Body fat 16.8% (normal for age 16.5–20.5%)
Heart Rate:	46 bpm
Blood Pressure:	108/68

Bush's cholesterol was 174 (last year 178), his HDL was 60 (last year 56), and the LDL 101 (last year 100). "He exercised for a total of 26:02 minutes achieving a maximum heart rate of 179 bpm with a 1-minute recovery of 148 bpm. No signs or symptoms of cardiovascular pathology were noted. Stress cardiogram was normal. Screening ultrasound of the abdominal aorta was normal." The president's PSA was 0.6, meaning he did not have to worry about prostate cancer. The report concluded that the president "remains in excellent health and 'fit for duty.' All data suggests that he will remain so for the duration of his presidency."[37]

Bush's fixation on physical activity was unique. Exercise had helped him stop drinking after he turned forty, and it was the way he managed stress. At the ranch he constructed a number of bike trails, and cycling several hours a day had become a way of life. "Riding helps clear my head," he told Steve Holland of Reuters.[38] Bush often invited others to join him on the bike trails. But he insisted on riding in front. That gave him the illusion of solitude.

Ready for a bike ride.

Bush used that solitude to think about Iraq. "The summer of 2006 was the worst period of my presidency," he wrote in his memoirs. "I thought about the war constantly. . . . For the first time, I worried we might not succeed. If Iraq split along sectarian lines, our mission would be doomed. . . . We had to stop that from happening. . . . I made a conscious decision to show resolve, not doubt, in public. . . . If I had concerns about the direction of the war, I needed to make changes in the policy, not wallow in public." [39]

Bush returned to Washington in mid-August convinced that changes in Iraq were necessary. On August 17, he convened a meeting of the NSC in the White House. Generals Abizaid and Casey participated via a video linkup as did Ambassador Khalilzad. "The situation seems to be deteriorating," said the president. "I want to be able to say that I have a plan to punch back. Can America succeed? If so, how? How do our commanders answer that?" [40]

General Abizaid was the first to reply. "The region is in a sour mood," he told the president. "The way we are focusing on this problem is too military. We need to help them help themselves." Rumsfeld agreed. "Help them help themselves." General Casey saw the problem the same way. "Enduring success will only be achieved by the Iraqis. There's steady progress, but it needs another four to six months." Casey pointed out there were three problems: The Sunni insurgency; the al Qaeda network that had sprung up in Iraq after the invasion; and the sectarian war between Shiites and Sunnis. Each was different, and each required a separate solution. Only the Iraqis could achieve this.

Bush was not persuaded. His month's reflection at the ranch had convinced him that a more aggressive approach was necessary. In his view, the Rumsfeld-Abizaid-Casey strategy was not working. It was certainly going to cost Republicans in the coming congressional elections. "We must succeed," said the president. "If they [the Iraqis] can't do it, we will. If the bicycle teeters, we're going to put the hand back on. We have to make damn sure we cannot fail." Bush's use of Rumsfeld's bicycle seat metaphor was deliberate. "I wanted to send a message to the team that I was thinking differently," said the president. [41]

Abizaid held firm. "Don't underestimate the sectarian problem," he told the president. "There's a sectarian line that divides the whole Arab world. It runs right through Iraq. Religion is a way of life, and so a sectarian divide can be profound." Abizaid, in a careful military way, was pointing out to the commander in chief that history might be against the democratic Iraq he was envisioning.[42]

After the meeting, Bush instructed NSC director Hadley to proceed with the review of the strategy in Iraq—the one that had been in the works since the June meeting at Camp David. "I wanted them to challenge every assumption behind our strategy and generate new options," said the president. "I soon came to view them as my personal band of warriors."[43] In effect, Bush was bypassing military leadership and substituting the NSC staff. The nitty-gritty of Iraq policy would be formulated in the White House. Bush also recognized the need for new military leadership, both on the ground in Iraq and in the Pentagon. Abizaid, Casey, and Rumsfeld were not on the president's wavelength. They wanted to leave the future of Iraq up to the Iraqis. They believed U.S. forces were an irritant that inflamed the insurgency and made the violence worse. Saddam Hussein may have been an evil man, but he held Iraq together as a secular state—perhaps the most secular in the Middle East. Now that he was gone, sectarian strife had taken over, and it was something only the Iraqis could solve.

But Bush was set on bringing Western-style democracy to Iraq. He felt the loss of American lives personally and was determined that the soldiers and marines who had been killed in Iraq must not have died in vain. He also saw a democratic Iraq as an American ally in the Middle East, analogous perhaps to South Korea in the Far East. The president was strongly supported both by Cheney and Rice, and the NSC staff was absolutely compliant. Bush hesitated to make the changes he now believed were necessary. To replace the military leadership before the election would be admitting that he had erred, and would give the Democrats an important issue. And at this point, he did not have replacements in mind.

Throughout the fall, Bush was asked repeatedly by reporters whether he contemplated any changes in Iraq. And the president consistently defended the current policy. His response at his press conference on September 15 was typical. Asked by Peter Baker, then with *The Washington Post*, what was happening in Iraq, Bush did not reveal what he was thinking.

> *Baker:* Mr. President, you've often used the phrase "stand up/stand down" to describe your policy when it comes to troop withdrawals from Iraq. . . . The Pentagon now says they've trained 294,000 Iraqi troops and expect to complete their program of training 325,000 by the end of the year. But American troops are not coming home and there are more there than there were previously. Is the goalpost moving?
>
> *Bush:* No, no, the enemy is changing tactics and we are adjusting. That's what's happening. I asked General Casey today, "Have you got what you need?" And he said, "Yes, I've got what I need."

"That's the way I will continue to conduct the war," said Bush.

> I'll listen to the generals. Maybe it's not the politically expedient thing to do . . . but you can't make decisions based upon politics. . . . And the fundamental question you have to ask is, can the President trust his commanders on the ground? . . . And I'm going to tell you, I've got great confidence in General John Abizaid and General George Casey. These are extraordinary men who understand the difficulties of the task and understand there is a delicate relationship between self-sufficiency on the Iraqis' part and the U.S. presence. . . . And so to answer your question, the policy still holds. The "stand up / stand down" still holds, and so does the policy of me listening to our commanders.[44]

When asked about Rumsfeld, the president was equally supportive. Asked at his press conference the following month whether he intended to replace the secretary of defense (the question was also asked by Peter Baker), Bush was effusive in his praise for Rumsfeld.

> I've asked him to do some difficult tasks as Secretary of Defense, one, wage war in two different theaters in this war on terror and at the same time, asked him to transform our military posture around the world

and our readiness here at home. . . . And I'm satisfied of how he had done all his jobs. He is a smart, tough, capable administrator.

Peter, the ultimate accountability rests with me. . . . If people are unhappy about it, look right at the President. I believe our generals did the job I asked them to do. They're competent, smart, capable men and women. And this country owes them a lot of gratitude and support.[45]

The president repeated the message in an Oval Office interview with several reporters on November 1, six days before the congressional elections. Seated in a wing chair in front of a table with a bowl of roses, Bush said he wanted both Rumsfeld and Cheney to remain with him until the end of his presidency. "Both of these men are doing fantastic jobs and I strongly support them," said the president.[46]

Bush was holding his cards close to his chest. The White House staff was working around the clock to fashion a new strategy in Iraq, but the president gave no hint of what was coming. Shortly before the election, Mitch McConnell, the Republican whip in the Senate, came to see Bush. McConnell's wife, Elaine Chao, was secretary of labor, and had been in the cabinet since Bush took office in 2001. The McConnells and the Bushes were close socially and the senator wanted to level with the president about the upcoming election. "Mr. President," said McConnell, "your unpopularity is going to cost us control of Congress."

"Well, Mitch, what do you want me to do about it?"

"Mr. President, bring some troops home from Iraq."

Bush declined. "Mitch, I believe our presence in Iraq is necessary to protect America, and I will not withdraw troops unless military conditions warrant." In his memoirs, Bush reflected on the meeting. "What I did not tell him was that I was seriously considering the opposite of his recommendation. Rather than pull troops out, I was on the verge of making the toughest and most unpopular decision of my presidency: deploying tens of thousands of more troops into Iraq with a new strategy, a new commander, and a mission to protect the Iraqi people and help enable the rise of democracy in the heart of the Middle East."[47]

The fact is, Rumsfeld was ready to resign. At the age of seventy-four, he was the oldest secretary of defense in American history.* He and Chao were the only two members of Bush's original cabinet still in office, and Rumsfeld had already submitted his resignation twice after the exposure of the atrocities at Abu Ghraib. He recognized that the Democrats would likely win control of at least one house of Congress, and he would become a whipping boy for those who disagreed with the administration's policy in Iraq. He also recognized that the president's views were shifting. Bush's reference to putting his hand back on the bicycle seat at the August 17 NSC meeting could not have been clearer. Shortly afterward, Rumsfeld told the president, "Maybe you need fresh eyes on the problem." Bush understood what the secretary of defense was saying.[48]

In early October, Rumsfeld indicated to his friend Cheney what he was planning. After a meeting in the Oval Office, he and Cheney walked out together talking. "The good news is that there are only 794 days left until the end of the term," said Cheney.

"Dick, there are 794 days left for you. Not for me," Rumsfeld replied.[49]

Both Bush and Rumsfeld wanted the transition to be as smooth as possible. "Don Rumsfeld is one of the true professionals who understands Washington about as well as anybody, that you serve at the pleasure of the president, and there's nothing personal," Bush told Bob Woodward.[50] The problem was there was no obvious successor. Over the years Bush had considered Fred Smith of FedEx, Condoleezza Rice, James Baker, and Senator Joe Lieberman, but they were either unavailable, as was the case with Smith, or not quite the right fit.

In late October the situation changed. Laura was out of town, and Bush was having dinner with Jack Morrison, an old chum from Andover and Yale whom he had appointed to the President's Foreign Policy Advisory Board. Bush told Morrison he was looking for a successor for

---

* General George C. Marshall was seventy when he served as Truman's secretary of defense from 1950 to 1951 during the Korean War. Henry L. Stimson, who was secretary of war during World War II, was the exception. Stimson was seventy-three when FDR appointed him in 1940 and served for five years. He retired at the age of seventy-eight.

Rumsfeld but needed someone who was both acceptable to the military and confirmable by the Senate.

"What about Bob Gates?" asked Morrison.

"How do you know Bob Gates?" Bush asked.

"I don't really. I spent a day with him a couple of weeks ago at Texas A&M and came away very impressed."[51]

Bush was surprised he hadn't thought of Gates himself. He had been his father's CIA director and was now president of Texas A&M where by all accounts he was doing a good job. Texas A&M was home to the George H. W. Bush presidential library. Indeed, the elder Bush had often spoken to George W. about Gates's leadership at the university.[52] Gates was also a member of the Baker-Hamilton Commission studying the problems in Iraq and was therefore familiar with the issues. As soon as Morrison left the White House that evening, Bush placed a telephone call to his father. "Do you think Gates would do it," he asked, "and do you think he would be good?"

"One, I think he would do it," Bush 41 replied. "Second, I think he'd be very good."[53]

Bush believed he had found an ideal replacement. In 2005, Gates had declined an offer to become the first director of national intelligence but secretary of defense might be different. Bush instructed Hadley to sound out Gates. Gates was interested. White House chief of staff Josh

Bolten followed up. The president wanted to meet with Gates as soon as possible, said Bolten. A meeting was scheduled at the ranch for Sunday, November 5. Gates drove from College Station, met White House deputy chief of staff Joe Hagin in a grocery store parking lot in McGregor, about twenty minutes from the ranch, and was clandestinely driven to the ranch, where he went to Bush's office rather than the house.

Bush arrived promptly at nine, having excused himself from Lau-

Robert Gates

ra's sixtieth birthday celebration in the main house. After exchanging pleasantries, they got down to business. Bush told Gates, "We're in the middle of war, and I need your leadership. What we have been doing is not working. We're going to change our strategy. I need a new face. Would you be interested?"[54]

Gates said he was. Bush told Gates he was thinking about a significant surge in U.S. forces in Iraq and that he intended to replace the commanders with men more amenable to the idea. According to Gates, the president also talked about his concern for Afghanistan and the challenge that Iran posed. And he told Gates he insisted on candor from his senior advisers. The two hit it off. Gates told the president he thought a surge was necessary but that it should be linked to Iraqi performance. The discussion lasted about an hour. At the end, Bush leaned forward and asked Gates if he had any more questions.

Gates said no. Bush smiled and said, "Cheney?" Gates returned the smile. Bush chuckled and said, "He is a voice, an important voice, but only one voice."[55] The president was attempting to ease whatever concerns Gates might have had. At that point he formally offered the job to Gates and Gates accepted.

Later Sunday afternoon, as he was flying back to Washington on Air Force One, Bush called Cheney to break the news. Cheney was at the vice president's home in the former Naval Observatory when the call arrived. Bush said he had decided to replace Rumsfeld as secretary of defense, had offered the job to Bob Gates, and Gates had accepted.

"I disagree with your decision," Cheney replied. "I think Don is doing a fine job. But it's your call."[56]

The president anticipated that Cheney would protest, and he let it pass. "Dick, would you like to be the one to tell Don, or should I ask Josh Bolten to make the call?" That was the way Bush operated. He was unwilling to deliver the message himself. He did not want to be the bearer of bad news or set up a possible confrontation. Whenever he replaced a senior official—Paul O'Neill, Colin Powell—he delegated the task of informing that person to someone else.

"I'll do it, Mr. President. I owe Don an awful lot and he should hear it from me."[57]

Cheney reached Rumsfeld by phone that evening. The secretary and his wife, Joyce, were having a quiet dinner with their friends Ginger and Jim Newmyer and the Newmyers' close friends, Diana and Robert McNamara. Rumsfeld excused himself to take the call.

"Don," said Cheney. "The president has decided to make a change. He wants to see you Tuesday."

"Fair enough," Rumsfeld replied. "I'll prepare a letter of resignation. It makes sense."

"We're going to lose the House of Representatives, and the next two years are going to be rough," said Cheney.

"I agree. It's not helpful for the military if I stay. Fresh eyes are a good thing."[58] Rumsfeld told Cheney that he had been considering resigning, especially if the Democrats won either the House or the Senate. "I'm just too much of a target."[59]

Tuesday, November 7, was election day. Rumsfeld met with Bush in the Oval Office at ten o'clock. As Rumsfeld recalls, the president was visibly uncomfortable. "I tried to make it easier for him." He gave Bush a single sheet of paper. It was his resignation.

> *Dear Mr. President:*
>
> *With my resignation as Secretary of Defense comes my deep appreciation to you for providing me this unexpected opportunity to serve.*
>
> *I leave with great respect for you and for the leadership you have provided during a most challenging time for our country. . . .*
>
> *It has been the highest honor of my long life to have been able to serve our country at such a crucial time in our history and to have had the privilege of working so closely with the truly amazing young men and women in uniform. . . .*
>
> *It is time to conclude my service.*
>
> Respectfully,
Donald Rumsfeld[60]

Bush was moved. "This is hard for me," said the president. "You are a pro. You're a hell of a lot better than others in this town." The president then asked about Rumsfeld's wife. "Is Joyce all right?"

"Joyce is fine. And she's ready. She even typed the letter for me."

Rumsfeld said it was evident that Bush was still concerned. "Look," he told the president. "Joyce and I are tracking with you on this."[61]

Bush and Rumsfeld talked briefly about Bob Gates and the situation in Iraq. The president did not indicate he was considering any major changes. Knowing that he was departing, Rumsfeld had sent Bush a final memorandum on Iraq the day before.* It would be his final input. There was no indication that the president had read it. Bush said he was considering bringing General Abizaid back to the White House to help coordinate the war effort, and would nominate General Casey to become Army chief of staff when his tour in Iraq ended. That was that. "After twenty minutes we stood up and shook hands."[62]

The meeting with Rumsfeld had been difficult. The congressional elections that day would be worse. The president had campaigned in eighteen states during the last five weeks of the campaign, speaking on behalf of Republican candidates. The party controlled the House 232–202, and had a 10-seat advantage in the Senate: 55 Republicans, 44 Democrats, and Independent Jim Jeffords of Vermont, who caucused

---

* Rumsfeld's November 6 memo on Iraq spells out the differences between his thinking (and that of Abizaid and Casey) and the emerging White House position. "In my view it is time for a major adjustment," said the secretary. He then listed a number of positive options that could be taken and a number he thought were undesirable. Among the positive options were:

- Conduct an accelerated draw-down of U.S. bases. We have already reduced from 110 to 55 bases. Plan to get down to 10 to 15 bases by April 2007 and 5 bases by July 2007.
- Withdraw U.S. forces from vulnerable positions—cities, patrolling, etc.
- Begin modest withdrawals of U.S. and Coalition forces (start "taking our hand off the bicycle seat"), so Iraqis know they have to pull up their socks, step up, and take responsibility for their country.
- Recast the U.S. military mission—go minimalist.

The negative options included:

- Move a large fraction of all U.S. forces into Baghdad to attempt to control it.
- Increase Brigade Combat Teams and U.S. forces in Iraq substantially.
- Set a firm withdrawal date.
- Assist in accelerating an aggressive federalism plan, moving toward three separate states—Sunni, Shia, and Kurd.

Rumsfeld's memo can be found in the Rumsfeld Papers, online.

with the Democrats. Bush had enjoyed congressional majorities for the past six years.

In his speeches, Bush painted the Democrats as weak in the war on terror—"the party of cut and run"—and determined to raise taxes. "The difference between our parties could not be clearer," he told voters in Macon, Georgia, on October 10. "If you want to keep the tax cuts we passed, vote Republican on November 7th." [63] In the final days of the campaign, the president was especially bitter about the Democratic stance on Iraq. "The Democrat[ic] goal is to get out of Iraq. The Republican goal is to win in Iraq." [64] And he enjoyed mocking House Democratic leader Nancy Pelosi.

> She said, "The president says that fighting them there"—she's talking about Iraq—"makes it less likely we will have to fight them here. The opposite is true. Because we're fighting them there, it may become more likely we will have to fight them here."

"We do not create terrorists by fighting terrorists," said Bush.

> The best way to protect you is to stay on the offense and bring the terrorists to justice wherever we find them. Our goal in Iraq is clear. It's victory.
>
> If you listen to the debate about Iraq, the Democrat[ic] plan for success, well, they don't have a plan for success. It's a serious party in the midst of a war, and they have no plan for success.[65]

The 2006 congressional election was the last political campaign in which Bush would participate actively. He enjoyed speaking to partisan crowds and lambasting the opposition. He particularly relished referring to the party of Jefferson, Jackson, and Franklin Roosevelt as the "Democrat Party." Nothing was more insulting to Democrats. Aside from the grammatical error (a noun is not an adjective), the term was contemptuous of the long heritage of the Democratic Party. It was first used by Harold Stassen in the 1940 presidential election (Stassen was Wendell Willkie's campaign manager), and has been used off and on by Republican politicians ever since, but never so much as during the Bush administration.

Republican congressional leaders like Tom DeLay and John Boehner regularly called the Democratic Party the "Democrat Party," and the GOP platform in the 2004 presidential election did so as well. The president did the same in delivering his 2007 State of the Union message to Congress.[66] Bush was well aware of how offensive the term was to Democrats, and later joked about it.* But on the campaign trail, he was consistent in his usage. That may have delighted devout Republican audiences, but it energized Democrats to exact revenge.

Indeed the Democrats did their utmost to turn the election into a national referendum on Bush and his decision to take the country to war in Iraq. Republican candidates by contrast tended to stress local issues and distance themselves from the president. On the Monday before the election, Bush flew to Pensacola, Florida, to speak at a rally for Charlie Crist, who was running to succeed Jeb as governor. Crist was scheduled to introduce the president. But he didn't show. Rather than appear with Bush, Crist chose to campaign in Jacksonville with John McCain.[67] Crist's action was not untypical. With Bush's approval rating in the low 30s, many Republican candidates saw his endorsement as the kiss of death.

Once again, Bush was out of touch with the mood of the country. Ken Mehlman, the chairman of the Republican National Committee, told the president that the Republicans were going to lose twenty-four seats in the House. Bush did not believe it. Nor did Karl Rove, who insisted the poll numbers were changing in their favor. According to Rove, recent polls in twenty key districts indicated that sixteen now favored the Republicans, and three were even. He told Bush the party would maintain its control over both the House and Senate, but with smaller majorities.[68]

---

* After the 2006 election, House Democrats invited Bush to address their caucus. The president began his speech by saying, "Now look, my diction isn't all that good. I've been accused of occasionally mangling the English language. And so I appreciate your inviting the head of the Republic party." Michael Abramowitz, "At Democratic Meeting, Bush Appeals for Cooperation," *Washington Post*, February 3, 2007.

Bush watched the election returns that evening from the family quarters in the White House. He was joined by Laura, Karl and Darby Rove, former commerce secretary Don Evans, Ken Mehlman, and Josh Bolten. Early returns from Kentucky—the first state to report—were grim. In the key third district, five-term veteran Anne Northup, a staunch supporter for whom Bush had campaigned, was going down to defeat. In nearby Indiana, where the polls also closed early, three Republican incumbents, Chris Chocola, John Hostettler, and Mike Sodrel were also going down. In New Hampshire, voters defeated both Republican incumbents, Charles Bass and Jeb Bradley. Overall, the Republicans would lose 30 seats in the House, giving the Democrats a 233–202 majority.

In the Senate, the outcome was equally devastating as six Republican incumbents were defeated. In addition to Rick Santorum in Pennsylvania and Mike DeWine in Ohio, the Republicans lost seats in Missouri, Montana, and Rhode Island. Perhaps the most telling defeat was in the normally red state of Virginia, where former navy secretary James Webb upended George Allen, a potential contender for the GOP presidential nomination in 2008. Allen, a former governor of Virginia (and son of the great NFL coach of the Los Angeles Rams and Washington Redskins, George Allen), had defeated Chuck Robb for the Senate seat in 2000, and was already planning his presidential campaign. No more. The final results gave the Democrats control of the Senate 50–49, plus Independent Bernie Sanders of Vermont, who caucused with the Democrats. Remarkably, the Democrats did not lose a single seat in either the House or Senate, making 2006 the first election in American history in which a party retained all of its congressional seats.[69]

For Bush, the personal loss was even greater. The president had campaigned personally for twenty-six candidates in October and November. Over half were defeated. Of the five senatorial candidates with whom Bush campaigned, only one survived. Politically, it was clear the president had hit rock bottom.

Exit polls confirmed that voters were primarily concerned about Bush's performance as president and the war in Iraq. But there were other issues as well. Public discontent with Congress was rampant.

Various scandals, some involving convicted lobbyist Jack Abramoff, others involving serious personal lapses, had ushered in what Democrats called a "culture of corruption." There was also discontent with Congress's lack of productivity.[70] The exit polls suggested many voters were sympathetic with traditional Democratic issues such as more accessible health care, a raise in the minimum wage, and the protection of Social Security. Many Republican candidates—and contrary to Bush's views—also antagonized Latino voters with a hard-line stance on immigration. While that might appeal to the party's base, it cost Republicans dearly in states like Arizona, where the party dropped two seats, one held by six-term incumbent John Hayworth. Finally, the Democratic campaign was exceedingly well run and well financed, led by Rahm Emanuel in the House, and Chuck Schumer in the Senate.

Bush went to bed early that evening. Mehlman had been right. Rove was wrong. The Democrats would control the 110th Congress.

CHAPTER TWENTY-ONE

Bush Takes Command

Our troops in Iraq have fought bravely. They have done everything we asked them to do. Where mistakes have been made, the responsibility rests with me.

George W. Bush

January 10, 2007

Bush was stunned by the election results, but he put on a good face. At a White House news conference the following day the president was exceptionally gracious as he called for bipartisan support. "This isn't my first rodeo," said Bush. "This is not the first time I've been in a campaign where people have expressed themselves and in different kinds of ways. But I have learned that if you focus on the big picture, which in this case, is our nation and the issues we need to work together on, you can get stuff done."

Asked by CNN White House correspondent Suzanne Malveaux how he could work with incoming House speaker Nancy Pelosi, who, as Malveaux put it, had called Bush "incompetent, a liar, the emperor with no clothes, and dangerous," the president took the high road. "I've been around politics a long time," Bush replied. "I understand when campaigns end, and I know when governing begins."

Look, people say unfortunate things at times. But if you hold
grudges in this line of work, you're never going to get anything done. . . .
This was a close election. If you look at it race by race, it was close. The
cumulative effect, however, was not too close. It was a thumping. But
nevertheless, the people expect us to work together.[1]

Old habits were hard to break. Bush repeatedly referred to the opposition as the "Democrat Party," and had difficulty admitting that
dissatisfaction with the war in Iraq had been a major factor in the
Republican defeat.

The high point of the news conference was the president's announcement that Donald Rumsfeld would be stepping down as secretary of defense to be replaced by Robert Gates. This was a surprise. One
week before, in an interview with three veteran reporters in the Oval
Office, Bush had said that he expected Cheney and Rumsfeld to remain with him for the remainder of his term. Now Rumsfeld was out.
"After a series of thoughtful conversations," said the president, "Secretary Rumsfeld and I agreed that the timing is right for new leadership
at the Pentagon. . . . Don Rumsfeld has been a superb leader during a
time of change. Yet he also appreciates the value of bringing in a fresh
perspective during a critical period in this war."

> *Q:* Does the departure of Don Rumsfeld signal a new direction in
>   Iraq?
> *President:* Well, there is certainly going to be new leadership at
>   the Pentagon. And as I mentioned in my comments, Secretary
>   Rumsfeld and I agreed that sometimes it's necessary to have a fresh
>   perspective, and Bob Gates will have a fresh perspective.

Bush was then asked by one of the reporters with whom he had met
the week before whether the timing of Rumsfeld's replacement was
related to the election results. Bush said no. He did not have a replacement lined up when he met with the reporters, said the president, and
he also "did not want to inject a major decision about this war into the
final days of the campaign."

I had been talking with Don Rumsfeld over a period of time about fresh perspective. He likes to call it fresh eyes. He himself understands that Iraq is not working well enough, fast enough. . . . And so he and I both agreed in our meeting yesterday that it was appropriate that I accept his resignation. And so the decision was made. Actually, I thought we were going to do fine yesterday [in the election]. Shows how much I know.[2]

Working with a Democratic majority in the House and Senate would prove a challenge for Bush, but his immediate concern was Iraq. The present strategy was not working. The military—Rumsfeld, Abizaid, and Casey—wanted to wind down. So did much of the public. And certainly the new Democratic leadership on Capitol Hill. Bush believed otherwise. As he saw it, to withdraw from Iraq without having established a stable democratic government would be an admission of defeat. In the president's mind, the answer was to increase U.S. forces significantly and bring order out of chaos. But to do so, the ground had to be prepared. Rumsfeld was now gone, and Gates would have fresh eyes, but the rationale for more troops had to be articulated convincingly.

At this point, Bush was very much alone. As Karen Hughes put it, "He really felt strongly that it was his sheer force of will that was holding the line between winning and losing the war. That everybody else was ready to abandon it, and that only his force of will was keeping us there."[3]

The day after the election, Bush invited Cheney, Rice, and Hadley to come upstairs to the family quarters to discuss how they might go forward. He needed support, and Cheney provided it. "Do not waver," said the vice president. Bush was relieved. He instructed Hadley and Rice to prepare a formal review of Iraq strategy. The president was not explicit about what he wanted, but it was obvious that he was considering increasing the number of American forces in Iraq.

Bush was confident he had the solution. And he appreciated the support Cheney, Rice, and Hadley provided. The following day, November 10, in a routine videoconference with Casey and Khalilzad in

Bush addresses Iraq Study Group, November 13, 2006.

Baghdad, the president's new determination was apparent. Both Casey and Khalilzad gave their usual reports, and Bush made clear his dissatisfaction with the lack of progress. According to Casey, the president was irritated and unmistakably cold. In all of their previous video-conferences, Bush had been warm and friendly. But not today. He was icy and borderline rude. "Wow," Casey said to Khalilzad afterward. "That was something. I wonder what is going to come out of this?"[4] Bush had decided to jettison the wind-down strategy that Abizaid, Casey, and Khalilzad supported, and he was dismissing their advice. "He was noticeably colder," Casey recalled.[5]

On Monday, November 13, Bush met with the Iraq Study Group, co-chaired by former secretary of state James Baker and former Democratic congressman Lee Hamilton of Indiana, who during his time in Congress had chaired the House Committee on Foreign Affairs. The Study Group had been created by Congress on March 15, 2006, to assess the situation in Iraq and provide policy recommendations. It was a blue-ribbon, bipartisan panel—five Republicans, five Democrats—composed of senior public figures whose recommendations would be difficult to ignore.* Bush regarded the panel warily. He instructed the

---

*   In addition to Baker, the Republican members of the Study Group were Edwin Meese, Sandra Day O'Connor, Robert Gates, and former senator Alan Simpson. Democrats were Hamil-

administration to cooperate by providing the necessary support, but he sensed that the ultimate purpose of the Study Group was to provide a face-saving strategy for leaving Iraq.[6]

Bush spoke to the Study Group authoritatively. "He was not seeking advice from us," said William Perry. "He was telling us what his view of the war was. The president held forth on his views on how important the war was, and how it was tough, how we had to stay together. It was a Churchillian type of thing. Blood, sweat, and tears and all that. . . . It is quite clear that he had this image of a great global struggle, and he was presiding over it, and Iraq was just one element of that, and that the people who were wavering on Iraq did not see the big picture the way he saw it."[7]

For Bush, the war in Iraq was a test of will. "If you don't think this is an ideological struggle, then my comments are wasted," he told the Study Group. The president put the blame on al Qaeda. "They are fomenting sectarian violence. . . . Our job is to find them and kill them." Asked by Lee Hamilton what constituted victory, Bush replied, "The word that captures what we want to achieve is victory. We want an ally in the war on terror, a government that can govern, sustain, and defend itself."

The president appeared deeply committed. "The consequences of defeat would be disaster for future generations. You won't know the moment when you achieve victory. Victory is when the government is functioning, when there is an oil law, when the army is capable of stability. That is a signal of progress. An end to violence, an end to sectarian violence—that won't happen." Members of the Study Group were struck by the fact that Bush never defined what it meant to win and never laid out what the United States ultimately intended. When Edwin Meese, who had been attorney general under Ronald Reagan, asked the president about reconstruction, Bush replied, "We've pretty well run our string on reconstruction. Congress won't spend any more."

---

ton, Leon Panetta, Vernon Jordan, former secretary of defense William Perry, and Chuck Robb. When Gates was appointed secretary of defense, he was replaced on the Study Group by Lawrence Eagleburger.

Asked by Chuck Robb if he needed more troops in Iraq, the president replied that if the commanders recommended it, he would be inclined to accept it.

"I am as frustrated as the American people," Bush concluded.

> If I didn't think it was worth it, we would leave. We need to win an ideological victory. I am not making excuses, but we cannot improve in the short term. . . . Your report can make a significant contribution here, if you deal with the tendencies toward isolationism in this country. We need to deal with a psychology of engagement in international affairs and position this country so that it remains a leader. The United States has to take the lead on all these tough issues, or it just won't happen.[8]

Bush left the meeting convinced the Iraq Study Group was going to recommend some form of American withdrawal. That was why it had been created, and Baker and Hamilton were going to follow through. To counter the Study Group's expected recommendation, and to swing public opinion, the president needed his own study report supporting a surge in troop strength. The instructions he had given to Hadley and Rice now became crucial. He needed support, and he needed it as soon as possible.

To prepare the way, an unidentified White House spokesman briefed the press. The following day, *The Washington Post* carried a front-page article headlined "Bush Initiates Iraq Policy Review Separate from Baker's Group." Written by Robin Wright, the *Post* article noted that the decision by the president "changes the dynamics of what happens next to U.S. policy deliberations. The administration will have its own working document as well as recommendations from the independent bipartisan commission to consider as it struggles to prevent further deterioration in Iraq." As Wright noted, "the White House review would provide the president with alternatives so that he would feel less pressure to adopt the recommendations of the Iraq Study Group."[9]

Bush was convinced that only by increasing U.S. forces in Iraq could defeat be avoided. He was supported by the NSC staff, who characterized it as a policy to "double down."* But before he could adopt such a policy, or announce it publicly, the president had to bring the rest of the administration on board. That would not be easy. The review group he established was divided. Condi Rice and the State Department representatives advocated reducing the American presence in Iraq and adopting "a more traditional state-to-state relationship." Vice President Cheney's office proposed backing the Shiites and Kurds and forgetting about the Sunnis. That was dubbed "the 80 percent solution," reflecting the fact that the Shiites and Kurds constituted 80 percent of Iraq's population. Representatives of the military services preferred to continue the strategy of Abizaid and Casey: "Leave to win." The Defense Department's civilian leadership agreed: "Accelerate the transition to self-reliance." And the intelligence community waffled. "No approach stands out as clearly preferable to the others, and all entail significant risks and dangers to the United States."[10]

It was in this context that Bush assembled his principal advisers at five o'clock the Sunday after Thanksgiving. Perhaps to encourage informality and the free exchange of ideas, Bush decided to hold the meeting in the White House Solarium—a cozy setting on the third floor of the executive mansion with sweeping views of the nation's capital. Eisenhower had often used it when he met with his senior advisers during the Cold War, Clinton had prepared for his testimony in the Monica Lewinsky investigation there, and Bush hoped the informal setting would be conducive to arriving at a consensus.

The president was disappointed. As Rice observed afterward, "the discussion was raucous and intense but led to no final consensus."[11] The meeting began with a summary of conditions in Iraq by J. D. Crouch, deputy director of the National Security Council. Crouch focused on

---

* The concept of a surge traces to a position paper prepared by former Navy Captain William J. Luti, the senior director for defense on the NSC staff. Entitled "Changing the Dynamics in Iraq," it was presented to Hadley on October 11, 2006. Luti suggested the United States could "surge" five additional brigades to Iraq to maintain order in Baghdad. In addition to increasing the number of U.S. forces in Iraq, the paper also recommended increasing the overall size of the Army and Marine Corps. For a discussion, see Bob Woodward, *The War Within: A Secret White House History, 2006–2008* (New York: Simon & Schuster, 2008), 170–71.

past misconceptions. The president and the White House had assumed that political progress would diminish the violence. The opposite was true. Until the violence was brought under control, there would be no political progress. The administration had assumed that the majority of Iraqis supported coalition efforts to bring democracy to Iraq. Iraqis were increasingly disillusioned with coalition efforts. Finally, the administration had been wrong about the interest of other countries in the region in a stable Iraq, about the ability of the Iraqi security forces to handle the problem, and about the possibility of engaging in dialogue with insurgent elements. None of these assumptions was correct. The question was what to do now. Summarizing what he called an "emerging consensus," Crouch said the ultimate goal was still to "accelerate the transfer of security responsibility to the Iraqis," but to do so they should "consider a significant surge in U.S. forces." [12]

In the discussion that followed, Rice was skeptical of a surge. "What if we can't do anything about the violence with more American forces?" asked Rice. Rumsfeld, who remained secretary pending Gates's confirmation, said, "The Iraqis need to pull up their socks." [13] General Peter Pace, chairman of the Joint Chiefs, was also unconvinced. From the military point of view, he doubted if the American forces could pull it off. [14] The discussion lasted for two hours. Bush mostly listened. At the end he said he would take the views expressed into account and would announce his decision in mid-December. The president had his work cut out. A surge was still very much just an idea on the drawing board. There was little administration support.

Bush was dejected. At this point, the only support for a surge came from the White House staff; Stephen Hadley, his assistants on the NSC; and Josh Bolten. These were people who understood the president's thinking and were eager to please him. But they had little knowledge of the situation on the ground. Rice and the State Department, the chairman of the Joint Chiefs, and the uniformed services still wanted to leave Iraq as soon as possible. Bush was not deterred. He was commander in chief and the final decision would be his. The day after meeting with his advisers, the president flew to Estonia and then Latvia for a NATO summit meeting. When the summit concluded, he flew to

Amman, Jordan, to meet with Iraqi prime minister Nouri al-Maliki. If Bush was going to double down, he needed to be sure of Maliki's support. Before leaving Latvia, Bush tipped his hand. Speaking at the University of Riga, the president said he was prepared to make changes in Iraq. "But there is one thing I am not going to do. I'm not going to pull our troops off the battlefield before the mission is complete." [15]

Maliki was waiting for the president when he arrived in Amman. With Casey's help, the prime minister had prepared a plan by which the Iraqis would take control of maintaining order in Baghdad. Bush was impressed. "I knew his army and police were not ready for such a major undertaking. What mattered was that Maliki recognized the problem of sectarian violence and was showing a willingness to lead." [16]

Bush asked to speak with Maliki privately. Only their translators remained. For the first time, the president mentioned the possibility of a surge. He laid his cards on the table. "The political pressure to abandon Iraq is enormous," Bush told the prime minister, "but I am willing to resist that pressure if you are willing to make some hard choices. I'm willing to commit tens of thousands of additional American troops to help you retake Baghdad. But you need to give me certain assurances." [17]

Maliki was enthusiastic. Bush then ticked off a number of requirements. There must be no political interference with military operations, Iraqi forces had to treat Shiite and Sunni militants evenhandedly, and, as the situation improved, Maliki had to address the problem of political reconciliation among Shiites, Sunnis, and Kurds. The prime minister agreed. "On every point, Maliki gave me his word that he would follow through." [18]

On the flight back to Washington, Bush breathed a sigh of relief. With Maliki on board, a surge now seemed feasible. There were risks, of course. It would be unpopular initially, casualties might be high, and the fighting would be difficult. But Bush believed he had found the solution. "The surge was our best chance, maybe our last chance, to accomplish our objectives in Iraq." [19]

Other pieces were falling into place. After the meeting with Maliki, Rice went to a conference on the shore of the Dead Sea in Jordan with the foreign ministers of the Gulf States, Saudi Arabia, and Egypt.

The New York Times had recently published two front-page articles by David Sanger suggesting that the Baker-Hamilton Iraq Study Group was going to recommend a drawdown of American troops in Iraq.[20] Each of the foreign ministers implored Rice not to do so. They were terrified that if the United States left Iraq, all Sunni states would become vulnerable. "It hurts me as an Arab to say this," the Egyptian foreign minister told Rice, "but you need to increase your presence and finish the job. We will all be done if you don't."[21] From that point on, Rice became more prepared to accept the surge that Bush was planning.

At seven o'clock on the morning of December 6, the ten members of the Baker-Hamilton Iraq Study Group filed into the White House Cabinet Room to deliver their report to the president. Subtitled *The Way Forward—A New Approach*, the document reflected the work of a unanimous panel. The first line of the report was devastating. "The situation in Iraq is grave and deteriorating." The ninety-six-page report made seventy-nine recommendations as to how the situation could be improved but the bottom line was clear: the United States should gradually draw down its forces and turn responsibility over to the Iraqis. It was an endorsement of the Rumsfeld-Pace-Abizaid-Casey strategy, and was intended to encourage Bush to withdraw. "A responsible exit," in the words of co-chairman Lee Hamilton.[22] The report also recommended opening diplomatic discussions with Iran and Syria as well as intensifying efforts to resolve the Israeli-Palestinian dispute. Finally, in a sop to Chuck Robb, the report provided the president with limited support for a brief surge if the ultimate purpose was to facilitate the withdrawal of U.S. forces.

> Because of the importance of Iraq to our regional security goals and our ongoing fight against al-Qaeda, we considered proposals to make a substantial increase (100,000 to 200,000) in the number of U.S. troops in Iraq. We rejected this course because we do not believe that the needed levels are available for a sustained deployment. Further, adding more American troops could conceivably worsen those aspects of the security problem that are fed by the view that the U.S. presence is intended to

be a long-term "occupation." *We could, however, support a short-term redeployment or surge of American combat forces to stabilize Baghdad, or to speed up the training and equipping mission, if the U.S. commander in Iraq determines that such steps would be effective.*[23] (Emphasis added.)

Each member of the Study Group spoke briefly. Baker said, "There is no magic formula that will solve the problems of Iraq. But to give the Iraqi government a chance to succeed, United States policy must be focused more broadly than on military strategy alone or on Iraq alone." Co-chairman Hamilton followed. "We do not know if it can be turned around, but we think we have an obligation to try; and if the recommendations that we have made are effectively implemented, there is at least a chance that you can see a stable government in Iraq."[24]

The unanimity of the Study Group was extraordinary. Former senator Alan Simpson (R., Wy.) told the president that the recommendations were not intended to embarrass him. Leon Panetta said the report represented the work of five Democrats and five Republicans. "This report gives you at least the opportunity to try to begin to repair the divisions that have taken place and try to unify the country."[25] There was no mention of the goal of establishing democracy in Iraq, no allusion to "victory," or the centrality of Iraq in the war on terror. As Congressman Frank Wolf (R., Va.) noted, "There is almost a biblical thing about wise elderly people. They can speak the truth."[26]*

Bush listened to each speaker, asked an occasional question, and at eight o'clock, one hour after the session began, welcomed the press into the Cabinet Room and made a formal statement.

"I have just received the Iraq Study Group report, prepared by a distinguished panel of our fellow citizens," said the president. "This report gives a very tough assessment of the situation in Iraq. It is a report that brings some really very interesting proposals, and we will take every proposal seriously, and we will act in a timely fashion."

Bush had already decided upon the direction of march. He was

---

* Congressman Wolf was the author of the original congressional resolution that established the Study Group on March 15, 2006.

going to order a surge. But he utilized the report to seek bipartisan support. "The country, in my judgment, is tired of the pure political bickering that happens in Washington, and they understand that on this important issue of war and peace, it is best for our country to work together."

> This report will give us all an opportunity to find common ground, for the good of the country, not for the good of the Republican party or the Democrat[ic] party, but for the good of the country.

It was the president's strongest appeal for bipartisan support since the invasion of Iraq three years ago. And he lavished praise on the Study Group members. "I can't thank you enough," said the president. "You could have been doing a lot of other things. You could have had a lot more simple life than to allow your government to call you back into service, and you've made a vital contribution to the country. . . . We applaud your work. I will take it very seriously, and we'll act on it in a timely fashion."[27]

Press coverage was overwhelmingly favorable. To many it seemed as though a major change in direction might be at hand. "Iraq Panel Proposes Major Strategy Shift," said *The Washington Post*. *The New York Times* carried a front-page headline, "Panel Urges Basic Shift in U.S. Policy in Iraq." Tim Russert of NBC News called the report "powerful, passionate, bipartisan, and unanimous. I think it is not only a wakeup call for the Bush White House, but the whole country."[28] On the other hand, Washington's neoconservative community was appalled. "It's a deeply irresponsible report," said *Weekly Standard* editor Bill Kristol on Fox News. "The key is to win the war, not to have everyone sitting around Washington feeling good that 'Hey, we've got a bipartisan document.'"[29]

Bush finessed the Study Group report. Having lunch with James Baker later that day, the president asked Baker, "Can we get to where you want us to be without doing something in the meantime?" It was obvious to Baker that Bush was planning to increase American forces in Iraq, at least temporarily. He told Bush to consult page 73 of the report. Bush later said, "He's the guy who reminded me of whatever page it [the surge] was on."[30] For Bush, there was no question at this point but that a surge was the answer. Maliki was agreeable, Rice was coming around, and Gates had been confirmed by the Senate as secretary of defense. He would take office on December 18. But the military was not yet convinced, and their support was essential. Indeed, on December 8, two days after the Study Group report, Rumsfeld sent Bush a memo that restated the views of the senior military command to "accelerate the transition" in Iraq—exactly the opposite of what Bush desired.

According to the memo, which had the approval of the chairman and the Joint Chiefs of Staff, United States forces in Iraq should shift their main effort to support Iraqi Security Forces, reduce the number of U.S. bases from fifty-five to twenty, and "formally conclude" its mission by December 2007. "No increase in the level of U.S. forces can substitute for successful diplomacy in the region and getting the Iraqi government to act."[31] This was exactly what Bush did not want to hear.

Despite the military's objections, Bush remained convinced that a surge was essential. To buttress the case, NSC director Hadley organized a second seminar for the president on December 11, similar to the one at Camp David in June. Five speakers appeared, led by Professor Eliot Cohen, a leading neoconservative intellectual of the Johns Hopkins School of Advanced International Studies, and retired General Jack Keane, former Army vice chief of staff who was now at the American Enterprise Institute.* The purpose of the seminar was to restate the arguments for sending additional troops to Iraq. Cohen led off with a vigorous attack on current policy and suggested there had been no accountability for failure. "One of the biggest problems is leadership," said Cohen. "I have the greatest respect for General Casey, but you need different leadership in Iraq," he told Bush.

"So who would you put in?" asked the president.

"Petraeus," said Cohen, a reference to Lieutenant General David

---

* The other participants were retired generals Barry McCaffrey and Wayne Downing, and Professor Stephen Biddle.

Petraeus, who was commanding the Army's Combined Arms Center at Fort Leavenworth and was a darling of the neoconservative establishment.[32]*

Retired General Keane followed Cohen and gave an equally vehement presentation. "Time is running out," he told the president. "All of the recommendations that are being made in and around town—and also by the Iraq Study Group—none of these actually solve the crisis." The answer was to adopt a counterinsurgency approach to protect the population, and that would require more American combat troops. "Don't let people tell you that this is going to break the back of the Army and the Marine Corps, because it will not. These forces are available. We can extend tours." Keane agreed with Cohen that Casey should be replaced and that Petraeus was the best alternative. "If you are going to put new generals in, then hold them accountable for their performance. And tell them you're holding them accountable and you expect them to be successful."[33]

Bush was buoyed by Keane's presentation. If he was going to over-

---

*   David Petraeus enjoyed a mixed reputation. He was well regarded by many, particularly in the journalistic community, but disdained by others, especially in the military establishment, who regarded him as too blatantly ambitious—a Republican Wesley Clark. In 2004, he was passed over for promotion to lieutenant general by the military. But on May 5 of that year, he was promoted to the three-star rank by recommendation to the president by the secretary of defense, and assigned to head the Office of Security Transition—Iraq. (Personal interview with Donald Rumsfeld, September 22, 2014.) From that point, his career took off.

[Personal note: After being cashiered as director of the CIA following the exposure of his extramarital affair with Paula Broadwell, Petraeus invited me to dinner at the Cosmos Club in Washington. Before I left home that evening, my wife told me not to mention Eisenhower's affair with Kay Summersby. As the dishes were being cleared after the first course, Petraeus raised the subject. "How did Ike handle the Kay Summersby affair?" Much of the rest of the meal was devoted to my explaining how Eisenhower had put the affair behind him and successfully run for president in 1952.

The reason for Petraeus's interest was evident. Before his dismissal from the CIA, he was being touted as a replacement for Shirley Tilghman, who was stepping down as president of Princeton. The alumni rumor circuit was buzzing with the possibility. And as president of Princeton, he would be in an ideal position to seek the Republican presidential nomination in 2016, just as Eisenhower had done in 1952 when he was president of Columbia. At the end of the meal I asked General Petraeus whether the Obama administration had taken advantage of his affair to cut his head off. He smiled, but did not reply.]

rule the military and order a surge, it helped to have the Army's former vice chief of staff leading the way. "Keane is great as a validator,"
Hadley said afterward, and it was clear that Keane had now become
a front man for the administration. The military command structure,
well aware of Keane's political maneuvering, was apoplectic. "I guess
you have to resign from the military and go to work for AEI if you
are going to give military advice to the president," said General Abizaid.[34]

The following day, Tuesday, December 12, Bush conferred once
more with Casey and Abizaid. Both generals were strongly opposed to
a surge and continued to urge an accelerated transfer of responsibility
to the Iraqis. Casey told the president that additional troops might have
a temporary effect but would "extend the time it takes to pass security
responsibility to the Iraqis." A surge would also increase American casualties and would not have a decisive effect on the situation. As Casey
saw it, the core problem in Iraq was reconciling the interests of the
different ethnic and sectarian factions, and he had sufficient troops to
accomplish that.

> I believe that I had asked for the troops I needed to accomplish our
> objectives, and that if the prime minister delivered on his pledges to the
> president to allow our forces and the I[raq] S[ecurity] F[orces] to operate
> freely without political interference, we would bring security to Bagh-
> dad by the summer. I felt that additional troops beyond that would risk
> introducing them into a very confusing and difficult operational envi-
> ronment without a plan for how their introduction would contribute to
> the accomplishment of our strategic objectives. I remained adamantly
> opposed to that.[35]

Casey realized that the president was not listening. Abizaid shared
Casey's view. At one point the president told Abizaid, "I know, you're
going to tell me you're against the surge." When Abizaid said yes, Bush
turned away. In closing, he defended the surge. It would help keep a
lid on, said the president. "It buys time for the Maliki government and
the Iraqi Security Forces. It also helps here at home, since for many the

measure of success is reduction in violence." Abizaid and Casey made no reply.[36]

Bush needed military support. As commander in chief he could order a surge. But it would be far better if the military high command agreed. On Wednesday, December 13, the president went to the Pentagon to meet with the Joint Chiefs of Staff. "I opened by telling them I was there to hear their opinions and ask their advice."[37] For the president to visit the Joint Chiefs in their lair at the Pentagon was out of the ordinary. Bush had done so immediately after 9/11, but presidents traditionally called the generals to the White House if there was something to discuss. By visiting the generals on their home turf, Bush was hoping to impress them with his determination and the importance he attached to the issue. He realized it was going to be a tough sell, and so he took Cheney with him. The vice president could be the heavy. Bush had already decided upon a surge, and he wanted to bring the generals along.

General Peter Pace began the discussion by saying the chiefs believed that American forces in Iraq should shift to a more advisory and training role, in effect accelerating the transition to Iraqi control. Bush said he understood. "The question is when do you shift to advising. You don't want to do it too early." Pace said he thought Iraqi troops could handle it. "We need to get the Iraqi Security Forces in charge."

At that point Cheney jumped in. "We're betting the farm on Iraqi Security Forces," said the vice president. "Wouldn't it be better to make a push with our own forces to get it done?" Cheney then articulated the consequences of losing in Iraq and how it would destabilize the region. "Suddenly it will be very dangerous to be a friend of the United States. There's an awful lot riding on this."[38]

The president went around the table. Each chief spoke.* They had concerns about Maliki. They worried that sending more troops to Iraq would diminish the ability to respond to possible crises elsewhere, and

---

* In addition to Pace, the Joint Chiefs included Admiral Michael Mullen, chief of naval operations; General Peter Schoomaker, Army chief of staff; General Michael Moseley, Air Force chief of staff; and General James Conway, Marine Corps commandant.

they thought other government agencies should be doing more in Iraq. The most articulate spokesman for the chiefs was the Army chief of staff, General Peter Schoomaker. Schoomaker, a veteran of special operations, had been brought back from retirement by Rumsfeld in 2003 to succeed Eric Shinseki as chief of staff and had presided over the lengthy deployment of U.S. forces in Iraq and Afghanistan—the multiple tours, the retention and recruiting problems that entailed, the toll on equipment, and the casualties.

Schoomaker questioned whether a surge could be mounted without calling up more National Guard and Reserve units. He also questioned whether a surge would bring the level of violence down, noting there had been a number of troop increases in the past, usually before Iraqi elections, and the violence had not subsided. And if it would not transform the situation, why do it? "I don't think you have the time to surge and generate enough force for this thing to continue to go," Schoomaker told Bush.

The president was offended. He saw the general's comment as a political jab. "I am the president," Bush told Schoomaker. "I've got the time. Thanks very much for the political advice. But I will take care of the politics. That's my job."[39]

"Fine, Mr. President," Schoomaker replied. "You're the president." But he did not back off. "I'm concerned this is going to break the Army." A surge of five brigades, which the administration was planning, some 25,000 men, would actually involve fifteen brigades, said Schoomaker. Five in Iraq whose tours would be extended, another five whose rotation would have to be accelerated, and another five to take their place in line.

Bush was getting hot under the collar. "Let me tell you what's going to break the Army," he replied. "What's going to break the Army is a defeat like we had in Vietnam that broke the Army for a generation." Looking directly at Schoomaker, the president said, "Pete, you don't agree with me, do you?"

"No, I don't agree with you," Schoomaker replied. "I just don't see it. I just don't. But I know right now it's going to be fifteen brigades. And how we're going to get those brigades I don't know. This is going to require more than we can generate. You're stressing the force, Mr. President, and these kids just see deployments to Iraq or Afghanistan for the indefinite future."

"We have to send a signal," Bush replied. The president recognized that the military was not on board, and that his presence at the Pentagon had not convinced them. He also accepted the possibility that Schoomaker had a legitimate point. If he was going to order a surge, the Army and the Marine Corps might need more men. To take the sting out of the exchange, Bush said he would ask Congress to increase the size of the Army and the Marine Corps. That should alleviate the pressure. He also said he would increase the number of civilians in Iraq.[40]

Meeting with reporters at the Pentagon immediately afterward, Bush said, "Today I heard some opinions that mean a lot to me, and these are opinions from those that wear the uniform. These generals have spent a lot of time thinking about this issue. . . . And it was a fascinating discussion we had. These are smart people and capable people and people whose judgment I listen to. And at the appropriate time, I will stand up in front of the nation and say, 'Here's where we are headed.'"[41] The upshot of his meeting with the chiefs was that Bush recognized he needed more time. He had planned to announce the surge in mid-December, but the opposition of the Joint Chiefs forced him to delay. He would wait for Gates to assume his duties, and he hoped the military would come around.

Despite Bush's courtship, the Joint Chiefs remained unconvinced. The day after meeting with the president, General Schoomaker testified on Capitol Hill before the Commission on the National Guard and Reserve, and said openly that "the Army will break under the strain of war-zone rotations." Schoomaker voiced skepticism about an additional infusion of U.S. ground troops into Iraq, and noted that his colleagues on the Joint Chiefs agreed. Afterward he told reporters, "We should not surge without a purpose, and that purpose should be measurable and get us something."[42]

For Bush, the challenge was clear. He was determined to bring the Joint Chiefs on board. And it was now apparent that the only means to do so involved asking Congress to increase the size of the Army and Marine Corps. On December 19, the president invited several reporters from *The Washington Post* into the Oval Office and confirmed that he would support a force increase. "We need to reset our military," said the president. "I'm inclined to believe that we do need to increase our troops—the Army, the Marines. And I talked about this to Secretary Gates [Gates was sworn in as secretary the day before], and he is going to spend some time talking to the folks in the building, come back with a recommendation to me about how to proceed forward on this idea."[43]

Bush offered no specifics, but White House officials later said the administration was preparing plans to increase the nation's permanent active duty military by as many as seventy thousand additional troops. This was an expensive proposition. According to Army figures, every additional ten thousand soldiers cost $1.2 billion a year. Since 9/11, Congress had approved over $500 billion for the wars in Afghanistan and Iraq, and the administration was already asking for a supplemental $100 billion in military funding. That exceeded the total cost of the Vietnam War, which, adjusted for inflation, cost $549 billion.[44]

Bush also confirmed to the *Post* reporters that he was considering a short-term surge in Iraq, which the generals had been resisting. The president said he did not interpret the Democratic victories in the congressional elections as a mandate to leave Iraq but as a call to find new ways to make the mission succeed. He also disavowed his pre-election boast that we were winning in Iraq. "We're not winning," said the president, but "we're not losing."[45]

For Bush to advocate an increase in the size of the Army and Marine Corps meant that he was reversing what had been administration policy for the last six years. The president had favored a leaner military. When John Kerry proposed an increase of 40,000 troops during the 2004 campaign, Bush had dismissed it. As recently as June the president had publicly rejected adding more troops because the restructuring that Rumsfeld had presided over "is enabling our military to get more war-fighting capability from current end strength."[46] Now, to bring the Chiefs along, that policy was being abandoned.

Bush also recognized that personnel shifts were necessary. Gates had replaced Rumsfeld, and the new secretary was supportive of a surge. But Abizaid, Casey, and Schoomaker remained opposed. They had to be replaced. The president did not want to make it obvious that he was relieving those who disagreed. Instead, he found face-saving measures to replace the high command. Abizaid, who had been at Central Command since the inception of the war on terror, first as deputy to Tommy Franks, then as his successor, was offered the position of director of national intelligence in Washington. Many would see that as a promotion. Abizaid chose to retire instead. Casey had been in command in Iraq ever since he replaced Ricardo Sanchez in May of 2004. He was due for reassignment. Pete Schoomaker, who had come out of retirement to become Army chief of staff, was nearing the end of his four-year term. Bush decided to kill two birds with one stone. Schoomaker would be allowed to go back into retirement, and Casey would be named to succeed him as chief of staff. And to replace Casey, the president would name Petraeus. In effect, the president would be fielding a new team. Those who had opposed the surge would be out, and Casey as chief of staff could contribute his considerable administrative skills to the war effort from Washington.

Casey was not expecting to leave Iraq until spring. Schoomaker's term did not expire until summer. To expedite the changeover, Bush decided to send Gates to Iraq to break the news to Casey. He also wanted Gates to examine the situation in Iraq and report his assessment. The secretary departed Washington on December 19—the day after he was sworn in.

Gates remained in Iraq three days. What he found was disconcerting. Both Maliki and Kurdish leader Jalal Talabani were opposed to a surge. An influx of more American troops ran counter to their expectations of an Iraqi takeover and would have a negative effect on public opinion. Why enlarge the American footprint? Abizaid and Casey were equally opposed. They could take two brigades if necessary, but not five. To do so would undermine much of what had been accomplished. Both also worried how the additional forces could be supported. Peter Pace, who accompanied Gates, agreed. If there was to be a surge, it should be limited to 10,000 troops.[47]

Gates arrived back in Washington on December 23, and the following morning went to Camp David to brief the president. Bush and his family were spending Christmas at the presidential retreat. Gates said the commanders in Iraq were convinced that it was important to turn security responsibilities over to the Iraqis. "I believe we are at a pivot point," said Gates. The Iraqis, he said, appeared to be ready to take over security responsibilities with strong U.S. support. Maliki was "very queasy" about a surge because it was counter to Iraqi expectations. And if there was a surge, the American commanders did not want more than 10,000 men, two brigades. "It would be difficult to resource a more aggressive approach . . . without imposing it on an Iraqi government clearly reluctant to see a large increase in the footprint of U.S. forces in Iraq. Forcing it on a balky Iraqi government would undermine much of what has been accomplished over the past two years." Gates pointed out that a redeployment of troops already in Iraq would be more acceptable to the Maliki government.

Gates concluded by reminding the president that the major concern was the pivot point—the turning over of responsibility to the Iraqis. "As they gain confidence and show success, we can begin to stand down. Ultimately, Pete Pace, John Abizaid, George Casey and I believe we probably have enough U.S. forces and Iraqi capability in place to avoid a catastrophe. The worst case is that we continue to make very little progress."[48]

Bush was disappointed with Gates's report. But he did not dismiss it. The question of a surge was no longer in doubt. What had not been decided was its size. The military now seemed ready to accept two brigades plus two Marine battalions that could be sent to Anbar province. Bush's National Security Council staff, the vice president, and Bush himself favored five brigades. The issue came to a head at a meeting of the NSC at the ranch in Crawford on December 28. When Gates presented General Casey's two-brigade proposal, Bush shot it down. "No, I am going to commit five brigades," said the president. "If I go to the American people and say I am going to commit two and more if I need it, what I am really telling them is I don't know what I'm doing."[49] As commander in chief, Bush had considered Gates's report over Christ-

mas and decided to reject it. He said he would call Maliki and ascertain
the prime minister's support for the surge. "Maliki needs to make clear
he wants coalition forces and help," said the president.[50]

Bush was in command at the meeting. He had wrestled with the
decision and was satisfied with his conclusion. The commander in
chief had decided that it would be five brigades. Bush instructed Rice
to increase civilian resources in Iraq, and said he was going to recommend that Congress increase the size of the Army and Marine Corps
by ninety thousand troops. That was twenty thousand more than the
services expected. At the end of the meeting the president announced
his changes in the batting order. General David Petraeus would succeed Casey in Iraq, Casey would succeed Schoomaker as Army chief of
staff, and Zalmay Khalilzad, the American ambassador in Baghdad,
would become ambassador to the U.N. Bush also said that General
Abizaid was retiring and would be replaced, but his replacement had
not yet been chosen.* The president was ordering a five-brigade surge
in Iraq and fielding a new team to conduct it.

After the meeting, Bush spoke briefly to the press at the ranch. "I'm
making good progress toward coming up with a plan that we think
will help us achieve our objective," said the president. "As I think about
this plan, I always have our troops in mind. There's nobody more important in this global war on terror than the men and women who
wear the uniform. . . . As we head into the new year, my thoughts are
with them."[51]

Bush recognized what needed to be done. On the morning of January 4, the president held a private videoconference with Maliki. Other
than interpreters, no aides were present. "A lot of people here don't
think we can succeed," Bush told the prime minister. "I'll put my neck

---

* On January 3, Gates recommended Admiral William J. "Fox" Fallon to the president to
head Central Command. Fallon was the commander of Pacific Command and a seasoned combat veteran. He had flown combat missions in Vietnam, commanded a carrier wing during the
first Gulf War and a naval battle group during Bosnia. He had also served as vice chief of naval
operations and then as commander of the Atlantic Fleet. Gates believed that Petraeus needed
a strong hand to guide him, and he thought Fallon would provide that. Robert Gates, *Duty:
Memoirs of a Secretary at War* (New York: Alfred A. Knopf, 2014), 47.

out if you put out yours."[52] Maliki agreed. He would support the surge. At a press conference that afternoon with visiting German chancellor Angela Merkel, the president was asked about his conversation with Maliki. "You spoke for nearly two hours today with Iraq's prime minister. Do you both agree now on the need to send more U.S. troops to Iraq to deal with the rising violence?"

"I did have a good conversation with Prime Minister Maliki," Bush replied. "It did last nearly two hours. . . . One thing I was looking for was will—to determine whether or not he had the will necessary to do the hard work to protect his people. And I told him, 'You show the will, we will help you.' "[53]

The day after speaking with Maliki, Bush officially announced his command reshuffling. "I am pleased to accept the recommendations of Secretary Gates for several key positions in our nation's armed forces," said the president. "General George Casey has been a strong and effective commander of the multinational force in Iraq. I look forward to working with him in his new role as chief of staff of the United States Army. General Casey will succeed General Peter Schoomaker, who has done an outstanding job in helping transform the U.S. Army to confront the challenges of the 21st century. I wish General Schoomaker all the best as he retires from active duty after a distinguished career."

Bush then announced that Lieutenant General David Petraeus would be succeeding Casey in Iraq. "General Petraeus is a soldier of vision and determination. . . . I am confident General Petraeus has the right experience, leadership skills, and judgment to be an outstanding commander of M[ulti] N[ational] F[orce]—I[raq]." The president concluded by saying that Admiral William Fallon would be succeeding General John Abizaid at Central Command. Abizaid, said Bush, "has earned the respect and admiration of a grateful nation, and his service is a model for those who wear our country's uniform. As he retires, I express my deep appreciation for all he has done for America."[54] Bush was generous and appreciative to those being replaced. What was important was that a new team take the field, and that would now happen.

On January 6, Maliki obliged the president by announcing his support for the surge. Speaking to an Iraqi television audience to commemorate Iraq Army Day, the prime minister said coalition forces would be providing additional backing for the Iraqi army as it undertook a new security plan to bring order to Baghdad. "The Baghdad security strategy will not be a shelter to the outlaws regardless of their political or religious affiliation, and we shall punish anyone who thwarts the strategy or presses their sectarian or partisan agenda. . . . Let's fold up the black past and work together to build a free, democratic, and diverse Iraq without discrimination or marginalization."[55]

On January 10, the president announced the surge to the nation. Speaking from the White House Library at nine p.m., Bush took personal responsibility for past failures. "Where mistakes have been made, the responsibility rests with me." The president said he had thought the Iraqi elections in 2005 would be a turning point, that the violence would end, and the troops could be brought home. The opposite occurred. The destruction of the Golden Mosque of Samarra by Sunni extremists unleashed "a vicious cycle of sectarian violence that continues today."

"It is clear that we need to change our strategy in Iraq," said Bush. The most pressing need was to reestablish security, especially in Baghdad. "Eighty percent of Iraq's sectarian violence occurs within thirty miles of the capital." The president said the Iraqi government was going to commit eighteen army brigades to restore order in Baghdad, but they needed help.

> This will require increasing American force levels. So I have committed more than 20,000 additional American troops to Iraq. The vast majority of them, five brigades, will be deployed to Baghdad. These troops will work alongside Iraqi units and be embedded in their formations. Our troops will have a well-defined mission: to help Iraqis clear and secure neighborhoods, to help them protect the local population, and to help ensure that the Iraqi forces left behind are capable of providing the security that Baghdad needs.
>
> This new strategy will not yield an immediate end to suicide bombings, assassinations, or IED attacks. . . . Yet over time, we can expect to see Iraqi troops chasing down murderers, fewer brazen acts of terror,

and growing trust and cooperation from Baghdad's residents. When this happens, daily life will improve. . . . Victory will not look like the ones our fathers and grandfathers achieved. There will be no surrender ceremony on the deck of a battleship. But victory in Iraq will bring something new to the Arab world: a functioning democracy that polices its territory, upholds the rule of law, respects fundamental human liberties, and answers to its people.

As was his habit, Bush concluded by invoking the Almighty. "We will go forward with trust that the Author of Liberty will guide us through these trying hours." [56]

Bush spoke for twenty-one minutes. He was swimming upstream. Recent opinion polls indicated that 70 percent of Americans thought the war was going badly, sixty-one percent opposed sending more troops, and 54 percent wanted to withdraw all troops immediately.[57] Bush was betting the ranch on the surge, and took personal responsibility. Laura said it was "the loneliest of George's decisions." [58] Robert Gates compared it to Gerald Ford's decision to pardon Richard Nixon. Both flew in the face of public opinion.[59]

The historical context is significant. Bush was overruling the entire military chain of command: the commander in Iraq, his superior at Central Command, the Joint Chiefs of Staff, and the secretary of defense. Presidents, as commander in chief, can do that. In the summer of 1942, Franklin Roosevelt overruled Secretary of War Henry Stimson and General Marshall and ordered the Army to invade North Africa that autumn.[60] In October 1948, Harry Truman overruled the Joint Chiefs and National Security Council and ordered the Air Force to provide the planes General Lucius Clay needed to continue the Berlin Airlift.[61] Dwight Eisenhower twice overruled the Joint Chiefs and NSC when they advocated the use of nuclear weapons: first to relieve the embattled French garrison at Dien Bien Phu, then to attack Chinese forces assembling to invade the offshore islands of Quemoy and Matsu. Both times Ike said no.[62] Like his predecessors, Bush took command. And like them, he had no second thoughts about his decision.[63]

AIDS

*I ask the Congress to commit $15 billion over the next
five years . . . to turn the tide against AIDS in the most
afflicted nations of Africa and the Caribbean.*

George W. Bush
January 28, 2003

Bush's prime-time televised speech on Iraq did little to change public opinion. A *Washington Post*/ABC News poll conducted immediately
afterward showed that 61 percent of Americans still opposed sending
more troops to Iraq, and 52 percent said they were strongly opposed.[1]
The New York Times captured the mood of the country when it noted
that the president offered no plan to bring the war in Iraq to a close.
"President Bush told Americans last night that failure in Iraq would
be a disaster. The disaster is Mr. Bush's war, and he has already failed.
Last night was his chance to stop offering more fog and be honest with
the nation, and he did not take it."[2]*

---

* The *Times* continued: "Americans needed to hear a clear plan to extricate United States
troops from the disaster that Mr. Bush created. What they got was more gauzy talk of victory in
the war on terrorism and of creating a 'young democracy' in Iraq. In other words, a way for this

On Capitol Hill, reaction was swift. Except for Senators McCain, Lieberman, and Graham, Bush found little support. Senator Chuck Hagel called the plan for a surge "the most dangerous foreign policy blunder in this country since Vietnam." Republican senator George Voinovich of Ohio said, "I've gone along with the president on this, and I bought into his dream. And at this stage of the game, I just don't think it's going to happen."[3] Senator John Warner, former chairman of the Armed Services committee, introduced a resolution opposing the surge, and conservative senators like Sam Brownback of Kansas, Norm Coleman of Minnesota, and Lisa Murkowski of Alaska also expressed doubt.[4]

Across the aisle, Joe Biden, chairman of the Foreign Relations Committee, noted that 3,009 American military personnel had been killed in Iraq and another 22,000 wounded. "And there seems to be no end in sight." Biden said that the entire military chain of command opposed the surge. "And so did our greatest soldier-statesman, Colin Powell."[5]

The young Barack Obama, then in his first term as senator from Illinois, noted that a surge in Iraq "would do nothing to solve the sectarian violence there. In fact, I think it will be the reverse. I think it takes pressure off the Iraqis to arrive at the sort of political accommodation that every observer believes is the ultimate solution to the problems we face there."[6] Congressional opposition to the surge would become even more manifest in February when the military appropriation bills came forward.

Despite the opposition, Bush remained convinced he was right. "I know the decision is unpopular," he told members of the White House staff the following week. "People say Bush needs to see the world as it is. Well, I've been here six years now and I see the world as it is, maybe better than most. The world as it is, that world needs America to lead. You know why? Because nothing happens if we don't lead."[7]

To engender support for the surge, Bush sought to use his State of the Union address to Congress on January 23 as a springboard. It was

---

president to run out the clock and leave his mess for the next one." *New York Times*, January 11, 2007.

tough going. The president's approval rating stood in the low 30s, and opposition to the surge now ran at 65 percent. And the Democrats controlled both Houses. Bush was undeterred. "This war is more than a clash of arms," said the president. "It is a decisive ideological struggle. And the security of our nation is in the balance.

> Every one of us wishes this war were over and won. Yet it would not be like us to leave our promises unkept, our friends abandoned, and our own security at risk. Ladies and gentlemen, on this day, at this hour, it is still within our power to shape the outcome of this battle. Let us find our resolve and turn events toward victory.

Bush said he had carefully weighed the options available and had chosen to increase American forces in Iraq "because it provides the best chance for success. . . . Our country is pursuing a new strategy in Iraq, and I ask you to give it a chance to work." The president then announced that he was asking Congress to increase the size of the Army and Marine Corps by 92,000. "The war on terror we fight today is a generational struggle that will continue long after you and I have turned our duties over to others. And that's why it's important to work together so our nation can see this great effort through."[8]

Congressional response was tepid. Bush's remarks on Iraq were greeted with silence from the Democratic side of the chamber. Even Republicans were skeptical of Bush's strategy. And so was the military. Journalist Howard Fineman pointed out that many in the military believed our presence in Iraq had inflamed hatred, not doused it, and had significantly eroded America's moral authority. "The dollar is down, the Euro is up; America, sadly, is regarded by much of the world as almost as great a threat to peace as the 'evil' people we have been fighting for six years."[9]

The official Democratic response to the State of the Union was given by newly elected senator James Webb of Virginia, a Marine veteran of Vietnam whose son was serving in Iraq. "The president took us into this war recklessly," said Webb. "We are now, as a nation, held hostage to the predictable—and predicted—disarray that has followed. . . . We need a new direction. . . . Not a precipitous withdrawal. . . . But an immediate shift toward a strong regionally based diplomacy, a policy that takes our soldiers off the streets of Iraq's cities, and a formula that will in short order allow our combat forces to leave Iraq." [10]

House speaker Nancy Pelosi and Senate majority leader Harry Reid issued a joint statement immediately after Bush spoke criticizing the troop increase in Iraq and promising to hold nonbinding votes on it. "While the president continues to ignore the will of the country, Congress will not ignore this president's failed policy. His plan will receive an up-or-down vote in both the House and Senate, and we will continue to hold him accountable for changing course in Iraq." [11]

Bush was clearly out of touch with the mood of the country. Shielded by an intensely loyal White House staff, and buttressed by the input of conservative Washington think tanks, the president was determined to pursue the surge. Like many presidents, he was beset by the loneliness of command. Bush often compared himself to Abraham Lincoln, whose bust he kept in the Oval Office. During his eight years in the White House, Bush read fourteen biographies of Lincoln. "Thinking about what Lincoln went through lends some of that perspective to things. I'm no Lincoln, but I'm in the same boat." [12] As Bush saw it, Lincoln persisted in the Civil War despite enormous casualties because he believed he was waging war for a just cause. Bush felt similarly about the war in Iraq. [13]

Bush's 2007 State of the Union was remarkable, not just for his unyielding defense of the surge, but for his renewed commitment to lead the global fight against AIDS. This is an often overlooked aspect of Bush's presidency, and it is one that deserves continued respect. Speaking to Congress, Bush said, "American foreign policy is more than a matter of war and diplomacy. Our work in the world is also based on a timeless truth. To whom much is given, much is required." *

> We must continue to fight HIV/AIDS, especially on the continent of Africa. Because you funded our Emergency Plan for AIDS Relief, the number of people receiving life-saving drugs has grown from 50,000 to

---

* The president was paraphrasing the Gospel according to St. Luke, 12:48: "For unto whomsoever much is given, of him shall be much required."

more than 800,000 in three short years. I ask you to continue funding
our efforts to fight HIV/AIDS.[14]

By 2007, Bush's determination to fight AIDS in Africa had become
a hallmark of his administration, and it is one of his most enduring
accomplishments. His interest in the issue began in 1990 when he was
sent by his father to The Gambia to represent the United States at a ceremony marking the twenty-fifth anniversary of The Gambia's independence. Bush was struck by the poverty and suffering he encountered.
In the 2000 campaign, Condoleezza Rice called his attention to the humanitarian crisis HIV/AIDS posed for sub-Saharan Africa. Millions of
people had died of the disease, said Rice, and in some countries one out
of every four adults was infected. If nothing was done, the number of
infected was expected to exceed 100 million by 2010. When Bush took
office in 2001, the United States was spending roughly $500 million a
year to combat global AIDS, but the effort was uncoordinated. Bush
immediately chose to step in. "I decided to make confronting AIDS in
Africa a key element in my foreign policy." [15]

The first opportunity arose when Bush met with U.N. secretary-
general Kofi Annan in March 2001. Both agreed on the urgent need
to confront the AIDS pandemic. Annan suggested creating a Global
Fund to Fight HIV/AIDS, tuberculosis, and malaria under the United
Nations. Bush was initially reluctant, but at the urging of Colin Powell
and Health and Human Services secretary Tommy Thompson, agreed
to be the first contributor to the fund with an initial pledge of $200 mil-
lion. Bush announced his decision in a Rose Garden ceremony with
Annan and Nigerian president Olusegun Obasanjo on May 11, 2001.
"I am today committing the United States of America to support a new
worldwide fund with a founding contribution of $200 million," said the
president. "This $200 million will go exclusively to a global fund, with
more to follow as we learn where our support can be most effective." [16]

In 2002, Bush increased the American contribution to the U.N. fund
to $500 million, but did not feel that was sufficient. He also believed the
U.N. Fund was slow to act. "I couldn't stand the idea of innocent people
dying while the international community delayed. I decided it was time
for America to launch a global AIDS initiative of our own." [17] Bush

directed deputy chief of staff Josh Bolten to assemble a team of experts to look into the problem and recommend how the United States could proceed most effectively. Led by Dr. Anthony Fauci, director of the National Institute of Allergy and Infectious Diseases at the National Institutes of Health, Bolten's team recommended spending $500 million over a five-year period to provide medication to HIV-infected pregnant women in Africa to reduce the chances of their transmitting the virus to their babies. Under the plan, one million mothers living in the highly infected area of Africa and the Caribbean would be treated annually. That would save the lives of at least 150,000 babies. Bush agreed immediately. "Let's get started right now," he told Bolten.

On June 19, 2002, Bush announced the International Mother and Child HIV Prevention Initiative in another Rose Garden ceremony. "The global devastation of HIV/AIDS staggers the imagination," said the president. "The disease has already killed over twenty million people, and it's poised to kill at least forty million more. . . . In the hardest hit countries of sub-Sahara Africa as much as one-third of the adult population is infected with HIV." The president said that one of the best ways to fight AIDS was to prevent mothers from passing on the virus to their children. "Worldwide, close to 2,000 babies are infected with HIV every day, during pregnancy, birth, or through breast feeding." To combat that, Bush said the administration was making $500 million available immediately. "Our initiative will focus on twelve countries in Africa and others in the Caribbean where the problem is most severe and where our help can make the greatest difference. . . . This major commitment of my government to prevent mother-to-child HIV transmission is the first of this scale by any government anywhere. . . . And as we see what works, we will make more funding available." [18]

The Mother and Child HIV Prevention Initiative was an important first step. But as Bush saw it, it was only a first step. "This is a good start," the president told Bolten, "but it's not enough. Go back to the drawing board and think even bigger." [19]

As Bolten recalls, "He wanted to do something game-changing. Something that, instead of at the margins assuaging everybody's conscience, might actually change the trajectory of this disease which, from the reports we were getting, was headed to destroy a whole continent."[20] Dr. Fauci's team went back to work. At Bush's direction, the team worked in secret. Not even Colin Powell or Tommy Thompson was informed. Nor was Condoleezza Rice. Fauci's team focused on the use of antiretroviral lifesaving drugs. Thanks to advances in drug technology, the cost of treating one AIDS patient with reliable drugs had shrunk from $1,000 a month to $25, less than a dollar a day. On December 4, 2002, Fauci's team made its final presentation to Bush and his principal advisers in the Roosevelt Room of the White House. The plan was ambitious and controversial. It would provide lifesaving drugs to two million people, prevent seven million new infections, and provide care for ten million AIDS victims and the children they left behind. It would cost $15 billion over five years, and would be the largest health initiative to combat a single disease in world history.

Budget director Mitch Daniels was skeptical, especially with the escalating costs of the war on terror and the upcoming invasion of Iraq. Others doubted whether the drugs could be delivered effectively. Representatives from Atlanta's Centers for Disease Control, smarting because they had not been consulted previously, dismissed the plan as "half-baked."[21]

On the other hand, Bolten and Rice were strongly in favor. Rice became emotional. "My mother was diagnosed with cancer when I was a teenager," she said. "She got treatment and lived until I was thirty. You bet those years meant something to me—and they would mean something to every African child whose mother lives to take care of them."[22]

At the end of the meeting Bush called on his speechwriter, Michael Gerson. "Gerson, what do you think?" asked the president.

"If we can do this and don't, it will be a source of shame," Gerson replied.

Bush was convinced. He not only approved the plan, but decided to announce it in his 2003 State of the Union address. And he selected the countries to be included: twelve in sub-Saharan Africa and two in the Caribbean.* For Bush, the decision to approve what became

---

*   Botswana, Ivory Coast, Ethiopia, Guyana, Haiti, Kenya, Mozambique, Namibia, Nigeria, Rwanda, South Africa, Tanzania, Uganda, and Zambia. At the subsequent request of Congress, Vietnam was added.

known as PEPFAR—the President's Emergency Plan for AIDS Relief—was one of the most exhilarating of his eight years in the White House. "This is one of those moments when we can actually change the lives of millions of people, a whole continent," he told a White House aide when the meeting concluded. "How can we not take this step?"[23]

After making his decision, Bush instructed everyone at the meeting to keep the decision a secret. He wanted to save it for his State of the Union address. "If word leaked out, there would be a turf war among government agencies for control of the money. Members of Congress would be tempted to dilute the program's focus by redirecting funds for their own purposes. I didn't want PEPFAR to end up hamstrung by bureaucracy and competing interests."[24]

On January 28, 2003, Bush unveiled PEPFAR to the nation. Some on the White House staff had made a last-minute effort to delete the announcement from the State of the Union address—"Americans don't want to hear about giving money to foreigners; they care about kitchen-table issues that affect their families"—but Bush was resolute. The State of the Union setting provided the largest audience the president would have, and he was determined to launch the program in that setting.

"Today on the continent of Africa, nearly thirty million people have the AIDS virus, including three million children under the age of fifteen. There are whole countries of Africa where more than one-third of the adult population carries the infection. More than four million require immediate drug treatment. Yet across that continent, only 50,000 AIDS victims—only 50,000—are receiving the medicine they need." Bush said that because AIDS was considered a death sentence in Africa, many did not seek treatment. "Almost all who do are turned away. Many hospitals tell people, 'You've got AIDS. We can't help you. Go home and die.' In an age of miraculous medicines, no person should have to hear those words."

Bush was glowing with warmth. "AIDS can be prevented," he told Congress. "Seldom has history offered a greater opportunity to do so much for so many. . . . To meet a severe and urgent crisis abroad, tonight I propose the Emergency Plan for AIDS Relief, a work of mercy beyond all current international efforts to help the people of Africa. . . . I ask the Congress to commit $15 billion over the next five years . . . to turn the tide against AIDS in the most afflicted nations of Africa and the Caribbean."[25]

George W. Bush's announcement of PEPFAR in his 2003 State of the Union was in many ways the high-water mark of his eight years in the White House. Americans across the political spectrum were captivated by the president's determination to take on a pressing humanitarian task of such magnitude. World opinion responded in a similar fashion, and the affected countries of sub-Saharan Africa and the Caribbean were deeply appreciative. Add to that the fact that the Iraq War had not yet begun. At that moment, Bush enjoyed universal respect.

In the House chamber, Bush received a prolonged standing ovation from both sides of the aisle. The legislation was introduced in the House on March 17 by Henry Hyde of Illinois, chairman of the International Relations Committee. It was co-sponsored by Tom Lantos of California, the ranking Democrat on the committee, and the unlikely pair of Barbara Lee (D., Calif.) and Dave Weldon (R., Fla.). Barbara Lee anchored the left wing of the Democratic Party in the House (she was the only member of Congress to vote against the use of force resolution after 9/11), and Dr. Dave Weldon occupied a similar position on the Republican right. The bill was voted out of the International Relations committee favorably on April 2, and to aid passage Bush invited members of Congress to the East Room of the White House on April 28, and delivered an impassioned speech urging immediate action. "Confronting the threat of AIDS is important work, and it is urgent work," said the president. "In the three months since I announced the Emergency Plan [in his State of the Union], an estimated 760,000 people have died from AIDS, 1.2 million people have been infected, and more than 175,000 babies have been born with the virus. Time is not on our side."[26]

Following the meeting at the White House, the bill was brought to the House floor on May 1, and after a brief debate was passed 375–41.

Bush signing the PEPFAR legislation, May 27, 2003.

Of the forty-one members who voted against, forty were Republicans.* In the Senate the bill was shepherded through by majority leader Bill Frist, Dick Lugar, chairman of the Foreign Relations committee, and Joe Biden, the ranking Democrat on the committee. The Senate debate was equally brief, and the bill was passed by voice vote (no roll call) in the early morning hours of May 16. Bush signed the bill establishing PEPFAR in a White House ceremony on May 27. "The legislation I sign today launches an emergency effort that will provide $15 billion over the next five years to fight AIDS abroad. This is the largest single upfront commitment in history for an international public health initiative involving a specific disease." After thanking everyone involved, Bush launched into a brief description of what was involved in PEPFAR, and demonstrated once again his deep commitment to the cause.

> We will purchase low-cost antiretroviral medications and other drugs that are needed to save lives. We will set up a broad and efficient network to deliver drugs to the farthest reaches of Africa, even by motorcycle or bicycle. We will train doctors and nurses and other health care professionals so they can treat HIV/AIDS patients. We will renovate and, where necessary, build and equip clinics and laboratories. We will support the care of AIDS orphans by training and hiring child-care workers. We will provide home-based care to ease the suffering of people living with AIDS.

---

* The sole Democrat voting against PEPFAR was Bennie Thompson of Mississippi's Second District.

"This is a massive undertaking," said the president, and it was time to get started. "The suffering in Africa is great. The suffering in the Caribbean is great. The United States of America has the power and we have the moral duty to help. And I am proud that our blessed and generous nation is doing that."[27]

PEPFAR proved a resounding success. An early Stanford University study indicated that the program had prevented about 1.1 million deaths in Africa during its first three years, and had reduced the death rate from AIDS by roughly 10 percent.[28] In the spring of 2007, PEPFAR director Dr. Mark Dybul, a highly respected figure in the AIDS community, recommended to Bush that when the five-year funding of the program expired, the United States should double its commitment for the next five years. The fight against AIDS was going well, he said, but with twice as much money available they could possibly turn the corner in fighting the disease. Bush agreed. Speaking in the Rose Garden on May 30, 2007, the president announced that he was asking Congress to increase the American commitment from $15 billion to $30 billion over the next five years.

> This money will be spent wisely through the establishment of partnership compacts with host nations. These compacts would insure that U.S. funds support programs that have the greatest possible impact and are sustainable for the future. America will work with governments, the private sector, and faith and community-based organizations around the world to meet measurable goals: to support treatment for nearly 2.5 million people, to prevent more than twelve million new infections, and to support care for twelve million people, including more than five million orphans and vulnerable children.

Bush went on to say that the PEPFAR program was bringing many villages back to life in Africa, and for the first time referred to the "Lazarus effect"—a reference to the Gospel of St. John in which Jesus raised Lazarus from the dead—and was the terminology now being used by AIDS workers in Africa to describe how many victims left for dead were being restored to life through the use of medication provided by the United States.[29]

Bush's request to Congress again enjoyed bipartisan support. Congressmen Hyde and Lantos had both died, and the resulting legislation was titled the Tom Lantos and Henry Hyde United States Global Leadership Against HIV/AIDS, Tuberculosis, and Malaria Reauthorization Act of 2008. Thirty-nine billion dollars was appropriated to fight AIDS, $4 billion for tuberculosis, and $5 billion for malaria—a total of $48 billion—over a period of five years.[30] The House passed the measure on April 2, 2008, by a vote of 308–116, and the Senate passed it on July 16, 80–16.

Bush signed the bill into law in a White House ceremony on July 30, 2008.[31] After expressing his appreciation to the congressional leadership, the president spoke briefly. "PEPFAR is the largest commitment by any nation to combat a single disease in human history," said Bush.

> With this bill, America will continue PEPFAR for another five years. . . . With this legislation, America is showing its tremendous regard for the dignity and worth of every human being. This afternoon, I want to speak directly to those around the world who have, or think they may have, HIV: A positive diagnosis does not have to be a reason for shame. So don't let shame keep you from getting tested or treated. Your life is treasured by the people who love you. It is precious in the eyes of God. It matters to the people of the United States.[32]

Bush's dedication to the global fight against AIDS is a remarkable chapter in his presidency and is unique to him. By the time he left office in 2009, PEPFAR had treated over two million people and provided care for ten million. Protective assistance had been provided during sixteen million pregnancies, and more than 57 million had benefited from AIDS testing and counseling. As Condoleezza Rice noted, PEPFAR will always "be remembered as one of the greatest acts of compassion by any country in history."[33] And George W. Bush deserves the credit.

Like most start-up government programs, PEPFAR was marred initially by several glitches. To head the program, Bush named former

Eli Lilly chief executive Randall Tobias. Tobias was a competent executive but had little knowledge of AIDS or Africa. Worse, he much preferred brand-name drugs rather than the much cheaper generic versions.[34] He also deplored the use of condoms, stressing abstinence instead.[35] Tobias remained head of PEPFAR until 2006, when he was replaced by Mark Dybul.* At that point PEPFAR began using generics, which reduced the cost of providing medication for a patient to less than 40 cents a day.

A second and perhaps more serious problem pertained to the statutory requirement in the 2003 Act that 20 percent of the funds be used for prevention, and that of those a third (6.7 percent of the total funds appropriated) be used to promote abstinence before marriage and fidelity. Since these programs were largely administered by faith-based organizations, they were seen as ideologically driven, especially since there was no reliable scientific evidence that they reduced the spread of AIDS.[36] Bush strongly supported the abstinence and fidelity provisions, but made no protest when the Democratic 110th Congress stripped them from PEPFAR's renewal.[37]

A related problem involved the act's requirement that all organizations receiving funding sign a pledge explicitly agreeing to oppose prostitution. Specifically, the act stated no funds could be given to an organization "that does not have a policy explicitly opposing prostitution and sex trafficking."[38] This provision was seen by many as the equivalent of a loyalty oath. It also ignored the fact that prostitution is legal in Ethiopia, the Ivory Coast, Mozambique, and Nigeria—four of the countries covered by PEPFAR. It is also legal in Canada, Germany, France, Great Britain, Mexico, Brazil, Argentina, Chile, the Netherlands, Switzerland, Belgium, Austria, and two dozen other countries as well as the state of Nevada.

In 2013, the Supreme Court, in an opinion written by Chief Jus-

---

* After leaving PEPFAR, Tobias was appointed director of foreign assistance and chief administrator of the Agency for International Development with the rank of deputy secretary of state. He resigned April 27, 2007, after being linked to the D.C. Madam scandal of Deborah Jeane Palfrey. Glenn Kessler, "Rice Deputy Quits After Query About Escort Service," *Washington Post*, April 28, 2007.

tice Roberts, held the requirement unconstitutional—a violation of the
First Amendment. Roberts said the law requires recipients "to pledge
allegiance to the Government's policy of eradicating prostitution. As to
that, we cannot improve upon what Justice Jackson wrote for the Court
seventy years ago:

> If there is any fixed star in our constitutional constellation, it is that no
> official, high or petty, can prescribe what shall be orthodox in politics,
> nationalism, religion, or other matters of opinion or force citizens to
> confess by word or act their faith therein.*

These were minor flaws. Overall, PEPFAR remains an amazing
achievement. And Bush's crusade against AIDS became a deeply felt
family affair. As president, Bush visited sub-Saharan Africa twice
to monitor the workings of PEPFAR, and Laura went five times.
Their twin daughters were also strongly committed. Barbara, after
graduating from Yale in 2004, abandoned her plans to become an architect and went to work for an AIDS clinic at the Red Cross Children's Hospital in Cape Town, South Africa, and then in Botswana
and Tanzania. Jenna, after finishing her studies at the University of
Texas, worked as an intern for UNICEF in Paraguay and Panama.
In 2008, Barbara and Jenna, joined by five others, founded the Global
Health Corps, a nonprofit volunteer organization that sends recent
college graduates to work in clinics in sub-Saharan Africa and other
depressed areas.† Barbara became—and remains—the CEO of the
Global Health Corps, and Jenna wrote a bestselling book about the
life of a young girl in Paraguay who was born with AIDS. Entitled
Ana's Story, the book was published by HarperCollins in 2007.[39] (Jenna
divided her royalties between the girl whose life she chronicled and
UNICEF.) "Laura and I are very proud of our daughters," said Bush.

---

* Chief Justice Roberts was quoting Jackson's decision in *West Virginia Board of Education v.
Barnette*, 319 U.S. 624, 642 (1943). The case challenging the PEPFAR requirement was *Agency
for International Development v. Alliance for Open Society International*, 570 U.S. 417 (2013).

† In 2014, the Global Health Corps placed 128 fellows in 59 different venues.

"They have become professional women serving a cause greater than themselves." [40]

After visiting Tanzania, Rwanda, Ghana, Liberia, and Benin in February 2008, Bush and Laura sat together on the return flight. They agreed that it was the best trip of their presidential years. "There was a new palpable sense of energy and hope across Africa," said Bush. "The outpouring of love for America was overwhelming." [41] In contrast to the negative public reception Bush often received in many European capitals, in Africa there was nothing but appreciation.

Eugene Robinson of *The Washington Post*, scarcely a friend of the Bush administration, may have said it best when he wrote that "if Africa is gaining ground against AIDS, history will note that it was Bush, more than any other individual, who turned the tide. The man who called himself the Decider will be held accountable for a host of calamitous decisions. But for opening his heart to Africa, he deserves nothing but gratitude and praise." [42]

Bush's fight against AIDS was an important exception, but it was an exception. Throughout 2007 his presidency continued to plummet. His approval ratings dropped to 30 percent. Fewer than one in three Americans said they approved his performance in the White House. The problem was exacerbated on April 1, when Matthew Dowd, a prominent member of Bush's inner circle, broke publicly with the president. Dowd had been the original author of the Republican election strategy of appealing to the base. He had joined Bush's staff in Texas in 1999, and by 2004 had become the president's primary political strategist. In a lengthy interview with Jim Rutenberg of *The New York Times*, Dowd expressed his disappointment with Bush's leadership. He criticized the president's "my way or the highway" mentality, which he felt was reinforced by "a shrinking circle of inner aides." And he found fault with Bush's handling of Katrina, Cindy Sheehan, Abu Ghraib, and particularly the war in Iraq. "I really like him," Dowd told Rutenberg, "which is why I'm so disappointed in things. I think he has become more, in my view, secluded and bubbled in." [43]

A more serious problem pertained to the precipitous dismissal of eight United States attorneys by the Bush administration for what appeared to be political purposes. This was a first in American history. There are ninety-three U.S. attorney positions throughout the United States. They are appointed by the president, confirmed by the Senate, and are responsible for representing the United States in federal court proceedings in their jurisdiction. And though appointed by the president, they are not political appointees but professional officers with an ethos and code of conduct of their own. Traditionally, all U.S. attorneys resign when a president's term expires, but remain in office until their replacement is named. If the incoming president is from a different political party, almost all of the resignations are accepted. Reagan replaced eighty-nine of the ninety-three U.S. attorneys in his first two years in office, Clinton replaced all ninety-three, and George W. Bush replaced eighty-eight in his first two years.[44] But there is no precedent for a U.S. attorney to be dismissed in the middle of his term by the president who appointed him, except for misconduct—and those examples are rare.

All of the eight U.S. attorneys dismissed by Bush had been appointed by him and had been in office for more than four years. But after the 2004 election, the Bush White House, in conjunction with the Justice Department, began to consider replacing those U.S. attorneys who were not considered politically reliable. The initial thrust came from White House counsel Harriet Miers, who wrote a memo to the Justice Department in February 2005 suggesting that all U.S. attorneys be replaced.[45] The Justice Department considered that excessive— particularly since most U.S. attorneys were strong supporters of the president. Kyle Sampson, chief of staff to Attorney General Gonzales, wrote Miers that a "limited number of U.S. attorneys could be targeted for removal and replacement, mitigating the shock to the system that would result from an across the board firing."[46] On September 6, 2006, Sampson sent a second memo to Miers suggesting that if they did remove a number of U.S. attorneys, they should utilize the Patriot Act when they appointed replacements so as to avoid the necessity of Senate confirmation.*

---

* The Patriot Act extension, which Bush signed into law on March 9, 2006, contained a provision, put there at White House request, that permitted the attorney general to fill U.S. attorney

The issue came to a head during the 2006 midterm elections. Bush told Gonzales he had received complaints that some U.S. attorneys were not pursuing voter fraud investigations. The complaints came from Republican officials who were demanding investigations into a number of Democratic campaigns. Gonzales was instructed to look into it.[47] On November 27, 2006, Gonzales met with his senior advisers to review a list of the U.S. attorneys who might be dismissed. The list had been prepared by Sampson in consultation with the White House.[48] There were seven names on the list.* All had been appointed by Bush at least four years previously, but were considered not sufficiently in tune with Republican policy. Karl Rove joined the assault when he insisted that H. E. "Bud" Cummins, U.S. attorney in Arkansas, also be removed to make a place for his former aide and protégé, thirty-seven-year-old Timothy Griffin.[49] Seven of the eight U.S. attorneys slated for removal had received highly positive job performance evaluations by Justice Department examiners.[50]

Miers approved the list on December 4, 2006. "We're a go for the U.S. Atty plan," her deputy emailed the Justice Department. "W[hite] H[ouse] leg[islative affairs], political, and communications have signed off and acknowledged that we have to be committed to following through once the pressure comes."[51] On December 7, the Department of Justice informed seven of the U.S. attorneys they were being dismissed. Cummings in Arkansas had been notified earlier. All were shocked. Nothing like this had ever happened before. But they dutifully submitted their resignations.

Initially there was little outcry. The Justice Department did not announce the dismissals publicly, and the mainstream press did not report

---

vacancies without the necessity of Senate confirmation. The new appointees could serve indefinitely. This represented a major change since under existing law a U.S. attorney nominated by the president could serve only 120 days without Senate confirmation after which the post became vacant and could be filled by the judges of the United States District Court. 28 U.S.C. 8546.

*   David Iglesias (New Mexico); Kevin V. Ryan (Northern California); John McKay (Western Washington); Paul K. Charlton (Arizona); Carol Lam (Southern California); Daniel Bogden (Nevada); Margaret Chiara (Western Michigan).

them.* The first rumblings came when senators discovered that the replacement U.S. attorneys would be appointed by the attorney general under the Patriot Act and would not be subject to Senate confirmation. "We have no idea why this is happening," said Senator Dianne Feinstein (D., Calif.), "but we believe that this use of expanded executive authority to appoint interim replacements clearly undermines essential constitutional checks and balances." [52] Feinstein, joined by Patrick Leahy (D., Vt.) and Mark Pryor (D., Ark.), immediately introduced legislation to repeal that portion of the Patriot Act that gave the attorney general the power to appoint U.S. attorneys. The measure was passed by the Senate 94–2 on March 20, the House passed its own version 329–78 on March 26, and then adopted the Senate bill on May 22 by a vote of 306–114. It was signed into law by President Bush without ceremony on June 17, 2007. [53]

The political basis of the dismissals was not immediately recognized. Attorney General Gonzales testified before the Senate Judiciary Committee on January 18. He denied any political motives and said all of the removals were routine personnel decisions based on performance evaluations. "What we're trying to do is ensure that for the people in each of these respective districts, we have the very best possible representative for the Department of Justice. I would never, ever make a change in a United States attorney for political reasons. I just would not do it." [54]

Gonzales's testimony heightened interest in the issue. The press began to inquire, and by February it was evident that eight U.S. attorneys had been relieved. At this point, the political aspects began to loom large. On February 6, deputy attorney general Paul McNulty appeared before a closed session of the Senate Judiciary Committee. McNulty told the committee that seven of the eight U.S. attorneys who were dismissed were let go for "performance related" issues not political reasons. The eighth, Bud Cummins of Arkansas, was removed

---

*   The first reporting of the firings was by Josh Marshall and his team on TalkingPointsMemo blog, a liberal New York website. Paul McLeary, "How TalkingPointsMemo Beat the Big Boys on the U.S. Attorney Story," *Columbia Journalism Review*, March 15, 2007.

to make room for Timothy Griffin, a protégé of Karl Rove at the insistence of Harriet Miers. "The indisputable fact is that United States attorneys serve at the pleasure of the president. They come and they go for lots of reasons," said McNulty.[55]

McNulty's testimony added fuel to the fire. Not only because of the reason he gave for the removal of Bud Cummins in Arkansas, but because he indicated that the other seven U.S. attorneys were not performing satisfactorily. When McNulty's comments were publicized, the dismissed attorneys were shocked and began to speak with reporters. At least six of the seven had recently received outstanding job performance ratings by the Justice Department, and were angered when the deputy attorney general said otherwise.[56] They recognized the president's right to dismiss them, but were unwilling to be labeled incompetent.

It was in this context that both the Senate and House of Representatives began investigations. On March 6, six of the dismissed U.S. attorneys were called to testify on Capitol Hill. Senator Patrick Leahy, chairman of the Judiciary Committee, compared their dismissals to Nixon's firing of Watergate prosecutor Archibald Cox in the Saturday Night Massacre, except that this time there was no Elliot Richardson or William Ruckelshaus to resign in protest.[57]

In their testimony before the committee, the attorneys made clear they did not wish to speculate as to why they had been removed. But they all agreed they did not know. In the questioning that followed, it became evident that there were indeed political issues that underlay the dismissals.* Perhaps the most telling exchange was when Senator

---

* John McKay of the Western District of Washington had run afoul of the Republican establishment when he failed to bring indictments against Democrats in the 2004 Washington gubernatorial race. Carol Lam of the Southern District of California was placed in the Republican doghouse after the conviction of Congressman Randy "Duke" Cunningham, and the continuing investigation of those who assisted him. David Iglesias of New Mexico had run afoul of Senator Pete Domenici and Representative Heather Wilson over his refusal to bring indictments against Democrats in the 2006 congressional election. Paul Charlton of Arizona had encountered disfavor for his refusal to prosecute minor marijuana violations as well as his stance on immigration, which offended two Arizona Republican congressmen. Cummins in Arkansas was dismissed to make room for Rove's former aide. Senate Judiciary Committee Hearing, Dismissal of U.S. Attorneys, March 6, 2007. House Judiciary Committee, Subcommittee on Commercial

Charles Schumer asked each of the former attorneys, "Based on every-thing you know sitting here today, do you believe you were fired for any failure of performance, as alleged by the Justice Department?" Each answered "No."[58]

The following day, Gonzales published an op-ed in USA Today hoping to quell the controversy. Said Gonzales:

> We have never asked a U.S. attorney to resign in an effort to retaliate against him or her. . . . Like me, U.S. attorneys are political appointees, and we all serve at the pleasure of the president. If U.S. attorneys are not executing their responsibilities in a manner that furthers the man-agement and policy goals of departmental leadership, it is appropriate they be replaced. . . . While I am grateful for the public service of these seven U.S. attorneys, they simply lost my confidence. I hope that this episode ultimately will be recognized for what it is: an overblown per-sonnel matter.[59]

Gonzales's comments made matters worse. Emails released that day by the Department of Justice revealed extensive communication between the attorney general's office and Harriet Miers's office in the White House pertaining to the dismissals. On March 12, Kyle Sampson resigned as Gonzales's chief of staff, supposedly because he had not informed senior Justice Department officials of the White House contacts. In retrospect, it appears that Sampson was being set up to take the blame. Additional documents that were released shortly afterward made it abundantly clear that Gonzales and the senior leadership at Justice were fully aware of the White House con-tacts.*

---

and Administrative Law, Dismissal of U.S. Attorneys, March 6, 2007. The full transcripts of both hearings are published online by The Washington Post.

*   In his testimony before the Senate Judiciary Committee on March 29, Sampson said that Gonzales had been repeatedly advised of the pending dismissals. "I don't think that the attorney general's statement that he was not involved in any discussion about U.S. attorney removals is accurate," said Sampson. David Johnston and Eric Lipton, "Ex-Aide Disputes Gonzales Stand over Dismissals," New York Times, March 30, 2007.

"Mistakes were made," said Gonzales at a press conference on May 13. "I accept that responsibility and my pledge to the American people is to find out what went wrong here, to access accountability, and to make improvements so that the mistakes in this instance do not occur again in the future." [60]

The president was on a state visit to Latin America at the time. Asked about Gonzales's statement at a press conference in Mexico City, Bush expressed his support. "I talked to him this morning," said the president.

> We talked about his need to go up to Capitol Hill and make it very clear to members of both political parties why the Justice Department made the decisions it made. And he's right: Mistakes were made. And I'm frankly not happy about them.
>
> The Justice Department recommended a list of U.S. attorneys. I believe the reasons were entirely appropriate. And yet the issue was mishandled to the point now where you are asking me questions about it in Mexico, which is fine. I mean, if I were you, I'd ask the same questions. . . . Al was right; mistakes were made, and he's going up to Capitol Hill to correct them. [61]

Bush attempted to calm the waters. When he returned to Washington he met with the press. The president said he regretted the confusion that had occurred and said he hoped to resolve it. First, he had instructed the attorney general to testify before Congress and explain how the decisions to remove the U.S. attorneys were made. Second, he was giving Congress more than three thousand pages of internal Justice Department documents related to the issue. And third, he was making members of the White House staff available to Congress for private interviews, but not under oath or by subpoena.

> Q: Why not? Since you say nothing wrong was done by your staff, why not just clear the air and let Karl Rove and other senior aides testify in public, under oath? There has been a precedent for previous administrations doing that.

Bush: Well, some have; some haven't. Michael [Abramowitz,
     Washington Post], I'm worried about precedents that would make
     it difficult for somebody to walk into the Oval Office and say,
     "Mr. President, here's what's on my mind."

Abramowitz followed up by asking Bush if he would "go to the
mat" if the Democrats pressed for on-the-record testimony from the
White House staff. "Absolutely," Bush replied. When Kelly O'Donnell
of NBC News asked whether the fact that the U.S. attorneys in San
Diego, Arizona, and Nevada were investigating Republican wrongdoing had something to do with their dismissal, Bush dodged the question. "It may give the appearance of something," he replied, but the
Justice Department in its testimony on Capitol Hill would set the record straight. "We would like the people to hear the truth. And Kelly,
your question is one I'm confident will be asked of people up there. And
the Justice Department will answer that question in an open forum for
everybody to see." [62]

Gonzales went to Capitol Hill to testify before the Senate Judiciary Committee on April 19. He had over three weeks to prepare his
testimony, and was brimming with confidence as he stepped into the
committee room. It was short lived. What he had assumed would be
a tour de force turned into a public relations disaster. Sixty-four times
Gonzales said, "I don't recall," or "I have no recollection," or "I have no
memory," when asked about the details of a decision. [63] "Mr. Gonzales
came across as a dull-witted apparatchik," said *The New York Times* editorially. "If Attorney General Alberto Gonzales had gone to the Senate
yesterday to convince the world that he ought to be fired, it's hard to
imagine how he could have done a better job." [64]

Republicans as well as Democrats asked Gonzales to step down.
Republican senator Tom Coburn of Oklahoma, a conservative voice
usually in tune with the administration, was brutal. The entire matter
"was handled incompetently," he told Gonzales. "The communication
was atrocious. It was inconsistent. It's generous to say there were mis-
statements. And I believe you ought to suffer the consequences that
these others have suffered. And I believe the best way to put this behind
us is your resignation."

Gonzales: Senator, I don't know whether or not that puts everything
  behind us, quite frankly. I am committed—I know mistakes were
  made here. And I'm committed to fix those mistakes.
Coburn: Well, Mr. Attorney General, you set the standard. You said
  leadership skills, management skills. They were sorely lacking
  in this instance. And the responsibility is to start with a clean
  slate . . . to heal this country, to restore the confidence of this
  country. . . . I like you as an individual, but I think mistakes
  have consequences.[65]

Gonzales testified for almost five hours. Not one senator offered support. "Mr. Attorney General, most of this is a stretch," said Lindsey Graham of South Carolina. "Why is your story changing?" asked Iowa's Charles Grassley. "Significantly, if not totally, it varies with the facts," observed Arlen Specter of Pennsylvania, the committee's ranking Republican. "Really deplorable," said John Cornyn, an old friend of Gonzales from Texas.[66] The Democrats were even more outspoken. Committee chairman Leahy summed up the hearing when he told Gonzales that his testimony confirmed that "politics have entered the Justice Department to an unprecedented extent. And if left unchecked, it would just become a political arm of the White House."[67]

As if to confirm Leahy's analysis, White House spokeswoman Dana Perino said President Bush "was pleased with the attorney general's testimony today," and continues to have "full confidence" in him. "After hours of testimony in which he answered all of the senators' questions and provided thousands of pages of documents, he again showed that nothing improper occurred," said Perino. "He admitted the matter could have been handled much better, and he apologized for the disruption of the U.S. attorneys involved, as well as for the lack of clarity in his initial responses." Perino added that the president appreciated the work Gonzales was doing "to help keep our citizens safe from terrorists, our children safe from predators, our government safe from corruption, and our streets free from gang violence."[68]

Three days later, Bush spoke directly to reporters in the White House.

The attorney general went up and gave a very candid assessment and answered every question he could possibly answer, honestly answer, in a way that increased my confidence in his ability to do the job.

One of the things that's important for the American people to understand is that the attorney general has a right to recommend to me to replace U.S. attorneys: U.S. attorneys serve at the pleasure of the president. In other words, we have named them, and I have the right to replace them with someone else.[69]

After Bush spoke, Senator Leahy noted that if Gonzales's performance at the hearing increased the president's confidence in him, "then he's setting the bar fairly low."[70] What Leahy—and most of the press—overlooked, is that Gonzales was doing exactly what Bush wanted him to do: helping to obscure the role the White House played in the dismissal of the U.S. attorneys, particularly the input of Karl Rove and Harriet Miers.

The issue intensified during the summer of 2007. The House and Senate Judiciary committees both sought documents and emails from the White House pertaining to the dismissals; Bush asserted executive privilege and declined to provide them; and both Josh Bolten and Harriet Miers (who had resigned and returned to Texas) refused to respond to congressional subpoenas to testify, citing a presidential directive not to do so. Fred Fielding, who had succeeded Miers as White House counsel, said the president was acting "to protect a fundamental interest of the presidency" by preserving the confidentiality of internal deliberations, including communications "with others inside and outside the Executive Branch."[71]

It was in this context that Karl Rove, who had been subpoenaed as well, decided to submit his resignation. Rove decided it was time to move on. There was no election pending, his family required attention, and he wanted to establish his financial independence. In early August, Rove told Bush he would be leaving. "I feel like I'm deserting you in time of war," he told the president.[72] Bush accepted Rove's decision, but with obvious regret. Speaking at a Rose Garden ceremony on August 13, the president said Rove was leaving to spend more time with his family. "We've been friends for a long time, and we're still going to be friends. I would call Karl Rove a dear friend. . . . And so I thank my friend. I'll be on the road behind you here in a little bit."[73] Rove, for his part, was unusually emotional at the ceremony. With a quivering voice he replied, "I'm grateful to have been a witness to history. It has been the joy and honor of a lifetime."[74] For both Bush and Rove, it was a heartfelt occasion. Later that day Rove, his wife, Darby, and their son, Andrew, accompanied Bush and Laura on Air Force One back to Texas.

With Gonzales, the situation was more complicated. In his testimony and public statements, the attorney general had done his utmost to conceal the political motivation behind the dismissal of the U.S. attorneys. It was not an easy assignment, and Gonzales had not handled it as well as he might have. There was no question about his loyalty to the president. On the other hand, the public response had been devastating. Gonzales's repeated memory lapses and the contradictions in his testimony made it obvious that he was in over his head as attorney general. Bush was reluctant to make a change, but eventually recognized the necessity to do so. When Bolten raised the matter in early August, Bush acquiesced. "We have a big agenda that the attorney general needs to carry for us," Bolten told Bush, "and Alberto can't carry it anymore."[75]

As with the dismissals of Paul O'Neill, Colin Powell, and Donald Rumsfeld, Bush was reluctant to tell Gonzales himself. Instead, he left it to Bolten to inform him. Bolten did as instructed, and tried to soften the blow. "Alberto, this makes us all heartsick, but the best thing you can do for the president right now is resign."

"I want to talk to the president," Gonzales replied.[76] Unlike O'Neill, Powell, and Rumsfeld, Gonzales was unwilling to fold his hand and quietly depart. He was carrying out the president's wishes, and did not feel he should be punished for doing so. Bolten understood. He arranged a meeting, and Gonzales flew to Texas to meet Bush at the ranch on August 26. This was a first for the president. Bush was forced to tell Gonzales to his face that his time was up. It was not easy. But he did so, and Gonzales recognized that he had no alternative.

Gonzales handled the matter well. He flew back to Washington

Bush and Laura meeting with Attorney
General Alberto Gonzales and his wife,
Rebecca, at the ranch, August 26, 2007.

to announce his res-
ignation, taking full
responsibility. "Yes-
terday I met with
President Bush and
informed him of my
decision to conclude
my government ser-
vice as Attorney Gen-
eral of the United
States effective as of
September 17, 2007."
It was a brief state-
ment, and Gonzales took no questions from the press. "I often remind
our fellow citizens that we live in the greatest country in the world and
that I have lived the American dream. Even my worst days as attorney
general have been better than my father's best days. Public service is
honorable and noble, and I am profoundly grateful to President Bush
for his friendship and for the many opportunities he has given me to
serve the American people."[77]

Bush played his part equally well. There was no suggestion that
Gonzales had been pushed out. "This morning," said the president,
"Attorney General Alberto Gonzales announced he will leave the Department of Justice, after two and a half years of service to the department. Al Gonzales is a man of integrity, decency and principle, and
I have reluctantly accepted his resignation, with great appreciation for
the service that he has provided for our country."

And it was Bush, not Gonzales, who displayed testiness. "After
months of unfair treatment that has created a harmful distraction at
the Justice Department," said the president, "Judge Gonzales decided
to resign his position, and I accept his decision. It's sad that we live in
a time when a talented and honorable person like Alberto Gonzales
is impeded from doing important work because his good name was
dragged through the mud for political reasons."[78]

On September 17, Bush nominated Michael Mukasey, a retired federal judge from New York, to succeed Gonzales as attorney general. But the U.S. attorney affair was not over. On September 29, 2008, the Justice Department inspector general and the Office of Professional Responsibility issued a joint 358-page report that found a number of the dismissals had been politically motivated and improper. "Our investigation found significant evidence that political partisan considerations were an important factor," said the inspector general. But the IG and the OPR said they were unable to "fully develop the facts" because of "the refusal by certain key witnesses to be interviewed by us, as well as by the White House's decision not to provide internal White House documents to us." Accordingly, the inspector general and Office of Professional Responsibility recommended that the attorney general appoint a special counsel to conduct a further investigation to determine whether any criminal offense had been committed by Gonzales and other high-ranking Justice Department officials.

The next day, Attorney General Mukasey appointed Nora Dannehy, a career Justice Department lawyer, as special counsel to investigate the matter. "Ms. Dannehy is a well-respected and experienced career prosecutor who has supervised a wide range of investigations and prosecutions during her lengthy career," said Mukasey, "and I am grateful to her for her willingness to serve in this capacity."[79]

Nora Dannehy's investigation lasted almost two years. She issued a final report on July 21, 2010. Dannehy concluded that while the politically motivated removal of some U.S. attorneys violated Justice Department principles, no crime had been committed that warranted prosecution. She also found that there was "insufficient evidence to establish that persons knowingly made material false statements to the OIG/OPR or Congress, or corruptly endeavored to obstruct justice."[80]

Obama's attorney general Eric Holder accepted Dannehy's findings. There would be no prosecutions. So ended the U.S. attorney affair.

CHAPTER TWENTY-THREE

Quagmire of the Vanities

We're kicking ass.

George W. Bush
September 5, 2007

Bush remained focused on Iraq. And the news was not good. As the surge troops began to arrive in Iraq in the spring of 2007, American casualties spiraled upward. Eighty-one were killed in March, 104 in April, and 126 in May, the highest monthly total since 2004.[1] June saw another 101 killed in action. For the first time since the war began the United States suffered triple-digit losses for three consecutive months. Iraqi casualties were also increasing. Twenty-five hundred in April; twenty-eight hundred in May.[2] With no end in sight.

An equally serious problem pertained to the passage of a $124 billion supplemental appropriations bill to fund the war in Iraq. The Democrats now controlled both the House and the Senate and were unwilling to underwrite Bush's failed strategy. Under the bill that came forward, American troops would be required to begin withdrawing from Iraq by October 1, 2007, and all combat troops would have to be out six months later. "This war has dragged on too long," said Senator Daniel Inouye (D., Hawaii), chairman of the Appropriations Committee. "I think we should remind ourselves that we've been in this war longer than we were in World War II, and we thought that was an eternity."[3]*

Bush was in no mood to compromise. "An artificial timetable of withdrawal would say to the enemy, just wait them out. It would say to the Iraqis, don't do the hard things necessary to achieve our objectives. And it would be discouraging for our troops."[4]

Despite Bush's objections, the House passed the measure 218–208, the evening of April 25. Two hundred and sixteen Democrats and 2 Republicans voted in favor; 195 Republicans and 13 Democrats opposed. "Our troops must be given all they need to do their jobs," said Speaker Nancy Pelosi, "but they must be brought home responsibly, safely, and soon."[5] The Senate added its approval (51–46) the following day. Two Republicans, Chuck Hagel of Nebraska and Gordon Smith of Oregon, joined 48 Democrats and Independent Bernie Sanders of Vermont voting in favor. "On Iraq, the American people want a new direction, and we are providing it," said Senator Patty Murray (D., Wash.), a leader of the conference committee that reported the bill.[6] Senator Murray was correct. A *New York Times*/CBS News poll taken immediately before the vote indicated that the American public favored withdrawal 64 to 32 percent.[7]

On May 1, Bush vetoed the bill—his second veto in six years.† It was the fourth anniversary of the president's "Mission Accomplished" speech from the flight deck of the *Abraham Lincoln*. Bush seemed unaware of the irony. "It makes no sense to tell the enemy when you plan to start withdrawing," said the president. "Setting a deadline for withdrawal is setting a date for failure, and that would be irresponsible."[8]

The Democrats lacked the votes to override Bush's veto. The House took up the measure on May 2, and debate lasted sixty minutes. "The president said Congress is substituting our judgment for the

---

* Senator Inouye was a highly decorated combat veteran of World War II, and had lost an arm fighting in Italy with the 442nd Regimental Combat Team—an all-Nisei unit assigned to the Fifth Army. Initially awarded the Distinguished Service Cross for bravery in action, the award was later upgraded to the Medal of Honor.

† On July 19, 2006, Bush had vetoed the Stem Cell Research Enhancement Act, H.R. 810. His veto was sustained 235–193, also on July 19.

judgments of commanders in the field 6,000 miles away," said Pelosi. "Wrong again, Mr. President. We are substituting our judgment for your judgment sixteen blocks down Pennsylvania Avenue."[9] Congressman Rahm Emanuel, chairman of the Democratic caucus, was more explicit. "President Bush calls the Democratic plan to change direction in Iraq a prescription for chaos and confusion. But if there is one thing we know for sure, it's that the man responsible for chaos and confusion in Iraq is the president, who has yet to demonstrate competence or command."[10]

The argument for sustaining Bush's veto was made by minority leader John Boehner. "In my view, and in others, al Qaeda has made Iraq the central front in their war with us."[11] Boehner made little effort to defend Bush's leadership. When the roll was called, 220 Democrats and 2 Republicans voted to override the president's veto; 196 Republicans joined by 7 Democrats voted against. Since the House failed to achieve the required two-thirds majority, Bush's veto was sustained. There would be no deadline for the withdrawal of American forces.

Less than an hour after the House vote, Bush met with congressional leaders in the White House to work out a funding compromise. "I thank the leaders from Congress for coming down to discuss the Iraq funding issue," said the president. "Yesterday was a day that highlighted differences. Today is a day where we can work together to find common ground. . . . I think it's very important we do this as quickly as we possibly can. I'm confident that we can reach an agreement."[12] The revised supplemental appropriations bill with no date for American withdrawal from Iraq was passed by both Houses of Congress on May 24, and signed by the president the following day.[13] Recognizing that Bush was not going to veto the bill, the Democrats attached the Fair Minimum Wage Act of 2007 as a rider, raising the minimum wage in the United States from $5.15 an hour to $7.25 by 2009. Bush got his funding, but the Democrats raised the minimum wage.

The bill also contained eighteen performance benchmarks to measure the progress in Iraq. Introduced by Senator John Warner, the benchmarks explicitly stated that "the United States strategy in Iraq, hereafter, shall be conditioned on the Iraqi government meeting benchmarks."

The benchmarks in-
cluded requirements to
reduce the level of sectarian violence and increase
the number of Iraqi secu-
rity units capable of operating independently. The
president was required
to report to Congress the
progress the Iraqi gov-
ernment was making to
meet the benchmarks.[14]
Bush got the money he

With General David Petraeus in the
Oval Office, January 26, 2007.

needed to continue the war through September, but Congress was no
longer providing a blank check.

Bush saw the Democratic opposition to the war in Iraq as politics.
But he recognized his time was running out. He needed results. And
he needed them quickly. To replace Ambassador Zalmay Khalilzad
the president named Ryan Crocker, a veteran diplomat familiar with
the Middle East. "Ryan gained my respect quickly," said Bush. "He
had a knack for detecting problems and heading them off.... He
worked seamlessly with General Petraeus."[15] And for Bush, Petraeus
was the key to victory in Iraq. Having overruled the military command structure and ordered the surge, Bush was now dependent upon
Petraeus to produce results. He was confident the general could do so.
After four years of war, Bush believed that like Lincoln, he had found
his Grant.

Not surprisingly, Bush established a direct personal relationship
with Petraeus. He spoke to the general and Ambassador Crocker every
Monday morning at 8:30 (3:30 p.m. Baghdad time), and sometimes
more often. These were command conferences, but quickly took on a
personal dimension. "I believed a close personal relationship and frequent contact were critical to making the new strategy succeed," said
Bush. "The conversations gave me a chance to hear firsthand reports on
conditions in Iraq. They allowed Petraeus and Crocker to share frustra-

tions and push for decisions from the commander in chief." [16] In effect, Bush was bypassing the military chain of command—just as Lincoln sometimes did.

Bush also developed an informal, backchannel line of communication with Petraeus. The go-between was retired General Jack Keane at the American Enterprise Institute. In the spring and summer of 2007, Keane made three lengthy visits to Baghdad, where he consulted with Petraeus and then reported his findings to Bush and Cheney. "You tell Petraeus, don't let the chain of command filter out any requests," Bush instructed Keane. "If he needs anything, you just tell me. You get the word to me." [17] Formally, Petraeus reported to Admiral William Fallon at Central Command, and through Fallon to the secretary of defense and the chairman of the Joint Chiefs. In practice, he reported directly to the president.

To facilitate his control of the war, Bush reorganized the staff of the National Security Council. The Iraqi conflict and the Afghan effort were stripped out from NSC director Stephen Hadley and placed under a "war czar" who reported directly to the president. Not since Franklin Roosevelt installed Admiral William Leahy as his personal chief of staff in the White House during World War II has a president become so directly involved in formulating military strategy. To fill the position, Bush tapped Lieutenant General Douglas Lute, who was the chief operations officer of the Joint Staff in the Pentagon. By moving Lute from the Joint Staff to the White House, Bush was visibly asserting his command of the war in Iraq. He was also facilitating his ability to deal directly with Petraeus in Baghdad. If Petraeus was having difficulty with his superiors (especially Admiral Fallon), he could bring the matter directly to Lute in the White House, and Lute could take the matter to the president. This process also short-circuited the military chain of command. But after four years of unsuccessful effort in Iraq, Bush was ready for a change.*

---

* Both the military and Secretary of Defense Gates were uncomfortable with the role Lute began to play, which continued into the Obama administration. As Gates noted in his memoirs, "The National Security [Council] Staff had, in effect, become an operational body with its own policy agenda, as opposed to a coordination mechanism. And this, in turn, led to micromanagement far beyond what was appropriate. . . . I told General Jim Mattis at Central Command that

Bush also replaced Peter Pace as chairman of the Joint Chiefs of Staff. Pace was the last holdover from the Rumsfeld era, and had opposed the surge from the beginning. If Bush was fielding a new team with a new strategy, why retain Pace? The term of the chairman of the Joint Chiefs is two years. Omar Bradley was the first chairman back in 1949, and the tradition was established that each chairman would serve two terms, or four years.* Pace was the sixteenth chairman and had been appointed to succeed Air Force General Richard Myers in 2005. His term expired September 30, 2007. But in the spring of 2007, the administration announced that Pace would be succeeded by Admiral Michael Mullen, the chief of naval operations, when his term expired. The reason ostensibly was that Pace would face a grueling confirmation fight in the Senate. But that was window dressing. "I knew I had, for all practical purposes, sacrificed Peter Pace to save the surge," Gates wrote in his memoirs. "I was not proud of that."[18] Bush was also uncomfortable about replacing Pace, and later awarded him the Presidential Medal of Freedom to assuage his regret.[19] But with Pace gone, Bush's new team was now complete.

Meanwhile in Iraq the tour of U.S. servicemen had been extended from twelve to fifteen months—a serious blow to morale. Bush saw the move as necessary, if that was what Petraeus needed. He also had trouble understanding why it should pose a problem. "Why do people join the military if they don't want to fight and defend the country?" he asked the Joint Chiefs.[20] It was a curious query for the man who as a young Yale graduate in the 1960s had avoided service in Vietnam by enrolling in the National Guard.

The absence of good news from Iraq saw Bush's popularity plummet further. On June 26, Senator Dick Lugar of Indiana, the ranking Republican on the Foreign Relations Committee, broke publicly with

---

if Lute ever called him again to question anything, Mattis was to tell him to go to hell." Robert M. Gates, *Duty: Memoirs of a Secretary at War* (New York: Alfred A. Knopf, 2014), 482.

* There were two exceptions: Army General Lyman Lemnitzer, who was appointed by Eisenhower in 1960, was not reappointed by Kennedy when his term expired in 1962, and General Maxwell Taylor, whom Kennedy appointed in 1962, was sent by Johnson to Vietnam as ambassador in 1964 (replacing Henry Cabot Lodge), and was not reappointed.

the president in a fifty-minute speech on the Senate floor. Said Lugar, "The costs and benefits of continuing down the current path outweigh the potential benefits that might be achieved. Persisting indefinitely with the surge strategy will delay policy adjustments that have a better chance of protecting our vital interests over the long term." [21]

Two days after Lugar spoke, the Senate defeated Bush's long cherished plan to overhaul the nation's outdated immigration system. The issue was whether to invoke cloture and end debate so the reform measure could be voted on. Only forty-six senators—well short of the sixty required—voted to do so. And of those forty-six, only twelve were Republicans. "The bill now dies," said Senator Dianne Feinstein, who had helped write the measure. [22] Bush had worked hard to achieve passage of the legislation, and had spent the morning before the vote calling Republican senators to ask for their support. The fact that he was unable to win them over was a reflection of his diminished standing in Washington. "Congress's failure to act is a disappointment," said Bush afterward. "A lot of us worked hard to see if we couldn't find common ground, and it didn't work." [23]

Throughout his public life, both as governor of Texas and as president, Bush had been strongly committed to achieving immigration reform. In his memoirs, he cites his childhood experience with the family housekeeper, Paula Rendón, a recent arrival from Mexico, as kindling his interest in the issue. "Paula became like a second mother to my younger brothers and sister and me," said Bush. "She worked hard, taking care of our family in Texas and her own in Mexico. Eventually she bought a home and moved her family to Houston." [24] Bush was thinking about Paula when during the 2000 Republican presidential primaries he famously told the editorial board of the *Cedar Rapids Gazette*, "Family values don't stop at the Rio Grande." [25] Bush became fond of the phrase, and used it repeatedly.

During his first term, Bush concentrated on tax reform and No Child Left Behind, and then the wars in Afghanistan and Iraq. Immigration reform was left on a back burner. But following his reelection, Bush renewed his interest. In the spring of 2005 he dispatched Karl Rove and Homeland Security Adviser Frances Townsend to canvass the Republican leadership on Capitol Hill. They received a chilly reception in the House. Republican lawmakers wanted to talk about securing the border. Resolving the status of illegal immigrants was a nonstarter. In the Senate, on the other hand, Bush found considerable support. Senators John Cornyn (R., Tex.) and Jon Kyl (R., Ariz.) were strongly in favor of revising the nation's immigration laws, as were John McCain, Arlen Specter, Lindsey Graham, and Ted Kennedy.

Bush decided to press ahead. On May 15, 2006, he made a prime-time television speech to the nation laying out his proposals. "We are a nation of laws, and we must enforce our laws," said the president. "We are also a nation of immigrants, and we must uphold that tradition, which has strengthened our country in so many ways."[26] Bush then laid out a five-point program that included increased border security; a temporary guest worker program "that would create a legal path for foreign workers to enter our country in an orderly way, for a limited period of time"; closer inspection of the workforce, including tamper-proof identity cards for foreign workers; increased efforts to assimilate immigrants, especially by instruction in English; and perhaps most important, a path to citizenship for the twelve million illegal immigrants already in the United States.

> Some in this country argue that the solution is to deport every illegal immigrant, and that any proposal short of this amounts to amnesty. I disagree. It is neither wise nor realistic to round up millions of people, many with deep roots in the United States, and send them across the border. There is a national middle ground between granting an automatic path to citizenship for every illegal immigrant, and a program of mass deportation. That middle ground recognizes that there are differences between an illegal immigrant who crossed the border recently and someone who has worked here for many years, has a home, a family, and an otherwise clean record.[27]

Bush concluded his address by asking Congress to enact a comprehensive immigration reform bill as soon as possible. And he suggested that the tone of the debate be respectful. "Feelings run deep on this issue, and as we work it out, all of us need to keep some things in mind. We cannot build a unified country by inciting people to anger or playing on anyone's fears, or exploiting the issue of immigration for political gain."[28]

Ten days after Bush spoke, the Senate passed an immigration bill introduced by Chuck Hagel and Mel Martinez that incorporated the president's proposals. Not surprisingly, it failed passage in the House of Representatives. That was in 2006, when the Republicans were in control of both Houses. After the 2006 election, Bush worked with Senator Kennedy and the Democratic leadership to reintroduce the legislation.* But the year interval between its first passage in the spring of 2006 and 2007 had allowed the opposition to mobilize. Led by right-wing talk show hosts such as Sean Hannity, the opposition fanned the flames of chauvinism and xenophobia, warning of a Third World invasion. "We will not surrender America," became a battle cry. Both Ted Kennedy and Bush urged Harry Reid to wait until after the July 4th weekend to call the cloture vote, believing they could mobilize the sixty votes necessary. Reid declined to do so. The cloture vote failed, and immigration reform was dead. Bush was profoundly disappointed, but there was nothing more he could do.

Closely related to Bush's desire for immigration reform was his determination to expand the area of American free trade. When he was

---

* Known as the Comprehensive Immigration Reform Act of 2007 (S.1348), the bill would have increased the number of Border Patrol agents by twenty thousand, added 370 miles of fencing to the border with Mexico, and instituted an "Employment Eligibility Verification System" that would provide a central databank for all immigrant workers living in the United States. The bill would also have established the "Z visa," which would be given to everyone living in the United States without a visa. This would allow holders to remain in the United States for the remainder of their life, as well as giving them the right to a Social Security number. After eight years, anyone with a Z visa could apply for a Permanent Residence Card, and after five additional years could apply for citizenship. The bill also would have established a "Y visa" for temporary workers who could remain in the United States for two years.

The Senate fight for S.1348 led by Ted Kennedy was later made into a documentary movie by Shari Robertson and Michael Camerini entitled *The Senators' Bargain*, and premiered on HBO, March 24, 2010. It was also featured at the 2010 Human Rights Watch Film Festival at Lincoln Center in New York City.

inaugurated in January 2001, the United States had free trade agreements with only three countries: Israel, which had been designated under Ronald Reagan in 1985; plus Canada and Mexico under the North American Free Trade Agreement (NAFTA) negotiated under George H. W. Bush and ratified under Bill Clinton in 1994. When Bush left office in January 2009, the United States had concluded free trade agreements with an additional seventeen countries, including the six nations of Central America.* "Americans should never fear competition," said Bush. "Our country has always thrived when we've engaged the world with confidence in our values and ourselves."[29]

Working through U.S. trade representative Robert Zoellick, Bush concluded free trade agreements with Chile and Singapore in September 2003. These were breakthrough agreements. The first with countries of South America and Asia, and Singapore was America's twelfth largest trading partner. "I signed this legislation today," said Bush, "fully expecting many more free trade agreements. We're now negotiating with Australia and Morocco, five nations in Central America, and the South African Customs Union."[30] Morocco was added in July of 2004, and Australia in August. The following year, Bush concluded the Central America Free Trade Agreement (CAFTA) with Costa Rica, El Salvador, Guatemala, Honduras, Nicaragua, and the Dominican Republic. Congressional opposition was fierce, especially from members representing sugar-producing states, but Bush pressed relentlessly for passage and was successful. An agreement with Bahrain was added in 2006, and with Peru and Oman just before Bush left office in 2009. Three agreements negotiated by Bush were left unratified when his term ended: Colombia, Panama, and South Korea (America's sixth largest trading partner). Democrats in the 110th Congress were reluctant to ratify the agreements because of the entrenched opposition of many American trade unions, especially the UAW. When the Republicans regained control of the House of Representatives after the 2010 elections, the agreements with Co-

---

* On September 23, 2001, President Bush signed a free trade agreement with Jordan that had been negotiated under President Clinton.

lombia, Panama, and South Korea were ratified and signed by President Obama in October 2011.

"One of the enduring lessons of the Great Depression," said Bush, "is that global protectionism is a path to global economic ruin."[31] Under Bush, America's world trade increased from $2.5 trillion in 2001 to $4 trillion in 2008—an increase of 60 percent. And of the $4 trillion, 40 percent was with free trade partners.[32] "Expanding trade and investment has been one of the highest priorities of my administration," he told the Asia-Pacific Economic Cooperation Business Summit meeting in Lima, Peru, just before leaving office.[33] Bush believed ardently in free markets and was always opposed to government intervention. That was a cherished belief on his part. Robert Zoellick also deserves substantial credit for successfully negotiating the agreements.

Despite his success on free trade, Bush's defeat on immigration reform sent shockwaves through the White House. If the president could not muster Republican votes on an issue to which he was so closely attached, what did that portend for the situation in Iraq? Would more Republican senators follow Lugar and defect? George Voinovich of Ohio had already done so, and on July 4, Pete Domenici told constituents in Albuquerque, New Mexico, that he too was unwilling to continue along the present course. The United States, said Domenici, needs a strategy "that will move our troops out of combat operations and on the path to coming home."[34] Bush believed it was urgent to prevent further defections. Petraeus was due to report to Congress in September, and the president needed to hold the line until then.

Speaking to an audience in Cleveland on July 10, Bush said that the additional troops sent to Iraq had just arrived, and needed time to have an effect. "I believe that it's in this nation's interests to give the commander a chance to fully implement his operations. And I believe Congress ought to wait for General Petraeus to come back and give his assessment of the strategy he is putting in place before they make any decisions."[35]

Two days later, Bush met with the press in the White House. "Before I answer some of your questions, I'd like to provide the American people with an update on the situation in Iraq," said the president.

"Since America began military operations in Iraq, the conflict there has gone through four major phases. The first phase was the liberation of Iraq from Saddam Hussein. The second was the return of sovereignty to the Iraqi people and free elections. The third was the tragic escalation of sectarian violence sparked by the bombing of the Golden Mosque in Samarra. We've entered the fourth phase: deploying reinforcements and launching new operations to help Iraqis bring security to their people."

Bush said he was sending Congress a preliminary report dealing with the eighteen benchmarks that had been established to measure progress in Iraq,* and that made clear "why a drawdown of forces that is not linked to the success of our operations would be a disaster." Of the eighteen benchmarks, the president said the Iraqis had made satisfactory progress in eight areas, were lagging in eight, and two were too mixed to be characterized one way or the other. "Those who believe that the battle in Iraq is lost will likely point to the unsatisfactory performance on some of the political benchmarks. Those of us who believe the battle of Iraq can and must be won see the satisfactory performance on several of the security benchmarks as a cause for optimism. Our strategy is built on the premise that progress on security will pave the way for political progress. So it is not surprising that political progress is lagging behind the security gains we are seeing."

Bush noted this was a preliminary report, and that in September General Petraeus and Ambassador Crocker would provide Congress with a more comprehensive assessment. In his view it was essential that Congress wait until they heard from Petraeus before taking action. "To begin withdrawing before our commander tells us we are ready would be dangerous for Iraq, for the regime, and for the United States."

In the question period that followed, the president was asked repeatedly about Iraq. And he consistently stressed the importance of waiting

---

* *Initial Benchmark Assessment Report on Iraq*, July 12, 2007. These were the benchmarks added by Senator Warner to the supplemental appropriations bill that Congress passed in May, http://2001-2009.state.gov/p/nea/rls/rpt/88195.htm.

until Petraeus returned and testified before making any change in the surge policy. "I'm going to wait for David to come back—David Petraeus to come back and give us a report on what he sees. And then we'll use that data—his report to work with the military chain of command and Members of Congress to make another decision if need be." It was clear throughout the press conference that Bush was primarily worried about peremptory action by Congress. Asked by Jim Axelrod of CBS News if he was still committed to vetoing any troop withdrawal deadline, Bush was emphatic that he would do so.

> I don't think Congress ought to be running the war. I think they ought to be funding the troops. I'm certainly interested in their opinion, but trying to run the war through resolution is a prescription for failure, as far as I am concerned, and we can't afford to fail.

More significantly, Bush sought to shift responsibility for the debacle in Iraq from himself to the American military establishment. Asked by Wendell Goler of Fox News why the country should trust his vision of victory in Iraq since he had failed to anticipate the sectarian divisions that tore the country apart after the removal of Saddam Hussein, Bush placed the blame on Tommy Franks.

> My primary question to General Franks was, do you have what it takes to succeed? And do you have what it takes to succeed after you succeed in removing Saddam Hussein? And his answer was, yes.
>
> Now, history is going to look back to determine whether or not there might have been a different decision made. But at the time, the only thing I can tell you, Wendell, is that I relied upon our military commanders to make the proper decisions about troop strength. And I can remember a meeting with the Joint Chiefs, who said, "We've reviewed the plan." I remember—and they seemed satisfied with it. I remember sitting in the Situation Room downstairs here at the White House and I went to commander and commander. . . . I said to each of them, do you have what it takes? Are you satisfied with the strategy? And the answer was, yes.[36]

What Bush did not say was that it was he who changed the military's mission in Iraq when he announced from the flight deck of the *Abraham Lincoln* on May 1, 2003, that the United States was going to bring democracy to the country. That was not the original battle plan, and it was not what the military had prepared for. The State Department, the Defense Department, and the military leadership had assumed that after removing Saddam they would remain for a few months and then withdraw, leaving the Iraqis to organize a successor government for themselves. They did not anticipate that American troops would become occupiers. But Bush changed course. On his own authority he shifted from simply removing Saddam and destroying his supposed weapons of mass destruction to establishing democracy in Iraq. Secretary of Defense Donald Rumsfeld questioned the shift at the time but was overruled.* Whether Bush grasped the fact that it was he who changed the American mission in Iraq is unclear. What is clear is that he was now attempting to place the blame for the catastrophe on the military.

Congress paid little heed to Bush's warnings. Later that afternoon the House of Representatives voted 223–201 to require the United States to begin the withdrawal of combat troops within 120 days and to have all combat forces out of Iraq by April 1, 2008. This was the second time within three months that the House had voted to begin the withdrawal of troops, and it was essentially a party-line vote. Only four Republicans voted in favor; only ten Democrats voted against. The Democratic leadership argued that the interim benchmark report Bush provided that morning confirmed the need to begin the withdrawal of U.S. forces; Republicans contended the Democrats were playing politics. "The Democrats want to wave a magic wand and make this war go away," said Congressman David Dreier of California.[37]

In the Senate, Bush was able to hold on. Once again, the Demo-

---

* In his memoirs Rumsfeld wrote, "The reason so many countries supported us, and the reason two successive U.S. presidents and the Congress of the United States supported regime change in Iraq was because of the security threat posed by Saddam Hussein. Bringing democracy to Iraq had not been among the primary rationales [for the invasion]." *Known and Unknown* (New York: Sentinel, 2011), 499.

crats failed to achieve the sixty votes necessary to invoke cloture. After an all-night debate on July 17–18, the Democrats could muster only fifty-two votes. Four Republicans joined the Democrats,* but Lugar, Voinovich, and Domenici supported the president. Failure to close off debate meant that the House bill would not be voted on.

Throughout the summer of 2007, Bush continued to concentrate on Iraq. Speaking to the Veterans of Foreign Wars national convention in Kansas City on August 22, the president likened the fighting in Iraq to the World War II conflict with Japan, the war in Korea, and the fighting in Vietnam. "In Asia, we saw freedom triumph over violent ideologies after the sacrifice of tens of thousands of American lives, and that freedom has yielded peace for generations. . . . The question now that comes before us is this: Will today's generation of Americans resist the allure of retreat, and will we do in the Middle East what the veterans in this room did in Asia?" Although the United States did not prevail in Vietnam, Bush found a lesson there as well. "Unlike in Vietnam, if we withdraw [from Iraq] before the job is done, the enemy would follow us home. And that is why for the security of the United States of America, we must defeat them overseas so we do not face them in the United States of America."[38]

For Bush, the war in Iraq was an ideological struggle between good and evil. "The struggle has been called a clash of civilizations. In truth, it is a struggle for civilization."[39] Speaking six days later to the American Legion in Reno, Nevada, Bush called the fighting in Iraq "the first ideological war of the 21st century. . . . The murderers and beheaders are not the true face of Islam; they are the face of evil. They seek to exploit religion as a path to power and a means to dominate the Middle East." And he upped the ante. Withdrawal from Iraq, said Bush, would leave "a region already known for instability under the shadow of nuclear holocaust."[40]

Bush spent most of the month of August at his ranch in Crawford. On Thursday, August 23, his sojourn was briefly interrupted when the

---

* The four Republicans voting for cloture were Chuck Hagel of Nebraska, Gordon Smith from Oregon, and Maine's two senators, Susan Collins and Olympia Snowe.

nation's intelligence community released the National Intelligence Estimate dealing with the situation in Iraq. Representing the consensus of America's sixteen intelligence agencies, the report was far from reassuring. "There have been measurable but uneven improvements in Iraq's security situation," said the NIE, but "the overall level of violence, including attacks on and casualties among civilians remains high; Iraq's sectarian groups remain unreconciled; AQI [al Qaeda in Iraq] retains the ability to conduct high-profile attacks; and to date, Iraqi political leaders remain unable to govern effectively."[41] Bush made no comment about the report, and Democrats enthusiastically embraced it as further evidence that the president's policy had failed. "We need to stop refereeing this civil war, and start getting out now," said New York senator Hillary Clinton, who was beginning her campaign for the Democratic presidential nomination.[42]

Bush returned to Washington in late August, stopping briefly in Louisiana to review recovery efforts from Hurricane Katrina. Having dinner at Dooky Chase's refurbished restaurant the evening of Tuesday, August 28, the president was graciousness itself. "We're thrilled that you would allow us to come and taste your beautiful food in this spectacular room. We love your art, but more importantly, we love your spirit."[43] The following day, Bush spoke three times, first at the Martin Luther King Charter School, then at the River Garden Housing Complex, and finally in Bay St. Louis, Mississippi. The federal government had already spent $114 billion on relief efforts, and the bitterness of the immediate aftermath of Katrina appeared to be over. Bush spoke of Governor Kathleen Blanco in glowing terms: "She had done what leaders are supposed to do, and when she sees a problem, addresses them head on. . . . And you've done so, Governor, I congratulate you for your leadership."[44] Bush was equally appreciative of Mississippi governor Haley Barbour when speaking in Bay St. Louis. "He's taken a problem on, and he's coordinated it and managed it in a way that you'd expect your chief executive to do. And so, Governor, I want to congratulate you on a job well done."[45]

Back in Washington, Bush turned to Iraq. The situation seemed to be improving. On Thursday, August 30, the president met with Gates, the military leadership, Cheney, and members of the White House staff preparatory to a videoconference with Petraeus and Ambassador Crocker the following day. The meeting had been organized by Gates. "I wanted him [Bush] to know beforehand what he would hear so he wouldn't have to react on the spur of the moment. . . . I also wanted the president to be able to ask questions, including political ones that might be less convenient (or inappropriate) to ask in the larger forum the next day."[46] Gates led the discussion. The news from Iraq was positive, he said. American military casualties had declined from 126 in May to 84 in August—a drop of 33 percent. Iraqi civilian deaths had fallen from 2,796 to 2,384 over the same period. More importantly perhaps, in Baghdad civilian casualties had declined by almost half—from 1,341 to 738.[47] Gates said the changed situation allowed them to start thinking about a gradual drawdown of forces, except around Baghdad. Cheney was skeptical. Would a drawdown put us on a path where we could not succeed? he asked. General Pace responded. "No. They put us on a path where we can."[48] Bush appeared satisfied, and appreciated Gates's effort to bring him up to speed before the videoconference with Petraeus.

The following morning at 8:30 Bush and the full National Security Council met with Petraeus and Crocker by teleconference. They were joined by Admiral Fallon from CENTCOM headquarters in Florida. Petraeus reviewed the situation once more, and said it looked as though they had turned the corner. He said he did not plan to replace the Marine Expeditionary Unit in Anbar province when its tour ran out in September, and believed he could reduce his strength by five brigade-combat teams and two Marine battalions between December and June 2008. That would bring U.S. forces in Iraq down to the same level as before the surge. Bush pressed Petraeus to be sure the recommendations were his and not those of Admiral Fallon or the Joint Chiefs. Petraeus assured him the recommendations were his.

Bush appeared satisfied. "The plan should be this," he said. "Keep a boot on the neck and get us in place for the long term."[49] The president said he was in no rush to bring the troops home, but understood what Petraeus was saying. After two hours the conference adjourned.

Bush wanted to see for himself. On Sunday evening, September 2, he secretly departed the White House in an unmarked vehicle (rather than a helicopter), and headed to Andrews Air Force Base without police escort or motorcade. At Andrews he boarded Air Force One in its hangar and the plane rolled out for takeoff after dark. Bush was scheduled to go to Australia for an Asia-Pacific Economic Conference in Sydney the following day, but stepped up his departure so he could visit Iraq.

Rather than land at the military airbase outside Baghdad, the president's plane touched down at Al Asad in Anbar province, a remote, well-fortified desert installation where some ten thousand troops were stationed. It was Bush's third visit to Iraq, and again he remained on territory held by the U.S. military. The president stayed for seven hours. During that time he met with Petraeus and Crocker, then with the Iraqi leadership—President Jalal Talabani, Prime Minister Nouri al-Maliki, two vice presidents, the deputy prime minister, and the president of the Kurdistan region—and then with the Sunni tribal chiefs who had recently switched sides. Bush later described them as a "rough-hewn, earthy bunch. Their friendly animated mannerisms reminded me of local officials in West Texas. But instead of jeans and boots, they were wearing full-length robes and colorful headdresses."[50]

After the meetings, Bush spoke to the press. Progress was being made, he said. "General Petraeus and Ambassador Crocker tell me if the kind of success we are now seeing continues, it will be possible to maintain the same level of security with fewer American forces."[51] Bush spent several hours mingling with the troops, and that evening before departing for Sydney, spoke to the garrison in a formal setting. "Because of your hard work, because of your bravery and sacrifice, you are denying al Qaeda a safe haven from which to plot and plan and carry out attacks against the United States of America. . . . We've come to tell you the American people are standing with you. They're grateful for your sacrifice. As Commander in Chief, I'm proud to be in your presence this Labor Day. I ask God's blessings on you and your family, and may God continue to bless America."[52]

Bush's visit to the base in Anbar proved a two-edged sword. The president may have profited from speaking to Petraeus and the Iraqi leaders in person, but it was also seen by many as a publicity stunt on the eve of Petraeus's testimony to Congress. *The New York Times* characterized Bush's visit as "Another Iraq Photo Op."[53] The president never set foot on Iraqi soil outside a fully protected military facility. Regardless of Bush's rhetoric, the United States was an occupying power. Joschka Fischer, the now former German foreign minister and vice chancellor, put it best when he contrasted Bush's visits to Iraq with those of Iranian president Mahmoud Ahmadinejad. When Bush visited the country, said Fischer, it was a state secret and he had to enter through the back door. "When Ahmadinejad wants to visit Baghdad, the visit was announced two weeks beforehand, he arrives in the brightest sunshine and travels in an open car through a cheering crowd to downtown Baghdad.[54]*

Bush was exhilarated by his stopover at Al Asad. Arriving in Australia, he was asked by deputy prime minister Mark Vaile about the situation in Iraq. "We're kicking ass," Bush replied. The president's crude comment did little to enhance his reputation. When Bush's remarks were reported in the *Sydney Morning Herald*, the Australians were stunned. As American diplomat Kurt Campbell wrote, "The president's increasingly diminishing number of red state supporters still rally to such incendiary words, but even the most ardent Australian

---

* Iranian president Mahmoud Ahmadinejad paid a state visit to Baghdad on March 1, 2008—the first by a Middle East head of state since the American invasion in 2003. As *The Washington Post* noted, "The pomp and ceremony, in public and on television, sharply contrasted with the surprise visits to Iraq by President Bush and former British prime minister Tony Blair."

Patrick Cockburn, writing in *The Independent*, was more explicit. "In contrast to President George Bush's furtive visits to U.S. military bases in Iraq, Mr. Ahmadinejad's delegation seemed to take pleasure in pre-announcing the two-day visit, landing at Baghdad airport in daylight, and driving by road to the Green Zone." CNN reported, "Ahmadinejad shunned the security measures followed by many other leaders on visits to Baghdad; riding from Baghdad's airport in a civilian style sedan—and not an armored vehicle or helicopter—to central Baghdad. His official meeting with [President] Talabani was at the presidential house outside the heavily fortified International [Green] Zone."

"Iranian Leader in Baghdad, Hails 'New Chapter' in Ties with Iraq," *Washington Post*, March 3, 2008; Patrick Cockburn, "Visit Trumpets Iran's Power in Iraq," *The Independent*, March 3, 2008; "Iran President on Landmark Iraq Visit," CNN.com, March 3, 2008.

supporters of the U.S. and Bush were a little sheepish after this most recent example of Bush's bravado."[55]

General Petraeus and Ambassador Crocker returned to Washington to testify before Congress on Monday, September 10, and Tuesday the 11th. Petraeus was greeted that Monday morning by a full-page ad in *The New York Times* bearing the headline: GENERAL PETRAEUS OR GENERAL BETRAY US. Beneath the headline was a picture of Petraeus and the caption, "Cooking the Books for the White House."[56] The ad had been placed by MoveOn.org, a liberal activist group and political action committee. It backfired badly and made Petraeus a momentary hero.

In his testimony, Petraeus told Congress "the military objectives of the surge are, in large measure, being met. . . . Though the improvements have been uneven across Iraq, the overall number of security incidents in Iraq has declined in eight of the past twelve weeks, with the number of incidents in the last two weeks at the lowest levels since June 2006." Petraeus said that based on the progress that had been made, "I believe that we will be able to reduce our forces to the pre-surge level of brigade-combat teams by next summer without jeopardizing the security gains that we have fought so hard to achieve." He went on to say that while the situation remained complex and difficult, over time he thought "it is possible to achieve our objectives." But he warned that "a premature drawdown of our forces would likely have devastating consequences."[57]

Petraeus and Crocker testified for six and a half hours on Monday before the joint House Foreign Affairs and Armed Services committees, and for seven hours on Tuesday before the Senate Foreign Relations Committee and then the Senate Armed Services Committee. Democrats, while praising Petraeus's military service, largely dismissed his testimony as a White House publicity gimmick.[58] The exchanges were sharp. Congressman Robert Wexler (D., Fla.) accused Petraeus of "cherry-picking statistics" and "massaging information," and compared his testimony to that of General William Westmoreland in 1967 when he assured Congress that American forces were making progress in Vietnam. In the Senate, the questioning was equally harsh. John Warner, ranking Republican on the Armed Services Committee, asked

Petraeus whether the current strategy in Iraq was "making America safer." Petraeus dodged the question. "Sir, I believe this is the best course of action to achieve our objections in Iraq."

"Does that make America safer?" asked Warner.

"Sir, I don't know, actually," Petraeus replied.[59]

Petraeus's testimony made little impact on public opinion. A *USA Today*/Gallup poll taken immediately afterward showed virtually no change in American attitudes toward the war.[60] That was not significant. What was important was that Petraeus had provided Bush with a basis for claiming the surge had been a success, and that the withdrawal of troops could begin. As Richard Haass, president of the Council on Foreign Relations, put it, Petraeus had "co-opted the reductions argument." The bottom line, Haass observed, was that "the administration has probably bought itself sixteen more months of what looks like the status quo."[61]

Bush watched much of the general's testimony on television and was overjoyed. As soon as the hearings concluded, the White House announced the president would speak to the nation about Iraq on Thursday evening. Prior to his speech, Bush invited the congressional leadership to the White House to discuss the war. Bush was in a triumphal mood. "Of course, al Qaeda needs new recruits," said the president, "because we're *killin'* 'em. We're *killin'* 'em all." Senator Reid was appalled. Bush, he thought, looked on the war in Iraq "as if it were some kind of sporting event or action movie. Sometimes it seems as if he really has no idea of the gravity of his words and decisions."[62] Nancy Pelosi was equally upset. The president's approach to the situation in Iraq, she said, was "an insult to the intelligence of the American people."[63]

It was in this climate that Bush spoke to the nation the evening of September 13. "In the life of all free nations, there come moments that decide the direction of a country and reveal the characteristics of its people," said the president. "We are now at such a moment." Bush spoke for eighteen minutes. He reiterated what Petraeus reported, and said the surge had proved a success.

Because of this success, General Petraeus believes we have now reached the point where we can maintain our security gains with fewer American forces. . . . I have accepted General Petraeus's recommendations. The principle guiding my decision on troop levels in Iraq is "return on success." The more successful we are, the more American troops can return home.

Some say the gains we are making in Iraq come too late. They are mistaken. It is never too late to deal a blow to al Qaeda. It is never too late to advance freedom. And it is never too late to support our troops in a fight they can win.[64]

The surge was successful in that it provided Bush with a rationale to begin the withdrawal of American troops. "Return on success." U.S. troop strength stood at 168,000 when the president spoke. By the end of his term in January 2009 it had decreased to 145,000. American casualties were down as well. From a high of 126 in May 2007, to only 25 in December of that year, and 16 in January 2009 when Bush's term ended. Iraqi civilian deaths had declined as well. From 2,481 in August 2007, to 987 in December of that year, and 372 in January 2009.[65]

Bush's willingness to begin the withdrawal of U.S. forces dampened public interest in Iraq. Prior to Petraeus's testimony and Bush's speech, television networks devoted roughly 25 percent of the news coverage to the war. By mid-2008, it was down to 3 percent. Antiwar rallies in March 2008 on the fifth anniversary of the American invasion attracted less than a thousand people in Washington and less than five hundred in San Francisco. Similar demonstrations during the Vietnam War attracted as many as 250,000. "I think the debate has moved on," said Secretary Gates.[66]

Iraq also receded as a political issue. At the Democratic presidential debate in Hanover, New Hampshire, on September 26, neither Hillary Clinton nor Barack Obama pressed for the immediate removal of U.S. troops from Iraq. Asked by moderator Tim Russert whether he would pledge to have all troops out by 2013, Obama said he thought it would be irresponsible to do so. "We don't know what contingency will be out there." Senator Clinton was equally reluctant. "Well, Tim, it is my goal to have all our troops out by the end of my first term [2013]. But

I agree with Barack, it is very difficult to know what we're going to be inheriting."[67]*

A more important question pertains to the surge itself. It coincided with the decline in violence in Iraq but was it the sole cause of the decline? Without denigrating the combat efficiency of the American military, the answer appears to be no. It certainly helped, but it was not the decisive factor. Far more important were the Anbar Awakening that began in late 2006, and the decision of the militant Shiite cleric Moqtada al-Sadr in August 2007 to order his Mahdi Army to stand down. Indeed, Prime Minister Maliki, when asked by the German magazine *Der Spiegel* in July 2008 why the violence in Iraq had declined, did not even mention the surge.[†]

The Anbar Awakening commenced in late 2006 following an attempt to form the Islamic State of Iraq (ISI) by al Qaeda leader Abu Omar al-Baghdadi. ISI was a precursor of ISIS (the Islamic State of Iraq and Syria), and Sunni tribal leaders in Anbar saw little point in declaring a separate state and ceding leadership to al Qaeda.[68] Al Qaeda had seriously overplayed its hand. Determined to impose their view of an Islamic state, Baghdadi and his al Qaeda followers placed rigid restrictions on daily life, beheaded their adversaries, and sought control of the province's oil revenue. Anbar is Iraq's largest province, occupying about a quarter of the total land area, is predominantly Sunni in population, and for almost four years had served as a sanctuary for al Qaeda. But confronted with al Qaeda's excesses, the indigenous tribal leadership rebelled.[‡] Caught between the Shiite government of Maliki and the ISI of

---

* The only Democrat who continued to press for the immediate withdrawal of troops from Iraq was Congressman Dennis Kucinich of Ohio. "To me, it is fairly astonishing to have Democrats who took power in the House and the Senate in 2006, to stand on this stage and tell the American people that this war will continue to 2013 and perhaps past that." Transcript, Democratic Presidential Debate on MSNBC, *New York Times*, September 26, 2007.

† Among the reasons Maliki cited were the Anbar Awakening, the role of Iraqi Security Forces, public revulsion at the excesses of al Qaeda, the economic recovery, and the cooperation of Moqtada al-Sadr. "The Tenure of Coalition Troops Should Be Ended," interview with Nouri al-Maliki, *Der Spiegel*, July 19, 2008.

‡ The Anbar Awakening began in late 2006 when a number of Sunni sheikhs, tired of extreme violence, formed the al-Anbar Salvation Council. The council made significant progress

Baghdadi, the Sunni leadership of Anbar reached out to the American military for assistance. Credit Petraeus for recognizing the opportunity and bringing the Sunnis on board. Sunni leaders were paid generously for their support, and Baghdadi and al Qaeda were driven out, taking refuge in northern Iraq near the Syrian border.*

The decision of Shiite cleric Moqtada al-Sadr on August 29, 2007, to order his Mahdi Army off the streets was equally significant and unexpected. Credit in this instance goes to Iran, which had decided to back the Maliki government fully. Iran had played a crucial role among Iraqi Shiites in helping Maliki become prime minister, and now mediated a cease-fire between the government and al-Sadr. The Bush administration was aware of the role Iran played, but never publicly acknowledged it.[69]

Another factor, perhaps equally important, was that after two years of violent sectarian bloodshed, Baghdad was now virtually separated into discrete Shiite and Sunni districts. Most of Baghdad was Shiite, with small enclaves of Sunni. That de facto sectarian segregation minimized daily friction. Said differently, the ethnic cleansing of both Sunni and Shiite neighborhoods encouraged normal life without violence.

The fact that the surge was not solely responsible for the decline in violence in Iraq in no way diminishes its importance. By coinciding with the decline it provided Bush with a rationale for beginning the drawdown of American forces. Bush considered the surge a success. That was all he needed. The president continued to monitor the fighting in Iraq, and relished receiving the daily body counts of Iraqi dissidents killed by coalition forces. Harry Reid was correct: Bush to some extent

---

in banishing al Qaeda from Anbar province and provided an incentive and protective shield for recruiting tribesmen into the police force. The Salvation Council represented twenty-five tribes, and assisted in recruiting 6,000 tribesmen into the provincial police, and also formed a 2,500-man "emergency brigade." Based on the success of the Anbar Salvation Council, in 2008 two hundred Sunni tribal sheikhs announced the formation of the Iraqi Awakening Sahwa Party. See Peter J. Manson, *Iraq in Transition: The Legacy of Dictatorship and the Prospects for Democracy* (Washington, D.C.: Potomac Books, 2009), 216.

* Abu Omar al-Baghdadi was killed in April 2010 when U.S. and Iraqi forces rocketed his home near Tikrit. He was succeeded as head of ISI by Abu Bakr al-Baghdadi on May 16, 2010. On April 8, 2013, Abu Bakr al-Baghdadi announced the formation of the Islamic State of Iraq and Syria (ISIS).

looked on the war in Iraq as an athletic contest and the body count provided a scorecard. Bush also bonded with David Petraeus. When Admiral Fallon retired in March 2008,* Petraeus was named CENTCOM
commander. To replace Petraeus, the president named General Ray
Odierno, who had been deputy to Petraeus earlier. "Lincoln discovered
Generals Grant and Sherman," said Bush. "Roosevelt had Eisenhower
and Bradley. I found David Petraeus and Ray Odierno."[70]

As 2008 began, Prime Minister Maliki stepped up his efforts to have
coalition forces withdraw from Iraq. "So far the Americans have had
trouble agreeing to a concrete timetable for withdrawal," said Maliki,
"because they feel it would appear tantamount to an admission of defeat. But that isn't the case at all. If we come to an agreement, it is not
evidence of a defeat, but of a victory, of a severe blow we have inflicted
on al Qaeda and the militants."[71] As it turned out, Maliki held the high
ground. The United Nations mandate for coalition troops to remain in
Iraq expired at the end of 2008. If a new agreement was not reached,
U.S. forces would have to withdraw.

Negotiations for a Status of Forces Agreement (SOFA) similar to
those governing the presence of American troops on the territory of
many other countries began in early 2008, but proved difficult. The
most contentious issue was the length of time American forces would
remain in Iraq. Bush was reluctant to set a date. The issue came to a
head during a videoconference in November. Maliki pressed for a firm
timetable. A withdrawal of U.S. troops would not be seen as a defeat,
he told Bush, but as a victory. With his term drawing to a close, Bush
agreed. American troops would begin to pull back from urban areas

---

* Relations between Fallon and Petraeus were always tense, but were not related to Fallon's
retirement. The problem was a lengthy article in *Esquire* magazine by Thomas P. M. Barnett, a
former professor at the Naval War College, about Fallon entitled "The Man Between War and
Peace." The article detailed Fallon's objections to the Bush administration policy regarding Iran
and suggested that only Fallon stood between Bush and war with that country. Fallon warned
Washington that the article was coming and shortly after it appeared quietly submitted his resignation. "The current embarrassing situation, public perception of differences between my views
and administration policy, and the distraction this causes from the mission make this the right
thing to do," Fallon wrote Secretary Gates. Robert M. Gates, *Duty: Memoirs of a Secretary at War*
(New York: Alfred A. Knopf, 2014), 188.

on January 1, 2009, and
would complete the
process by June 30. All
troops would be with-
drawn from Iraq by the
end of 2011. In Bush's
view, the success of the
surge made the with-
drawal possible. It was
not a complete victory,
but it was certainly not
a retreat in the face of
the enemy.

Signing the Status of Forces Agreement with Prime
Minister Maliki in Baghdad, December 14, 2008.

In December 2008, Bush made his fourth trip to Iraq to sign the
agreement. It would be Bush's final visit to Baghdad, and in contrast to
previous visits, he was received at a gala reception. "I remember what
it was like in 2006, and it was bad," Bush told Maliki. "Now it's better.
And you did it."

"We did it together," Maliki replied.[72]

The signing ceremony was elaborately staged, and the room was
packed with journalists and government officials. Bush and Maliki addressed the audience from adjacent lecterns. When Bush concluded his
remarks the scene was interrupted when an Iraqi journalist stood up
and threw his shoe at Bush, shouting: "This is a gift from the Iraqis.
This is a farewell kiss, you dog." Bush saw the shoe coming and deftly
dodged it. The twenty-eight-year-old journalist, Muntadhar al-Zaidi,
then threw his second shoe. "This is from the widows, the orphans,
and those who were killed in Iraq."[73] Maliki reached out and deflected
it. Throwing a shoe at someone is the worst possible insult in Iraq and
is meant to show contempt and disrespect. It means that the target is
even lower than the shoe, which is always on the ground and dirty.
Bush was not hit, and later joked about the incident. "If you want the
facts, it's a size 10 shoe he threw. Thank you for your concern; do not
worry about it."[74]

The shoe-throwing incident dominated Bush's final visit to Baghdad. Maliki was shaken and apologized profusely. Bush appeared un-perturbed. "Having a shoe thrown at me by a journalist ranked as one of my more unusual experiences," he wrote in his memoirs.[75] But to the members of the president's traveling entourage, it was clear that the event had shaken him. When Bush boarded Air Force One later that evening, his bounce was gone.[76]

George W. Bush's decision to invade Iraq in March 2003 was a tragic error. It was compounded by his follow-on decision to install Western-style democracy, and the ensuing military occupation that en-tailed. The tragic loss of life, the instability, the sectarian strife, and the rise of ISIS are all in many respects attributable to those decisions. Over four thousand American soldiers had been killed in Iraq by the time Bush left office, and over thirty thousand wounded. Iraqi deaths ex-ceeded 100,000. Another two million Iraqis had fled to other countries. And the direct military cost to the United States approached $600 bil-lion.* In the immediate aftermath of 9/11, America's international pres-tige had rarely been higher. When Bush left office in 2009, respect for the United States had rarely been lower.

From Iraq, Bush flew to Afghanistan. It was a surprise, un-announced visit, and the president said he wanted to say goodbye to President Hamid Karzai and pay a final visit to the troops stationed there. Unlike Iraq, Afghanistan was not occupied by coalition forces. The troops were there at the pleasure of the Afghan government, which was sovereign. Karzai had been elected president in 2004, the econ-omy was expanding rapidly, four million refugees had returned home, and the education system—which now admitted girls to school—was moving ahead. But there were also major problems. Corruption was rampant, and Afghanistan had become the world's principal producer of opium, accounting for 92 percent of the global supply of heroin in 2007.[77] Even more serious, the Taliban had regrouped and now con-

---

* According to official figures released by the Pentagon, total U.S. casualties from April 2003 to January 2009 were 4,238. Wounded totaled 30,740. The Iraqis reported 106,008 civilian deaths, and 8,890 military fatalities. U.S. expenditures for the war at the end of 2008 were esti-mated at $526 billion. See icasualties.org, 2009.

trolled much of the southern and eastern parts of the country adjacent to Pakistan.

To some extent, the Bush administration was partially responsible for these conditions. By not deploying sufficient forces to seal the border with Pakistan in December 2001, the administration had allowed Osama bin Laden and the al Qaeda leadership, plus remnants of the Taliban, to escape into Pakistan, where the Taliban refitted and reorganized. Also, in the aftermath of victory, too few coalition troops remained in Afghanistan. From 2001 through 2003, U.S. forces in Afghanistan numbered only eight thousand. Coalition partners added another five thousand. But many of the troops, especially from coalition partners, were primarily involved in training missions and were unavailable for combat. Bush's 2003 decision to invade and occupy Iraq also diminished the importance of Afghanistan, particularly in the mind of the military. Beginning in 2004, the number of troops was increased, but could not keep pace with the progress of the Taliban. By 2006 the situation had become critical. The Taliban was on the offensive, and the number of incidents was skyrocketing.

To his credit, Bush recognized the problem and took action. "I decided that America had to take on more responsibility, even though we were about to undertake a major new commitment in Iraq as well."[78] At the president's direction, U.S. forces in Afghanistan were increased to 31,000. Support for the Afghan government was intensified, funding for various reconstruction projects was doubled, and the Afghan army was expanded. But the violence continued.

By 2008, defeat had become a possibility. The Taliban was operating in thirty-three of Afghanistan's thirty-four provinces, and IED (Improvised Explosive Device) attacks had risen to 7,200 annually—as opposed to 80 in 2003. "The news out of Afghanistan is truly alarming," said *The New York Times* on August 21, 2008. "The number of United States and NATO casualties is mounting so quickly, that unless something happens soon this could be the deadliest year of the Afghan war. Kabul, the seat of Afghanistan's pro-Western government, is increasingly besieged. And Taliban and foreign Qaeda fighters are consolidating their control over an expanding swath

Soldiers of the 10th Mountain Division in Afghanistan.

of territory sprawling across both sides of the porous Afghanistan-Pakistan border."[79]

Bush was determined not to allow the Afghanistan effort to fail. As one of his last projects he ordered a review of the administration's strategy by the NSC. When the study called for a more robust effort by the United States, including an additional twenty thousand troops, Bush agreed. But with his term drawing to a close, he was reluctant to order the addition without clearing it with the incoming Obama administration. When Bush's NSC adviser Stephen Hadley inquired, he was told that the Obama administration would prefer to handle it when they took office. Bush agreed. "I decided the new strategy would have a better chance of success if we gave the new team an opportunity to revise it as they saw fit and then adopt it as their own."[80]*

Bush remained in Afghanistan less than five hours. He visited

---

* The Obama administration not only agreed with the buildup of U.S. forces but increased it even more. By mid-2011, there were over 100,000 U.S. troops in Afghanistan plus 42,000 coalition forces. "This is a war we have to win," Obama said during the 2008 campaign. For the text of Obama's remarks, see *New York Times*, July 15, 2008.

the troops at Bagram Air Base, and then went by helicopter to Kabul where President Karzai was waiting. After a brief discussion they met the press. "I was thinking, right before we landed, how much Afghanistan has changed since I have been president," said Bush.

> In 2001, the Taliban were brutally repressing the people of this country.... And American troops proudly liberated the people of Afghanistan.... There has been a lot of progress since 2001 ... but there are a lot of tough challenges.... I told the President you can count on the United States—just like you've been able to count on this administration, you'll be able to count on the next administration as well.... It has been a privilege to work with you over these years. I have come to admire you, I appreciate your service, and I wish you and the people of Afghanistan all the very best.[81]

As Bush boarded the helicopter for his return flight, he was reflective. "I knew I was leaving behind unfinished business. I wanted badly to bring bin Laden to justice. The fact that we did not ranks among my great regrets."[82]

Financial Armageddon

I felt like the captain of a sinking ship.

George W. Bush

As president, George Bush sought to establish what he called the ownership society. He was especially fond of the term, and in 2002 began using it as a substitute for compassionate conservatism to describe his domestic agenda.[1]* The slogan was more popular with the GOP's conservative base than compassionate conservatism, and by the end of his first term Bush was using it almost exclusively. FDR had the New Deal, Truman had the Fair Deal, LBJ had the Great Society, Ronald Reagan had his New Federalism, and George W. Bush had the Ownership Society.

For the first six years of his presidency, Bush seemed to be making

---

* The term was coined by the Cato Institute, a libertarian Washington research center, in the late 1990s. As defined by the institute, an ownership society "values responsibility, liberty, and property. Individuals are empowered by freeing themselves from dependence on government handouts and making them owners instead, in control of their own lives and destinies. In the ownership society, patients control their own health care, parents control their children's education, and workers control their retirement savings." http://www.dailykos.com/stories/989424/full_content.

progress pursuing his goal. After a brief recession in 2001, the American economy appeared to be thriving and the benefits were widely shared. Although the wars in Iraq and Afghanistan, plus the massive tax cuts in 2001 and 2002, had caused the federal deficit to soar—from a surplus of $128 billion when Bush took office to a shortfall of $248 billion in 2006—personal income had grown from $8.5 trillion to $11.3 trillion (an increase of 33 percent) during that period. Unemployment stood at 4.6 percent, new home construction exceeded two million units annually, and mortgage foreclosures stood at a record low of less than one percent.[2]

Speaking to the Republican convention in New York City following his renomination in 2004, Bush said that the priority for his administration in its second term would be "to build an ownership society, because ownership brings security and dignity and independence." He then laid out plans to increase home ownership, make health care plans privately owned, review the tax code, and amend Social Security to provide for personal accounts. "In all of these proposals, we seek to provide not just a government program, but a path to greater opportunity, more freedom and more control over your own life."[3]

Bush repeated the message in his inaugural address in January 2005. Once more he pledged to build an ownership society. "We will widen the ownership of homes and businesses, retirement savings, and health insurance, preparing our people for the challenge of life in a free society. By making every citizen an agent of his or her own destiny, we will give our fellow Americans greater freedom from want and fear, and make our society more prosperous and just and equal."[4] In his State of the Union address that February, the president boasted that "home ownership is at its highest level in history," and went on to advocate the establishment of private retirement accounts for younger workers. "Here's why the personal accounts are better," said Bush. "Your money will grow, over time, at a greater rate than anything the current system can deliver. . . . You'll be able to pass along the money that accumulates . . . to your children and/or grandchildren. And best of all the money in the account is yours, and the government can never take it away."[5]

As it turned out, Congress was uninterested in tampering with Social Security, Bush's proposals to reform the tax code and abolish inheritance taxes fell on deaf ears, and his efforts to further privatize the
health care system went nowhere. The one element of the ownership
society that seemed to fall on fertile ground was increased home ownership. By the end of 2005, home ownership in the United States stood
at a record 69 percent—69 percent of all Americans lived in their own
home. Over six million homes were sold that year, at a median price of
$240,000—almost double what it was ten years before—and minority
ownership had soared.[6] Bush called for an increase in the number of
minority homeowners by 5.5 million families by the end of the decade,
and in 2003 had signed into law the American Dream Downpayment
Act to help forty thousand families each year with their down payment
and closing costs.[7]

In 2005, thirty-year mortgage rates averaged 5.9 percent. Buyers
with modest incomes or poor credit ratings were able to purchase
homes with no down payment, mortgages were frequently written
to require interest-only payments, and interest was often adjustable.
Many of these were subprime mortgages.* Local banks unloaded their
subprime mortgages to Wall Street investment houses, who in turn
packaged them into highly leveraged subprime-mortgage-backed securities sold to eager investors. This created a housing bubble of im-
mense proportions, but it went largely unrecognized. So long as house
prices continued to rise, the danger of a collapse in this market appeared remote.

The Bush administration and the Federal Reserve were largely unaware of the fragility of the housing market. Alan Greenspan, chairman
of the Federal Reserve, speaking to the Economic Club of New York

---

* Subprime mortgages involve more than simply low-income purchasers. Many factors go into
the underwriting process of a home mortgage, including the purchaser's income, credit history,
credit score, employment history, as well as the property value and appraisal. A subprime mortgage is one that comes out of the underwriting process with a low grade. Income is important
but not decisive. A borrower with a low income could be party to a prime mortgage when all of
the factors are considered, just as a high-income borrower could be party to a subprime mortgage.

on May 20, 2005, denied there was a housing bubble. There might be a few local bubbles—he called them "froth"—but they did not pose a national problem. "Even if there are declines in price," said Greenspan, "the significant run-up to date has so increased

Ben Bernanke

equity in homes that only those who have purchased very recently . . . are going to have problems."[8]

Princeton professor Ben Bernanke, then head of the president's Council of Economic Advisers, was equally dismissive. After briefing Bush on the economy at the ranch in Crawford on August 9, 2005, Bernanke met with the White House press corps. Asked by a reporter whether the housing bubble had been discussed and whether he was concerned about it, Bernanke replied:

> We talked some about housing. There's a lot of good news about housing. The rate of home ownership is at a record level, affordability still pretty good. The issue of the housing bubble is one that people have—whether there is a housing bubble is one that people have raised. Housing prices have certainly come up quite a bit. But I think it's important to point out that house prices are being supported in very large part by very strong fundamentals. . . . We have a strong economy, we have lots of jobs, employment, high incomes, very low mortgage rates, growing population, and shortages of land and housing in many areas. And those supply-and-demand factors are a big reason for why housing prices have risen as much as they have.[9]

Bush saw the issue the same way. Attending a meeting on the national economy organized by the chamber of commerce of Loudoun County, Virginia, on January 19, 2006, Bush was asked about the

Henry Paulson

cost of housing. "Economies should cycle," the president replied. "If houses get too expensive, people will stop buying them. . . . Let the market function properly. Your kind of question has been asked throughout the history of homebuilding. . . . Things cycle. That's just the way it works." [10]

Alan Greenspan stepped down as chairman of the Federal Reserve on January 31, 2006. He had been appointed by Ronald Reagan to succeed Paul Volcker in 1987, and had won the nation's respect for having presided over an extended period of economic growth. To replace Greenspan, Bush nominated Bernanke. Testifying before the Joint Economic Committee of Congress prior to his confirmation, Bernanke made clear once again that he did not believe the national housing boom was a bubble about to burst. House prices may have risen by 25 percent in the last two years, he told Congress, but these increases "largely reflect strong economic fundamentals." [11] The Senate confirmed Bernanke by voice vote (no roll call) on January 31, 2006.

In June 2006, Bush replaced Treasury Secretary John Snow with Henry Paulson, head of the legendary Wall Street firm of Goldman Sachs. Paulson was Bush's third secretary of the treasury. Paul O'Neill, the president's first secretary, did not hit it off with Bush or the White House staff and was replaced after two years by Snow, the chief executive of CSX railroad. Snow, like O'Neill, also did not win many friends in the White House, and after three and a half years was shown the door. As Bush expressed it, "both John and I felt it was time for a fresh face." [12] Paulson was initially reluctant to take the post, but eventually agreed. Unlike his predecessors, Paulson insisted that he, not the White

House staff, would preside over the administration's economic policy, and Bush agreed. Also unlike his predecessors, Paulson was a financier, not an industry executive. He understood markets and how Wall Street functioned. Paulson was confirmed unanimously by the Senate following a brief confirmation hearing before the Senate Finance Committee. He was not asked about a housing bubble, nor did he comment on one.[13]

Just as Bush met frequently with his national security advisers at Camp David, he convened a session there with his financial team on August 18, 2006, to review the economy. The housing bubble was not discussed. Edward Lazear, who had succeeded Bernanke as chairman of the Council of Economic Advisers, led off with a discussion of wages and tax initiatives. Rob Portman, head of the office of Management and Budget, dissected the federal budget. And Al Hubbard, director of the National Economic Council, spoke about entitlements. Then it was Paulson's turn. Paulson had been in office little more than a month, and chose to speak about crisis management. "I explained that we had to be prepared to deal with everything from terror attacks and natural disasters to oil price shocks, the collapse of a major bank, or a sharp drop in the value of the dollar. . . . I was convinced we were due for another disruption."[14]

When Bush pressed Paulson for specifics, the treasury secretary talked about the enormous amount of leverage that had crept into the financial system, and then gave a quick primer on hedge funds and how they operated. "We can't predict how the next crisis will come, but we need to be prepared." Paulson said it was impossible to know what might trigger a big disruption, but it was like a forest fire. How the blaze started was less important than containing it. "I was right to be on guard," Paulson wrote later, "but I misread the cause and the scale of the coming disaster. Notably absent from my presentation was any mention of the problems in housing or mortgages."[15]

The housing market crested in 2005, and started to become choppy in 2006. Prices remained high—averaging over $250,000 nationally— but demand was slackening. Housing starts hit a peak of 192,000 in August 2005, but a year later were down to 146,000 and by December

2006 to 112,000. And the backlog of unsold houses had increased by 20 percent.[16] More ominously, mortgage foreclosures were mushrooming. In the first quarter of 2005, only 188,000 homes were in foreclosure proceedings. By the last quarter of 2006, the number had risen to 346,000, an increase of 84 percent. In Detroit, one of every twenty-one houses faced foreclosure; in Atlanta, one of every twenty-three; and in Dallas, one of every twenty-six.[17]

Because prices remained high, the weakness of the housing sector was not generally recognized. But the subprime market, which had expanded from 5 percent of the mortgage market in 1994 to 20 percent in 2006—an estimated $2 trillion—was in turmoil. On February 7, 2007, HSBC Holdings, the world's third largest bank, said it was setting aside $10.6 billion to cover losses in its subprime portfolio in the United States. On April 2, New Century Financial, the nation's largest subprime lender, filed for bankruptcy. Other lenders in the subprime market were in trouble. The administration showed little concern. Paulson, speaking in New York on April 20, 2007, said the housing market was bottoming out, and that the subprime problem was unlikely to spread. "I don't see subprime mortgage troubles imposing a serious problem. I think it's going to be largely self-contained."[18] At the Federal Reserve, Bernanke was equally unconcerned. Speaking at the Federal Reserve Bank of Chicago on May 17, 2007, Bernanke said, "We believe the effect of troubles in the subprime sector on the broader housing market will likely be limited, and we do not expect significant spillovers from the subprime market to the rest of the economy or to the financial system."[19]

As Bernanke later wrote in his memoirs, "Seen from the vantage point of early 2007, the economy's good performance, combined with the relatively small size of the subprime mortgage market and what appeared to be a healthy banking system, led me and others at the Fed to conclude that subprime problems . . . were unlikely to cause major economic problems."[20]

The housing market continued to shrink. In March 2007, sales were down 13 percent from the previous year and prices down 6 percent. Holders of subprime mortgages were desperate. American Home Mortgage, a midsize mortgage lender, declared bankruptcy on August 6,

2007. Ten days later, Countrywide Financial Corporation, the nation's largest across-the-board mortgage firm, narrowly escaped bankruptcy by securing emergency loans from backup banks totaling $11.5 billion. And it was not just the mortgage firms that were in trouble. Investment banks and hedge funds, heavily leveraged with subprime mortgages, could find no buyers for their securities.

Bush met with his economic advisers at the Treasury Department on August 8, and afterward spoke to the press. There was no indication that the subprime crisis had been considered at the meeting. "My administration follows a simple philosophy," said the president. "Our economy prospers when we trust the American people with their own paychecks. . . . Since 2003, our economy has added more than 8.3 million new jobs and almost four years of uninterrupted growth. The economy continues to grow at a steady pace, and during the most recent quarter, it grew at an annual rate of 3.4 percent." Bush went on to say he appreciated that Paulson—"one of the world's most successful investment bankers"—had joined his administration. "Here's how he [Paulson] puts it. He said, 'This is far and away the strongest global economy I've seen in my business lifetime.' In other words, not only is our economy strong, but so is [sic] the economies around the world."[21]

On August 9, 2007, the day after Bush spoke to the press, BNP Paribas, France's largest bank, announced it was halting withdrawals from three of its investment funds because of their exposure to the U.S. subprime mortgage market. Citing "a complete evaporation of liquidity" in the subprime market, BNP Paribas said it had become impossible to value assets invested in the funds.[22] The European Central Bank responded immediately by opening lines of credit to all European banks exposed to the American mortgage market. Within hours, forty-nine of Europe's banks had borrowed 94.8 billion euros—$130 billion. After BNP Paribas's announcement, world stock markets plummeted. In New York, the Dow Jones Industrial Average, which had climbed to record levels in July, experienced its second largest decline in the past five years.

Later that day, Bush held a press conference in the White House. He began by boasting about the economy—apparently oblivious to the collapse of the subprime mortgage market. "Real after tax income has grown by an average of more than $3,400 per person since I took office," said the president. "The American economy is the envy of the world. . . . Our economy is growing in large part because America has the most ambitious, educated, and innovative people in the world, men and women who take risks, try out new ideas, and have the skills and courage to turn their dreams into new technologies and new businesses." Most of the questions that followed during the press conference dealt with the war in Iraq. But toward the end of the session David Gregory of NBC News asked about the volatility of the financial markets and falling house prices. "Is this a correction or a crisis, in your view?"

Bush replied that he had been briefed by his economic advisers as to whether there would be a precipitous decline in the housing market or a soft landing "and it appears at this point that it looks like we're headed for a soft landing. And that's what the facts say." [23]

As the housing market continued to decline and as more mortgages were foreclosed, the Democrats in Congress stepped up their criticism of the administration. Bush responded on August 31 by announcing a limited plan to assist homeowners facing foreclosure. "The recent disturbances in the subprime mortgage industry are modest," said the president. "But if you are a family—if your family is one of those having trouble making the monthly payments, this problem doesn't seem modest at all." Bush went on to say that the government had a limited role to play. "It's not the government's job to bail out speculators or those who made a decision to buy a home they knew they could never afford." He then laid out a limited program to expand the Federal Housing Administration's ability to guarantee loans for borrowers with modest incomes and to revise the tax code to make it easier to restructure mortgages. Bush also said that he had instructed Treasury Secretary Paulson and Alphonso Jackson, the secretary of housing and urban development, to launch a "foreclosure avoidance initiative to help struggling homeowners find a way to refinance."

After he had concluded his remarks, Bush was asked by a reporter about hedge funds and banks overexposed to the subprime market. "That's a bigger problem," said the reporter. "Have you got a plan?"

Bush did not answer the question. He said "Thank you," and walked away.[24] His initial response to the subprime mortgage meltdown was similar to his initial response to Hurricane Katrina. He watched it happen.

That same day, Ameriquest, which had been the nation's largest subprime lender in 2005, went out of business. With $45 billion in mortgage loans outstanding, most of which were subprime, Ameriquest was no longer viable. Its assets were sold to Citigroup for an undisclosed price. Ironically, Ameriquest was for many years the name of the stadium in which the Texas Rangers, Bush's old team, played baseball.

In his memoirs, Bush notes that "the global pool of cash, easy monetary policy, booming housing market, insatiable appetite for mortgage-backed assets, complexity of Wall Street financial engineering, and leverage of financial institutions created a house of cards. This precarious structure was fated to collapse as soon as the underlying card—the nonstop growth in housing prices—was pulled out. But few saw it at the time—including me."[25]

By the end of 2007, the housing market was in a nosedive. The median price had fallen to $217,800, and new construction was down 24.8 percent from its peak—the second largest decline on record.[26] Perhaps more revealing, over 2.2 million foreclosures—default notices, auction sale notices, and bank repossessions—had been filed on 1,285,873 residential properties, an increase of 75 percent over 2006.[27] Bush responded on December 6, by announcing a voluntary plan—the HOPE NOW Alliance—to freeze interest rates on subprime mortgages for five years. The plan would be funded by private industry. "HOPE NOW is an example of Government bringing together members of the private sector to voluntarily address a national challenge, without taxpayer subsidies or without Government mandates," said Bush.[28] The effect was minimal. "This is a Band-Aid when the patient needs major surgery," noted a leading financial publication.[29]

Two weeks later, Bush restated his views on the housing downturn in Fredericksburg, Virginia. "People are concerned around this country about housing," said the president. "Here's my attitude on housing. One, the Government should never bail out lenders; two, some people bought a house that they shouldn't have been in the market to buy; three, there are speculators who thought they could get one of these reset mortgages, and flip it, make some money." Bush went on to say that the mortgage market had changed. Mortgages had been bundled. "So the savings and loan doesn't own the mortgage anymore, or the bank doesn't own the mortgage anymore. The local lending institute doesn't own the mortgage anymore. It's owned by some international group, perhaps, or it's bundled into an asset. And so there is hardly anyone to negotiate with. And so lenders aren't sure where to turn. They have creditworthiness; they may get pinched as their interest rates reset." [30]

As if to confirm Bush's assessment, in early March of 2008 the venerable firm of Bear Stearns, one of Wall Street's big five investment banks,* faced a severe liquidity crisis. Bear Stearns was a major underwriter of subprime securities, and was heavily leveraged. With the market in precipitous decline, many of the firm's clients began to withdraw their money, and many of its creditors demanded more collateral for their loans. To accommodate the requests, Bear Stearns used its cash reserves, and by the afternoon of Thursday, May 15, had just $2 billion in cash left, not nearly enough to meet its obligations when the market opened Friday morning.

"This is the real thing," Paulson told Bush. "We're in danger of having a firm go down." [31]

Bush was initially reluctant to assist Bear Stearns. "In a free market economy, firms that fail should go out of business." Bush believed that if the government stepped in, it would set a precedent. "Other firms would assume they would be bailed out, which would embolden them to take more risks." [32]

Paulson and Bernanke at the Federal Reserve initially agreed with Bush that Bear Stearns should be allowed to fail, but a quick inspec-

---

*   Bear Stearns was the smallest of the five, which included Goldman Sachs, Morgan Stanley, Merrill Lynch, and Lehman Brothers. Under the Glass-Stegall Act that had been enacted during the first one hundred days of FDR's New Deal, the investment banks were divorced from commercial banking. This separation was repealed by passage of the Gramm-Leach-Bliley Act of 1999, creating a giant financial supermarket that was largely unregulated, somewhat analogous to that which existed in 1929.

tion of Bear Stearns's books by federal officials in New York convinced them otherwise. Bear Stearns was far too interconnected. As Paulson put it, "Bear had hundreds, maybe thousands, of counterparties—firms that lent it money or with which it traded stocks, bonds, mortgages, and other securities. These firms . . . all had myriad counterparties of their own. If Bear fell, all these counterparties would be scrambling to collect their loans and collateral." It would be a domino effect. Paulson believed that if Bear Stearns went down, it would take many other firms with it.[33]

Bush reluctantly agreed. "While I was concerned about creating a moral hazard, I worried more about a financial collapse."[34] Working through the night of May 15, Paulson and Bernanke made an arrangement with Jamie Dimon, the CEO of JPMorgan Chase, which was Bear Stearns's clearing bank. Utilizing a never before used portion of the Federal Reserve Act of 1932 that empowered the Fed to extend credit to financial institutions other than banks "in unusual and exigent circumstances," the Federal Reserve loaned money to JPMorgan, who would pass it along to Bear Stearns.* That would provide Bear with sufficient liquidity to get through trading on Friday.

A more serious problem was to find a permanent solution for Bear's lack of liquidity before the Asian financial markets opened Sunday evening. Working through the weekend, Paulson and Bernanke hammered out an agreement with Jamie Dimon whereby JPMorgan would buy Bear Stearns for a knockdown price of $2 a share, a total of $236 million. (At the height of the housing market in January 2007, Bear Stearns stock sold for $173 a share—a capitalization of almost $20 billion.) In addition, the Federal Reserve would provide $30 billion and assume ownership of Bear Stearns's mortgage portfolio.† Dimon

---

* Section 13(3) of the Federal Reserve Act of 1932 states, "In unusual and exigent circumstances, the Board of Governors of the Federal Reserve System by the affirmative vote of not less than five members, may authorize any Federal reserve bank . . . to discount for any individual, partnership or corporation, notes, drafts, and bills of exchange when such notes, drafts, and bills of exchange are endorsed or otherwise secured to the satisfaction of the Federal reserve bank." Act of July 21; 1932, 47 Stat. 715.

† The Federal Reserve established a free-standing entity, Maiden Lane LLC, and Maiden Lane took control of Bear Stearns's mortgage assets. (Maiden Lane is the name of a small

later sweetened the offer to $10 a share, and the Bear Stearns board accepted.

Bush was relieved that a financial crisis had been avoided. "Can we say we are going to get our money back?" he asked Paulson.

"We might, but that will depend on the market," Paulson replied.

Bush said a lot of people were going to object to what they had just done. "You'll have to explain it," he told Paulson. "You've got credibility." [35]

Throughout the spring of 2008 the housing market continued its decline. Prices were down 21 percent from their highs two years before, and many homeowners were "underwater"—the amount of their mortgage exceeded the value of their property. Mortgage foreclosures were also rising rapidly. The Sun Belt was particularly hard hit. In Stockton, California, 9.5 percent of all houses were in foreclosure; in Las Vegas, 8.9 percent, and in San Bernardino, California, 8.1 percent. [36] On July 11, 2008, IndyMac Bank, one of the largest financial institutions in the Los Angeles area and the seventh largest mortgage originator in the United States, went bankrupt. With $32 billion in assets, it was the fourth largest bank failure in American history. [37]

A much more serious problem pertained to the two real estate giants that operated under government sponsorship: the Federal National Mortgage Association (Fannie Mae) and the Federal Home Loan Mortgage Corporation (Freddie Mac). As the nation's largest mortgage lenders funding roughly two thirds of the home loans in America, they had suffered enormous losses and many believed they were on the verge of going under. Officially, Fannie and Freddie were private companies. They were chartered by the government to encourage home ownership and to provide a profit for their shareholders. Their debt, estimated at $5.2 trillion, traded on global financial markets as though the United States government had guaranteed it (which it had not). If Fannie and Freddie went under, it would not only create enormous havoc in finan-

---

street alongside the New York Federal Reserve.) The Fed actually provided $28.8 billion and JPMorgan put up $1.5 billion to buy the mortgages. These were considered "loans" that would be repaid to the Fed and JPMorgan as Maiden Lane sold off the mortgages. Final Report of the National Commission on the Causes of the Financial and Economic Crisis in the United States, *The Financial Crisis: Inquiry Report* (New York: PublicAffairs, 2011), 290.

cial markets, but would seriously undermine the creditworthiness of the American government.

To meet the emergency, Bush asked Congress for authority to invest federal funds in Fannie and Freddie to provide them with sufficient liquidity to meet the crisis. That was what Paulson recommended, and Bush agreed. "We've got to get this done," said the president.[38] The Democratic Congress was supportive, and even raised the debt ceiling to accommodate the president's request. On July 23, 2008, the Housing and Economic Recovery Act (HERA) passed the House 272–152, and three days later cleared the Senate 72–13. Under the legislation, the federal government was given a free hand to support Fannie and Freddie, the secretary of the treasury was given oversight responsibility, and the two firms would remain private corporations.

The enactment of HERA did not stop the bleeding. Both Fannie and Freddie continued to suffer heavy losses, and by September it was evident that they could not survive on their own. Paulson recommended to Bush that the two firms be placed under government "conservatorship." The government would assume an 80 percent ownership stake in each firm, a new management team would be installed, and they would be provided access to $200 billion in ready cash. Once again, Bush agreed. "It won't look good, but we are going to do what we need to do to save the economy."[39]

On Sunday, September 7, 2008, Paulson announced the takeover. It was the largest government intervention in private financial markets since the Great Depression. The public response was overwhelmingly favorable. When the markets opened on Monday, the Dow closed up 300 points. Billionaire Warren Buffett was quoted as saying that the takeover was "exactly the right decision for the country." Even *The Wall Street Journal*, ever critical of government intervention, endorsed the plan.[40] For a brief moment, it appeared as though the financial panic had been contained.*

---

* Fannie and Freddie returned to profitability in May 2012, with $4.5 billion that month. They have remained profitable, and by the end of 2014 had provided the Treasury with $225.4 billion. Gretchen Morgenson, "After Crisis: A Cash Flood and Silence," *New York Times*, February 15, 2015.

That was not the case. As soon as the pressure on Fannie and Freddie was relieved, investors turned their attention to Lehman Brothers, one of Wall Street's most hallowed institutions. Lehman had $600 billion in assets, but like Bear Stearns, was heavily leveraged and highly exposed to the mortgage market. In 2007, Lehman Brothers had made the greatest profit in its 158-year history, but with the mortgage meltdown it now faced a severe liquidity crisis. As stock markets around the world resumed their tumble, Lehman's shares were hit by waves of selling. On Tuesday, September 9, 2008, Lehman's stock dropped by 45 percent. On Wednesday it dropped another 7 percent. By the end of the week, Lehman's shares were selling for $3.65, a small fraction of their earlier value. The decline in its stock price placed a severe strain on Lehman's liquidity. Without an immediate infusion of cash, the firm could not meet its obligations when the markets reopened on Monday.

The solution was to find a buyer for Lehman similar to JP Morgan Chase's emergency takeover of Bear Stearns in March. Paulson went to New York on Friday to oversee the negotiations. Two banks were interested—Bank of America and Barclays—but both made it clear that any deal would be contingent upon the government's agreement to absorb Lehman's toxic mortgage assets. The Federal Reserve had provided $30 billion in the case of Bear Stearns, and just last weekend had put up $200 billion to rescue Fannie and Freddie. It seemed a reasonable expectation.

For whatever reason, Paulson declined to do so. He recognized the need to remove Lehman's mortgage assets, but insisted that the financial industry, not the government, should provide the funds to do so. Negotiations went nowhere. Without government support the banks were uninterested, and Lehman filed for bankruptcy early Monday morning.*

Bush followed Paulson's lead throughout the Lehman crisis, and so

---

* After Lehman Brothers declared bankruptcy, Barclays bought Lehman's North American investment banking operations and its presence on Wall Street for $250 million. It also paid $1.5 billion for Lehman's headquarters building and other real estate. Several months later, when the market had stabilized, Barclays showed a profit of $3.5 billion on the transaction. James B. Stewart, "Eight Days: The Battle to Save the American Financial System," *The New Yorker*, September 21, 2009.

the question arises why Paulson was unwilling to provide government support for Lehman as it had for Bear Stearns, Fannie, and Freddie. Sometime later Paulson and Bernanke made the argument that they lacked legal authority to bail out Lehman, but that was not true. Section 13(3) of the Federal Reserve Act, which was used to rescue Bear Stearns, is a virtual carte blanche for the Fed "in unusual and exigent circumstances." The answer is perhaps more personal. Paulson told Bernanke and New York Fed president Timothy Geithner that he did not want to be known as Mr. Bailout. "I'm being called 'Mr. Bailout.' I can't do it again."[41]

"This was one of the few times," said Geithner,

> when there was any distance between Hank and me. There was even some distance between Ben and me. I sensed their advisers pulling them toward political expedience. . . . The natural human instinct in a financial crisis, and especially the political instinct, is to avoid unpopular intervention, to let the market work its will, to show the world you're punishing the perpetrators. But letting the fire burn out of control is much more economically damaging, and ultimately more politically damaging, than taking the decisive actions necessary to prevent it from spreading . . . into the core of the system. By pledging not to take any more risk, I thought we risked fanning the flames.[42]

Another reason, rarely mentioned, may have been the age-old animosity between Goldman Sachs, Paulson's old firm, and Lehman Brothers. This was not simply a commercial rivalry, but often personal and very bitter. Whatever the reason, the failure to rescue Lehman Brothers launched the financial meltdown that followed. Christine Lagarde, then France's finance minister (and now the managing director of the International Monetary Fund), said Paulson's decision was horrendous. "For the equilibrium of the world's financial system, this was a genuine error."[43] Peter Wallison, a member of the congressionally established Financial Crisis Inquiry Commission, called Paulson's refusal "perhaps the greatest financial blunder ever."[44]

Bush accepted Paulson's decision. When his cousin George

Walker IV, a direct descendant of their common great-grandfather the renowned financier George Herbert Walker, and a member of Lehman's executive committee, called the White House that evening and attempted to speak with Bush, he declined to take the call. "I'm sorry, Mr. Walker. The president is not able to take your call at this time," said the operator.[45] But he took Paulson's call. "Will we be able to explain why Lehman is different from Bear Stearns?" asked the president.

"Without JP Morgan as a buyer for Bear, it would have failed," Paulson replied. "We just couldn't find a buyer for Lehman."[46] Paulson was partially right. No banks wanted to buy. But if the Fed had bought Lehman's toxic assets, as they did for Bear, there is little doubt that a buyer could have been found.

Paulson's error in not bailing out Lehman Brothers was immediately evident when world stock markets opened Monday. A tsunami of selling hit stocks, driving prices to new lows. In New York, the Dow was down almost 5 percent. Financial stocks were hit even harder. Hedge funds withdrew money from investment banks and credit markets dried up. The most extreme flight of capital was from the American Insurance Group (AIG), an insurance giant that had become heavily involved in insuring mortgage-backed securities. With the housing market in free fall, and with liquidity drying up, AIG faced bankruptcy. Its stock plummeted 60 percent on Monday, and without major assistance it clearly could not survive. If AIG went down, the entire financial system would be imperiled, given the extent to which the insurance conglomerate was intertwined with the world's major financial institutions.

"How did we get to this point?" Bush asked Paulson at a White House meeting Monday afternoon. Paulson did his best to explain the interconnectedness of the financial system to the president. "If we don't shore up AIG, we will likely lose several more financial institutions. Morgan Stanley, for one."

Bush found it hard to believe that an insurance company could be so interconnected but Paulson persisted. Eventually, the president surrendered. "Someday you guys are going to have to tell me how we ended up with a system like this and what we need to do to fix it."[47] With

Bush's approval and Treasury support, the Federal Reserve provided AIG with $85 billion that day in return for 80 percent control of the company. The money was technically a loan that AIG would repay when the market recovered.

"There was nothing appealing about the deal," said Bush. "It was basically a nationalization of America's largest insurance company. Less than forty-eight hours after Lehman filed for bankruptcy, saving AIG would look like a glaring contradiction. But that was a hell of a lot better than a financial collapse."[48]

Why did Bush agree to bail out AIG but not Lehman Brothers? Because that is what Paulson and Bernanke recommended. Throughout the financial crisis Bush relied on the judgment of his secretary of the treasury and the chairman of the Federal Reserve, and did not insert his personal opinion. That practice differed fundamentally from his approach to diplomatic and military issues. As commander in chief, Bush relished both the responsibility and the authority that went with the position. He did not hesitate to overrule diplomats and generals, and did not shy from initiating policy himself. The decision to bring democracy to Iraq in 2003, and the surge in 2007, are good examples of the president's determination to take charge. But in the economic meltdown of 2008, Bush recognized that the issues were exceedingly complex, and their ramifications even more so. They were beyond his expertise. As president, he continued to make the final decisions. But he trusted the judgment of Paulson and Bernanke, and relied on their advice even when it ran counter to many of his cherished beliefs. Bush was aware of that and had no regrets. "Putting a world class investment banker and an expert on the Great Depression in the nation's top two economic positions were among the most important decisions of my presidency," Bush wrote in his memoirs.[49]

Bush was tired. This was the eighth year of his presidency, most of his original staff had departed, his approval ratings had dropped to the high 20s, he was consumed with the fighting in Iraq and Afghanistan, and both presidential candidates—John McCain and Barack Obama— were pointedly ignoring him. "I felt like the captain of a sinking ship," said Bush.[50]

A more interesting question is why Paulson and Bernanke recommended bailing out AIG after they had stood by and allowed Lehman Brothers to fail. Both argue that AIG was more central to the functioning of world financial markets than Lehman, and that the magnitude of the loss would have been crippling. That may have been true, but if Lehman had been saved, the pressure might not have been so great on AIG in the first place. Or perhaps they had belatedly recognized they erred in not saving Lehman. A cabinet member should be able to live with being called "Mr. Bailout." Princeton economics professor Alan Blinder, a former vice chairman of the Federal Reserve Board, suggests a third reason. "A significant share of the original loan [to AIG] passed through directly to Goldman Sachs, making it look like a backdoor deal for Goldman, Paulson's old firm." [51]*

Whatever the reason, the financial markets continued their nosedive. The bailout of AIG had little effect. The following day the Dow Jones fell 4.1 percent; its lowest close in three years. And capital markets had dried up. Banks stopped lending to each other and there was a run on money market accounts as investors moved their money into short-term Treasury bills. "It was becoming clear that the markets were going into anaphylactic shock, and we needed to do something," said Bernanke. [52] The Fed could no longer cope with the crisis alone. The government needed to step in with massive assistance. Paulson agreed. There was no other way out. They immediately went to the White House to lay the case for intervention before the president.

Bush had been scheduled to fly to Alabama and Florida on a GOP fundraising trip, but canceled his flight to meet with Paulson and Bernanke. At 3:30 on Thursday, September 18, they convened in the Roosevelt Room of the White House. They were joined by Dick Cheney, Josh Bolten, Securities and Exchange Commission chairman Chris Cox, and Tim Geithner from the New York Fed. The meeting lasted forty-five minutes.

---

* Paulson received a waiver of conflict-of-interest regulations from the Treasury Department's legal ethics officer. "The magnitude of the government's interest" outweighed any ethical concerns. Over the next several days, Paulson's calendar indicates that he spoke to Lloyd Blankfein, his successor at Goldman Sachs, twenty-four times. Gretchen Morgenson and Don Van Natta, Jr., "Paulson's Calls to Goldman Tested Ethics," *New York Times*, August 8, 2009.

"Mr. President," said Paulson, "we are witnessing a financial panic. Money market funds are on the verge of breaking up. Companies are taking drastic measures to preserve their finances. The situation is extraordinarily serious."[53] Paulson then laid out a four-point program. The Treasury would guarantee all money market mutual funds—a $3.5 trillion undertaking; the SEC would temporarily ban the short-selling of financial stocks; the Federal Reserve would attempt to add liquidity to the commercial paper market; and perhaps most important, the Treasury would buy the toxic mortgage assets from endangered financial firms. This would cost at least $500 billion, and would require congressional approval.

"What happens if we don't," Bush asked.

"We're looking at an economy worse than the Great Depression," Paulson responded.

Bush was stunned. "Worse than the Great Depression? Do you agree with that?" he asked Bernanke.

"I do, Mr. President," Bernanke replied. "In terms of the financial system, we have not seen anything like this since the 1930s, and it could get worse."[54]

Bernanke's answer was all Bush needed. After a few more questions, he endorsed what Paulson proposed. "I was furious the situation had reached this point," said Bush, but he recognized this was an emergency. "The market had ceased to function . . . and the consequences of inaction would be catastrophic."

"Get to work," the president told Paulson and Bernanke. "We are going to solve this. We are going to get through this. We have to get through this."[55]

Bush adjourned the meeting and went across the hall to the Oval Office. Several members of his staff followed. "If we're really looking at another Great Depression," said the president, "you can be damn sure I'm going to be Roosevelt, not Hoover."[56]

That evening, Paulson and Bernanke met with the congressional leadership from both parties in Speaker Pelosi's office on Capitol Hill. In a curious twist, the administration case was laid out by Bernanke, whose standing with members of Congress was now higher than Paulson's. The Fed chief drew parallels to the Great Depression, and said that if Congress did not act, "this is going to be worse." The financial system was "only a matter of days" away from "a meltdown," and the government's tools were insufficient to meet the crisis.[57] Paulson followed and laid out the four-point program the president had approved. The members were shocked. Paulson avoided putting a precise figure on how much money would be required, but said it was "several hundred billion." Pelosi and the Republican leadership assured Bernanke and Paulson that Congress would do whatever was necessary. Senate majority leader Harry Reid wasn't so sure. "It takes me forty-eight hours to get the Republicans to flush the toilet."[58] The meeting lasted ninety minutes. The congressional leaders asked Paulson and Bernanke to submit a written plan as soon as possible, and then went before the press where they promised to do "whatever it takes."[59]

On Friday, September 19, the Treasury announced that from that day forward all money market mutual funds would be insured in their entirety; the SEC banned short-selling of financial stocks; and the Fed added liquidity to the commercial paper market. The legislation to allow the government to buy the toxic mortgage assets proved more difficult. Just before the markets opened Friday morning, Paulson issued a statement outlining a Troubled Asset Relief Program—TARP—which would remove "illiquid assets that are weighing down our financial institutions and threatening our economy." This would require congressional approval.

Paulson's announcement triggered a spontaneous rally on Wall Street, and the Dow immediately rose 400 points. At 10:45 Friday morning, Bush spoke to the country from the Rose Garden. He was flanked by Bernanke, Paulson, and SEC chairman Cox. "This is a pivotal moment for America's economy," said the president. "In our Nation's history, there have been moments that require us to come together across party lines to address major challenges. This is such a moment." Bush then laid out the steps being taken and emphasized the importance of enacting TARP as soon as possible. "Our system of free enterprise rests on the conviction that the Federal Government should interfere in the marketplace only when necessary. Given the precarious state of today's financial markets and their vital importance to the daily lives of the American people, Government intervention is not only warranted, it is essential." [60]

On Capitol Hill, despite the efforts of the congressional leadership, TARP ran into immediate difficulty. Under the three-page draft act that Paulson submitted, the Treasury was authorized to spend $700 billion to purchase "mortgage related assets." [61] There were no strings attached. House Republicans balked. Cheney was delegated the task of bringing them on board. On Tuesday, September 23, the vice president went to Capitol Hill to speak to the House Republican caucus. He was given a standing ovation. But his presentation convinced no one, and the questions afterward were uniformly hostile. "I left the session thinking that if the vote had been held that day, we'd have been lucky to have fifty Republicans with us," said Cheney. [62]

To rally public opinion and bring pressure on Congress, Bush delivered a prime-time television address on September 24. "I'm a strong believer in free enterprise, so my natural instinct is to oppose Government intervention," said the president. "I believe that companies that make bad decisions should be allowed to go out of business. Under normal circumstances, I would have followed this course. But these are not normal circumstances." After describing how the meltdown had occurred and what the government was proposing, Bush concluded on a personal note. "I understand the frustrations of responsible Americans who pay their mortgages on time, file their tax returns every April 15th, and are reluctant to pay the cost of excesses on Wall Street. But given the situation we are facing, not passing a bill now would cost those Americans much more later." [63] How much Bush's speech helped is unclear. His approval rating had reached a low point, and for many Americans the financial collapse was simply another manifestation of his ineptitude.

The presidential campaign complicated matters further. Election day was six weeks away, and McCain was trailing Obama by several percentage points. To gain momentum, McCain chose to distance himself from Bush. Speaking in Scranton, Pennsylvania, on Monday, September 22, the Republican candidate took issue with the TARP proposal. "I am greatly concerned that the plan gives a single individual [the secretary of the treasury] unprecedented power to spend one trillion—trillion—dollars without any meaningful accountability. Never before in the history of our nation has so much power and money been concentrated in the hands of one person."[64] McCain's comments sent shock waves through the White House. Presidential political adviser Barry Jackson called the Arizona senator "a stupid prick."[65]

Two days later, September 24, a few hours before Bush was to address the nation, McCain called the president and asked for an immediate White House conference with congressional leaders to discuss the rescue effort. Bush was furious. Negotiations with Congress were at a delicate stage, and now McCain was attempting to horn in. Bush asked McCain to wait until he could discuss the matter with Paulson. McCain rejected the idea. He told Bush he was going to issue a statement immediately, and would suspend his campaign and fly back to Washington to work on the crisis. Bush was appalled but felt he had no alternative but to convene the meeting with congressional leaders McCain requested. The Republican candidate had gone public, and left the president little choice. "I could see the headlines," Bush told his staff. " 'Even Bush thinks McCain's idea is a Bad One.' "[66]

Before announcing the meeting, Bush called Obama. "McCain asked for this meeting and I think I have to give him this meeting and I need you to be here." Bush assured Obama that it was not a political trap. Obama agreed to attend. "Any time the president calls, I will take it," he replied.[67]

Bush scheduled the meeting for 4 p.m. the following day. He had no idea what McCain was going to say, nor did anyone else. The president opened the discussion by stressing the importance of immediate congressional action to pass the TARP legislation. "If money isn't loosened up, this sucker could go down."[68] Paulson then gave an update on the financial situation, stressing even more the necessity to put TARP in place as soon as possible.

Observing protocol, Bush then turned to House speaker Nancy Pelosi. "Mr. President," Pelosi replied, "Senator Obama is going to speak for us today." It was immediately clear that the Democrats had prepared for the meeting. Obama spoke without notes, stressed the importance of immediate action and said the Democratic leadership had been working closely with Secretary Paulson to improve the proposed legislation. He ended with what amounted to a challenge to McCain. "On the way here, we were on the brink of a deal. Now there are those who think we should start from scratch. . . . If we are indeed starting over, the consequences could well be severe."[69]

When Obama finished, Bush turned to McCain. "I think it is fair if I give you a chance to speak next," said the president.

"I'll wait my turn," McCain replied. The meeting was dumbstruck. McCain had called for the meeting, but evidently had nothing to offer. "It was an incredible moment," Paulson remembered.[70] At that point the discussion went off the track. Bush thought it was a farce. "Tempers flared. Voices were raised. Some barbs were thrown. I was watching a verbal food fight, which would have been comical except that the stakes were so high."[71]

Eventually Obama interrupted. "Can I hear from Senator McCain," he asked.

McCain responded by speaking in glib generalities. Cheney remembered that McCain "added nothing of substance. It was entirely unclear why he'd returned to Washington and why he wanted the congressional leadership called together. I left the Cabinet Room when the meeting was over thinking the Republican presidential ticket was in trouble."[72]

Bush was equally unimpressed. He leaned over to Pelosi and whispered, "I told you you'd miss me when I am gone."[73] The discussion deteriorated further. After another ten minutes, Bush stood up and took his leave. "Well, I've clearly lost control of this meeting. It's over."[74] Bush was amused and at the same time distraught. What was McCain up to? "That was the most ridiculous meeting I've ever been part of," he told his aides.[75]

Over the weekend, the Bush White House, Cheney, Paulson, and the congressional leadership worked to assemble the support necessary to pass TARP. On Monday, September 29, the House of Representatives put the measure to a vote. Members strode to the well of the House to cast their ballot. Bush watched on television. Midway through it was obvious the measure was going down. At 2:07 p.m. the final vote was cast. TARP was defeated 205–228. Republicans voted against it 133–65—slightly more than two to one. Democrats voted in favor 140–95. But that was not enough to put the measure across.

Global stock markets went into an immediate tailspin. Within minutes the Dow Jones Industrial Average dropped 777 points, its largest one-day loss in history. The S&P 500 dropped 8.8 percent. Over $1.2 trillion in stock market value was wiped out—also a one-day record. "I knew the vote would be a disaster," said Bush later. "My party played the leading role in killing TARP. Now Republicans would be blamed for the consequences."[76]

At this point, Bush took command. Paulson and Bernanke were the financial experts, but the Bush White House knew the political game better than they. "We've got to get this done," said the president. They needed thirteen more votes in the House to pass TARP, and the arm-twisting began. At Bush's direction, the campaign was managed by White House chief of staff Josh Bolten. "Give me the ball for a few days," he told Paulson, "and let me see if we can corral the votes."[77] Fortunately, the stock market collapse had rattled the opposition, and now the administration added several sweeteners to the bill: the FDIC would increase individual bank deposit insurance from $100,000 to $250,000. That would relieve those who worried that their deposits were no longer safe. Other sweeteners included extending a number of tax breaks that were due to expire, energy provisions to assist individual homeowners, and a mental health parity bill that required insurers to cover mental health costs just as they did other health care costs.

In consultations with the congressional leadership, it was decided to take the measure to the Senate first, where the support was greater. To emphasize the importance of the vote, majority leader Harry Reid insisted on a roll call with the senators sitting at their desks—a rarely used historic procedure. On Wednesday evening, October 1, the roll was called. The measure passed 74–25. Thirty-four Republicans joined 40 Democrats voting in favor. Both Obama and McCain voted yes.*

Two days later, on October 3, the revised bill came before the House.

---

* The only senator not voting was Ted Kennedy of Massachusetts, who was fatally ill with cancer.

Bush spent the morning calling individual members, and this time the TARP measure was approved, 263–171. A majority of Republicans still voted against (91–108), but 24 had changed their votes in favor. Among Democrats, the vote was 172–63, with 33 who had originally voted against the bill now supporting the measure. House officials immediately carried the bill to the White House, and less than two hours after the vote, Bush signed the Emergency Economic Stabilization Act of 2008 into law.

"There were moments this week when some thought the Federal Government could not rise to the challenge," said the president. "But thanks to the hard work of members of both parties in both Houses—and the spirit of cooperation between Capitol Hill and my administration—we completed this bill in a timely manner." Bush went on to say that he knew many Americans had concerns about the bill, and he understood those concerns. "As a strong supporter of free enterprise, I believe Government intervention should occur only when necessary. In this situation, action is clearly necessary. And ultimately, the cost to taxpayers will be far less than the initial outlay."[78]

After speaking in the Rose Garden, Bush went next door to the Treasury, where he congratulated everyone on the victory just won. "Sometimes people in Government never get thanked for all the hours they keep. I want to thank you for giving me a chance to come by, and looking forward to getting this plan in place."[79]

Passage of the Emergency Economic Stabilization Act did not end the financial crisis. But it arrested the meltdown. In that sense, TARP was a success.[80] Rather than buying the toxic assets, the $700 billion appropriated was funneled into the banks to provide immediate capital. That was what Bernanke recommended, and Bush and Paulson agreed. The Treasury bought nonvoting preferred stock, and that provided the banks with money to lend.

Paulson announced the plan on October 13, and the markets responded with enthusiasm. The Dow Jones increased 936 points that day, its largest one-day increase ever. The crisis was not over, but banks began to lend once more, and the panic that gripped the market began to recede. Bush deserves credit for pushing TARP through Congress. He also deserves credit for recognizing that his cherished ideas of unfettered free enterprise were inadequate to meet the crisis the nation faced. He (and his principal financial advisers) can be criticized for not recognizing the crisis as it emerged, and for the failure to regulate the financial markets adequately. He also may have erred in not saving Lehman Brothers, which might have lessened the meltdown. But when the chips were down, Bush kept his head and did what was required. The bold decision to guarantee money market funds combined with the TARP legislation did not end the crisis. But they bought enough time for reason to reassert itself and banish the unbridled fear that had prevailed.

After he left office, Bush summed up the financial meltdown with remarkable candor. "My administration and the regulators underestimated the extent of the risks taken by Wall Street. The rating agencies created a false sense of security by blessing shaky assets. Financial firms built up too much leverage and hid some exposure with off-balance sheet accounting. Many new products were so complicated that even their creators didn't fully understand them. For all of these reasons, we were blindsided by a financial crisis that had been more than a decade in the making."[81] That is an honest assessment. And the manner in which Bush handled the crisis turned out remarkably well. Critics might say he was growing into the job. Ideology was replaced by pragmatism.

CHAPTER TWENTY-FIVE

Finis

———

In the presidency, as in life, you have to play the hand you're dealt.

George W. Bush

Throughout 2008, Bush's approval rating hovered in the high 20s—dropping to an all-time low of 26.5 percent in October, just before the presidential election. Other presidents have suffered low ratings. Harry Truman's approval dropped significantly during his second term, Lyndon Johnson's fell as a result of the Vietnam War, and Richard Nixon suffered appreciably prior to his resignation. But not since Herbert Hoover in the early 1930s has a president been more unpopular than Bush, or for such an extended period.

Among age groups, Bush was least popular with those under thirty. According to data assembled by the Pew Research Center, that was not because of the war in Iraq but because of Bush's views on social and religious issues. Younger voters were more tolerant of gay rights and far less committed to the fundamentalist moral views of the president. Karl Rove had trumpeted anti-gay themes to rally conservative Christians behind Bush in the 2004 election. By 2008, that strategy worked against the president, particularly among younger voters.[1]

John McCain on the campaign trail.

And it was not just young voters. According to Gallup polls, only 3 percent of Democrats approved the job Bush was doing—another record low.[2] Never in recent American history has political opposition transformed itself into such deep personal animosity. As Peter Baker of *The New York Times* has pointed out, the slogan "Bush Lied, People Died" became an article of faith for many.[3] Pundits and scholars regularly debated whether Bush would go down in history as the worst president ever.*

For John McCain, who had clinched the Republican nomination in the late spring of 2008, Bush's unpopularity posed a serious problem. Not since Adlai Stevenson won the Democratic nomination in 1952 has the nominee of a sitting president's party not been part of the administration. That afforded McCain the opportunity to criticize Bush, and he made the most of it. Prior to the Republican convention in September, the McCain campaign regularly ran television ads declaring, "We're worse off than we were four years ago," and "We can't afford four more years of the same."[4] Speaking at a campaign rally in Missouri just before the convention opened, McCain told the crowd, "I promise, if you are sick and tired of the way Washington operates, you need only be patient for a couple of more months. Change is coming! Change is coming! Change is coming!"[5]

The Republican convention, which was scheduled to convene in

---

* A poll of historians conducted by the History News Network and published on November 6, 2008, found that 98.2 percent of those polled considered the Bush presidency a failure, and 61 percent believed Bush to be the worst president in American history. Robert S. McElvaine, "HNN Poll: 61% Historians Rate the Bush Presidency Worst," History News Network, George Mason University. Also see Sean Wilentz, "The Worst President in History?," *Rolling Stone*, April 19, 2006.

St. Paul, Minnesota, on September 1, presented a more serious problem for the McCain campaign. Bush was president and—despite his low poll numbers—still popular with many party regulars, particularly the conservative base. He could not be snubbed. At least, not overtly. But as Senator Joe Lieberman, who had been reelected in 2006 as an Independent and who was now supporting McCain, noted, Bush had become "an albatross." [6]

The simplest solution would be for the president to be out of the country when the convention met. Perhaps in Africa dealing with AIDS. That was suggested to the White House and immediately rejected. [7] But Bush understood McCain's problem. "If I were running," he told old friends, "I would be saying the same thing. 'Bush screwed it up!' You cannot, I don't care who you are, embrace George W. Bush." [8] Nevertheless, the president insisted on speaking at the convention. So did Dick Cheney. In many respects, that was even worse. And the McCain campaign had little choice. To minimize the damage, both Bush and Cheney were scheduled to speak Monday night, September 1, the first day of the convention. They were told to be brief. Ten minutes each should suffice. Praise the nominee, go light on the Bush record.

Fortunately for McCain, nature intervened. Another hurricane, this time named Gustav, hit the Gulf coast just as the convention was about to begin. With Katrina very much in mind, McCain canceled the first night of the convention and hurried to Louisiana and Mississippi to inspect the damage. This was the night when the president and vice president were scheduled to speak. They too were canceled. The damage on the Gulf coast proved far less severe than Katrina—this time the levees held—and the convention resumed on Tuesday. McCain profited by being on the scene when the storm hit, and more importantly, by having a reason to remove Bush and Cheney from the program. Bush was allowed to address the convention by satellite from the White House on Tuesday night, and Cheney was dropped altogether. As a further indignity, Bush's speech was scheduled to be shown to the delegates before the television networks began their live coverage of the convention. According to friends, Bush was furious that McCain had used the storm to deny him the opportunity of speaking to the delegates in person. He also felt slighted at not being on national television. But he played the role he was assigned.

Bush was the first sitting president not to attend his party's convention since Lyndon Johnson missed the Democratic convention in Chicago in 1968.* At 9:54 p.m. on Tuesday, September 2, Bush appeared on a giant television screen in the auditorium of the Xcel Energy Center in St. Paul. The delegates applauded politely. Bush spoke for eight minutes.

> I know what it takes to be President. In these past eight years, I've sat at the Resolute desk and reviewed the daily intelligence briefings, the threat assessments, and the reports from our commanders on the front lines. I've stood in the ruins of buildings knocked down by killers and promised the survivors I would never let them down. I know the hard choices that fall solely to a president. John McCain's life has prepared him to make those choices. He is ready to lead this nation.[9]

For the remainder of the speech, Bush touted McCain's ability to handle the job. "John is a man who thinks for himself. He's not afraid to tell you when he disagrees. Believe me, I know. [Laughter.] No matter what the issue, this man is honest and speaks straight from the heart." Bush concluded on a note of personal reflection. "In the time the Oval Office has been in my trust, I've kept near my desk reminders of America's character, including a painting of a west Texas mountain lit by the morning sun. It reminds me that Americans have always lived on the sunrise side of the mountain. We are a nation that looks to the new day with confidence and optimism. And I am optimistic about our future because I believe in the goodness and wisdom of the American people."[10]

When Bush concluded, the lights came on and the prime-time television coverage of the convention began. The president was followed by

---

* During the administration of Franklin D. Roosevelt, the Republicans always invited Herbert Hoover to speak at their conventions—1936, 1940, and 1944. Given Hoover's dismal standing in the country, the Democrats always looked forward to his appearance.

Senator Joe Lieberman, former senator Fred Thompson of Tennessee, Senator Norm Coleman from Minnesota, and House minority leader John Boehner. Not one mentioned Bush in his presentation. When the convention was shown a video about 9/11, former New York mayor Rudy Giuliani and former defense secretary Donald Rumsfeld were featured. Bush was not mentioned. And in his acceptance speech on the evening of September 4, McCain not only did not mention Bush by name, but once again spoke as if he were running against him. "I fight to restore the pride and principles of our party," said McCain. "We were elected to change Washington, but we allowed Washington to change us. . . . We need to change the way government does almost everything. . . . We have to catch up to history, and we have to change the way we do business in Washington." [11] *

During the campaign itself, McCain avoided any endorsement of Bush or the president's policies. In the final debate with Obama at Hofstra University in New York, when the Democratic candidate accused McCain of supporting Bush's economic policies, the Arizona senator responded, "Senator Obama, I am not President Bush. If you wanted to run against President Bush, you should have run four years ago." [12]

Bush understood he had become a pariah. Later he said he preferred McCain to Obama, but did not campaign for him. "Mostly because he didn't ask. I understood he had to establish his independence. I also suspected he was worried about the polls. I thought it looked defensive for John to distance himself from me. . . . But the decision was his." [13]

The convention gave McCain a brief bounce in the polls—partially attributable to the fresh face of Sarah Palin as his running mate—but by mid-September, Obama regained the lead and retained it through election day.† The fact is, the economic meltdown had made the out-

---

* In contrast to the treatment of the president, Laura was welcomed at the convention and appeared jointly on the program with Cindy McCain asking for support for the victims of Hurricane Gustav.

† Bush was unimpressed with McCain's choice of Palin as his running mate. "I'm sure I've met her," he told his staff. "What is she, the governor of Guam? . . . Just wait a few days until the bloom is off that rose. This woman is being put into a position she is not even remotely prepared for. She hasn't spent one day on the national level. Neither has her family. Let's wait and see how

come inevitable. McCain's strong suit was national security and terrorism. His response to the economic crisis was erratic and unfocused, and
won little respect. He was also seventy-two years old, one of the oldest
presidential nominees in history, and eight years older than Bush. To
vote for McCain meant setting the clock back a generation. By contrast,
Obama was forty-seven and represented a new generation.

When the votes were counted on November 4, Obama defeated
McCain in a landslide by ten million votes, carrying twenty-seven
states and the District of Columbia, and winning 365 electoral votes to
McCain's 173.* Bush immediately called Obama to congratulate him.
There was no bitterness. Bush was deeply impressed that an African
American had been elected president. As he watched the returns come
in on television that evening, he was struck by the sight of black men
and women openly crying at Obama's victory.[14]

On Wednesday morning, Bush spoke to the nation. "All Americans
can be proud of the history that was made yesterday," said the president.

> They showed a watching world the vitality of America's democracy and
> the strides we have made toward a more perfect union. They chose a
> president whose journey represents a triumph of the American story, a
> testament to hard work, optimism, and faith in the enduring promise
> of our nation.
>
> It will be a stirring sight to watch President Obama, his wife Mi-
> chelle, and their beautiful girls step through the doors of the White
> House. I know millions of Americans will be overcome with pride
> at this inspiring moment that so many have waited so long. I know
> Senator Obama's beloved mother and grandparents would have been
> thrilled to watch the child they raised ascend the steps of the Capitol
> and take his oath to defend the Constitution of the greatest nation on
> the face of the earth.[15]

---

she looks five days out." Matt Latimer, *Speech-Less: Tales of a White House Survivor* (New York:
Three Rivers Press, 2009), 273.
*   The final vote count showed Obama with 69,498,516 votes to McCain's 59,948,323. Ralph
Nader received 739,034, and two dozen other candidates split the remaining 1,127,947.

Bush meets with President-elect Barack Obama in the Oval Office, November 10, 2008.

The president immediately invited Obama and Michelle to the White House, and did his utmost to insure a smooth transition. Several months earlier Bush had established a Transition Coordinating Council under Josh Bolten to manage the changeover, and on Thursday, November 6, met with the full White House staff and the cabinet to emphasize the importance of a smooth transition. Once again, Bush was gracious and congratulatory. "Over the next 75 days," he told the staff, "all of us must ensure that the next president and his team can hit the ground running." Bush then ticked off the steps being taken by Bolten's team. "These measures represent an unprecedented effort to ensure that the executive branch is prepared to fulfill its responsibility at all times. . . . As January 20 draws near, some of you may be anxious about finding a new job or a new place to live. I know how you feel. But between now and then we must keep our attention on the task at hand, because the American people expect no less." [16]

True to his word, the changeover between the Bush administration and the incoming Obama team was the smoothest of any presidential transition involving different political parties in American history. Perhaps McCain deserves some credit for that, however inadvertently.

Had he not been so hostile to Bush during the campaign, the president might have found it more difficult to establish cordial relations with Obama.

Responding to Bush's invitation, Obama and Michelle arrived at the White House on the Monday following the election. Obama went with Bush into the Oval Office, and Laura gave Michelle a tour of the residence. Both couples hit it off. Laura invited Michelle to bring her daughters and mother back for another visit, and the president and Obama sat together for several hours. "Barack was gracious and confident," Bush recalled. "He asked questions about how I structured my day and organized my staff." Bush gave Obama a quick review of foreign policy issues, and mentally compared the president-elect to himself when he had met with Bill Clinton in 2001. "I could see the sense of responsibility start to envelop him," said Bush.[17] The financial meltdown was being brought under control, and Obama was aware of the issues, having stayed in touch with Paulson throughout the campaign.* But it was not clear sailing. The automobile industry was now in serious trouble. Bush assured Obama that he would not let the automobile companies fail, and the two parted on friendly terms. As for the auto companies, Bush told his staff, "I won't dump this mess on him."[18]

Bailing out the American auto industry presented another difficult decision for Bush. He had opposed President Carter's rescue of Chrysler in 1979, and believed the government had no business supporting the car companies. Once again, the magnitude of the impending disaster changed his mind. The president's economic advisers, including Paulson, chairman of the Council of Economic Advisers Ed Lazear, and Commerce Secretary Carlos Gutierrez, believed that the failure of the American auto industry would reduce the nation's gross domestic product by hundreds of billions of dollars, cost a million jobs, and decrease tax revenue by at least $150 billion.[19]

---

*   When awoken by his wife on election night and told that Obama had won, Paulson said he "went back to sleep comforted by the knowledge that our president-elect fully understood the threat our economy still faced." Henry M. Paulson, *On the Brink: Inside the Race to Stop the Collapse of the Global Financial System* (New York: Business Plus, 2010), 392.

The crisis in the auto industry had been long in the making. To maximize profits, the Big Three—General Motors, Ford, and Chrysler—had shifted increasingly to the production of SUVs and large pickup trucks rather than smaller fuel-efficient cars. The profit margin on an SUV was 15 to 20 percent, versus as little as 3 percent on a small car. That was fine so long as gasoline remained affordable, but an energy crisis had caused fuel prices to spike, reaching $4 a gallon in 2008. At that point the sales of SUVs and large pickups plummeted. In addition, many new cars were purchased with money from home equity loans; in 2007, about two million. Such funding dried up during the financial crisis, as did other forms of credit.

The annual capacity of the U.S. auto industry was seventeen million vehicles. In 2008, only ten million were produced. That was also a reflection of the inability of the U.S. automakers to compete with foreign companies. In 1998, Detroit's Big Three commanded 70 percent of the American market. By 2008, their share had shrunk to 53 percent. U.S. production costs were uncompetitive as a result of the high wages and elaborate health care arrangements the carmakers had negotiated with the United Auto Workers, as well as high pension costs. Finally, the severe downturn in the stock market had significantly reduced the capital assets of the Big Three, and their cash reserves were dangerously low. Bankruptcy appeared inevitable.

Bush initially sought to provide the money the auto industry needed by tapping into a $25 billion fund that had been established earlier in the year to assist the car companies in producing more fuel-efficient vehicles. Under an arrangement negotiated with House speaker Nancy Pelosi, the Treasury would be authorized to loan $14 billion from the fund to General Motors and Chrysler until March 2009. (Ford said it had sufficient cash reserves and did not need federal assistance.) Bush would be authorized to appoint a financial director—a "car czar"—who would be empowered to ensure that GM and Chrysler restructured themselves to become commercially viable. If they failed to do so, the loans would be called and the companies would be forced into bankruptcy. As White House press secretary Dana Perino expressed it, "Long-term financing must be conditioned on the principle that taxpayers should only assist automakers executing a credible plan for long-term viability." [20]

On December 10, the Bush-Pelosi proposal passed the House of Representatives 237–170, largely along party lines. Thirty-two Republicans, mainly from states with auto plants, joined 205 Democrats voting in favor, while 20 Democrats voted with 150 Republicans against. [21] But in the Senate the bill immediately ran into trouble. Republicans balked at supporting the bill without steep cuts in pay and benefits for the autoworkers. The bill was flawed, said minority leader Mitch McConnell, because "it promises taxpayers money today for reforms that may or may not come tomorrow." [22] When Harry Reid asked for cloture to bring the bill to a vote, he could muster only fifty-two of the sixty votes required. Just as with their initial consideration of the TARP legislation, Congress once again turned the president down. Only this time it was the Senate that wielded the ax.

Once again, Bush responded to the defeat by pledging to take action. After expressing his disappointment that Congress had failed to pass the rescue legislation, the president emphasized the consequences of failing to respond to the crisis in the auto industry. "A precipitous collapse of this industry would have a severe impact on our economy, and it would be irresponsible to further weaken or destabilize our economy at this time." Speaking through the White House press office, Bush said that "Under normal economic circumstances we would prefer that markets determine the ultimate fate of private firms. However, given the current weakened state of the U.S. economy, we will consider other options if necessary—including the use of the TARP program—to avert a collapse of troubled automakers." [23]

The day after the Senate vote, Bush left the White House for Texas to deliver the commencement address at Texas A&M, and then undertook his final visit to Iraq and Afghanistan. The question of what to do about the auto industry remained unresolved. When the president returned to Washington in mid-December, he immediately took up the issue. Several on the White House staff, as well as Vice President Cheney, argued that the question was not as serious as the Wall Street meltdown and that the auto companies should be allowed to fail. Others, including Paulson, Gutierrez, and Lazear, argued that without federal funds the auto companies would be forced to liquidate. Bankruptcy was not an option because there was no private financing available to permit them to restructure. Having listened to the arguments for an hour and a half, Bush said he would think about it. Paulson urged him to think fast, because time was running out.

Bush wrestled with the questions for two days. Appearing at an open forum of the American Enterprise Institute at the Mayflower Hotel on the morning of December 18, he was frank about what was involved. "I haven't made up my mind yet," Bush told the audience.

> This is a difficult time for a free market person. Under ordinary circumstances, failed entities—failing entities should be allowed to fail.
>
> I have concluded these are not ordinary circumstances, for a lot of reasons. Our financial system is interwoven domestically, internationally. And we got to the point where, if a major institution were to fail, there is great likelihood there would be a ripple effect throughout the world. . . . And so I analyzed that and decided I didn't want to be the President during a depression greater than the Great Depression or the beginning of a depression greater than the Great Depression.

As for the automobile industry, Bush said,

> The autos obviously are very fragile and I've laid out a couple of principles. One, I'm worried about a disorderly bankruptcy and what it would do to the psychology and the markets. They're beginning to thaw, but there's a lot of uncertainty. I'm also worried about putting good money after bad; that means whether or not these autos will be viable in the future. And frankly, there's one other consideration, and that is, I feel an obligation to my successor. I've thought about what it would be like to become President during this period. I believe that good policy is not to dump him a major catastrophe on his first day in office.[24]

Bush's oral presentation clarified his thinking. That afternoon he instructed Paulson to proceed with the bailout using money from

TARP. Under the plan that Bush approved, General Motors would be provided with federal loans of $13.4 billion and Chrysler $4 billion. The money would carry the companies through March. GM and Chrysler would have to come up with viable restructuring plans by then, but there would be no "car czar" to oversee the operation. If the companies failed to produce, the loans would be called and the companies forced into bankruptcy.

Bush announced his decision before the markets opened Friday morning, December 19, 2008. "If we were to allow the free market to take its course now, it would almost certainly lead to disorderly bankruptcy and liquidation for the automakers. Under ordinary economic circumstances, I would say this is the price that failed companies must pay, and I would not favor intervening to prevent the automakers from going out of business. But these are not ordinary circumstances." The president went on to describe current economic conditions and how the auto industry had been affected. He then laid out what he had decided to do, and what the auto companies would be required to do in return. "The actions I am announcing today represent a step that we wish were not necessary. But given the situation, it is the most effective and responsible way to address this challenge facing our nation. By giving the auto companies a chance to restructure, we will shield the American people from a harsh economic blow at a vulnerable time. And we will give American workers an opportunity to show the world once again they can meet challenges with ingenuity and determination and bounce back from tough times and emerge stronger than before."[25]

Bush's decision to intervene on behalf of General Motors and Chrysler was unpopular at the time,* but saved the American auto industry. It also avoided another financial meltdown and the follow-on ripple effect that would have damaged other parts of the manufacturing sector. Bush was not happy about the decision but recognized its necessity.

---

* According to a CNN/Opinion Research Corporation poll, only 37 percent of Americans supported the decision of the president at the time. By 2012, it was supported by 56 percent. Elspeth Reeve, "Most Americans Now Think Auto Bailout Was a Good Idea," *The Atlantic Wire*, February 2012. In 2008, Mitt Romney, who was to run against Obama in 2012, wrote an op-ed for *The New York Times* (October 19) entitled "Let Detroit Go Bankrupt."

"It was frustrating," he wrote, "to have the automakers' rescue be my last major economic decision. But with the market not yet functioning, I had to safeguard American workers' families from a widespread collapse. I also had my successor in mind. I decided to treat him the way I would like to have been treated if I were in his position." [26]

Obama, for his part, immediately embraced the president's decision. "I do want to emphasize to the Big Three automakers the people's patience is running out, and they should seize this opportunity over the next several weeks to come up with a plan that is sustainable. And that means they're going to have to make some hard choices." [27]

In many respects, and despite his unpopularity, 2008 was the high point of Bush's presidency. His approval ratings may have hovered in the high 20s, but his decisions to rescue Wall Street and the auto industry were essential to the survival of the American economic system. Bush was very much alone at this point. Cheney had become simply another vice president and was no longer the president's principal adviser. Rove and Gonzales were gone, and most of the White House staff was new. Bush wrestled with the problems on his own. Contrary to his deeply held belief in free enterprise, he intervened with TARP to provide liquidity to the financial markets and then bailed out GM and Chrysler with bridging loans to keep them afloat. In both instances, he was opposed by the majority of his own party in Congress. He also concluded an agreement with Iraqi prime minister Nouri al-Maliki to withdraw all U.S. forces by 2011. This too was contrary to his long cherished belief in American global leadership, but was essential to preserve the independence of Iraq. And he went out of his way to insure a smooth and orderly transition with the incoming Obama administration. In all four instances, Bush deserves credit for addressing the issues head-on, regardless of ideology.

The year 2008 brought pleasures as well as challenges. In May, Bush's daughter Jenna was married at the ranch in Crawford to Henry Hager, a former aide to Karl Rove. Jenna did not want a White House wedding, preferring the informality of the Texas setting. The ceremony was conducted by Bush's old friend the Reverend Kirbyjon Caldwell from Houston, and a mariachi band played the wedding march

Barbara, Laura, Henry Hager, Jenna, and Bush
at Jenna and Henry's wedding, May 10, 2008.

as the president, with tears in his eyes, walked Jenna down the aisle. The wedding was strictly a family affair and none of the White House staff attended. Jenna's sister, Barbara, was the maid of honor, her grandfather, George H. W. Bush, read from the scriptures, and Hager's parents spoke briefly about the joys of marriage. After the ceremony there was a festive dinner under a large tent that had been erected at the ranch, guests danced to music provided by local musicians, and then gathered around a firepit to savor the experience. Bush remained up until the last guests departed about 1:00 a.m.—a remarkable testament to his enthusiasm. As he noted, "After my eight years in the presidency, our family had emerged not only stronger, but bigger, too."[28]

In August of 2008, Bush attended the 29th Olympic Games in Beijing—the first American president to attend the Olympics in a foreign country. From the time Bush announced his intention to go to the Games he was under fire from human rights advocates and critics across the political spectrum for lending support to the Chinese regime. Bush was unimpressed. "It's an athletic event," he noted at a press conference in Toyako, Japan, on July 6. "I don't need the Olympics to express my concerns. . . . I happen to believe not going to the opening ceremony would be an affront to the Chinese people, which may make it more difficult to be able to speak frankly with the Chinese leadership. . . . I'm looking forward to cheering the athletes. I think it would be good for these athletes who have worked hard to see their President waving that flag."[29] Bush's judgment proved correct. The opening ceremony in

Beijing was attended by every major head of government or head of state, and watched by a television audience estimated at four billion.[30]

Before he left for Beijing, Bush hosted some two dozen members of the U.S. Olympic team at a Rose Garden ceremony at the White House on July 21, and then spoke to the press. "Today we honor skill

With China's president Hu Jintao
at the Beijing Olympics.

and discipline," said the president. "America's Olympians have two very important things in common: God-given talent and an appreciation for the hard work required to achieve true excellence."[31] When the ceremony was over, Bush invited the athletes to the Oval Office, where he shook hands with each one, spoke briefly about his or her accomplishments, and wished them luck in Beijing. That evening Bush and Laura hosted a dinner for the athletes and the U.S. Olympic Committee in the White House.

Bush and Laura spent four days and four nights in Beijing, and were accompanied by former president George H. W. Bush and Barbara. The elder Bush had been appointed by Richard Nixon as American diplomatic representative to Beijing some thirty-three years earlier, and was delighted to be returning. Also in the president's party were his daughter Barbara, his brother Marvin, his sister, Doro, and Roland and Lois Betts. Roland was W's classmate at Yale, a DKE buddy, and his partner in the purchase of the Texas Rangers in 1989. China's president, Hu Jintao, publicly thanked Bush for not politicizing the Olympic Games, and invited the entire Bush family to a lavish luncheon in the Forbidden City. It was, as Bush recalled, "a Bush family reunion like none before or since."[32]

Cheering for the U.S. swim team.
Laura, left; Barbara, right.

While in Beijing, Bush spoke at the dedication of a new American embassy—the Chinese had just opened a new embassy in Washington—and emphasized the importance of China to the United States. "The relationship between our nations is constructive and cooperative and candid. We'll continue to be candid about our mutual global responsibilities. . . . Candor is most effective where nations have built a relationship of respect and trust. I've worked hard to build that respect and trust. I appreciate the Chinese leadership that have worked hard to build that respect and trust."[33]

Bush spent his time in Beijing watching the games and cheering the American athletes. He saw the United States beat China in basketball, watched swimmer Michael Phelps win his first gold medal in the 200-meter freestyle (Phelps would win eight golds—an Olympic record), and cheered madly as the United States came from behind to defeat France in the freestyle relay. He also went for a test ride on the Laoshan Olympic mountain bike course, and then visited with the American beach volleyball team of Misty May-Traenor and Kerri Walsh. "Biking was really, really difficult," he told reporters afterward. "That's why I am an amateur, and they are professionals."[34] Overall, the United States led the medal count with 110 to China's 100. But the Chinese won 51 gold medals—a new Olympic record—to 36 for the United States.

Throughout his presidency, Bush followed athletic events closely, and the Beijing Olympics was no exception. He saw athletics as a unifying force bringing the world together. Asked by Bob Costas of NBC

Sports in Beijing whether good relations with China—"an authoritarian state with a dismal human rights record"—was contrary to America's interests, Bush was explicit in pointing out the benefits. "In the long run," said the president, "America better remain engaged with China and understand that we can have a cooperative and constructive, yet candid relationship. It's really important for future presidents to understand the relationship between China and the region, and it is important to make sure that America is engaged with China, even though we may have some disagreements." [35]

Bush worked hard to improve his relationship with President Hu Jintao. In October, French president Nicolas Sarkozy suggested to Bush that he convene a meeting of G-7 countries—Britain, France, Germany, Italy, Canada, Japan, and the United States—to deal with the economic crisis. Bush liked the idea, but since the financial meltdown was global, thought it would be more effective to convene a meeting of the leaders of the G-20, representing almost 90 percent of the world's economy. In addition to the G-7 countries, the G-20 included China, Russia, India, Indonesia, Brazil, Mexico, Saudi Arabia, Argentina, South Africa, South Korea, Turkey, and Australia.* Bush dispatched invitations to the leaders of those countries to meet in Washington on November 14–15 for the first ever Summit on Financial Markets and the World Economy. Said White House press secretary Dana Perino, "The leaders will review progress being made to address the current financial crisis, advance a common understanding of its causes, and, in order to avoid a repetition, agree on a common set of principles for reform of the regulatory and institutional regimes for the world's financial sectors." [36]

The meeting was a resounding success. Bush welcomed the leaders, and the White House staff did its utmost to fashion a unanimous agreement. A major assist must go to Chinese president Hu Jintao, who spoke convincingly of the need to take immediate action and laid out four priorities for reforming the international financial system: better

---

* The twentieth member of the G-20 is the European Union, which is represented by the European Commission and the European Central Bank.

international cooperation in regulating the system, reform of international financial institutions, improving regional financial cooperation, and improving the international currency system.[37] When the meeting concluded on the 15th, the leaders signed a joint statement—the Washington Declaration—affirming that they had reached an agreement on the root causes of the crisis; reviewed what countries had done to meet the crisis; agreed on common principles for reforming the financial markets; and reaffirmed their commitment to the free market.[38] Bush's economic summit for the G-20 was a resounding success. The Obama administration has followed with seven more such meetings, but it was Bush who began the process. The meeting sent a powerful signal that the world's principal nations would not turn inward when confronting a financial crisis but would cooperate with one another to resolve it.

As part of the presidential transition, Barack Obama asked Bush if it would be possible for him to meet with all the ex-presidents. Bush was happy to oblige, and organized a White House luncheon in the Oval Office on January 7. Bush and Obama were joined by Jimmy Carter, Bill Clinton, and George H. W. Bush. The luncheon lasted over two hours, each former president ordered his lunch à la carte from the White House mess, and the tone was convivial and friendly. "All the gentlemen here understand both the pressures and possibilities of this office," said Obama before the meeting. "For me to have the opportunity to get advice, good counsel and fellowship with these individuals is extraordinary, and I just want to thank the president for hosting us."[39]

Bush was equally effusive. "We all want you to succeed," he replied. "Whether we're Democrat or Republican we care deeply about this country. And to the extent we can, we look forward to sharing our experiences with you. All of us who have served in this office understand that the office transcends the individual."[40]

Immediately after the luncheon, Bush met with Brit Hume of Fox News for a lengthy and reflective interview. Asked about his feelings toward Obama, Bush was remarkably positive. "I liked him," the president told Hume. "The man is obviously a charismatic person. And I wish him all the best. The reason we had the dinner, or the lunch— we call them dinners in Texas—the lunch at the White House was so

Bush, President-elect Obama, and former presidents George H. W. Bush, Bill Clinton, and Jimmy Carter at the White House lunch, January 7, 2009.

that he could hear from the current president and the former presidents that we wanted him to succeed. And he is an engaging person, and I am impressed by the priority he places on his family."

Later in the interview, Bush and Hume were joined by the president's father. Asked by Hume about the ex-presidents' club—"Are all the old political differences set aside?"—the elder Bush agreed that they were. "I think every member of that club realizes there can be only one president. He's not going to be turning to you every day saying, 'What will I do now?' . . . He doesn't need a lot of advice from former presidents. . . . And so I don't think there is much to it except collegiality and the idea that you want to be out there if he needs support."

Asked about the transition, President Bush was enthusiastic. "I think he's [Obama] had a very good transition. I think Josh Bolten, my chief of staff, and the people that work here in the White House have also had a good transition, because they've reached out to the president-elect's team at all levels. And the message is, we want this to be a seamless move from us leaving and you coming in, and we want you to succeed."

Hume asked Bush's father if he agreed. "Yes, totally, totally," the former president replied.

> Why be out there looking like you're carping and criticizing and know everything? I've heard what the president [Bush 43] said about president-elect Obama. I feel the same way: Support him where you can, and don't go out there criticizing and carping. You look small yourself for one thing, but that's not the main reason. The main reason is that he needs support. And if it's something you disagree with violently, sit on the sidelines and shut up.[41]

At his final press conference the following week, Bush reflected on the meeting of the former presidents with Obama. "To have two guys who are nearly 85, two 62-year-olders, and a 47-year-old, is a classic generational statement. And one common area, in at least the four of us—we all had different circumstances and experiences—but we've all experienced what it means to assume the responsibility of the presidency." Bush went on to make light of the "burdens of the office," and then in response to a question from Sheryl Stolberg of *The New York Times* talked about what he saw as his mistakes: putting the "Mission Accomplished" banner on the *Abraham Lincoln* in 2003, his response to Katrina, and his failure to press immigration reform immediately after the 2004 election. "There have been disappointments. Abu Ghraib obviously was a huge disappointment. Not having weapons of mass destruction was a significant disappointment. I don't know if you want to call those mistakes or not, but things didn't go according to plan, let's put it that way."[42]

It was a similarly thoughtful Bush who delivered his farewell address on January 15, five days before Obama's inauguration.

> Like all who have held this office before me, I have experienced setbacks. And there are things I would do differently if given the chance.

Yet I have always acted with the best interests of our country in mind. I have followed my conscience and done what I thought was right. You may not agree with some of the tough decisions I have made, but I hope you can agree that I was willing to make tough decisions.[43]

Shortly before ten o'clock on the morning of January 20, Bush and Laura greeted Barack and Michelle Obama on the North Portico of the White House and invited them in for the traditional inauguration day coffee between outgoing and incoming presidents. Bush had become fond of Obama and went out of his way to insure the incoming president was comfortable that morning. On the ride up Pennsylvania Avenue, the two chatted amiably and Bush refrained from giving Obama additional advice. This was a day to celebrate, and Bush understood that.

When they arrived at the Capitol, they made their way separately to the speaker's office, where they waited until being introduced on the platform. David Axelrod, Obama's political aide, was in the room and caught Bush's eye. "Axelrod," said the president, "I've been watching you. I've been watching you, and I think you're all right. You're going to do just fine. You're in for the ride of your life. Just hang on and really enjoy it, 'cause it'll go by faster than you can imagine."[44] It was the personal side of Bush, transcending the intensity of political differences.

Obama began his inaugural address by thanking Bush for his support. "I stand here today humbled by the task before us, grateful for the trust you have bestowed, mindful of the sacrifices borne by our ancestors. I thank President Bush for his service to our nation, as well as the generosity and cooperation he has shown throughout this transition."[45] Obama's speech was not overly partisan and scarcely critical of the Bush administration. Instead, he focused on America's heritage and how it applied to the problems facing the nation. "Our challenges may be new, the instruments with which we meet them may be new, but those values upon which our success depends, honesty and hard work, courage and fair play, tolerance and curiosity, loyalty and patriotism— these things are old." Bush could have said exactly the same. "That was a hell of a speech," he told Rahm Emanuel when Obama concluded.[46]

When the ceremony was over, the Obamas escorted Bush and

Michelle and Barack Obama escort Bush and Laura to the waiting
helicopter at the east front of the Capitol, January 20, 2009.

Laura through the Rotunda of the Capitol to the East Front, and down
the steps to the presidential helicopter, Marine One. Already aboard
were Bush 41 and Barbara, ready to accompany George and Laura to
Andrews Air Force Base, where they would board Air Force One for
the final flight to Texas. As Laura noted, "The love of the Bush family
had come full circle; the pride George had felt for his parents, they felt
in return for their son. They too had made this journey we were about
to begin and had found unexpected joys in the years beyond."[47]

Bush and Obama embraced and bid each other farewell. "We will
brief you from time to time," said Obama. "There is no need for that,"
Bush replied. "I have served my time, and I don't want you to feel like
you need to waste a lot of time on me."[48]

At Andrews Air Force Base, over a thousand members of Bush's staff,
their families, and friends, were waiting to say goodbye to the former
president and Laura. Bush spoke briefly, said he was "proud to have had
a front-row seat to history" at Obama's swearing in, and then boarded

Air Force One (redesignated Special Air Mission 28000) for the return to Midland. In addition to his parents and daughters, Bush and Laura were joined on the plane by many former aides from Texas including Karl Rove, Karen Hughes, Alberto Gonzales, and Margaret Spellings. It was a nonstop party. Bush was relieved his job was over and was very huggy. "He was

Bush glances out the window of his helicopter after departing the U.S. Capitol en route to Andrews Air Force Base following the inauguration of President Obama.

hugging everybody," a former aide recalled. "A little weepy, but mostly just hugging people."[49]

In Midland, a crowd of twenty thousand supporters was waiting in Centennial Plaza to welcome Bush home. It was an emotional moment. "It is good to be home," said the former president. "Laura and I may have left Texas, but Texas never left us." There was no bitterness. "Today was a great day for America and a good man took the oath of office, and we offer our prayers for his success." Bush said that for himself, "the days have been long, but the years are short. When I walked out of the Oval Office this morning, I left with the same values I took to Washington eight years ago. When I go home tonight and look into the mirror, I'm not going to regret what I see. . . . The presidency was a joyful experience, but nothing compares with Texas at sunset. It is good to be home."[50]

Bush was sixty-two when he left office, and was determined to lead a private life. "When I saw his [Obama's] hand go up," he told friends, "I thought 'Free at Last.'"[51] Bush took no part in the congressional elections of 2010 and 2014, or in Mitt Romney's bid for the presidency in 2012. He addressed the GOP convention that year, but as in 2008 it was

The Bush home in Dallas.

by video hookup and not in person. With the exception of immigration reform—which he continued to advocate—he scrupulously avoided taking stands on public issues and devoted himself to private causes, particularly the fight against AIDS and malaria in Africa.

Initially, Bush concentrated on writing his memoirs and establishing his presidential library. He and Laura purchased a large house in the Preston Hollow neighborhood of North Dallas,* not far from where they lived when he directed the Texas Rangers, and began alternating between there and the ranch in Crawford. Bush's memoirs, *Decision Points*, were published in 2010 and sold more than two million copies. The presidential library, located on the campus of Southern Methodist University, opened in April 2013. Once again the ex-presidents came together for the occasion. "To know the man is to like the man, because he is comfortable in his own skin," said President Obama. "He knows

---

* The Bush house is at 10141 Daria Place. According to the Dallas Central Appraisal District, the house has 8,505 square feet, four bedrooms, four and a half baths, and sits on a lot of 1.134 acres. It also contains servant's quarters, a cabana, and a detached garage. When they purchased the house in December 2008, Bush and Laura took out a mortgage of $3,074,239 from the Community National Bank in Midland. The cost of the house was apparently $3 million, and closing costs $74,239. Taxes are $68,000 annually. Also see Leslie Easton and Ben Casselwan, "Bushes Buy Dallas Home for Residence," *Wall Street Journal*, December 5, 2008.

who he is. He doesn't put on any pretenses. He takes his job seriously, but he doesn't take himself too seriously. He is a good man."[52] The Bush Library is second in size to the Reagan Library in Simi Valley, California, and combines the official National Archives library containing the president's White House records with the George W. Bush Institute, a public policy institute focusing on contemporary issues.[53]

Bush and Laura traveled extensively, going to Africa frequently on behalf of PEPFAR, but avoiding Europe because of continued public disapproval. In 2011, Bush canceled a trip to Geneva—that would have been his first post-presidential visit to the continent—because human rights groups planned major protests and warned they would attempt to have him arrested.[54] Like Bill Clinton, Bush also began to speak privately to elite host groups, charging fees between $100,000 and $150,000 for each appearance. Two and a half years after leaving office he had delivered 140 such speeches, earning over $15 million.[55]

Once again Bush and Laura became regulars at home games of the Texas Rangers, and the former president took up golf. He had given up the sport while in the White House out of deference to the troops at war, but now resumed with a vengeance. "He's a golf-a-holic now," said his friend from Midland, Charlie Younger. Bush would go to the golf course early in the morning and often play with the first people who showed up. "I decided I was going to get better at golf, not just play golf," he told writer Walter Harrington. Bush's game did improve, but not as much as he wanted. "That's the problem with the game. It requires discipline, patience, and focus . . . a couple of areas where I could use some improvement."[56]

The former president also devoted considerable time to his family. Both his father and mother were in failing health, and Bush set about to look after them. In 2014, he published a tribute to his father—*41: A Portrait of My Father*—a deeply moving personal account of their relationship. "Dad and I spoke frequently throughout my presidency, although not necessarily about the topics that some people have assumed. In the limo after a State of the Union address or another big speech, I would often get a call from the White House operator: 'Mr. President, your father is on the line.' Dad would offer an encouraging and comforting word."[57] The book is personal and extremely well written, a tribute both to the subject and the author.*

Like Dwight Eisenhower and Winston Churchill, Bush also took up painting. Churchill began painting during World War I after he had been relieved as First Lord of the Admiralty following the disaster at Gallipoli. Eisenhower began while he was president of Columbia. With Bush it was much the same. "He was desperate for a pastime," said Laura.[58] Bush's hobby was discovered when a Romanian computer expert hacked into the email accounts of Bush's family members and then leaked images of the paintings to American websites. The revelation that Bush had become a painter helped erode some of the hostility that had surrounded him and made him seem more likable. As art critic Alastair Sooke wrote in the London *Telegraph*, "Bush paints in a similar fashion to the way he talks—affecting a folksy, homespun, plain-speaking tone, with just enough ham-fisted strangeness and bungling mistakes to keep things interesting."[59] At one point, Bush was painting five to six hours a day, and in April 2014 exhibited the portraits of more than twenty-four world leaders he had known at the Bush Institute on the SMU campus. "Painting has changed my life in an unbelievably positive way," Bush told Rick Klein of ABC News.[60]

Unlike Clinton and Carter, Bush did not miss the presidency. "I really don't," he told an audience in Houston in 2011. "I actually found my freedom by leaving Washington."[61] Speaking with *USA Today* two years later, Bush said, "There is no need to defend myself. I did what I did and ultimately history will be the judge."[62] He recognized he had made mistakes, and he let it go at that.

George W. Bush may not have been America's worst president.

---

* "I did not use e-mail during my presidency," wrote George W. Bush, "but Dad would often write a corny joke to my senior aides, knowing they would bring it into the Oval Office to brighten my day. For example, in 2007, he sent this along: 'An eighty year old man was arrested for shoplifting. When he went before the judge, he asked him what he had stolen. "A can of peaches." The judge asked how many peaches were in the can. "Six," he replied. "Then I will give you six days in jail," the judge said. Then the man's wife spoke up: "He stole a can of peas too."'" George W. Bush, *41: A Portrait of My Father* (New York: Crown, 2014), 267.

His accomplishments were noteworthy. His decisions in 2008 to rescue Wall Street and the American automobile industry were acts of genuine courage and statesmanship. The country suffered a severe economic recession, but thanks to Bush it avoided a repeat of the Great Depression. Together with Vladimir Putin he reduced the nuclear arsenal each country maintains, and with Hu Jintao improved American relations with China. He expanded American free trade, and almost singlehandedly led the global fight against AIDS. Domestically, he extended Medicare to include prescription drugs for seniors, improved educational standards with No Child Left Behind, and fought hard for immigration reform. It is also true that he kept the country safe after 9/11. But that ignores the fact that he was warned of a possible terrorist attack prior to 9/11 and ignored those warnings. He also overreacted to 9/11. The events that day were tragic, but did not warrant the blank check given to the National Security Agency to violate the privacy Americans enjoy, nor did it justify the enhanced interrogation procedures employed by the CIA. And it certainly did not justify the rendition of suspected terrorists to countries known to practice torture or the holding of others at black sites overseas without access to legal safeguards.

Bush's religious certitude and his singular determination became serious problems. In 2001 he scuttled the Clinton administration's efforts to bring a nonnuclear North Korea back into the family of nations, and two years later led the United States into an unwarranted war with Iraq. Saddam Hussein may have been a ruthless dictator, but he kept the lid on violent extremists and was no threat to the United States. Iraq was not implicated in the events of 9/11, and al Qaeda had no presence in the country. There was also no ISIS under Saddam and there were no weapons of mass destruction. By attacking Iraq and overthrowing Saddam Hussein the United States upset the delicate equilibrium between Shiites and Sunnis that existed in the Middle East. The casualties and the cost—estimated in excess of $3 trillion—have been disastrous. But even worse is the continued instability of the region. Bush wanted to bring democracy to Iraq. That was naïve given the deep sectarian, ethnic, and tribal fissures that existed. What he achieved was to create the conditions for the continuing insurrection that is led today by ISIS fundamentalists. Whether George W. Bush was the worst president in American history will be long debated, but his decision to invade Iraq is easily the worst foreign policy decision ever made by an American president.

Acknowledgments

This book is dedicated to Professors John E. Seaman and Sanford A. Lakoff. John, a 1954 classmate of mine at Princeton, read the manuscript of every chapter of every book I have written, beginning with *The Defense of Berlin* in 1963. A professor of English for many years at the University of the Pacific, John passed away in December 2013. His editorial commentary was invaluable. Sandy was a colleague of mine at the University of Toronto in the 1960s, and has read every chapter of every biography I have written, beginning with *Lucius D. Clay*. Currently the Edward A. Dickson professor emeritus of political science at the University of California, San Diego, Sandy's erudition and vast knowledge of the historical and political literature has saved me from numerous errors. By dedicating this book to them, I hope to acknowledge my gratitude for their friendship and support.

Once again, my primary indebtedness is to Rhonda Mullins of Marshall University. Rhonda has typed the manuscript for my last three biographies—*FDR, Eisenhower,* and *Bush.* That is not easy. I write in longhand on yellow legal pads. Over the years the legibility has decreased. Rhonda nevertheless reads what I have written, types it, and gives me clean copy every morning. She has typed dozens of drafts of each book, and does so faultlessly and without complaint. It has been a privilege for me to work with her. I am also deeply indebted to Kristen Pack of Marshall University. Kristen served as illustrations editor, prepared the bibliography, and did an indefatigable job as my research assistant. She too deserves credit and recognition.

Once again my editor is Bob Bender at Simon & Schuster. Bob was my editor for *Grant*, and we are back together. Bob reads the manuscript carefully, and his suggestions are invaluable. He is also a wonderful person. I would also like to thank Lisa Healy, the senior production editor at Simon & Schuster; art director Allison Forner, who arranged the cover; Elisa Rivlin of the legal department, who read the manuscript for possible problems; senior publicity manager Maureen Cole; marketing manager Ebony LaDelle; associate editor Johanna Li, who is Bob Bender's assistant; and especially copy editor Fred Chase. Mr. Chase is the finest copy editor in the business and I am grateful to him.

I am also deeply indebted to the "Gang of Thirteen"—old friends, former classmates, and colleagues—who have read the manuscript and offered suggestions. Each reader brings a different perspective, and their suggestions have been invaluable. To the "Gang of Thirteen": Richard Arndt, Paul Ehrlich, Ellen Feldman, Beth Fischer, Henry Graff, Peter Krogh, Sandy Lakoff, Peter Matson, Harry Moul, George Packard, John Seaman, and Kelly and David Vaziri.

My agent is Peter Matson of Sterling Lord Literistic. Peter is a master at navigating the shoals of publishing, and I am very grateful to him. I began my writing career with Sterling Lord in 1962. It's nice to be back.

Finally, I would like to express my appreciation to the History Department at Columbia University and the Institute for the Study of Diplomacy at Georgetown University. I spent 2011 and 2012 at Columbia as a senior scholar, and 2013 and 2014 at Georgetown as a visiting scholar. An academic institution is a wonderful place at which to write and I am deeply grateful.

Notes

Abbreviation Used in the Notes

PPPUS-GWB   *Public Papers of the Presidents of the United States: George W. Bush,*
2001–2008 (Washington, D.C.: Government Printing Office,
2003–2012).

Preface

1 U.S. Census Bureau, *Statistical Abstract of the United States: 2011*, Tables 467, 474, 501, 514, 584, 729. The federal budget had not been in balance since the last year of the administration of Dwight Eisenhower. Under Bill Clinton, budget deficits were systematically reduced, and in 1998 the federal budget showed a surplus ($69.3 billion) for the first time since 1960. The surpluses for 1999, 2000, and 2001 were $125 billion, $236 billion, and $128 billion respectively.

2 The United States' national debt doubled from 2001 to 2009, going from $5.7 trillion to $11.8 trillion, and from 56 percent of GDP to 83.4 percent. Federal personal income tax receipts dropped from $1.005 trillion in 2001 to $915.3 billion in 2009, while corporate income taxes dropped from $207.3 billion to $138.2 billion. During the same period, the mortgage foreclosure rate went from 1.2 percent on an annual basis to 4.6 percent, while the delinquency rate on subprime mortgages climbed to 25.5 percent. New home construction sagged from 1.6 million units in 2001 to 554,000 in 2009. At the beginning of 2001, the Standard & Poor's 500 Composite Index stood at 1,320. By 2009 it was down to 903—a decline of 31.6 percent. The Dow Jones Industrial Average dropped from 10,787 to 8,776, or 18.6 percent, during the same period. The U.S. dollar fell to .71 euro and 90 yen, declines of 33 and 23 percent respectively. *Statistical Abstract of the United States: 2011*, Tables 468, 473, 584, 729, 964, 1163, 1206.

3 Robert Draper, *Dead Certain: The Presidency of George W. Bush* (New York: Free Press, 2007), 419 (Bush's emphasis).

4 I am indebted to Professor Beth A. Fischer of the University of Toronto for the thought behind this paragraph.

5 See Joseph E. Stiglitz and Linda J. Bilmes, *The Three Trillion Dollar War: The True Cost of the Iraq Conflict* (New York: W. W. Norton, 2008).

6 Bush's remark was made on *Meet the Press with Tim Russert*, NBC, February 8, 2004, msnbc.com, transcript.

7 I am indebted to Zbigniew Brzezinski for this observation. See Brzezinski, *Second Chance: Three Presidents and the Crisis of American Superpower* (New York: Basic Books, 2006), 193.

8 The basic planning document of the Department of Defense is a classified study entitled *Defense Planning Guidance* that is rewritten every two years and serves as the basis for coming defense budgets. It was drafted in 1991 by Wolfowitz and Libby, and was adopted by Defense Secretary Cheney in 1992, who, in the words of one Defense Department official, "took ownership of it." It was declassified by Cheney just before leaving office in January 1993, and entitled "Defense Strategy for the 1990s: The Regional Defense Strategy." The quotation is from Zalmay Khalilzad, cited in James Mann, *Rise of the Vulcans: The History of Bush's War Cabinet* (New York: Viking, 2004), 213.

9 United States military spending in fiscal year 2009, the last year for which the Bush administration was responsible, totaled $711 billion. According to figures compiled by the International Institute of Strategic Studies, that exceeded the defense spending of the next forty-five countries combined. The United States spent 5.8 times more than China, 10.2 times more than Russia, and 98.6 times more than Iran. *The Military Balance 2011*, 471–77.

10 The statement is that of Fred Glimp, the legendary Harvard dean of admissions, quoted in Elizabeth Mitchell, *W: Revenge of the Bush Dynasty* (New York: Hyperion, 2000), 200.

11 Ibid.

12 Kevin Phillips, *American Dynasty: Aristocracy, Fortune, and the Politics of Deceit in the House of Bush* (New York: Penguin, 2004), 137.

13 Letter, George Herbert Walker Bush to Jean Edward Smith, December 1, 1997.

Chapter One: The Wilderness Years

The epigraph is from the original draft of George W. Bush's commencement address at Yale, marking the graduation of his daughter Barbara. It was deleted before delivery. Kitty Kelley, *The Family: The Real Story of the Bush Dynasty* (New York: Doubleday, 2004), 271.

1 Barbara Bush to the *Smith Alumnae Quarterly*, quoted in Kitty Kelley, *The Family: The Real Story of the Bush Dynasty* (New York: Doubleday, 2004), 93.

2 The final returns showed Benton with 431,413 to Prescott Bush's 430,311. Congressional Quarterly, *Guide to U.S. Elections* (Washington, D.C.: Congressional Quarterly, 1975), 488.

3 *Time*, April 4, 1952.

4 Prescott Bush had a remarkable singing voice, was president of the Yale Glee Club as an undergraduate, and a member of the All-Time Wiffenpoof Quartet in which he sang second bass. Bill Minutaglio, *First Son: George W. Bush and the Bush Family Dynasty* (New York: Times Books, 1999), 20.

5 *Hartford Courant*, October 5, 1952.

6 In 1952, Bush received 559,465 votes to Ribicoff's 530,505. Congressional Quarterly, *Guide to U.S. Elections*, 488.

7 Kitty Kelley interview with Warren, January 8, 2003, quoted in Kelley, *The Family*, 64.

8 Herbert S. Parmet, *George Bush: The Life of a Lone Star Yankee* (New York: Scribner, 1997), 45.

9 Joe Hyams, *Flight of the Avenger* (New York: Berkley, 1992), 44.

10 George Bush, with Victor Gold, *Looking Forward* (New York: Doubleday, 1987), 31.

11 *Yale Daily News*, September 22, 1947.

12 FDR's remark was made to his cousin W. Sheffield Cowles while returning from Europe on the *George Washington* with President Woodrow Wilson in 1919. Letter, Cowles to Nathan Miller, March 18, 1980, in Miller, *FDR: An Intimate History* (New York: Doubleday, 1983), 35, 513.

13 "Modest" is a relative term. The three-story Bush house on Grove Lane in Greenwich had eight bedrooms and a full assortment of maids, cooks, and chauffeurs. Minutaglio, *First Son*, 21.

14 Kelley, *The Family*, 46–47.

15 Ibid., 44.

16 Ibid., 292–93.

17 Ibid., 68.

18 Ibid., 69.

19 "I was Neil Mallon's chief adviser and consultant in connection with every move that he made," Prescott Bush said in his oral history at Columbia University. Columbia Oral History Project (COHP).

20 Richard Ben Cramer, "How Bush Made It," *Esquire*, June 1991. (Barbara's emphasis.)

21 Harry Hunt III, "George Bush, Plucky Lad," *Texas Monthly*, June 1983.

22 Minutaglio, *First Son*, 26. H. G. Bissinger's marvelous *Friday Night Lights* (Reading, Mass.: Addison-Wesley, 1990) is set in Odessa, Texas.

23 George H. W. Bush, *Looking Forward*, 58; Minutaglio, *First Son*, 39.

24 Parmet, *George Bush*, 81.

25 Minutaglio, *First Son*, 35.

26 George W. Bush, *Decision Points* (New York: Crown, 2010), 6.

27 Donnie Radcliffe, *Simply Barbara Bush: A Portrait of America's Candid First Lady* (New York: Warner, 1989), 128.

28 Bill Minutaglio interview with Charles Sanders, August 1998, in Minutaglio, *First Son*, 56.

29 Bill Minutaglio interview with John Ellis, February 10, 1999, in ibid., 58.

30 G. W. Bush, *Decision Points*, 11.

31 Kitty Kelley interview with Torbert Macdonald, July 18, 2003, in Kelley, *The Family*, 256.

32 Bill Minutaglio interview with Bill Semple, October 1998, in Minutaglio, *First Son*, 62.

33 Kitty Kelley interview with Conway Downing, February 15, 2002, in Kelley, *The Family*, 257.

34 Kelley, *The Family*, 257.

35 Ibid., 260.

36 G. W. Bush, *Decision Points*, 15.

37 Peter Schweizer and Rochelle Schweizer, *The Bushes: Portrait of a Dynasty* (New York: Doubleday, 2004), 166.

38 Ibid., 166–67.

39 In 1964, the year that George W. Bush entered Yale, four hundred students turned out for an introductory socializer at DKE (which had been founded at Yale in 1844). The following year, only two hundred attended. Within a year of Bush's graduation, the 1969 Class Book was referring to fraternities as a "benign irrelevancy." By the early 1970s, all of the organizations on Fraternity Row had failed financially and were forced to turn over their houses to the university. Carter Wiseman, "In the Days of DKE and S.D.S.," *Yale Alumni Magazine*, February 2001.

40 Walter Isaacson, "My Heritage Is Part of Who I Am," *Time*, August 7, 2000.

41 Jacob Weisberg, *The Bush Tragedy* (New York: Random House, 2008), 41.

42 Bill Minutaglio interview with Bob Wei, September 1998, in Minutaglio, *First Son*, 110.

43 *Public Papers of the Presidents, Lyndon B. Johnson, 1968*, President's Address to the Nation Announcing Steps to Limit the War in Vietnam and Reporting His Decision Not to Seek Reelection, March 31, 1968 (Washington, D.C.: Government Printing Office, 1971), 469–76.

44 Kitty Kelley interview with Mark I. Soler, July 2003, in Kelley, *The Family*, 295.

45 Bill Minutaglio interview with Doug Hannah, September 3, 1998, in Minutaglio, *First Son*, 115–16.

46 Ibid., 116.

47 George W. Bush, *A Charge to Keep: My Journey to the White House* (New York: William Morrow, 1999), 50. (Emphasis added.)

48 George W. Bush, *Decision Points*, 16. Also see Molly Ivins and Lou Dubose, *Shrub: The Short but Happy Political Life of George W. Bush* (New York: Vintage, 2000), 4. Compare, George W. Bush, *A Charge to Keep*, 51.

49 *Houston Post*, November 7, 1993.

50 Russ Baker, *Family of Secrets: The Bush Dynasty, America's Invisible Government, and the Hidden History of the Last Fifty Years* (New York: Bloomsbury Press, 2009), 139.

51 Elizabeth Mitchell, *W: Revenge of the Bush Dynasty* (New York: Hyperion, 2000), 121.

52 Bill Minutaglio interview with Norman Dotti, December 1998, in Minutaglio, *First Son*, 126.

53 *Los Angeles Times*, July 4, 1999.

54 Kelley, *The Family*, 299.

55 Ibid.

56 George W. Bush, "I Was Young and Irresponsible," *Dallas Morning News*, November 15, 1998.

57 Press Release, Office of Information, 147 Combat Crew Training Group, Texas Air National Guard, March 24, 1970, reproduced in Glenn W. Smith, *Unfit Commander* (New York: Regan Books, 2004), 314–15.

58 111th Fighter Interceptor Squadron, Promotion of Officer, November 3, 1970, reproduced in ibid., 212.

59 Bill Minutaglio interview with Doug Hannah, September 3, 1998, quoted in Minutaglio, *First Son*, 232.

60 The comment is that of Jim Bath, in Kenneth T. Walsh, "From Boys to Men," *U.S. News & World Report*, May 3, 2004.

61 Inge Honneus, quoted in Baker, *Family of Secrets*, 144.

62 Monica Crowley, *Nixon Off the Record: His Candid Commentary on People and Politics* (New York: Random House, 1996), 46.

63 *Washington Evening Star*, February 20, 1972.

64 The comment is that of Dean Page Keeton, quoted in Kelley, *The Family*, 300.

65 Kelley, *The Family*, 300.

66 Schweizer and Schweizer, *The Bushes*, 193.

67 I have intentionally omitted the names of the young woman and the doctor involved. The incident is treated extensively by Russ Baker in *Family of Secrets* at pages 145–47.

68 President George H. W. Bush later rewarded Ensenat by appointing him ambassador to Brunei. President George W. Bush appointed him chief of protocol in the Department of State.

69 Kelley, *The Family*, 301.

70 Baker, *Family of Secrets*, 147–48.

71 Kelley, *The Family*, 301; Baker, *Family of Secrets*, 151.

72 Baker, *Family of Secrets*, 149.

73 Kelley, *The Family*, 304.

74 *Boston Globe*, October 31, 2000. General (ret.) Turnipseed also said he was a Republican and supported Bush for president.

75 Bush's efficiency report is reproduced in Smith, *Unfit Commander*, 270–71.

76 The incident is widely reported by Bush biographers. See Kelley, *The Family*, 306.

77 Ibid., 306–7.

78 Ibid., 308.

79 G. W. Bush, *A Charge to Keep*, 58.

80 Kelley, *The Family*, 307–8.

81 Kevin Phillips, *American Dynasty: Aristocracy, Fortune, and the Politics of Deceit in the House of Bush* (New York: Penguin, 2004), 45. Also see J. H. Hatfield, *Fortunate Son: George W. Bush and the Making of an American President* (New York: Soft Skull Press, 2000), 313–18.

82 Meg Laughlin, "Former Workers Dispute Bush's Pull in Project P.U.L.L.," Knight Ridder, October 23, 2004.

83 Ibid. In 1974, George H. W. Bush arranged for PULL to receive federal funding under the Law Enforcement Alliance of America legislation. See John Calhoun, staff assistant to the president to George H. W. Bush, August 16, 1974, Gerald R. Ford Presidential Library.

84 G. W. Bush, *A Charge to Keep*, 59.

85 Kelley, *The Family*, 308–9.

86 Mica Schneider and Douglas Harbrecht, "George W.'s Business School Days," *Bloomberg Businessweek*, February 15, 2001.

87 Kelley, *The Family*, 310.

88 Russ Baker, interview with Bill White, November 14, 2006, in Baker, *Family of Secrets*, 323. After graduation, Bush never activated his Harvard School alumnus email account and did not attend class reunions. Schneider and Harbrecht, "George W's Business School Days," *Bloomberg Businessweek*, February 15, 2001.

89 Don Balz and Paul Duggan, "Bush Alters Answer on Drug Questions," *Washington Post*, August 19, 1999.

Chapter Two: Turnaround

The epigraph is George W. Bush's warning to Lee Atwater. Bush is paraphrasing Sonny Corleone in *The Godfather*. Elizabeth Mitchell, *W: Revenge of the Bush Dynasty* (New York: Hyperion, 2000), 213.

1 George W. Bush, *Decision Points* (New York: Crown, 2010), 23.

2 George W. Bush, *A Charge to Keep* (New York: William Morrow, 1999), 56.

3 Bill Minutaglio interview with Robert McCleskey, October 1998, in Minutaglio, *First Son* (New York: Times Books, 1999), 170.

4   G. W. Bush, *Decision Points*, 25.

5   *Washington Post*, July 30, 1999, citing records on file at the Securities and Exchange Commission.

6   Lois Romano and George Lardner, Jr., "Young Bush, a Political Natural, Revs Up," *Washington Post*, July 29, 1999.

7   Skip Hollandsworth, "Born to Run: What's in a Name?," *Texas Monthly*, May 1994. In his post-presidential memoirs, Bush backed away from "European-style socialism" and speaks of "welfare-state Europe." *Decision Points*, 38.

8   G. W. Bush, *Decision Points*, 38.

9   *Washington Post*, July 30, 1999.

10 Elizabeth Mitchell, *W: Revenge of the Bush Dynasty* (New York: Hyperion, 2000), 162.

11 Laura Bush, *Spoken from the Heart* (New York: Scribner, 2010), 94.

12 G. W. Bush, *Decision Points*, 26.

13 Laura Bush, *Spoken from the Heart*, 95.

14 Ibid., 64–65.

15 See Minutaglio, *First Son*, 183.

16 G. W. Bush, *Decision Points*, 27.

17 Peter Schweizer and Rochelle Schweizer, *The Bushes: Portrait of a Dynasty* (New York: Doubleday, 2004), 260.

18 *New York Times*, July 31, 2000.

19 The quotations are from G. W. Bush's *Decision Points*, 26, and *A Charge to Keep*, 81.

20 Laura Bush, *Spoken from the Heart*, 99.

21 G. W. Bush, *Decision Points,* 39. The line was originally used by Poppy when he ran against Ralph Yarborough for the Senate in 1964.

22 Ibid., 40.

23 Schweizer and Schweizer, *The Bushes*, 259.

24 Minutaglio, *First Son*, 190; Laura Bush, *Spoken from the Heart*, 101.

25 *Washington Post*, July 29, 1999.

26 G. W. Bush, *Decision Points*, 41.

27 *Washington Post*, July 30, 1999.

28 Minutaglio, *First Son*, 199.

29 G. W. Bush, *A Charge to Keep*, 84.

30 Ibid.

31 Laura Bush, *Spoken from the Heart*, 105.

32 G. W. Bush, *Decision Points*, 28.

33 G. W. Bush, *A Charge to Keep*, 85.

34 Laura Bush, *Spoken from the Heart*, 107.

35 "Bush Has Fared Well Despite Firm's Troubles," *Dallas Morning News*, May 7, 1994.

36 *Washington Post*, July 30, 1999.

37 G. W. Bush, *Decision Points*, 30.

38 *Washington Post*, July 30, 1999.

39 Ibid.

40 J. H. Hatfield, *Fortunate Son: George W. Bush and the Making of an American President* (New York: Soft Skull Press, 2000), 70.

41 G. W. Bush, *Decision Points*, 81.

42 G. W. Bush, *A Charge to Keep*, 136.

43 G. W. Bush, *Decision Points*, 81.

44 Ibid., 32–33.

45 Quoted in Kelley, *The Family*, 427.

46 *Washington Post*, July 30, 1999.

47 Molly Ivins and Lou Dubose, *Shrub: The Short but Happy Political Life of George W. Bush* (New York: Vintage, 2000), 27.

48 *Washington Post*, July 30, 1999.

49 Kelley, *The Family*, 202.

50 Laura Bush, *Spoken from the Heart*, 118.

51 G. W. Bush, *Decision Points*, 34.

52 Laura Bush, *Spoken from the Heart*, 118.

53 Ibid., 118–19.

54 Bill Minutaglio interview with Joseph O'Neill, July 1998, in Minutaglio, *First Son*, 210.

55 Laura Bush, *Spoken from the Heart*, 118.

56 G. W. Bush, *Decision Points*, 34.

57 Kelley, *The Family*, 428.

58 Ivins and Dubose, *Shrub*, 31–37.

59 G. W. Bush, *A Charge to Keep*, 64.

60 Kelley, *The Family*, 432.

61 Mitchell, *W: Revenge of the Bush Dynasty*, 213.

62 Minutaglio, *First Son*, 206.

63 John Brady, *Bad Boy: The Life and Politics of Lee Atwater* (New York: Addison-Wesley, 1997), 138–39.

64 *Washington Post*, July 31, 1999.

65 Hatfield, *Fortunate Son*, 765; Kelley, *The Family*, 446.

66 Jon Meacham, *Destiny and Power: The American Odyssey of George Herbert Walker Bush* (New York: Random House, 2015), 705.

67 *Newsweek*, June 29, 1987.

68 Schweizer and Schweizer, *The Bushes*, 341.

69 Laura Bush, *Spoken from the Heart*, 121–22.

70 *Proceedings of the 1988 Republican National Convention*.

71 *Houston Chronicle*, August 16, 1988.

72 G. W. Bush, *Decision Points*, 44–45.

73 The comment is that of Pug Ravenel, quoted in Brady, *Bad Boy*, 177.

74 G. W. Bush, *A Charge to Keep*, 198.

75 G. W. Bush, *Decision Points*, 45.

76 Mitchell, *W: Revenge of the Bush Dynasty*, 217.

Chapter Three: "Don't Mess with Texas"

The epigraph is one of George W. Bush's "fixed stars" designed to guide young people through life. *A Charge to Keep* (New York: William Morrow, 1999), 207.

1 Lois Romano and George Lardner, Jr., "Bush's Move Up the Majors," *Washington Post*, July 31, 1999.

2 Ibid.

3 Bill Minutaglio interview with Kent Hance, October 8, 1998, in Minutaglio, *First Son* (New York: Times Books, 1999), 243.

4 J. H. Hatfield, *Fortunate Son: George W. Bush and the Making of an American President* (New York: Soft Skull Press, 2000), 93.

5 *Washington Post*, July 31, 1999.

6 *Dallas Morning News*, April 28, 1989.

7 Nicholas Kristof, "Road to Politics Ran Through a Texas Ballpark," *New York Times*, September 24, 2000.

8 *Dallas Times-Herald*, July 20, 1986.

9 Kevin Sack, "George Bush the Son Finds That Oil and Blood Do Mix," *New York Times*, May 8, 1999.

10 G. W. Bush, *A Charge to Keep* (New York: William Morrow, 1999), 199.

11 Russ Baker, *Family of Secrets: The Bush Dynasty, America's Invisible Government, and the Hidden History of the Last Fifty Years* (New York: Bloomsbury, 2009), 360–63.

12 Elizabeth Mitchell, *W: Revenge of the Bush Dynasty* (New York: Hyperion, 2000), 247.

13 Ibid.

14 *New York Times*, September 24, 2000.

15 *Dallas Morning News*, May 7, 1989.

16 *New York Times*, May 8, 1999. In his post-presidential memoirs, Bush acknowledges Ueberroth's assistance. "I am particularly grateful," the former president wrote, "to Commissioner Peter Ueberroth, American League President Bobby Brown, and Jerry Reinsdorf of the Chicago White Sox for their help in navigating the buying process." George W. Bush, *Decision Points* (New York: Crown, 2010), 46n.

17 G. W. Bush, *A Charge to Keep*, 201.

18 Minutaglio, *First Son*, 244.

19 *Dallas Morning News*, August 2, 1989.

20 George Lardner, Jr., and Lois Romano, "Bush Name Helps Fuel Oil Dealings," *Washington Post*, July 30, 1999.

21 Molly Ivins and Lou Dubose, *Shrub: The Short but Happy Political Life of*

George W. Bush (New York: Vintage, 2000), 32–33; Baker, *Family of Secrets*, 354–56; Hatfield, *Fortunate Son*, 102–5; Kitty Kelley, *The Family: The Real Story of the Bush Dynasty* (New York: Random House, 2004), 552–54; Minutaglio, *First Son*, 251–52; Mitchell, *W: Revenge of the Bush Dynasty*, 264–66.

22 *Washington Post*, July 30, 1999.

23 Ibid.

24 *New York Times*, November 24, 2000.

25 Ibid.

26 G. W. Bush, *A Charge to Keep*, 206–7.

27 Ibid., 206.

28 *Washington Post*, July 30, 1999.

29 Hatfield, *Fortunate Son*, 114.

30 G. W. Bush, *A Charge to Keep*, 204.

31 Ibid.

32 Ibid., 205–8.

33 Peter Goldman, Thomas M. DeFrank, Mark Miller, Andrew Murr, and Tom Mathews, *Quest for the Presidency, 1992* (College Station: Texas A&M University Press, 1994), 303–7.

34 Hatfield, *Fortunate Son*, 106.

35 Mitchell, *W: Revenge of the Bush Dynasty*, 271.

36 Hatfield, *Fortunate Son*, 107.

37 Ibid.

38 Ibid., 108.

39 Mitchell, *W: Revenge of the Bush Dynasty*, 274.

40 Hatfield, *Fortunate Son*, 108.

41 Kelley, *The Family*, 521.

42 Ibid., 529.

43 Ibid., 530.

44 Mitchell, *W: Revenge of the Bush Dynasty*, 290.

45 G. W. Bush, *Decision Points*, 50.

46 Laura Bush, *Spoken from the Heart* (New York: Scribner, 2010), 129.

47 I am indebted to Kitty Kelley for the snapshot comparison of George W. and Jeb. *The Family*, 540–41.

48 Keynote Address, 1988 Democratic National Convention. In her speech, Richards noted that Ginger Rogers did everything Fred Astaire did. "She just did it backwards and in high heels."

49 Mitchell, *W: Revenge of the Bush Dynasty*, 306–7. The same story, told by Indiana basketball coach Bobby Knight to NBC's Connie Chung on nationwide TV, helped seal Knight's fate at IU.

50 Hatfield, *Fortunate Son*, 121.

51 Quoted in Kelley, *The Family*, 542.

52 *Washington Post*, July 31, 1999.

53 Hatfield, *Fortunate Son*, 140.

54 G. W. Bush, *A Charge to Keep*, 90.

55 Ivins and Dubose, *Shrub*, 43.

56 Minutaglio, *First Son*, 274.

57 Hatfield, *Fortunate Son*, 122.

58 Minutaglio, *First Son*, 274.

59 Don Balz, "Team Bush: The Iron Triangle," *Washington Post*, July 23, 1999.

60 *Dallas Observer*, May 13, 1999.

61 G. W. Bush, *Decision Points*, 51–52.

62 *Washington Post*, July 23, 1999.

63 Ibid.; G. W. Bush, *Decision Points*, 54.

64 *Washington Post*, July 23, 1999.

65 Ibid., July 31, 1999.

66 Hatfield, *Fortunate Son*, 123–24.

67 *Washington Post*, July 31, 1999; Mitchell, *W: Revenge of the Bush Dynasty*, 296.

68 Kelley, *The Family*, 549.

69 G. W. Bush, *A Charge to Keep*, 31.

70 Ibid., 36–37.

71 Hatfield, *Fortunate Son*, 127.

72 Ibid., 129.

73 *Washington Post*, July 31, 1999.

74 Hatfield, *Fortunate Son*, 130.

75 Mitchell, *W: Revenge of the Bush Dynasty*, 307–8.

76 *Houston Chronicle*, May 3, 1994.

77 *Texarkana Gazette*, May 4, 1994.

78 G. W. Bush, *Decision Points*, 54.

79 Ibid.

80 Ivins and Dubose, *Shrub*, 49.

81 Minutaglio, *First Son*, 286.

82 *Washington Post*, July 31, 1999.

83 *New York Times*, November 9, 1994.

84 Kelley, *The Family*, 541.

85 Peter Schweizer and Rochelle Schweizer, *The Bushes: Portrait of a Dynasty* (New York: Doubleday, 2004), 429.

86 Ibid., 426.

87 Kelley, *The Family*, 555.

Chapter Four: Governor

The epigraph is from the Methodist hymn "A Charge to Keep," written by Charles Wesley in 1762.

1 Bill Minutaglio, *First Son: George W. Bush and the Bush Family Dynasty* (New York: Times Books, 1999), 297.

2 I am indebted to Jacob Weisberg for this observation. *The Bush Tragedy* (New York: Random House, 2008), 127–28.
3 Inaugural Address of Governor George W. Bush, Austin, Texas, January 18, 1995.
4 *Dallas Morning News*, September 24, 1995.
5 David Aikman, *Man of Faith: The Spiritual Journey of George W. Bush* (Nashville: W Publishing Group, 2004), 108.
6 G. W. Bush, *A Charge to Keep* (New York: William Morrow, 1999), 45.
7 Ben Ames Williams, "A Charge to Keep," *The Country Gentleman*, January 26, February 2, February 9, February 16, 1918. The painting appears in the February 16 issue at page 19.
8 Weisberg, *The Bush Tragedy*, 115, 125.
9 Paul Burka, "The W. Nobody Knows," *Texas Monthly*, June 1999.
10 Elizabeth Mitchell, *W: Revenge of the Bush Dynasty* (New York: Hyperion, 2000), 325.
11 Burka, "The W. Nobody Knows."
12 Minutaglio, *First Son*, 295.
13 Molly Ivins and Lou Dubose, *Shrub: The Short but Happy Political Life of George W. Bush*, 85.
14 G. W. Bush, *Decision Points*, 57.
15 Bill Minutaglio interview with Bob Bullock, February 15, 1999, in Minutaglio, *First Son*, 298.
16 Bill Minutaglio interview with Pete Laney, February 12, 1999, in ibid., 299.
17 G. W. Bush, *A Charge to Keep*, 112.
18 Ibid., 113.
19 G. W. Bush, *Decision Points*, 57.
20 G. W. Bush, *A Charge to Keep*, 115.
21 Mitchell, *W: Revenge of the Bush Dynasty*, 318.
22 G. W. Bush, *A Charge to Keep*, 121.
23 *Houston Chronicle*, April 27, 1995.
24 James Moore and Wayne Slater, *Bush's Brain: How Karl Rove Made George W. Bush Presidential* (Hoboken, N.J.: John Wiley & Sons, 2003), 232.
25 Laura Bush, *Spoken from the Heart* (New York: Scribner, 2010), 146.
26 G. W. Bush, *Decision Points*, 59.
27 G. W. Bush, *A Charge to Keep*, 129–30.
28 J. H. Hatfield, *Fortunate Son: George W. Bush and the Making of an American President* (New York: Soft Skull Press, 2000), 241.
29 *Austin American-Statesman*, November 21, 1997.
30 Hatfield, *Fortunate Son*, 241.
31 Ibid., 242.
32 Ibid.
33 Ibid., 187.
34 Ibid., 245.

35 *New York Times*, August 20, 1995.
36 R. G. Ratcliffe, "Courtship of Hispanic Voters Paid Off for Bush," *Houston Chronicle*, February 28, 1999.
37 G. W. Bush, *A Charge to Keep*, 224.
38 Minutaglio, *First Son*, 317.
39 Kelley, *The Family*, 567.
40 Laura Bush, *Spoken from the Heart*, 155.
41 Lawrence McQuillan and Judy Keen, "Texas White House a Refuge from Stress," *USA Today*, April 13, 2001.
42 Hatfield, *Fortunate Son*, 257.
43 G. W. Bush, *Decision Points*, 62.
44 Peter Schweizer and Rochelle Schweizer, *The Bushes: Portrait of a Dynasty* (New York: Doubleday, 2004), 458.
45 G. W. Bush, *Decision Points*, 61.
46 Ibid.
47 Stephen Mansfield, *The Faith of George W. Bush* (New York: Penguin, 2004), 108.
48 CBS News interview, August 11, 1996.

Chapter Five: The 2000 Election

The epigraph is a comment by Jay Leno on the *Tonight Show* the evening after the first Bush-Gore debate. Ronald Elving, "Bush Gets Pleasant October Surprise," *Congressional Quarterly*, October 25, 2000.
 1 Bob Woodward, *State of Denial: Bush at War, Part III* (New York: Simon & Schuster, 2006), 3. The dialogue evidently is based on a series of interviews Woodward conducted with Prince Bandar.
 2 Ibid., 5.
 3 James Mann interview with Martin Anderson, February 12, 2002, quoted in Mann, *Rise of the Vulcans: The History of Bush's War Cabinet* (New York: Viking, 2004), 249.
 4 Ibid.
 5 Condoleezza Rice, *No Higher Honor* (New York: Crown, 2011), 1.
 6 Woodward, *State of Denial*, 6.
 7 Mann, *Rise of the Vulcans*, 250.
 8 Rice, *No Higher Honor*, 2.
 9 *Austin American-Statesman*, March 3, 1999.
10 Dana Milbank, "What 'W' Stands For," *The New Republic*, April 26 and May 3, 1999.
11 Karl Rove, *Courage and Consequence* (New York: Threshold, 2010), 125.
12 Ibid., 127.
13 Milbank, "What 'W' Stands For," 68.
14 Ibid.
15 Ibid., 70.

16 Karen Hughes, *Ten Minutes from Normal* (New York: Viking, 2004), 96.

17 Rove, *Courage and Consequence*, 134.

18 Ibid., 134–35.

19 Ibid., 140.

20 George W. Bush, *Decision Points* (New York: Crown, 2010), 21.

21 Hughes, *Ten Minutes from Normal*, 128.

22 Ibid., 129.

23 G. W. Bush, *Decision Points*, 73.

24 Robert Draper, *Dead Certain: The Presidency of George W. Bush* (New York: Free Press, 2007), 64.

25 Rove, *Courage and Consequence*, 154.

26 Ibid., 156.

27 G. W. Bush, *Decision Points*, 67.

28 Dick Cheney, *In My Time* (New York: Threshold, 2011), 255.

29 Ibid., 258.

30 G. W. Bush, *Decision Points*, 68.

31 Cheney, *In My Time*, 259; G. W. Bush, *Decision Points*, 69.

32 Bush, *Decision Points*, 69.

33 Eric Schmitt, "The 2000 Campaign: The Running Mate," *New York Times*, July 26, 2000.

34 Draper, *Dead Certain*, 90.

35 Bill Turque interview with Joe Siscoe, in Turque, *Inventing Al Gore: A Biography* (New York: Houghton Mifflin, 2000), 40.

36 During his freshman and sophomore years at Harvard, Gore finished in the bottom 20 percent of his class. Patrick Healy, "Matters of Honor," *Boston Globe*, October 8, 2001.

37 According to Gore's roommate John Tyson, "I wouldn't say it was necessarily pressure [from Gore's parents] but they certainly wanted him to know that his father was running for reelection. That's all they had to say." Bill Turque interview with John Tyson, in Turque, *Inventing Al Gore*, 63.

38 Gail Sheehy, "Gore: The Son Also Rises," *Vanity Fair*, March 1988, 194.

39 Bill Turque interview with John Warnecke, in Turque, *Inventing Al Gore*, 101. According to Warnecke, Gore was "paranoid about getting busted. He'd go around the room and close all the curtains and turn the lights out so no one could see."

40 Bill Turque interview with Speaker Stan Rogers, quoted in *Inventing Al Gore*, 128.

41 Bob Zelnic, *Gore: A Political Life* (Washington, D.C.: Regnery, 1999), 165.

42 Ibid., 156.

43 Ibid., 148.

44 Louis Menand, "After Elvis," *The New Yorker*, October 26, 1998.

45 Gerald M. Pomper, "The Presidential Election," in *The Election of 2000* (New York: Chatham House, 2001), 140–41. As the campaign progressed, Clinton's

approval rating rose even higher. In December, the CNN/*USA Today*/Gallup poll showed a 66 percent job approval rating, the highest of any president in his final month in office. Ronald Reagan was second with 63 percent and Eisenhower third with 59 percent.

46 Robert G. Kaiser, "Academics Say It's Elementary Gore Wins," *Washington Post*, August 31, 2000; Adam Clymer, "And the Winner Is Gore," *New York Times*, September 4, 2000. Also see Kaiser, "Is This Any Way to Pick a Winner?," *Washington Post*, May 26, 2000.

47 Dana Milbank, *Smashmouth: Notes from the 2000 Campaign Trail* (New York: Basic Books, 2001), 310.

48 *New York Times*, August 18, 2000.

49 "Don't worry, Jim," Eisenhower told his press secretary James Hagerty before a press conference dealing with Formosa, "If that question comes up, I'll just confuse them." For the text of Ike's successful effort to obfuscate the question of a nuclear response to an attack on Quemoy and Matsu, see Jean Edward Smith, *Eisenhower in War and Peace* (New York: Random House, 2012), 659–70.

50 Jacob Weisberg has written three books compiling George W. Bush's grammatical errors. See *George W. Bushisms: The Slate Book of the Accidental Wit and Wisdom of Our 43rd President* (New York: Fireside, 2001); *George W. Bushisms: New Ways to Harm Our Country* (New York: Fireside, 2005); *The Ultimate George W. Bushisms: Bush at War with the English Language* (New York: Fireside, 2007).

51 Milbank, *Smashmouth*, 321.

52 *Boston Globe*, September 18, 2000.

53 Frank Bruni, *Ambling into History: The Unlikely Odyssey of George W. Bush* (New York: HarperCollins, 2002), 187.

54 Frank Newport, "Presidential Race Close as Final Debate Nears," Gallup News Service, October 17, 2000. Newport's article reprints a summary of all Gallup pre-election polls.

55 *New York Times*, October 12, 2000.

56 Hughes, *Ten Minutes from Normal*, 165.

57 Bruni, *Ambling into History*, 128, 130.

58 Maureen Dowd, "Freedom Face-Off," *New York Times*, June 16, 1999. Continuing her *Wizard of Oz* imagery, Dowd suggested that George W. Bush was the Scarecrow: "charming, limber, cocky, fidgety, seeking to stuff his head with a few more weighty thoughts."

59 Bruni, *Ambling into History*, 143.

60 Kitty Kelley, *The Family: The Real Story of the Bush Dynasty* (New York: Doubleday, 2004), 587–88.

61 Turque, *Inventing Al Gore*, 369.

62 *New York Times*, October 28, 2000; *Newsweek*, November 20, 2000.

63 In 1992, 68 percent of the voters had incomes below $50,000, and in 1996,

61 percent did. In 2000, only 47 percent reported incomes less than $50,000, which is a far greater change than the growth in income during those eight years. Pomper, "The Presidential Election," 144, 153.

64 G. W. Bush, *Decision Points*, 76.

65 Rove, *Courage and Consequence*, 190.

66 G. W. Bush, *Decision Points*, 76.

Chapter Six: The Rule of Law

The epigraph is from Bush's speech in the chamber of the Texas House of Representatives following the Supreme Court's decision in *Bush v. Gore. New York Times*, December 14, 2000.

1 G. W. Bush, *Decision Points* (New York: Crown, 2010), 77.

2 The ten counties of the Florida Panhandle voted as follows (in percentage terms):

	Bush	Gore	Nader
Bay	65.7	32.1	1.4
Calhoun	55.5	41.7	.8
Escambia	62.6	35.1	1.5
Gulf	57.8	39.0	1.4
Holmes	67.8	29.4	1.3
Jackson	56.1	42.1	.8
Okaloosa	73.7	24.0	1.4
Santa Rosa	72.1	25.4	1.4
Walton	66.5	30.8	1.4
Washington	62.2	34.9	1.2

Division of Elections of the State of Florida.

3 Karen Hughes, *Ten Minutes from Normal* (New York: Viking, 2004), 173.

4 The dialogue was recorded by Bush, who then gave his notes to Karen Hughes. Ibid., 175.

5 Dick Cheney, *In My Time* (New York: Threshold, 2011), 288–89.

6 Jeffrey Toobin, *Too Close to Call: The Thirty-Six-Day Battle to Decide the 2000 Election* (New York: Random House, 2001), 25.

7 G. W. Bush, *Decision Points*, 78.

8 Cheney, *In My Time*, 289. "If the Gore campaign had been any kind of a professional operation," said Cheney, "they would have realized how close the vote was and wouldn't have conceded in the first place. But to concede and then take it back was amateur hour."

9 G. W. Bush, *Decision Points*, 78.

10 Hughes, *Ten Minutes from Normal*, 176.

11 G. W. Bush, *Decision Points*, 79.

12 In New Hampshire, Bush received 273,558 votes to Gore's 266,348. Nader polled 22,198. In Nevada, it was 301,575 for Bush, 279,978 for Gore. In West

Virginia, 336,475 for Bush, 295,497 for Gore. Richard M. Scammon, Alice V. McGillivay, and Rhodes Clark, *America Votes 24: A Handbook of Contemporary American Election Statistics* (Washington, D.C.: CQ Press, 2001), 9.

13 Henry C. Kenski, Brooks Aylor, and Kate Kenski, "Explaining the Vote in a Divided Country: The Presidential Election of 2000," in Robert E. Denton, Jr., *The 2000 Presidential Campaign* (Westport, Conn.: Praeger, 2002), 255.

14 I am indebted to George Will for this point.

15 Thomas Edsall, "Voter Values Determine Political Affiliation, *Washington Post*, March 26, 2001.

16 G. W. Bush, *Decision Points*, 80.

17 Laura Bush, *Spoken from the Heart* (New York: Scribner, 2010), 163.

18 G. W. Bush, *Decision Points*, 82.

19 Karen DeYoung, *Soldier: The Life of Colin Powell* (New York: Alfred A. Knopf, 2006), 296.

20 The commission, consisting of six Republican and three Democratic appointees, issued a unanimous report to Congress in 1998 critical of the CIA. "The Threat to the United States," *Report of the Commission to Assess the Ballistic Missile Threat to the United States: Executive Summary* (Washington, D.C.: Government Printing Office, July 15, 1998).

21 Commission to Assess United States National Security Space Management and Organization.

22 When Rumsfeld joined Searle in 1977, its stock sold for $12.50 a share. When he sold the company to Monsanto in 1985, it was worth $65 a share. Rumsfeld remained at General Instrument Corporation for three years. He took the company public at $15 a share, and later sold his interest at $40 a share, earning $24 million in the process. See James Mann, *Rise of the Vulcans: The History of Bush's War Cabinet* (New York: Viking, 2004), 231.

23 Condoleezza Rice, *No Higher Honor* (New York: Crown, 2011), 18; Bradley Graham, *By His Own Rules: The Ambitions, Successes, and Ultimate Failures of Donald Rumsfeld* (New York: PublicAffairs, 2009), 201, 204; Karl Rove, *Courage and Consequence* (New York: Threshold, 2010), 220; Donald Rumsfeld, *Known and Unknown* (New York: Sentinel, 2011), 275. "I said he would be a fine director of the CIA," Shultz recalled, "but that they should really want him to be secretary of defense. What you need at Defense are three things: You need somebody who knows how to manage something big; somebody who knows the Congress and somebody who can fight a war, who's tough." Shultz interview with James Mann, February 2, 2002, in Mann, *Rise of the Vulcans*, 269.

24 Robert Draper, *Dead Certain: The Presidency of George W. Bush* (New York: Free Press, 2007), 282. Brent Scowcroft, when consulted, offered a mixed judgment on Rumsfeld. "He's capable and smart," Scowcroft told Cheney, "but he is a difficult person to work with." Scowcroft interview with Bradley Graham, April 6, 2007, in Graham, *By His Own Rules*, 201.

25 Graham interview with Andrew Card, January 11, 2008, in ibid., 202.

26 Rove, *Courage and Consequence*, 220.

27 Rumsfeld, *Known and Unknown*, 279.

28 Ibid., 281.

29 Ibid., 281, 283.

30 G. W. Bush, *Decision Points*, 85.

31 Bradley Graham interview with Dick Cheney, November 20, 2007, in Graham, *By His Own Rules*, 202.

32 Andrew Cockburn, *Rumsfeld: His Rise, Fall, and Catastrophic Legacy* (New York: Scribner, 2007), 97.

33 "Bush Nominates Donald Rumsfeld as Secretary of Defense," CNN, December 28, 2008, transcript.

34 When O'Neill assumed the direction of Alcoa in 1987, the company reported earnings of $1.1 million on sales of $8 billion. In 2000, Alcoa earned $1.5 billion on sales of $23 billion. Ron Suskind, *The Price of Loyalty: George W. Bush, the White House, and the Education of Paul O'Neill* (New York: Simon & Schuster, 2004), 6.

35 Cheney, *In My Time*, 298.

36 C. Vann Woodward, *Reunion and Reaction: The Compromise of 1877 and the End of Reconstruction* (New York: Doubleday, 1936), 23.

37 Elaine Sciolino, *New York Times*, November 10, 2000.

38 Political Staff of the *Washington Post, Deadlock: The Inside Story of America's Closest Election* (New York: PublicAffairs, 2001), 72.

39 *New York Times*, November 11, 2000.

40 Advisory Opinion, Division of Elections, 00–13 "Manual Recount Procedures and Partial Certification of County Returns," November 13, 2000.

41 Florida Attorney General, Advisory Legal Opinion, "Manual Recount of Ballots, Error in Voter Tabulations," November 14, 2000.

42 *Siegel v. LePore*, 120 F. Supp. 2d 1041 (S.D. Fla. 2000).

43 *Palm Beach County Canvassing Board v. Harris*, Supreme Court of Florida, SC00-2346 (November 21, 2000).

44 *Marbury v. Madison*, 1 Cranch 137 (1803).

45 *New York Times*, November 27, 2000.

46 Ibid.

47 *New York Times*, December 2, 2000.

48 Ibid.

49 *Bush v. Palm Beach County Canvassing Board*, 531 U.S. 70, December 4, 2000.

50 *Gore v. Harris*, 772 So. 2d 1243 (2000).

51 101 F. 3d 1565 (11th Cir., 2000).

52 *Bush v. Gore*, 531 U.S. 1046 (2000). The Court's per curiam read as follows:
    The application for a stay presented to Justice Kennedy and by him referred to the Court is granted, and it is ordered that the mandate of

the Florida Supreme Court, case No. SC00-2431, is hereby stayed pending further order of the Court. In addition, the application for stay is treated as a petition for a writ of certiorari, and the petition for a writ of certiorari is granted. The case is set for oral argument on Monday, December 11, 2000 at 11 a.m., and a total of 1½ hours is allotted for oral argument.

53 Ibid., 1046.
54 *Bush v. Gore*, Brief of Respondent Albert Gore, Jr.
55 Toobin, *Too Close to Call*, 263.
56 *Bush v. Gore*, 531 U.S. 98 (2000).
57 Ibid. Compare Justice Scalia dissenting in *United States v. Virginia*, 518 U.S. 515, 596 (1996):

The Supreme Court of the United States does not sit to announce "unique" disposition. Its principal function is to announce precedent—that is, to set forth principles of law that every court in America must follow. . . . That is the principal reason we publish our opinions.

58 *Bush v. Gore*, 531 U.S. 98, 134–35 (2000).
59 Ibid., 144–58.
60 Ibid., 135–43.
61 Toobin, *Too Close to Call*, 238.
62 *Bush v. Gore*, 531 U.S. 98, 128–29.

Chapter Seven: Inauguration

Bush's quote in the epigraph is from a statement he made to White House counsel Alberto Gonzales upon entering office. See Barton Gellman, *Angler: The Cheney Vice Presidency* (New York: Penguin, 2008), 99, 415. Congressman Rangel's quote is in Thomas Oliphant, *Utter Incompetents: Ego and Ideology in the Age of Bush* (New York: St. Martin's Press, 2007), 16.

1 Mike Allen and Edward Walsh, "Bush Calls for Unity, Civility," *Washington Post*, January 21, 2001.
2 R. W. Apple, Jr., "The Inauguration: Tradition and Legitimacy," *New York Times*, January 21, 2001.
3 *PPPUS-GWB, 2001*, Vol. 1, Inaugural Address, January 20, 2001, 1–3.
4 *Washington Post*, January 21, 2001. Also see Frank Bruni and David E. Sanger, "The Inauguration: Bush Calls for Civility," *New York Times*, January 21, 2001.
5 James Bennet, "C.E.O., U.S.A.," *New York Times Magazine*, January 21, 2001.
6 David Gergen, "Stubborn Kind of Fellow," *Compass*, 15 (Fall 2003).
7 Bob Woodward, *Bush at War* (New York: Simon & Schuster, 2002), 255; Donald F. Kettl, *Team Bush: Leadership Lessons from the Bush White House* (New York: McGraw-Hill, 2003), 41.
8 Lou Cannon and Carl M. Cannon, *Reagan's Disciple: George W. Bush's Troubled Quest for a Presidential Legacy* (New York: PublicAffairs, 2008), 242.

9　John P. Burke, *Becoming President: The Bush Transition, 2000–2003* (Boulder: Lynne Rienner, 2004), 77.

10　Mike Allen, "Hughes Keeps White House in Line," *Washington Post*, March 19, 2001.

11　Lou Dubose, Jan Reid, and Carl M. Cannon, *Boy Genius: Karl Rove, the Brains Behind the Remarkable Political Triumph of George W. Bush* (New York: PublicAffairs, 2003), 194.

12　John Steinbeck, *Travels with Charley* (New York: Viking, 1962), 228.

13　Ron Suskind, "Faith, Certainty, and the Presidency of George W. Bush," *New York Times Magazine*, October 17, 2004.

14　Jeffrey Goldberg, "Breaking Ranks: What Turned Brent Scowcroft Against the Bush Administration," *The New Yorker*, October 31, 2005.

15　Peggy Noonan, "Republicans Break the Ice," *Wall Street Journal*, February 2, 2013.

16　Nicholas Lemann, "Without a Doubt," *The New Yorker*, October 14, 2002.

17　Cannon and Cannon, *Reagan's Disciple*, 235; Richard Lowry, "A Question of Competence," *National Review*, April 2, 2007.

18　Personal interview with Richard Armitage, January 30, 2013.

19　Personal interview with David Frum, January 9, 2013.

20　Bascom Nolly Timmons, *Garner of Texas: A Personal History* (New York: Harper, 1948), 176. Also see O. C. Fisher, *Cactus Jack: A Biography of John Nance Garner* (Waco: Texian Press, 1978), 6.

21　Jody C. Baumgartner, *The American Vice Presidency Reconsidered* (Westport, Conn.: Praeger, 2006), 135. Also see James K. Libbey, *Dean Alben: Mr. Barkley of Kentucky* (Lexington: University of Kentucky Press, 1979), 345.

22　Robert Caro, *The Passage of Power: The Years of Lyndon Johnson* (New York: Alfred A. Knopf, 2012).

23　Herbert Parmet interview with Nicholas Brady, quoted in Parmet, *George Bush: The Life of a Lone Star Yankee* (New York: Scribner, 1997), 263.

24　Dick Cheney, *In My Time* (New York: Threshold, 2011), 305.

25　Ibid.

26　Shirley Anne Warshaw, *The Co-Presidency of Bush and Cheney* (Stanford: Stanford University Press, 2009), 84.

27　Eric Schmitt, "Cheney Assembles Formidable Team," *New York Times*, February 3, 2001.

28　Dana Milbank, "For Number Two, the Future Is Now," *Washington Post*, February 3, 2001.

29　Sheryl Gay Stolberg, "In Glimpses, Private Soul Contemplates Public Legacy," *New York Times*, August 31, 2008.

30　Carl M. Cannon, "The Point Man," *National Journal*, October 11, 2002.

31　Barton Gellman interview with Josh Bolten, in Gellman, *Angler: The Cheney Vice Presidency* (New York: Penguin, 2008), 51.

32 R. W. Apple, Jr., "The Inauguration: Tradition and Legitimacy," *New York Times*, January 20, 2001.

33 George W. Bush Monthly Approval Ratings, http://www.gallup.com/poll/116500/presidential-approval-ratings-george-bush.aspx.

34 Karl Rove, *Courage and Consequence* (New York: Threshold, 2010), 229.

35 Alan Greenspan, *The Age of Turbulence: Adventures in a New World* (New York: Penguin, 2007), 215.

36 Gary Mucciaroni and Paul Quirk, "Deliberations of a Compassionate Conservative: George W. Bush's Domestic Presidency," in *The George W. Bush Presidency*, Colin Campbell and Bert A. Rockman, eds. (Washington, D.C.: CQ Press, 2004), 165.

37 George W. Bush, acceptance speech, Republican National Convention, August 3, 2000.

38 Greenspan, *The Age of Turbulence*, 215.

39 Ron Suskind, *The Price of Loyalty: George W. Bush, the White House, and the Education of Paul O'Neill* (New York: Simon & Schuster, 2004), 117.

40 Greenspan, *The Age of Turbulence*, 221.

41 Suskind, *The Price of Loyalty*, 219.

42 Ibid., 127.

43 Greenspan, *The Age of Turbulence*, 217.

44 Gellman, *Angler*, 72.

45 Ibid.

46 *PPPUS-GWB, 2001,* Vol. 1, Remarks on Transmitting Tax Relief Bill to the Congress, February 8, 2001, 65–66.

47 The House split Bush's proposal into three parts. The tax cut itself was approved March 8, 230–198 with only 10 Democrats voting in favor. The child credit and reduced marriage penalty were approved March 29, 288–144, with 64 Democrats voting in favor. The phase-out of the inheritance tax was approved April 4, 274–154, with 58 Democrats voting in favor and 3 Republicans opposed. See John C. Fortier and Norman J. Ornstein, "President Bush: Legislative Strategist," in *The George W. Bush Presidency*, Fred I. Greenstein, ed. (Baltimore: Johns Hopkins University Press, 2003), 149.

48 *PPPUS-GWB, 2001,* Vol. 1, Remarks on Signing the Economic Growth and Tax Relief Reconciliation Act of 2001, June 7, 2001, 621.

49 James T. Patterson, "Transformative Economic Policies: Tax Cutting, Stimuli, and Bailouts," in *The Presidency of George W. Bush: A First Historical Assessment*, Julian E. Zelizer, ed. (Princeton: Princeton University Press, 2010), 124.

50 Daniel Altman, *Neoconomy: George Bush's Revolutionary Gamble with America's Future* (New York: PublicAffairs, 2004), 72.

51 W. Elliot Brownlee, *Federal Taxation in America: A Short History* (Cambridge: Cambridge University Press, 2004), 223.

52 Greenspan, *The Age of Turbulence*, 223–24.

53 Ibid.

54 U.S. Department of Commerce, *Statistical Abstract of the United States, 2011*, Table 468, Federal Budget Debt (Washington, D.C.: Government Printing Office, 2010).

55 George W. Bush, Address Accepting the Presidential Nomination at the Republican National Convention in Philadelphia, August 3, 2000.

56 The ABC/*Washington Post* poll of March 9–11, 2000, gave Gore and Bush 44 percent each on the question of education. Later polls conducted by Howard University and the Kaiser Foundation showed Bush ahead. See John C. Fortier and Norman J. Ornstein, "President Bush: Legislative Strategist," in Greenstein, ed., *The George W. Bush Presidency*, note 7, 284.

57 Frederick M. Hess and Patrick J. McGuinn, "George W. Bush's Education Legacy: The Two Faces of No Child Left Behind," in Robert Maranto, Tom Lansford, and Jeremy Johnson, eds., *Judging Bush (Studies in the Modern Presidency)* (Stanford: Stanford University Press, 2009), 161.

58 John R. Boehner, "Making the Grade: In the Hands of Parents, Information Is Like Rocket Fuel for Education Reform," *National Review*, April 6, 2001.

59 *Thirteen Days* was released in February 2001. It starred Kevin Costner as JFK's aide Kenny O'Donnell, and was directed by Roger Donaldson. Bruce Greenwood played President Kennedy.

60 George W. Bush, *Decision Points* (New York: Crown, 2010), 275.

61 *PPPUS-GWB, 2001,* Vol. 1, Remarks at Merritt Elementary School, Washington, D.C., January 25, 2001, 17–19.

62 Robert Draper, *Dead Certain: The Presidency of George W. Bush* (New York: Free Press, 2007), 116.

63 Hess and McGuinn, "George W. Bush's Education Legacy," 163.

64 Dana Milbank, "With Fanfare, Bush Signs Education Bill," *Washington Post*, January 9, 2002.

65 Thomas Oliphant, *Utter Incompetents: Ego and Ideology in the Age of Bush* (New York: St. Martin's Press, 2007), 74; Rove, *Courage and Consequence*, 239.

66 G. W. Bush, *Decision Points*, 277.

67 George W. Bush acceptance speech, Republican National Convention, August 3, 2000.

68 *PPPUS-GWB, 2001,* Vol. 1, Inaugural Address, January 20, 2001, 1–3.

69 Executive Order 13198, Agency Responsibilities with Respect to Faith-Based and Community Initiatives, 66 *Federal Register* 8497; Executive Order 13199, Establishment of White House Office of Faith-Based and Community Initiatives, 66 *Federal Register* 8499.

70 *PPPUS-GWB, 2001,* Vol. 1, Remarks on Signing Executive Orders with Respect to Faith-Based and Community Initiatives, January 29, 2001, 26–27.

71 *Wall Street Journal*, February 14, 2001.

72 Kevin M. Kruse, "Compassionate Conservatism: Religion in the Age of George W. Bush," in Zelizer, ed., *The Presidency of George W. Bush*, 234.

73 Letter, John J. DiIulio to George W. Bush, April 2002, quoted in John J. DiIulio, "Why Judging Bush Is Never as Easy as It Seems," in Maranto, Lansford, and Johnson, eds., *Judging Bush*, 294–310.

74 David Kuo, *Tempting Faith: An Inside Story of Political Seduction* (New York: Free Press, 2006), 201–12.

75 David Frum, *The Right Man: An Inside Account of the Bush White House* (New York: Random House, 2003), 27–28.

76 Draper, *Dead Certain*, 106.

77 G. W. Bush, *Decision Points*, 111–12.

78 Nancy Reagan to George W. Bush, April 2001, quoted in ibid., 106.

79 *Newsweek*, July 9, 2001. According to a *Washington Post*/ABC poll on July 26, 63 percent of Americans favored stem cell research, 33 percent opposed, and 4 percent were undecided. Among college graduates, 76 percent were in favor. Seventy-seven percent of those earning above $75,000 favored it, while only 54 percent of those earning less than $30,000 did so. *Washington Post*, July 26, 2001.

80 *New York Times*, July 22, 2001.

81 Draper, *Dead Certain*, 124.

82 *PPPUS-GWB, 2001,* Vol. 1, News Conference with Prime Minister Tony Blair, Halton, England, July 19, 2001, 878.

83 G. W. Bush, *Decision Points*, 117.

84 Ibid., 118.

85 *PPPUS-GWB, 2001,* Vol. 1, Address to the Nation on Stem Cell Research, August 9, 2001, 953–56.

86 George W. Bush, "Stem Cell Science and the Preservation of Life," *New York Times*, August 12, 2001.

87 "Abortion Foes Split over Plan on Stem Cells," *New York Times*, August 12, 2001.

88 G. W. Bush, *Decision Points*, 119.

89 *Washington Post*, August 14, 2001.

90 Suskind, *The Price of Loyalty*, 70.

91 I am indebted to Ron Suskind for this observation. See Suskind, "Faith, Certainty, and the Presidency of George W. Bush." David Gergen makes a similar observation. See Gergen, "Stubborn Kind of Fellow," *Compass*, 18 (Fall, 2003).

Chapter Eight: March of the Hegelians

The epigraph is attributed to Karl Rove in Ron Suskind, "Faith, Certainty, and the Presidency of George W. Bush," *New York Times Magazine*, October 17, 2004. Also see Mark Danner, "Words in a Time of War," in Andras Szanto, *What Orwell Didn't Know* (New York: PublicAffairs, 2009), 17.

 1 Hegel's thought is succinctly stated in Volume 3 of his *The Idea of History and Its Realization* at page 31: "Reason governs the world and has consequently governed its history. In relation to this Reason, which is universal and sub-

stantial, in and for itself, all else is subordinate, subservient, and the means for its actualization. Moreover, this reason is immanent in historical existence and reaches its own perfection in and through this existence."

2 Ron Suskind, "Faith, Certainty, and the Presidency of George W. Bush," *New York Times Magazine*, October 17, 2004.

3 In 1970 I hired Allan Bloom and Walter Berns away from Cornell on behalf of the Department of Political Economy at the University of Toronto. Allan was a gifted lecturer and always had a coterie of graduate students surrounding him. He was a credit to the department, although his strong attachment to philosophical absolutes, even more strongly expressed, occasionally made him a difficult colleague. He remained at Toronto for nine years, returning to the University of Chicago in 1979.

4 Saul Bellow, *Ravelstein* (New York: Penguin, 2000), 58.

5 Allan Bloom, *The Closing of the American Mind* (New York: Simon & Schuster, 1987), 141–42.

6 Interview with Yale professor emeritus Joseph LaPalombara, August 14, 2012. Wolfowitz wrote his dissertation on the dangers of nuclear proliferation in the Middle East, focusing on the production of plutonium as a by-product of nuclear-powered desalination stations. Paul D. Wolfowitz, "Nuclear Proliferation in the Middle East: The Politics and Economics of Proposals for Nuclear Desalting," PhD diss., University of Chicago, June 1972.

7 At the time, the Arms Control and Disarmament Agency was headed by Fred Iklé, a hawk from the RAND Corporation and a close friend of Wohlstetter, who had been appointed by Nixon to assuage congressional fears about the recently negotiated ABM treaty with the Soviet Union.

8 James Mann, *Rise of the Vulcans: The History of Bush's War Cabinet* (New York: Viking, 2004), 79–83.

9 Wolfowitz was urged by his former mentor Fred Iklé that it was time to leave. "Paul, you got to get out of there. We want you in the new administration." James Mann interview with Fred Iklé in ibid., 98.

10 Wolfowitz was strongly recommended to Cheney by Indiana senator Dick Lugar, who had worked closely with Wolfowitz during Ferdinand Marcos's closing days in the Philippines when Wolfowitz was assistant secretary of state. Ibid., 170–71.

11 The authorization to use force carried in the Senate by a thin margin of 52–47. Only 10 Democrats voted in favor. Republicans Mark Hatfield (Oregon) and Charles Grassley (Iowa) voted against. The measure carried the House 250–183, 32 Democrats voting in favor. For an analysis of the events leading to the congressional vote of authorization, see Jean Edward Smith, *George Bush's War* (New York: Henry Holt, 1991).

12 Colin Powell, *My American Journey* (New York: Ballantine, 1995), 516.

13 Secretary of Defense Dick Cheney, "Defense Strategy for the 1990s: The

Regional Defense Strategy" (Washington, D.C.: Department of Defense, 1993), 4.

14 Statement of Principles, Project for the New American Century, June 3, 1997.

15 Open Letter to the Honorable William J. Clinton, January 26, 1998, Project for the New American Century.

16 Andrew Bacevich, "Trigger Man," *The American Conservative*, June 6, 2005.

17 Personal interview with George Packard, January 14, 2013.

18 Bob Woodward, *State of Denial: Bush at War, Part III* (New York: Simon & Schuster, 2006), 12; Sebastian Mallaby, "The Character Question," *Washington Post*, August 30, 2004.

19 I am grateful to Professor Beth Fischer of the University of Toronto for calling this to my attention. See Robert MacFarlane in "Understanding the End of the Cold War, 1980–1987: An Oral History Conference," Brown University, May 7–10, 1998, Nina Tannenwald, ed., 66–68.

20 Ron Suskind, *The Price of Loyalty: George W. Bush, the White House, and the Education of Paul O'Neill* (New York: Simon & Schuster, 2004), 70.

21 Elisabeth Bumiller, *Condoleezza Rice: An American Life* (New York: Random House, 2007), 136–37. Cheney said he never personally asked to chair the NSC meetings. Personal interview, May 13, 2013.

22 Donald Rumsfeld, *Known and Unknown* (New York: Sentinel, 2011), 325.

23 Amy B. Zegart, *Flawed by Design: The Evolution of the CIA, JCS, and NSC* (Stanford: Stanford University Press, 1999), 87.

24 Ivo H. Daalder and I. M. Destler, *In the Shadow of the Oval Office* (New York: Simon & Schuster, 2009), 252, 278; Bumiller, *Condoleezza Rice*, 134.

25 Karen DeYoung, *Soldier: The Life of Colin Powell* (New York: Alfred A. Knopf, 2006), 328–29.

26 Peter Rodman, an NSC veteran, former special assistant to Henry Kissinger, and assistant secretary of defense for international security affairs under Rumsfeld, offers a similar assessment. "When I served in the Nixon administration," wrote Rodman, "the NSC staff's most important product was a memorandum to Nixon laying out options for his decision. Bush 43's NSC crafted laborious statements of broad policy attempting to capture interagency consensus. . . . [Stephen] Hadley told the NSC staff that good governance required this pursuit of consensus." Peter W. Rodman, *Presidential Command: Power, Leadership, and Foreign Policy from Richard Nixon to George W. Bush* (New York: Alfred A. Knopf, 2009), 249–50.

27 Rumsfeld, *Known and Unknown*, 318–29.

28 Bumiller, *Condoleezza Rice*, 134.

29 "There is not enough time while I am president to prepare the way for an agreement with North Korea," said Clinton on December 28, 2000. John Lancaster, "Clinton Rules Out Visit to North Korea," *Washington Post*, December 29, 2000.

30 Press Conference, Secretary Colin Powell and Swedish Foreign Minister, Anna Lindh, March 6, 2001, State Department transcript.

31 *Washington Post*, March 7, 2001.

32 Powell remarks, March 7, 2001, Federal News Service transcript.

33 *PPPUS-GWB, 2001*, Vol. 1, Press Conference, President Bush and President Kim Dae-jung, March 7, 2001, 203.

34 Bob Woodward, *Bush at War* (New York: Simon & Schuster, 2002), 340.

35 Richard N. Haass, *War of Necessity, War of Choice: A Memoir of Two Iraq Wars* (New York: Simon & Schuster, 2009), 176–77.

36 Don Oberdorfer, *The Turn: From the Cold War to a New Era* (New York: Poseidon, 1991), 299.

37 Statement of high-level White House official, presumably Karl Rove, quoted in Mann, *Rise of the Vulcans*, 229.

38 Christine Todd Whitman, *It's My Party Too: The Battle for the Heart of the GOP and the Future of America* (New York: Penguin, 2005), 176.

39 Suskind, *The Price of Loyalty*, 109.

40 Whitman, *It's My Party Too*, 172.

41 Suskind, *The Price of Loyalty*, 120.

42 Whitman, *It's My Party Too*, 121.

43 For the full text of Bush's reply to Hagel, see *PPPUS-GWB, 2001*, Vol. 1, 235.

44 Whitman, *It's My Party Too*, 176.

45 Ibid., 178.

46 Karen DeYoung, *Soldier*, 328.

47 Condoleezza Rice, *No Higher Honor* (New York: Crown, 2011), 42.

48 Whitman, *It's My Party Too*, 178. Whitman goes on to say that "The roots of our difficulties in forging a strong multinational alliance to fight terrorism go all the way back to how we handled Kyoto as well as other international issues."

49 Suskind, *The Price of Loyalty*, 130.

50 Haass, *War of Necessity, War of Choice*, 185.

51 *PPPUS-GWB, 2001*, Vol. 1, Exchange with Reporters Following Discussions with Egyptian President Hosni Mubarak, April 2, 2001, 354.

52 Evan Thomas and Melinda Lu, "A Crash in the Clouds," *Newsweek*, April 16, 2001.

53 *PPPUS-GWB, 2001*, Vol. 1, Remarks to the American Society of Newspaper Editors, April 5, 2001, 368.

54 Letter from Ambassador Prueher to Minister of Foreign Affairs Tang, April 11, 2001, www.whitehouse.gov/news/release/2001/04/20010411-1.html.

55 BBC online, April 9, 2001.

56 Karen Hughes, *Ten Minutes from Normal* (New York: Viking, 2004), 207.

57 Rumsfeld, *Known and Unknown*, 315.

58 George W. Bush Interview, *Washington Post*, April 25, 2001.

59 Neil King, "Bush Leaves Taiwan Policy in Confusing State," *Wall Street Journal*, April 26, 2001.

60 *PPPUS-GWB, 2001,* Vol. 1, Statement on the Renewal of Normal Trade Relations Status for China, June 1, 2001, 605.

61 Ibid., "Remarks on Global Climate Change," June 11, 2001, 634–37.

62 Laura Bush, *Spoken from the Heart* (New York: Scribner, 2010), 188.

63 *PPPUS-GWB, 2001,* Vol. 1, Bush-Aznar News Conference, Madrid, Spain, June 12, 2001, 638–48.

64 Ibid.

65 *PPPUS-GWB, 2001,* Vol. 1, President's News Conference with Lord Robertson, Brussels, Belgium, June 13, 2001, 650–55.

66 *PPPUS-GWB, 2001,* Vol. 1, News Conference with European Union Leaders in Göteborg, Sweden, June 14, 2001, 659–64.

67 Laura Bush, *Spoken from the Heart,* 189.

68 For the text of Bush's address to Warsaw University, see *PPPUS-GWB, 2001,* Vol. 1, 677–81.

69 *PPPUS-GWB, 2001,* Vol. 1, President's News Conference with President Aleksander Kwasniewski, Warsaw, Poland, June 15, 2001, 670–75.

70 Bob Woodward, *State of Denial,* 47–48.

71 Rice, *No Higher Honor,* 62.

72 G. W. Bush, *Decision Points,* 196.

73 Rice, *No Higher Honor,* 62.

74 Draper, *Dead Certain,* 132.

75 *PPPUS-GWB, 2001,* Vol. 1, President's News Conference with President Putin, Brdo Castle, Slovenia, June 16, 2001, 685–93.

76 Ibid.

77 Ibid.

78 Draper, *Dead Certain,* 133.

79 Personal interview with Dick Cheney, May 13, 2013.

Chapter Nine: Asleep at the Switch

The epigraph is a statement CIA director George Tenet made in testimony to the Senate Select Committee on Intelligence, February 12, 2001. George Tenet, *At the Center of the Storm: My Years at the CIA* (New York: HarperCollins, 2007), 144.

1 Craig Unger, *House of Bush, House of Saud* (New York: Scribner, 2004), 234.

2 Elsa Walsh, "The Prince," *The New Yorker,* March 24, 2003, 58.

3 Jane Perlez, "Bush and Sharon Differ on Ending Violence," *New York Times,* June 27, 2001.

4 Jane Perlez, "Bush Senior, on His Son's Behalf, Reassures Saudi Leader," *New York Times,* July 15, 2001.

5 Craig Unger, *The Fall of the House of Bush* (New York: Scribner, 2007), 211.

6 *PPPUS-GWB, 2001,* Vol. 2, July 16, 2001, 852.

7 Laura Bush, *Spoken from the Heart* (New York: Scribner, 2010), 191–92.

8 Jane Perlez, "Rice on Front Line in Foreign Policy Role," *New York Times,* August 19, 2001.

9   Bob Woodward, *Bush at War* (New York: Simon & Schuster, 2002), 14.

10 Barbara Slavin and Bill Nichols, "Powell Finds Steep Learning Curve in New Job," *USA Today*, July 19, 2001; Acel Moore, "Is Powell the Invisible Man in the Bush Administration?," *Philadelphia Inquirer*, September 11, 2001.

11 Johanna McGeary, "Odd Man Out," *Time*, September 10, 2001.

12 Karen DeYoung, *Soldier: The Life of Colin Powell* (New York: Alfred A. Knopf, 2006), 337.

13 *PPPUS-GWB, 2001,* Vol. 2, Bush-Putin Press Conference, Genoa, June 22, 2001, 888–91.

14 Karen Hughes, *Ten Minutes from Normal* (New York: Viking, 2004), 224–25.

15 George W. Bush, *Decision Points* (New York: Crown, 2010), 116.

16 Hughes, *Ten Minutes from Normal*, 225.

17 Christopher Andersen, *George and Laura: Portrait of a Marriage* (New York: HarperCollins, 2002), 254.

18 Ibid., 255.

19 Hughes, *Ten Minutes from Normal*, 226.

20 Andersen, *George and Laura*, 257–58.

21 Terry H. Anderson, *Bush's Wars* (New York: Oxford University Press, 2011), 64. The text of the August 6 briefing is reprinted in *The 9/11 Commission Report* (New York: W. W. Norton, 2004), 261–62.

22 *9/11 Commission Report*, 262.

23 Frank Rich, "Thanks for the Heads Up," *New York Times*, May 25, 2002. Also see Bob Woodward and Don Eggen, "August Memo Focused on Attack in U.S.," *Washington Post*, May 18, 2002.

24 Barton Gellman, "A Strategy's Cautious Evolution," *Washington Post*, January 20, 2002.

25 Richard A. Clarke, *Against All Enemies: Inside America's War on Terror* (New York: Free Press, 2004), 229–30.

26 Ibid., 231–32.

27 George Tenet, *At the Center of the Storm: My Years at the CIA* (New York: HarperCollins, 2007), 144–45.

28 Anderson, *Bush's Wars*, 63; Bob Woodward, "Two Months Before 9/11, an Urgent Warning to Rice," *Washington Post*, October 1, 2006.

29 Sidney Blumenthal, *The Clinton Wars* (New York: Farrar, Straus & Giroux, 2003), 796.

30 Unger, *House of Bush, House of Saud*, 237.

31 *PPPUS-GWB, 2001,* Vol. 2, Question and Answer Session with Students at Crawford Elementary School, August 23, 2001, 1014.

32 President's News Conference, Crawford, Texas, August 24, 2001, ibid., 1018–27, 1020.

33 Robert G. Kaiser and David B. Ottaway, "Saudi Leader's Anger Revealed Shaky Ties," *Washington Post*, February 10, 2002.

34 Walsh, "The Prince," 59.
35 Kaiser and Ottaway, "Saudi Leader's Anger," *Washington Post*, February 10, 2002.
36 Walsh, "The Prince," 59.
37 Ibid.
38 Kaiser and Ottaway, "Saudi Leader's Anger," *Washington Post*, February 10, 2002.
39 Ibid.
40 *Washington Post*, August 7, 2001; Unger, *House of Bush, House of Saud*, 237.
41 G. W. Bush, *Decision Points*, 302.
42 Laura Bush, *Spoken from the Heart*, 193–94.
43 Hughes, *Ten Minutes from Normal*, 230.
44 Laura Bush, *Spoken from the Heart*, 194.
45 Bob Woodward, *State of Denial: Bush at War, Part III* (New York: Simon & Schuster, 2006), 76.
46 Walsh, "The Prince," 59.
47 Woodward, *State of Denial*, 77.
48 Kaiser and Ottaway, "Saudi Leader's Anger," *Washington Post*, February 10, 2002.
49 Ibid.
50 Karl Rove, *Courage and Consequence* (New York: Threshold, 2010), 244–50.
51 G. W. Bush, *Decision Points*, 127.
52 Robert Draper, *Dead Certain: The Presidency of George W. Bush* (New York: Free Press, 2007), 136.
53 G. W. Bush, *Decision Points*, 127.
54 *PPPUS-GWB, 2001,* Vol. 2, Remarks at Booker Elementary School, Sarasota, Florida, September 11, 2001, 1098.
55 Draper, *Dead Certain*, 139.
56 Woodward, *Bush at War*, 16.
57 Ibid., 17.
58 Rove, *Courage and Consequence*, 253.
59 G. W. Bush, *Decision Points*, 130.
60 Rove, *Courage and Consequence*, 255.
61 G. W. Bush, *Decision Points*, 132.
62 Donald Rumsfeld, *Known and Unknown* (New York: Sentinel, 2011), 342.
63 *PPPUS-GWB, 2001,* Vol. 2, Remarks at Barksdale Air Force Base, September 11, 2001, 1098–99.
64 Rove, *Courage and Consequence*, 260.
65 Woodward, *Bush at War*, 19.
66 G. W. Bush, *Decision Points*, 134.
67 Clarke, *Against All Enemies*, 21.
68 Woodward, *Bush at War*, 27.

69 Ibid.

70 Rove, *Courage and Consequence*, 263.

71 G. W. Bush, *Decision Points*, 138.

72 Laura Bush, *Spoken from the Heart*, 265.

73 Woodward, *Bush at War*, 30.

74 *PPPUS-GWB, 2001,* Vol. 2, Address to the Nation, September 11, 2001, 1099–1100.

75 David Frum, *The Right Man: An Inside Account of the Bush White House* (New York: Random House 2003), 126.

76 Woodward, *Bush at War*, 31–32.

77 Tenet, *At the Center of the Storm*, 171. Also see Condoleezza Rice, *No Higher Honor* (New York: Crown, 2011), 77; Clarke, *Against All Enemies*, 23.

78 Clarke, *Against All Enemies*, 24.

79 Woodward, *Bush at War*, 32.

80 Kurt Eichenwald, *500 Days: Secrets and Lies in the Terror Wars* (New York: Touchstone, 2012), 51.

81 Rumsfeld, *Known and Unknown*, 346–47. Also see *The 9/11 Commission Report*, 330.

82 Clarke, *Against All Enemies*, 24.

83 Ibid., 24–25.

84 G. W. Bush, *Decision Points*, 138.

85 Laura Bush, *Spoken from the Heart*, 265.

86 Ibid.

87 G. W. Bush, *Decision Points*, 139.

88 Woodward, *Bush at War*, 37.

89 James Harding, "Conflicting Views from Two Bush Camps," *Financial Times*, March 20, 2003; Woodward, *Bush at War*, 205.

90 I am indebted to Professor Robert Jervis for this observation. Jervis, "Understanding the Bush Doctrine," Vol. 118 *Political Science Quarterly*, 363, 379, Fall 2003.

91 *PPPUS-GWB, 2001,* Vol. 2, Remarks at National Day of Prayer, September 14, 2001, 1108–9.

92 William F. McCombs, *Making Woodrow Wilson President* (New York: Fairview Publishing Co., 1921), 180–81.

93 Margaret MacMillan, *Paris 1919: Six Months That Changed the World* (New York: Random House, 2001), 6.

94 David Lloyd George, *The Truth About the Peace Treaties*, Vol. 1 (London: V. Gollancz, 1938), 223–24.

Chapter Ten: Toppling the Taliban

The epigraph is a nineteenth-century English hymn composed by Sabine Baring-Gould in 1865 and set to music by Arthur Sullivan (of Gilbert and Sullivan fame) in 1871.

1 Robert McNamara, *In Retrospect: The Tragedy and Lessons of Vietnam* (New York: Random House, 1995), 39.

2 Jacob Weisberg, *The Bush Tragedy* (New York: Random House, 2008), 146. Weisberg cites an interview with Kenneth Adelman, a close friend of Wolfowitz, as the source of the observation.

3 *Texas v. White*, 74 U.S. 700 (1869). According to Chief Justice Salmon P. Chase, the Constitution created "an indestructible Union composed of indestructible States." Secession was illegal, and Texas had never left the Union.

4 United Nations Security Council Resolution 678, November 29, 1990; Congressional Joint Resolution, January 12, 1991, Public Law 102-1.

5 Eisenhower's remark was in a speech he delivered to the Canadian Club in Ottawa, June 10, 1946. See Jean Edward Smith, *Eisenhower in War and Peace* (New York: Random House, 2012), ix.

6 Bob Woodward, *Bush at War* (New York: Simon & Schuster, 2002), 38.

7 George W. Bush, *Decision Points* (New York: Crown, 2010), 139.

8 Ibid., 140.

9 *PPPUS-GWB, 2001,* Vol. 2, Remarks to the Press, September 12, 2001, 1100–1101.

10 National Center for Health Statistics, "Death from Each Cause, by 5-Year Age Groups, Race, and Sex: United States, 2001. In 2001, there was 2,416,425 deaths from all causes, averaging 6,620 per day. Also see *National Vital Statistics Report 52*, No. 9, November 7, 2003, Table E, "Deaths and Percentage of Total Deaths for the 10 Leading Causes of Death, by Race, United States, 2001."

11 I am indebted to Barton Gellman for this observation. Gellman, *Angler: The Cheney Vice Presidency* (New York: Penguin, 2008), 132.

12 Tom Daschle, *Like No Other Time: The 107th Congress and the Two Years That Changed America Forever* (New York: Crown, 2003), 121.

13 Woodward, *Bush at War*, 45.

14 Daschle, *Like No Other Time*, 122.

15 Weisberg, *The Bush Tragedy*, 207.

16 Ibid., 208.

17 Chester A. Crocker, "Engaging Falling States," *Foreign Affairs* (September/October 2003), 32–44. Professor Crocker's article was one of the first to question the war on terror. As he pointed out, "Terrorism is a tool, not an actor." An even sharper critique was published by Professor Crocker in

Survival (Spring 2005), "A Dubious Template for US Foreign Policy," 51–70. Again, "The impossibility of 'defeating terrorism'—especially when defined so indiscriminately—makes it the ideal adversary for decision-makers who describe themselves as wartime leaders."

18 John le Carré, "The United States Has Gone Completely Mad," *The Times* (London), January 15, 2003.

19 Stefan Halper and Jonathan Clarke, *America Alone: The Neo-Conservatives and the Global Order* (New York: Cambridge University Press, 2004), 207.

20 Attendees included the president and vice president, Powell and Armitage from State; Rumsfeld and Wolfowitz from Defense; Ashcroft and deputy attorney general Larry Thompson from Justice; Andrew Card; Libby and Edelman from Cheney's office; Alberto Gonzales and John Bellinger from the Office of the White House counsel; George Tenet, John McLaughlin, and Cofer Black from the CIA; Generals Chairman Hugh Shelton and Richard Myers representing the Army and the Air Force from the Joint Chiefs; Robert Mueller and Dale Watson from the FBI; Rice, Hadley, and Richard Clarke from the NSC. Secretary of the Treasury Paul O'Neill was absent, flying back from Tokyo.

21 Condoleezza Rice, *No Higher Honor* (New York: Crown, 2011), 80.

22 Woodward, *Bush at War*, 44.

23 Richard A. Clarke, *Against All Enemies* (New York: Free Press, 2004), 30.

24 Woodward, *Bush at War*, 43.

25 Dick Cheney, *In My Time* (New York: Threshold, 2011), 331.

26 Clarke, *Against All Enemies*, 30–31.

27 Ibid., 32.

28 Douglas J. Feith, *War and Decision: Inside the Pentagon at the Dawn of the War on Terrorism* (New York: HarperCollins, 2008), 12.

29 Ron Suskind, *The Price of Loyalty: George W. Bush, the White House, and the Education of Paul O'Neill* (New York: Simon & Schuster, 2004), 185.

30 Woodward, *Bush at War*, 52.

31 George Tenet, *At the Center of the Storm: My Years at the CIA* (New York: HarperCollins, 2007), 176.

32 Woodward, *Bush at War*, 51–52.

33 Feith, *War and Decision*, 14.

34 Ibid., 15–16.

35 G. W. Bush, *Decision Points*, 146.

36 *PPPUS-GWB, 2001,* Vol. 2, Remarks at National Day of Prayer, September 14, 2001, 1108–9.

37 Ibid.

38 Woodward, *Bush at War*, 46.

39 G. W. Bush, *Decision Points*, 142.

40 Max Blumenthal, "The Christian Right's Humble Servant," Alter.Net, November 14, 2004.

41 Eric Foner, *The Fiery Trial: Abraham Lincoln and American Slavery* (New York: W. W. Norton, 2010), 169.

42 G. W. Bush, *Decision Points*, 147.

43 Ibid., 148.

44 *PPPUS-GWB, 2001*, Vol. 2, Remarks at World Trade Center Site in New York City, September 14, 2001, 1110.

45 G. W. Bush, *Decision Points*, 149.

46 Ibid., 150.

47 107th Congress, 1st Session, S. J. Res. 23, "Authorization for Use of Military Force," September 14, 2001.

48 Italics added. The White House request is reproduced in Daschle, *Like No Other Time*, 123.

49 *PPPUS-GWB, 2001*, Vol. 2, Remarks to Reporters at Camp David, September 15, 2001, 1111–12.

50 G. W. Bush, *Decision Points*, 188.

51 Woodward, *Bush at War*, 78.

52 Terry H. Anderson, *Bush's Wars* (New York: Oxford University Press, 2011), 76.

53 Woodward, *Bush at War*, 76. Treasury Secretary O'Neill was alarmed when he read Tenet's draft that evening at Camp David. "I hope the president reads this carefully," O'Neill recalled. "It's kind of his job. You can't forfeit this much responsibility to unelected officials. But I knew he wouldn't." Suskind, *The Price of Loyalty*, 190–91.

54 Karen DeYoung, *Soldier: The Life of Colin Powell* (New York: Alfred A. Knopf, 2006), 352; Woodward, *Bush at War*, 83.

55 G. W. Bush, *Decision Points*, 189.

56 Ibid.

57 Woodward, *Bush at War*, 81.

58 Ibid., 87–88.

59 G. W. Bush, *Decision Points*, 189.

60 Woodward, *Bush at War*, 88.

61 G. W. Bush, *Decision Points*, 190.

62 Woodward, *Bush at War*, 91.

63 *PPPUS-GWB, 2001*, Vol. 2, Remarks to Reporters Upon Arrival at the White House, September 16, 2001, 1114–7.

64 G. W. Bush, *Decision Points*, 191.

65 Woodward, *Bush at War*, 97–98.

66 Ibid., 99.

67 *PPPUS-GWB, 2001*, Vol. 2, Exchange with Reporters in the Pentagon," September 17, 2001, 1120.

68 Woodward, *Bush at War*, 101.

69 *PPPUS-GWB, 2001*, Vol. 2, Exchange with Reporters at the White House, September 18, 2001, 1125–28.

70 Ibid., Address Before a Joint Session of Congress, September 20, 2001, 1140–44.

71 Alastair Campbell, *The Blair Years: The Alastair Campbell Diaries* (New York: Alfred A. Knopf, 2007), 573.

72 Anderson, *Bush's Wars*, 76. Also see Murray Wass, "Key Bush Intelligence Briefing Kept from Hill Panel," *National Journal*, November 22, 2005.

73 Woodward, *Bush at War*, 118.

74 G. W. Bush, *Decision Points*, 195.

75 Tommy Franks, with Malcolm McConnell, *American Soldier* (New York: HarperCollins, 2004), 271–72.

76 Ibid., 281.

77 Woodward, *Bush at War*, 204.

78 *PPPUS-GWB, 2001,* Vol. 2, Address to the Nation Announcing Strikes Against al Qaeda Training Camps and Taliban Military Installations in Afghanistan, October 7, 2001, 1201–2.

79 Robert Draper, *Dead Certain: The Presidency of George Bush* (New York: Free Press, 2007), 158–59.

80 Woodward, *Bush at War*, 277.

81 Donald Rumsfeld, *Known and Unknown* (New York: Sentinel, 2011).

82 Franks, *American Soldier*, 315.

Chapter Eleven: *L'État, c'est moi*

The chapter title is a statement attributed to Louis XIV of France ("The state, it is I") made to the Parliament of Paris, April 13, 1655. The epigraph is a comment of George W. Bush to the writer Bob Woodward. *Bush at War* (New York: Simon & Schuster, 2002), 145–46.

1 Chester Crocker, "A Dubious Template for US Foreign Policy," *Survival* (Spring 2005), 52.

2 Ron Suskind, *The One Percent Doctrine: Deep Inside America's Pursuit of Its Enemies Since 9/11* (New York: Simon & Schuster, 2006), 97–98.

3 The Justice Department order was issued by Michael Creppy, chief U.S. immigration judge (not a judicial position). Creppy also prohibited immigration court administrators from listing detainees' names or cases on public dockets. In the litigation that followed, two U.S. Courts of Appeals issued conflicting judgments, and the Supreme Court declined to hear the case. The result was that the government got its way. *Detroit Free Press v. Ashcroft*, 303 F. 3d. G81 (6th Cir. 2002); *North Jersey Media Group v. Ashcroft*, 308 F. 3d 198 (3rd Cir. 2002).

4 Charlie Savage, *Takeover: The Return of the Imperial Presidency and the Subversion of American Democracy* (New York: Little, Brown, 2007), 96.

5 Executive Order 13233, November 1, 2001.

6 George W. Bush, *Decision Points* (New York: Crown, 2010), 154.

7 18 U.S.C. 1385. The act, as amended, prohibits the use of the armed forces of the United States domestically. It does not prohibit use of the National Guard or the Coast Guard.

8 50 U.S.C. 1801–11. Also see Savage, *Takeover*, 129. If engaged in "hot pursuit," the government may eavesdrop first and submit the request for a warrant later, but there must be evidence to justify the eavesdropping.

9 Savage, *Takeover*, 129.

10 G. W. Bush, *Decision Points*, 164.

11 Daniel Klaidman, Stuart Taylor, Jr., Evan Thomas, "Palace Revolt," *Newsweek*, February 6, 2006.

12 Office of Legal Counsel Memorandum Opinion, September 25, 2001, "The President's Constitutional Authority to Conduct Military Operations Against Terrorists and Nations Supporting Them," https://www.justice.gov/sites/default/files/olc/opinions/2001/09/31/op-olc-v025-p0188_0.pdf. (Emphasis added.)

13 Office of Legal Counsel, Memorandum Opinion, September 25, 2001, "Constitutionality of Amending Foreign Intelligence Surveillance Act to Change the 'Purpose' Standard for Searches,"www.justice.gov/sites/default/files/opa/legacy/2009/03/09/memoforeignsurveillanceact09252001.pdf.

14 Jack L. Goldsmith, *The Terror Presidency: Law and Judgment Inside the Bush Administration* (New York: W. W. Norton, 2007), 97.

15 The ten memoranda, all classified "Secret," were dated October 4, 2001; November 2, 2001; February 25, 2003; March 11, 2004; March 12, 2004; March 15, 2004; March 16, 2004; March 30, 2004; July 16, 2004; August 9, 2004. They remain a subject of litigation in a suit filed by the American Civil Liberties Union, *ACLU v. DOJ*, 06-cv-0214 (D.D.C.).

16 "President Discusses War on Terrorism and Operation Iraqi Freedom," Cleveland, Ohio, March 6, 2006, White House website.

17 Dana Priest, "Covert CIA Program Withstands New Furor," *Washington Post*, December 30, 2005.

18 G. W. Bush, *Decision Points*, 163.

19 Kurt Eichenwald, *500 Days: Secrets and Lies in the Terror Wars* (New York: Simon & Schuster, 2012), 105.

20 G. W. Bush, *Decision Points*, 164.

21 Eichenwald, *500 Days*, 106.

22 Bruce Fein, opening statement, Senate Judiciary Committee, *Wartime Executive Powers at the NSA's Surveillance Authority*, February 28, 2006.

23 Jim Lehrer interview with Vice President Cheney, *The NewsHour with Jim Lehrer*, PBS, October 12, 2001.

24 *PPPUS-GWB, 2001,* Vol. 2, Exchange with Reporters Following Discussions with Prime Minister Berlusconi, October 15, 2001, 1239.

25 Jacob Weisberg, *The Bush Tragedy* (New York: Random House, 2008), 191; Eichenwald, *500 Days*, 129.

26 David Frum, *The Right Man: An Inside Account of the Bush White House* (New York: Random House, 2008), 179.

27 Laura Bush, *Spoken from the Heart* (New York: Scribner, 2010, 219.

28 The other dead, aside from Stevens and the two postal employees, included a New York hospital worker and a ninety-four-year-old woman in Oxford, Connecticut.

29 Weisberg, *The Bush Tragedy*, 192.

30 Personal interview with Donald Rumsfeld, October 2, 2013.

31 Weisberg, *The Bush Tragedy*, 193.

32 Goldsmith, *The Terror Presidency*, 72.

33 Jane Mayer, *The Dark Side: The Inside Story of How the War on Terror Turned into a War on American Ideals* (New York: Random House, 2008), 5.

34 I am indebted to Katrina vanden Heuvel for pointing this out. "It's Not a 'War' on Terror," *The Nation*, September 8, 2006.

35 *PPPUS-GWB, 2001,* Vol. 2, Remarks on Signing the USA Patriot Act of 2001, October 26, 2001, 1306–7.

36 Goldsmith, *The Terror Presidency*, 74.

37 A draft of the Domestic Security Enhancement Act was leaked to the Center for Public Integrity on February 7, 2003. The center posted it on its website, and a firestorm of criticism ensued. A brief analysis is provided online by Alex James, "Pertinent Political." Also see Adam Clymer, "Justice Dept. Draft on Wider Powers Draws Quick Criticism," *New York Times*, February 8, 2003.

38 *Afroyim v. Rusk,* 387 U.S. 253 (1967). The case involved a naturalized American who had voted in an Israeli election, which under the law at the time meant a forfeiture of American citizenship. The Court overturned that law.

39 Mayer, *The Dark Side*, 48; Woodward, *Bush at War*, 80.

40 Military Order of November 13, 2001, "Detention Treatment and Trial of Certain Non-Citizens in the War Against Terrorism," 66 *Federal Register* 57831–36.

41 *PPPUS-GWB, 2001,* Vol. 2, Remarks Following a Cabinet Meeting, November 19, 2001, 1425–26.

42 Military Order of November 13, 2001, section 1(f).

43 William Safire, "Seizing Dictatorial Power," *New York Times*, November 15, 2001.

44 Jeremy Rabkin, "After Guantánamo: The War over the Geneva Convention," *The National Interest* (Summer 2002), 4.

45 Mayer, *The Dark Side*, 88.

46 Barton Gellman and Jo Becker, "A Different Understanding with the President," *Washington Post*, June 24, 2007.

47 Ibid.

48 *ex parte Quirin,* 317 U.S. 1 (1942). The Court's per curiam decision was 8–0,

Justice Frank Murphy not participating. Two of the defendants, George John Dasch and Ernest Peter Burger, cooperated with U.S. authorities and President Roosevelt commuted their sentences, thirty years for Dasch, life imprisonment for Burger. In 1948 President Truman ordered their release from prison and they were deported to the American occupation zone of Germany.

49 Eichenwald, *500 Days*, 145.

50 Memorandum Opinion, Office of the Legal Counsel, "Legality of the Use of Military Commissions to Try Terrorists," November 6, 2001. The memorandum was signed by Deputy Attorney General Patrick F. Philbin, but it was written by Yoo.

51 Eichenwald, *500 Days*, 152.

52 Ibid., 154.

53 Gellman and Becker, "A Different Understanding with the President."

54 Condoleezza Rice, *No Higher Honor* (New York: Crown, 2011), 106.

55 *PPPUS-GWB, 2001,* Vol. 2, Exchange with Reporters Upon Arrival at Waco, Texas, November 13, 2001, 1404–6.

56 Ibid.

57 Ibid., Remarks with President Putin at Crawford High School, November 15, 2001, 1413.

58 Ibid., Exchange with Reporters Upon Arrival in Waco, November 13, 2001, 1405.

59 Karen Hughes, *Ten Minutes from Normal* (New York: Viking, 2004), 285.

60 *PPPUS-GWB, 2001,* Vol. 2, Remarks with President Putin at Crawford High School, November 15, 2001, 1417.

61 Tommy Franks, with Malcolm McConnell, *American Soldier* (New York: HarperCollins, 2004), 346–56.

62 Peter Baker, *Days of Fire: Bush and Cheney in the White House* (New York: Doubleday, 2013), 185–86.

63 Frum, *The Right Man*, 224.

64 Ibid., 233.

65 State of the Union Address, January 29, 2002, http://georgewbush-white house.archives.gov.

66 I am indebted to Robert Draper for this expression. *Dead Certain: The Presidency of George W. Bush* (New York: Free Press, 2007), 169.

Chapter Twelve: The Torture Trail

The epigraph is a question George W. Bush put to George Tenet shortly after the arrest of Abu Zubaydah, a key lieutenant of Osama bin Laden. James Risen, *State of War: The Secret History of the CIA and the Bush Administration* (New York: Free Press, 2006), 22.

1 *New York Times*, February 13, 2002.

2 *Die Welt*, February 6, 2002.

3 James Mann, *Rise of the Vulcans: The History of Bush's War Cabinet* (New York: Viking, 2004), 321.

4 Condoleezza Rice, *No Higher Honor* (New York: Crown, 2011), 151.

5 Robert Draper, *Dead Certain: The Presidency of George W. Bush* (New York: Free Press, 2007), 169.

6 Howard Kurtz, "Straight Man," *Washington Post Magazine*, May 19, 2002.

7 Military Order of November 13, 2001, 66 *Federal Register*, November 16, 2001, 57831–36.

8 Donald Rumsfeld, *Known and Unknown* (New York: Sentinel, 2011), 557, 565–66.

9 Department of Defense, Press Conference, Donald Rumsfeld, December 27, 2001.

10 General Richard B. Myers, *Eyes on the Horizon: Serving on the Front Lines of National Security* (New York: Threshold, 2009), 200. Also see Douglas J. Feith, *War and Decision: Inside the Pentagon at the Dawn of the War on Terrorism* (New York: HarperCollins, 2009), 160.

11 Kurt Eichenwald, *500 Days: Secrets and Lies in the Terror Wars* (New York: Touchstone, 2012), 196–97.

12 Alan Crowell, "U.S. Thumbs Its Nose at Rights, Amnesty Says," *New York Times*, May 26, 2005. Lord Johan Steyn, a judge on Britain's highest court (Queen's Bench), got it exactly right. In a memorial lecture at the British Institute of International and Comparative Law, he said, "The purpose of holding the prisoners at Guantánamo Bay was and is to put them beyond the rule of law, beyond the protection of any court, and at the mercy of the victors." November 26, 2005.

13 Department of Defense News Briefing by Secretary Rumsfeld and General Myers, January 11, 2002.

14 Office of Legal Counsel, Department of Justice, "Application of Treaties and Laws to al Qaeda and Taliban Detainees," January 9, 2002, in Karen J. Greenberg and Joshua L. Dratel, *The Torture Papers: The Road to Abu Ghraib* (New York: Cambridge University Press, 2005), 38–79.

15 Memorandum for Chairman of the Joint Chiefs of Staff, January 19, 2002, in Greenberg and Dratel, eds., *The Torture Papers*, 80. Rumsfeld added that "The Combatant Commanders shall, in detaining Al Qaeda and Taliban individuals under control of the Defense Department, treat them humanely and, *to the extent appropriate and consistent with military necessity*, in a manner consistent with the principles of the Geneva Conventions of 1949." (Emphasis added.)

16 Myers, *Eyes on the Horizon*, 203.

17 "Schlesinger Report: Final Report of the Independent Commission to Review DoD Detainment Operations," in Greenberg and Dratel, eds., *The Torture Papers*, 947.

18 David Hackett Fischer, *Washington's Crossing* (New York: Oxford University Press, 2004), 379.

19 General Orders No. 100, *Instructions for the Government of Armies of the United States in the Field*, Arts. 15, 16, 49, 56, 75, 80 (Washington, D.C.: War Department, 1863).

20 Army Field Manual 30–15, *Military Intelligence Examination of Enemy Personnel* 5 (Washington, D.C.: War Department, 1943).

21 "In addition," said MacArthur, "I have directed the forces under my command to abide by the detailed provisions of the prisoner of war convention." Joseph P. Bailke, "United Nations Peace Operations: Applicable Norms and the Application of the Law of Armed Conflict," 50 *Air Force Law Review* (2001), 50.

22 84th Congress, 1st Session, U.S. Senate, Committee on Foreign Relations, *Geneva Conventions for the Protection of War Victims*, Executive Report No. 9, page 32.

23 At the end of the Gulf War, the International Committee of the Red Cross said the treatment of POWs by U.S. forces was "the best compliance with the GPW [the third Geneva Convention] in any conflict in history." Department of Defense, Conduct of the Persian Gulf War, Final Report to Congress, Appendix L (1992).

24 The War Crimes Act passed the Senate unanimously on August 2, 1996, and by voice vote (no roll call) in the House on July 29. It was signed into law by President Clinton, August 21, 1996. Pub. Law 104-192; 110 Stat. 2104; 18 U.S.C. 2441.

25 Myers, *Eyes on the Horizon*, 202, 204.

26 Jane Mayer interview with Richard Armitage, in Mayer, *The Dark Side*, 125.

27 Karen DeYoung, *Soldier: The Life of Colin Powell* (New York: Alfred A. Knopf, 2008), 365.

28 Eichenwald, *500 Days*, 218.

29 DeYoung, *Soldier*, 369.

30 Ibid.

31 Joseph Margulies, *Guantánamo and the Abuse of Presidential Power* (New York: Simon & Schuster, 2006), 72.

32 Memorandum, William H. Taft IV to John C. Yoo, January 11, 2002, U.S. Department of State.

33 Alberto R. Gonzales, Memorandum for the President, "Decision re Application of the Geneva Convention on Prisoners of War to the Conflict with al Qaeda and the Taliban," January 25, 2002, in Greenberg and Dratel, eds., *The Torture Papers*, 118–21.

34 Ibid.

35 Rowen Scarborough, "Powell Wants Detainees to Be Declared POWs," *Washington Times*, January 26, 2002.

36 DeYoung, *Soldier*, 370.

37 Eichenwald, *500 Days*, 229; DeYoung, *Soldier*, 370–71.

38 Myers, *Eyes on the Horizon*, 205.

39 Rumsfeld, *Known and Unknown*, 565.
40 Myers, *Eyes on the Horizon*, 205–6.
41 Eichenwald, *500 Days*, 230.
42 Katharine Seeley and David Sanger, "A Nation Challenged: Bush Reconsiders Stand on Treating Captives of War," *New York Times*, January 28, 2002.
43 DeYoung, *Soldier*, 371.
44 Presidential Order, "Humane Treatment of al Qaeda and Taliban Detainees," February 7, 2007, in Greenberg and Dratel, eds., *The Torture Papers*, 134–35.
45 Jack Goldsmith, *The Terror Presidency: Law and Judgment Inside the Bush Administration* (New York: W. W. Norton, 2007), 375.
46 *Hamdan v. Rumsfeld*, 548 U.S. 557, 631 (2006).
47 Dana Priest and Barton Gellman, "U.S. Denies Abuse but Defends Interrogations," *Washington Post*, December 26, 2002.
48 Article 3, "Convention Against Torture and Other Cruel, Inhumane or Degrading Treatment or Punishment," December 10, 1984, 1465 U.N.T.S. 85, S. Treaty Doc. No. 100–20.
49 United Nations, Universal Declaration of Human Rights.
50 Article 7, International Covenant on Civil and Political Rights.
51 Ronald Reagan, Message to Congress, May 20, 1988.
52 101st Congress, 2nd Session, *Congressional Record*, October 27, 1990, 517486.
53 Ibid., 5174487.
54 Ibid., 5174891.
55 Public Law 105-227 2242(a) (1998).
56 Department of Justice, Office of Legal Counsel, Memorandum for William J. Haynes II, General Counsel, Department of Defense, "The President's power as Commander in Chief to transfer captured terrorists to control and custody of foreign nations," March 13, 2002.
57 Ron Suskind, *The One Percent Doctrine: Deep Inside America's Pursuit of Its Enemies Since 9/11* (New York: Simon & Schuster, 2006), 116.
58 George W. Bush, *Decision Points* (New York: Crown, 2010), 169.
59 James Risen, *State of War: The Secret History of the CIA and the Bush Administration* (New York: Free Press, 2006), 22.
60 G. W. Bush, *Decision Points*, 169.
61 Ibid.
62 Ibid.
63 Anthony Lewis, "Making Torture Legal," *New York Review of Books*, July 15, 2004.
64 Department of Justice, Office of Legal Counsel, Memorandum for Alberto R. Gonzales, Counsel to the President, August 1, 2002, "Standards of Conduct for Interrogation Under 18 U.S.C. § 2340-2340A," reprinted in Greenberg and Dratel, eds., *The Torture Papers*, 172–222.
65 I am indebted to Jane Mayer for this formulation. *The Dark Side*, 171.

66 Senate Select Committee on Intelligence, *The CIA Torture Report: Unclassi-fied: Findings and Conclusions* (Washington, D.C.: United States Senate, 2014).

Chapter Thirteen: Waging Aggressive War: The Prelude

The epigraph is from President George W. Bush's address to the nation delivered in Cincinnati, October 7, 2002. *PPPUS-GWB, 2002,* Vol. 2, 1751–57.

1 George W. Bush, *Decision Points* (New York: Crown, 2010), 229.

2 Ibid., 234.

3 The CNN/*USA Today*/Gallup poll was taken January 11–14, 2002. Also see Bruce Morton, "Selling an Iraq–al Qaeda Connection," CNN.com.

4 Tommy Franks, with Malcolm McConnell, *American Soldier* (New York: HarperCollins, 2004), 369.

5 Ibid., 372–73.

6 Karen DeYoung, *Soldier: The Life of Colin Powell* (New York: Alfred A. Knopf, 2006), 377.

7 Hearing of the House International Relations Committee, State Department Budget, February 6, 2002, Federal News Service transcript.

8 Franks, *American Soldier*, 369–77.

9 Dick Cheney, *In My Time* (New York: Threshold, 2011), 371.

10 Ibid., 372–73.

11 Ibid., 371.

12 Ibid., 379.

13 *PPPUS-GWB, 2002,* Vol. 1, 444.

14 Bob Woodward, *Plan of Attack* (New York: Simon & Schuster, 2004), 115.

15 The Goldwater-Nichols Act, Public Law 99-433, 10 U.S.C. 162, was signed into law by President Reagan, October 1, 1986.

16 *PPPUS-GWB, 2002,* Vol. 1, Interview with the United Kingdom ITV Network, April 4, 2002, 556.

17 Ibid., News Conference with Prime Minister Tony Blair, April 6, 2002, 564 65.

18 Michael R. Gordon and General Bernard E. Trainor, *Cobra II: The Inside Story of the Invasion and Occupation of Iraq* (New York: Pantheon, 2006), 50.

19 Ibid., 50–51.

20 *PPPUS-GWB, 2002,* Vol. 1, News Conference with Chancellor Gerhard Schroeder, Berlin, May 22, 2002, 851. (Emphasis added.)

21 Ibid., News Conference with President Jacques Chirac, Paris, May 26, 2002, 901. (Emphasis added.)

22 Ibid., News Conference with President Putin, Moscow, May 24, 2002, 861.

23 Condoleezza Rice, *No Higher Honor* (New York: Crown, 2011), 173–75.

24 Woodward, *Plan of Attack*, 131.

25 *PPPUS-GWB, 2002,* Vol. 1, Commencement Address at the United States Military Academy, June 1, 2002, 917–21. (Emphasis added.)

26 Elisabeth Bumiller, "U.S. Must Act First to Battle Terror," *New York Times*, June 2, 2002.

27 Scott McClellan, *What Happened: Inside the Bush White House and Washington's Culture of Deception* (New York: PublicAffairs, 2008), 134.

28 Gordon and Trainor, *Cobra II*, 52.

29 Richard Haass, *War of Necessity, War of Choice: A Memoir of Two Iraq Wars* (New York: Simon & Schuster, 2009), 213–14.

30 *The Sunday Times* (London), May 1, 2005.

31 Alastair Campbell, *The Blair Years: The Alastair Campbell Diaries* (New York: Alfred A. Knopf, 2007), 530.

32 Franks, *American Soldier*, 392–93.

33 Ibid., 393.

34 Cheney, *In My Time*, 386.

35 Franks, *American Soldier*, 393.

36 DeYoung, *Soldier*, 401–2.

37 G. W. Bush, *Decision Points*, 238.

38 Peter Baker, *Days of Fire: Bush and Cheney in the White House* (New York: Doubleday, 2013), 208.

39 Woodward, *Plan of Attack*, 152.

40 Senator Chuck Hagel interview on *Face the Nation*, CBS, August 4, 2002, Federal News Service transcript.

41 Brent Scowcroft interview on *Face the Nation*, CBS, August 4, 2002, Federal News Service transcript.

42 Brent Scowcroft, "Don't Attack Saddam," *Wall Street Journal*, August 15, 2002.

43 Woodward, *Plan of Attack*, 160.

44 Baker, *Days of Fire*, 209.

45 G. W. Bush, *Decision Points*, 238.

46 Cheney, *In My Time*, 388.

47 Rice, *No Higher Honor*, 179.

48 James Baker, "The Right Way to Change a Regime," *New York Times*, August 25, 2002.

49 DeYoung, *Soldier*, 406.

50 Woodward, *Plan of Attack*, 161.

51 For the text of Cheney's remarks, see "Vice President Speaks to VFW 103rd National Convention," White House press release, August 26, 2002.

52 Thomas E. Ricks, *Fiasco: The American Military Adventure in Iraq* (New York: Penguin, 2006), 50.

53 George Tenet, *At the Center of the Storm: My Years at the CIA* (New York: HarperCollins, 2007), 315–16.

54 The CNN/*USA Today*/Gallup poll was published on September 5, 2002, reflecting sentiment gathered the week before.

55 Elisabeth Bumiller, "Traces of Terror: The Strategy," *New York Times*, September 7, 2002.

56 Elisabeth Bumiller, *Condoleezza Rice: An American Life* (New York: Random House, 2007), 191.

57 Letter, George W. Bush to Dennis Hastert, "America Intends to Lead," September 4, 2002, http://www.edition.cnn.com/2002/ALLPOLITICS/09/04/bush.letter/index.html.

58 Michael Isikoff and David Corn, *Hubris: The Inside Story of Spin, Scandal, and the Selling of the Iraq War* (New York: Crown, 2006), 24.

59 Ibid., 25.

60 *PPPUS-GWB, 2002,* Vol. 2, Remarks Following a Meeting with Congressional Leaders, September 4, 2002, 1523–25.

61 Michael Gordon and Judith Miller, "U.S. Says Hussein Intensifies Quest for A-Bomb Parts," *New York Times*, September 8, 2002.

62 *Meet the Press*, NBC, September 8, 2002.

63 *Late Edition*, CBS, September 8, 2002.

64 *PPPUS-GWB, 2002,* Vol. 2, Address to the Nation from Ellis Island, September 11, 2002, 1570–72.

65 George W. Bush, *Decision Points*, 20. Also see Ari Fleischer, *Taking Heat: The President, the Press, and My Years at the White House* (New York: William Morrow, 2005), 282.

66 Robert Draper, *Dead Certain: The Presidency of George W. Bush* (New York: Free Press, 2007), 183.

67 *PPPUS-GWB, 2002,* Vol. 2, Address to the United Nations, September 12, 2002, 1572–76.

68 Karen DeYoung and Mike Allen, "Bush Urges UN to Join Action Against Iraq," *Washington Post*, September 13, 2002.

69 *PPPUS-GWB, 2002,* Vol. 2, The President's Radio Address, September 14, 2002, 1582–83.

70 *PPPUS-GWB, 2002,* Vol. 2, Remarks Prior to Discussions with Prime Minister Silvio Berlusconi, September 14, 2002, 1584–86.

71 *PPPUS-GWB, 2002,* Vol. 2, Remarks to Employees of Sears Manufacturing Company in Davenport, Iowa, September 16, 2002, 1586–92.

72 *PPPUS-GWB, 2002,* Vol. 2, Remarks at a Luncheon for Representative Jim Nussel, September 16, 2002, 1592–98.

73 *PPPUS-GWB, 2002,* Vol. 2, Remarks at a Luncheon for Senatorial Candidate Lamar Alexander, September 17, 2002, 1601–7.

74 Text of Proposed Resolution on Iraq, Reuters, September 19, 2002.

75 Brian Knowlton, "President Asks Congress to Back Force Against Iraq," *New York Times*, September 20, 2002.

76 McClellan, *What Happened*, 139–41.

77 *The National Security Strategy of the United States of America*, The White House, September 20, 2002.

78 Ibid.
79 I am indebted to Elisabeth Bumiller for this observation. *Condoleezza Rice*, 194.
80 The operative portions of H.J. Res. 114–5 read as follows:

SEC. 3. AUTHORIZATION FOR USE OF UNITED STATES ARMED FORCES.

(a) AUTHORIZATION—The President is authorized to use the Armed Forces of the United States as he determines to be necessary and appropriate in order to—

(1) defend the national security of the United States against the continuing threat posed by Iraq; and

(2) enforce all relevant United Nations Security Council resolutions regarding Iraq.

(b) PRESIDENTIAL DETERMINATION—In connection with the exercise of the authority granted in subsection (a) to use force the President shall, prior to such exercise or as soon thereafter as may be feasible, but no later than 48 hours after exercising such authority, make available to the Speaker of the House of Representatives and the President pro tempore of the Senate his determination that—

(1) reliance by the United States on further diplomatic or other peaceful means alone either (A) will not adequately protect the national security of the United States against the continuing threat posed by Iraq or (B) is not likely to lead to enforcement of all relevant United Nations Security Council resolutions regarding Iraq; and

(2) acting pursuant to this joint resolution is consistent with the United States and other countries continuing to take the necessary actions against international terrorist and terrorist organizations, including those nations, organizations, or persons who planned, authorized, committed or aided the terrorist attacks that occurred on September 11, 2001.

(c) WAR POWERS RESOLUTION REQUIREMENTS—

(1) SPECIFIC STATUTORY AUTHORIZATION—Consistent with section 8(a)(1) of the War Powers Resolution, the Congress declares that this section is intended to constitute specific statutory authorization within the meaning of section 5(b) of the War Powers Resolution.

(2) APPLICABILITY OF OTHER REQUIREMENTS—Nothing in this joint resolution supersedes any requirement of the War Powers Resolution.

81 *PPPUS-GWB, 2002,* Vol. 2, Remarks Announcing Bipartisan Agreement on Joint Resolution to Authorize Force Against Iraq, October 2, 2002, 1707–8.
82 Director of Central Intelligence, White Paper, "Iraq's Weapons of Mass Destruction," October 2002. (Emphasis added.)
83 On July 9, 2004, the Senate Select Committee on Intelligence issued a 511-page report documenting the errors in the CIA's NIE. "Most of the major key judg-

ments were either overstated, or were not supported by, the underlying intelligence reporting." The committee report was unanimous. All nine Republicans and eight Democrats agreed that the CIA had erred. "In the end, what the President and the Congress used to send the country to war was information provided by the intelligence community, and that information was flawed," said Senator Pat Roberts of Kansas, the committee's Republican chairman. Douglas Jehl, "Judging Intelligence: The Report: Senators Assail CIA Judgments on Iraq's Arms as Deeply Flawed," *New York Times*, July 10, 2004.

84 Ibid.

85 Paul R. Pillar, "Intelligence, Policy, and the War in Iraq," *Foreign Affairs* (March/April 2006).

86 CNN/*USA Today*/Gallup poll, October 3–6, 2002, Gallup News Service, Lydia Saad, "Top Ten Findings About Public Opinion and Iraq."

87 *PPPUS-GWB, 2002,* Vol. 2, Address to the Nation on Iraq, October 7, 2002, 1751–57.

88 *Congressional Record*, 107th Congress, 2d Session, S10234.

89 Ibid., S10262.

90 *PPPUS-GWB, 2002,* Vol. 2, Remarks on House of Representatives Action on Resolution Authorizing the Use of Military Force against Iraq, October 10, 2002, 1778.

91 Elisabeth Bumiller and Carl Hulse, "Threats and Responses: Bush Will Use Congress Vote to Press U.N.," *New York Times*, October 12, 2002.

Chapter Fourteen: Invasion

The epigraph is from General H. Norman Schwarzkopf's commencement address at the United States Military Academy, May 15, 1991. The address is available on YouTube.

1 Ari Fleischer, *Taking Heat: The President, the Press, and My Years at the White House* (New York: William Morrow, 2005), 285.

2 Thomas E. Ricks, *Fiasco: The American Military Adventure in Iraq* (New York: Penguin, 2006), 66.

3 Donald Rumsfeld, *Known and Unknown* (New York: Sentinel, 2011), 434.

4 Bob Woodward, *Plan of Attack* (New York: Simon & Schuster, 2004), 207–8.

5 Ricks, *Fiasco*, 74.

6 Rumsfeld, *Known and Unknown*, 480.

7 Woodward, *Plan of Attack*, 206.

8 Donald Rumsfeld, "Iraq: An Illustrative List of Potential Problems to Be Considered and Addressed," October 15, 2002, the Rumsfeld Archive, online.

9 Rumsfeld, *Known and Unknown*, 481.

10 *PPPUS-GWB, 2002,* Vol. 2, Remarks at Cedar Rapids, Iowa, November 4, 2002, 2012–19. The other nineteen speeches can be found at pages 1904–2036.

11 For the text of Security Council Resolution 1441, see *The Iraq Papers*, John

Ehrenberg, J. Patrice McSherry, José Ramós Sánchez, and Caroleen Marji Sayej, eds. (New York: Oxford University Press, 2010), 96–99.

12 George W. Bush, *Decision Points* (New York: Crown, 2010), 241.

13 *PPPUS-GWB, 2002,* Vol. 2, Remarks on the Passage of a United Nations Security Council Resolution on Iraq, November 8, 2002, 2053–54.

14 Rumsfeld, *Known and Unknown*, 439–40.

15 Tommy Franks, with Malcolm McConnell, *American Soldier* (New York: HarperCollins, 2004), 410–11.

16 Rumsfeld, *Known and Unknown*, 452.

17 Thomas E. Ricks, "Projection on Fall of Hussein Disputed: Ground Forces Chiefs and Pentagon at Odds," *Washington Post*, December 18, 2002.

18 Thomas E. Ricks, "Gen. Schwarzkopf Is Skeptical About U.S. Action in Iraq," *Washington Post*, January 29, 2003.

19 *New York Times*, December 8, 2002.

20 *PPPUS-GWB, 2002,* Vol. 2, President's Radio Address, December 7, 2002, 2170–71.

21 Colin Powell, News Conference, December 19, 2002, *New York Times*, December 20, 2002. To accompany Powell's press conference, the State Department released a list of "Illustrative Examples of Omissions from the Iraqi Declaration to the United Nations Security Council." These included:
   • Failure to fully list all anthrax on hand.
   • Failure to explain missile fuel on hand.
   • Failure to acknowledge "efforts to procure uranium from Niger. Why is the Iraqi regime hiding their uranium procurement?"
   • No information about VX nerve gas. "What is the Iraqi regime trying to hide by not providing this information?"
   • "The Iraqi declaration provides no information about its mobile biological weapons agent facilities. What is the Iraqi regime trying to hide about their mobile biological facilities?"
   "Threats and Responses: U.S. Catalogs 'Material Omissions,'" *New York Times*, December 20, 2002.

22 Personal interview, January 29, 2014. Also see Peter Baker, *Days of Fire: Bush and Cheney in the White House* (New York: Doubleday, 2013), 266.

23 George Tenet, *At the Center of the Storm: My Years at the CIA* (New York: HarperCollins, 2007), 359–62.

24 Peter Baker interview with John McLaughlin, in Baker, *Days of Fire*, 239.

25 Woodward, *Plan of Attack*, 249.

26 Tenet, *At the Center of the Storm*, 361–62.

27 Woodward, *Plan of Attack*, 249.

28 Ibid., 250.

29 G. W. Bush, *Decision Points*, 243.

30 *PPPUS-GWB, 2003,* Vol. 1, Remarks to the Troops at Fort Hood, Texas, January 3, 2003, 20–24.

31 Ari Fleischer, *Taking Heat*, 296.

32 Ibid., 296–97.
33 Woodward, *Plan of Attack*, 257–58.
34 Hans Blix, *Disarming Iraq* (New York: Pantheon, 2004), 111.
35 Dick Cheney, *In My Time* (New York: Threshold, 2011), 394.
36 Woodward, *Plan of Attack*, 267.
37 Karen DeYoung, *Soldier: The Life of Colin Powell* (New York: Alfred A. Knopf, 2006), 429–31.
38 Woodward, *Plan of Attack*, 270–71.
39 Ed Cray, *General of the Army: George C. Marshall, Soldier and Statesman* (New York: Cooper Square Press, 1990), 661.
40 DeYoung, *Soldier*, 431.
41 Julia Preston, "Threats and Responses: An Attack on Iraq Not Yet Justified," *New York Times*, January 20, 2003.
42 DeYoung, *Soldier*, 434.
43 Kurt Eichenwald, *500 Days: Secrets and Lies in the Terror Wars* (New York: Touchstone, 2012), 458–59.
44 *Encyclopaedia Britannica,* 11th ed. (New York: University of Cambridge Press, 1910), 190.

> The Book of Revelation, Chapter 20, verses 7–10, reads as follows:
> [7] And when the thousand years are expired, Satan shall be loosed out of his prison.
> [8] And shall go out to deceive the nations which are in the four quarters of the earth, Gog and Magog, to gather them together to battle: the number of whom is as the sand of the sea.
> [9] And they went up to the breadth of the earth, and compassed the camp of the saints about, and the beloved city: the fire came down from God out of heaven, and devoured them.
> [10] And the devil that deceived them was cast into the lake of fire and brimstone, where the beast and the false prophet are, and shall be tormented day and night for ever and ever.

45 Eichenwald, *500 Days*, 461.
46 Jim Henley, "Europe's Big Two Unite for Versailles Lovefest," *The Guardian*, January 23, 2003. Also see Eichenwald, *500 Days*, 571, and the sources cited therein.
47 *PPPUS-GWB, 2003,* Vol. 1, Exchange with Reporters, January 21, 2003, 70.
48 Department of Defense, January 22, 2003, news transcript, Rumsfeld Papers, online.
49 Blix, *Disarming Iraq*, 138–41.
50 Mohamed ElBaradei, "The Status of Nuclear Inspections in Iraq," International Atomic Energy Agency, Vienna, Austria, March 7, 2003.
51 DeYoung, *Soldier*, 439.
52 *PPPUS-GWB, 2003,* Vol. 1, State of the Union Address, January 28, 2003, 82–90.

53 Baker, *Days of Fire*, 243.
54 Rumsfeld, *Known and Unknown*, 453.
55 Kori Schake interview with Peter Baker, in Baker, *Days of Fire*, 243.
56 Alastair Campbell, *The Blair Years: The Alastair Campbell Diaries* (New York: Alfred A. Knopf, 2007), 660.
57 Bush's comments were recorded by David Manning, Blair's foreign policy adviser, and reported subsequently by Don Van Natta, Jr. in the *New York Times*, "Bush Was Set on Path to War, Memo by British Advisor Says," March 27, 2006.
58 Ibid.
59 *Newsweek* poll, Richard Wolffe and Daniel Klaidman, February 17, 2003.
60 Editorial, *Washington Post*, February 6, 2003; editorial, *New York Times*, February 6, 2003.
61 United Nations press release, February 5, 2003.
62 *New York Times*, February 11, 2003. Also see Peter Finn, "US-Europe Rift Widens over Iraq," *Washington Post*, February 11, 2003.
63 *New York Times*, February 15, 2003.
64 Ibid.
65 *San Francisco Chronicle*, February 13, 2003.
66 Robert C. Byrd, "We Stand Passively Mute," remarks to the Senate, February 12, 2003, reprinted in Ehrenberg et al., eds., *The Iraq Papers*, 102–5.
67 Senate Armed Services Committee Hearing, February 25, 2003.
68 Michael R. Gordon and General Bernard E. Trainor, *Cobra II: The Inside Story of the Invasion and Occupation of Iraq* (New York: Pantheon, 2006), 102.
69 House Budget Committee Hearing, February 27, 2003.
70 Andrew Bacevich, "Trigger Man," *American Conservative*, June 5, 2005.
71 Franks, *American Soldier*, 428–29.
72 Woodward, *Plan of Attack*, 331.
73 Franks, *American Soldier*, 429–30.
74 Woodward, *Plan of Attack*, 332.
75 *New York Times*, May 5, 2003.
76 *PPPUS-GWB, 2003,* Vol. 1, President's News Conference, March 6, 2003, 244–54.
77 For text of the resolution, see Ehrenberg et al., eds., *The Iraq Papers*, 143–45.
78 For the text of Blix's report, see ibid., 106–10. Also see Blix, *Disarming Iraq*, 208–10.
79 *New York Times*, March 8, 2003; Blix, *Disarming Iraq*, 210–11.
80 Eichenwald, *500 Days*, 488–89, and the sources cited therein.
81 The episode is recounted in Gordon and Trainor, *Cobra II*, 164, based on interviews with those who witnessed the showing.
82 Woodward, *Plan of Attack*, 347. Also see Fleischer, *Taking Heat*, 322–23.
83 Eichenwald, *500 Days*, 494.

84 Woodward, *Plan of Attack*, 358. Also see Campbell, *The Blair Years*, 678–79.

85 *PPPUS-GWB, 2003,* Vol. 1, President's News Conference with Prime Minister Barroso, President Aznar, and Prime Minister Blair, Azores, March 16, 2003, 267–74.

86 Fleischer, *Taking Heat*, 324–25.

87 Woodward, *Plan of Attack*, 365.

88 Ibid., 368–69.

89 *PPPUS-GWB, 2003,* Vol. 1, Address to the Nation on Iraq, March 17, 2003, 277–80.

90 Ibid., Letter to Congressional Leaders on Conclusion of Diplomatic Efforts with Regard to Iraq, March 18, 2003, 280.

91 House of Commons Debates, Iraq, March 18, 2003.

92 Baker, *Days of Fire*, 257; Woodward, *Plan of Attack*, 378–79.

93 Franks, *American Soldier*, 431; Baker, *Days of Fire*, 257.

94 Woodward, *Plan of Attack*, 379.

Chapter Fifteen: "Mission Accomplished"

The epigraph is from George W. Bush's speech on the flight deck of the USS *Abraham Lincoln*, May 1, 2003. *PPPUS-GWB, 2003,* Vol. 1, 410–13.

 1 *PPPUS-GWB, 2003,* Vol. 1, Address to the Nation on Iraq, March 19, 2003, 281–82.

 2 Tommy Franks, with Malcolm McConnell, *American Soldier* (New York: HarperCollins, 2004), 433.

 3 Donald Rumsfeld, *Known and Unknown* (New York: Sentinel, 2011), 499.

 4 Franks, *American Soldier*, 440–41.

 5 Dominique de Villepin, Address to the U.N. Security Council, March 19, 2003, reprinted in John Ehrenberg, J. Patrice McSherry, José Ramón Sánchez, and Caroleen Marji Sayej, eds., *The Iraq Papers* (New York: Oxford University Press, 2010), 151–54.

 6 Joschka Fischer address to the U.N. Security Council, March 19, 2003, in ibid., 154–57.

 7 Chinese Foreign Ministry statement on the War in Iraq, March 20, 2003, in ibid., 157.

 8 Vladimir Putin, press statement on Iraq, April 3, 2003, in ibid., 159–61.

 9 Kofi Annan, interview, Australian Broadcasting Company, September 16, 2004, in ibid., 161–62.

10 Todd S. Purdum, *A Time of Our Choosing: America's War with Iraq* (New York: Times Books, 2003), 119.

11 Bob Woodward, *State of Denial: Bush at War, Part III* (New York: Simon & Schuster, 2006), 154.

12 Alastair Campbell, *The Blair Years: The Alastair Campbell Diaries* (New York: Alfred A. Knopf, 2007), 685–86.

13 *PPPUS-GWB, 2003,* Vol. 1, Remarks at MacDill Air Force Base, Tampa, Florida, March 26, 2003, 297–300.
14 Ibid., Remarks at Camp Lejeune, North Carolina, April 3, 2003, 317–20.
15 Ari Fleischer, *Taking Heat: The President, the Press, and My Years in the White House* (New York: HarperCollins, 2005), 336–37.
16 Woodward, *State of Denial,* 155.
17 Franks, *American Soldier,* 517.
18 George W. Bush, *Decision Points* (New York: Crown, 2010), 250.
19 Peter Baker, *Days of Fire: Bush and Cheney in the White House* (New York: Doubleday, 2013), 265.
20 Terry H. Anderson, *Bush's Wars* (New York: Oxford University Press, 2011), 136; Thomas E. Ricks, *Fiasco: The American Military Adventure in Iraq* (New York: Penguin, 2006), 134.
21 *PPPUS-GWB, 2003,* Vol. 1, Videotaped Remarks to the Iraqi People, April 10, 2003, 330–31.
22 Frank Rich, "And Now, 'Operation Iraqi Looting,'" *New York Times,* April 27, 2003.
23 *New York Times,* April 12, 2003.
24 Ricks, *Fiasco,* 136.
25 Rich, "And Now, 'Operation Iraqi Looting,'" *New York Times,* April 27, 2003. On March 3, 2003, well before the invasion, *The Washington Post* carried a lengthy article by Guy Gugliotta warning of the possible looting. After the 1991 Gulf War, "Nine of the 13 regional museums in both north and south were raided by mobs who stole things straight from the cases. . . . Mesopotamian antiquities began flooding international art markets, a phenomenon virtually unknown before the war."
26 Donald Rumsfeld, "Beyond Nation-Building," remarks at the *Intrepid* Sea-Air-Space Museum, New York City, February 14, 2003.
27 Michael R. Gordon and General Bernard E. Trainor, *Cobra II: The Inside Story of the Invasion and Occupation of Iraq* (New York: Pantheon, 2006), 458–59; Lt. Gen. Ricardo S. Sanchez, *Wiser in Battle: A Soldier's Story* (New York: HarperCollins, 2008), 168.
28 Bill Sammon, *Misunderestimated: The President Battles Terrorism, Media Bias, and the Bush Haters* (New York: HarperCollins, 2004), 255–56.
29 Ibid., 261.
30 Ibid., 267.
31 Craig Unger, *Boss Rove: Inside Karl Rove's Secret Kingdom of Power* (New York: Scribner, 2012), 72.
32 *PPPUS-GWB, 2003,* Vol. 1, Address to the Nation from the USS *Abraham Lincoln,* May 1, 2003, 410–13.
33 Ricks, *Fiasco,* 145.
34 *PPPUS-GWB, 2003,* Vol. 1, Remarks to Employees of United Defense Industries, Santa Clara, California, May 2, 2003, 413–14.

35 Karl Rove, *Courage and Consequence* (New York: Threshold, 2010), 361–71.
36 National Security Presidential Directive 24, January 20, 2003. For a para-phrase of the text, see Douglas J. Feith, *War and Decision: Inside the Penta-gon at the Dawn of the War on Terrorism* (New York: HarperCollins, 2008), 616–17.
37 Rumsfeld, *Known and Unknown*, 488.
38 Personal interview with Donald Rumsfeld, March 31, 2014.
39 Rumsfeld, Memorandum for Secretaries of the Military Departments; Chair-man of the Joint Chiefs of Staff; Under Secretary of Defense for Policy; Under Secretary of Defense (Comptroller); Commander, U.S. Central Command; General Counsel, Department of Defense; Directors of the Defense Agencies; Directors of the DOD Field Activities, April 2, 2003, Rumsfeld Papers, online.
40 When Rumsfeld asked Garner what he proposed to do about de-Baathification, Garner said he would remove two people in each ministry and major government office—the top Baathist and the chief personnel of-ficer. Rumsfeld said, "That sounds fine with me until we get you a policy." Ricks, *Fiasco*, 105, 155.
41 *PPPUS-GWB, 2003,* Vol. 1, Address to the Nation on Iraq from the USS *Abraham Lincoln*, May 1, 2003, 411.
42 Rumsfeld, *Known and Unknown*, 498.
43 Woodward, *State of Denial*, 168–69.
44 Rumsfeld, *Known and Unknown*, 505.
45 Letter, Donald Rumsfeld to Andrew Card, April 24, 2003, Rumsfeld Papers, online.
46 Peter Baker interview with Paul Bremer, in Baker, *Days of Fire*, 220.
47 *PPPUS-GWB, 2003,* Vol. 1, Remarks on the Appointment of L. Paul Bremer as Presidential Envoy to Iraq, May 6, 2003, 440–41.
48 L. Paul Bremer, *My Year in Iraq* (New York: Simon & Schuster, 2006), 12.
49 Rumsfeld, *Known and Unknown*, 506.
50 Ibid., 506–7.
51 Ricks, *Fiasco*, 161.
52 Ricks, *Fiasco*, 163.
53 Sanchez, *Wiser in Battle*, 178.
54 Baker, *Days of Fire*, 273.
55 Ricks, *Fiasco*, 170.
56 *PPPUS-GWB, 2003,* Vol. 2, Exchange with Reporters, July 2, 2003, 815–19.
57 Robert Draper, *Dead Certain: The Presidency of George W. Bush* (New York: Free Press, 2007), 209.
58 G. W. Bush, *Decision Points*, 261.
59 Sanchez, *Wiser in Battle*, 227.
60 Ibid.
61 Frank Rich, *The Greatest Story Ever Sold* (New York: Penguin, 2006), 95.
62 Wolfowitz interview with Sam Tanenhaus in *Vanity Fair*, July 2003.

63 Tenet, *At the Center of the Storm: My Years at the CIA* (New York: Harper-Collins, 2007), 401–2.

64 Woodward, *State of Denial*, 218.

65 Ibid., 228.

66 Ibid., 337.

67 Tenet, *At the Center of the Storm*, 408; Woodward, *State of Denial*, 277.

68 David Kay at Senate Hearing, January 28, 2004, CNN.com, transcript.

69 Baker, *Days of Fire*, 308; Woodward, *State of Denial*, 289.

70 *Washington Post*, February 3, 2004.

71 *Meet the Press*, NBC, February 8, 2004, transcript.

72 Report of the Iraq Study Group, October 6, 2004.

73 icasualties.org, based on figures provided by the Department of Defense.

Chapter Sixteen: Four More Years

The epigraph is a statement Bush made to the Republican Governors Association on February 23, 2004. *PPPUS-GWB, 2004,* Vol. 1, 258.

 1 Karen DeYoung, *Soldier: The Life of Colin Powell* (New York: Alfred A. Knopf, 2006), 490–91.

 2 Ibid. (Italics in original.)

 3 Ed Cray, *General of the Army: George C. Marshall, Soldier and Statesman* (New York: Cooper Square Press, 1990), 144–45.

 4 Karen DeYoung interview with Alma Powell, in DeYoung, *Soldier*, 510.

 5 Peter Baker, *Days of Fire: Bush and Cheney in the White House* (New York: Doubleday, 2013), 230.

 6 G. W. Bush, *Decision Points* (New York: Crown, 2010), 90.

 7 Baker, *Days of Fire*, 331.

 8 Dick Cheney, *In My Time* (New York: Threshold, 2011), 417–18.

 9 Baker, *Days of Fire*, 282.

10 Cheney, *In My Time*, 418.

11 G. W. Bush, *Decision Points*, 86; Baker, *Days of Fire*, 285.

12 G. W. Bush, *Decision Points*, 87.

13 Ibid.

14 "Vatican Calls Prison Abuse a Bigger Blow to U.S. than Sept. 11," *USA Today*, May 12, 2004.

15 Colin Powell on *Larry King Live*, CNN, May 5, 2004; Edward Kennedy, "The Prisoner Abuse Resolution," May 10, 2004, *Congressional Record*, 108th Congress, 2nd Session, 55058.

16 Donald Rumsfeld, *Known and Unknown* (New York: Sentinel, 2011), 547.

17 G. W. Bush, *Decision Points*, 89.

18 Donald Rumsfeld, Resignation, May 9, 2003, Rumsfeld Papers, online.

19 G. W. Bush, *Decision Points*, 89.

20 Rumsfeld, *Known and Unknown*, 551.

21 Ibid.

22 Seymour M. Hersh, "The Gray Zone," *The New Yorker*, May 24, 2004.

23 "The Taguba Report," March 2004, in Karen J. Greenberg and Joshua L. Dratel, eds., *The Torture Papers: The Road to Abu Ghraib* (New York: Cambridge University Press, 2005), 417–18.

24 Ibid., 416.

25 Seymour M. Hersh, "The General's Report," *The New Yorker*, June 25, 2007. Also see Hersh, *Chain of Command: The Road from 9/11 to Abu Ghraib* (New York: HarperCollins, 2004).

26 Investigation of the Abu Ghraib Detention Facility and 205th Military Intelligence Brigade, Major General George B. Fay, Investigating Officer, in Greenberg and Dratel, eds., *The Torture Papers*, 1022.

27 AR15-6 Investigation of the Abu Ghraib Prison and the 205th Military Intelligence Brigade, Lieutenant General Anthony R. Jones, in Greenberg and Dratel, eds., *The Torture Papers*, 1007.

28 The Schlesinger Report, Final Report of the Independent Panel to Review DoD Detention Operations, August 2004, in Greenberg and Dratel, eds., *The Torture Papers*, 909.

29 Dan Fromkin, "General Accuses WH of War Crimes," *Washington Post*, June 18, 2008.

30 For O'Neill's views, see Ron Suskind, *The Price of Loyalty: George W. Bush, the White House, and the Education of Paul O'Neill* (New York: Simon & Schuster, 2004).

31 G. W. Bush, *Decision Points*, 85.

32 Bob Davis, "Bush Economic Aide Says the Cost of Iraq War May Top $100 Billion," *Wall Street Journal*, September 16, 2002.

33 George Tenet, *At the Center of the Storm: My Years at the CIA* (New York: HarperCollins, 2007), 480.

34 *PPPUS-GWB, 2004,* Vol. 1, Remarks on Resignation of George J. Tenet as Director of Central Intelligence, June 3, 2004, 985.

35 Baker, *Days of Fire*, 293.

36 Ibid., 294.

37 Robert Draper, *Dead Certain: The Presidency of George W. Bush* (New York: Free Press, 2007), 230. Dowd's emphasis.

38 *PPPUS-GWB, 2004,* Vol. 1, State of the Union Address, January 20, 2004, 81–89.

39 Laura Bush, *Spoken from the Heart* (New York: Scribner, 2010), 303.

40 *PPPUS-GWB, 2004,* Vol. 1, Remarks in the Roosevelt Room, February 24, 2004, 263–64.

41 Gallup poll, February 16–17, 2004, online.

42 Jane Mayer, *The Dark Side: The Inside Story of How the War on Terror Turned into a War on American Ideals* (New York: Doubleday, 2008), 289. Also see Baker, *Days of Fire*, 315–16. (Comey's emphasis.)

43 G. W. Bush, *Decision Points*, 172.

44   Mayer, *The Dark Side*, 290; Baker, *Days of Fire*, 316–17.
45   Unclassified Report on the President's Surveillance Program, 29.
46   G. W. Bush, *Decision Points*, 173–74.
47   Ibid., 174.
48   Thomas E. Ricks, *Fiasco: The American Military Adventure in Iraq* (New York: Penguin, 2006), 327.
49   Ibid., 326.
50   Ibid., 332–33.
51   Lt. Gen. Ricardo S. Sanchez, *Wiser in Battle: A Soldier's Story* (New York: HarperCollins, 2008), 332–33.
52   Ibid., 336.
53   Ibid., 350.
54   Ricks, *Fiasco*, 342.
55   Sanchez, *Wiser in Battle*, 371.
56   Bill Sammons, *Strategery: How George W. Bush Is Defeating Terrorists, Outwitting Democrats, and Confounding the Mainstream Media* (Washington, D.C.: Regnery, 2006), 23–24.
57   *PPPUS-GWB, 2004,* Vol. 1, The President's News Conference, April 13, 2004, 557.
58   Scott McClellan, *What Happened: Inside the Bush White House and Washington's Culture of Deception* (New York: PublicAffairs, 2008), 205.
59   *PPPUS-GWB, 2004,* Vol. 1, 568–69.
60   Ibid., 569.
61   Gallup poll, May 6, 2004.
62   Republicans gained seats in Arizona (2), Florida (2), Georgia (2), Texas (2), Colorado (1), North Carolina (1), and Nevada (1). They lost seats in Mississippi (1), Ohio (1), Oklahoma (1), and Indiana (1). The only Democratic state to gain an electoral vote was California (1). Losses occurred in New York (2), Pennsylvania (2), Connecticut (1), Wisconsin (1), Illinois (1), and Michigan (1).
63   Paul Alexander, *The Candidate: Behind John Kerry's Remarkable Run for the White House* (New York: Riverhead Books, 2004), 113.
64   G. W. Bush, *Decision Points*, 287.
65   Ibid., 288–89.
66   Ibid., 289.
67   Draper, *Dead Certain*, 237.
68   G. W. Bush, *Decision Points*, 288.
69   Karl Rove, *Courage and Consequence* (New York: Threshold, 2010), 381.
70   Draper, *Dead Certain*, 238.
71   Sammon, *Strategery*, 16.
72   *New York Times*, May 15, 2004.
73   *PPPUS-GWB, 2004,* Vol. 1, Remarks at Fort Lewis Washington, June 18, 2004, 1085; Draper, *Dead Certain*, 242.

74 Sammon, *Strategery*, 62.
75 Democratic Convention Proceedings.
76 Campaign 2004, "Race Too Close to Call," *USA Today*/CNN/Gallup poll results, March–November 2004.
77 Draper, *Dead Certain*, 240.
78 Republican Convention Proceedings.
79 Ibid.
80 *PPPUS-GWB, 2004*, Vol. 2, Remarks Accepting the Presidential Nomination at the Republican National Convention, September 2, 2004, 1855–63.
81 *USA Today*/CNN/Gallup poll results, March–November 2004.
82 Sammon, *Strategery*, 94.
83 Rove, *Courage and Consequence*, 389.
84 Sammon, *Strategery*, 168.
85 Draper, *Dead Certain*, 256.
86 Ibid.
87 Rove, *Courage and Consequence*, 392–93.
88 Evan Thomas and the Staff of *Newsweek, Election 2004: How Bush Won and What You Can Expect in the Future* (New York: PublicAffairs, 2004), 159.
89 Ronald Kessler, *Laura Bush: An Intimate Portrait of the First Lady* (New York: Broadway, 2007), 189.
90 Peter Baker interview with Matthew Dowd, in Baker, *Days of Fire*, 345.
91 Ibid., 346.
92 Cheney-Edwards debate, official transcript.
93 The *USA Today*/CNN/Gallup poll of registered voters, October 9, 2004, showed Bush and Kerry still even, this time at 48 percent.
94 Baker, *Days of Fire*, 349.
95 *PPPUS-GWB, 2004,* Vol. 3, Presidential Debate in Tempe, Arizona, October 13, 2004, 2479–2502.
96 Cheney, *In My Time*, 425.
97 Sammon, *Strategery*, 176–77.
98 G. W. Bush, *Decision Points*, 289.
99 Osama bin Laden audiotape, aired October 30, 2004, aljazeera.com, November 1, 2004.
100 Sammon, *Strategery*, 184.
101 *USA Today*/CNN/Gallup poll of likely voters, October 29–31, 2004.
102 *PPPUS-GWB, 2004,* Vol. 3, Remarks in Dallas, Texas, November 1, 2004, 2930–33.
103 Ibid., 2933–35, Exchange with Reporters in Crawford, Texas, November 2, 2004.
104 Rove, *Courage and Consequence*, 396.
105 Sammon, *Strategery*, 187.
106 Baker, *Days of Fire*, 357.

107 Sammon, *Strategery*, 264.

108 Michael Barone, *The Almanac of American Politics, 2006* (Washington, D.C.: National Journal, 2005), 21–36; CNN, "Election Results, 2004."

Chapter Seventeen: Katrina

The epigraph is a comment the president made to FEMA director Michael Brown upon inspecting hurricane damage in Mobile, Alabama, September 2, 2005. *PPPUS-GWB, 2005,* Vol. 2, 1385.

1 *PPPUS-GWB, 2004,* Vol. 3, Remarks at Victory Celebration, November 3, 2004, 2936–37.

2 Scott McClellan, *What Happened: Inside the Bush White House and Washington's Culture of Deception* (New York: PublicAffairs, 2008), 236.

3 Ibid., 237.

4 Ibid., 238.

5 *PPPUS-GWB, 2004,* Vol. 3, President's News Conference, November 4, 2004, 2943.

6 Karen DeYoung, *Soldier: The Life of Colin Powell* (New York: Alfred A. Knopf, 2006), 511.

7 Peter Baker, *Days of Fire: Bush and Cheney in the White House* (New York: Doubleday, 2013), 361.

8 Condoleezza Rice, *No Higher Honor* (New York: Crown, 2011), 293.

9 Deborah Schoeneman, "Condi's Slip," *New York,* April 26, 2004. The comment was made at a dinner party hosted by Philip Taubman, Washington bureau chief of *The New York Times,* and his wife, Felicity Barringer, a *Times* correspondent. Rice was overheard saying, "As I was telling my husb-," before she corrected herself.

10 Robert Draper, *Dead Certain: The Presidency of George W. Bush* (New York: Free Press, 2007), 256.

11 McClellan, *What Happened,* 243.

12 DeYoung, *Soldier,* 7.

13 For the text of Ashcroft's letter, see John Ashcroft, *Never Again* (New York: Center Street, 2006), 282–84.

14 *PPPUS-GWB, 2004,* Vol. 3, Remarks on the Nomination of Bernard B. Kerik to be Secretary of Homeland Security, December 3, 2004, 3037–38. For details of the White House security check, see Mike Allen, "On Kerik Nomination, White House Missed Red Flags," *Washington Post,* December 15, 2004.

15 Bill Sammon, *Strategy: How George Bush Is Defeating Terrorists, Outwitting Democrats, and Confounding the Mainstream Media* (Washington, D.C.: Regnery, 2006), 212.

16 Bob Woodward, *State of Denial: Bush at War, Part III* (New York: Simon & Schuster, 2006), 371.

17 *PPPUS-GWB, 2005,* Vol. 1, Inaugural Address, January 20, 2005, 66–69.
18 Draper, *Dead Certain,* 289.
19 Ibid., 290.
20 *PPPUS-GWB, 2005,* Vol. 1, State of the Union Address, February 2, 2005, 113–21.
21 Baker, *Days of Fire,* 380–81.
22 Tom Hamburger and Peter Wallsten, *One Party Country: The Republican Plan for Dominance in the 21st Century* (New York: Wiley, 2006), 201–6.
23 *Bush v. Gore,* 531 U.S. 98 (2000).
24 *Roe v. Wade,* 410 U.S. 113 (1973).
25 *Lawrence v. Texas,* 539 U.S. 588 (2003).
26 *Hamdi v. Rumsfeld,* 542 U.S. 507 (2004).
27 Ibid., 540.
28 *PPPUS-GWB, 2005,* Vol. 2, Address to the Nation Announcing the Nomination of John G. Roberts to be an Associate Justice of the Supreme Court, July 19, 2005, 1247–48.
29 Baker, *Days of Fire,* 404.
30 *PPPUS-GWB, 2005,* Vol. 2, President's News Conference, Crawford, Texas, August 11, 2005, 1326.
31 McClellan, *What Happened,* 279–80.
32 FEMA briefing, August 28, 2005, transcript, online.
33 Ibid.
34 *PPPUS-GWB, 2005,* Vol. 2, Remarks on Hurricane Katrina and the Iraqi Constitution, August 28, 2005, 1353–55.
35 Ibid., 1355–1365. Remarks in a discussion on Medicare in El Mirage, Arizona, August 29, 2005.
36 Christopher Cooper and Robert Block, *Disaster: Hurricane Katrina and the Failure of Homeland Security* (New York: Times Books, 2006), 160–61.
37 McClellan, *What Happened,* 276–77.
38 *PPPUS-GWB, 2005,* Vol. 2, Remarks on the 60th Anniversary of V-J Day in San Diego, California, August 30, 2005, 1373–78.
39 Douglas Brinkley, *The Great Deluge: Hurricane Katrina, New Orleans, and the Mississippi Gulf Coast* (New York: HarperCollins, 2006), 339.
40 David D. Kirkpatrick and Scott Shana, "Ex-FEMA Chief Tells of Frustration and Chaos," *New York Times,* September 5, 2005.
41 Brinkley, *The Great Deluge,* 394.
42 McClellan, *What Happened,* 274.
43 Brinkley, *The Great Deluge,* 406.
44 Ibid., 407.
45 McClellan, *What Happened,* 281.
46 Howard Fineman, "A Storm-Tossed Boss," *Newsweek,* September 19, 2005.
47 *New York Times,* September 1, 2005.

48   McClellan, *What Happened*, 283.
49   Michael D. Brown, testimony, Senate Homeland Security and Government Affairs Committee, February 10, 2006. Also see "An Early Alarm from New Orleans," *New York Times*, February 10, 2006.
50   *PPPUS-GWB, 2005,* Vol. 2, Remarks on the Aftermath of Hurricane Katrina in Mobile, Alabama, September 2, 2005, 1384–85.
51   Ibid.
52   Baker, *Days of Fire*, 411.
53   On page 413 of *Days of Fire*, Peter Baker quotes Bush as saying that if he sent federal troops without a request from Blanco, it "could unleash holy hell" in the South. "I wanted to overrule them all. But at the time I worried that the consequences could be a constitutional crisis, and possibly a political insurrection as well." See G. W. Bush, *Decision Points*, 321.
54   Brinkley, *The Great Deluge*, 568.
55   Peter Baker interview with Governor Blanco, in Baker, *Days of Fire*, 412–13.
56   G. W. Bush, *Decision Points*, 323.
57   *PPPUS-GWB, 2005,* Vol. 2, President's Radio Address, September 3, 2005, 1391–93.
58   Pervaze A. Sheikh, "The Impact of Hurricane Katrina on Biological Resources," Congressional Research Service.
59   G. W. Bush, *Decision Points*, 310.
60   CNN/*USA Today*/Gallup poll, George W. Bush Monthly Approval Ratings, online.
61   Peter Baker interview with Steve Schmidt, in Baker, *Days of Fire*, 414.
62   McClellan, *What Happened*, 290–91.

Chapter Eighteen: Perils of a Second Term

The epigraph is from President Bush's signing statement overturning the McCain anti-torture amendment, December 30, 2005, *PPPUS-GWB, 2005,* Vol. 2, 1901–3.
   1   George W. Bush, *Decision Points* (New York: Crown, 2010), 98.
   2   *PPPUS-GWB, 2005,* Vol. 2, Remarks Announcing the Nomination of John Roberts, September 5, 2005, 1395. (Judicial scholars will recognize the president's error. He should have said "Chief Justice of the United States.")
   3   Day One of Roberts Hearings, *Washington Post*, September 13, 2005, transcript.
   4   *PPPUS-GWB, 2005,* Vol. 2, Remarks Announcing the Nomination of Harriet E. Miers, October 4, 2005, 1502–4.
   5   *Weekly Standard* website, October 4, 2005.
   6   *Washington Post*, October 7, 2005.
   7   George Will, "Can This Nomination Be Justified?," *Washington Post*, October 5, 2005.

8 *PPPUS-GWB, 2005,* Vol. 2, The President's Radio Address, October 8, 2005, 1535–36.

9 Ibid. Interview with Matt Lauer on the *Today* show, NBC, October 11, 2005, 1539–40.

10 Bill Sammon, *Strategery: How George Bush Is Defeating Terrorists, Outwitting Democrats, and Confounding the Mainstream Media* (Washington, D.C.: Regnery, 2006), 300. In his memoirs, Bush wrote that he put his friend in an impossible situation. "If I had it to do over again, I would not have thrown Harriet to the wolves of Washington." *Decision Points*, 101.

11 Mark Stefanski, "Alito Disavows Conservative Alumni Group," *Daily Princetonian*, January 13, 2006.

12 Peter Baker, *Days of Fire: Bush and Cheney in the White House* (New York: Doubleday, 2013), 426.

13 Peter Baker, "Bush Vows to Keep Focus on His Political Agenda," *Washington Post*, October 29, 2005.

14 *PPPUS-GWB, 2005,* Vol. 2, Remarks on Resignation of the Vice President's Chief of Staff, I. Lewis Libby, October 28, 2005, 1625.

15 Dan Fromkin, "The Cloud over Cheney," *Washington Post*, February 21, 2002.

16 *PPPUS-GWB, 2007,* Vol. 1, Interview with Members of the White House Press Pool in Heilgendamm, Germany, June 6, 2007, 697.

17 United States Court of Appeals, D.C. Circuit, *United States v. I. Lewis Libby*, Case 07-3036, July 2, 2007.

18 G. W. Bush, *Decision Points*, 103.

19 Ibid., 104.

20 *PPPUS-GWB, 2007,* Vol. 2, Statement on Granting Executive Clemency to I. Lewis Libby, July 2, 2007, 908–9.

21 G. W. Bush, *Decision Points*, 105.

22 Scott McClellan, *What Happened: Inside the Bush White House and Washington's Culture of Deception* (New York: PublicAffairs, 2008), 216.

23 Ibid., 218.

24 Ibid., 297.

25 American military casualties in Iraq:

	Killed	Wounded
2003	580	2607
2004	906	7813
2005	897	5942

Source: http://icasualties.org/Iraq

26 "Bush Reaches New Lows in Washington Post-ABC Poll," *Washington Post*, November 4, 2005.

27 McCain Torture Amendment, Senate Amendment 1977 to HR 2863, Department of Defense authorization bill for the fiscal year ending September 30, 2006, July 24, 2005, 109th Congress, 1st session.

28 Baker, *Days of Fire*, 428.
29 Letter, General John Shalikashvili et al. to Senator John McCain, October 2, 2005, posted on McCain's website October 3, 2005, and published in *Executive Intelligence Review*, October 14, 2005.
30 Letter, Colin Powell to John McCain, October 5, 2004, *Executive Intelligence Review*, October 14, 2005.
31 Powell on *Larry King Live*, October 18, 2005 extract, donklephant.com/2005 /10/19/powell-on-mccain/.
32 McCain statement introducing Senate amendment 1977, October 5, 2005, http://www.mccain.senate.gov/public/index.cfm/speeches.
33 Press briefing with Scott McClellan, October 5, 2005, *The American Presidency Project*, John T. Wooley and Gerhard Peters, eds., University of California, Santa Barbara.
34 McCain Closing Statement, Senate Amendment, 1977, October 5, 2005.
35 Eric Schmitt, "White House Seeks Exception in Abuse Ban," *New York Times*, October 25, 2005.
36 Charlie Savage, "McCain Fights Exception in Torture Ban," *Boston Globe*, October 26, 2005.
37 Dana Priest, "CIA Holds Terror Suspect in Secret Prisons," *Washington Post*, November 2, 2005.
38 Jane Mayer, *The Dark Side: The Inside Story How the War on Terror Turned Into a War on American Ideals* (New York: Doubleday, 2008), 320.
39 *PPPUS-GWB, 2005,* Vol. 2, President's New Conference in Panama City, Panama, November 7, 2005, 1667–71.
40 *Hamdan v. Rumsfeld* 548 U.S. 577 (2006).
41 Jack Murtha news conference, U.S. Capitol, November 17, 2005, Federal News Service transcript.
42 Sammon, *Strategery*, 321.
43 *PPPUS-GWB, 2005,* Vol. 2, Exchange with Reporters in Beijing, November 20, 2005, 1751–56.
44 Ibid.
45 Dana Priest and Robin Wright, "Cheney Fights for Detainee Policy," *Washington Post*, November 7, 2005.
46 *PPPUS-GWB, 2005,* Vol. 2, Remarks on the War on Terror at the United States Naval Academy, November 30, 2005, 1782–90.
47 Ibid., Remarks to the Council on Foreign Relations, December 7, 2005, 1820–27.
48 Ibid., Remarks to the World Affairs Council of Philadelphia, December 12, 2005, 1836–49.
49 Ibid., Remarks to the Woodrow Wilson International Center for Scholars, Washington, D.C., December 14, 2005, 1851–56.
50 *New York Times*, December 15, 2005.
51 *PPPUS-GWB, 2005,* Vol. 2, Remarks Following Meeting with Senators John McCain and John Warner, December 15, 2005, 1859–60.

52 Eric Schmitt, "President Backs McCain Measure on Inmate Abuse," *New York Times*, December 16, 2005.

53 James Risen and Eric Lichtblau, "Bush Lets U.S. Spy on Callers Without Courts," *New York Times*, December 16, 2005.

54 James Risen, *State of War: The Secret History of the CIA and the Bush Administration* (New York: Free Press, 2006).

55 Joe Hagen, "The United States of America vs. Bill Keller," *New York*, September 10, 2006.

56 Eric Lichtblau, *Bush's Law: The Remaking of American Justice* (New York: Pantheon, 2008), 205–7.

57 Ibid., 208.

58 Hagen, "The United States of America vs. Bill Keller."

59 Lichtblau, *Bush's Law*, 210.

60 *PPPUS-GWB, 2005,* Vol. 2, The President's Radio Address, December 17, 2005, 1870–71.

61 Ibid., Address to the Nation on Iraq and the War on Terror, December 18, 2005, 1872–75.

62 *Washington Post*/ABC News poll, December 19, 2005.

63 *White House Press Release*, President's Statement on the Department of Defense, Emergency Supplemental Appropriations to Address Hurricanes in the Gulf of Mexico, and Pandemic Influenza Act, 2006, December 30, 2005.

64 *PPPUS-GWB, 2005,* Vol. 2, Statement on Signing the Department of Defense, Emergency Supplemental Appropriations to Address Hurricanes in the Gulf of Mexico, and Pandemic Influenza Act, 2006, December 30, 2005, 1901–3.

65 I am indebted to Charlie Savage for this succinct description. *Takeover: The Return of the Imperial Presidency and the Subversion of American Democracy* (New York: Back Bay Books, 2007), 266.

66 Charlie Savage interview with Senator Lindsey Graham, in ibid., 226–27.

Chapter Nineteen: The Mess in Mesopotamia

The Duke of Wellington, as British prime minister, was warning hawkish members of Parliament against ill-considered military interventions abroad. His comments are quoted in *Familiar Short Sayings of Great Men*, 6th ed., compiled by Samuel Arthur Bent (Boston: Ticknor & Co., 1887).

1 *Clinton v. New York*, 524 U.S. 417 (1998).

2 List of all signing statements issued by George W. Bush, 2001–2008, is available at http://www.coherentbabble.com/listGWBall.pdf.

3 Charlie Savage, *Takeover: The Return of the Imperial Presidency* (New York: Back Bay Books, 2007), 230.

4 Charlie Savage, "Bush Shuns Patriot Act," *Boston Globe*, March 24, 2006.

5 *PPPUS-GWB, 2006,* Vol. 1, Remarks on Signing the USA Patriot Act Improvement and Reauthorization Act, March 9, 2006, 426–30, 1395.

6 Ibid., 430.

7 Savage, *Takeover*, 237.

8 Ibid., 238.

9 Ibid., 239–40.

10 Ibid., 240.

11 Savage, "Bush Shuns Patriot Act."

12 Charlie Savage, "3 Democrats Slam President," *Boston Globe*, May 2, 2006.

13 Savage won the Pulitzer for seven articles on signing statements published in *The Boston Globe* in 2006, and twelve supporting articles.

14 President Bush vetoed the following bills: Stem Cell Research Enhancement Act of 2005 (July 19, 2006); US Troop Readiness, Veterans' Care, Katrina Recovery, and Iraq Accountability (May 1, 2007); Stem Cell Research Enhancement Act of 2007 (June 20, 2007); Children's Health Insurance Program Reauthorization Act of 2007 (October 3, 2007); Water Resources Development Act of 2007 (November 2, 2007, veto overridden); Appropriations: Labor, Health and Human Services, Education, 2008 (November 13, 2007); Children's Health Insurance Program Reauthorization Act of 2007 (December 12, 2007); National Defense Authorization Act for FY2008 (December 28, 2007); Intelligence Authorization Act for Fiscal Year 2008 (March 8, 2008); Food, Conservation, and Energy Act of 2008 (May 21, 2008, veto overridden); Food, Conservation, and Energy Act of 2008 (June 18, 2008, veto overridden); Medicare Improvement for Patients and Providers Act of 2008 (July 15, 2008, veto overridden).

15 Report of the American Bar Association Task Force on Presidential Signing Statements and the Separation of Powers Doctrine, http://www.abanet.org/media/docs/signstatereport.pdf.

16 Bob Woodward, *State of Denial: Bush at War, Part III* (New York: Simon & Schuster, 2008), 451.

17 *PPPUS-GWB, 2003,* Vol. 1, Address to the Nation on Iraq from the USS *Abraham Lincoln*, May 1, 2003, 410–19.

18 http://icasualties.org., U.S. killed and wounded, Operation Iraqi Freedom.

19 http://icasualties.org/Iraq/IraqiDeaths.aspx.

20 Woodward, *State of Denial*, 313.

21 Ibid., 336.

22 Donald Rumsfeld, *Known and Unknown* (New York: Sentinel, 2011), 676.

23 Patrick Cockburn, *The Occupation: War and Resistance in Iraq* (London: Verso, 2006), 166.

24 Woodward, *State of Denial*, 326.

25 Ibid., 416.

26 Ibid., 373.

27 *PPPUS-GWB, 2005,* Vol. 1, Address to the Nation on the Iraqi Election, January 30, 2005, 110.

28 icasualties.org, Operation Iraqi Freedom; Monthly Civilian Deaths from Violence, 2003.

29 *Larry King Live*, May 30, 2005, CNN.com, transcript.

30 In April 2005, 52 American servicemen were killed in action; in May the figure rose to 88. Similarly, Iraqi casualties totaled 1,145 in April versus 1,394 in May. http://icasualties.org, Operation Iraqi Freedom.

31 Dick Cheney, *In My Time* (New York: Threshold, 2011), 433–34.

32 Woodward, *State of Denial*, 398.

33 Ibid.

34 Ibid., 399.

35 Kevin Whitelaw, Ilana Ozernoy, and Terrence Samuel, "Hit by Friendly Fire," *U.S. News & World Report*, June 27, 2005.

36 Mark Thompson, "America's Broken-Down Army," *Time*, April 5, 2007.

37 Terry H. Anderson, *Bush's Wars* (New York: Oxford University Press, 2011), 191.

38 Robert Draper, *Dead Certain: The Presidency of George W. Bush* (New York: Free Press, 2007), 350.

39 *PPPUS-GWB, 2005,* Vol. 2, Remarks on the Vote Approving the Iraqi Constitution, October 16, 2005, 1553.

40 Saad N. Jawad, "The Iraqi Constitution: Structural Flaws and Political Implications," LSE Middle East Centre Paper Series 101, November 2013, 22.

41 Ibid., 23.

42 Jean Edward Smith, *Lucius D. Clay: An American Life* (New York: Henry Holt, 1990), 541; also see Andrew Arato, *Constitution Making Under Occupation: The Politics of Imposed Revolution in Iraq* (New York: Columbia University Press, 2009), 33.

43 Rumsfeld, *Known and Unknown*, 667.

44 Woodward, *State of Denial*, 415.

45 *PPPUS-GWB, 2005,* Vol. 2, Remarks on the War on Terror, Tobyhanna, Pennsylvania, November 11, 2005, 1699–1708.

46 Rumsfeld, *Known and Unknown*, 679.

47 Edward Wong, "Turnout in the Iraqi Election Is Reported at 70 Percent," *New York Times*, December 22, 2005.

48 *PPPUS-GWB, 2005,* Vol. 2, Remarks Following a Meeting with Iraqi Out-of-Country Voters, December 15, 2005, 1858–59.

49 Anderson, *Bush's Wars*, 197.

50 *PPPUS-GWB, 2006,* Vol. 1, Statement on the Bombing of the Golden Mosque in Samarra, Iraq, February 22, 2006, 329.

51 Walter Pincus, "1,000 Iraqis a Day Flee Violence," *Washington Post*, November 24, 2006.

52 CNN/*USA Today*/Gallup poll, March 15, 2006; Anderson, *Bush's Wars*, 199.

53 *PPPUS-GWB, 2006,* Vol. 1, President's News Conference, March 21, 2006, 527–28.

54 Cockburn, *The Occupation*, 157.

55 "Billions Wasted in Iraq," *60 Minutes*, CBS News, February 9, 2006.
56 Ali A. Allawi, *The Occupation of Iraq: Winning the War, Losing the Peace* (New Haven: Yale University Press, 2007), 367.
57 Richard A. Oppel, Jr., "In Iraq, Oil Profits Help Feed Insurgency," *New York Times*, March 22, 2008.
58 Anderson, *Bush's Wars*, 196.
59 iCasualties.org.
60 George W. Casey, Jr., *Strategic Reflections: Operation Iraqi Freedom, July 2004–February 2007* (Washington, D.C.: National Defense University Press, 2012), 104.
61 Peter Baker interview with John Negroponte, in Baker, *Days of Fire*, 449.
62 Baker, *Days of Fire*, 453. Also see Draper, *Dead Certain*, 398.
63 *PPPUS-GWB, 2006,* Vol. 1, Remarks on the Nomination of Robert J. Portman to be Director of the Office of Management and Budget, April 18, 2006, 736.
64 Graham Fuller, former vice chairman of the CIA's National Intelligence Council, quoted in *International Herald Tribune*, April 15, 2006.
65 Iraqi clerical spokesman, quoted in the *Los Angeles Times*, May 7, 2006.
66 Brian Knowlton, "Bush Makes Public Parts of Report on Terrorism," *New York Times*, September 26, 2006.
67 Ibid.
68 *New York Times*, August 27, 2014. Senator Rand Paul made the same point in a *Wall Street Journal* op-ed on August 28, 2014.
69 Peter W. Galbraith, *The End of Iraq: How American Incompetence Created a War Without End* (New York: Simon & Schuster, 2006), 9.
70 Woodward, *State of Denial*, 456.
71 G. W. Bush, *Decision Points*, 367.
72 Baker, *Days of Fire*, 457.
73 Laura Bush, *Spoken from the Heart* (New York: Scribner, 2010), 383–84.
74 Baker, *Days of Fire*, 457.
75 Woodward, *State of Denial*, 334.
76 G. W. Bush, *Decision Points*, 75.
77 Ibid., 368.
78 Bob Woodward, *The War Within: A Secret White House History, 2006–2008* (New York: Simon & Schuster, 2008), 4.
79 Ibid., 5.
80 Baker, *Days of Fire*, 465.
81 *PPPUS-GWB, 2006,* Vol. 1, Remarks on the Death of Senior Al Qaeda Associate Abu Musab al-Zarqawi, June 8, 2006, 1099–1100.
82 Baker, *Days of Fire*, 459.
83 Casey, *Strategic Reflections*, 104–5; also see Baker, *Days of Fire*, 465; Rumsfeld, *Known and Unknown*, 695.

84 Woodward, *The War Within*, 10.

85 Rumsfeld, *Known and Unknown*, 696.

86 Baker, *Days of Fire*, 466.

87 G. W. Bush, *Decision Points*, 166.

88 Woodward, *The War Within*, 4.

89 T. E. Lawrence, "Twenty-seven Articles," *The Arab Bulletin*, August 20, 1917.

90 Woodward, *The War Within*, 4. Also see G. W. Bush, *Decision Points*, 367.

91 *PPPUS-GWB, 2006,* Vol. 1, The President's News Conference, June 14, 2006, 1132.

Chapter Twenty: Rummy Walks the Plank

The epigraph is from Justice John Paul Stevens's opinion of the Court in *Hamdan v. Rumsfeld*, 548 U.S. 557, 628 (2006).

1 *Youngstown Sheet & Tube v. Sawyer*, 343 U.S. 579 (1952).

2 *United States v. Nixon*, 418 U.S. 683 (1974).

3 Charlie Savage, "Justices Deal Bush Setback on Tribunals," *Boston Globe*, June 30, 2006.

4 *Hamdan v. Rumsfeld*, 548 U.S. 557 (2006).

5 Ibid.

6 *Hamdan v. Rumsfeld*, 344 F. Supp. 2d 152 (D.C. 2004).

7 *Hamdan v. Rumsfeld*, 415 F. 3d 33 (D.C. Cir. 2005).

8 Stevens's emphasis. *Hamdan v. Rumsfeld*, 548 U.S. 557, 649 (2006). Stevens was joined by Justices Souter, Ginsburg, Breyer, and Kennedy. Justices Scalia, Thomas, and Alito dissented.

9 For the texts of the Geneva Conventions, see 6 *United States Treaties and Other International Acts* 3115 (Convention I), 3219 (Convention II), 3517 (Convention III), and 3317 (Convention IV). Also see Charlie Savage, *Takeover: The Return of the Imperial Presidency and the Subversion of American Democracy* (New York: Little, Brown, 2007), 276.

10 War Crimes Act, 18 USG 2441; Pub. Law 104–192; 110 Stat. 2104.

11 Defense Department Directive 2310. 01E, July 6, 2006. Also see Donald Rumsfeld, *Known and Unknown* (New York: Sentinel, 2011), 594.

12 Condoleezza Rice, *No Higher Honor* (New York: Crown, 2011), 501.

13 George W. Bush, *Decision Points* (New York: Crown, 2010), 178.

14 *PPPUS-GWB, 2006,* Vol. 2, President's News Conference in Chicago, July 7, 2006, 1339.

15 Peter Baker, *Days of Fire: Bush and Cheney in the White House* (New York: Doubleday, 2013), 484.

16 Jane Mayer, *The Dark Side: The Inside Story of How the War on Terror Turned into a War on American Ideals* (New York: Doubleday, 2008), 325.

17 Ibid., 324; Baker, *Days of Fire*, 484.

18 Mayer, *The Dark Side*, 324; Baker, *Days of Fire*, 484.

19 Rice, *No Higher Honor*, 502.

20 Ibid.

21 Baker, *Days of Fire*, 485.

22 *PPPUS-GWB, 2006,* Vol. 2, Remarks on Terror, September 6, 2006, 1612–20.

23 Baker, *Days of Fire*, 486.

24 *PPPUS-GWB, 2006,* Vol. 2, Remarks on Terror, 1612–20.

25 Baker, *Days of Fire*, 486.

26 *PPPUS-GWB, 2006,* Vol. 2, Remarks on Terror, 1616.

27 Mayer, *The Dark Side*, 326.

28 Baker, *Days of Fire*, 486.

29 *PPPUS-GWB, 2006,* Vol. 2, Remarks on Terror, 1619.

30 Ibid.

31 Letter, General Joseph Hoar, USMC, et al., to Senators John Warner and Carl Levin, September 12, 2006. The generals were joined by William H. Taft IV, who had been the State Department's chief legal officer for the first four years of Bush's presidency.

32 Letter, General John W. Vessey to Senator John McCain, September 12, 2006.

33 Letter, General Colin L. Powell to Senator John McCain, September 13, 2006.

34 *New York Times*, "Rushing Off a Cliff," September 28, 2006.

35 *PPPUS-GWB, 2006,* Vol. 2, Remarks on Signing the Military Commissions Act of 2006, October 17, 2006, 1857–59.

36 *Boumediene v. Bush*, 533 U.S. 723, 59 (2008). In *Marbury v. Madison*, 1 Cranch 137, 177 (1803), Chief Justice Marshall established the authority of the Supreme Court to exercise judicial review, i.e., to declare an act of Congress unconstitutional if it conflicted with the Constitution. Said Marshall, "It is emphatically the province and duty of the judicial department to say what the law is." For a discussion, see Jean Edward Smith, *John Marshall: Definer of a Nation* (New York: Henry Holt, 1996), 307–25.

37 "Report on President Bush's Physical Examination," *New York Times*, August 1, 2006.

38 Steve Holland, Reuters, August 5, 2006.

39 G. W. Bush, *Decision Points*, 367–68.

40 Woodward, *The War Within*, 88–90. Also see G. W. Bush, *Decision Points*, 370.

41 G. W. Bush, *Decision Points*, 371; Woodward, *The War Within*, 90–94.

42 Woodward, *The War Within*, 97.

43 G. W. Bush, *Decision Points*, 371.

44 *PPPUS-GWB, 2006,* Vol. 2, President's News Conference, September 15, 2006, 1655–60.

45 Ibid., President's News Conference, October 25, 2006, 1911.

46 Terrence Hunt, "Bush Says Rumsfeld and Cheney Should Stay in Office Until the End," Associated Press, November 1, 2006.

47 G. W. Bush, *Decision Points*, 355.

48 Ibid., 93. Also see Woodward, *The War Within*, 196.

49 Rumsfeld, *Known and Unknown*, 706.

50 Woodward, *The War Within*, 197.

51 Ibid., 198. Also see Baker, *Days of Fire*, 490–91.

52 Woodward, *The War Within*, 198.

53 Jon Meacham interview with GHWB, quoted in Meacham, *Destiny and Power: The American Odyssey of George Herbert Walker Bush* (New York: Random House, 2015), 584.

54 Woodward, *The War Within*, 202.

55 Robert M. Gates, *Duty: Memoirs of a Secretary at War* (New York: Alfred A. Knopf, 2014), 6–7.

56 Baker, *Days of Fire*, 499.

57 Dick Cheney, *In My Time* (New York: Threshold, 2011), 443.

58 Rumsfeld, *Known and Unknown*, 706.

59 Cheney, *In My Time*, 443.

60 Donald Rumsfeld, Letter of Resignation, November 6, 2006, Rumsfeld Papers, online.

61 Rumsfeld, *Known and Unknown*, 707.

62 Ibid., 707–8.

63 *PPPUS-GWB, 2006,* Vol. 2, Remarks at Reception for Congressional Candidate Michael A. Collins in Macon, Georgia, October 10, 2006, 1807–13.

64 Ibid., Remarks at a Georgia Victory Rally, Statesboro, Georgia, October 30, 2006, 1946–53.

65 Ibid., Remarks at a Texas Victory Rally, Sugarland, Texas, October 30, 2006, 1953–60.

66 Libby Copeland, "President's Sin of Omission: Dropped Syllable in Speech Riles Democrats," *Washington Post*, January 24, 2007.

67 Baker, *Days of Fire*, 500. Also see Robert Draper, *Dead Certain: The Presidency of George W. Bush* (New York: Simon & Schuster, 2007), 369.

68 Draper, *Dead Certain*, 365.

69 Gary C. Jacobson, *A Divider, Not a Uniter: George W. Bush and the American People* (New York: Longman, 2011), 192.

70 "Public Disillusionment with Congress at Record Levels," Pew Research Center for the People and the Press, April 20, 2006.

Chapter Twenty-One: Bush Takes Command

The epigraph is from George W. Bush's address to the nation on military operations in Iraq, January 10, 2007, *PPPUS-GWB, 2007,* Vol. 1, 16–20.

1 *PPPUS-GWB, 2006,* Vol. 2, President's News Conference, November 8, 2006, 2052–64.

2 Ibid.

3 Peter Baker, *Days of Fire: Bush and Cheney in the White House* (New York: Doubleday, 2013), 507.

4 Bob Woodward, *The War Within: A Secret White House History, 2006–2008* (New York: Simon & Schuster, 2008), 207.

5 Baker, *Days of Fire*, 508.

6 The fact that the Study Group was chaired by James Baker and vigorously supported by Brent Scowcroft caused Bush to be especially suspicious of its motives. For a discussion, see Craig Unger, *The Fall of the House of Bush* (New York: Scribner, 2007), 341.

7 Bob Woodward interview with William Perry. Woodward, *The War Within*, 214.

8 Iraq Study Group Record, November 13, 2006. Also see Woodward, *The War Within*, 209–14.

9 Robin Wright, "Bush Initiates Iraq Policy Review Separate from Baker's Group," *Washington Post*, November 15, 2006.

10 For a discussion of the SECRET papers submitted to the president's research group, see Woodward, *The War Within*, 230–39. Woodward evidently was given access to the documents.

11 Condoleezza Rice, *No Higher Honor* (New York: Crown, 2011), 542.

12 Woodward, *The War Within*, 245. Also see Baker, *Days of Fire*, 511–12.

13 Woodward, *The War Within*, 246.

14 Baker, *Days of Fire*, 512.

15 *PPPUS-GWB, 2006,* Vol. 2, Remarks of the President at Latvia University in Riga, November 28, 2006, 2127–33.

16 G. W. Bush, *Decision Points*, 374.

17 Ibid.

18 Ibid.

19 Ibid., 375.

20 David Sanger, "Panel to Weigh Overture by U.S. to Iran and Syria," *New York Times*, November 27, 2006; David Sanger and David S. Cloud, "Iraq Panel to Recommend Pullback of Combat Troops," *New York Times*, November 30, 2006.

21 Rice, *No Higher Honor*, 543.

22 Cullen Murphy and Todd S. Purdum, "Farewell to All That: An Oral History of the Bush White House," *Vanity Fair*, February 2009.

23 *The Iraq Study Group Report: The Way Forward—A New Approach* (New York: Vintage, 2006), 73.

24 Alan Abramowitz and Robin Wright, "Iraq Panel Proposes Major Shift in Strategy," *Washington Post*, December 7, 2006.

25 David Montgomery, "Footnote to History: Rituals of Delivering the Iraq Report," *Washington Post*, December 7, 2006.

26 Ibid.

27 *PPPUS-GWB, 2006,* Vol. 2, Remarks Following a Meeting With the Iraq Study Group, December 6, 2006, 2150–51.

28 Montgomery, "Footnote to History." Also see Abramowitz and Wright, "Iraq Panel Proposes Major Strategy Shift"; "Panel Urges Basic Shift in U.S. Policy in Iraq," *New York Times,* December 7, 2006.

29 Montgomery, "Footnote to History."

30 Robert Draper, *Dead Certain: The Presidency of George W. Bush* (New York: Free Press, 2007), 403.

31 Memo, "Iraq Policy: Proposal for the New Phase," Rumsfeld to Bush, December 8, 2006. Retrievable as footnote 5, Chapter 50, end notes, Rumsfeld Papers, online.

32 Baker, *Days of Fire,* 516.

33 Woodward, *The War Within,* 280–81.

34 Baker, *Days of Fire,* 517.

35 George W. Casey, Jr., *Strategic Reflections: Operation Iraqi Freedom, July 2004–February 2007* (Washington, D.C.: National Defense University Press, 2012), 143–44.

36 Woodward, *The War Within,* 284.

37 G. W. Bush, *Decision Points,* 376.

38 Dick Cheney, *In My Time* (New York: Threshold, 2011), 451–52.

39 Baker, *Days of Fire,* 520.

40 Woodward, *The War Within,* 288–89.

41 *PPPUS-GWB, 2006,* Vol. 2, Remarks Following Meeting with Senior Military Officers, The Pentagon, December 13, 2006, 2175–79.

42 Ann Scott Tyson, "General Says Army Will Need to Grow," *Washington Post,* December 15, 2006.

43 Peter Baker, "U.S. Not Winning War in Iraq, Bush Says for 1st Time," *Washington Post,* December 20, 2006. Also see Peter Baker, "Bush to Expand Size of Military," *Washington Post,* December 19, 2006.

44 Baker, "U.S. Not Winning War in Iraq, Bush Says for 1st Time."

45 Ibid.

46 Ibid.

47 Robert Gates, *Duty: Memoirs of a Secretary at War* (New York: Alfred A. Knopf, 2014), 41–43.

48 Gates's talking points are reproduced in Michael R. Gordon and General Bernard E. Trainor, *Endgame: The Inside Story of the Struggle for Iraq, from George W. Bush to Barack Obama* (New York: Vintage, 2012), 306–7. Also see Gates, *Duty,* 42–43.

49 Baker, *Days of Fire,* 522.

50 Woodward, *The War Within,* 306.

51 *PPPUS-GWB, 2006,* Vol. 2, Remarks Following a Meeting with the National Security Council, Crawford, Texas, December 28, 2006, 2225.

52 G. W. Bush, *Decision Points*, 377–78.

53 *PPPUS-GWB, 2007,* Vol. 1, President's News Conference with Chancellor Angela Merkel, January 4, 2007, 4–9.

54 Ibid., Statement on United States Military Personnel Recommendations of Secretary of Defense Robert M. Gates, January 5, 2007, 11.

55 Solomon Moore, "Maliki Unveils Effort to End Bloodshed," *New York Times,* January 7, 2007.

56 *PPPUS-GWB, 2007,* Vol. 1, Address to the Nation on Military Operations in Iraq, January 10, 2007, 16–20.

57 *USA Today*/CNN/Gallup poll, January 5–7, 2007.

58 Laura Bush, *Spoken from the Heart* (New York: Scribner, 2010), 241.

59 Gates, *Duty*, 48.

60 Jean Edward Smith, *FDR* (New York: Random House, 2007), 561.

61 Jean Edward Smith, *Lucius D. Clay: An American Life* (New York: Henry Holt, 1990), 503–4.

62 Jean Edward Smith, *Eisenhower in War and Peace* (New York: Random House, 2012), 610–11, 655–56.

63 Gates, *Duty*, 49.

Chapter Twenty-Two: AIDS

The epigraph is from Bush's State of the Union address, January 28, 2003, *PPPUS-GWB, 2003,* Vol. 1, 85.

 1 Jon Cohen and Dan Balz, "Poll: Most Americans Opposed to Bush's Iraq Plan," *Washington Post*, January 11, 2007.

 2 Editorial, *New York Times,* January 11, 2007.

 3 Bob Woodward, *The War Within: A Secret White House Diary, 2006–2008* (New York: Simon & Schuster, 2008), 316.

 4 Robert Gates, *Duty: Memoirs of a Secretary at War* (New York: Alfred A. Knopf, 2014), 54.

 5 Senate Foreign Relations Committee, Opening Remarks by Senator Biden, January 11, 2007.

 6 Woodward, *The War Within*, 315–16.

 7 Peter Baker, *Days of Fire: Bush and Cheney in the White House* (New York: Doubleday, 2013), 528.

 8 *PPPUS-GWB, 2007,* Vol. 1, President's State of the Union Address, January 23, 2007, 42–50.

 9 Howard Fineman, "President Bush Defends His Iraq Stance," MSNBC, January 24, 2007, online.

10 "Democratic Response of Senator James Webb to the President's State of the Union Address," *New York Times*, January 23, 2007.

11 Peter Baker and Michael Abramowitz, "Bush Urges Congress, Nation to Give His Iraq Plan a Chance," *Washington Post*, January 24, 2007.

12 Baker, *Days of Fire*, 527–28.

13 George W. Bush, *Decision Points* (New York: Crown, 2010), 368.
14 *PPPUS-GWB, 2007,* Vol. 1, President's State of the Union Address, January 23, 2007, 49.
15 G. W. Bush, *Decision Points*, 335.
16 *PPPUS-GWB, 2001,* Vol. 1, Remarks Following Discussions With President Olusegun Obasanjo of Nigeria and U.N. Secretary-General Kofi Annan, May 11, 2001, 513–15.
17 G. W. Bush, *Decision Points*, 337.
18 *PPPUS-GWB, 2002,* Vol. 1, Remarks Announcing the International Mother and Child HIV Prevention Initiative, June 19, 2002, 1012–14.
19 G. W. Bush, *Decision Points*, 338.
20 Sheryl Gay Stolberg, "In Global Battle on AIDS, Bush Creates Legacy," *New York Times,* January 5, 2008.
21 Michael J. Gerson, *Heroic Conservatism: Why Republicans Need to Embrace America's Ideals (And Why They Deserve to Fail if They Don't)* (New York: HarperCollins, 2007), 2.
22 Ibid., 2–3.
23 Bush to Jay Lefkowitz, quoted in Baker, *Days of Fire*, 236.
24 G. W. Bush, *Decision Points*, 340.
25 *PPPUS-GWB, 2003,* Vol. 1, President's State of the Union Address, January 28, 2003, 85.
26 *PPPUS-GWB, 2003,* Vol. 1, Remarks on the Global HIV/AIDS Initiative, April 28, 2003, 392–95.
27 Ibid., Remarks on Signing the United States Leadership Against HIV/AIDS, Tuberculosis, and Malaria Act, May 27, 2003, 541–44.
28 Eran Bendavid and Jayanta Bhattacharya, "PEPFAR in Africa: An Evaluation of Outcomes," 150 *Annals of Internal Medicine*, May 19, 2009, 688–95.
29 *PPPUS-GWB, 2007,* Vol. 1, Remarks on the President's Emergency Plan for AIDS Relief, May 30, 2007, 640–42.
30 HR 5501, 110th Congress, 2nd Session.
31 Public Law 110–293; 122 Stat. 2918.
32 *PPPUS-GWB, 2008,* Vol. 2, Remarks on signing the Tom Lantos and Henry Hyde United States Global Leadership Against HIV/AIDS, Tuberculosis, and Malaria Reauthorization Act, July 30, 2008, 1066–69.
33 Condoleezza Rice, *No Higher Honor* (New York: Crown, 2011), 229.
34 Paul Clement, "Popping the PEPFAR Bubble," *Los Angeles Times,* February 21, 2008.
35 *New York Times,* April 10, 2011.
36 Thomas J. Coates, "Science vs. Assumption in Public Health Policy: Abstinence Alone Is Not the Answer," *San Francisco Chronicle*, May 25, 2005.
37 "International HIV/AIDS, Tuberculosis, and Malaria: Key Changes to U.S. Programs and Funding," Congressional Research Service, August 25, 2008.

38 7631(f), the United States Leadership Against HIV/AIDS, Tuberculosis, and Malaria Act of 2003, 117 Stat. 711.

39 Jenna Bush, *Ana's Story: A Journey of Hope* (New York: HarperCollins, 2007).

40 G. W. Bush, *Decision Points*, 344.

41 Ibid., 352–53.

42 Eugene Robinson, "George W. Bush's Greatest Legacy—His Battle Against AIDS," *Washington Post*, July 26, 2012.

43 Jim Rutenberg, "Ex-Aide Says He's Lost Faith in Bush," *New York Times*, April 1, 2007.

44 David Savage, "A History of Replacing U.S. Attorneys," *Los Angeles Times*, March 23, 2007.

45 Dan Eggen and John Solomon, "Firings Had Genesis in White House," *Washington Post*, March 13, 2007.

46 Ibid.

47 Ibid.

48 David Johnston and Eric Lipton, "Gonzales Meets with Advisers on Dismissals," *New York Times*, March 24, 2007.

49 Eric Lichtblau and Eric Lipton, "E-Mail Reveals Rove's Key Role in '06 Dismissals," *New York Times*, August 12, 2009.

50 Eggen and Solomon, "Firings Had Genesis in White House," *New York Times*, March 13, 2007.

51 Allegra Hartley, "How the U.S. Attorneys Were Fired," *U.S. News & World Report*, March 30, 2007.

52 Press Release, Senators Dianne Feinstein, Patrick Leahy, and Mark Pryor, issued by Senator Feinstein's office, January 11, 2007.

53 Public Law 110–34.

54 Dan Eggen, "Prosecutor Firings Not Political, Gonzales Says," *Washington Post,* January 19, 2007.

55 Hartley, "How the U.S. Attorneys Were Fired."

56 Kevin Johnson, "Prosecutor Fired So Ex-Rove Aide Could Get His Job," *USA Today,* February 6, 2007.

57 U.S. Senate, Judiciary Committee, Hearing on Dismissal of U.S. Attorneys, 11–12, *Washington Post*, transcript, online.

58 Ibid., 40.

59 Alberto Gonzales, "They Lost My Confidence," *USA Today*, March 7, 2007.

60 Department of Justice, Media Availability with Attorney General Gonzales, March 13, 2007, transcript.

61 *PPPUS-GWB, 2007,* Vol. 1, News Conference with President Felipe de Jesús Calderón Hinojosa in Merida, Mexico, March 14, 2007, 310.

62 Ibid., Remarks on the Department of Justice and an Exchange with Reporters, March 20, 2007, 334–36.

63 Dana Milbank, "Maybe Gonzales Won't Recall His Painful Day on the Hill," *Washington Post*, April 20, 2007.

64 Editorial, "Gonzales v. Gonzales," *New York Times*, April 20, 2007.

65 Text, "Gonzales Testifies Before Senate Panel," Part II, 32, C.Q. Transcripts wire, April 19, 2007.

66 Milbank, "Maybe Gonzales Won't Recall His Painful Day on the Hill."

67 Text, "Gonzales Testifies Before Senate Panel," Part III, 35, C.Q. Transcripts wire, April 19, 2007.

68 William Branigin, "Gonzales Defends Actions on U.S. Attorney Firings," *Washington Post*, April 19, 2007.

69 *PPPUS-GWB, 2007*, Vol. 1, Remarks Following a Meeting with Military Leaders, April 23, 2007, 465–66.

70 Jim Rutenberg and Neil A. Lewis, "Bush Reaffirms His Support for Gonzales," *New York Times*, April 23, 2007.

71 Peter Baker and Dan Essen, "New Privilege Claim by Bush Escalates Clash over Firings," *Washington Post*, July 10, 2007.

72 Peter Baker, "An Exit Toward Soul-Searching," *Washington Post*, October 7, 2007.

73 *PPPUS-GWB, 2007*, Vol. 2, Remarks on the Resignation of Karl Rove, August 13, 2007, 1072.

74 Terrence Hunt, "Rove to Leave White House Aug. 31," *Washington Post*, August 13, 2007.

75 Baker, *Days of Fire*, 561.

76 Ibid.

77 Text, "Gonzales Statement on His Resignation," *New York Times*, August 27, 2007.

78 *PPPUS-GWB, 2007*, Vol. 2, Remarks on the Resignation of Attorney General Alberto R. Gonzales in Waco, Texas, August 27, 2007, 1109.

79 Department of Justice, Statement by Attorney General Michael B. Mukasey on the Report of an Investigation into the Removal of Nine U.S. Attorneys in 2006, September 29, 2008. (The ninth U.S. attorney covered by the investigation was Todd Graves of the Western District of Missouri, who resigned March 10, 2006.)

80 Letter, Assistant Attorney General Ronald Weich to Representative John Conyers, Jr., Chairman, House Judiciary Committee, July 21, 2010.

Chapter Twenty-Three: Quagmire of the Vanities

The epigraph is a statement made by George W. Bush to Australian deputy prime minister Mark Vaile upon his arrival in Sydney, Australia, September 5, 2007, CNN, September 7, 2007.

1 George W. Bush, *Decision Points* (New York: Crown, 2010), 380.

2 Monthly Civilian Deaths from Violence, 2003 Onwards, http://www.iraq bodycount.org/database.

3 Carl Hulse, "Democrats Back Date for Start of Iraq Pullout," *New York Times*, April 24, 2007.

4 *PPPUS-GWB, 2007,* Vol. 1, Exchange with Reporters, April 23, 2007, 465.

5 Carl Hulse and Jeff Zeleny, "War Bill Passes House, Requiring Iraqi Pullout," *New York Times*, April 26, 2007.

6 Hulse, "Democrats Back Date for Start of Iraq Pullout."

7 Carl Hulse, "Senate Passes Bill Seeking Iraq Exit; Veto Is Expected," *New York Times*, April 27, 2007.

8 *PPPUS-GWB, 2007,* Vol. 1, Remarks on Returning Without Approval to the House of Representatives the "U.S. Troop Readiness, Veterans' Care, Katrina Recovery, and Iraq Accountability Appropriations Act, 2007," May 1, 2007, 513–14.

9 *Congressional Record*, 110th Congress, 1st Session, H4317, H4322, May 2, 2007.

10 Sheryl Gay Stolberg and Jeff Zeleny, "House Fails to Override Bush Veto on Iraq," *New York Times*, May 2, 2007.

11 *Congressional Record*, 110th Congress, 1st Session, H4322, May 2, 2007.

12 *PPPUS-GWB, 2007,* Vol. 1, Remarks Prior to Meeting with Congressional Leaders, May 2, 2007, 532.

13 U.S. Troop Readiness, Veterans' Care, Katrina Recovery, and Iraq Accountability Appropriations Act of 2007, Public Law 110-028; 121 Stat. 112.

14 According to the Act, the eighteen benchmarks provided by Senator Warner were as follows:

(A) The United States strategy in Iraq, hereafter, shall be conditioned on the Iraqi government meeting benchmarks, as told to members of Congress by the President, the Secretary of State, the Secretary of Defense, and the Chairman of the Joint Chiefs of Staff, and reflected in the Iraqi Government's commitments to the United States, and to the international community, including:

(i) Forming a Constitutional Review Committee and then completing the constitutional review.

(ii) Enacting and implementing legislation on de-Baathification.

(iii) Enacting and implementing legislation to ensure the equitable distribution of hydrocarbon resources of the people of Iraq without regard to the sect or ethnicity of recipients, and enacting and implementing legislation to ensure that the energy resources of Iraq benefit Sunni Arabs, Shia Arabs, Kurds, and other Iraqi citizens in an equitable manner.

(iv) Enacting and implementing legislation on procedures to form semi-autonomous regions.

(v) Enacting and implementing legislation establishing an Independent High Electoral Commission, provincial elections law, provincial council authorities, and a date for provincial elections.

(vi) Enacting and implementing legislation addressing amnesty.

(vii) Enacting and implementing legislation establishing a strong militia disarmament program to ensure that such security forces are accountable only to the central government and loyal to the Constitution of Iraq.

(viii) Establishing supporting political, media, economic, and services committees in support of the Baghdad Security Plan.

(ix) Providing three trained and ready Iraqi brigades to support Baghdad operations.

(x) Providing Iraqi commanders with all authorities to execute this plan and to make tactical and operational decisions, in consultation with U.S. commanders, without political intervention, to include the authority to pursue all extremists, including Sunni insurgents and Shiite militias.

(xi) Ensuring that the Iraqi Security Forces are providing even handed enforcement of the law.

(xii) Ensuring that, according to President Bush, Prime Minister Maliki said "the Baghdad security plan will not provide a safe haven for any outlaws, regardless of [their] sectarian or political affiliation."

(xiii) Reducing the level of sectarian violence in Iraq and eliminating militia control of local security.

(xiv) Establishing all of the planned joint security stations in neighborhoods across Baghdad.

(xv) Increasing the number of Iraqi security forces units capable of operating independently.

(xvi) Ensuring that the rights of minority political parties in the Iraqi legislature are protected.

(xvii) Allocating and spending $10 billion in Iraqi revenues for reconstruction projects, including delivery of essential services, on an equitable basis.

(xviii) Ensuring that Iraq's political authorities are not undermining or making false accusations against members of the Iraqi Security Forces.

(B) The President shall submit reports to Congress on how the sovereign Government of Iraq is, or is not, achieving progress towards accomplishing the aforementioned benchmarks, and shall advise the Congress on how that assessment requires, or does not require, changes to the strategy announced on January 10, 2007.

15 G. W. Bush, *Decision Points*, 381.

16 Ibid., 382.

17 Peter Baker, *Days of Fire: Bush and Cheney in the White House* (New York: Doubleday, 2013), 565. Compare Bob Woodward, *The War Within: A Secret White House Diary, 2006–2008* (New York: Simon & Schuster, 2008), 389–90. Keane's role as a go-between was facilitated by Vice President Cheney, who knew Keane from his time as secretary of defense during the first Gulf War. As Cheney stated in his memoirs, "Because of the ongoing resistance inside

the Pentagon and at Central Command to the surge strategy, I wanted to ensure that General Petraeus's thoughts and concerns made it all the way up the chain of command"—i.e., to the commander in chief. Dick Cheney, *In My Time* (New York: Threshold, 2011), 457.

18 Robert M. Gates, *Duty: Memoirs of a Secretary at War* (New York: Alfred A. Knopf, 2014), 66. Also see Thomas E. Ricks, *The Gamble: General Petraeus and the American Military Adventure in Iraq* (New York: Penguin, 2009), 199.

19 G. W. Bush, *Decision Points*, 386.

20 Gates, *Duty*, 73.

21 Jeff Zeleny, "G.O.P. Senator Splits with Bush over Iraq Policy," *New York Times*, June 27, 2007.

22 Robert Pear and Carl Hulse, "Immigration Bill Fails to Survive Senate Vote," *New York Times*, June 28, 2007.

23 *PPPUS-GWB, 2007,* Vol. 1, Remarks on the Senate's Failure to Pass Immigration Reform Legislation, June 28, 2007, 829–30.

24 G. W. Bush, *Decision Points*, 301.

25 "GOP's Bush Calls for Increasing Legal Immigration Levels," *Middle American News*, February 2000.

26 Text, President's Speech on Immigration, reprinted in the *New York Times*, May 15, 2006.

27 Ibid.

28 Ibid.

29 G. W. Bush, *Decision Points*, 308.

30 *PPPUS-GWB, 2003,* Vol. 2, Remarks at the Signing Ceremony for Legislation to Implement the Chile and Singapore Free Trade Agreements, September 3, 2003, 1081–83.

31 "At Summit, Bush Touts Free-Trade," CNNPolitics.com, November 22, 2008.

32 Letter, Robert B. Zoellick to Jean Edward Smith, January 25, 2012.

33 *PPPUS-GWB, 2008,* Vol. 2, Remarks at the Asia-Pacific Economic Cooperation Business Summit, Lima, Peru, November 22, 2008, 1386–91.

34 John Rogin, "Sen. Domenici Is Latest Republican to Step Away from Bush on Iraq," *New York Times*, July 5, 2007.

35 *PPPUS-GWB, 2007,* Vol. 2, Remarks to the Greater Cleveland Partnership, July 10, 2007, 933.

36 Ibid., President's News Conference, July 12, 2007, 951–65.

37 Martha Angle, "Defying Bush, House Passes New Deadline for Withdrawal from Iraq," *New York Times*, July 12, 2007.

38 *PPPUS-GWB, 2007,* Vol. 2, Remarks to the Veterans of Foreign Wars Convention in Kansas City, Missouri, August 22, 2007, 1099–1106.

39 Ibid.

40 Ibid., Remarks at the American Legion Convention in Reno, Nevada, August 28, 2007, 1116–24.

41 National Intelligence Estimate, "Prospects for Iraq's Stability: Some Security Progress but Political Reconciliation Elusive," National Intelligence Council, August 2007.

42 Mark Mazzetti, "Report Offers Grim View of Iraqi Leaders," *New York Times*, August 24, 2007.

43 *PPPUS-GWB, 2007,* Vol. 2, Remarks Following a Dinner with Elected Officials and Community Leaders in New Orleans, Louisiana, August 28, 2007, 1125.

44 Ibid., Remarks on Hurricane Katrina Recovery Efforts in New Orleans, August 29, 2007, 1126–30.

45 Ibid., Remarks on Gulf Coast Recovery in Bay St. Louis, Mississippi, August 29, 2007, 1131–33.

46 Gates, *Duty*, 71.

47 Iraq Body Count, http://www.iraqbodycount.org/analysis/numbers/2007/.

48 Gates, *Duty*, 72.

49 Baker, *Days of Fire*, 562.

50 G. W. Bush, *Decision Points*, 384.

51 *PPPUS-GWB, 2007,* Vol. 2, Remarks Following Meeting with Iraqi Leaders at Al Asad Air Base, Iraq, September 3, 2007, 1157–58.

52 Ibid., Remarks to United States Military Personnel at Al Asad Air Base, September 3, 2007, 1159–60.

53 *New York Times*, September 5, 2007.

54 Joschka Fischer, quoted in Cullen Murphy and Todd S. Purdum, "Farewell to All That: An Oral History of the Bush White House," *Vanity Fair*, February 4, 2009. Fischer, a visiting professor at Princeton at the time, was quoting a Saudi diplomat.

55 Nicholas Kristof, "On the Ground," *New York Times*, September 11, 2007.

56 *New York Times*, September 10, 2007.

57 General David H. Petraeus, "Report to Congress on the Situation in Iraq," 10–11 September 2007. http://burgess.house.gov/uploadedfiles/petraeus%20testimony.pdf.

58 David S. Cloud and Thom Shanker, "Petraeus Warns Against Quick Pullback in Iraq," *New York Times*, September 11, 2007.

59 Transcript, "Crocker, Petraeus Testify Before the Senate Armed Services Committee on Iraq," September 11, 2007, C.Q. Transcripts wire, 23.

60 Prior to Petraeus appearing before Congress, 60 percent of Americans favored withdrawal "regardless of what is going on in Iraq at the time." After Petraeus spoke, 59 percent did. Susan Page, "Poll: Public Not Swayed by Petraeus," *USA Today*, September 18, 2007.

61 Council on Foreign Relations, "Haass: Petraeus, Crocker Blunt Congressional Criticism on Iraq," September 11, 2007.

62 Harry Reid, *The Good Fight: Hard Lessons from Searchlight to Washington* (New York: Penguin, 2008), 10–11.

63 David E. Sanger, "Officials Cite Long-Term Need for U.S. in Iraq," *New York Times*, September 12, 2007.

64 *PPPUS-GWB, 2007,* Vol. 2, Address to the Nation on Military Operations in Iraq, September 13, 2007, 1194–98.

65 "U.S. Ground Forces End Strength," Global Security.org; icasualties.org.

66 Ricks, *The Gamble*, 254–55.

67 Democratic Presidential Debate on MSNBC, at Dartmouth College, Hanover, New Hampshire, *New York Times*, September 26, 2007, transcript.

68 Steven Simon, "The Price of the Surge," *Foreign Affairs*, May/June 2008.

69 Patrick Cockburn, "Iraq: Violence Is Down—But Not Because of America's Surge," *The Independent*, September 14, 2008.

70 G. W. Bush, *Decision Points*, 389.

71 *Der Spiegel* Interview with Nouri al-Maliki, "The Tenure of Coalition Troops in Iraq Should be Limited," July 19, 2008.

72 Baker, *Days of Fire*, 622.

73 Steven Lee Myers and Alissa J. Rubin, "Iraqi Journalist Hurls Shoes at Bush and Denounces Him on TV as a Dog," *New York Times*, December 15, 2008.

74 Sudarsan Raghavan and Dan Eggen, "Shoe-Throwing Mars Bush's Baghdad Trip," *Washington Post*, December 15, 2008.

75 G. W. Bush, *Decision Points*, 392.

76 Baker, *Days of Fire*, 624.

77 Ian S. Livingston and Michael O'Hanlon, *Afghanistan Index* 18 "Annual Opium Production in Afghanistan, 1990–2013" (Washington, D.C.: Brookings Institution, 2014). Also see James Risen, *State of War: The Secret History of the CIA and the Bush Administration* (New York: Free Press, 2006).

78 G. W. Bush, *Decision Points*, 211.

79 *New York Times*, August 21, 2008.

80 G. W. Bush, *Decision Points*, 218.

81 The White House, Office of the Press Secretary, "President Bush Participates in Press Availability with President Karzai in Afghanistan," December 15, 2008.

82 G. W. Bush, *Decision Points*, 220.

Chapter Twenty-Four: Financial Armageddon

The epigraph is from George W. Bush, *Decision Points* (New York: Crown, 2010).

1 Bush's first use of the term "ownership society" came in a speech he delivered to the National Summit on Retirement Savings meeting in Washington, D.C., on February 28, 2002. Said the president: "I want America to be an ownership society, a society where a life of work becomes a retirement of independence." *PPPUS-GWB, 2002,* Vol. 1, 309.

2 U.S. Census Bureau, *Statistical Abstract of the United States: 2011*, Tables 467, 677, 584, 964, 1194 (Washington, D.C.: Government Printing Office, 2010).

3   Text, "President Bush's Acceptance Speech to the Republican National Convention," 5, *Washington Post*, September 2, 2004.

4   *PPPUS-GWB, 2005,* Vol. 1, Inaugural Address, January 21, 2005, 68.

5   Ibid., President's State of the Union Address, February 2, 2005, 116.

6   U.S. Bureau of the Census, *Statistical Abstract of the United States: 2011*, Tables 965, 970, 972, 987.

7   The White House, Record of Achievement, Expanding Home Ownership. https://georgewbush-whitehouse.archives.gov/infocus/achievement/chap7.html.

8   Edmund L. Andrews, "Greenspan Is Concerned About 'Froth' in Housing," *New York Times*, May 21, 2005. Also see "Greenspan: 'Local Bubbles' Build in Housing Sector," *USA Today*, May 20, 2005.

9   Press Briefing by Director, National Economic Council, Al Hubbard, and Chairman, Council of Economic Advisers, Ben Bernanke, Crawford, Texas, August 9, 2005. White House Archives.

10 *PPPUS-GWB, 2006,* Vol. 1, Remarks on the National Economy, Sterling, Virginia, January 19, 2006, 90.

11 Nell Henderson, "Bernanke: There's No Housing Bubble," *Washington Post*, October 27, 2005.

12 George W. Bush, *Decision Points* (New York: Crown, 2010), 449.

13 United States Senate, Committee on Finance, Confirmation hearing of Henry M. Paulson, June 27, 2006.

14 Henry M. Paulson, Jr., *On the Brink: Inside the Race to Stop the Collapse of the Global Financial System* (New York: Business Plus, 2010), 45–47.

15 Ibid.

16 The housing statistics are drawn from the United States Census Bureau website.

17 RealtyTrac website, January 1, 2007.

18 Henry Paulson, Speech to the Committee of 100, New York City, April 20, 2007. Reuters, April 20, 2007.

19 Text, Ben S. Bernanke, Speech at the 43rd Annual Conference on Bank Structure and Competition, Chicago, Illinois, May 17, 2007, "The Subprime Mortgage Market."

20 Ben S. Bernanke, *The Courage to Act: A Memoir of a Crisis and Its Aftermath* (New York: Norton, 2015), 136.

21 *PPPUS-GWB, 2007,* Vol. 2, Remarks Following a Meeting with Economic Advisers, August 8, 2007, 1050–52.

22 Sebastian Boyd, "BNP Paribas Freezes Funds as Loan Losses Roil Markets," Bloomberg.com, August 9, 2007. The three funds closed, Parvest Dynamics ABS; BNP Paribas ABS Euribor; and BNP Paribas ABS Eonia, had 1.6 billion euros ($2.2 billion) in assets.

23 *PPPUS-GWB, 2007,* Vol. 2, President's News Conference, August 9, 2007, 1052–64.

24 Ibid., Remarks on Home Ownership Financing and an Exchange with Reporters, August 31, 2007, 1150–53.

25 G. W. Bush, *Decision Points*, 449.

26 Martin Crutsinger, "Existing Single-Family Home Sales Drop," *USA Today*, January 24, 2008.

27 "U.S. Foreclosure Activity Increases 75 Percent in 2007," *RealtyTrac*, January 30, 2008; "Number of Foreclosures Soared in 2007," Associated Press, January 29, 2008.

28 *PPPUS-GWB, 2007*, Vol. 2, Remarks Following Meeting with Secretary of the Treasury Henry M. Paulson, and Secretary of Housing and Urban Development Alphonso R. Jackson, December 6, 2007, 1527–30.

29 "Putting a Freeze to Mortgage Meltdown," *Marketplace*, December 6, 2007.

30 *PPPUS-GWB, 2007*, Vol. 2, Remarks on the National Economy, Fredericksburg, Virginia, December 17, 2007, 1555–68.

31 Paulson, *On the Brink*, 96.

32 G. W. Bush, *Decision Points*, 453.

33 Paulson, *On the Brink*, 99.

34 G. W. Bush, *Decision Points*, 453.

35 Paulson, *On the Brink*, 113.

36 "Foreclosures Up a Record 81% in 2008," CNNMoney.com.

37 Damian Paletta and David Enrich, "Crisis Deepens as Big Bank Fails," *Wall Street Journal*, July 12, 2008.

38 Paulson, *On the Brink*, 152.

39 Ibid., 166.

40 John Cassidy, "Anatomy of a Meltdown," *The New Yorker*, December 1, 2008.

41 David Wessel, *In Fed We Trust: Ben Bernanke's War on the Great Panic* (New York: Crown Business, 2009), 14.

42 Timothy F. Geithner, *Stress Test: Reflections on the Financial Crisis* (New York: Crown, 2014), 180.

43 Henry Samuel and Harry Wallop, "Christine Lagarde Warned Hank Paulson to Bail Out Lehman Brothers," *Daily Telegraph*, October 16, 2008; Joe Nocera and Edmund L. Andrews, "Struggling to Keep Up as the Crisis Raced On," *New York Times*, October 23, 2008.

44 Peter J. Wallison, *Hidden in Plain Sight: What Really Caused the World's Worst Financial Crisis and Why It Could Happen Again* (New York: Encounter Books, 2015), 324.

45 Lawrence G. McDonald, *Colossal Failure of Common Sense: The Inside Story of the Collapse of Lehman Brothers* (New York: Three Rivers Press, 2009), 323–24.

46 G. W. Bush, *Decision Points*, 457.

47 Paulson, *On the Brink*, 235–37.

48 G. W. Bush, *Decision Points*, 458.

49 Ibid., 452.

50 Ibid., 458.

51 Alan S. Blinder, *After the Music Stopped: The Financial Crisis, the Response, and the Work Ahead* (New York: Penguin, 2013), 137.

52 Wessel, *In Fed We Trust*, 199–200.

53 Paulson, *On the Brink*, 255–56.

54 Baker, *Days of Fire*, 610.

55 G. W. Bush, *Decision Points*, 439–46. Also see Paulson, *On the Brink*, 257.

56 G. W. Bush, *Decision Points*, 440.

57 Wessel, *In Fed We Trust*, 203–04.

58 James B. Stewart, "Eight Days: The Battle to Save the American Financial System," *The New Yorker*, September 21, 2009.

59 Wessel, *In Fed We Trust*, 205.

60 *PPPUS-GWB, 2008,* Vol. 2, Remarks on the National Economy, September 19, 2008, 1212–14.

61 The text of the three-page draft proposal is reprinted in *The New York Times*, September 21, 2008.

62 Dick Cheney, *In My Time* (New York: Threshold, 2011), 508.

63 *PPPUS-GWB, 2008,* Vol. 2, Address to the Nation on the National Economy, September 25, 2008, 1237–40.

64 Paulson, *On the Brink*, 279.

65 Baker, *Days of Fire*, 612.

66 G. W. Bush, *Decision Points*, 461.

67 Ibid.

68 Baker, *Days of Fire*, 614.

69 Paulson, *On the Brink*, 297.

70 Ibid.

71 G. W. Bush, *Decision Points*, 462.

72 Cheney, *In My Time*, 509.

73 Jonathan Alter, *The Promise: President Obama, Year One* (New York: Simon & Schuster, 2011), 12.

74 Paulson, *On the Brink*, 299.

75 Baker, *Days of Fire*, 615.

76 G. W. Bush, *Decision Points*, 463.

77 Paulson, *On the Brink*, 326.

78 *PPPUS-GWB, 2008,* Vol. 2, Remarks on Economic Stabilization, October 3, 2008, 1267–68.

79 Ibid., Remarks Following a Visit to the Treasury Department, October 3, 2008, 1269.

80 Blinder, *After the Music Stopped*, 178.

81 G. W. Bush, *Decision Points*, 420.

Chapter Twenty-Five: *Finis*

The epigraph is from George W. Bush, *Decision Points* (New York: Crown, 2010), 459.

1 Gary C. Jacobson, *A Divider, Not a Uniter: George W. Bush and the American People* (New York: Longman, 2011), 245–52.

2 Gary C. Jacobson, "The 2008 Presidential and Congressional Elections; Anti-Bush Referendums and the Prospects for the Democratic Majority," 124 *Political Science Quarterly* (Spring 2009), 12.

3 Peter Baker, *Days of Fire: Bush and Cheney in the White House* (New York: Doubleday, 2013), 599.

4 Jacobson, *A Divider, Not a Uniter*, 256.

5 Peter Baker, "Party in Power, Running as if It Weren't," *New York Times*, September 5, 2008.

6 Baker, *Days of Fire*, 599.

7 John Heileman and Mark Halperin, *Game Change: Obama and the Clintons, McCain and Palin, and the Race of a Lifetime* (New York: HarperCollins, 2010), 366.

8 Baker, *Days of Fire*, 599.

9 *PPPUS-GWB, 2008,* Vol. 2, Satellite Remarks to the Republican National Convention, September 2, 2008, 1170–71.

10 Ibid.

11 John McCain's Acceptance Speech, September 4, 2008, *New York Times*, September 4, 2008, transcript.

12 Jim Rutenberg, "Candidates Clash over Character and Policy," *New York Times*, October 15, 2008.

13 G. W. Bush, *Decision Points*, 466.

14 Ibid., 467.

15 *PPPUS-GWB, 2008,* Vol. 2, Remarks on the 2008 Presidential Election, November 5, 2008, 1349–50.

16 Ibid., Remarks to White House Staff, November 6, 2008, 1350–51.

17 G. W. Bush, *Decision Points*, 468.

18 Ibid.

19 Ibid. Also see Henry W. Paulson, *On the Brink: Inside the Race to Stop the Collapse of the Global Financial System* (New York: Business Plus, 2010), 424.

20 David M. Herszenhorn, "Deal to Rescue American Automakers Is Moving Ahead," *New York Times*, December 9, 2008.

21 David M. Herszenhorn and David E. Sanger, "House Passes Auto Rescue Plan," *New York Times*, December 11, 2008.

22 David M. Herszenhorn and David E. Sanger, "Senate Abandons Automaker Bailout Bid," *New York Times*, December 12, 2008.

23 Statement by Press Secretary Dana Perino, The White House Office of the Press Secretary, December 12, 2008.

24 *PPPUS-GWB, 2008,* Vol. 2, Remarks to the American Enterprise Institute and a Question-and-Answer Session, December 18, 2008, 1476–91.

25 Ibid., Remarks on the United States Auto Industry, December 19, 2008, 1499–1501.

26 G. W. Bush, *Decision Points*, 469.

27 David E. Sanger, David M. Herszenhorn, and Bill Vlasic, "Bush Aids De-

troit, but Hard Choices Wait for Obama," *New York Times*, December 19, 2008.

28 G. W. Bush, *Decision Points*, 63.

29 *PPPUS-GWB, 2008,* Vol. 2, President's News Conference with Prime Minister Yasuo Fukuda of Japan, Toyako, Japan, July 6, 2008, 993–99.

30 Edward Cody, Maureen Fan, and Jill Drew, "A Spectacular Opening to the 29th Olympiad," *Washington Post*, August 9, 2008.

31 *PPPUS-GWB, 2008,* Vol. 2, Remarks to the 2008 United States Olympiad and Paralympic Team, July 21, 2008, 1039–41.

32 G. W. Bush, *Decision Points*, 429. Also see Associated Press, "Bush First President to See Olympics on Foreign Soil," August 2, 2008.

33 *PPPUS-GWB, 2008,* Vol. 2, Remarks at Dedication Ceremony for the United States Embassy in Beijing, China, August 8, 2008, 1127–28.

34 Calum MacLeod, "At Olympics, President Bush Enjoys a Day at the Beach," *USA Today*, August 9, 2008.

35 *PPPUS-GWB, 2008,* Vol. 2, Interview with Bob Costas of NBC Sports in Beijing, August 11, 2008, 1134–37.

36 "White House to Host Summit on World Economy," *Wall Street Journal*, October 22, 2008.

37 Chinese Ministry of Finance, "Hu Jintao Addresses the G-20 Summit on Financial Markets and the World Economy in Washington," November 16, 2008.

38 The White House, "Summit on Financial Markets and the World Economy," Washington, D.C., November 14–15, 2008.

39 Kenneth R. Baznet, "All the Presidents' Lunch: Barack Obama Meets Past Presidents," *New York Daily News*, January 7, 2009.

40 Ibid.

41 *PPPUS-GWB, 2008,* Vol. 2, Interview with Brit Hume of Fox News, January 7, 2009, 1531–42.

42 Ibid., President's News Conference, January 12, 2009, 1552–1563.

43 Ibid., Farewell Address to the Nation, January 15, 2009, 1577–1580.

44 David Axelrod, *Believer: My Forty Years in Politics* (New York: Penguin, 2015), 339.

45 Text, Barack Obama's Inaugural Address, *New York Times*, January 20, 2009.

46 Peter Baker, "On Plane to Texas, Critiques of the Speech," *New York Times*, January 23, 2009. Some of Bush's inner circle, Karen Hughes, Marc Thiessen, and Dan Bartlett, were critical of Obama's speech and thought he was shooting at Bush. Other former aides, such as Ari Fleischer, Peter Wehner, and Mark McKinnon, found nothing objectionable.

47 Laura Bush, *Spoken from the Heart* (New York: Scribner, 2010), 426.

48 Peter Baker interview with David Axelrod, in Baker, *Days of Fire*, 637.

49 Baker, *Days of Fire*, 638.

50 G. W. Bush, *Decision Points*, 475; Jim Rutenberg, "Bushes Have a Warm

Homecoming in Texas," *New York Times*, January 21, 2009; Laura Bush, *Spoken from the Heart*, 429.

51 Baker, *Days of Fire*, 642.

52 The White House, Office of the Press Secretary, Remarks by President Obama at Dedication of the George W. Bush Presidential Library, April 25, 2013.

53 Dan Balz, "Obama, Ex-Presidents Gather to Dedicate George W. Bush Library," *Washington Post*, April 25, 2013.

54 Ewen MacAskill and Afu Hirsch, "George Bush Calls Off Visit to Switzerland," *Guardian*, February 6, 2011.

55 Peter Stone, "After Skipping Ground Zero Event with Obama, Bush Made Three Paid Speeches," Center for Public Integrity, May 20, 2011. Bush's speaking arrangements were made by the Washington Speakers Bureau, a commercial booking agency. Bush's speaking income, while significant, pales when compared to that of Bill Clinton, who earned $65 million for his speaking between 2001 and 2009.

56 Baker, *Days of Fire*, 543.

57 George W. Bush, *41: A Portrait of My Father* (New York: Crown, 2014), 266–67.

58 Mark K. Updegrove, "President George W. Bush and Laura Bush Reflect on the Twins, Bush's Newfound Passion for Painting, and More," *Parade*, April 19, 2013.

59 Alastair Sooke, "George W. Bush Paintings: All the Hallmarks of Outsider Art," *The Telegraph*, April 4, 2014.

60 Rick Klein, "George W. Bush: Painting Has Changed My Life," "The Note," ABC News, April 24, 2014.

61 Peter Baker, "Bush Dips Toe Back into Washington," *New York Times*, May 15, 2012.

62 George W. Bush interview with *USA Today*, April 21, 2013.

Bibliography

Abrams, Elliott. *Tested by Zion: The Bush Administration and the Israeli-Palestinian Conflict*. New York: Cambridge University Press, 2013.

Aikman, David. *Man of Faith: The Spiritual Journey of George W. Bush*. Nashville: W Publishing Group, 2004.

Alexander, Paul. *The Candidate: Behind John Kerry's Remarkable Run for the White House*. New York: Riverhead Books, 2004.

Allawi, Ali A. *The Occupation of Iraq: Winning the War, Losing the Peace*. New Haven: Yale University Press, 2007.

Alter, Jonathan. *The Promise: President Obama, Year One*. New York: Simon & Schuster, 2011.

Altman, Daniel. *Neoconomy: George Bush's Revolutionary Gamble with America's Future*. New York: PublicAffairs, 2004.

Andersen, Christopher. *George and Laura: Portrait of a Marriage*. New York: HarperCollins, 2002.

Anderson, Terry H. *Bush's Wars*. New York: Oxford University Press, 2011.

Annan, Kofi, with Nader Mousavizadeh. *Interventions: A Life in War and Peace*. New York: Penguin, 2012.

Arato, Andrew. *Constitution Making Under Occupation: The Politics of Imposed Revolution in Iraq*. New York: Columbia University Press, 2009.

Ashcroft, John. *Never Again: Securing America and Restoring Justice*. New York: Center Street, 2006.

Atkinson, Rick. *In the Company of Soldiers: A Chronicle of Combat in Iraq*. New York: Henry Holt, 2004.

Axelrod, David. *Believe: My Forty Years in Politics*. New York: Penguin, 2015.

Baker, Nicholson. *Checkpoint*. New York: Alfred A. Knopf, 2004.

Baker, Peter. *Days of Fire: Bush and Cheney in the White House.* New York: Doubleday, 2013.

Baker, Russ. *Family of Secrets: The Bush Dynasty, America's Invisible Government, and the Hidden History of the Last Fifty Years.* New York: Bloomsbury, 2009.

Balz, Dan, and Haynes Johnson. *The Battle for America, 2008: The Story of an Extraordinary Election.* New York: Viking, 2009.

Bamford, James. *The Puzzle Palace: A Report on NSA, America's Most Secret Agency.* Boston: Houghton Mifflin, 1982.

Barone, Michael. *The Almanac of American Politics, 2006.* Washington, D.C.: National Journal, 2005.

Baumgartner, Jody C. *The American Vice Presidency Reconsidered.* Westport, Conn.: Praeger, 2006.

Bellow, Saul. *Ravelstein.* New York: Penguin, 2000.

Bent, Samuel Arthur, comp. *Familiar Short Sayings of Great Men*, 6th Edition. Boston: Ticknor & Co., 1887.

Bergen, Peter. *The Longest War: Inside the Enduring Conflict Between America and al-Qaeda.* New York: Free Press, 2011.

Bernanke, Ben S. *The Courage to Act: A Memoir of a Crisis and Its Aftermath.* New York: W. W. Norton, 2015.

Bissinger, H. G. *Friday Night Lights.* Reading, Mass.: Addison-Wesley, 1990.

Blair, Tony. *A Journey: My Political Life.* New York: Alfred A. Knopf, 2010.

Blinder, Alan S. *After the Music Stopped: The Financial Crisis, the Response, and the Work Ahead.* New York: Penguin, 2013.

Blix, Hans. *Disarming Iraq.* New York: Pantheon, 2004.

Bloom, Allan. *The Closing of the American Mind.* New York: Simon & Schuster, 1987.

Blumenthal, Sidney. *The Clinton Wars.* New York: Farrar, Straus & Giroux, 2003.

Bolger, Daniel P. *Why We Lost: A General's Inside Account of the Iraq and Afghanistan Wars.* New York: Houghton Mifflin Harcourt, 2014.

Brady, John. *Bad Boy: The Life and Politics of Lee Atwater.* New York: Addison-Wesley, 1997.

Bremer, L. Paul. *My Year in Iraq: The Struggle to Build a Future of Hope.* New York: Simon & Schuster, 2006.

Brinkley, Douglas. *The Great Deluge: Hurricane Katrina, New Orleans, and the Mississippi Gulf Coast.* New York: HarperCollins, 2006.

Brown, Michael, and Ted Schwarz. *Deadly Indifference: The Perfect (Political) Storm: Hurricane Katrina, the Bush White House, and Beyond.* Lanham, Md.: Taylor Trade Publishing, 2011.

Brownlee, W. Elliot. *Federal Taxation in America: A Short History.* Cambridge: Cambridge University Press, 2004.

Bruni, Frank. *Ambling into History: The Unlikely Odyssey of George W. Bush.* New York: HarperCollins, 2002.

Brzezinski, Zbigniew. *Second Chance: Three Presidents and the Crisis of American Superpower.* New York: Basic Books, 2006.

Bumiller, Elisabeth. *Condoleezza Rice: An American Life.* New York: Random House, 2007.

Burke, John P. *Becoming President: The Bush Transition, 2000–2003.* Boulder: Lynne Rienner, 2004.

Bush, Barbara. *Barbara Bush: A Memoir.* New York: Guideposts, 1994.

Bush, George, and Brent Scowcroft. *A World Transformed.* New York: Alfred A. Knopf, 1998.

Bush, George, with Victor Gold. *Looking Forward.* New York: Doubleday, 1987.

Bush, George W. *41: A Portrait of My Father.* New York: Crown, 2014.

——. *A Charge to Keep: My Journey to the White House.* New York: William Morrow, 1999.

——. *Decision Points.* New York: Crown, 2010.

——. *Public Papers of the Presidents of the United States: George W. Bush, 2001.* 2 vols. Washington, D.C.: Government Printing Office, 2003.

——. *Public Papers of the Presidents of the United States: George W. Bush, 2002.* 2 vols. Washington, D.C.: Government Printing Office, 2004.

——. *Public Papers of the Presidents of the United States: George W. Bush, 2003.* 2 vols. Washington, D.C.: Government Printing Office, 2006.

——. *Public Papers of the Presidents of the United States: George W. Bush, 2004.* 3 vols. Washington, D.C.: Government Printing Office, 2007.

——. *Public Papers of the Presidents of the United States: George W. Bush, 2005.* 2 vols. Washington, D.C.: Government Printing Office, 2009.

——. *Public Papers of the Presidents of the United States: George W. Bush, 2006.* 2 vols. Washington, D.C.: Government Printing Office, 2010.

——. *Public Papers of the Presidents of the United States: George W. Bush, 2007.* 2 vols. Washington, D.C.: Government Printing Office, 2011.

——. *Public Papers of the Presidents of the United States: George W. Bush, 2008.* 2 vols. Washington, D.C.: Government Printing Office, 2012.

Bush, Jenna. *Ana's Story: A Journey of Hope.* New York: HarperCollins, 2007.

Bush, Laura. *Spoken from the Heart.* New York: Scribner, 2010.

Campbell, Alastair. *The Blair Years: The Alastair Campbell Diaries.* New York: Alfred A. Knopf, 2007.

Campbell, Colin, and Bert A. Rockman, eds. *The George W. Bush Presidency.* Washington, D.C.: CQ Press, 2004.

Cannon, Lou, and Carl M. Cannon. *Reagan's Disciple: George W. Bush's Troubled Quest for a Presidential Legacy.* New York: PublicAffairs, 2008.

Caro, Robert. *The Passage of Power: The Years of Lyndon Johnson.* New York: Alfred A. Knopf, 2012.

Casey, George W. Jr. *Strategic Reflections: Operation Iraqi Freedom, July 2004–February 2007.* Washington, D.C.: National Defense University Press, 2012.

Chafee, Lincoln. *Against the Tide: How a Compliant Congress Empowered a Reckless President.* New York: Thomas Dunne Books, 2008.

Cheney, Dick. *In My Time.* New York: Threshold, 2011.

Cheney, Mary. *Now It's My Turn: A Daughter's Chronicle of Political Life.* New York: Threshold, 2006.

Chertoff, Michael. *Homeland Security: Assessing the First Five Years.* Philadelphia: University of Pennsylvania Press, 2009.

Chirac, Jacques. *My Life in Politics.* Translated by Catherine Spencer. New York: Palgrave Macmillan, 2012.

Christie, Ron. *Black in the White House: Life Inside George W. Bush's West Wing.* Nashville: Thomas Nelson, 2006.

Clarke, Richard A. *Against All Enemies: Inside America's War on Terror.* New York: Free Press, 2004.

Cockburn, Andrew. *Rumsfeld: His Rise, Fall, and Catastrophic Legacy.* New York: Scribner, 2007.

Cockburn, Patrick. *The Occupation: War and Resistance in Iraq.* London: Verso, 2006.

Cole, David. *The Torture Memos: Rationalizing the Unthinkable.* New York: The New Press, 2009.

Commission to Assess the Ballistic Missile Threat to the United States. *Report of the Commission to Assess the Ballistic Missile Threat to the United States: Executive Summary.* Washington, D.C.: Government Printing Office, 1998.

Congressional Quarterly. *Guide to U.S. Elections.* Washington, D.C.: Congressional Quarterly, 1975.

Cooper, Christopher, and Robert Block. *Disaster: Hurricane Katrina and the Failure of Homeland Security.* New York: Times Books, 2006.

Cray, Ed. *General of the Army: George C. Marshall, Soldier and Statesman.* New York: Cooper Square Press, 1990.

Crowley, Monica. *Nixon Off the Record: His Candid Commentary on People and Politics.* New York: Random House, 1996.

Daalder, Ivo H., and I. M. Destler. *In the Shadow of the Oval Office.* New York: Simon & Schuster, 2009.

Daschle, Tom. *Like No Other Time: The 107th Congress and the Two Years That Changed America Forever.* New York: Crown, 2003.

Denton, Robert E. Jr. *The 2000 Presidential Campaign: A Communication Perspective.* Westport, Conn.: Praeger, 2002.

DeYoung, Karen. *Soldier: The Life of Colin Powell.* New York: Alfred A. Knopf, 2006.

Dobbins, James F., Seth G. Jones, Benjamin Runkle, and Siddharth Mohandas. *Occupying Iraq: A History of the Coalition Provisional Authority.* Arlington, Va.: RAND, 2009.

Dobrynin, Anatoly. *In Confidence: Moscow's Ambassador to Six Cold War Presidents.* New York: Random House, 1995.

Draper, Robert. *Dead Certain: The Presidency of George W. Bush*. New York: Free Press, 2007.

Drogin, Bob. *Curveball: Spies, Lies, and the Con Man Who Caused a War*. New York: Random House, 2007.

Dubose, Lou, Jan Reid, and Carl M. Cannon. *Boy Genius: Karl Rove, the Brains Behind the Remarkable Political Triumph of George W. Bush*. New York: Public-Affairs, 2003.

Duelfer, Charles. *Hide and Seek: The Search for Truth in Iraq*. New York: Public-Affairs, 2009.

Ehrenberg, John, J. Patrice McSherry, José Ramós Sánchez, and Caroleen Marji Sayej, eds. *The Iraq Papers*. New York: Oxford University Press, 2010.

Eichenwald, Kurt. *500 Days: Secrets and Lies in the Terror Wars*. New York: Touchstone, 2012.

Encyclopaedia Britannica, 11th ed. New York: University of Cambridge Press, 1910.

Fehrenbach, T. R. *Lone Star: A History of Texas and the Texans*. New York: Da Capo, 2000.

Feith, Douglas J. *War and Decision: Inside the Pentagon at the Dawn of the War on Terrorism*. New York: HarperCollins, 2008.

Fischer, David Hackett. *Washington's Crossing*. New York: Oxford University Press, 2004.

Fisher, O. C. *Cactus Jack: A Biography of John Nance Garner*. Waco: Texian Press, 1978.

Fleischer, Ari. *Taking Heat: The President, the Press, and My Years at the White House*. New York: William Morrow, 2005.

Foner, Eric. *The Fiery Trial: Abraham Lincoln and American Slavery*. New York: W. W. Norton, 2010.

Franks, Tommy, with Malcolm McConnell. *American Soldier*. New York: Harper-Collins, 2004.

Friedman, Leon, ed. *The Laws of War: A Documentary History*. New York: Random House, 1972.

Frum, David. *The Right Man: An Inside Account of the Bush White House*. New York: Random House, 2003.

Galbraith, Peter W. *The End of Iraq: How American Incompetence Created a War Without End*. New York: Simon & Schuster, 2006.

Gates, Robert. *Duty: Memoirs of a Secretary at War*. New York: Alfred A. Knopf, 2014.

Geithner, Timothy F. *Stress Test: Reflections on the Financial Crisis*. New York: Crown, 2014.

Gellman, Barton. *Angler: The Cheney Vice Presidency*. New York: Penguin, 2008.

Gerhart, Ann. *The Perfect Wife: The Life and Choices of Laura Bush*. New York: Simon & Schuster, 2004.

Gerson, Michael J. *Heroic Conservatism: Why Republicans Need to Embrace America's Ideals (And Why They Deserve to Fail if They Don't)*. New York: Harper-Collins, 2007.

Gillespie, Ed. *Winning Right: Campaign Politics and Conservative Policies*. New York: Threshold, 2006.

Goldman, Peter, Thomas M. DeFrank, Mark Miller, Andrew Murr, and Tom Mathews. *Quest for the Presidency, 1992*. College Station: Texas A&M University Press, 1994.

Goldsmith, Jack L. *The Terror Presidency: Law and Judgment Inside the Bush Administration*. New York: W. W. Norton, 2007.

Gordon, Michael R., and General Bernard E. Trainor. *Cobra II: The Inside Story of the Invasion and Occupation of Iraq*. New York: Pantheon, 2006.

———. *Endgame: The Inside Story of the Struggle for Iraq, from George W. Bush to Barack Obama*. New York: Vintage, 2012.

Graham, Bradley. *By His Own Rules: The Ambitions, Successes, and Ultimate Failures of Donald Rumsfeld*. New York: PublicAffairs, 2009.

Graveline, Christopher, and Michael Clemens. *The Secrets of Abu Ghraib Revealed: American Soldiers on Trial*. Washington, D.C.: Potomac Books, 2010.

Greenberg, Karen J., and Joshua L. Dratel, eds. *The Torture Papers: The Road to Abu Ghraib*. New York: Cambridge University Press, 2005.

Greenspan, Alan. *The Age of Turbulence: Adventures in a New World*. New York: Penguin, 2007.

Greenstein, Fred I., ed. *The George W. Bush Presidency*. Baltimore: Johns Hopkins University Press, 2003.

Haass, Richard N. *War of Necessity, War of Choice: A Memoir of Two Iraq Wars*. New York: Simon & Schuster, 2009.

Halper, Stefan, and Jonathan Clarke. *America Alone: The Neo-Conservatives and the Global Order*. New York: Cambridge University Press, 2004.

Halperin, Mark, and John F. Harris. *The Way to Win: Taking the White House in 2008*. New York: Random House, 2006.

Hamburger, Tom, and Peter Wallsten. *One Party Country: The Republican Plan for Dominance in the 21st Century*. New York: Wiley, 2006.

Hatfield, J. H. *Fortunate Son: George W. Bush and the Making of an American President*. New York: Soft Skull Press, 2000.

Hayes, Stephen F. *Cheney: The Untold Story of America's Most Powerful and Controversial Vice President*. New York: HarperCollins, 2007.

Hegel, Georg Wilhelm Friedrich. *Reason in History, a General Introduction to the Philosophy of History*. Translated by Robert S. Hartman. New York: Bobbs-Merrill, 1953.

Heileman, John, and Mark Halperin. *Game Change: Obama and the Clintons, McCain and Palin, and the Race of a Lifetime*. New York: HarperCollins, 2010.

Hersh, Seymour M. *Chain of Command: The Road from 9/11 to Abu Ghraib*. New York: HarperCollins, 2004.

Horton, Scott. *Lords of Secrecy: The National Security Elite and America's Stealth Warfare.* New York: Nation Books, 2015.

Hughes, Karen. *Ten Minutes from Normal.* New York: Viking, 2004.

Hyams, Joe. *Flight of the Avenger.* New York: Berkley, 1992.

Iraq Study Group. *The Iraq Study Group Report: The Way Forward—A New Approach.* New York: Vintage, 2006.

Isikoff, Michael, and David Corn. *Hubris: The Inside Story of Spin, Scandal, and the Selling of the Iraq War.* New York: Crown, 2006.

Ivins, Molly, and Lou Dubose. *Shrub: The Short but Happy Political Life of George W. Bush.* New York: Vintage, 2000.

Jacobson, Gary C. *A Divider, Not a Uniter: George W. Bush and the American People.* New York: Longman, 2011.

James, Marquis. *The Raven: A Biography of Sam Houston.* Austin: University of Texas Press, 1929.

Jeffords, James M. *My Declaration of Independence.* New York: Simon & Schuster, 2001.

Johnson, Lyndon B. *Public Papers of the Presidents of the United States: Lyndon B. Johnson, 1968.* 2 vols. Washington, D.C.: Government Printing Office, 1971.

Joseph, Robert C. *Countering WMD: The Libya Experience.* Fairfax, Va.: National Institute Press, 2009.

Kelley, Kitty. *The Family: The Real Story of the Bush Dynasty.* New York: Doubleday, 2004.

Kessler, Glenn. *The Confidante: Condoleezza Rice and the Creation of the Bush Legacy.* New York: St. Martin's Press, 2007.

Kessler, Ronald. *Laura Bush: An Intimate Portrait of the First Lady.* New York: Broadway, 2007.

Kettl, Donald F. *Team Bush: Leadership Lessons from the Bush White House.* New York: McGraw-Hill, 2003.

Kitfield, James. *War and Destiny: How the Bush Revolution in Foreign and Military Affairs Redefined American Power.* Dulles, Va.: Potomac Books, 2005.

Kraus, Kendall. *The Assassination of George W. Bush: A Love Story.* New York: Lulu, 2007.

Kumar, Martha Joynt. *Before the Oath: How George W. Bush and Barack Obama Managed a Transfer of Power.* Baltimore: Johns Hopkins University Press, 2015.

Kuo, David. *Tempting Faith: An Inside Story of Political Seduction.* New York: Free Press, 2006.

Latimer, Matt. *Speech-Less: Tales of a White House Survivor.* New York: Three Rivers Press, 2009.

Libbey, James K. *Dear Alben: Mr. Barkley of Kentucky.* Lexington: University of Kentucky Press, 1979.

Lichtblau, Eric. *Bush's Law: The Remaking of American Justice.* New York: Pantheon, 2008.

Lindsey, Lawrence, with Marc Sumerlin. *What a President Should Know . . . but Most Learn Too Late: An Insider's View on How to Succeed in the Oval Office.* Lanham, Md.: Rowman & Littlefield, 2008.

Lloyd George, David. *The Truth About the Peace Treaties.* Vol. 1. London: V. Gollancz, 1938.

MacMillan, Margaret. *Paris 1919: Six Months That Changed the World.* New York: Random House, 2001.

Mann, James. *George W. Bush.* New York: Times Books, 2015.

——. *Rise of the Vulcans: The History of Bush's War Cabinet.* New York: Viking, 2004.

Mansfield, Stephen. *The Faith of George W. Bush.* New York: Penguin, 2004.

Manson, Peter J. *Iraq in Transition: The Legacy of Dictatorship and the Prospects for Democracy.* Washington, D.C.: Potomac Books, 2009.

Maraniss, David, and Ellen Nakashima. *The Prince of Tennessee: The Rise of Al Gore.* New York: Simon & Schuster, 2000.

Maranto, Robert, Tom Lansford, and Jeremy Johnson, eds. *Judging Bush (Studies in the Modern Presidency).* Stanford: Stanford University Press, 2009.

Margulies, Joseph. *Guantánamo and the Abuse of Presidential Power.* New York: Simon & Schuster, 2006.

Matlock, Jack. *Reagan and Gorbachev: How the Cold War Ended.* New York: Random House, 2004.

Mayer, Jane. *The Dark Side: The Inside Story of How the War on Terror Turned into a War on American Ideals.* New York: Random House, 2008.

McClellan, Scott. *What Happened: Inside the Bush White House and Washington's Culture of Deception.* New York: PublicAffairs, 2008.

McCombs, William F. *Making Woodrow Wilson President.* New York: Fairview Publishing Co., 1921.

McChrystal, General Stanley. *My Share of the Task: A Memoir.* New York: Penguin, 2013.

McDonald, Lawrence G. *Colossal Failure of Common Sense: The Inside Story of the Collapse of Lehman Brothers.* New York: Three Rivers Press, 2009.

McNamara, Robert. *In Retrospect: The Tragedy and Lessons of Vietnam.* New York: Random House, 1995.

Meacham, Jon. *Destiny and Power: The American Odyssey of George Herbert Walker Bush.* New York: Random House, 2015.

Meyer, Christopher. *DC Confidential: The Controversial Memoirs of Britain's Ambassador to the U.S. at the time of 9/11 and the Run-up to the Iraq War.* London: Orion, 2006.

Milbank, Dana. *Smashmouth: Notes from the 2000 Campaign Trail.* New York: Basic Books, 2001.

Miller, Mark Crispin. *Fooled Again: How the Right Stole the 2004 Election and Why They'll Steal the Next One Too (Unless We Stop Them).* New York: Basic Books, 2005.

Miller, Nathan. *FDR: An Intimate History.* New York: Doubleday, 1983.

Minutaglio, Bill. *First Son: George W. Bush and the Bush Family Dynasty.* New York: Times Books, 1999.

Mitchell, Elizabeth. *W: Revenge of the Bush Dynasty.* New York: Hyperion, 2000.

Moore, James, and Wayne Slater. *Bush's Brain: How Karl Rove Made George W. Bush Presidential.* Hoboken, N.J.: John Wiley & Sons, 2003.

Moran, Charles McMoran Wilson. *Churchill: Taken from the Diaries of Lord Moran.* Boston: Houghton Mifflin, 1966.

Myers, General Richard B. *Eyes on the Horizon: Serving on the Front Lines of National Security.* New York: Threshold, 2009.

National Commission on Terrorist Attacks Upon the United States. *The 9/11 Commission Report: Final Report of the National Commission on Terrorist Attacks Upon the United States.* New York: W. W. Norton, 2004.

National Commission on the Causes of the Financial and Economic Crisis in the United States. *The Financial Crisis: Inquiry Report.* New York: PublicAffairs, 2011.

Nevins, Allan. *Hamilton Fish: The Inner History of the Grant Administration.* New York: Frederick Ungar, 1937.

Obama, Barack. *Public Papers of the Presidents of the United States: Barack Obama, 2009.* 2 vols. Washington, D.C.: Government Printing Office, 2011.

Oberdorfer, Don. *The Turn: From the Cold War to a New Era.* New York: Poseidon, 1991.

Oliphant, Thomas. *Utter Incompetents: Ego and Ideology in the Age of Bush.* New York: St. Martin's Press, 2007.

Ottaway, David B. *The King's Messenger: Prince Bandar bin Sultan and America's Tangled Relationship with Saudi Arabia.* New York: Walker, 2008.

Parmet, Herbert S. *George Bush: The Life of a Lone Star Yankee.* New York: Scribner, 1997.

Paulson, Henry W. *On The Brink: Inside the Race to Stop the Collapse of the Global Financial System.* New York: Business Plus, 2010.

Phillips, Kevin. *American Dynasty: Aristocracy, Fortune, and the Politics of Deceit in the House of Bush.* New York: Penguin, 2004.

Political Staff of the *Washington Post. Deadlock: The Inside Story of America's Closest Election.* New York: PublicAffairs, 2001.

Pomper, Gerald M. *The Election of 2000.* New York: Chatham House, 2001.

Powell, Colin. *My American Journey.* New York: Ballantine, 1995.

Prugh, Major General George S. *Law of War: Vietnam, 1964–1973.* Washington, D.C.: Department of the Army, 1975.

Purdum, Todd S. *A Time of Our Choosing: America's War with Iraq.* New York: Times Books, 2003.

Radcliffe, Donnie. *Simply Barbara Bush: A Portrait of America's Candid First Lady.* New York: Warner, 1989.

Record, Jeffrey. *Wanting War: Why the Bush Administration Invaded Iraq.* Washington, D.C.: Potomac Books, 2010.

Reid, Harry. *The Good Fight: Hard Lessons from Searchlight to Washington.* New York: Penguin, 2008.

Rice, Condoleezza. *No Higher Honor.* New York: Crown, 2011.

Rich, Frank. *The Greatest Story Ever Sold.* New York: Penguin, 2006.

Ricks, Thomas E. *Fiasco: The American Military Adventure in Iraq.* New York: Penguin, 2006.

———. *The Gamble: General Petraeus and the American Military Adventure in Iraq.* New York: Penguin, 2010.

Risen, James. *State of War: The Secret History of the CIA and the Bush Administration.* New York: Free Press, 2006.

Rizzo, John. *Company Man: Thirty Years of Controversy and Crisis in the CIA.* New York: Scribner, 2014.

Robinson, Linda. *Tell Me How This Ends: General David Petraeus and the Search for a Way Out of Iraq.* New York: PublicAffairs, 2009.

Rodman, Peter W. *Presidential Command: Power, Leadership, and Foreign Policy from Richard Nixon to George W. Bush.* New York: Alfred A. Knopf, 2009.

Rothkopf, David J. *Running the World: The Inside Story of the National Security Council and the Architects of American Power.* New York: PublicAffairs, 2005.

Rove, Karl. *Courage and Consequence.* New York: Threshold, 2010.

Rozell, Mark J., and Gleaves Whitney, eds. *Religion and the Bush Presidency.* New York: Palgrave, 2007.

Rumsfeld, Donald. *Known and Unknown.* New York: Sentinel, 2011.

Sammon, Bill. *Misunderestimated: The President Battles Terrorism, Media Bias, and the Bush Haters.* New York: HarperCollins, 2004.

———. *Strategery: How George W. Bush Is Defeating Terrorists, Outwitting Democrats, and Confounding the Mainstream Media.* Washington, D.C.: Regnery, 2006.

Sanchez, Lt. Gen. Ricardo S. *Wiser in Battle: A Soldier's Story.* New York: HarperCollins, 2008.

Sands, Philippe. *Lawless World: Making and Breaking Global Rules.* London: Penguin, 2006.

Savage, Charlie. *Takeover: The Return of the Imperial Presidency and the Subversion of American Democracy.* New York: Little, Brown, 2007.

Scammon, Richard M., Alice V. McGillivay, and Rhodes Clark. *America Votes 24: A Handbook of Contemporary American Election Statistics.* Washington, D.C.: CQ Press, 2001.

Schmitt, Eric, and Thom Shanker. *Counterstrike: The Untold Story of America's Secret Campaign Against Al Qaeda.* New York: Times Books, 2011.

Schweizer, Peter, and Rochelle Schweizer. *The Bushes: Portrait of a Dynasty.* New York: Doubleday, 2004.

Senate Select Committee on Intelligence. *The CIA Torture Report: Unclassified: Findings and Conclusions.* Washington, D.C.: United States Senate, 2014.

Shelton, Hugh, with Ronald Levinson and Malcolm McConnell. *Without Hesitation: The Odyssey of an American Warrior.* New York: St. Martin's Press, 2010.

Smith, Glenn W. *Unfit Commander.* New York: Regan Books, 2004.

Smith, Jean Edward. *Eisenhower in War and Peace.* New York: Random House, 2012.

———. *FDR.* New York: Random House, 2007.

———. *George Bush's War.* New York: Henry Holt, 1991.

———. *Grant.* New York: Simon & Schuster, 2001.

———. *John Marshall: Definer of a Nation.* New York: Henry Holt, 1996.

———. *Lucius D. Clay: An American Life.* New York: Henry Holt, 1990.

Special Inspector General for Iraq Reconstruction. *Hard Lessons: The Iraq Reconstruction Experience.* Washington, D.C.: U.S. Independent Agencies and Commissions, 2009.

Steinbeck, John. *Travels with Charley.* New York: Viking, 1962.

Stiglitz, Joseph E., and Linda J. Bilmes. *The Three Trillion Dollar War: The True Cost of the Iraq Conflict.* New York: W. W. Norton, 2008.

Suskind, Ron. *The One Percent Doctrine: Deep Inside America's Pursuit of Its Enemies Since 9/11.* New York: Simon & Schuster, 2006.

———. *The Price of Loyalty: George W. Bush, the White House, and the Education of Paul O'Neill.* New York: Simon & Schuster, 2004.

Szanto, Andras. *What Orwell Didn't Know.* New York: PublicAffairs, 2009.

Tenet, George. *At the Center of the Storm: My Years at the CIA.* New York: HarperCollins, 2007.

Thiessen, Marc A. *A Charge Kept: The Record of the Bush Presidency, 2001–2009.* New York: Morgan James, 2009.

Thomas, Evan, and the Staff of *Newsweek.* *Election 2004: How Bush Won and What You Can Expect in the Future.* New York: PublicAffairs, 2004.

Timmons, Bascom Nolly. *Garner of Texas: A Personal History.* New York: Harper, 1948.

Toobin, Jeffrey. *Too Close to Call: The Thirty-Six-Day Battle to Decide the 2000 Election.* New York: Random House, 2001.

Turque, Bill. *Inventing Al Gore: A Biography.* Boston: Houghton Mifflin, 2000.

Unger, Craig. *Boss Rove: Inside Karl Rove's Secret Kingdom of Power.* New York: Scribner, 2012.

———. *The Fall of the House of Bush.* New York: Scribner, 2007.

———. *House of Bush, House of Saud.* New York: Scribner, 2004.

United States Army. *Military Intelligence Examination of Enemy Personnel.* Department of the Army. FM 30-15. Washington, D.C.: War Department, 1943.

United States Census Bureau. *Statistical Abstract of the United States: 2011 (130th edition).* Washington, D.C.: U.S. Census Bureau, 2011.

United States Congress. *Pearl Harbor Attack: Hearings Before the Joint Committee on the Investigation of the Pearl Harbor Attack.* 39 vols. Washington, D.C.: Government Printing Office, 1946.

United States Department of Commerce. *Statistical Abstract of the United States, 2011.* Washington, D.C.: Government Printing Office, 2010.

United States War Department. *General Order N. 100: Instructions for the Government of Armies of the United States in the Field.* Washington, D.C.: War Department, 1863.

Wallison, Peter J. *Hidden in Plain Sight: What Really Caused the World's Worst Financial Crisis and Why It Could Happen Again.* New York: Encounter Books, 2015.

Warshaw, Shirley Anne. *The Co-Presidency of Bush and Cheney.* Stanford: Stanford University Press, 2009.

Weisberg, Jacob. *The Bush Tragedy.* New York: Random House, 2008.

——. *George W. Bushisms: New Ways to Harm Our Country.* New York: Fireside, 2005.

——. *George W. Bushisms: The Slate Book of the Accidental Wit and Wisdom of Our 43rd President.* New York: Fireside, 2001.

——. *The Ultimate George W. Bushisms: Bush at War With the English Language.* New York: Fireside, 2007.

Wessel, David. *In Fed We Trust: Ben Bernanke's War on the Great Panic.* New York: Crown Business, 2009.

Whitman, Christine Todd. *It's My Party Too: The Battle for the Heart of the GOP and the Future of America.* New York: Penguin, 2005.

Wilson, Joseph. *The Politics of Truth: Inside the Lies That Led to War and Betrayed My Wife's CIA Identity: A Diplomat's Memoir.* New York: Carroll & Graf, 2004.

Wilson, Valerie Plame. *Fair Game: My Life as a Spy, My Betrayal by the White House.* New York: Simon & Schuster, 2007.

Woodward, Bob. *Bush at War.* New York: Simon & Schuster, 2002.

——. *Plan of Attack.* New York: Simon & Schuster, 2004.

——. *State of Denial: Bush at War, Part III.* New York: Simon & Schuster, 2006.

——. *The War Within: A Secret White House History, 2006–2008.* New York: Simon & Schuster, 2008.

Woodward, C. Vann. *Reunion and Reaction: The Compromise of 1877 and the End of Reconstruction.* New York: Doubleday, 1936.

Yoo, John. *The Powers of War and Peace: The Constitution and Foreign Affairs After 9/11.* Chicago: University of Chicago Press, 2005.

——. *War by Other Means: An Insider's Account of the War on Terror.* New York: Atlantic Monthly Press, 2006.

Zegart, Amy B. *Flawed by Design: The Evolution of the CIA, JCS, and NSC.* Stanford: Stanford University Press, 1999.

Zelizer, Julian E., ed. *The Presidency of George W. Bush: A First Historical Assessment.* Princeton: Princeton University Press, 2010.

Zelnick, Bob. *Gore: A Political Life.* Washington, D.C.: Regnery, 1999.

INDEX

Page numbers in *italics* refer to illustrations.

ABC, 197, 261, 404, 413
ABC News, 435, 467*n*
Abdullah, Crown Prince of Saudi Arabia,
    205–6, 213–15, 303, 337
Abizaid, John, 376, 376*n*, 387, 397, 398,
    476–77, 477*n*, 493–95, 511–12, 513,
    519, 519*n*, 526, 527, 530, 533, 538–39,
    543, 544, 545, 546
abortion issue, 22, 22*n*, 104, 391, 404, 428,
    449
Abraham, Spencer, 135, 135*n*, 136, *157*,
    419, 420
Abraham Lincoln, USS, 364–67, *366*, 368,
    375, 379, 477, 480, 577, 589, 652
Abramoff, Jack, 523
Abramowitz, Michael, 570
Abrams, Elliott, xviii, 180*n*
Abu Ghraib prison, Iraq, 299, 299*n*,
    384–89, *385*, 387*n*, 458–59*n*, 475, 515,
    563, 652
Adams, John, 149*n*
Adams, John Quincy, 124*n*, 149*n*
Adams, Sherman, 152
Addington, David, 109, 158

Adenauer, Konrad, 339
Adger, Sid, 17
Afghanistan, xvi, 201, 224, 229, 235–36,
    282, 327, 408, 417, 517, 542, 642
    detainees and, 282, 284–85, 288–90,
        299, 299*n*, 388, 500
    force surge and, 604, 604*n*
    Russia and, 248–49, 250
    Taliban resurgence and, 602–5
    U.S. operations in, 243–52, 243*n*, 250*n*,
        320, 356, 357, 400, 500, 582, 602–5,
        604
    see also Taliban
Africa, AIDS epidemic and, xix, 549,
    552–63, *558*, 657, 659
African Americans:
    Bob Jones University and, 106
    election of 1876 and, 137
    George W. Bush and, 78–79, 78–79*n*,
        95, 414
Afroyim v. Rusk (1967), 268
Agency for International Development
    (USAID), U.S., 561*n*
Agoglia, John, 373

Agriculture Department, U.S., 135, 419, 420

Ahmadinejad, Mahmoud, 594, 594n

AIDS (acquired immune deficiency
    syndrome), xix, 549, 552–63, 552n,
    558, 657, 659

Ailes, Roger, 48, 52, 66, 74

Air Force, U.S.:
    Berlin Airlift and, 372, 548
    Iraq war and, 327, 354

Alabama, 413, 624
    Hurricane Katrina and, 432, 436, 442n

Alaska, 51

Albert, King of the Belgians, 198

Alcoa, 134

Alexander, Lamar, 104, 110n, 319

al-Hawza, 396–97

Alien and Sedition Acts (1798), 267, 508

Alito, Samuel, 428n, 451

Al Jazeera, 397, 399, 412

Allawi, Ali, 374n, 480, 482

Allbaugh, Joe, 71–73, 73, 74, 85, 222
    election of 2000 and, 103, 106, 109, 121,
    146

Allen, George, 522

Allen, Thad, 442

Allison, Jimmy, 23

al Qaeda, xvi, 201, 204, 210–12, 221–22,
    228, 234, 235–36, 243, 244, 245, 246,
    247, 248, 249, 250–52, 254, 260, 262,
    271, 280, 283, 284–85, 288–91, 293,
    296–99, 298n, 299n, 311, 324, 324n,
    412, 429, 603
    Iraq and, 398, 494, 511, 528, 578, 591,
    593, 596, 597–99, 598–99n, 600, 659

American Airlines flight 11, 218

American Airlines flight 77, 218, 219

American Bar Association (ABA), 476

American Birth Control League, 2

American Civil Liberties Union (ACLU),
    267n

American Dream Downpayment Act
    (2003), 608

American Enterprise Institute, 129, 155,
    161, 495, 536, 538, 580, 643

American Home Mortgage, 612–13

American Insurance Group (AIG),
    622–24, 624n

American League, 56, 57

American Legion, 590

American Muslim Alliance, 135n

American Petroleum Information
    Corporation, 40

American Political Science Association,
    115

American Red Cross, 238

American Revolution, 285

Americans for Tax Reform, 426

American Society of Newspaper Editors,
    195

American Spectator, 135n

Amnesty International, 282

Ana's Story (Bush), 562

Anbar Awakening, 598–99, 598–99n

Anbar Salvation Council, 598–99n

Anderson, Martin, 101, 101n

Anderson, Ralph, 19

Andover, xvii, xix, 3–4, 8, 11–13, 12, 14,
    81–82, 112, 371, 515

Angola, 246

Annan, Kofi, 358, 553

anthrax, 261–63, 263n, 344

Anti-Ballistic Missile (ABM) Treaty
    (1972), 193, 201, 207, 275, 292

Arafat, Yasser, 205, 213, 216, 417

Arbusto Energy, 29, 37–38, 39–41

Archibald, C. Murphy, 24

Argentina, 561, 649

Arizona, 126n, 401, 523

Arkansas, 126n
    election of 2000 and, 120–21

Arlington, Tex., Rangers stadium and,
    63–64, 94

Armed Forces of the United States:
    annual expenditures and, xv, xix
    Geneva Conventions and, 284–86,
    284n, 286n, 287, 289, 290, 387, 501,
    505n
    stop-loss policies and, 484, 581

Armed Services Officer, The (Defense Dept.), 507n

Armey, Dick, 171, 315, 325

Armitage, Richard, 155, 176n, 181, 185–86, 222, 233, 287, 363, 382, 417, 422, 481–82

Armitage Associates, 176n

Arms Control and Disarmament Agency, U.S., 178

Army, U.S.:
  Abu Ghraib scandal and, 386–89, 387n
  Center of Military History of, 346
  expansion of, 530n, 537, 540–41, 542, 545, 551
  Hurricane Katrina and, 441–42
  Iraq invasion and, 356–61
  Iraq occupation and, 374, 375, 386–89, 387n, 396–99, 476–77, 482, 484, 493–95, 512, 540–41, 542, 544, 581
  Iraq surge and, 540–41, 542, 544
  Iraq war buildup and, 308, 327, 331, 346–47, 354
  waterboarding and, 297n

Army Field Manual on Intelligence Interrogation, 458, 458n, 501, 505n

Arthur Anderson & Co., 61n

Ashcroft, Janet, 394, 395

Ashcroft, John, 134, 136, 157, 167n, 224, 246, 254, 267, 272–73, 290, 316, 393–95, 412, 419–20

Asia-Pacific Economic Conference (APEC), 593

Asia-Pacific Economic Cooperation Business Summit, 586

Askari, Hassan Ali al-, 487

Atkinson, Rick, 359n

Atlantic, 495, 496n

Atwater, Lee, 48–49, 52–53, 55, 65, 65n, 66, 74

Austin American-Statesman, 92

Australia, 407, 585, 593, 594–95, 649

Austria, 561

auto industry bailout, 640–45, 644n, 659

Axelrod, David, 653

Axelrod, Jim, 588

"axis of evil," 277–78, 278n, 279–80, 307

Azar, Alex, 147n

Aznar, José María, 198, 352–53

Baath Party, 373, 375, 479

Bacevich, Andrew, 347

Baghdad, Iraq, 357, 360–61, 361, 421, 488
  Bush's visits to, 496–98, 496, 601–2, 601
  ethnic cleansing and, 599
  Green Zone in, 375n, 479, 497, 594n
  postwar looting and, 361–63, 361–62n
  U.S. surge and, 547–48

Baghdadi, Abu Bakr al-, 599n

Baghdadi, Abu Omar al-, 598–99, 599n

Bahrain, 46n, 60, 585

Baier, Bret, 498

Baines, Harold, 63

Baird, Zoe, 422n

Baker, Howard, 113

Baker, James, 38, 137, 152, 152n, 176n, 312, 424, 515
  Bush transition and, 132
  election of 2000 and, 126, 127, 137, 138, 139, 142, 146–47, 427
  Iraq Study Group and, 527, 527n, 529, 534, 535–36

Baker, Jim, 266

Baker, Peter, 513, 634

Baker-Hamilton Commission (Iraq Study Group), 516, 527–29, 527, 527–28n, 533–36, 534n, 537

Bakhsh, Abdullah Taha, 44

Ball, George L., 38

Ballpark at Arlington (Rangers stadium), 63–64, 94

Bandar bin Sultan, Prince, 99–100, 182, 213–15, 216, 336–37, 492

Banking Act of 1932, 617, 617n, 621

Bank of America, 620

banks, banking, 611, 620–22
  bank failures and, 618, 620, 620n
  deregulation and, 616n

banks, banking (*cont.*)
  investment versus commercial types of, 616*n*
  subprime mortgages and, 612–18, 620
  TARP and, 624–25, 626, 630, 631, 632
Barak, Ehud, 205
Barbour, Haley, 102, 409
  Hurricane Katrina and, 431, 432, 440, 591
Barclays, 620, 620*n*
Baring-Gould, Sabine, 228
Barkley, Alben, 155–56
Barnes, Ben, 17–18
Barnett, Ross, 440
Barnett, Thomas P. M., 600*n*
Barr, William, 257*n*
Barroso, José Manuel Durao, 352–53
Bartlett, Dan, 154, 312, 314, 436, 490
Bass, Charles, 522
Bass family, 46*n*
Bass Family Enterprises, 94*n*
Bauer, Gary, 105, 107
Bear Stearns, 616–18, 616*n*, 617–18*n*, 620, 621, 622
Beijing, China, 646–49, *647, 648*
Belgium, 198, 561
Bellinger, John, 506
Bellmon, Harry, 73
Bellow, Saul, 178, 178*n*
Benin, 563
Bennett, William J., 180*n*
Benson, Ezra Taft, 233*n*
Benton, William, 2
Bentsen, Lloyd, 18, 21
Berenson, Bradford, 273
Berger, Sandy, 211
Berlin Airlift (1948–1949), 372, 548
Berlusconi, Silvio, 262, 318
Bernanke, Ben, *609*
  AIG and, 623, 624
  Bear Stearns and, 616–17
  housing bubble and, 609, 610, 612
  TARP and, 624–26, 630, 631
  see also financial crisis of 2007–2008

Bernstein, Tom, 58
Betsy, Hurricane, 437–38, 437*n*
Betts, Lois, 647
Betts, Roland, 17, 58, 63, 358, 647
Betty Ford Clinic, 46
Bible, xviii, 339, 552*n*, 559
Biddle, Stephen, 536*n*
Biden, Joe, 325, 550, 558
"Bin Laden Determined to Strike in U.S." (CIA), 210
biological weapons, 261–65, 263*n*, 264*n*
biological weapons convention, 193
Birge, Robert, 13
birth control, 2*n*
Bishop, Thomas, 18
Black, Cofer, 212, 235–36, 243*n*
Black, Conrad, 176*n*
Black, Hugo, 268, 448
Blackmun, Harry, 428
Blackwater, 397
Blackwill, Robert, 176*n*, 181
Blair, Cherie, 206, 207, 305
Blair, Tony, 99, 171, 206, 248, 303, 305, 309, 343, 350, 351, *351,* 352–53, 354, 358–59, 594*n*
Blanco, Kathleen, Hurricane Katrina and, 431, 432, 436, 439–41, 591
Blankfein, Lloyd, 624*n*
Blasingame, Ken, 97
Blessit, Arthur, 42–43*n*
Blinder, Alan, 624
Blix, Hans, 336, 338, 340–41, *341,* 345, 349, 350, 353, 377
Bloom, Allan, 177–78
Blount, Winton, 23–24
Blum, Steven, 441
Blumenthal, Sidney, 85*n*, 113–14
BNP Paribas, 613
Bob Jones University, 106–7
Bodman, Samuel, 420
Boehner, John, 164, 165, 166, *166,* 521, 578, 637
Bogden, Daniel, 565*n*
Boies, David, 145, 145*n*

Bolten, Josh, 158, 490, 491, 492*n*, 497, 502, 516, 517, 522, 531, 554, 555, 572, 573, 624, 630, 639
Border Patrol, U.S., 584*n*
Bork, Robert, 449
Boskin, Michael, 101*n*
Bosnia, 286, 545*n*
Boston Globe, 24, 117, 476
Botswana, 555*n*, 562
Boumediene, Lakhdar, 484, 509*n*
Boumediene v. Bush (2008), 509*n*
Bowen, Stuart, 273, 489
Bradbury, Steven G., 296*n*
Bradley, Bill, 111, 451
Bradley, Jeb, 522
Bradley, Omar, 305, 581, 600
Brady, Nicholas, 156
Brandeis, Louis, 448
Brazil, 561, 649
Bremer, L. Paul, 370–75, *370,* 371*n*, 396, 398, 421, 479, 489
Brentwood Baptist Church, 78*n*
Brewster, Kingman, 14*n*
Breyer, Stephen, 144, 145, 146
Brezhnev, Leonid, 201
Brinkley, Douglas, 436
Britain, Great, 190, 418*n*, 561, 649
    Iraq invasion and, 357, 407
    Iraq war leadup and, 303, 309, 309*n*, 314*n*, 343, 350, 351, 352–53, 354
Broadwell, Paula, 537*n*
Brock, Bill, 112*n*
Brokaw, Tom, 105, 261
Brooks, Vincent, 361, 361*n*
Brown, Michael, 416, 431, 432, 434–35, 436, 438–39, 440, 442
Brown, Robert W. "Bobby," 56, 57, 58–59
Brownback, Sam, 550
Brown Brothers Harriman, 1, 8, 83
Brownell, Herbert, 127
Brown v. Board of Education (1954), 112*n*, 446
Bruni, Frank, 33, 82, 118
Buchanan, Pat, 424

Buckley, William F., Jr., 115
budget, federal, xv, 611
Buffett, Warren, 619
Bull Moose Party, 68
Bullock, Bob, 88–90, 91–92, 93, 94, 95*n*
Bumiller, Elisabeth, 308
Burck, William, 504
Burger, Warren, 147*n*, 427
Burka, Paul, 87
Burr, Aaron, 124*n*
Bush, Barbara (GWB daughter), 14, 39, *39, 43,* 74, 79, 265, 646, *646*
    AIDS issue and, 562–63
    Bush first inauguration and, 149
    drinking and, 208–9
    education and, 54, 70, 83, 91, 403, 562
    election of 2000 and, 121
    election of 2004 and, 402–3, 413
    European trip and, 206–7, 208
    father's idea of presidential run and, 97, 98
    9/11 attacks and, 219, 220
    Rangers games and, 62
Bush, Barbara Pierce, 1, 7–8, *7, 11,* 21, 25, 55, 68*n*, 132*n*, 647, 654, 657–58, 658*n*
    background of, 7
    election of 1992 and, 67
    George W. Bush's gubernatorial run and, 70, 74, 74*n*, 78, 79
    George W. Bush's idea of presidential run and, 98
    marriage and, 5
Bush, Columba Garnica Gallo, 47, 79
Bush, Dorothy "Doro," 10, *11,* 48, 492, 647
Bush, Dorothy Walker, 1–2, *2,* 6–7, 42
Bush, George (Jeb Bush son), 79
Bush, George H. W., *7, 11,* 38, *41,* 135, 138, 158, 176*n*, 179, 208, 212, 229, 237, *237,* 238, 254, 269, 287, 332, 399, 440, 449, 473, 473*n*, 553, 585, 646, 650–51, *651,* 654, 657–58
    athletics and, 5, 12, 13, 62
    Atwater and, 48–49, 52–53

Bush, George H. W. (*cont.*)
  awards and medals and, 5
  Bandar and, 99, 213, 337
  Billy Graham and, 42
  campaigning and, 94, 116–17
  China and, 132*n*, 647
  CIA and, xxii, 131*n*, 132*n*, 133*n*, 136
  Clinton and, 149*n*
  Cold War's end and, xxii
  congressional career and, 16–17, 30
  education and, 1, 3–4, 5–6, 8
  election of 1970 and, 21, 30, 31
  election of 1980 and, 37, 38
  election of 1988 and, 47–53, 65, 132
  election of 1992 and, 66–68, 114, 116,
    138, 383
  election of 1998 and, 96
  family background and, 6–7
  Gates and, 516
  George W. Bush's congressional bid
    and, 34, 35
  George W. Bush's decision to run for
    president and, 98
  George W. Bush's gubernatorial bid
    and, 70, 74, 74*n*, 79
  George W. Bush's "nomadic years"
    and, 22–26
  Godfather film and, 48*n*
  illnesses and, 65
  Iran-Contra and, 67
  Iraq war leadup and, 311, 312, 334–35
  Jennifer Fitzgerald and, 50, 50*n*
  marriage and, 5
  Middle East policy and, 204, 205–6,
    213
  neoconservatives and, 100, 176*n*
  NSC and, 174, 185, 308
  nuclear arms reduction and, 274, 306,
    306, 307
  oil business and, 8–11, 23, 29
  Overby and, 9–10, 29
  Persian Gulf War and, xvii, xxii, 46*n*,
    64, 108, 179–80, 230, 367
  presidency and, 46*n*, 64–66, 83

  presidential transition and, 127–28, 127*n*
  Rice's relationship with, 101, 418–19
  Richards and, 69, 69*n*, 74, 75–78
  RNC and, 24–25, 50, 72
  Rumsfeld and, 110, 131–32, 132*n*
  Senate campaign and, 21, 30, 31
  Skull and Bones and, 5–6, 15
  Sununu and, 51, 65, 66, 152, 153, 155
  Thomas and, 64, 427
  Trilateral Commission and, 34
  Ueberroth and, 56
  UN and, 21, 23, 24, 34, 48*n*
  vice presidency and, 38, 51, 108, 156
  Vietnam War and, 16–17, 20
  Wolfowitz and, 179, 180, 182, 229
  World War II and, 3, 4–5, *4*
Bush, George W.:
  abortion issue and, 104
  Abu Ghraib scandal and, 387, 563, 652
  addresses and speeches of, 1, 9, 172,
    221, 223–24, 224*n*, 237–39, *237*, 242,
    247–48, 251, 277–78, 307–8, 316–19,
    317, 323, 333, 353–54, 365–67, 416,
    417, 418, 418*n*, 422–25, 422*n*, 425,
    425, 432–33, 438, 449, 468–69, 482,
    486, 504–6, 547–48, 550–51, 552–53,
    555–57, 583–84, 596–97, 607, 626–27,
    638, 642, 652–53
  Afghanistan and, xvi, 229, 235–36,
    400, 417, 517, 580, 582, 602–5, 642
  African American voters and, 78–79,
    78–79*n*, 95, 414
  African trips and, 562, 657
  AIDS issue and, xix, 549, 552–63,
    552*n*, *558*, 657, 659
  al Qaeda potential threat and, 210–12
  approval ratings and, 158, 251, 277,
    442–43, 470, 471, 488, 489, 499, 521,
    551, 563, 581, 623, 627, 633–34, 634*n*,
    645
  athletics and, 12–13, 648–49, 657
  Atwater and, 48–49, 52–53, 55, 74
  auto industry bailout and, 640–45,
    644*n*, 659

"axis of evil" phrase and, 277–78, 278*n*, 279–80, 307

Bandar and, 99–100, 182, 213–15, 216, 492

baseball as love of, 54, 62, 62*n*

biological attack fear and, 262, 263–64, 265

biological weapons convention and, 193

birth of, 1

"black site" prisons and, 503–6, 659

Bullock and, 88–90, 91–92

cabinet meetings and, xviii, 169, 184, 202, 269, 280

campaign style of, 94, 119–20

Cheney and, *see* Cheney, Dick

childhood and youth of, 7, 8, 9, 10–11, *11*

China and, 194–97, 195*n*, 196*n*, 646–50, 659

Chinese seizure of U.S. plane and, 194–97, 195*n*, 196*n*

Cindy Sheehan and, 429–30, *429*, 563

climate change issue and, xix, 189–93, 197–98, 199, 311

compassionate conservatism and, xx, 95*n*, 96, 103–4, 163, 167, 229, 384, 390, 606

congressional race of 1978 and, xix, 29–30, 33–37, *34*, 113, 121, 425–26

Dallas homes and, 54–55, 54*n*, 82–83, 83*n*, 655, *655*, 655*n*

decisions and, ix, xvi, xvii, 63, 91, 151, 151*n*, 174, 280, 292, 326, 384, 469, 478, 490, 563, 623

detainee issue and, 280–99, 420, 457–61, 470–71, 499–509

drinking and, xix, 21, 22, 24, 25, 29, 41, 45–46, 47, 77, 122

drug use and, 22, 26, 77

DUI arrest and, 29, 36, 109, 121–22, 122*n*, 411–12

education of, xix, xx, 11–16, *12*, 13*n*, *15*, 26–27, 31, 32, 58, 81–82, 103, 112, 279, 515, 647

education policy and, xix, 87, 88–89, 90, 104, 142, 158, 163–67, *166*, 173, 204, 217, 390, 406, 426, 449, 582, 659

election of 1968 and, 18–19

election of 1970 and, 21

election of 1972 and, 23–24

election of 1988 and, 47–53

election of 1992 and, 66–68

election of 2000 and, *see* presidential election of 2000

election of 2002 and, 329–30

election of 2004 and, *see* presidential election of 2004

election of 2006 and, 499, 504, 512, 519–23, 521*n*, 524–25, 526, 542

election of 2008 and, 623, 624, 627, 633–38, 637–38*n*

enhanced interrogation techniques and, 296–99, 389, 444, 457–61, 466–67, 470–71, 472, 473, 474, 501, 503–6, 508–9, 659

European trips and, 197–202, 206–8, 306–7, *306*, 531–32

extraordinary renditions and, xvii, 293–96, 388, 659

faith-based initiatives and, 167–68

family background and, 1–2

farewell address and, 652–53

father's administration and, 64–66

fiftieth birthday party and, 91

financial crisis of 2007–2008 and, 231, 606–32, 645, 659

first cabinet and, *157*, 169, 202, 417

first inauguration and, 148–51, *149*, *151*

foreign policy and, 175–203, 204–6, 205*n*, 207–8, 209, 213–15, 229, 269, 646–50, 659

G-20 summit and, 649–50

Gates and, 516–17

Godfather and, 48, 48*n*

Gonzales firing and, 573–74, *574*

Gore compared with, 103, 111–12

governorship of Texas and, xx, 80–98, *81*, 99, 103, 163, 209, 466

Bush, George W. (*cont.*)
  Graham and, 42, 42–43*n*, *43*, 46, 82
  gubernatorial campaign of 1994 and,
    68–79, *73*, 74*n*, 121
  gubernatorial campaign of 1998 and,
    92–93, 94–96, 94*n*, 97, 121
  gubernatorial race of 1990 and, 54–56,
    60
  Harken stock sale and, 60–61, 60–61*n*
  health and, 509–10, *510*
  Hispanics and, 94–95, 104
  Hume interview and, 650–52
  Hurricane Katrina and, 416, 430–43,
    436, 444, 457, 563, 591, 652
  ideological advisers and, xviii
  immigration policy and, xix, 104, 215,
    417, 582–84, 584*n*, 586, 652, 659
  inaugurations as governor and, *81*, 82,
    99
  income and wealth of, 94, 94*n*
  intellectualism and, 14, 15
  Iran and, 246, 277–78, 517, 600*n*
  Iraq occupation and, 369–80, 396–99,
    417, 431, 432–33, 435, 443, 457,
    461–65, 476–98, 477*n*, *496*, 511–17,
    519, 524, 526–48, 576–82, 586–602,
    603, 614, 645
  Iraq surge and, 514, 517, 526, 529–48,
    549–52, 549–50*n*, 581, 586–88,
    592–99, 623
  Iraq visits and, 496–98, *496*, 593–94,
    594*n*, 601–2, *601*, 642
  Iraq war and, xvi–xvii, xviii, xix, 229,
    356–68, *361*, *366*, 469, 563
  Iraq war leadup and, 174, 234–35, 236,
    246, 248, 276–78, 300–355, *351*, *355*,
    452*n*, 659
  Jeb Bush and, 68, 68*n*, 70
  Jenna Bush's marriage and, 645–46,
    646
  Laura Bush's pregnancy and, 38–39, *39*
  legislation signed by, 162, 166, *166*, 209,
    266, 508–9, 558, *558*, 560, 564*n*, 566,
    578, 585, 585*n*, 608, 631

  Libby indictment and, 452–57, 455*n*
  McCain's distancing from, 634–37,
    639–40
  Maliki and, 496–98, *496*, 532, 536, 538,
    545–46, 593, 600–602, *601*, 645
  marriage of, xix, 32–33, *33*
  memoirs and, 42–43*n*
  Middle East policy and, 174, 204–6,
    205*n*, 213–15, 216, 417, 464, 478, 482,
    512, 514, 590, 659–60
  military commissions and, 269–74, 280,
    499–503, 506–9
  military service and, 17–20, *17*, 23, 24,
    26
  missile defense issue and, 193, 197, 198,
    201, 207, 275, 292
  "Mission Accomplished" declaration
    and, 363–67, *366*, 368, 375, 379, 477,
    480, 577, 652
  National Cathedral address and,
    237–39, *237*, 242
  NATO and, 197, 198–99, 200–201, 208,
    229, 248, 303, 304, 340, 402, 531, 603
  neoconservatives and, 100, 102, 175,
    176*n*, 535, 536–38
  9/11 attacks and, xvi, xviii–xix, 166,
    217–27, *217*, *220*, 224*n*
  "nomadic years" of, 21–27
  North Korea and, 182, 187–88, 659
  NSA warrantless surveillance program
    and, 467–69, 659
  NSC and, 174, 182, 183–84, 184*n*,
    186, 221–22, 224–25, 231, 233, 289,
    290, 302, 309–10, 312–13, 363, 397,
    511–12, 580, 580–81*n*, 592, 604
  nuclear arms reduction and, 274, 659
  Obama inauguration and, 653–54, *654*,
    655, *655*
  Obama's friendship with, 650–51, 653,
    654, 656–57
  Obama transition and, 639–40, *639*,
    645, 650–52, *650*, *651*
  oil industry and, xix, xx, 28–29, 37–38,
    39–41, 43–45, 46–47

Olympics and, 646–49, *647, 648*

ownership society and, 606–8, 606*n*

painting and, 658

Patriot Act and, 266–67, 473–74, 476

personalization of presidential power and, 152, 184, 184*n,* 188, 201, 202, 223, 225, 248, 293, 315, 370, 420

Petraeus's relationship with, 579–80, *579,* 600

policy details and, xvii–xviii, 182

post-presidency and, 655–60, *656*

Powell and, 193–94, 202, 207, 289, 292, 337–38, 383

Prairie Chapel Ranch and, 93, 96–97, 127, 172, 204, 209–15, 269, 273, 274–76, 305, 307, 312, 335, 368, 413, 429–33, 435, 436, 470, 509, 510, *510,* 512, 516–17, 544–45, 573, *574,* 609, 645–46, *646, 656*

preemptive war doctrine and, xvi, 242, 307–8, 313, 320–21, 320*n,* 356, 379

prescription drug issue and, xix, 117, 119, 142–43, 183, 384, 390–91, 426, 434, 659

presidential library and, 656–57

presidential primary of 2000 and, xx, 103–8, 405, 408, 582

presidential transition and, 127–36, 640

"presidents club" luncheon and, 650–52, *651*

President's Daily Briefing and, 182, 210, 248, 268–69, 275, 378

press conferences and, 75, 82, 103, 107, 122, 171, 187, 198, 200, 202, 213, 215, 247, 254, 262, 318, 349–50, 399–401, 417, 430, 488–89, 498, 512–14, 524–26, 546, 569–70, 571–72, 586–88, 613–15, 652

press relations and, 82, 119, 245

PULL and, 25–26

punctuality and, 87

Putin and, 199–202, *200,* 207–8, 248–49, 269, 274–76, 275*n,* 306, *306,* 307, 455, 659

regime change and, xviii–xix, 174, 276–78, 301, 305, 306, 313, 349–50, 366

regulation and, xix

religious views and, xviii, xix–xx, 42–43, 46, 104, 105, 169, 172, 188, 226–27, 231, 238, 278, 339, 345, 350, 351, 399, 399*n,* 492–93, 659

Rove and, *see* Rove, Karl

Rumsfeld's interview by, 132–33

Rumsfeld's resignation and, 513–19, 525–26

same-sex marriage issue and, 392–93, 407, 409, 410–11

school vouchers and, 165, 166

second cabinet and, 417–22

second inauguration and, 422–25, 422*n, 425,* 426, 607

second term perils and, 444–71

secrecy issue and, 254–55

shoe-throwing incident and, 601–2

siblings of, 10

signing statements and, 472–76

Skull and Bones and, 15

Social Security reform and, 417, 425–26, 457, 607–8

State of the Union addresses and, 277–78, 279, 307, 341, 341–42*n,* 351, 418, 418*n,* 425, 452*n,* 521, 550–51, 552, 555–57, 607

stem cell research issue and, 169–73, 172*n,* 208, 577*n*

Sununu and, 65–66

Supreme Court appointments and, 426–29, 428*n,* 444–51, 446*n, 447, 448,* 457

tax policy and, xvi, 92, 104, 158, 159–63, 204, 367, 417, 582, 607, 608, 614

terrorism issue and, 201

Terrorist Surveillance Program renewal and, 393–96

Texas Rangers and, xix, xx, 52, 54–55, 56–64, *59,* 70, 82, 93–94, 94*n,* 102, 647, 655, 657

Bush, George W. (*cont.*)
  Texas reform agenda and, 87, 88–89, 90
  threat matrix reports and, 265–66, 269
  tort reform and, 87, 89, 90, 417
  trade policy and, 584–86, 585*n*, 659
  UN and, 313–14, 317–18, *317*, 319, 325,
    329, 349, 353–54, 489
  U.S. attorney firings and, 563–75,
    564–65*n*, 566*n*
  vacations and, 209–15, 429–35, 509
  vetoes and, 472, 473, 476, 577, 577*n*, 578
  Vietnam War and, 17, 233, 581
  Vulcans and, 176–81, 176*n*, 197
  war on terror and, 221, 224, 227,
    228–52, 230*n*, 243*n*, 253–74, 307,
    466, 659–60
  Washington departure and, 654–55, *655*
  West Point address and, 307–8, 313
  White House routine and, 168–69
  White House staff and, 152–55, 175,
    184–85, 184*n*, 201, 202–3, 209, 254,
    269, 370, 443, 512, 531, 550, 645
  Wolfowitz-Cheney theory of power
    and, 181–82
  World Series of 2001 and, 251–52, *252*
  writings of, 42*n*, 656, 657–58, 658*n*
Bush, Jebby, 79
Bush, Jenna, 39, *39, 43,* 74, 79, 265
  AIDS issue and, 562–63
  Bush first inauguration and, 149
  drinking and, 208–9
  education and, 54, 70, 83, 91, 403, 562
  election of 2000 and, 121
  election of 2004 and, 402–3, 413
  father's idea of presidential run and,
    97, 98
  marriage of, 493, 645–46, *646*
  9/11 attacks and, 219, 220
  Rangers games and, 62
Bush, John Ellis "Jeb," 10, 11, *11,* 47, 180*n*,
    217
  campaigning and, 94
  election of 1994 and, 68, 70, 78–79
  election of 1998 and, 95–96

  election of 2000 and, 124, 125
  election of 2006 and, 521
  George W. Bush and, 68, 68*n,* 70
  Hurricane Katrina and, 430, 431, 432
Bush, Jonathan, 6–7, 37, 38
Bush, Laura Welch, xix, *41,* 51, 417, 418,
    492, 515, 573, 657
  AIDS issue and, 562, 657
  background of, 31
  Beijing Olympics and, 647
  Bush first inauguration and, 148, 149,
    151, *151*
  Bush's drinking and, 45–46
  Bush's fiftieth birthday and, 91–92
  Bush's idea of presidential run and,
    97, 98
  congressional race of 1978 and, 33–34,
    34
  Dallas homes and, 54–55, 54*n*, 83*n*,
    655, *655,* 655*n*
  daughters' drinking and, 209
  education of, 31, 32, 249
  education reform issue and, 164, 165
  election of 1992 and, 68
  election of 2000 and, 123, 127
  election of 2004 and, 402, 407, 409, 413
  election of 2006 and, 522
  European trips and, 198, 199, 206–8
  George W. Bush's gubernatorial
    campaign and, 70–71, 78, 79
  Hurricane Katrina and, 442
  Iraq invasion and, 359–60
  Iraq surge and, 548
  literacy issue and, 83, 216
  marriage of, xix, 32–33, *33*
  9/11 attacks and, 218–19, 220, 222–23,
    226
  Obamas and, 640, 653–54, *654*
  personal habits and, 87
  Prairie Chapel Ranch and, 93, 96–97,
    127, 204, 209–10, 274–75, 305, 335,
    413, 433, 470, 516–17, *574,* 646, *646*
  pregnancy of, 38–39, *39*
  Rangers and, 62

same-sex marriage issue and, 392
state dinners and, 215
Supreme Court nominees and, 428,
447, 450
teaching and librarian careers of, 32
war on terror and, 247, 248, 263, 265
White House routine and, 169
Bush, Marvin Pierce, 10, *11,* 25, 33, 75, 98,
492, 647
Bush, Neil Mallon, 10, *11,* 45, 47–48, 55
Bush, Noelle, 79
Bush, Prescott, 1–3, *2,* 6, 8, 10, 13, 83
McCarthy and, 3
Bush, Prescott, Jr., 6
Bush, Robin, 10
Bush, William "Bucky," 7
Bush Doctrine, 223, 423
Bush Exploration Company, 40–41
Bush-Overby Development Company,
9–10
Bush Tragedy, The (Weisberg), 85*n*
Bush v. Gore (2000), 145–46, 147, 428
Butterworth, Bob, 139
Byrd, Robert, 164*n,* 238, 345–46

Caldwell, Kirbyjon, 493, 645
California Law Review, 258*n*
Cambone, Stephen, 305
Camerini, Michael, 584*n*
Campbell, Alastair, 343, 358
Campbell, Kurt, 594
Camp David, Md., 47, 185, 199, 204, 209,
215, 242, 248, 305, 334, 358, 417–18,
456, 470, 492, 493, 494–96, 496*n,* 512,
536, 544, 611
Camp Lejeune, N.C., 359–60
Canada, 190, 222, 561, 585, 649
capital gains taxes, 162
carbon dioxide emissions, 189–93, 198
Card, Andrew, 129, 153, *157,* 169, 187, 190,
193, 208, 209, 210, 273, 276, 314, 334,
364, 371, 372, 378, 413, 417, 491–92*n*
Hurricane Katrina and, 431, 434, 436,
441, 441*n*

Iraq occupation and, 490, 491
Libby case and, 457
9/11 terror attacks and, 217, 220, 221,
223, 226
Powell resignation and, 419
Supreme Court nominees and, 427
TSP reauthorization and, 394–95
Caribbean, AIDS epidemic and, 549, 554,
555, 557, 559
Carl Gustaf, King of Sweden, 199
Carlucci, Frank, 127*n,* 183*n*
Carnahan, Mel, 134, 134*n*
Caro, Robert A., 156
Carter, Jimmy, 30, 38, 125, 133*n,* 137, 156,
163, 178, 183, 195, 237, 256, 405, 640,
650–51, *651,* 658
Case for Democracy, The (Sharansky), 422*n*
Casey, George, 356, 480, 484, 490, 493–95,
497–98, 511, 512, 513, 519, 519*n,*
526–27, 530, 532, 533, 537–39, 543,
544, 545, 546
Cato Institute, 606*n*
CBS, 261, 311, 384–85
CBS News, 98, 410, 588
CBS poll, 158
Cedar Rapids Gazette, 582
Celanese Corporation of America, 38
Census, U.S., 401
Center for Strategic and Budgetary
Assessments, 495
Center for Strategic and International
Studies, 176*n,* 487*n*
Centers for Disease Control and
Prevention (CDC), U.S., 435, 555
Central America Free Trade Agreement
(CAFTA), 585
Central Command (CENTCOM), U.S.,
245, 249, 301–3, 304, 309–10, 313,
351–52, 354–55, 356–58, 359, 361,
361–62*n,* 363, 373, 387, 397, 476,
494, 543, 545, 545*n,* 546, 548, 580,
580–81*n,* 592, 600
see also Abizaid, John; Fallon, William
J.; Franks, Tommy

Central Intelligence Agency (CIA), 131, 133, 480
  Abu Ghraib and, 387–89, 387n
  Afghanistan and, 235–36, 243, 244, 245, 246, 250, 495
  al Qaeda and, 204, 210–12, 243, 296–99, 298n, 299n, 429
  anthrax scare and, 261–62
  "black site" prisons and, 460–61, 466, 475, 503–6, 659
  detainees and, 292, 293, 387–89, 387n, 458, 460–61, 466, 475, 503–6
  domestic surveillance and, 256, 259n, 260
  enhanced interrogation techniques and, 297–99, 298n, 387–89, 387n, 458, 460–61, 466–67, 471, 501, 503–6, 508–9, 659
  George H. W. Bush and, xxii, 131n, 132n, 133n, 136
  Iraq war leadup and, 212, 248, 276, 310, 313–14, 321–24, 322n, 333–34, 337, 341–42n, 344, 377, 378
  Iraq WMD search and, 377–79, 382
  "Memorandum of Notification" and, 243, 243n
  National Intelligence Estimate and, 321–23, 322n, 491, 591
  Niger yellowcake report and, 341–42n, 452n, 454
  9/11 attacks and, 224, 225
  NSC and, 184n, 221–22
  Patriot Act and, 266, 267
  Petraeus and, 537n
  President's Daily Briefing and, 182, 210, 248, 268–69, 275, 378
  renditions and, xvii, 293, 388, 659
  Tenet and, see Tenet, George
Chafee, Lincoln, 162, 325, 508
Chalabi, Ahmed, 369, 373
"Changing the Dynamics in Iraq" (Luti), 530n
Chao, Elaine, 134–35, 157, 420, 514, 515

Charge to Keep, A (Bush), 42–43n, 84, 122n
Charge to Keep, A (Koerner), 84–85, 84n, 85, 85n
"Charge to Keep, A" (Wesley), 80, 84, 84n
"Charge to Keep, A" (Williams), 85
Charlie Wilson's War, 495
Charlton, Paul K., 565n, 567n
Chavez, Linda, 134, 422n
Chelsea Piers club, 58
Cheney, Dick, 109, 128, 152n, 154, 157, 158n, 159, 188–89, 203, 206, 209, 216, 280, 381, 423
  auto industry bailout and, 642, 645
  Bush administration staff and, 156–58
  Bush's relationship with, 128, 384, 389, 453, 456, 463–64, 514, 525, 645
  Bush tax cuts and, 160–61
  Bush transition and, 128, 129, 133, 134, 142
  China and, 194, 195n
  climate change issue and, 191, 192
  Defense Department and, xviii, 179, 303, 332n, 383
  detainee issue and, 289n, 291, 503–6
  draft deferments and, 110n, 405, 462
  DUI arrests and, 109, 122n
  election of 2000 and, xxi, 101, 102, 108–11, 125, 332
  election of 2004 and, 406–7, 409–10, 411
  election of 2008 and, 635
  financial crisis and, 624, 627, 629
  Ford and, 131, 131n, 152, 383
  health and, 111
  House and, 108, 110–11n, 179
  Hurricane Katrina and, 430–31, 434
  Iraq occupation and, 372, 378, 462–63, 477n, 482–83, 490, 496, 512, 526, 580, 592
  Iraq surge and, 530, 539, 544
  Iraq war leadup and, 175–76, 234, 245, 248, 302–4, 312, 313–14, 315, 316, 334, 336–37, 376

Libby indictment and, 452–57

military commissions and, 271–74, 501–3

Murtha and, 462, 463

9/11 attacks and, 219–20, 219*n*, 220, 221, 224, 224*n*, 225

North Korea and, 187, 188

NSC and, 183–84, 184*n*, 265

Persian Gulf War and, 108, 175–76, 179, 332*n*, 357

resignation offers and, 383–84, 389

Rice's conflicts with, 183–84, 503–4

Rumsfeld and, xviii, 110, 131, 386, 515, 517–18

stem cell research and, 170

Supreme Court nominees and, 427, 445

war on terror and, 230, 234, 260, 261, 265, 393–94, 396, 465, 466–67, 467*n*

White House briefings and, 169

Wolfowitz and, xviii, 179–80, 181–82

Cheney, Liz, 109, 110

Cheney, Lynne, 110

Cheney, Mary, 110, 392, 410, 411

Chertoff, Michael, 422, 434, 435, 438–39, 440, 442

Chiara, Margaret, 565*n*

Chicago, University of, 171, 178

Chicago Tribune, 169

Chicago White Sox, 63

Chile, 561, 585

Chiles, Eddie, 52, 57, *59*

Chiles, Fran, 57

Chiles, Lawton, 68

China, People's Republic of, 206, 330, 338, 344, 349, 350, 548, 646–50, 659

    climate change and, 190

    George H. W. Bush and, 132*n*, 647

    George W. Bush and, 194–97, 195*n*, 196*n*, 646–50, 659

    Nixon and, 180

    Olympics and, 646–49, *647, 648*

    U.S. plane seizure and, 194–97, 195*n*, 196*n*

Chirac, Jacques, 247, 306–7, 338–40, 344–45

Chocola, Chris, 522

Christian Coalition, 173

Christian fundamentalists, 104, 106–7, 130, 168, 419, 633

Christopher, Warren, 114*n*, 125, 137–38, 139, 146

Chrysler, 640, 641, 644, 645

Church, Frank, 256, 256*n*

Churchill, Winston S., 206, 279–80, 352, 658

Cincinnati Reds, 40

Civil Rights Commission, U.S., 134

civil rights movement, 3, 440

Civil War, U.S., 80, 229, 285, 552

Clark, Vern, 327

Clark, Wesley, 402, 537*n*

Clarke, Richard, 211–12, 221, 225, 234–35

Clay, Lucius D., 127, 372, 372*n*, 383, 396–97*n*, 485, 548

Clean Air Act (1970), 191

Clement, Edith Brown, 428*n*

Cleveland, Grover, 149*n*, 444

Cleveland Browns, 102

climate change, xix, 189–93, 197–98, 199, 311

Clinton, Bill, xviii, xix, 77, 91, 128, 136, 138, 159, 180, 182, 184*n*, 185, 199, 208, 211, 212, 229, 249, 254, 259*n*, 269, 287, 399, 422*n*, 473, 473*n*, 564, 585, 585*n*, 640, 650–51, *651,* 657, 658, 659

    Bush inauguration and, 148–49, 150, 151

    election of 1992 and, 67, 114

    election of 1996 and, 93, 126, 126*n*, 127, 163

    election of 2000 and, xx, 115–16, 121, 363

    election of 2004 and, 405

    George H. W. Bush and, 149*n*

    impeachment and, xx, 115, 444

    International Criminal Court and, 193

Clinton, Bill (*cont.*)
  Lewinsky and, xx, 115, 444, 530
  Middle East and, 204–5, 205*n*, 215
  North Korea and, 187, 188, 189
  Reagan Democrats and, 114
  stem cell research and, 170
  VP running mate search and, 114*n*
Clinton, Hillary, 149–50, 154, 325, 405,
    591, 597–98
CNN, 82, 273, 316, 361, 399, 463, 482–83,
    594*n*
CNN/*Time* poll, 118*n*
Coalition Provisional Authority (CPA),
    373, 374, 396, 398, 479, 489
Coast Guard, U.S., 442
Coats, Dan, 130
Coburn, Tom, 570–71
Cockburn, Patrick, 594*n*
Cogan, John, 101*n*
Cohen, Eliot, 180*n*, 495, 536, 537
Coke County, Tex., 10
Cold War, xxii, 181, 188, 189, 199, 211,
    307, 530
Coleman, Norm, 550, 637
College Republicans, 72
Collins, Susan, 458, 590*n*
Colombia, 246, 474, 585–86
Colorado, 401
Columbia University, Eisenhower and,
    180, 537*n*, 658
Comey, James, 266, 393–95, 452*n*
Commerce Department, U.S., 129, 420,
    640
Commission on the National Guard and
    Reserves, U.S., 541
Compass Bank of Dallas, 83*n*
compassionate conservatism, xx, 95*n*, 96,
    103–4, 163, 167, 229, 384, 390, 606
Comprehensive Immigration Reform Act
    of 2007, 584, 584*n*
Comprehensive Test Ban Treaty (1996),
    193
Conaway, Michael, 40
Concerned Alumni of Princeton, 451, 451*n*

Congo, 246
Congress, U.S., xix, 30, 152*n*, 304, 608,
    614
  Abu Ghraib scandal and, 386, 475
  AIDS issue and, 552–53, 555–57, 555*n*,
    558*n*, 559, 560
  Army and Marine Corps expansion
    and, 541, 542, 545, 551
  auto industry bailout and, 641, 642, 645
  Bush's address to joint session of,
    247–48
  Bush's State of the Union messages
    and, 277–78, 279, 307, 341, 341–42*n*,
    351, 418, 418*n*, 425, 452*n*, 521,
    550–51, 552, 555–57
  Bush tax cuts and, 161–62, 204
  citizenship issue and, 268, 268*n*
  election of 2002 and, 330
  election of 2006 and, 515, 518, 519–23,
    542, 598*n*
  financial crisis of 2007–2008 and, 619,
    625–26, 627, 628–31, 642, 645
  Geneva Conventions and, 283*n*, 286
  Hurricane Katrina and, 438–39
  immigration reform and, 582–84, 584*n*
  Iraq occupation and, 375, 377, 386, 477,
    527, 528, 576–79, 581–82, 586, 587,
    587*n*, 588, 589–90, 590*n*, 594, 595–96
  Iraq Study Group and, 527, 534*n*
  Iraq surge and, 541, 542, 545, 550,
    551–52, 595–96
  Iraq war authorization and, 319,
    321–22, 323, 324–25
  Iraq war leadup and, 301, 314–16,
    319, 321–22, 323, 324–25, 335–36,
    345–46, 353, 354
  Joint Economic Committee and, 610
  military commissions and, 501*n*, 502,
    503, 506–8, 509*n*
  No Child Left Behind and, 164–66,
    204, 449
  Persian Gulf War and, 179
  prescription drug issue and, 390–91,
    390*n*

Rumsfeld and, 130, 132
signing statements and, 472–76
trade policy and, 585–86
U.S. attorney firings and, 564,
    564–65*n*, 566–68, 568*n*, 569, 572
Vietnam War and, 595
war declarations and, 229–30
war on terror and, 232, 240–42,
    240–41*n*, 254, 255, 256–57, 258, 260,
    261, 266, 272, 471
Watergate and, 255, 256
see also House of Representatives, U.S.;
    Senate, U.S.
Congressional Budget Office (CBO), 159,
    160, 162–63
Connally, John, 18
Constitution, U.S., 143, 144, 455, 456, 470
electoral vote and, 109, 109*n*, 124*n*, 142
Fifth Amendment to, 255, 267*n*
First Amendment to, 267*n*, 562
Fourteenth Amendment to, 76, 268, 428
Fourth Amendment to, 255, 260, 267*n*,
    473
signing statements and, 472–76,
    472–73*n*
Sixth Amendment to, 255
Supremacy Clause and, 288, 288*n*
Twelfth Amendment to, 109*n*, 111,
    124*n*
Twenty-third Amendment to, 124*n*
war on terror and, 253–74, 267*n*, 268*n*,
    509*n*
Contract with America, 163
Convention Against Torture (1987),
    294–95, 294*n*, 299
Conway, James, 397, 539*n*
Cooley, Denton, 111
Coolidge, Calvin, xviii
Cooper, Matthew, 452*n*
Cooper, Washington, 83–84
Coppola, Francis Ford, 48*n*
Cordesman, Anthony, 487*n*
Corn, David, 342*n*
Cornell University, 177, 177*n*

Cornyn, John, 571, 583
Corzine, Jon, 460*n*
Costa Rica, 585
Costas, Bob, 648
Cottrell, Comer, 58
Council of Economic Advisers, 609, 611,
    640
Council on Foreign Relations, 205, 464,
    596
Country Gentleman, 85, 85*n*
Countrywide Financial Corporation, 613
Court of Appeals, U.S., 144
Cox, Archibald, 567
Cox, Chris, 624, 626
Craddick, Tom, 71
Craig, Larry, 240*n*
Crist, Charlie, 521
Crocker, Chester, 254
Crocker, Ryan, 373*n*, 579–80, 587, 592,
    593, 595
Crouch, J. D., 436, 530–31
Crowe, Russell, 351–52
Crowe, William, 131*n*
Crowley, Candy, 82
Crowley, Monica, 65*n*
Cruz, Ted, 147*n*
CSX railroad, 610
Cuba, 281, 281*n*
Cuban Missile Crisis (1962), 164, 343–44
Cummins, H. E. "Bud," 565, 566–67,
    567*n*
Cunningham, Randy "Duke," 567*n*
Cuomo, Mario, 37, 114*n*

Daley, Bill, 125
Daley, Richard, 139, 139*n*
Dallas, Tex., 54–55, 54*n*, 82–83, 83*n*, 655,
    655, 655*n*
Dallas Cowboys, 18
Dallas Jewish Federation, 60
Dallas Morning News, 20, 40, 78, 83, 90,
    97, 122*n*
Dallas Observer, 72
Dallas Times-Herald, 57

Dam, Kenneth, 225–26
Daniels, Mitch, *157,* 555
Dannehy, Nora, 575
Dark Winter war game, 264–65, 264*n*
Daschle, Tom, 231–32, 261–62, 263*n,* 315, 325
Davis, Edmund J., 81*n*
Davis, Lanny, 103
Davis, Shelby Cullom, 451
Davis Cup, 6
D-Day (June 6, 1944), 357*n*
Dean, Howard, 401–2
Dearlove, Richard ("C"), 309
debt, federal, 159, 163
Decision Economics, 161
Decision Points (Bush), 42*n,* 656
Decter, Midge, 180*n*
Defense Advisory Board, 181, 181*n*
Defense Department, U.S., 127*n,* 131*n,* 176*n,* 507*n,* 515*n,* 542
    Abu Ghraib scandal and, 386, 388–89
    Afghanistan and, 245, 250*n*
    anthrax scare and, 263*n*
    Cheney and, xviii, 179, 303, 332*n,* 383
    CIA Memorandum of Notification and, 243*n*
    detainees and, 280–81, 282, 287, 290, 291, 293, 386, 388–89
    Gates and, *see* Gates, Robert
    Geneva Conventions and, 284, 284*n,* 287–92
    Iraq invasion and occupation and, 359*n,* 361*n,* 368–70, 370*n,* 371, 372, 380, 386, 388–89, 477, 484, 485–86, 496, 498, 530, 580, 580–81*n,* 589
    Iraq surge and, 530, 548
    Iraq war leadup and, 245, 300–301, 302, 310, 314, 327–29, 328*n,* 331, 332, 336–37, 340, 342, 346–48, 355
    military commissions and, 273
    "moral waivers" and, 484
    neoconservatives and, 175, 176*n*
    9/11 attacks and, 220, 222, 224, 224*n*
    NSC and, 184*n*
    Office of Reconstruction and Humanitarian Assistance and, 361–62*n,* 368, 370
    Rumsfeld and, *see* Rumsfeld, Donald
    stop-loss and enlistment bonus programs and, 484, 581
    Wolfowitz and, xviii, 176*n,* 179, 181, 305, 332, 347
Defense Intelligence Agency (DIA), U.S., 133
"Defense Strategy for the 1990s" (Cheney and Wolfowitz), 180, 182
deficit, federal, 607
DeLay, Tom, 165, 171, 521
Dellinger, Walter, 257*n*
Delta Kappa Epsilon (DKE), 14–15, 17, 58, 129, 647
Democratic National Committee (DNC), 35
Democratic National Convention of 1988, 69
DeMuth, Christopher, 155
Denmark, 407
Depression, Great, xvii, 443, 586, 619, 623, 625–26, 643, 659
derivatives, xvi
desegregation, 112*n,* 446
Desert Storm, Operation (1991), 46*n,* 301, 332, 336
detainee issue, 273, 279–99, *282,* 289*n,* 293*n,* 420, 457–61, 466, 470–71, 499–509, 501*n,* 509*n*
    Abu Ghraib and, 299, 299*n,* 384–89, *385,* 387*n,* 458–59*n,* 475, 515, 563, 652
Devenish, Nicolle, 431
Dewey, Thomas E., 383
Dewine, Mike, 522
DeWitt, William O., Jr., 40–41, 52, 57, 58
DeWitt, William O., Sr., 40
DeYoung, Karen, 290, 318, 382
Dickerson, John, 399–401
Dickey, Jay, 170*n*
Dickey Amendment (1996), 170, 170*n*

Dien Bien Phu, Battle of (1954), 548
Die Welt, 279
DiIulio, John J., 167–68, 168*n*
Dimon, Jamie, 617–18
Dirksen, Everett, 112*n*
diseases:
    AIDS and, xix, 549, 552–63, 552*n*, *558,*
        657, 659
    malaria and, xix, 553, 560, 561
    stem cell research and, 169–73, 170*n*,
        172*n*, 173*n*, 208, 577*n*
District of Columbia, 124, 124*n*
dividend taxes, 162
Dixie Chicks, 82
D magazine, 66
Dobrynin, Anatoly, 189*n*
Dobson, James C., 173
Doerflinger, Richard, 173
Doe v. Ashcroft (2004), 267*n*
Dole, Bob, 48, 51, 102, 120, 130, 132, 132*n*,
    163
Dole, Elizabeth, 104
Domenici, Pete, 567*n*, 586, 590
Domestic Policy Council, 154
domestic surveillance, xvii, 255–61, 256*n*,
    258*n*, 259*n*, 393–96, 420, 467–69, 659
Dominican Republic, 585
Dotti, Norman, 19
Douglas, William O., 137, 448
Dowd, Matthew, 368, 392, 406, 409, 563
Dowd, Maureen, 119
Dow Jones Industrial Average, 613, 619,
    622, 624, 626, 630, 631
Downing, Conway, 13
Downing, Wayne, 536*n*
draft, conscription, 110*n*
Draper, William H., 38
Dreier, David, 589
Dresser Industries, 8, 9
Duelfer, Charles, 379, 400
Dukakis, Michael, 51–52, 77, 113
Dulles, John Foster, xviii, 286, 463, 463*n*
Dwyer, Jim, 359*n*
Dybul, Mark, 559

Eastwood, Clint, 215
Ebbets Field, 64
Economic Club of New York, 608–9
economy, U.S.:
    auto industry bailout and, 640–45,
        644*n*, 659
    G-20 Summit and, 649–50
    housing bubble and, xvi, 608–15,
        618–19, 622
    see also financial crisis of 2007–2008
Edelman, Eric, 233
education:
    Bush presidency and, xix, 142, 158,
        163–67, *166*, 173, 204, 217, 390, 406,
        426, 449, 582
    Bush's Texas reform agenda and, 87,
        88–89, 90
    funding issue and, 75–76
    No Child Left Behind and, xix,
        164–67, *166*, 173, 204, 217, 390, 406,
        426, 449, 582, 659
Education Department, U.S., 135, 163,
    164, 167*n*, 419
Edwards, John, 402, 405, 409–10
E.F. Hutton, 38
Egypt, 293, 303, 532–33
82nd Airborne Division, U.S., 357, 441–42
Eisenhower, David, 242
Eisenhower, Dwight D., 35, 116, 127, 128,
    136, 149*n*, 152, 154, 156, 179, 199,
    230, 286, 305, 352, 357*n*, 440, 444,
    445*n*, 447, 463, 463*n*, 473, 478–79,
    478*n*, 488, 530, 581*n*, 600
    athletics and, 13
    Camp David and, 242
    China and, 197
    Columbia and, 180, 537*n*, 658
    election of 1952 and, 3
    election of 1956 and, 383
    election of 1960 and, 121
    NSC and, xvii–xviii, 183, 233, 233*n*,
        548
    reading and, 169
Eisenhower, Mamie, 242

ElBaradei, Mohamed, 341, *341,* 345, 349, 350–51, 353, 377
elections:
of 1800, 124*n*
of 1824, 124*n*
of 1876, xxi, 136–37, 142*n*
of 1912, 67, 68, 227
of 1928, 72, 120
of 1930, 92
of 1932, xx, 103
of 1934, 29, 329
of 1936, 422, 636*n*
of 1940, 383, 520, 636*n*
of 1944, 383, 636*n*
of 1950, 2
of 1952, 2–3, 537*n,* 634
of 1956, 120, 383
of 1960, 121, 139, 139*n*
of 1964, 391
of 1968, 18–19, 108, 126, 636
of 1970, 21, 30, 31
of 1972, 23–24, 72, 392
of 1974, 113
of 1976, 30, 34, 108, 125, 131*n,* 133*n,* 383, 392
of 1978, xix, 29–30, 33–37, *34,* 113, 121, 425–26
of 1980, 37, 38, 178
of 1982, 37
of 1984, 73, 113
of 1988, 47–53, 65, 69, 113–14, 115, 132, 132*n*
of 1990, 54–56, 60, 113
of 1992, 66–68, 114, 116, 121, 138, 383
of 1994, xx, 68–79, *73,* 74*n,* 121
of 1996, 93, 102, 120, 121, 126, 126*n,* 127, 130, 163
of 1998, xx, 92–93, 94–96, 94*n,* 97, 121
of 2000, *see* presidential election of 2000
of 2002, 329–30, 392
of 2004, *see* presidential election of 2004

of 2006, 499, 504, 507, 511, 512, 514, 515, 518, 519–23, 521*n,* 524–25, 526, 542, 565, 567*n,* 598*n,* 635
of 2008, 405, 522, 597–98, 598*n,* 604*n,* 623, 624, 627, 633–38, *634,* 637–38*n,* 639–40, 640*n*
of 2010, 655
of 2012, 655–56
of 2014, 655
likability factor and, 126
Elementary and Secondary Education Act (1965), 163
Eli Lilly, 561
Elizabeth II, Queen of England, 68, 206
Ellis, John, 11–12, 98
Ellis, Nancy Bush, 33, 67
El Salvador, 407, 585
Emanuel, Rahm, 523, 578, 653
Emergency Economic Stabilization Act of 2008, 631
Emilio, 95
Emma E. Booker Elementary School (Sarasota, Fla.), 166, 217, *217*
End of Iraq, The (Galbraith), 491
Enduring Freedom, Operation (2001–2014), 357
Energy Department, U.S., 135, 135*n,* 419, 420
Engelbrecht family, 93
Engler, John, 110*n*
Enron Corporation, 94*n*
Ensenat, Donald, 23, 200
environment, xix
Environmental Protection Agency (EPA), U.S., 189, 190–93, 420
Esquire, 600*n*
Estonia, 531
Estrada, Miguel, 147*n*
Ethiopia, 555*n,* 561
European Central Bank, 613, 649*n*
European Commission, 649*n*
European Union (EU), 199, 279, 649*n*
evangelical Christians, 104, 339, 399*n,* 419

Evans, Don, 45, 106, 125–26, 129, *157,*
  420, 522
Evans, Mrs. Don, 45
Evins, Joe, 113
Executive Office Building (EOB), 157
ex parte Quirin (1942), 272
Export-Import Bank, U.S., 38
extraordinary renditions, xvii, 293–96,
  388, 659

Face the Nation, 311
Fagan, Shawn, 147*n*
Fair Deal, 606
Fair Minimum Wage Act of 2007, 578
faith-based initiatives, 167–68
Fallon, William J., 545*n,* 546, 580, 592,
  600, 600*n*
Fallujah, Iraq, 397–99, 480–81, 480*n*
Falwell, Jerry, 173
Farley, James A., 72, 103
Faubus, Orval, 440
Fauci, Anthony, 554, 555
Fay, George R., 388
Federal Aviation Administration (FAA),
  9/11 attacks and, 220, 222, 226
Federal Bureau of Investigation (FBI):
  al Qaeda threat and, 211, 212
  anthrax scare and, 263
  background checks and, 421
  Hoover and, 420
  Libby case and, 452*n,* 453, 454
  Patriot Act and, 266, 267, 473–74
  threat matrix reports and, 265–66, 269
  TSP reauthorization and, 394, 395
Federal Deposit Insurance Corporation
  (FDIC), U.S., 630
Federal Election Commission (FEC),
  U.S., 368
Federal Emergency Management Agency
  (FEMA), 117, 222
  Hurricane Katrina and, 431–32,
    434–36, 438–39, 440, 442
Federal Home Loan Mortgage Corporation
  (Freddie Mac), 618–20, 619*n,* 621

Federal Housing Administration (FHA),
  U.S., 614
Federalist Society, 140, 450
Federal National Mortgage Association
  (Fannie Mae), 618–20, 619*n,* 621
Federal Reserve Bank of Chicago, 612
Federal Reserve Bank of New York, 621,
  624
Federal Reserve System, U.S., 159,
  160–61, 617–18*n*
  AIG and, 623, 624
  Bear Stearns and, 616–18, 617–18*n*
  housing bubble and, 608–9, 610, 612
  Lehman Brothers and, 620–22, 624
  TARP and, 625, 626
FedEx, 129, 515
Fein, Bruce, 261
Feingold, Bruce, 266*n*
Feinstein, Dianne, 299, 566, 582
Feith, Douglas, xviii, 235, 287, 305, 314*n,*
  332, 375*n*
Feldman, Ellen, 54*n*
Feldman, Hervey, 54*n*
Fenway Park, 64
Ferguson, James, 69*n*
Ferguson, Miriam Amanda "Ma," 69,
  69*n*
Fielding, Fred, 572
Fifth Amendment (1791), 255, 267*n*
Financial Crisis Inquiry Commission, 621
financial crisis of 2007–2008, xvi, xvii,
  231, 606–32, 645, 659
  AIG and, 622–24, 624*n*
  bankruptcies and, 612–13
  Bear Stearns and, 616–18, 616*n,*
    617–18*n,* 620, 621, 622
  Fannie Mae and Freddie Mac and,
    618–20, 619*n,* 621
  Lehman Brothers and, 620–22, 620*n,*
    623, 624, 632
  money markets and, 624–25, 626
  subprime mortgages and, 231, 608,
    608*n,* 612–18, 620
  TARP and, 624–32, 642, 643–44

financial industry, regulation and, xvi, xix, 616*n*

Financial Times, 191, 205

Financial World, 93

Fineman, Howard, 50, 551

1st Armoured Division, British, 357

1st Cavalry Division, U.S., 441–42

1st Marine Division, U.S., 397

1st Marine Expeditionary Force, U.S., 357, 359

First Amendment (1791), 267*n,* 562

Fischer, David Hackett, 285

Fischer, Joschka, 279, 338, 358, 594

Fitzgerald, Jennifer, 50, 50*n*

Fitzgerald, Patrick J., 452*n,* 454

Fitzwater, Marlin, 48

Flanigan, Tim, 147*n*

Fleischer, Ari, 223, 280, 326, 352, 353, 360, 362, 376, 377

Florida, 624
    election of 1876 and, 136
    election of 2000 and, xxi, 116*n,* 123–27, 135*n,* 136–47, 138*n,* 142*n,* 147*n,* 401, 427, 521
    election of 2004 and, 411, 413
    election of 2006 and, 521
    Hurricane Betsy and, 437*n*
    Hurricane Katrina and, 430, 431, 432, 442*n*
    Panhandle section of, 123–24
    see also Bush, John Ellis "Jeb"

Florida Supreme Court, election of 2000 and, 141, 142, 142*n,* 143–45, 146, 147*n*

Focus on the Family, 173

Forbes, 46*n*

Forbes, Steve, 104, 107, 180*n*

Ford, 641

Ford, Gerald R., 30, 35, 108, 125, 130–31, 131*n,* 132*n,* 133*n,* 152, 152*n,* 156, 237, 383, 449, 500, 548

Ford, John, 43*n*

Foreign Affairs, 323*n*

Foreign Affairs Reform and Restructuring Act (1998), 295

Foreign Intelligence Surveillance Act (FISA) (1978), 255–57, 256*n,* 259, 260, 261, 266, 267

Fornea, Stan, 493

Fortas, Abe, 445

Fort Detrick, Md., 263, 263*n*

41: A Portrait of My Father (Bush), 657–58, 658*n*

442nd Civil Affairs Battalion, U.S., 396

442nd Regimental Combat Team, U.S., 577*n*

Fourteenth Amendment (1868), 76, 268, 428

4th Infantry Division, U.S., 348

Fourth Amendment (1791), 255, 260, 267*n,* 473

Fox, 232

Fox, Vicente, 215

Fox News, 48, 121, 361, 413, 498, 535, 588, 650

France, 190, 247, 478–79, 561, 649
    Iraq war leadup and, 314*n,* 330, 338–40, 344–45, 348–49, 350, 351, 353

Francisco, Noel, 147*n*

Frankfurter, Felix, 448

Franks, Tommy, 249–51, *250,* 252, 276–77, 284–85, 301–3, 304, 304*n,* 305–6, 308, 313, 326–27, 331, 342, 347–48, 351, 353, 354–55, 357–58, 359, 359*n,* 360, 363, 368, 374, 477, 477*n,* 543, 588
    see also Central Command (CENTCOM), U.S.

Franks, Trent, 391

Freedom of Information Act (FOIA) (1966), 254

Friedrich, Carl, 485

Frist, Bill, 110*n,* 170, 384, 391, 450, 458, 459, 558

Frum, David, 155, 168, 263, 277, 278*n*

Fukuyama, Francis, 180*n*

Fuller, Craig, 48

G-7 countries, 649
G-8 countries, 190–91, 206–7, 248
G-20 countries, 649–50, 649*n*
Gaddis, John Lewis, 422*n*
Galbraith, Peter, 491
Gallagher, Sean, 147*n*
Gallup poll, 158, 167, 393, 408, 634
Gambia, The, 553
Garner, Jay, 368–70, 373–74, 373*n*, 477, 479
Garner, John Nance, 128, 155, 383
Garnett, Rick, 147*n*
gasoline, xv, xvi
Gates, Bill, 162
Gates, Robert, 516–17, *516*, 519, 525, 527–28*n*, 531, 536, 542
    Iraq and, 543–45, 545*n*, 546, 548, 580–81*n*, 591–92, 597, 600*n*
Gaulle, Charles de, 339, 478, 479
gay rights, 104, 106, 633
G.D. Searle, 130
Geithner, Timothy, 621, 624
General Election Legal and Accounting Compliance funds (GELAC), 120
General Instrument Corporation, 130
General Motors (GM), 641, 644, 645
Generated Start war plan, 301–3, 306, 308, 309
Geneva, Switzerland, Reagan-Gorbachev summit at (1985), 182–83, 188, 199
Geneva Convention Relative to the Treatment of Prisoners of War (1929), 285
Geneva Conventions (1949), 271, 272, 273, 280, 283, 284–86, 284*n*, 286*n*, 287–93, 299, 387, 458, 460, 461, 471, 499–503, 505, 505*n*
    Common Article 3 of, 283*n*, 291–93, 295, 499, 500–501, 506–8, 509*n*
George Bush's War (Smith), xxii
George W. Bush Institute, 657, 658
George W. Bush Presidential Library and Museum, 656–57

Georgia, 401, 422*n*
Gephardt, Dick, 111, 321, 325, 402
Gergen, David, 151, 264
Germany, 190, 229, 346, 372–73*n*, 396–97*n*, 478–79, 485, 561, 649
    Iraq war leadup and, 314*n*, 339–40, 344–45, 348–49
Germany, Nazi, 229
Gerson, Michael, 171, 223, 277, 278*n*, 307, 313, 314, 316, 317, 324, 413, 423, 490, 555
Ghana, 563
G.H. Walker and Company, 6
G.I. Bill of Rights (Servicemen's Readjustment Act of 1944), 5
Gibson, Charles, 197, 404
Gibson, Dunn & Crutcher, 140
Gilead Sciences, 130
Gillespie, Edward, 419, 490
Gingrich, Newt, 163
Ginsburg, Ruth Bader, 144, 145, 146
Giuliani, Rudolph, 239, 240, 406, 421, 637
Gladiator, 351–52
Glass-Stegall Act (1933), 616*n*
Glenn, Edwin F., 297*n*
Global Fund to Fight HIV/AIDS, Tuberculosis, and Malaria, 553
Global Health Corps, 562, 562*n*
global warming, 189–93, 197–98
Godfather, The, 48, 48*n*
Goldberg, Jeffrey, 155
Golden Mosque of Samarra, 487, 487*n*, 490, 494, 547
Goldman Sachs, 610, 616*n*, 621, 624, 624*n*
Goldsmith, Jack, 258, 393, 394, 395
Goldsmith, Peter, 309, 343, 351
Goldwater, Barry S., 392
Goldwater-Nichols Defense Reorganization Act (1986), 304, 305, 331, 332*n*
Goler, Wendell, 588
golf, 2, 6, 657

Gonzales, Alberto, 129, 153, 154, 158, 289,
    291, 394–95, 420, 421, 427, 447, 502,
    503, 504, 655
    resignation of, 573–74, *574,* 575
    U.S. attorney firings and, 564–65, 566,
        568–69, 568*n,* 570–72, 573
Gonzales, Rebecca, *574*
Good Morning America, 404
Goodpaster, Andrew, 154, 447
Gorbachev, Mikhail, 99, 182–83, 182*n,*
    188–89, 189*n,* 199, 274
Gore, Albert, Jr., 97, 128, 159
    background of, 112
    Bush compared with, 103, 111–12
    campaigning and debating
        awkwardness and, xxi, 114, 116, 118,
        119
    concession to Bush and, 124–25
    drug use and, 113
    education of, 112, 113
    election of 1988 and, 113–14
    election of 1992 and, 67, 114
    election of 2000 and, *see* presidential
        election of 2000
    election of 2004 and, 405
    exaggeration of accomplishments and,
        117, 118
    House election and, 113
    Senate election and, 113
    vice presidency and, 114, 156
    Vietnam and, 112, 117
Gore, Albert, Sr., 111–12, 112*n*
Gore, Mary Elizabeth Aitcheson
    "Tipper," 112, 114, 116, 117
Goss, Porter, 460
Gow, Robert H., 23
Graham, Billy, 42, 42–43*n, 43,* 46, 82
Graham, Bob, 114*n*
Graham, Lindsey, 458, 471, 550, 571, 583
Graham, Mrs. Billy, *43*
Gramm, Phil, 55
Gramm-Leach-Bliley Act (1999), 616*n*
Grant, Ulysses S., 149*n,* 579, 600
Grassley, Charles, 571

Great Society, 114, 315, 426, 606
Green, Fitzhugh, 8
Greenberg, Stan, 127
Green Party, election of 2000 and, 116,
    116*n*
Greenspan, Alan, 134, 159, 160–61, 162,
    608–9, 610
Greenwich, Conn., 1–2, 6, 8
Green Zone (Baghdad, Iraq), 375*n,* 479,
    497, 594*n*
Gregory, David, 82, 614
Grenada, 286
Griffin, Timothy, 565, 567
Griswold v. Connecticut (1965), 2*n*
Groenhuijsen, Charles, 340
gross domestic product (GDP), xv–xvi,
    114, 115, 162, 162*n,* 163, 640
Guantánamo Naval Base, Cuba, xvii,
    270*n,* 280–83, 281*n, 282,* 291, 387,
    388, 458–59*n,* 500, 503, 506, 509*n*
Guatemala, 585
Gulf of Tonkin Resolution (1964), 241,
    311, 350
Gulfport, Miss., 433
Gurney, Edward, 18
Gustav, Hurricane, 635, 637*n*
Guter, Donald, 270
Gutierrez, Carlos, 420, 640, 643
Guyana, 555*n*

Haass, Richard, 193–94, 308, 596
habeas corpus, writs of, 500, 508, 509
Hadi, Ali al-, 487
Hadley, Stephen, 176*n,* 181, 211, 226, 233,
    314, 360, 363, 419, 429, 468, 483, 490,
    494, 495, 496, 502, 503, 504, 512, 516,
    580, 604
    Iraq policy review and, 526, 529
    Iraq surge and, 530*n,* 531, 536, 538
Hagel, Chuck, 110*n,* 191, 192, 311, 325,
    458, 483–84, 550, 577, 584, 590*n*
Hager, Henry, 493, 645–46, *646*
Hagin, Joe, 364, 430, 516
Haig, Alexander, 178–79, 188, 371

Haiti, 244, 286, 555*n*
Haldeman, H. R., 152
Halleck, Charles, 130
Halliburton, 108, 109, 303
"Halloween Massacre" (1975), 130–31,
    131*n*, 132*n*
Hamburg, Margaret, 264
Hamdan, Salim Ahmed, 499, 500, 501,
    501*n*
Hamdan v. Rumsfeld (2006), 293*n*, 461,
    499–503, 501*n*, 506
Hamdi v. Rumsfeld (2004), 428
Hamilton, Alexander, 136
Hamilton, Lee, 114*n*, 527, 527–28*n*, 528,
    529, 533, 534
Hance, Kent, 30, 35–36, 36*n*, 55, 113,
    121
Hanifl, David, 19
Hannah, Doug, 16, 21
Hannity, Sean, 584
Harding, Warren G., xviii
Harken Energy, 44, 46*n*, 58
    Bush's liquidation of stock in, 60–61,
        60–61*n*
Harken Oil and Gas, 44–45, 46–47, 49
Harrington, Walter, 657
Harris, Katherine, 139, 140, 141, 142
Harris, William D., 24
Harrison, Benjamin, 149*n*
Hart, Gary, 49–50
Hartford Courant, 3
Harvard Business School, xix, 26–27,
    174, 279
Harvard Management Corporation, 44,
    60*n*
Harvard University, 5, 13, 44, 60*n*, 112,
    176*n*
Hastert, Dennis, 314–15, 391, 423
Hatch, Orrin, 170, 258*n*
Hayden, Michael, 259–60, 259*n*, 468
    "black sites" issue and, 503, 504
Hayes, Rutherford B., xxi, 136, 142*n*
Hayworth, John, 523
Head Start, 111*n*

Health and Human Services Department
    (HHS), U.S., 135, 167*n*, 173*n*, 420–21
healthcare, xix, 117, 119, 142–43, 183,
    384, 390–91, 390*n*, 426, 434, 608,
    630
Heclo, Hugh, 151*n*
hedge funds, 611, 613, 614, 622
Hegel, Georg Wilhelm Friedrich, 175
Helms, Jesse, 240*n*, 295
Henderson, Donald, 265
Henderson, Muriel, 25–26
Herald Tribune, 169
Heritage Homestead, 96
Herman, Ken, 75
Hersh, Seymour, 388
Heymann, David, 96
Hickok, Eugene, 165
Hicks, Tom, 93–94, 94*n*
Hiler, Bruce A., 61
Hill, Calvin, 15
Hilton, James, 242
Hispanics:
    George W. Bush and, 94–95, 104
    immigration reform issue and, 523
History News Network, 634*n*
HIV (human immunodeficiency virus),
    552, 553, 554, 558, 560
Hoar, Joseph, 507
Hockaday School, 54, 70
Hoffmann, Roy, 408
Holder, Eric, 575
Holland, Steve, 510
Hollenbeck, Ralph, 396
Hollinger International, 176*n*
Hollings, Fritz, 50
Homeland Security Department (DHS),
    U.S., 421–22
    Hurricane Katrina and, 434, 435,
        438–39, 440, 442
Homeland Security Presidential
    Directive 3, 316*n*
Honduras, 585
Honoré, Russel, 441
Hoon, Geoff, 309

Hoover, Herbert, xviii, 4, 120, 149*n*, 443, 633, 636*n*
Hoover, J. Edgar, 420
Hoover Institution, 101, 101*n*
Hopkins, Harry, xvii, 201
Horton, Phil, 177*n*
Horton, Willie, 52
Hostettler, John, 522
House of Representatives, U.S.:
  AIDS issue and, 557–58, 558*n*, 560
  Appropriations Committee of, 29
  Armed Services Committee and, 595
  auto industry bailout and, 641, 642
  Budget Committee of, 347
  Bush tax cuts and, 161
  Cheney and, 108, 110–11*n*, 179
  Education Committee and, 164, 165
  election of 2000 and, 159
  election of 2002 and, 330
  election of 2006 and, 518, 519, 521–22, 523, 526, 598*n*
  financial crisis of 2007–2008 and, 619, 627, 629–31
  Foreign Affairs Committee and, 527, 595
  Gates confirmation and, 536
  Gore, Jr. and, 113
  Gore, Sr. and, 112*n*
  Hance and, 36*n*
  immigration reform and, 583, 584
  International Relations Committee and, 301, 557
  Iraq occupation and, 461–63, 576, 577–78, 589, 590, 595, 598*n*
  Iraq surge and, 552, 595
  Iraq war leadup and, 301, 314–16, 321, 324–25, 335–36
  Judiciary Committee and, 572
  Mahon and, 29–30
  military commissions and, 508
  No Child Left Behind and, 165, 166, 204
  Patriot Act and, 266*n*, 566
  prescription drug issue and, 390*n*, 391

presidential elections and, 124*n*, 137
Rumsfeld and, 130, 132
torture issue and, 460, 465
trade policy and, 585–86
Transportation Committee and, 135
U.S. attorney firings and, 567, 572
war on terror and, 232, 240, 240–41*n*, 255, 266*n*
see also Congress, U.S.; Senate, U.S.
Housing and Economic Recovery Act (HERA) (2008), 619
Housing and Urban Development Department (HUD), U.S., 135, 167*n*, 614
housing market:
  construction starts and, 607, 611–12
  economic bubble and, xvi, 608–15, 618–19, 622
Houston, Sam, 82–84, *83*
Houston, Tex., 11, *11*
Houston Chronicle, 51, 77, 78, 95
Houston Post, 75
Howard, Arlene, 240, *241*
Howard, George, 239
Howe, Louis, 72, 103
Hoyer, Steny, 508
HSBC Holdings, 612
Hubbard, Al, 27, 611
Hughes, Charles Evans, 448
Hughes, Karen, 43*n*, *73*, 74, 77, 85, 129, 172*n*, 187, 208, 215, 426, 490, 506, 526, 655
  background of, 73
  compassionate conservative phrase and, 95*n*
  election of 1984 and, 73
  election of 2000 and, 103, 106, 119, 121
  election of 2004 and, 409
  military commissions and, 502
  9/11 attacks and, 223
  White House staff and, 153–54, 155, 157–58, 209, 254, 312
Hu Jintao, 647, *647*, 649–50, 659
Hull, Cordell, xvii

"Humane Treatment of al Qaeda and Taliban Detainees" (Bush), 291

Humanitarian Law Project v. Ashcroft (2004), 267*n*

Hume, Brit, 650–52

Humphrey, Hubert H., 126, 183

Hungar, Tom, 147*n*

Hunt, H. L., 18

Hussein, Saddam, xvi, xvii, 179–81, 230, 234–35, 236, 244, 248, 277, 300, 301, 303, 305–6, 307, 309, 310, 311, 315, 316, 317, 318, 320, 321, 324, 330, 331, 332, 333, 336, 340, 344, 353–54, 356, *361,* 368, 373, 378–79, 380, 382*n,* 400, 401, 469, 477, 489, 512, 588, 589, 589*n,* 659

Hussein, Uday, 359

Hybrid war plan, 309–10, 309*n*

Hyde, Henry, 557, 560

IEDs (Improvised Explosive Devices), 603

Ifill, Gwen, 409

Iglesias, David, 565*n,* 567*n*

Iklé, Fred, 180, 362

Illinois, election of 1960 and, 139, 139*n*

immigrants, immigration, xix, 3, 104, 215, 417, 582–84, 584*n,* 586, 652, 659

income inequality issue, 162

Independent, 594*n*

India, 181, 190, 649

Indiana, 413, 522

Individuals with Disabilities Education Act (IDEA) (1990), 159*n*

Indonesia, 179, 649

IndyMac Bank, 618

Ingraham, Laura, 232

inheritance taxes, 160, 161, 608

Inouye, Daniel, 576–77, 577*n*

Insurrection Act (1807), 440, 441

Intelligence Identities Protection Act (1982), 452*n*

Interior Department, U.S., 134, 420

Internal Revenue Service (IRS), U.S., Bob Jones University and, 106

International Atomic Energy Agency (IAEA), 341, 345, 350–51, 452*n*

International Committee of the Red Cross, 270, 283*n*

International Covenant on Civil and Political Rights (1966), 294

International Criminal Court (ICC), 193, 292

International Criminal Tribunal, 271

International Derrick and Equipment Company (IDECO), 8–9

International Monetary Fund (IMF), 621

International Mother and Child HIV Prevention Initiative, 554

Internet, 117, 468

Intifada, 205

Iowa:
election of 2000 and, 104–5, 109
election of 2004 and, 401–2, 411, 412, 413, 414
Republican primary of 1988 and, 51

Iran, 482, 517, 533
"axis of evil" phrase and, 277–78
George W. Bush and, 246, 277–78, 517, 600*n*
Iraq and, 594, 594*n,* 599
9/11 attacks and, 225, 235
Persian Gulf War and, 179–80
war on terror and, 246

Iran-Contra scandal, 67, 183*n,* 444, 453

Iran hostage crisis (1979–1980), 137–38, 195

Iraq:
Abu Ghraib prison and, 299, 299*n,* 384–89, *385,* 387*n,* 458–59*n,* 475, 515, 563, 652
al Qaeda and, 398, 494, 511, 528, 578, 591, 593, 596, 597–99, 598–99*n,* 600, 659
aluminum tube issue and, 316, 318, 341, 350–51
Anbar province and, 397, 544, 592–94, 598–99, 598–99*n*
"axis of evil" phrase and, 277–78

Iraq (*cont.*)

benchmarks for U.S. actions in, 578–79, 587, 587*n*, 589

casualty figures and, 380, 380*n*, 478, 482, 490, 550, 592, 597, 602, 602*n*

civil war in, 487–88, 490, 492, 493, 511–12, 547, 588, 591

constitution and, 484–85, 487*n*

corruption and, 489–90

cost of U.S. invasion of, 602, 602*n*

CPA and, 373, 374, 396, 398, 479, 489

de-Baathification and, 373, 375, 479

democratization and, 369–70, 374, 380, 477, 478, 479, 481, 482, 484–86, 490, 493, 512, 514, 531, 534, 589, 589*n*, 602, 623

disbanding of Iraqi army and, 373, 479

displaced persons and refugees and, 488

elections and, 482, 484–85, 486, 547

George W. Bush and, xvi–xvii, xviii–xix, 174, 229, 234–35, 236, 246, 248, 252, 659

insurgency and, 367, 373, 375, 376*n*, 396–99, 480–83, 480–81*n*, 487, 489, 493, 511, 531

international opposition to invasion of, 338–40, 344–46, 348–49, 350, 351, 353, 358

Iran and, 594, 594*n*, 599

leadup to U.S. invasion of, 174, 234–35, 236, 246, 248, 276–78, 300–355, *355*

9/11 attacks and, 225, 248, 300

nuclear program and, 316, 318, 320, 322, 324, 341–42, 341*n*, 345, 350–51, 382*n*, 452*n*

parliament and, 486, 487*n*

Persian Gulf War and, xvii, xxii, 46*n*, 64, 108, 175–76, 179–80, 230, 249, 276, 286, 325, 332*n*, 356, 357, 364, 367, 368, 378, 382*n*, 545*n*

postwar reconstruction and, 361–62*n*, 368–70, 528

Republican Guard and, 276

Senior Leadership Council and, 373*n*, 374

Status of Forces Agreement and, 600–601, *601*, 645

terrorism and, 277–78, 309, 311, 314*n*, 324*n*, 329, 366–67

transitional government and, 484

UN weapons inspections and, 330, 331, 332, 333, 336, 338, 339, 340–41, *341*, 344–45, 349, 350–51

U.S. force drawdown and, 363, 369, 374, 376, 530, 532–33, 576–79, 587, 588, 589–90, 590*n*, 592, 595, 596, 597, 598*n*, 599, 600–601, 645

U.S. force surge and, 514, 517, 526, 529–48, 530*n*, 549–52, 549–50*n*, 576, 581–82, 586–88, 592–99, 623

U.S. invasion and occupation of, xvi–xix, 5, 61, 64, 229, 356–80, 359*n*, *361*, 361*n*, *366*, 370*n*, 371*n*, 374*n*, 375*n*, 376*n*, 386, 387*n*, 388–89, 396–99, 415, 417, 431–35, 443, 453, 457, 461–65, 476–98, 477*n*, 480–81*n*, *487*, *496*, 511–17, 519, 524, 526–48, 555, 563, 576–82, 580–81*n*, 586–602, 587*n*, 590*n*, 603, 614

U.S. invasion plans for, 326–27, 331, 336, 342–43, 347–48

war on terror and, 338, 366, 398, 491, 494, 534

weapons of mass destruction and, 264, 265, 276–78, 309, 313–14, 316–17, 318, 320, 321–24, 322*n*, 330–31, 333–34, 336, 341, 344, 350–51, 353–54, 359, 366–67, 376–80, 381–82, 382*n*, 400–401, 418, 589, 652, 659

Wolfowitz and, 178, 180–81, 211–12, 234, 244, 305, 332, 347, 357, 375, 377

Iraq Body Count, 380*n*

Iraqi Awakening Sahwa Party, 599*n*

Iraqi Freedom, Operation (2003), 355, 356–61, 364, 365, 368, 377

Iraqi Integrity Commission, 489
Iraqi Security Forces (ISF), 421, 469, 495, 531, 536, 538, 539, 598n
Iraqiyya party, 482
Iraq Study Group (Baker-Hamilton Commission), 516, 527–29, 527, 527–28n, 533–36, 534n, 537
Iraq Survey Group, 377–79
"Iron Triangle" (Rove, Allbaugh, Hughes), 73, 74, 103, 106, 121
Isaacson, Walter, 15
Isikoff, Michael, 315, 342n
Islamic State of Iraq (ISI), 598–99, 599n
Islamic State of Iraq and Syria (ISIS), xvii, 491, 598, 599n, 602, 659–60
Israel, 100, 174, 204–5, 213–15, 216, 417, 533, 585
Italy, 190, 229, 407, 649
Ivanov, Igor, 338, 344–45, 349
Ivanov, Sergei, 201
Ivins, Bruce, 263, 263n
Ivins, Molly, 47, 71, 77
Ivory Coast, 555n, 561

Jaafari, Ibrahim al-, 482, 487
Jackson, Alphonso, 614
Jackson, Andrew, 124n, 149n, 520
Jackson, Barry, 628
Jackson, Henry "Scoop," 176n
Jackson, Jesse, 113
Jackson, Robert H., 448, 562, 562n
James, Marquis, 84n
Japan, 190, 229, 285, 321, 346, 435, 590, 649
Jefferson, Thomas, 124n, 136, 149n, 168, 520
Jeffords, Jim, 159, 159n, 325, 508, 519–20
Jerusalem Post, 176n
Jeter, Derek, 251
Jews, Judaism, 95
Jiang Zemin, 195
jihad, xvii, 376, 491
Johanns, Mike, 420

John Paul II, Pope, 171, 206, 208, 348
Johns Hopkins, 265
Johns Hopkins Center for Civilian Biodefense Strategies, 264
Johns Hopkins School of Advanced International Studies, 101, 178, 180, 495, 536
Johnson, Andrew, 149n
Johnson, Claudia Alta Taylor "Lady Bird," 32
Johnson, Clay, 153, 154
Johnson, Lyndon B., 16, 49, 88, 112n, 114, 128, 137, 156, 163, 183, 184n, 209, 229, 230, 249, 256, 311, 315, 350, 426, 437–38, 445, 491, 492, 581n, 606, 633, 636
Joint Chiefs of Staff, U.S., 131, 131n, 184, 185, 235, 236, 244, 284n, 304–5, 304n, 327, 331, 332n, 342, 357, 458, 502, 507, 531, 536, 539–42, 539n, 548, 580, 581, 588, 592
Jones, Anthony R., 388
Jones, Bob, III, 106–7, 107n
Jones, James L., 327, 331
Jordan, 293, 303, 532, 585n
Jordan, Barbara, 79n
Jordan, Vernon, 528n
JPMorgan Chase, 617–18, 618n, 620, 622
Juan Carlos, King of Spain, 198
Jubeir, Adel, 215
Jumper, John P., 327
Justice Department, U.S., 451, 475
  anthrax scare and, 263
  Ashcroft and, 134, 136, 167n, 224, 246, 254, 272–73, 290, 316, 393–95, 412, 419–20
  CIA Memorandum of Notification and, 243n
  detainee issue and, 290, 291, 420
  Gonzales and, see Gonzales, Alberto
  military commissions and, 269, 271, 272–73, 420
  9/11 attacks and, 224

Justice Department, U.S. (*cont.*)
    Office of Legal Counsel (OLC) of,
        257–59, 257*n*, 258*n*, 260, 272, 283,
        288, 289, 293, 295–96, 296*n*, 298–99,
        298*n*, 299*n*, 323, 393, 448, 505
    Patriot Act and, 267, 564, 564–65*n*, 566
    Plame case and, 452*n*
    Roberts and, 427
    secrecy issue and, 254
    terrorism threat alerts and, 316, 316*n*,
        412
    Terrorist Surveillance Program
        reauthorization and, 393–96
    threat matrix reports and, 266
    U.S. attorney firings and, 564–75,
        564–65*n*, 566*n*, 567*n*, 568*n*

Kabul, Afghanistan, 252, 603, 605
Kagan, Donald, 180*n*
Kagan, Frederick, 495
Kaplan, Robert, 495, 496*n*
Karl Rove & Co., 94*n*, 134
Karpinski, Janis, 389
Karzai, Hamid, 252, 277, 602, 605
Kashmir, 246
Kass, Leon, 171
Katrina, Hurricane, 231, 416, 430–43,
    433, 436, 437*n*, 441*n*, 444, 457, 563,
    591, 635, 652
    death and damage totals in, 442, 442*n*
Katzenbach, Nicholas, 257*n*
Kay, David, 377–78, 379, 382*n*
Keane, Jack, 536, 537–38, 580
Keating, Frank, 110*n*, 264
Keating, Timothy, 354
Keck, Tom, 220
Kefauver, Estes, 112*n*
Keller, Bill, 467, 468
Kelley, Bill, 147*n*
Kelley, Kitty, 19
Kemp, Jack, 48
Kempe, Paul, 83*n*
Kempe, Susan, 83*n*
Kempton, Murray, 463*n*

Kennebunkport, Maine:
    Bush family compound in, 29, 41–42,
        41, 43, 68n, 101–2, 204, 205–6, 215,
        455
    Bush-Rice meeting at, 101–2
    Walker estate at, 6
Kennedy, Anthony, 144, 145, 147*n*, 449,
    509
Kennedy, Edward M. "Ted," 164–66,
    166, 218, 325, 385, 405, 451, 583, 630*n*
Kennedy, John F., 128, 139*n*, 150, 156,
    164, 184*n*, 230, 420, 440, 581*n*
Kennedy, Joseph P., 6, 98
Kennedy, Robert F., 420
Kennedy, Vicki, 164
Kennedy v. Mendoza-Martinez (1963),
    268*n*
Kentucky, 126*n*, 413, 422*n*, 522
Kenya, 555*n*
Kerik, Bernard, 421–22, 422*n*
Kerrey, Bob, 114*n*, 404
Kerrick, Don, 212
Kerry, John F., *403*
    election of 2004 and, 402–15, 422,
        457–58, 542
    flip-flop charge and, 403–4, 406–7
    Iraq war authorization and, 325
    Vietnam War and, 402, 404, 405,
        407–8
Keyes, Alan, 105, 107, 111*n*
KGB (Soviet State Police), 200*n*
Khalilzad, Zalmay, 180*n*, 373*n*, 494, 511,
    526–27, 545
Khomeini, Ruhollah, 180
Khrushchev, Nikita S., 199
Killian, Jerry B., 20
Kim Dae-jung, 186, 187, 188
Kim Jong Il, 188
Kimmons, John, 505*n*
King, Alan, 396
King, Larry, 78, 385, 482–83
King, Martin Luther, Jr., 16
King, Rodney, 440
Kinkaid School, 11, 12

Kissinger, Henry, 131*n*, 195*n*, 206, 371, 424
Kitty Hawk, USS, 346
Koerner, W. H. D., 84–85, *85, 85n*
Koh, Harold, 258*n*, 500
Korea, North, 182, 186–88, 186*n*, 187*n*, 189, 229–30, 264, 659
 "axis of evil" phrase and, 277–78
Korea, South, 186, 187, 188, 585–86, 649
Korean War, 229–30, 286, 305, 327, 500, 507, 515*n*, 590
Kosovo, 208, 286, 363, 402
Krauthammer, Charles, 449
Kristof, Nicholas, 56
Kristol, William, 448–49, 535
Kucinich, Dennis, 598*n*
Kuhn, Bowie, 35
Kurdish Alliance, 482
Kurds, 303, 328, 332, 343, 368, 378, 482, 485, 486, 487*n*, 530, 532, 593
Kuwait, 303, 336, 348, 351
Kyl, Jon, 110*n*, 583
Kyoto Protocol (1997), 189–93, 197, 198, 199, 292, 311

Labor Department, U.S., 134–35, 167*n*, 367, 420, 422*n*
Ladd, Ernie, 25, 26
Laden, Osama bin, 204, 210, 211, 212, 222, 224, 232, 234, 236, 246–47, 252, 261, 262, 296, 408, 412, 500, 603, 605
Lagarde, Christine, 621
Laghi, Pio, 348
Laikind, Jeffrey, 44
Lam, Carol, 567*n*
LaMontagne, Margaret, 153, 154, 169–70
Landon, Alf, 422
Landry, Tom, 54
Laney, Pete, 88, 89, 90
Lantos, Tom, 557, 560
Larry King Live, 459, 482–83
Late Edition, 316
Latinos:
 George W. Bush and, 94–95, 104
 immigration reform issue and, 523

Latvia, 531, 532
Lauder, Ronald, 199
Lauer, Matt, 450
Lawrence, T. E., 497
Lawrence v. Texas (2003), 428
Lay, Kenneth, 94*n*
Lay, Linda, 94*n*
Lazarus effect, 559–60
Lazear, Edward, 611, 640, 643
Lea, Tom, 92
Leahy, Patrick, 263*n*, 476, 566, 567, 571, 572
Leahy, William, 580
Leavitt, Michael, 420–21
le Carré, John, 232
Lee, Barbara, 240–41*n*, 557
LeHand, Missy, 72, 154
Lehman Brothers, 616*n*, 620–22, 620*n*, 623, 624, 632
Lehrer, Jim, 408
Lehrman, Lewis, 37–38
Lemnitzer, Lyman, 581*n*
Leno, Jay, 99, 405
Levin, Carl, 346, 481
Lewinsky, Monica, xx, 115, 444, 530
Lewis, Anthony, 298
Lewis, Terry, 140
Libby, I. Lewis "Scooter," xviii, 157, 180*n*, 187, 233, 314, 334
 indictment and, 452–57, 452*n*, 455*n*
Liberia, 563
Lichtblau, Eric, 467, 468, 470, 476
Lieber, Francis, 285
Lieber Code (General Orders 100) (1863), 285, 292
Lieberman, Joe, xxi, 115–16, *115,* 402, 422, 515, 550, 635, 637
Liedtke, Hugh, 10, 35
LIFE Today, 98
Limbaugh, Rush, 345, 375–76
Lincoln, Abraham, 136, 229, 239, 406, 552, 579, 580
Lindh, Anna, 187
Lindsey, Larry, 129, 389

Little Rock, Ark., 440
Lloyd George, David, 227
Lodge, Henry Cabot, 581*n*
Logan International Airport, 218
London School of Economics, 485
London *Sunday Times,* 309*n*
London *Telegraph,* 658
Los Angeles, Calif., 440
Los Angeles Times, 19
Lost Horizon (Hilton), 242
Lott, Trent, 321, 391, 439
Louisiana, 126*n,* 136, 635
    Hurricane Betsy and, 437*n*
    Hurricane Katrina and, 430, 431, 432,
        433, 434–42, 591
Louisiana National Guard, 439–42
Love Canal disaster, 117
Love Story (Segal), 117
Luce, Tom, 71
Lugar, Dick, 558, 581–82, 586, 590
Lussier, John, 364–65
Lute, Douglas, 580, 580–81*n*
Luti, William J., 530*n*
Luttig, Michael, 427, 428, 428*n,* 451

MacArthur, Douglas, 286, 305, 372
MacArthur, Mrs. Douglas, 35
McBride, Andrew, 147*n*
McCaffrey, Barry, 536*n*
McCain, Bridget, 107
McCain, Cindy, 107, 637*n*
McCain, John:
    anti-torture amendment and, 457–60,
        459*n,* 465, 466, 467, 470–71, 472, 473,
        476
    Bush tax cuts and, 162
    election of 2000 and, xx, 105–8, 107*n,*
        110, 111, 405, 408
    election of 2004 and, 404–5, 406, 408,
        457–58
    election of 2006 and, 521
    election of 2008 and, 623, 627, 634–38,
        634, 638*n,* 639–40
    immigration reform and, 583

    Iraq surge and, 550
    military commissions and, 507
    TARP and, 627–29, 630
    Vietnam War and, 107, 404, 405,
        459–60
McCall Publishing Company, 7
McCallum, Robert, 14
McCarran-Walter Immigration Act
    (1952), 3
McCarthy, Joseph R., 3
McCarthyism, 3
McClellan, Scott, 153, 154, 308, 400, 417,
    418, 418*n,* 492*n*
    Hurricane Katrina and, 431, 436, 443
    Libby case and, 456–57
    McCain anti-torture amendment and,
        459
    Murtha and, 462, 463
McCleskey, Robert, 29
McCombs, William, 227*n*
McConnell, Mitch, 135, 426, 508, 514, 642
Macdonald, Torbert, 12
McFarlane, Robert C. "Bud," 182–83
McGovern, George, 72, 114, 392
McKay, John, 565*n,* 567*n*
McKellar, Kenneth, 112*n*
McKiernan, David, 354, 374
McKinley, William, 444
McKinnon, Mark, 368
McLaughlin, John (CIA official), 334
McLaughlin, John (journalist), 55
McLaughlin Group, 55
McMahon, Brien, 2
Macmillan, Harold, 352
MacMillan, Margaret, 227
McNamara, Robert S., 229, 249, 332*n,* 350
McNulty, Paul, 566–67
Macomber, John D., 38
Mahdi Army, 398, 598, 599
Mahon, George, 29–30, 32, 35, 113
Maiden Lane LLC, 617–18*n*
Makin, John, 161
malaria, xix, 553, 560, 561
Malek, Fred, 58

Maliki, Nouri al-, 487, 490, 496–98, *496,* 532, 536, 538, 539, 543, 544, 545–47, 593, 598, 598*n,* 599, 600–602, *601,* 645

Mallon, Neil, 8

Manning, John, 147*n*

Man Who Shot Liberty Valance, The, 43*n*

Marbury v. Madison (1803), 141, 509

Marcus, Sandy, 54

Marine Corps, U.S.:
   expansion of, 530*n,* 537, 541, 542, 545, 551
   Iraq invasion and occupation and, 308, 331, 357, 359–60, 373, 397, 398, 480, 482, 512, 592
   Iraq surge and, 544

Marine One, 222, 269, 273, 360, 411, 496, 654, *655*

Marius, Caius, 84

Marriott, 58

Marsh & McLennan, 58, 371

Marshall, George C., 305, 337–38, 357*n,* 382, 507, 507*n,* 515*n,* 548

Marshall, James, 465*n*

Marshall, John, 141, 147, 428*n,* 446, 446*n,* 448, 509

Marshall, Josh, 566*n*

Marsh Crisis Consulting, 371

Martin, Fred, 114

Martinez, Mel, 135, *157,* 584

Martin Luther King Day, 111*n*

Matalin, Mary, 49, 65, 67, 157–58

Matlock, Jack, 182–83, 182*n*

Matthews, Chris, 232

Mattis, James, 373, 397, 398, 580–81*n*

Maura, Fred, 26

Mauro, Garry, 93, 94, 95, 97

Mayfield, Brandon, 267*n*

Mayfield, Max, 431–32, 433

Mayfield v. Gonzales (2007), 267*n*

May-Traenor, Misty, 648

Mazar-e-Sharif, Afghanistan, 252

Meacham, Jon, 50

Medicare, 150, 384, 390, 390*n,* 434, 659

Meese, Edwin, 527*n,* 528

Meet the Press, 316, 378–79

Mehlman, Ken, 368, 490, 521, 522, 523

"Memorandum of Notification," 243, 243*n*

"Memorandum on Interrogation of al Qaeda Operative [Zubaydah]" (OLC), 298–99, 298*n,* 299*n*

Menand, Louis, 114

Meredith, James, 440

Merkel, Angela, 546

Merrill Lynch, 616*n*

Merritt, James, 238

Mexico, 94–95, 215, 561, 582, 584*n,* 585, 649

Meyer, Christopher, 206

Meyer, Eugene, 10

Miami-Dade County Republican Party, 68

Miami Herald, 78

Michigan:
   election of 2000 and, 123, 135*n*
   Republican primary of 2000 and, 108

Middlebrooks, Donald M., 140

Middle East:
   Bush and, 174, 204–6, 205*n,* 213–15, 216, 417, 464, 478, 482, 512, 514, 590, 659–60
   Clinton and, 204–5, 205*n,* 215
   neoconservatives and, 175, 369
   see also specific countries

Midland, Tex., xix, 9–11, 28–31, 32, 33, 35, 36, 37, 42*n,* 51, 92, 655, 656*n*

Miers, Harriet, 86, 129, 153, 154, 155, 169, 427, 441*n,* 453, 502
   Supreme Court nomination and, 447–51, *448,* 457
   U.S. attorney firings and, 564, 565, 567, 568, 572

Mies van der Rohe, Ludwig, 96–97

Milbank, Dana, 103, 166

military commissions, 269–74, 270*n,* 280, 292, 293, 420, 499–503, 501*n,* 506–9, 508*n,* 509*n*

Military Commissions Act (2006), 501*n*, 506–9, 509*n*

Military Commissions Act (2009), 509*n*

Military Intelligence, U.S., 387–89, 387*n*

Miller, George, 165, *166*

Mineta, Norman, 135, 136, *157*, 222, 226, 420

Minnesota Twins, 56

Mirror, 343

Mississippi, 413, 440, 635

   Hurricane Katrina and, 430, 431, 432, 433, 436, 439, 442, 591

Missouri, 126*n*, 522

Mitscher, Marc, 5

Mobile, Ala., 439

Mohammed, Khalid Sheikh, 505

Mondale, Walter, 114, 156, 183

money market funds, 624–25, 626

Monroe, James, 473*n*

Montana, 522

Moon, Sun Myung, 289

Moore, Michael, 462

Morgan Stanley, 616*n*, 622

Mori, Dan, 270*n*

Morocco, 293, 585

Morrison, Jack, 515–16

mortgage-backed securities, 608, 622, 627

   rating agencies and, 632

mortgage industry, 607–8, 609, 611

   bankruptcies in, 612–13, 618

   bundling and, 616

   foreclosures and, 607, 612, 614, 618

   Lehman Brothers and, 620

   subprime mortgages and, 231, 608, 608*n*, 612–18, 620

   TARP and, 626

Mosbacher, Rob, 71

Mosbacher, Robert, 71

Moseley, Michael, 354, 539*n*

Mosul, Iraq, 480–81*n*

MoveOn.org, 595

Moynihan, Daniel Patrick, 295

Mozambique, 555*n*, 561

MSNBC, 232

Mubarak, Hosni, 303

Mueller, Robert, 265, 394, 395

Muhayya, Salih Ali bin, 214

Mukasey, Michael, 574–75

Mullen, Michael, 539*n*, 581

Murchison, Clint, Jr., 18

Murkowski, Lisa, 550

Murray, Patty, 577

Murtha, Jack, 461–63, 465, 476, 477*n*

Musharraf, Pervez, 105, 243

Muslims, Islam, xvii, 135*n*, 245, 328, 332, 343, 367, 373, 378, 396–99, 399*n*, 479, 480–82, 484, 485, 486, 487, 487*n*, 491, 511, 530, 532, 547, 590, 593, 598–99, 598–99*n*, 659

Myers, Richard, 244, 276, 287, 289, 290, 331, 336, 337, 581

My Lai massacre (1968), 385

Nader, Ralph, xxi, 116, 116*n*, 126, 135*n*, 638*n*

Nagin, Ray, 431

Namibia, 555*n*

Nashville Tennessean, 113, 117

National Archives, U.S., 657

National Book Festival, 216

National Cathedral (Washington, D.C.), 237–39, *237*

National Center for Health Statistics, 231

National Day of Prayer and Remembrance (September 14, 2001), 237

National Economic Council, 611

National Enquirer, 261

National Guard, U.S., 17–18, *17*, 20, 24, 26, 439–42

   Iraq occupation and, 479, 540, 541

National Guard Bureau, U.S., 441

National Hurricane Center, U.S., 431–32

National Institute of Allergy and Infectious Diseases, U.S., 554

National Institutes of Health (NIH), U.S., 172*n*, 173*n*, 554

National Intelligence Estimate (NIE), 321–23, 322n, 491, 591
National Museum, Iraqi, 361–63, 361–62n
National Rifle Association (NRA), 193
National Right to Life Committee, 173
National Security Act of 1947, 152n
National Security Agency (NSA), U.S.:
    Patriot Act and, 267
    surveillance and, 256, 256n, 259–61, 259n, 393–96, 420, 467–69, 659
National Security Council (NSC), U.S., 152n, 174, 176n, 183n, 187, 548
    Afghanistan and, 604
    biological attacks and, 265
    CIA Memorandum of Notification and, 243n
    Clarke and, 211, 234–35
    Counterterrorism and Security Group of, 211
    detainee issue and, 287, 289, 290, 503–4
    Eisenhower and, xvii–xviii, 183, 233, 233n, 548
    George H. W. Bush and, 174, 185, 308
    George W. Bush and, 174, 182, 183–84, 184n, 186, 221–22, 224–25, 231, 233, 289, 290, 302, 309–10, 312–13, 363, 397, 511–12, 580, 580–81n, 592, 604
    Iraq occupation and, 363, 369, 370n, 397, 495, 496, 511–12, 529–31, 530n, 544, 580, 580–81n, 592
    Iraq surge and, 529–31, 530n, 544–45
    Iraq war leadup and, 276, 302, 309–10, 312–13, 327–28, 342–43
    9/11 attacks and, 221–22, 224–25
    war on terror and, 230n, 243n, 271, 272, 273
National Security Letters, 267n
National Security Strategy of the United States of America, The, 320, 320n
Naval Medical Center (Bethesda, Md.), 484, 509
Navy, U.S.:
    George H. W. Bush and, 3, 4–5, 4
    Iraq war buildup and, 327, 346, 354

NBC, 82, 105, 261
NBC News, 452n, 502, 535, 570, 614
NBC Sports, 648–49
Negroponte, John, 480, 490
Neidig, William J., 85n
Neiman Marcus, 54
neoconservatives, xxi, 100, 102, 175, 176n, 369, 535, 536–38
Netherlands, 407, 561
Nevada, 561
    election of 2000 and, 126, 401
    election of 2004 and, 413
New Century Financial, 612
New Deal, 128, 426, 606, 616n
New Federalism, 606
New Frontier, 128
New Hampshire:
    Democratic primary of 2004 and, 402
    election of 2000 and, 116n, 126, 126n
    election of 2004 and, 414
    election of 2006 and, 522
    Republican primary of 1988 and, 51, 65, 132n
    Republican primary of 2000 and, 105–6
New Mexico, 412, 413, 414
Newmyer, Ginger, 518
Newmyer, Jim, 518
New Orleans, La., Hurricane Katrina and, 430, 431, 433, 434–42
New Republic, 103
Newsweek, 50, 170, 257, 315, 344
New York, 401
New Yorker, 114, 155
New York Times, 33, 44, 56, 60, 66, 78, 82, 94, 111, 118, 119, 143, 159, 169, 172, 173, 179, 206, 207, 212, 270, 298, 308, 312, 314, 316, 322, 325, 344, 359n, 404, 438, 446n, 452n, 466–69, 491, 508, 533, 535, 549, 549–50n, 563, 570, 594, 595, 603, 634, 652
New York Times/CBS News poll, 577
Nicaragua, 585
Nicholson, James, 420

Niger, 341–42*n*, 351, 452*n*, 454
Nigeria, 555*n*, 561
9/11 Commission, 219*n*, 324*n*
1984 (Orwell), 248
Nishikawa v. Dulles (1958), 268*n*
Nixon, Richard M., 19, 21, 35, 50, 65*n*,
    103, 120, 128, 134, 152, 156, 158, 201,
    256, 548, 633, 647
  China policy and, 180
  election of 1956 and, 383
  election of 1960 and, 121, 139, 139*n*
  election of 1968 and, 108, 126
  election of 1972 and, 24, 72
  NSC and, 183
  Pentagon Papers and, 468
  Watergate and, 24, 396, 444, 453, 500, 567
Nixon, Tricia, 20
No Child Left Behind Act (2001), xix,
    164–67, *166*, 173, 204, 217, 390, 406,
    426, 449, 582, 659
Noonan, Peggy, 155
Norquist, Grover, 135*n*, 426
North, Oliver, 453
North American Free Trade Act
    (NAFTA), 406, 585
North Atlantic Treaty Organization
    (NATO), Bush and, 197, 198–99,
    200–201, 208, 229, 248, 303, 304, 340,
    402, 531, 603
North Carolina, 401
Northern Alliance, 235, 243, 250, 250*n*,
    251, 252
Northup, Anne, 522
Norton, Gale, 134, *157*, 420
nuclear arms reduction, 274, 306, *306*,
    307, 659
Nunn, Sam, 264
Nuremberg war crimes trials, 271

Oak Ridge Boys, 82
Obama, Barack H., 173*n*, 255*n*, 259*n*,
    405, 444, 496*n*, 509*n*, 537*n*, 550, 575,
    586, 597–98, 604, 604*n*, 623, 627,
    628–29, 630

  auto industry bailout and, 645
  Bush's friendship with, 650–51, 653,
      654, 656–57
  election of 2008 and, 637, 638, 638*n*,
      640, 640*n*
  inauguration and, 652, 653–54, *654*,
      655, *655*
  transition and, 639–40, *639*, 645,
      650–52, *650*, *651*
Obama, Michelle, 638, 639, 640, 653, 654,
    654
Obasanjo, Olusegun, 553
O'Connor, Sandra Day, 143, 144, 145,
    147*n*, 427–28, 428*n*, 444, 447, 449,
    451, 527*n*
Odessa, Tex., 8–9
Odierno, Raymond T. "Ray," 600
O'Donnell, Brett, 409
O'Donnell, Kelly, 502
Office of Homeland Security, U.S., 247
Office of Management and Budget
    (OMB), U.S., 134, 492*n*, 611
Office of Reconstruction and
    Humanitarian Assistance (ORHA),
    U.S., 361–62*n*, 368, 370
Office of Strategic Initiatives, 154
Ohio, 126*n*, 135*n*, 411, 412, 413, 422*n*, 522
Oklahoma, 402
Olson, Theodore "Ted," 139–40, 141, 143,
    145, 257*n*
Olympic Games (2008), 646–49, *647*,
    648
Oman, 585
Omar, Mullah, 252
O'Melveny & Myers, 137
101st Airborne Division, U.S., 357, 440
O'Neill, Jan, 31, 45
O'Neill, Joe, 31, 45, 46, 492
O'Neill, Paul, 134, 136, *157*, 160–61, 184,
    189, 191, 192–93, 235, 243, 246, 389,
    419, 517, 573, 610
OPEC (Organization of Petroleum
    Exporting Countries), 29, 40
OPLAN 1003 Victory, 327, 342

Organisation for Economic Cooperation
    and Development (OECD), 162*n*
Orwell, George, 248, 253
Othman, Mahmoud, 489
Overby, John, 9–10, 29

Pace, Peter, 531, 533, 539*n*, 543, 544, 581,
    592
Packard, George, 181
Paige, Roderick, 135, *157, 166,* 419
Pakistan, 105, 201, 224, 235, 243, 603
Palestinians, 204–6, 213–15, 216, 417, 533
Palfrey, Deborah Jeane, 561*n*
Palin, Sarah, 637, 637–38*n*
Panama, 286, 562, 585–86
Panama Canal Zone, 73
Panetta, Leon, 528*n*, 534
Paola, Queen of the Belgians, 198
Pappas, Thomas, 389
Paraguay, 562
Parfitt, Harold, 73
Paris Commune of 1871, 478–79
Paris Peace Conference (1919), 227
Parliament, British, 351, 353, 354
Pass Christian, Miss., 437
Pataki, George, 239
Patten, Christopher, 279
Pattullo, George, 85*n*
Paul, Ron, 266*n*
Paul, Weiss, Rifkind, Wharton &
    Garrison, 58
Paulson, Henry "Hank," 610–11, *610,*
    612, 640, 640*n*
    AIG and, 622–23, 624
    auto industry bailout and, 643
    Bear Stearns and, 616–18, 621
    Goldman Sachs and, 610, 621, 624, 624*n*
    housing bubble and, 611, 612, 614
    Lehman Brothers and, 620–22, 624
    subprime crisis and, 613
    TARP and, 624–26, 627–30, 631
    see also financial crisis of 2007–2008
PBS, 409
PBS Newshour with Jim Lehrer, 261

Peace Corps, U.S., 135
Pearl Harbor, Hawaii, 2, 4, 135, 152*n,*
    229, 231, 464
Pell, Claiborne, 294–95
Pelosi, Nancy, 508, 520, 552, 577–78, 596,
    625–26, 628, 629, 641, 642
Pennsylvania, 123, 401, 412, 413, 522
Pennzoil, 10, 35, 145*n*
Pennzoil v. Texaco (1987), 145*n*
Pentagon, 9/11 attack and, 218–19, 220,
    221, 222, 226, 235, 239
Pentagon Papers, 468
Perino, Dana, 571, 641, 649
Perle, Richard, 176*n,* 181
Perot, Ross, 54, 67–68, 71, 78, 116
Perry, William, 528, 528*n*
Persian Gulf War, xvii, xxii, 46*n,* 64, 108,
    175–76, 179–80, 230, 249, 276, 286,
    325, 332*n,* 356, 357, 364, 367, 368,
    378, 382*n,* 545*n*
Persson, Göran, 199
Peru, 585, 586
Petraeus, David, 536–37, 537*n,* 543, 545,
    545*n,* 546, 579–80, *579,* 586, 587, 588,
    592, 593, 594, 595–97, 599, 600, 600*n*
Pew Research Center, 633
Phelps, Michael, 648
Philadelphia Inquirer, 207
Philip, Prince, Duke of Edinburgh, 206
Philip Gorman, 178*n*
Philip Morris, 86
Philippines, 297*n*
Phillips, Kevin, 26
Phillips, Thomas R., *81*
Pierce, Franklin, 7
Pierce, Marvin, 7
Pierce, Pauline, 7
Pike, Otis, 256
Pillar, Paul, 323, 323*n*
Planned Parenthood, 2
Plan of Attack (Woodward), 389
Podhoretz, Norman, 180
Poindexter, John, 183*n,* 453
Poland, 199, 407

Portman, Rob, 611

Portugal, 352–53

Posse Comitatus Act (1878), 255, 339–40

Powell, Alma, 382

Powell, Colin, 18*n,* 110, 131, 134, 136, *157,*
    228–29, 233, 243, 424, 573
  Abu Ghraib scandal and, 385
  Afghanistan and, 243, 244, 245, 249
  AIDS issue and, 553, 555
  Bush and, 193–94, 202, 207, 289, 292,
    337–38, 383
  China and, 194, 195
  climate change issue and, 189, 192, 193
  detainees and, 273, 287–90, 291, 292
  Iraq occupation and, 368, 370, 370*n,*
    372, 374, 381–82, 382*n*
  Iraq war leadup and, 234, 244, 245,
    248, 276, 301, 308, 312–13, 322*n,* 333,
    337–38, 341, 343–44, 345, 351, 377
  Iraq WMD search and, 378, 381–82,
    382*n*
  Joint Chiefs and, 131, 131*n,* 185, 332*n*
  military commissions and, 269, 271,
    507
  9/11 attacks and, 222, 224, 224*n,* 225
  North Korea and, 186–88, 187*n,* 189
  Patriot Act and, 267
  Persian Gulf War and, 179–80, 332*n,*
    357
  resignation of, 419, 426, 517
  resignation plans and, 381–83, 389,
    417
  torture issue and, 459
  UN and, 322*n,* 330, 338, 341, 343–44,
    344, 345, 377, 382, 553
  see also State Department, U.S.

Powell, Jonathan, 248

Prairie Chapel Ranch (Crawford, Tex.),
    93, 96–97, *96,* 127, 172, 204, 209–15,
    269, 273, 274–76, 303, 305, 307,
    312, 335, 368, 413, 418, 429–33, 435,
    436, 470, 509, 510, *510,* 512, 516–17,
    544–45, 573, *574,* 609, 645–46, *646,*
    656

preemptive war doctrine, xvi, xviii, 242,
    307–8, 313, 320–21, 320*n,* 328, 346,
    356, 379, 389

presidential election of 2000, xx–xxi, 40*n,*
    99–122, 159, 180, 190, 332, 363, 402,
    414, 522, 553
  Bush campaign funding and, 102–3,
    120, 120*n*
  Bush-Gore debates and, 117–19, 118*n,*
    160, 408, 493
  Bush motion to stop recount in, 139–40
  Bush's decision to run and, 99–102, 104
  Bush's DUI record and, 121–22, 122*n,*
    411–12
  Bush's VP candidate selection and,
    109–11, 110*n*
  Bush transition and, 127–36
  Democratic Convention and, 111, *115,*
    116
  Democratic primaries and, 111
  education issue and, 163
  electoral vote count and, 124, 126*n,* 144,
    146, 401
  Florida Supreme Court and, 141, 142,
    142*n,* 143–45, 146, 147*n*
  Florida vote count and, xxi, 116*n,*
    123–27, 135*n,* 136–47, 138*n,* 142,
    142*n,* 147*n,* 427
  Gore campaign and, 114–22, *115,* 126,
    126*n*
  Gore campaign funding and, 102, 120,
    120*n*
  Gore concession and, 124–25
  Gore's dissociation from Clinton and,
    115–16, 121, 126
  Iowa caucuses and, 104–5, 109
  McCain and, xx, 105–8, 107*n,* 110, 111,
    111*n*
  Michigan primary and, 108
  Muslim voters and, 135*n*
  Nader and, 116, 116*n,* 126, 135*n*
  national polls and, 118, 118*n,* 119, 121,
    126
  New Hampshire primary and, 105–6

popular vote and, 126
religious voters and, 168*n*
Republican Convention and, 111, 111*n*
Republican primaries and, xx, 103–8,
    405, 408, 582
Republican primary TV debates and,
    104–5
South Carolina primary and, 106–8
Supreme Court and, 141–42, 143,
    144–46, 147, 147*n*
voter demographics and, 126–27, 135*n*
presidential election of 2004, 40*n*, 367,
    381, 391–93, 401–15, 521, 542
bin Laden tape and, 412
Bush's "Mission Accomplished"
    declaration and, 365
Cheney and, 406–7, 409–10, 411
Democratic convention and, 405–6
electoral vote and, 414
ground campaigns and, 415
Iowa caucuses and, 401–2
Iraq occupation and, 381
Kerry flip-flop charge and, 403–4,
    406–7
McCain and, 404–5, 406, 408, 457–58
presidential debates and, 408–9, 410–11
redistricting and, 401
Republican convention and, 406–7, 607
Rove and, 368, 392, 404, 406, 409, 413,
    416, 633
Swift Boat ads and, 407–8
swing vote and, 392
vice presidential debate and, 409–10
voter demographics and, 414–15
Presidential Emergency Operations
    Center (PEOC), 219, 222–23, 224
Presidential Records Act (1978), 255
President's Daily Briefing, 182, 210, 248,
    268–69, 275, 378
President's Emergency Plan for AIDS
    Relief (PEPFAR) (2003), 552,
    556–63, *558*, 558*n*, 561*n*, 562*n*, 657
Prichard, Bob, xxii
Priest, Dana, 293, 460–61, 470, 476

Princeton University, 133, 451, 451*n*, 537*n*
Principi, Anthony, 135, *157*, 420
privatization, 115, 607–8
Project for the New American Century,
    xviii, 180, 180*n*
Prosper, Pierre-Richard, 271
prostitution, 561–62
Provide Comfort, Operation (1991), 368
Prudential-Bache, 38
Prueher, Joseph, 195
Pryor, Mark, 566
PULL (Professional United Leadership
    League), 25–26
Putin, Lyudmila, 307
Putin, Vladimir:
    Bush and, 199–202, *200*, 207–8,
        248–49, 269, 274–76, 275*n*, 306, *306*,
        307, 455, 659
    Iraq invasion and, 358
    KGB and, 200*n*

Quasha, Alan, 44
Quayle, Dan, 108, 128, 156, 180*n*, 383

Rabb, Max, 233*n*
racism, Republican primary of 2000 and,
    106–7
Raddatz, Martha, 435
Radhi, Radhi al-, 489
Rainwater, Richard, 58–59
Rangel, Charles, 149
Rangers Stadium (Ballpark at Arlington),
    63–64, 94
Ravelstein (Bellow), 178, 178*n*
Raven, The (James), 84*n*
Rea, Paul, 44
Reagan, Nancy, 170
Reagan, Ron, 405
Reagan, Ronald W., 13, 101, 108, 127,
    127*n*, 132, 138, 151*n*, 152, 152*n*, 156,
    158, 161, 176*n*, 179, 254, 287, 294,
    371, 428, 429, 444, 449, 451, 453, 473,
    473*n*, 507, 528, 585, 606, 610
    Bush congressional race and, 34, 35

Reagan, Ronald W. (*cont.*)
  election of 1976 and, 131*n*, 383
  election of 1980 and, 38
  election of 1984 and, 73
  foreign policy and, 182–83, 182*n*
  NSC and, 183, 183*n*, 184*n*, 185
  presidential library and, 657
  Soviet Union and, 178, 188–89, 189*n*
  U.S. attorneys and, 564
Reagan Democrats, 114
Reconstruction, 80, 81*n*, 82, 87, 136, 255
Reese, Jim, 30, 33, 34–35
Regan, Donald, 152, 182
Rehnquist, William, 142, 143, 144, 145,
    147*n*, 149, 257*n*, 423, 425, 426, 427,
    428, 445, 446, 446*n*, 448, 451
Reid, Harry, 476, 552, 584, 596, 599, 626,
    630, 642
Rendón, Paula, 582
Reno, Janet, 254
Reporter, 177*n*
Republican Guard, 276
Republican National Committee (RNC),
    419, 521
  Atwater and, 52–53, 55
  College Republicans and, 72
  George H. W. Bush and, 24–25, 50, 72
Republican National Convention of 2008,
    634–37
Republican Party, 95, 173, 406, 449, 493
  education issue and, 163–64
  neoconservatives and, 100
  Prescott Bush and, 3
  Rove and, 55
Reuters, 191, 378, 461, 510
Reynolds, Mercer, 40–41, 40*n*
Rhode Island, 522
Ribicoff, Abraham, 3
Rice, Condoleezza, 101*n*, 208, 210, 215,
    308, 381, 418, 426, 515
  Afghanistan and, 244, 249
  AIDS issue and, 553, 555, 560
  al Qaeda threat and, 211, 212
  Armitage and, 185–86

"axis of evil" phrase and, 280
"black sites" issue and, 503–4, 506
Bush transition and, 129, 131, 134
Cheney's conflicts with, 183–84, 503–4
China and, 194
climate change issue and, 190, 192
detainees and, 281, 287, 503–4, 506
election of 2000 and, 118–19
G-8 summit and, 207
George H. W. Bush's relationship
    with, 101, 418–19
Iraq occupation and, 370, 370*n*, 372,
    378, 398, 477*n*, 486, 490, 495, 496,
    512, 531, 545
Iraq policy review and, 526, 529, 530
Iraq surge and, 531, 532–33, 536
Iraq war leadup and, 248, 276, 310, 312,
    314, 316, 328*n*, 334
Kennebunkport meeting with Bush
    and, 101–2
military commissions and, 269, 273–74,
    502
national security advisor role and, 155,
    169, 174, 176, 181, 183, 185, 202–3
9/11 attacks and, 217, 218, 223, 224,
    224*n*, 226, 233
North Korea and, 187
NSC and, 184–85, 187
Putin and, 200
Rumsfeld and, 185, 486
Saudi crisis and, 214, 216
secretary of state position accepted by,
    417–18, 419, 420
terrorism issue and, 201
Vulcans and, 176, 176*n*, 181
Richards, Ann, xx, 68–70, 69, 69*n*, 74,
    75–78, 79*n*, 83, 88, 121
  Bush debate with, 77–78
  Bush "jerk" remark by, 76–77
  Democratic Convention of 1988 and, 69
  education funding issue and, 75–76
Richardson, Elliot, 567
Ricks, Thomas, 332, 367
Ridge, Tom, 110*n*, 130, 247, 421

Risen, James, 467, 470, 476
Rite-Aid, 37
Rizzo, John, 298n
Robb, Chuck, 522, 528n, 529, 533
Roberts, Jane, 447
Roberts, John G., Jr., 147, 147n, 293n,
    427–29, 428n, 444–46, 446n, 451,
    500, 562, 562n
Roberts, Pat, 322
Robertson, George, Lord, 198
Robertson, Pat, 51, 173
Robertson, Shari, 584n
Robinson, Eugene, 563
Robison, James, 98
Robson, Eleanor, 361
Rockefeller, Nelson A., 96n, 131n, 383
Rockefeller, Winthrop, 96n
Rockwell, Norman, 85
Roden, Randall, 13
Rodman, Peter, 180n
Roe v. Wade (1973), 22n, 391, 404, 428
Rogers, Kenny, 62
Romig, Thomas, 270
Romney, Mitt, 655
Roosevelt, Eleanor, 2, 294
Roosevelt, Franklin D., xvii, xx, 1, 4, 5,
    13, 72, 82, 92, 103, 128, 149n, 152,
    152n, 154, 155, 169, 201, 223, 242,
    266, 272, 329, 382, 383, 422, 424, 426,
    444, 478, 478n, 515n, 520, 548, 580,
    600, 606, 616n, 636n
Roosevelt, Theodore, 68
Rose, Edward "Rusty," 59, 59, 63
Rose, James M., 18
Rosenman, Sam, 103
Rove, Andrew, 573
Rove, Darby, 522, 573
Rove, Karl, 55, 73, 101, 129, 191, 207, 208,
    209, 252, 314, 365, 492n, 655
    background of, 72
    Bush's first gubernatorial campaign
        and, 71, 72, 74, 76
    Bush's governorship and, 85–86
    Bush transition and, 129, 134

election of 2000 and, 103, 106, 107, 108,
    111, 121, 123
election of 2004 and, 368, 392, 404, 406,
    409, 413, 416, 633
election of 2006 and, 521, 522, 523
faith-based initiatives and, 168
Hurricane Katrina and, 436, 437, 440
immigration reform and, 582–83
Iraq occupation and, 490
Iraq war leadup and, 326
9/11 attacks and, 217, 220, 221, 222
reality quote and, 175
resignation and, 572–73
stem cell research and, 171
Supreme Court nominees and, 427, 445
tax cut issue and, 160
U.S. attorney firings and, 565, 567, 569,
    572
White House staff and, 153, 154, 156
Rowen, Henry, 180n
Rozen, Miriam, 72
Rubin, Robert, 159
Ruckelshaus, William, 567
Rumsfeld, Donald, 131, 152, 157, 233, 235,
    265, 381, 420, 537n, 542, 573, 637
    Abu Ghraib scandal and, 384–86, 387,
        389, 515
    Afghanistan and, 234, 249, 250n, 251
    Bush's interview of, 132–33
    Cheney and, xviii, 110, 131, 386, 515,
        517–18
    China and, 196
    Defense Department and, see Defense
        Department, U.S.
    detainees and, 280–81, 284, 287, 290,
        502
    George H. W. Bush and, 110, 131–32,
        132n
    George W. Bush's congressional run
        and, 35
    "Halloween Massacre" of 1975 and,
        130–31, 131n, 132n
    House and, 130, 132
    Iraq invasion and, 357, 359n, 361

Rumsfeld, Donald (*cont.*)
  Iraq occupation and, 362, 363, 368–70,
    370*n*, 371, 372, 374, 375, 376, 376*n*,
    384–86, 387, 389, 477, 477*n*, 484,
    486, 490, 493, 496, 498, 511, 512, 519,
    519*n*, 531, 533, 536, 540, 589, 589*n*
  Iraq "Parade of Horribles" list and,
    327–29, 328*n*
  Iraq surge and, 531, 536
  Iraq war leadup and, 236, 244, 248,
    252, 276, 300–301, 302, 303, 304–5,
    308, 310, 327–29, 328*n*, 331, 336–37,
    340, 342, 347–48, 355
  military commissions and, 502
  9/11 attacks and, 220, 222, 224, 224*n*,
    225
  Patriot Act and, 267
  resignation and, 513–19, 525–26
  resignation offers and, 384–86, 386*n*,
    389, 390, 515
  Rice and, 185, 486
  war on terror term and, 230*n*
  Wolfowitz and, 180, 233, 305, 332, 347
Rumsfeld, Joyce, 131, 518–19
Running Start war plan, 306, 308, 309
Rushailo, Vladimir, 200
Rusk, Dean, 229, 350
Rusk v. Cort (1962), 268*n*
Russert, Tim, 316, 378–79, 452*n*, 535,
  597
Russian Federation, 190, 199–202, 264,
  292, 649
  Afghanistan and, 248–49, 250
  Iraq war leadup and, 330, 344–45,
    348–49, 350
Rutenberg, Jim, 563
Rwanda, 271, 555*n*, 563
Ryan, Kevin V., 565*n*
Ryan, Nolan, 62, 78, 82
Rye, N.Y., 5, 7

Saddam Fedayeen, 359
Sadler, Paul, 91
Sadr, Mohammed Sadiq al-, 396

Sadr, Moqtada al-, 396, 397, 398, 482, 598,
  598*n*, 599
Safire, William, 66, 270
St. Albans, 112
St. Andrew's Episcopal School, 83
St. Louis Browns, 40
Salon.com, 85*n*
Samarra, Iraq, Golden Mosque in, 487,
  487*n*, 490, 494, 547
same-sex marriage, 392–93, 407, 409,
  410–11
Sam Houston as Marius (Cooper), 83–84,
  83
Sammon, Bill, 399, 450
Sampson, Kyle, 564, 565, 568, 568*n*
*San Antonio Independent School Disctrict
  v. Rodriguez* (1971), 76
Sanchez, Ricardo, 374, 376, 387, 397,
  398–99, 480, 543
Sanders, Bernie, 522, 577
Sanders, Charles, 11
Sanger, David, 533
San Jacinto, USS, 4–5
Santorum, Rick, 522
Sarasota, Fla., 166, 217, 217*n*
Sarkozy, Nicolas, 649
Saturday Evening Post, 85, 85*n*
Saturday Night Massacre (1973), 395–96,
  567
Saudi Arabia, 100, 204–6, 213–15, 216,
  303, 336–37, 424, 492, 649
  Iraq surge and, 532–33
  terrorism financing and, 201, 235
Savage, Charlie, 476
Sawyer, Diane, 404
Scalia, Antonin, 143, 144, 145, 147*n*, 257*n*,
  427, 445, 449
Schake, Kori, 343
Schieffer, Bob, 63, 410
Schieffer, Thomas, 63
Schlesinger, James, 131*n*, 389, 483
Schlesinger Report (2004), 388–89
Schmidt, Steve, 443
Schneider v. Rusk (1964), 268*n*

Schoomaker, Peter, 539*n*, 540–41, 543,
    545, 546
Schriefer, Russ, 406
Schroeder, Gerhard, 300, 306, 340,
    344–45
Schumer, Chuck, 523, 568
Schwarz, David, 64
Schwarzenegger, Arnold, 406, 407
Schwarzkopf, H. Norman, 73, 326,
    332–33, 332*n*, 357, 364*n*
Scowcroft, Brent, 101, 204, 205–6, 311–12,
    314
Secret Service, U.S., 114, 208–9, 218–19,
    220, 223, 226, 266, 365, 429
Securities and Exchange Commission
    (SEC), U.S., 61, 624, 625, 626
Security Engineers Company, 9
Segal, Erich, 117
Semple, Bill, 12
Senate, U.S., 402, 445*n*, 610
    administration appointees and, 156
    AIDS issue and, 558, 560
    anthrax scare and, 261–62, 263*n*
    Appropriations Committee of, 483,
        576–77
    Armed Services Committee of, 130,
        346–47, 378, 458, 476, 477*n*, 483, 507,
        550, 595–96
    auto industry bailout and, 642
    Bush Supreme Court nominees and,
        427–29, 445, 446, 449, 450, 451
    Bush tax cuts and, 161–62
    Cheney and, 158*n*, 159
    Convention Against Torture and,
        294–95
    Education Committee and, 164, 165,
        218–19
    election of 1876 and, 137
    election of 2002 and, 330
    election of 2006 and, 519–20, 521–22,
        521*n*, 523, 526, 598*n*
    Finance Committee and, 611
    financial crisis of 2007–2008 and, 619,
        630, 630*n*
    Foreign Relations Committee and,
        294–95, 550, 558, 581–82, 595
    Geneva Conventions and, 283*n*,
        286
    George H. W. Bush and, 21, 30, 31,
        132*n*
    Gore, Jr. and, 113
    Gore, Sr. and, 112*n*
    immigration reform and, 582, 583, 584,
        584*n*
    Iraq occupation and, 476, 477*n*,
        483, 550, 552, 576–77, 578, 581–82,
        587*n*, 589–90, 590*n*, 595–96,
        598*n*
    Iraq surge and, 550, 552, 581–82,
        595–96
    Iraq war and, 322, 325, 335, 345–47,
        403
    Iraq WMD search and, 378
    Jeffords and, 159, 159*n*, 325, 508
    Judiciary Committee and, 258*n*,
        446, 450, 451, 476, 566–68, 568*n*,
        570–72
    Kerry and, 325, 402, 403, 451
    Kyoto Protocol and, 190
    Lieberman and, 115, 135*n*
    military commissions and, 507, 508,
        508*n*
    No Child Left Behind and, 165, 166,
        204
    Patriot Act and, 266*n*, 473–74, 566
    Prescott Bush and, 3
    prescription drug issue and, 391
    Select Committee on Intelligence of,
        299, 322
    Shinseki and, 346–47
    terrorism issue and, 212
    torture issue and, 299, 457–60
    U.S. attorney firings and, 564,
        564–65*n*, 566–68, 568*n*, 570–72
    war on terror and, 232, 240, 240*n*, 255,
        266*n*
    see also Congress, U.S.
Senators' Bargain, The, 584*n*

September 11, 2001 terror attacks,
    xviii–xix, 166, 217–27, *217, 220, 221,*
    406, 412, 429, 659
  aftermath of, 228–43, 230*n, 237*
  Bush's national address on, 223–24,
    224*n*
  death total and, 231
  global sympathy for U.S. after, xvi,
    228, 292
  Iraq and, 225, 248, 300
Sessions, William, 264
Sforza, Scott, 365
Shalikashvili, John, 458, 459
Sharansky, Natan, 422*n*
Sharif, Nawaz, 105
Sharon, Ariel, 205, 214
Shearer, Cody, 25
Sheehan, Cindy, 429–30, *429,* 563
Shelton, Hugh, 236, 243–44, 246
Sherman, William T., 600
Shia Muslims (Shiites), 328, 332, 343, 378,
    396–97, 398, 479, 480, 482, 485, 486,
    487, 487*n,* 491, 511, 530, 532, 598, 659
Shinseki, Eric, 327, 331, 342–43, 346–47,
    540
Shultz, George, 67, 101, 101*n,* 102, 131,
    134, 183*n,* 188, 370
Sidey, Hugh, 70
signing statements, 472–76, 472–73*n*
Silverado Savings & Loan, 47–48
Silver Screen Management, 58
Silvia, Queen of Sweden, 199
Simpson, Alan, 135, 527*n,* 534
Sinai, Allen, 161
Singapore, 585
Sistani, Ali, 482
Sixth Amendment (1791), 255
60 Minutes, 489
60 Minutes II, 384–85
Skull and Bones, 23, 129
  George H. W. Bush and, 5–6, 15
  George W. Bush and, 15
Slater, Wayne, 122*n*
"Slipper Tongue, The" (Neidig), 85*n*

Smith, Fred, 129, 130, 515
Smith, Gordon, 577, 590*n*
Smith, Michael, 309*n*
Smith Barney, 61
"smoking gun might be a mushroom
    cloud" phrase, 316, 324
Snow, Tony, 492*n*
Snowe, Olympia, 508*n,* 590*n*
Social Security, 115, 183, 417, 421–22,
    422*n,* 425–26, 457, 523, 584*n,* 607–8
Sodrel, Mike, 522
Sofia, Queen of Spain, 198
Soler, Mark, 16
Somalia, 286
Sonny Corleone, 48, 49
Sooke, Alistair, 658
Soros, George, 44, 46
Sosa, Sammy, 63
Souter, David, 144, 145, 146, 427, 449
South Africa, 555*n,* 562, 585, 649
South Carolina:
  election of 1876 and, 136
  election of 2004 and, 402, 413
  Republican primary of 2000 and, 106–8
Southern Manifesto, 112*n*
Southern Methodist University, 32, 656,
    658
Soviet Union, xvii, 176*n,* 178, 180, 182–83,
    182*n,* 188–89, 189*n,* 193, 201, 250,
    260, 372*n,* 495
Spain, 198, 350, 352–53
Spanish-American War, 281
Sparkman, John, 23, 24
Special Forces, U.S., 243, 246, 250, 251,
    252, 309*n,* 336, 348, 494
Specter, Arlen, 450, 571, 583
Spectrum 7, 40–41, 44, 46–47, 52
Spellings, Margaret, 419, 420, 490, 655
Spiegel, Der, 598
Stabenow, Debbie, 135
Standard & Poor's 500 Index, 630
Stanford University, 101, 101*n*
Stapleton, Craig, 58
Star Trek, 176

Stassen, Harold, 520
State Department, U.S., 383, 417, 478, 478n
   Baker and, 138, 176n
   "black sites" issue and, 506
   Bremer and, 371
   Christopher and, 138
   CIA Memorandum of Notification and, 243n
   detainees and, 273, 287–90
   Eisenhower and, xviii
   Hughes and, 426
   Iraqi constitution and, 485
   Iraq occupation and, 368, 370, 370n, 372, 380, 485–86, 487, 496, 530, 531, 589
   Iraq surge and, 530
   Iraq war leadup and, 234, 244, 245, 248, 276, 301, 308, 312–13, 314, 322n
   Kissinger and, 131n
   Marshall and, 337–38
   military commissions and, 271, 273
   9/11 attacks and, 222, 224, 224n, 225
   NSC and, 184n
   Powell and, see Powell, Colin
   Rice's appointment to, 417–18, 419, 420
   war on terror and, 228–29, 233, 234, 273
   Wolfowitz and, 178–79
Status of Forces Agreement (SOFA), 600–601, 601, 645
Staudt, Walter, 18
Steinbeck, John, 154
Steinbrenner, George, 252
stem cell research, 169–73, 170n, 172n, 173n, 208, 577n
Stem Cell Research Enhancement Act (2006), 577n
Stevens, John Paul, 144, 145, 147, 293, 447, 449, 500
Stevens, Robert, 261
Stevens, Ted, 483
Stevenson, Adlai E., 23, 343–44, 634
Stimson, Henry L., 4, 515n, 548

stock market:
   AIG and, 624
   auto industry and, 641
   housing bubble and, xvi, 613, 619
   Lehman failure and, 622
   regulation and, xix
   short-selling and, 625, 626
   subprime crisis and, 613, 620
   TARP and, 626, 630, 631
Stolberg, Sheryl, 652
Stowe, Matt, 147n
Strategic Air Command (SAC), U.S., 221
Strategic Arms Reduction Treaty (START) (1991), 274, 306, 306, 307
Strategic Petroleum Reserve, U.S., 117
Stratford of Texas, 23
Strauss, Bob, 35
Strauss, Leo, 177, 178
Straw, Jack, 309, 351
subprime mortgages, 231, 608, 608n, 612–18, 620
Sudan, 246
Sullivan, Mike, 134
Sulzberger, Arthur, Jr., 468
Summers, Larry, 159
Summersby, Kay, 537n
Summit on Financial Markets and the World Economy, 649–50
Sunni Muslims, 328, 332, 343, 367, 373, 396, 397–99, 479, 480, 481, 482, 484, 485, 486, 487, 491, 511, 530, 532, 547, 593, 598–99, 598–99n, 659
Sununu, John, 51, 65–66, 129, 152, 153, 155
Supreme Court, U.S., 140, 229, 445n
   abortion issue and, 22n
   birth control issue and, 2n
   Bush appointments and, 426–29, 428n, 444–51, 446n, 447, 448, 457
   citizenship issue and, 268, 268n
   detainee issue and, 292–93, 293n, 295, 499–503, 501n, 508, 509, 509n
   education funding issue and, 76
   election of 1876 and, 137

Supreme Court, U.S. (*cont.*)
  election of 2000 and, 141–42, 143,
    144–46, 147, 147*n*
  enhanced interrogation issue and, 461,
    501, 508
  military commissions and, 272, 501*n*,
    502, 503, 506, 508
  PEPFAR and, 561–62, 562*n*
  Roosevelt and, 152, 422, 424, 444
  school desegregation issue and, 112*n*,
    446
  signing statements and, 476
  Thomas nomination and, 64, 427
  writs of certiorari and, 141–42, 141*n*
Sweden, 199
Swift Boat Veterans for Truth, 407–8
Switzerland, 561
Sydney Morning Herald, 594
Syria, 225, 246, 293, 330, 533

Taft, William Howard, 4, 67, 448
Taft, William Howard, IV, 288–89
Taguba, Antonio, 387–88, 387*n*
Taiwan, 197
Talabani, Jalal, 543, 593, 594*n*
Taliban, 24, 201, 224, 235–36, 246, 249,
    250–52, 271, 277, 280, 283, 284–85,
    288–91, 293, 602–5
TalkingPointsMemo blog, 566*n*
Taney, Roger Brooke, 448
Tang Jiaxuan, 195, 338, 344
Tanzania, 555*n*, 562, 563
Tarrance, V. Lance, 30
Taubman, Phil, 468
taxes, taxation, xv, 76, 80, 92, 104, 162*n*,
    417, 582, 608, 614, 630
  Bush cuts and, xvi, 158, 159–63, 204,
    367, 607
Taylor, John, 101*n*
Taylor, Maxwell, 581*n*
Teeter, Robert, 48
Tenet, George, 136, 169, 174, 460
  Afghanistan and, 235–36, 244, 245,
    246, 249

al Qaeda threat and, 204, 210, 212
  Iraq war leadup and, 276, 310, 314, 322,
    322*n*, 333–34, 337, 341–42*n*, 344, 378
  Iraq WMD search and, 377
  9/11 attacks and, 221–22, 224, 225
  resignation and, 389–90
  "slam dunk" remark and, 334, 389
  war on terror and, 235–36, 243, 243*n*,
    260, 280
Tennessee, election of 2000 and, 120–21,
    126*n*
10th Mountain Division, U.S., *604*
Teresa, Mother, 107
terrorism, xvi–xvii, xviii–xix, 166, 201,
    204–27, 415, 659
  9/11 attacks and, *see* September 11,
    2001 terror attacks
  "war on terror" and, *see* war on terror
terrorism threat alerts, 316, 316*n*, 412
Terrorist Surveillance Program (TSP),
    U.S., 260, 393–96, 420
Texaco, 145*n*
Texas:
  abortion issue and, 22*n*
  Bush as governor of, xx, 80–98, *81, 99,*
    103
  constitution of, 81*n*
  education funding issue an, 75–76
  election of 2000 and, 401
  election of 2004 and, 412
  House speaker's power in, 88
  legislature and, 80, 87–91, 103
  lieutenant governor's power in, 87–88
  Permian Basin and, 9, 52
  state budget of, 81
  state capitol of, 82
  state government structure in, 80–81,
    81*n*
  taxes and, 80, 92
Texas, University of, 32, 47, 86, 96, 562
Texas, West Jameson field in, 10
Texas A&M, 93, 516, 642
Texas Air National Guard, 17–18, *17,* 20,
    24, 26

Texas Board of Pardons and Paroles,
    81n
Texas League, 56
Texas Monthly, 30, 86
Texas Rangers, xix, xx, 52, 54–55, 56–64,
    59, 70, 82, 93–94, 94n, 102, 647, 655,
    657
Texas Tech, 36, 36n
Texas v. White (1869), 229
Thatcher, Margaret, 99, 248
Theodore Roosevelt, USS, 346
3rd Infantry Division, U.S., 357
Thirteen Days, 164
Thomas, Clarence, 64, 144, 145, 147n,
    258n, 427, 449
Thomas, Helen, 488–89
Thompson, Benny, 558n
Thompson, Fred, 110n, 637
Thompson, Tommy, 135, 157, 170, 421,
    553, 555
threat matrix reports, 265–66, 269
372nd Military Police Company, U.S.,
    387
thunder runs, 360–61
Thurmond, Strom, 112n, 164n, 170
Tilden, Samuel, xxi, 136, 142n
Tilghman, Shirley, 537n
Time, 3, 15, 44, 46n, 59, 70, 160, 207, 399,
    452n
Times of London, 192, 232
Tito, 200
Tobias, Randall, 561, 561n
Today, 450
Tom Lantos and Henry Hyde United
    States Global Leadership Against
    HIV/AIDS, Tuberculosis, and
    Malaria Reauthorization Act of
    2008, 560, 561
Tonight Show, 405
Tora Bora, Afghanistan, 252
Toronto, University of, xxii
tort reform, 87, 89, 90, 417
Tower, John, 18, 36n, 127n, 179
Townsend, Frances, 582–83

trade policy, 406, 584–86, 585n, 659
"Transition 2000" (Bush transition team),
    190
Transportation Department, U.S., 135,
    222, 420
Treasury Department, U.S., 610, 613
    auto industry bailout and, 641
    Baker and, 138, 176n
    Bush tax cuts and, 160–61
    financial crisis of 2007–2008 and, 613,
        614, 619, 619n, 620–23, 624–26, 624n,
        627, 631
    war on terror and, 243, 246
    see also O'Neill, Paul; Paulson, Henry
        "Hank"
Tribe, Laurence, 140, 143, 145
Trilateral Commission, 34
Trop v. Dulles (1958), 268n
Troubled Asset Relief Program (TARP),
    624–32, 642, 643–44
Truman, Harry S., xvii, 6, 149n, 156, 229,
    260, 337, 383, 473, 500, 515n, 548,
    606, 633
Tsurumi, Yoshi, 27
Tucker, Mindy, 117
Turkey, 303–4, 336, 342, 348, 649
Turner, Althia, 26
Turner, Stansfield, 507
Turnipseed, William, 24
Twelfth Amendment (1804), 109n, 111,
    124n
Twenty-third Amendment (1961),
    124n

Udell, Maurice, 19
Ueberroth, Peter, 52, 56, 58–59, 60
Uganda, 555n
UNESCO (United Nations Educational,
    Scientific, and Cultural
    Organization), 317
UNICEF (United Nations Children's
    Emergency Fund), 562
Uniform Code of Military Justice
    (UCMJ), 270–71, 500

United Airlines flight 93, 219, 219*n*
United Airlines flight 175, 218
United Auto Workers (UAW), 585,
    641
United Bank National Association, 54*n*,
    58
United Bank of Midland, 54*n*
United Iraqi Alliance, 482, 486
United Nations, 178, 216, 229–30, 248,
    286, 321, 358
  AIDS issue and, 553
  Baker and, 138
  George H. W. Bush and, 21, 23, 24,
    34, 48*n*
  George W. Bush and, 313–14, 317–18,
    317, 319, 325, 329, 349, 353–54,
    489
  Iraq occupation and, 600
  Iraq war leadup and, 310, 312–13,
    317–18, 328, 330–31, 338, 341,
    343–45, *344,* 349, 350–51, 352–53,
    489
  Iraq weapons inspections and, 330, 331,
    332, 333, 336, 338, 339, 340–41, *341,*
    344–45, 349, 350–51, 377, 382*n*
  Powell and, 322*n,* 330, 338, 341,
    343–44, *344,* 345, 377, 382, 553
United Nations Commission on Human
    Rights, 294
United Nations Convention on the Law
    of the Sea (1982), 194
United Nations High Commissioner for
    Refugees, 488
United Negro College Fund, 2
United States:
  anthrax and, 264
  Clinton era prosperity and, 114–15
  domestic surveillance issue and, xvii,
    255–61, 256*n,* 258*n,* 259*n,* 393–96,
    420, 467–69, 659
  federal budget and, xv, 611
  federal debt and, 159, 163
  infrastructure investment and, xix
  military expenditures and, xv, xix

  tax rates and, 162*n*
  unemployment and, xv, xvi, 160, 367,
    607
  war on terror and constitutional rights
    in, 253–74, 267*n,* 268*n,* 509*n*
United States Code (USC), 142*n,* 144*n,*
    304*n*
United States Conference of Catholic
    Bishops, 173
United States Golf Association (USGA),
    2, 6
United States v. Nixon (1974), 500
Universal Declaration of Human Rights
    (1948), 294
UN Resolution 1441 (2002), 330, 333, 338,
    343, 345, 351, 353
USA Patriot Act (2001), 266–67, 266*n,*
    267*n,* 406, 422, 473–74, 476, 564,
    564–65*n,* 566
USA Today, 207, 568, 658
USA Today/CNN/Gallup poll, 300, 323,
    407, 409, 410
USA Today/Gallup poll, 596
U.S. News & World Report, 21, 483
U.S. Olympic Committee (USOC),
    647
USO (United Services Organization), 2

Vaile, Mark, 594
Valentine, Bobby, 63
Vanderbilt Law School, 113
Vanderbilt University, 113
Vatican, 348, 385, 420
Védrine, Hubert, 279
Veneman, Ann, 135, *157,* 419, 420
Vermont, 402, 522
Versailles, Treaty of (1919), 444
Vessey, John W., 507
Veterans Affairs Department, U.S., 135,
    390*n,* 420
Veterans of Foreign Wars (VFW), 313,
    376, 590
Vickers, Michael, 495, 496, 496*n*
Vietnam, 555*n*

Vietnam War, 16–20, 18*n*, 129, 229, 230, 241, 249, 286, 286*n*, 305, 311, 315, 326, 327, 332*n*, 349, 350, 360, 385, 437, 483, 484, 491, 492, 493, 507, 540, 545*n*, 550, 551, 581*n*, 590, 595, 597, 633
   Cheney and, 110*n*, 462, 463
   cost of, 542
   George W. Bush and, 17, 233, 581
   Gore, Jr. and, 112, 117
   Gore, Sr. and, 112*n*
   Kerry and, 402, 404, 405, 407–8
   McCain and, 107, 404, 405, 459–60
   Murtha and, 462
Villepin, Dominique de, 338, 344, 358
Virginia, 413, 522
Vitter, David, 440
Voinovich, George, 550, 586, 590
Volcker, Paul, 610
Voting Rights Act of 1965, 112*n*
Vulcans, 176–81, 176*n*, 188–89, 197

Wake Forest University, 118
Walker, Elsie, 68*n*, 78
Walker, George, IV, 621–22
Walker, George Herbert, 6, 6, 68*n*, 622
Walker, Helgi, 147*n*
Walker, Herbert, Jr., 10
Walker, Ray, 23
Walker Cup, 6
Wallace, Henry A., 383
Wallace, Mark, 431
Wallace, William Scott, 359*n*
Wallison, Peter, 621
Wall Street, 608, 610, 611, 620*n*, 627, 632, 645, 659
Wall Street Journal, 46*n*, 169, 311, 312, 389, 619
Walsh, Kerri, 648
Walt Disney Company, 58
Walters, Logan, xxi–xxii, 169
Walton, Reggie, 454–55
Wang Wei, 194, 195, 196
War by Other Means: An Insider's Account of the War on Terror (Yoo), 258*n*

War Crimes Act (1996), 286, 292, 293, 501, 506
Warnecke, John, 113
Warner, John, 458, 466, 467, 471, 483, 550, 578, 587*n*, 595–96
war on terror, 221, 224, 227, 228–52, 230*n*, 240–41*n*, 243*n*, 253–78, 307, 310, 393–96, 406, 412, 555, 659–60
   Abu Ghraib and, 299, 299*n*, 384–89, 385, 387*n*, 458–59*n*, 475, 515, 563, 652
   airline security and, 253, 253*n*
   anthrax scare and, 261–63, 263*n*
   biological attacks and, 261–65, 263*n*, 264*n*
   CIA "black site" prisons and, 460–61, 466, 475, 503–6, 659
   Constitution and, 253–74, 267*n*, 268*n*, 509*n*
   detainees and, *see* detainee issue
   domestic surveillance issue and, xvii, 255–61, 256*n*, 258*n*, 259*n*, 393–96, 420, 467–69, 659
   enhanced interrogation techniques and, 280, 296–99, 298*n*, 387–89, 387*n*, 444, 457–61, 458–59*n*, 465, 466–67, 467*n*, 470–71, 472, 473, 474, 501, 503–6, 508–9, 659
   extraordinary renditions and, xvii, 293–96, 388, 659
   FISA and, 255–57, 256*n*, 259, 260, 261, 266, 267
   FOIA and, 254
   Geneva Conventions and, 271, 272, 273, 280, 283, 283*n*, 284, 284*n*, 287–93, 295, 299, 387, 458, 461, 471, 499–503, 506–8, 509*n*
   Iraq invasion and occupation and, 338, 366, 398, 491, 494, 534
   mass media and, 254, 261
   military commissions and, 269–74, 270*n*, 280, 292, 293, 420, 499–503, 501*n*, 506–9, 509*n*

war on terror (*cont.*)
   Office of Legal Counsel and, 257–59,
      258*n,* 260, 272, 283, 288, 289, 293,
      295–96, 296*n,* 298–99, 298*n,* 299*n,*
      323, 393, 505
   Patriot Act and, 266–67, 266*n,* 267*n,*
      406, 422, 473–74, 476, 564, 564–65*n,*
      566
   torture and, 44, 280, 293–99, 293*n,*
      294*n,* 457–61, 458–59*n,* 465–67,
      470–71, 472, 473, 476, 501, 505,
      508
   *see also names of specific government
      agencies and persons*
War Powers Resolution (1973), 321
Warren, Earl, 268, 445, 445*n,* 448
Warren, George "Red Dog," 4
Washington, George, 136, 285, 472*n*
Washington Declaration (2008), 650
Washington Evening Star, 21
Washington Post, 37, 49, 63, 77, 113–14,
      166, 169, 187, 215, 293, 318, 331, 344,
      359*n,* 367, 378, 381–82, 461, 513, 529,
      535, 542, 563, 570, 594*n*
Washington Post/ABC News poll, 457,
      470, 549
Washington's Crossing (Fischer), 285
Washington Senators, 56–57
Washington Times, 266*n,* 289, 290, 399
Washington University, 119
waterboarding, 297–99, 297*n,* 461,
      505
Watergate scandal, 24, 255, 256, 396,
      444, 453, 500, 567
Way Forward, The—A New Approach
      (Iraq Study Group), 533–34
"Ways That Are Dark" (Pattullo), 85*n*
weapons of mass destruction (WMDs),
      xviii, 193, 261–65, 263*n,* 264*n,*
      276–78, 309, 313–14, 316–17, 318,
      320, 321–24, 322*n,* 330–31, 333–34,
      336, 341, 344, 350–51, 353–54, 359,
      366–67, 376–80, 381–82, 382*n,*
      400–401, 418, 589, 652, 659

Wear, Joseph, 6
Webb, James, 522, 551–52
Weber, Vin, 180*n*
Weekly Standard, 448, 535
Wehner, Peter, 453
Weicker, Lowell, 115
Weinberger, Caspar, 67, 176*n*
Weisberg, Jacob, 85*n*
Welch, Harold, 31
Welch, Jenna, 31, 39
Weldon, Dave, 557
Wesley, Charles, 80, 84, 84*n*
Western Company, 57
Westmoreland, William, 595
West Point (U.S. Military Academy),
      Bush's address at, 307–8, 313
West Virginia:
   election of 2000 and, 120–21, 126,
      126*n*
   election of 2004 and, 413
*West Virginia Board of Education v.
      Barnette* (1943), 562*n*
whistle blowers, 475
White, Bill, 27
White, John, 25, 26
White House:
   Bush staff at, 152–55
   offices in, *153*
White House Iraq Group (WHIG), 314,
      316
White House Office of Faith-Based and
      Community Initiatives, 167–68
Whitman, Christine Todd "Christie,"
      157, 189, 190–93
Wicker, Roger, 170*n*
Wilkes, Jim, 19
Wilkinson, J. Harvie, III, 428*n*
Will, George, 56, 173–74, 233*n,* 449
Williams, Ben Ames, 85
Williams, Brian, 42*n*
Williams, Clayton, 69–70
Williams, Scott, 374
Williams, Ted, 4, 51
Willis, Frank, 489

Willkie, Wendell, 520
Wills, Mark, 435
Wilson, Heather, 567*n*
Wilson, Joseph, 452*n*, 454
Wilson, Pete, 440
Wilson, Roger B., 134*n*
Wilson, Valerie Plame, 452, 452*n*, 454, 455*n*, 456
Wilson, Woodrow, 227, 227*n*, 444
Winston, David, 163
Witt, James Lee, 117
Wofford, Harris, 114*n*
Wohlstetter, Albert, 178
Wolf, Frank, 534, 534*n*
Wolfowitz, Jacob, 177
Wolfowitz, Paul, 101, 102, 118, 130, 176–82, 178*n*, 229, 233, 370
  Bloom and, 177–78
  Cheney and, xviii, 179–80, 181–82
  Defense Department and, xviii, 176*n*, 179, 181, 305, 332, 347
  Iraq invasion and, 357
  Iraq occupation and, 375
  Iraq war leadup and, 178, 180–81, 211–12, 234, 244, 305, 332, 347, 377
  Strauss and, 177, 178
  World Bank and, 426
Wood, Kimba, 422*n*
Woodrow Wilson Center, 464–65
Woodward, Bob, 152, 188, 247, 328, 389, 515
Woolsey, James, 264
Works Progress Administration (WPA), 242
World Affairs Council, 464
World Bank, 147, 426
World Health Organization (WHO), 264
WorldPublicOpinion.org, 481
World Series, 251–52, *252*
World Trade Center:
  bombing of (1993), 271
  Bush's visit to site of, 239–40, *239*
  terror attack on, 217–18, 226, 231

World War I, 285
World War II, 21, 135, 152*n*, 163, 229, 242, 272, 285, 305, 321, 327, 357*n*, 372*n*, 435, 444, 478–79, 507, 515*n*, 548, 577, 577*n*, 580, 590
  George H. W. Bush and, 3, 4–5, *4*
  Prescott Bush and, 2
Wright, Robin, 529
writs of certiorari, 141–42, 141*n*
Wyatt, Jerry, *33*
Wyoming, 111

Yale Corporation, 2
Yale Daily News, 5
Yale Law School, 258*n*, 451
Yale University, xvii, xix, 23, 129, 134, 219, 371, 403, 562
  Cheney and, 108
  George H. W. Bush and, 1, 3, 5–6
  George W. Bush and, 1, 13–16, 13*n*, *15*, 32, 58, 82, 103, 112, 515, 647
  legacy admissions and, 13–14, 14*n*
  Prescott Bush and, 2
  Skull and Bones and, 5–6
  Vietnam War and, 16
  Wolfowitz and, 178, 180
  women and, 15
Yarborough, Ralph, 21
yellowcake (mixed uranium oxides), 341–42*n*, 351, 452*n*, 454
Yeltsin, Boris, 199
Yemen, 235
Yoo, John C., 258*n*, *259*, 272, 393, 394, 420
Younger, Charles, 87, 657
Youngstown Sheet & Tube v. Sawyer (1952), 499–500
YouTube, 264
Y visas, 584*n*

Zaidi, Muntadhar al-, 601
Zakaria, Fareed, 205*n*
Zakaria, Toby, 378, 461

Zakheim, Dov, 176*n*, 181
Zambia, 555*n*
Zapata Off-Shore Drilling, 23
Zapata Petroleum Company, 10–11
Zarqawi, Abu Musab al-, 494
Zhukov, Georgy, 463*n*

Zinni, Anthony, 313–14
Zoellick, Robert, 147, *157*, 176*n*, 181, 585, 586
Zogby poll, 402
Zubaydah, Abu, 296–97, 299, 505
Z visas, 584*n*

Illustration Credits

The George Bush Presidential Library and Museum: 2, 4, 6, 7, 11, 15, 17, 33, 34, 41, 43

Darren McCollester/Newsmakers/Getty Images: 12

The George W. Bush Presidential Library and Museum: 39, 96, 149, 151, 157, 166, 220, 237, 239, 241, 252, 306, 317, 351, 355, 425, 436, 447, 448, 496, 510, 527, 558, 574, 579, 601, 639, 646, 647, 648, 651, 654, 655

Dallas Morning News: 59

Kenneth C. Zirkel: 69

Tom Lankes/*Austin American-Statesman*, via Associated Press: 73

The Texas State Library and Archives Commission: 81

Texas State Preservation Board: 83

Saturday Evening Post: 85

U.S. Air Force: 109

Associated Press/Doug Mills: 115

Paul J. Richards/AFP/Getty Images: 118

U.S. Department of Defense: 131, 177, 250, 282, 370, 516

Associated Press/Michel Euler: 137

Associated Press/Peter Dejong: 200

Sarasota Herald-Tribune: 217

CPL Jason Ingersoll, USMC: 221

Associated Press/Susan Walsh: 259

Lawrence Meledeth/IAEA: 341

Associated Press/Elise Amendola: 344

Goran Tomasevic/Reuters: 361

Associated Press/J. Scott Applewhite: 366

United States Congress: 403

U.S. Department of State: 418

Greg Heartsfield: 429

U.S. Coast Guard (Petty Officer 2nd Class Kyle Niemi): 433

National Archives and Records Administration: 453

Associated Press/Khalid Mohammed, Hameed Rasheed: 487

U.S. Army: 604

Shirley Li/Medill: 609

United States Treasury: 610

Associated Press/Carolyn Kaster: 634

Oscar Slotboom: 656

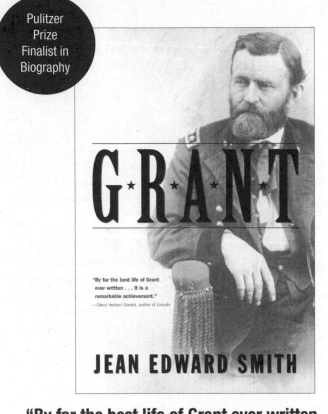